THE CATHOLIC BIBLICAL QUARTERLY MONOGRAPH SERIES

22

THE DWELLING OF GOD
The Tabernacle in the Old Testament, Intertestamental Jewish Literature, and the New Testament

by
Craig R. Koester

THE DWELLING OF GOD
The Tabernacle in the Old Testament, Intertestamental Jewish Literature, and the Old Testament

by
Craig R. Koester

The Catholic Biblical Association of America
Washington, DC 20064
1989

THE DWELLING OF GOD

©1989 The Catholic Biblical Association of America
Washington, DC 20064

PRODUCED IN THE UNITED STATES

Library of Congress Cataloging-in-Publication Data

Koester, Craig R., 1953–
    The dwelling of God : the tabernacle in the Old Testament,
intertestamental Jewish literature, and the New Testament / by Craig
R. Koester.
        p.   cm. — (The Catholic Biblical quarterly. Monograph series
; 22)
    Bibliography: p.
    Includes index.
    ISBN 0-915170-21-3
    1. Tabernacle—Typology—History of doctrines. 2. Bible—
Criticism, interpretation, etc. 3. Apocryphal books (Old
Testament)—Criticism, interpretation, etc. I. Title. II. Series.
BS680.T32K64   1989
220.6'4—dc20   89-9853
                                                    CIP

TABLE OF CONTENTS

PREFACE

The story of God's tent dwelling or "tabernacle" dominates the second half of the book of Exodus and is mentioned at other key points in both Old and New Testaments. Generations of Christian scholars have attempted to discern in the tabernacle a theological significance for the church of their own time. For Clement of Alexandria, Jerome, and others, the tabernacle represented the universe. Origen, Bede, and medieval exegetes maintained that it illustrated the virtues of Christian life, while various interpreters from the seventeenth through the early twentieth centuries presented the tabernacle as a type of Christ and the church. A glance at the brief history of exegesis compiled by B. Childs (*The Book of Exodus: A Critical, Theological Commentary* [OTL; Philadelphia: Westminster, 1974] 547–50) reveals that the list does not end here. While many of these interpretations are no longer compelling, they attest to a continued Christian fascination with Israel's ancient sanctuary.

In our own time, tabernacle imagery continues to play a role in Christian worship. For example, in Roman Catholic churches the consecrated host is placed in a receptacle called a "tabernacle," since in Christ "the Word became flesh and tabernacled among us" (John 1:14). On the other hand, store-front "tabernacles" continue a tradition with roots in the revivals of the American frontier, where meetings were held in a tent that was often called a "tabernacle," like the tent where God met with Israel in the wilderness.

Our study will focus on the role of the tabernacle in the earliest Christian sources, those of the NT. The work is a revised form of a doctoral dissertation that was accepted with distinction at Union Theological Seminary in New York in the fall of 1986. Raymond E. Brown directed the research with interest, insight, and pastoral concern. J. Louis Martyn read each draft and offered valuable suggestions at each stage. The other members of the committee were Thomas Robinson and Christopher Morse, who helped to sharpen a number of significant points. I would also like to thank Burton Visotzky, who introduced me to the "sea" of rabbinic literature. The revisions were completed alongside teaching responsibilities at Luther Northwestern Theological Seminary in St. Paul, Minnesota, where Terence Fretheim offered suggestions on the revised OT section and Donald Juel reviewed the work as a whole. Thomas Shoemaker, my student assistant, produced the indexes, carefully proofread the manuscript, and verified the references. I also want to thank Robert Karris for overseeing the publication process and the CBQMS reviewers for their suggestions on the manuscript. My greatest debt of gratitude, however, I owe to my wife, Nancy, for her support and good humor throughout the process. It is to her that this volume is dedicated.

The translations of OT materials are adapted from the RSV; the translations of NT texts are those of the author.

I

INTRODUCTION

The Jerusalem temple was the central cultic institution for Jews in the first century, and it also affected the development of early Christianity. NT scholars have produced significant studies on early Christian attitudes toward the temple, the use of temple and cultic imagery in the NT, and especially the concept of the Christian community as a temple.[1] Such studies have made important contributions to our understanding of early Christian life and thought.

The tabernacle has not received the same attention by NT scholars. There has been no special study of the significance of the tabernacle during the intertestamental and NT period.[2] The lack of attention is, perhaps, understandable, since the tabernacle was not a functioning institution during the first century. According to the OT, the tabernacle was constructed under Moses' direction, brought into the promised land, and finally brought to Jerusalem for the dedication of Solomon's temple. Afterward, the temple became Israel's chief sanctuary, and the tabernacle disappeared from view.

---

[1] Two of the most important studies are by H. Wenschkewitz, "Die Spiritualisierung der Kultusbegriffe Temple, Priester und Opfer im Neuen Testament," *Angelos* 4 (1932) 70-230; and G. Klinzing, *Die Umdeutung des Kultus in der Qumrangemeinde und im Neuen Testament* (SUNT 7; Göttingen: Vandenhoeck & Ruprecht, 1971). Other studies include K. Baltzer, "The Meaning of the Temple in the Lukan Writings," *HTR* 58 (1965) 263-77; J. C. Coppens, "The Spiritual Temple in the Pauline Letters and its Background," *Studia Evangelica* 6 (1969) 53-66; O. Cullmann, "L'opposition contre le temple de Jerusalem, motif commun de la theologie johannique et du monde ambiant," *NTS* 5 (1958-59) 157-73; B. Gärtner, *The Temple and the Community in Qumran and the New Testament* (SNTSMS 1; Cambridge: University, 1965); L. Gaston, *No Stone on Another: Studies in the Significance of the Fall of Jerusalem in the Synoptic Gospels* (NovTSup 23; Leiden: Brill, 1970); D. Juel, *Messiah and Temple: The Trial of Jesus in the Gospel of Mark* (SBLDS 31; Missoula, MT: Scholars, 1977); R. J. McKelvey, *The New Temple: The Church in the New Testament* (Oxford Theological Monographs; Oxford: Oxford, 1969); W. D. Davies, *The Gospel and the Land: Early Christianity and Jewish Territorial Doctrine* (Berkeley: University of California, 1974) 150-54, 185-94, 289-96; E. Schüssler Fiorenza, "Cultic Language in Qumran and in the NT," *CBQ* 38 (1976) 159-77.

[2] A beginning was made by W. Michaelis, *"skēnē, ktl.," TDNT* 7 (1971) 368-94.

But surprisingly, the tabernacle does appear at important points in the NT. According to the book of Acts, Stephen referred to the tabernacle shortly before his martyrdom and the extension of the Christian mission to Samaria (Acts 7:44–46), and James mentioned David's tent when the circumcision-free mission to Gentiles was formally approved (15:16). The prologue to John's gospel announces the incarnation by saying, "the Word became flesh and tabernacled among us" (John 1:14). The book of Revelation culminates in a vision of the new Jerusalem and the proclamation, "Behold the tabernacle of God" (Rev 21:3). The Epistle to the Hebrews conducts the NT's most extended discussion of Israel's cult *solely* in terms of the tabernacle; the temple is never mentioned.

Scholars have sometimes considered the tabernacle and temple to be virtually indistinguishable, but early Christians actually perceived the two sanctuaries in different ways. Stephen viewed the tabernacle favorably, yet roundly denounced Solomon's temple (Acts 7:47–50). The Fourth Evangelist used tabernacle imagery for the incarnate Word, but later indicated that the temple would be replaced by Jesus' resurrected body (John 2:21), and by worship in Spirit and in truth (4:21–23). The descent of the new Jerusalem signaled the presence of God's tabernacle among humankind, yet there was "no temple in the city" (Rev 21:22).

Our task will be to discern what the tabernacle, rather than the temple, meant to early Christians, and why they used tabernacle imagery as they did. The results of the study are intended to contribute to a clearer understanding of a number of important NT texts and to a broader discussion of early Christian attitudes toward Israel's cult and the use of cultic language in Christian theology. The methods used in this study have been shaped by earlier studies of cultic imagery in the NT. A sketch of the approaches taken in several important works will help to clarify the direction of our investigation.

In 1932 Hans Wenschkewitz published a study describing the "spiritualization" of the concepts of temple, priesthood, and sacrifice in the NT.[3] He perceived a cleft between cultic piety with its emphases on sacrifices, priests, and temples, and a more "spiritual" piety that was expressed in prayer and ethical conduct. "Spiritualization" he defined as the process by which language taken from the sacrificial cult was applied to more spiritual expressions of piety. By noting parallels between the uses of cultic language in the OT, later Jewish writings, Stoic works, and the NT, Wenschkewitz identified "spiritualization" as a common religious phenomenon expressed in all these texts. He acknowledged that the Christian use of cultic language for Jesus'

---

[3] "Die Spiritualisierung der Kultusbegriffe Temple, Priester und Opfer im Neuen Testament."

death had few precedents and reflected distinctive theological presupposi-
tions. Nevertheless, he concluded that both the Christian and non-Christian
sources manifested a common tendency to elevate cultic motifs to a higher
plane.

Nearly forty years later, Georg Klinzing published a study of cultic imagery in the Dead Sea Scrolls and the NT that marked a significant advance over
previous works.[4] Klinzing noted that the Dead Sea texts do not exhibit the
cleft between cultic and more spiritual forms of piety that was central to
Wenschkewitz's definition of spiritualization. He also tried to demonstrate
that the Qumran community's reinterpretation of the cult was decisively
shaped by a dispute with the Jerusalem priesthood and by a form of realized
eschatology, rather than the developing spiritual or ethical piety posited by
Wenschkewitz. After noting the parallels between the Dead Sea texts and the
NT, he concluded that Christians derived the notion of a community as a
temple from the theology of the Qumran community, and that both groups
based their reinterpretation of the cult on forms of realized eschatology.

Elizabeth Schüssler Fiorenza responded favorably to Klinzing's analysis
of individual texts, but insisted that "the category of *religionsgeschichtlich*
parallels and similarities does not methodologically suffice to understand the
theological differences" between NT texts and Jewish writings like those in
the Qumran library.[5] Such parallels also provide an insufficient basis on
which to define the relationship between the two communities. As an example of the inadequacy of the method, she noted that the Dead Sea community retained a priestly hierarchy, while the early church did not develop
one, even though both groups were supposed to have shared a common
worldview. She remarked that NT writers "do not so much reinterpret cultic
institutions and terminology but express a new reality in cultic language."[6]
Therefore she concluded that it is necessary to identify the social context and
the theological interest and function that cultic language had in different
Jewish and Christian groups.

The work of Oscar Cullmann and Raymond Brown underscores Schüssler Fiorenza's remarks about method. Cullmann tried to identify connections
between actual groups of people that had similar attitudes toward the
Jerusalem temple.[7] He observed that opposition to the temple was
characteristic of certain Jewish groups, the Samaritans, the Hellenists mentioned in Acts 6, and the Johannine community. He tried to trace possible

---

[4] *Die Umdeutung des Kultus in der Qumrangemeinde und im Neuen Testament.*

[5] "Cultic Language," 164.

[6] "Cultic Language," 162 n. 12.

[7] See esp. "L'opposition contre le temple de Jerusalem"; and more recently *The Johannine Circle: Its Place in Judaism, Among the Disciples of Jesus, and in Early Christianity*
(London: SCM, 1975) 39–56.

connections between the Hellenists and the Johannine Christians by noting similarities in theological outlook, their common interest in Samaria (Acts 8; John 4), and their mutual relationship to "heterodox" Jewish groups. He suggests that further traces of this "Johannine Circle" appear in Revelation and Hebrews, both of which exhibit opposition to the temple cult. Brown agrees that attitudes toward Israel's cult can be associated with certain groups of Christians and that these attitudes may provide clues to relationships between these groups.[8] Yet Brown also insists that Cullmann's synthesis overlooks many important theological differences between the texts and groups he discusses.[9]

Our investigation, therefore, will explore the distinctive social context and theological interests of texts that mention one of Israel's cultic institutions — the tabernacle. We will not assume that the use of cultic language by Jews and Christians manifests a common, underlying religious tendency. Both groups shared common scriptures and were informed by similar interpretive traditions, but belief in Jesus set Christians apart from non-Christian Jews and gave a distinctive stamp to early Christian writings. If NT texts express a "new reality," as Schüssler Fiorenza remarked, then we must ask why they do so in cultic language, especially the language of the tabernacle, which had been defunct for centuries.

In order to respond to this question, we first will describe the spectrum of biblical and extra-biblical traditions concerning the ancient Israelite tabernacle that was available to the authors of the NT. The value of this material for NT study has recently been highlighted by Donald Juel, who observed that

> Christianity began not as a scholarly proposal about the meaning of the Scriptures, but as a response to events focusing on a particular person, Jesus of Nazareth. The response required a language, and the language of Jesus' followers was that of the Bible (i.e., the OT) as read and interpreted in Jewish circles of the first century.[10]

---

[8] "Not Jewish Christianity or Gentile Christianity but Types of Jewish/Gentile Christianity," *CBQ* 45 (1983) 74-79; *The Community of the Beloved Disciple* (New York: Paulist, 1979) 38-39; *Antioch and Rome: New Testament Cradles of Catholic Christianity* (New York: Paulist, 1983) 1-9.

[9] See Brown's review of *The Johannine Circle* in *TS* 38 (1977) 157-59 and his *Community,* 38 and 176-78. Cf. the comments by W. A. Meeks in his review of Cullmann's work in *JBL* 95 (1976) 304-5; and the remarks by E. Haenchen in *The Acts of the Apostles* (Philadelphia: Westminster, 1971) 260-61 n. 3.

[10] *Messianic Exegesis: Christological Interpretation of the Old Testament in Early Christianity* (Philadelphia: Fortress, 1988) 14.

By describing the range of meanings associated with the tabernacle in the OT and in Jewish writings from about 200 B.C. to A.D. 150, we will be in a position to discern how and why early Christians utilized language concerning the ancient tent sanctuary for Christian theology.

Our discussion of the tabernacle in the NT begins by treating references to the tabernacle in their present literary contexts, with consideration of matters of composition and literary structure that affect the interpretation of the relevant passages. Special attention will be given to the theological interests that inform each author's view of the tabernacle. The second part of these chapters deals with ways in which the author appropriated and transformed the traditions available to him in his social context. Instead of noting the "parallels" between NT and extra-NT texts, we will attempt to locate extra-biblical materials that actually may have contributed to the NT author's view of the tabernacle. Several considerations govern the discussion of these antecedents. (1) Preference is given to materials that are slightly older or contemporary with the NT texts. Later materials are included only when they help to elucidate views that are evident in earlier sources. (2) Attempts will be made to define the relationship of NT passages to extra-biblical sources. For example, we will ask whether there is a relationship of literary dependence between two tabernacle texts or whether both depend on a common tradition. (3) Several different types of extra-biblical material may lie behind the same NT passage. Therefore attempts will be made to distinguish the types of material with the strongest affinities to the NT text from materials where the connections are less clear. (4) We will try to determine whether the various extra-biblical sources that may lie behind a text can plausibly be related to each other. For example, we will ask whether they were known at the same time in the same geographical area, and whether their perspectives are compatible with each other.

Our study of the tabernacle tradition will provide glimpses into a much larger process of early Christian self-definition. The NT texts considered here were written by Christians primarily for Christian readers in the late first century, most probably after the temple had been destroyed, when Jews were seeking ways to compensate for the loss of their cultic center. During this period, Christianity was becoming increasingly distinct from Judaism, but Christians continued to formulate their theology and identity by drawing on Jewish scriptures and traditions. The process entailed both appropriation and transformation of traditional materials. Here we will focus on one facet of the process, by attempting to trace how the story of Israel's ancient tabernacle became a suitable vehicle for Christian theology.

II

THE TABERNACLE IN THE OLD TESTAMENT

The OT accounts of Israel's tent-sanctuary appear to be summarized in God's word to David in 2 Sam 7:6. God said, "I have not dwelt in a house since the day I brought up the people of Israel from Egypt to this day, but I have been moving about in a tent for my tabernacle." Closer scrutiny, however, reveals that the biblical portrayal of God's tent-sanctuary is far from straightforward. God's tent or tabernacle appears in texts that weave together variegated strands of tradition and have differing theological interests. Since intertestamental and NT writings develop these diverse OT perspectives, it will be important to survey OT references to the tabernacle, noting the theological characteristics of the various texts, and the contexts within which they were written.

A. The Tabernacle in the Pentateuch

OT scholars have significantly enhanced our understanding of the tabernacle by delineating its traits in the various pentateuchal traditions. Authors of the NT and intertestamental literature, however, based their interpretations on the final form of the material. Therefore we will first discuss the tabernacle texts in their present form, before turning to the traditions that lie behind the present text.

Present Form of the Pentateuch

The story of the tabernacle begins at Mt. Sinai, after God's covenant with Israel was ratified (Exodus 24). God commanded Moses to take a free will offering from the people (25:1–7), then said,

> Let them build me a sanctuary that I may dwell in their midst. According to all that I show you concerning the pattern of the tabernacle, and of all its furniture, so you shall make it (25:8–9).

The remainder of the book of Exodus is devoted primarily to this sanctuary, which is called both a "dwelling" or "tabernacle" (מִשְׁכָּן) and the "tent of meeting" (אֹהֶל מוֹעֵד).

Prescriptions for the tabernacle are given in Exodus 25-31.[1] The sanctuary was to be made of wooden boards or frames draped with coverings of goat hair and leather. It was to be ten cubits high, ten cubits wide, and thirty cubits long. A veil suspended on four pillars would divide the tabernacle into a "holy of holies" (ten cubits long) and a forecourt (twenty cubits long). The ark of the covenant, mercy seat, and two cherubim would be placed in the holy of holies. A lampstand, incense altar, and table with twelve loaves of bread would stand in the forecourt. Around the tabernacle was to be a courtyard measuring fifty by one hundred cubits, which would contain a bronze altar and a laver for priestly ablutions. Aaron and his sons would attend the shrine.

The tabernacle would perform several functions. First, it would be a place of divine revelation, for God promised to speak to Moses in its holy of holies, "from above the mercy seat, from between the two cherubim that are upon the ark of the testimony" (25:22). Second, it would be where sacrifices would be offered and atonement made (29:38-43; 30:7-10). Third, God's presence in the tent would be a sign of his covenant faithfulness, since it would fulfill his promise to dwell with Israel and to be their God (25:8; 29:45-46). Israel's faithfulness would be expressed by obedience to God's commandments, especially the sabbath commandment which concludes the prescriptions for the tabernacle (31:12-17).[2]

Before the tabernacle could be built, however, Israel committed apostasy by fabricating a golden calf to worship (chap. 32). As a result, God threatened to withdraw from Israel (33:1-3). At this point the text says that Moses "used to take the tent and pitch it outside the camp, far off from the camp, and he called it the tent of meeting" (33:7). The passage seems incongruous because the tent of meeting had not been constructed at this point in the story, and the passage almost certainly preserves a fragment of an older tradition that will be discussed below. Nevertheless, in its present context, Exod 33:7-11 signals God's withdrawal from the Israelite camp in response to Israel's apostasy.[3] Signs of hope appeared as God continued to

---

[1] For detailed discussion of the tabernacle's structure see A. R. S. Kennedy, "Tabernacle," *Hastings Dictionary of the Bible* 4 (1911) 653-68; M. Haran, "The Priestly Image of the Tabernacle," *HUCA* 36 (1965) 191-226; G. H. Davies, "Tabernacle," *IDB* 4 (1962) 498-506 (On p. 500 Davies correctly states that there were four pillars between the holy of holies and forecourt, although the diagram on p. 499 pictures five pillars).

[2] On covenant faithfulness and the sabbath command see B. Childs, *The Book of Exodus: A Critical, Theological Commentary* (OTL; Philadelphia: Westminster, 1974) 541-42.

[3] See Childs, *Exodus,* 592-93; Davies, "Tabernacle," 504; R. W. L. Moberly, *At the*

descend in a pillar of cloud to meet with Moses, and at least some of the people went out to the tent to seek the Lord, suggesting that they repented of their apostasy.

Moses' intercession led to the restoration of God's covenant with Israel (chap. 34) and preparations were made immediately for the construction of the tabernacle, with the solemn reminder that the work must not be done on the sabbath (35:1-3). The account of the tabernacle's construction shows how Israel meticulously followed God's command, in sharp contrast to its previous apostasy.[4] The calf had been fabricated by Aaron at Israel's request (32:1), but the tabernacle was built according to divine command by Bezalel, whom God called and empowered by his spirit (35:30-36:1). The people had once given their gold for idolatry (32:3), but later brought more gold and free will offerings than were needed for the entire tabernacle (35:21; 36:2-7). The building of the calf led to a withdrawal of God's presence from the camp (33:7), but at the completion of the tabernacle God's glory filled the tent and remained there day and night (40:34-38).

In the remainder of the Pentateuch the tabernacle continued to perform the functions ascribed to it in Exodus. It was the place of revelation, where God made known the statutes concerning various types of offerings (Lev 1:1-17), confirmed Moses' singular status among the prophets (Num 12:1-9), and foretold Israel's future apostasy (Deut 31:14-21). It was the place where sacrifices were offered and atonement secured, making it possible for Israel to live in holiness (e.g., Lev 1:5; 4:7; 15:29-31; 16:1-34). God's presence in the tabernacle continued to remind Israel of his covenant with them and of the importance of faithful obedience to his commandments (Lev 26:9-13; Num 9:15-23).

PENTATEUCHAL TRADITIONS

Behind the present form of the Pentateuch lie older traditions concerning Israel's tent-sanctuary. The oldest tradition is variously ascribed to the E, J, or JE stratum of the Pentateuch.[5] The tradition first appears in Exod

---

Mountain of God: Story and Theology in Exodus 32-34 (JSOTSup 22; Sheffield: JSOT, 1983) 63-65, 110.

[4] Childs, *Exodus,* 542-43.

[5] On "E" see M. Haran, "The Nature of the *''ohel mo'edh'* in Pentateuchal Sources," *JSS* 5 (1960) 50-65, esp. 52-54; idem, *Temples and Temple Service: An Inquiry into the Character of Cult Phenomena and the Historical Setting of the Priestly School* (Oxford: Clarendon, 1978) 262-67; M. Görg, *Das Zelt der Begegnung: Untersuchung zur Gestalt der sakralen Zelttradition Altisraels* (BBB 27; Bonn: Hanstein, 1967) 138-70. On "J" see M. Noth, *A History of Pentateuchal Traditions* (Englewood Cliffs: Prentice-Hall, 1972) 244; idem, *Exodus: A Commentary* (OTL; Philadelphia: Westminster, 1962) 255; M. L. Newman, *The People of the Covenant*

33:7-11, which was noted above. The passage depicts the tent of meeting as a simple tent that stood outside the camp rather than at its center. The tent was attended by one man, Joshua the son of Nun, rather than by Aaron and his sons. This tent was not a place of sacrifice and apparently did not house the ark of the covenant.[6] God did speak to Moses there, but at the door of the tent, rather than in the holy of holies. Other traces of the tradition are found in Num 11:16-17 and 24-30 where God bestowed the spirit on the seventy elders, in Num 12:1-16 where God contended with Miriam and Aaron concerning the status of Moses, and in Deut 31:14-15 where Moses brought Joshua to be commissioned as his successor.

This tradition may stem from Israel's wilderness period,[7] and Menahem Haran suggests that it was associated with prophetic circles,[8] although the fragmentary nature of the material makes it difficult to reconstruct the context of transmission with certainty.[9] Theologically, this tradition transfers features of the Sinai theophany to the tent. The tent and the mountain were both located outside Israel's camp, and the people left the camp to meet God, who descended in a cloud (Exod 19:9, 17; 33:7, 9). Joshua served as Moses' attendant at the mountain and at the tent (24:13; 33:11), and the seventy elders who were endowed with the spirit at the tent were said to have seen God on the mountain in another ancient tradition (Num 11:24-25; Exod 24:9-11). Therefore, by means of the tent, the God who appeared at Sinai

---

(Nashville: Abingdon, 1962) 55. On "JE" see R. E. Clements, *God and Temple* (Philadelphia: Fortress, 1965) 37; Davies, "Tabernacle," 502.

[6] The relationship of the tent to the ark of the covenant has been widely debated. Those who insist that the ark and tent were originally separate institutions include R. Hartmann, "Zelt und Lade," *ZAW* 37 (1917-18) 209-44; G. von Rad, "The Tent and the Ark," *The Problem of the Hexateuch and Other Essays* (Edinburgh: Oliver and Boyd, 1966) 103-24; idem, *Old Testament Theology* (2 vols.; New York: Harper & Row, 1962-65) 1.234-41; Haran, "The Nature," 50-60; idem, *Temples,* 260-70. Those who argue that the tent housed the ark in the early tradition include W. Beyerlin, *Origins and History of the Oldest Sinaitic Traditions* (Oxford: Blackwell, 1965) 114-18; R. de Vaux, *The Bible and the Ancient Near East* (Garden City: Doubleday, 1971) 136-51; Görg, *Zelt,* 165-66. For an extensive survey of research see R. Schmitt, *Zelt und Lade als Thema alttestamentlicher Wissenschaft: Eine kritische forschungsgeschichtliche Darstellung* (Gütersloh: Mohn, 1972) 256-74.

[7] E.g., von Rad, "Tent," 117; de Vaux, "Ark," 138; Beyerlin, *Origins,* 147; K. Koch, "'ōhel," *TDOT* 1 (1974) 118-30, esp. 125.

[8] "Nature," 56-58; *Temples,* 267-69.

[9] A number of scholars locate the tent tradition in the south and the ark in the north of Palestine. See, e.g., Hartmann, "Zelt," 239-42; G. von Rad, *Studies in Deuteronomy* (SBT 9; London: SCM, 1953) 43; Newman, *People,* 55-71; Koch, *TDOT* 1.126. Others more plausibly locate the tent tradition in the north, at Shiloh or Shechem. See, e.g., Beyerlin, *Origins,* 118-19; Görg, *Zelt,* 166; Clements, *God and Temple,* 38.

continued to speak to his people after they departed from the mountain itself.[10]

The more elaborate shrine described in Exodus 25–31 and 35–40 is a literary creation of the priestly writer (P), whose work combines several types of material. First, the priestly writer recalls the ancient tent tradition by calling the sanctuary the "tent of meeting," prescribing a covering for it made of fabric and leather (26:7–14), and by indicating that it would be a portable sanctuary. Second, the extensive wooden framework and the designation "dwelling" or "tabernacle" (משכן) suggest that the writer also knew of semi-permanent sanctuaries associated with sites in Palestine.[11] Moreover, God's "tabernacle" was a reminder of his covenant faithfulness according to the Holiness Code, one of the priestly writer's sources (Leviticus 17–26; cf. 26:11). Third, the tabernacle incorporates features of Solomon's temple, especially the mercy seat and cherubim over the ark in the holy of holies, the lampstand, table, and incense altar in the forecourt, and the bronze altar and laver in the outer court. Moreover, the dimensions of the tabernacle are exactly half those of Solomon's temple, and both are oriented to the east.[12]

The priestly portrait of the tabernacle received its distinctive shape in the exilic or early postexilic period.[13] Although the temple had been destroyed, the priestly writer retained the idea that the cult was central to Israel's continued life as a people. He drew on the ancient tent tradition to show that God had bound himself to a people, not to a place or a kingdom, and could meet his people in many different locations.[14] By prefacing his accounts with creation narratives, the priestly writer showed that Israel's worship was anchored in the work of the creator. God's spirit was active when both the world and the tabernacle were made (Gen 1:2; Exod 31:3 and 35:31), and the construction of the tabernacle itself took place within the

---

[10] Cf. Haran, "Nature," 57, and *Temples,* 267–68; Koch, *TDOT* 1.124.

[11] See F. M. Cross ("The Tabernacle," *BA* 10 [1947] 45–68), who finds antecedents for P's tabernacle in David's tent, and M. Haran ("Shiloh and Jerusalem: The Origin of the Priestly Tradition in the Pentateuch," *JBL* 81 [1962] 14–24) who connects the tabernacle with traditions about the Shiloh shrine.

[12] See Haran, "Shiloh," 14–17 and *Temples,* 188–94; V. Fritz, *Tempel und Zelt: Studien zum Tempelbau in Israel und zu dem Zeltheiligtum der Priesterschrift* (WMANT 47; Neukirchen-Vluyn: Neukirchener, 1977) 148.

[13] E.g., Noth, *Exodus,* 17; F. M. Cross, *Canaanite Myth and Hebrew Epic: Essays in the History of the Religion of Israel* (Cambridge: Harvard, 1973) 323–24: J. Blenkinsopp, "The Structure of P," *CBQ* 38 (1976) 275–92, esp. 275. A notable exception is M. Haran, who argues for a preexilic date of composition. See esp. his "Behind the Scenes of History: Determining the Date of the Priestly Source," *JBL* 100 (1981) 321–33.

[14] Clements, *God and Temple,* 120–21; Fritz, *Temple,* 149–53; T. Fretheim, "The Priestly Document: Anti-Temple?" *VT* 18 (1968) 313–29, esp. 316.

pattern of sabbath rest that God established at creation (Gen 2:3; Exod 31:16–17; 35:1–3).[15]

The priestly prescriptions for the tabernacle anticipated the restoration of the temple cult in Jerusalem by insisting that a central sanctuary was essential for Israel and had been so since Sinai.[16] The priestly writer adapted the sanctuary to a wilderness setting by prescribing a structure of wood, fabric, and leather, but he also expected the shrine to have a bipartite design and gold and bronze furnishings like those of Solomon's temple. This account is not simply an attempt to legitimate an existing cult by projecting it back into the wilderness period, as some have argued, since the tabernacle's design is based to some extent on premonarchical traditions and does differ from Solomon's temple in numerous respects.[17] The priestly writer may have attempted to correct certain ideas associated with the temple, since he described a sanctuary that was designed by God and constructed by free will offerings, unlike Solomon's temple, which was a royal project that utilized forced labor.[18] He also indicated that God freely "met" with Israel in the tent but was not confined there.[19] Nevertheless, the priestly writer was probably not an opponent of the Jerusalem temple, since he did include temple features in his design and stated that in the tabernacle God's glory was *continually* present with his people (40:38).[20] Such a theology would assure Israel that God was present and could be worshiped in many different locations, and it would also foster hope for the restoration of the sanctuary in the future.

B. THE TABERNACLE IN ACCOUNTS OF ISRAEL IN THE LAND

The story of the tabernacle after Israel's entry into the promised land appears in two versions: the Deuteronomistic History and the work of the

[15] See esp. Blenkinsopp, "Structure," 281–83.

[16] Lev 17:1–9. Clements, *God and Temple,* 110–22; Koch, *TDOT* 1.129; cf. Noth, *Exodus,* 17; idem, *Pentateuchal Traditions,* 243–46.

[17] The retrojection hypothesis was classically formulated by J. Wellhausen, *Prolegomena to the History of Israel* (Edinburgh: Black, 1885) 17–51. Cf. Görg, *Zelt,* 34. This view is now widely acknowledged to be inadequate. See, e.g., Haran, "Shiloh,"17–18; idem, *Temples,* 194–97; Fritz, *Temple,* 148; Childs, *Exodus,* 530–32.

[18] Noted by Childs, *Exodus,* 541.

[19] Noth, *Pentateuchal Traditions,* 246; Koch, *TDOT* 1.129–30; cf. Fretheim, "Priestly Document," 328; Haran, *Temples,* 197 n. 14.

[20] The argument that P is anti-temple is most forcefully made by Fretheim ("Priestly Document"). On the continued presence of God in the sanctuary see Clements, *God and Temple,* 118. Also note that the reference to the tabernacle's incorporation into the temple in 1 Kgs 8:4 may be a priestly gloss. See J. Gray, *I and II Kings: A Commentary* (OTL; Philadelphia: Westminster, 1963) 194.

Chronicler. Although these accounts sometimes duplicate each other, they stem from different periods of time, reflect different theological interests, and can best be discussed separately.

JOSHUA–KINGS

The book of Joshua relates that when Israel had conquered much of the promised land, the tent of meeting was set up at Shiloh (Josh 18:1). There, at the door of the tent, land was allotted to seven tribes (18:1; 19:51). Soon afterward, the Transjordanian tribes built an altar east of the Jordan. The rest of Israel assembled at Shiloh and sent a delegation to the Transjordanian tribes charging them with apostasy and urging them to settle west of the Jordan "where the Lord's tabernacle now stands," rather than establish a second site for worship (22:19). The Transjordanian group insisted that their altar would not be used for burnt offerings, but would be a reminder that they too worshiped the God of Israel. They vowed not to sacrifice at an altar "other than the altar of the Lord our God that stands before his tabernacle" (22:29).

In subsequent narratives the tabernacle all but vanishes. The book of Judges refers to the "house of God" (בית האלהים) that was at Shiloh (Judg 18:31), but it never mentions the tent of meeting or tabernacle. In 1 Samuel the Shiloh sanctuary continues to be called a "house" (בית, 1 Sam 1:7, 24) and even a "temple" (היכל, 1:9). The MT of 1 Sam 2:22 does say that Eli's sons used to "lay with the women who served at the entrance to the tent of meeting." But since the tent of meeting is not mentioned in 4QSam[a] or the LXX version of the text it is probably a postexilic addition, which may have been inserted to establish a parallel between the actions of Eli's sons and those of Israel at Peor (Num 25:1–9).[21]

The tent tradition reappears in 2 Samuel, when David brings the ark of the covenant to his newly established capitol of Jerusalem and places it in the tent that he had pitched for it (2 Sam 6:17). There the ark was housed and sacrifices were offered as at Shiloh. David's tent was apparently a new one made for the occasion, but it indicates that the Jerusalem sanctuary stood firmly within the tradition of Israel's worship, despite the new location. By preserving the tent tradition, David presumably hoped to secure public acceptance of Jerusalem as a center for worship as well as political administration.[22]

In time, David proposed to build a temple or "house" for the ark. The

---

[21] See Cross, *Canaanite Myth,* 202 n. 34; P. K. McCarter, *I Samuel* (AB 8; Garden City: Doubleday, 1980) 81.

[22] Cross, "Tabernacle," 56–57; de Vaux, "Ark," 141; idem, *Ancient Israel* (New York: McGraw-Hill, 1965) 2.309; Görg, *Zelt,* 75–76; P. K. McCarter, *II Samuel* (AB 9; Garden City: Doubleday, 1984) 172.

prophet Nathan was initially favorable to the plan, (2 Sam 7:1-3), but that night God commanded him to tell David,

> Would you build me a house to dwell in? I have not dwelt in a house since the day I brought up the people of Israel from Egypt to this day, but I have been moving about in a tent for my tabernacle. In all the places where I have moved with all the people of Israel did I speak a word with any of the judges of Israel whom I commanded to shepherd my people Israel, saying, "Why have you not built me a house of cedar?" (7:5-7)

These verses seem to say that God's chosen dwelling was a tent and that he did not want a stationary house or temple to be built. But according to 7:13a, the prohibition against building a temple applied only to David, for God promised that a descendant of David would build a house for God's name.

When the temple was completed under Solomon, it became the legitimate successor to Israel's tent sanctuaries. At the time of its dedication, the priests "brought up the ark of the Lord, the tent of meeting, and all the holy vessels that were in the tent" (1 Kgs 8:4). Then "a cloud filled the house of the Lord so that the priests could not stand to minister because of the cloud; for the glory of the Lord filled the house of the Lord" (8:10-11). Historically, the tent mentioned in 8:4 must have been the tent that David made for the ark, not the Mosaic tabernacle. Nevertheless, by calling it "the tent of meeting," the text indicates that the Solomonic temple incorporated the Mosaic heritage. Similarly, the appearance of the cloud indicates that God was present in the temple as he had been in the tent in the wilderness (e.g., Exod 33:9; 40:34-35).[23]

The references to the tabernacle in these texts stem from multiple layers of tradition. The oldest level is probably the statement that God desired a tent rather than a temple (2 Sam 7:5-7), which may stem from the time of David.[24] Some interpreters have argued the tent sanctuary was theologically acceptable because it revealed God's freedom to "move about," while a temple was rejected because it implied that God was confined to a single location.[25] A more important element, however, is that the plan to build the temple was probably perceived as a presumptuous act, since God himself had never commanded anyone to build him a "house."[26] The divine preference

---

[23] On the tent of meeting and cloud see Gray, *Kings,* 194-95; de Vaux, *Ancient Israel,* 2.297, 325-26.

[24] On the origin and interpretation of 2 Sam 7:5-7 see Cross, *Canaanite Myth,* 241-55; McCarter, *II Samuel,* 209-31; Clements, *God and Temple,* 56.

[25] Cf. Fretheim, "Priestly Document," 322-28; Fritz, *Temple,* 98; McCarter, *II Samuel,* 199.

[26] M. Simon, "La prophétie de Nathan et le temple," *RHPR* 32 (1952) 41-58, esp. 50; M. Noth, "David and Israel in II Samuel 7," *The Laws of the Pentateuch and Other Studies*

was manifest in the long-standing tradition of Israel's tent sanctuaries, and by proposing to build a temple David arrogated a divine prerogative for himself. From a socio-political perspective, the temple threatened to become a royal shrine, which would undergird a view of kingship with its roots in Canaanite rather than in Israelite practice.[27] Therefore 2 Sam 7:5-7 was originally intended to prevent the construction of a temple.

In its present form, this material is part of the Deuteronomistic History (DtH), which includes Deuteronomy through Kings. Although the references to the tabernacle and tent of meeting in Joshua and 1 Kgs 8:4 may be priestly glosses,[28] the material can be interpreted in its present form. According to Deuteronomy 12, a programmatic passage, Moses commanded Israel to destroy the pagan altars in the land and promised that God would choose a place "to make his name dwell (שׁכן)"; there Israel would sacrifice when God had given them rest from their enemies (Deut 12:10-11). The references to the tabernacle in Joshua anticipate the fulfillment of this promise. The tent was set up at Shiloh only when most of "the land lay subdued" (Josh 18:1), and the insistence that the Transjordanian tribes sacrifice at the Shiloh tabernacle conveys the Deuteronomistic conviction that Israel must have only one national sanctuary (22:19, 29).[29] Nevertheless, the Shiloh sanctuary was not the fulfillment of the promise, for Israel continued to be plagued by enemies and turned to pagan practices.

In time Israel's self-will led to the establishment of a monarchy (1 Sam 12:12) and Saul, their first king, immediately overstepped the bounds of office by performing cultic functions (13:8-12). God rejected Saul and sought out David, "a man after his own heart" (13:13-14). Although David's plan to replace the tent sanctuary with a temple was presumptuous, God intervened (2 Sam 7:5-7) and, in the Deuteronomistic version, promised that David's heir would build "a house for [God's] name" (7:13a). Thus the Davidic dynasty and Solomonic temple rested on God's promise rather than human self-will. During Solomon's reign Israel enjoyed rest from its enemies and the temple was built (1 Kgs 5:4-5; 8:15-21), showing that "not one word

---

(Philadelphia: Fortress, 1967) 250-59, esp. 251; McCarter, *II Samuel,* 225-29. Cf. H. Gese, "Der Davidsbund und die Zionserwählung," *ZTK* 61 (1964) 10-26, esp. 21.

[27] De Vaux, *Ancient Israel,* 2.329-30; Clements, *God and Temple,* 59-60; Cross, *Canaanite Myth,* 233, 243.

[28] See M. Noth, *Das Buch Josua* (HAT 7; 2d ed.; Tübingen: Mohr/Siebeck, 1953) 11, 107-8; Fretheim, "Priestly Document," 314 n. 4; A. J. Soggin, *Joshua: A Commentary* (OTL; London: SCM, 1970) 189-90, 214-15; Blenkinsopp, "Structure," 287-89.

[29] Soggin, *Joshua,* 214.

has failed of all [God's] good promise, which he uttered by Moses his servant" (8:56).[30]

Within the present form of the DtH the tabernacle continues to be a place of revelation (Josh 18:1, 10; 19:51) and sacrifice (22:19, 29; 2 Sam 6:17-18). But above all, it shows God's fidelity to "all the people of Israel" prior to the fulfillment of his promise (2 Sam 7:7). Israel's sanctuary was central to its life as a people, and its character — first as a tent and later as a permanent house — was determined by the will of God, not human presumption.

The first edition of the DtH was probably compiled during the time of Josiah.[31] If the references to the tabernacle were included in this edition, they would have added support to Josiah's centralization of the cult. The present form of the DtH was produced during the exile. It demonstrated that Israel's well-being was inseparable from true worship of God, and that the destruction of the southern as well the northern kingdom was the result of the people's persistent infidelity. The exilic version of the DtH included the assurance of God's faithfulness to his promises, but did not attempt to define the shape of Israel's future.[32]

CHRONICLES

1 and 2 Chronicles is a postexilic rewriting of Israel's history that stresses the continuity between the Mosaic tabernacle and the Jerusalem temple cult. According to the Chronicler, the tabernacle that Moses built and the bronze altar made by Bezalel stood at Gibeon during David's reign (1 Chron 16:39; 21:29; 2 Chron 1:3-6, 13).[33] As in 2 Samuel, David brought the ark from Kiriath-jearim to Jerusalem and placed it in a tent (1 Chron 15:1; 16:1). There sacrifices were offered and the Levitical singers rejoiced that God's "steadfast love endures forever" (16:34). David's tent did not, however, replace the tabernacle. Zadok, who represented the Aaronic priesthood (6:8), continued to serve before the tabernacle at Gibeon, making burnt offerings in accordance with the law, and there, as in Jerusalem, God was praised for his steadfast love (16:39-41). David himself was not permitted

---

[30] See D. J. McCarthy, "II Samuel and the Structure of the Deuteronomic History," *JBL* 84 (1965) 131-38, esp. 134-35; Cross, *Canaanite Myth,* 241-55; McCarter, *II Samuel,* 217-20, 230-31.

[31] On the editions of the DtH see Cross, *Canaanite Myth,* 274-89; McCarter, *II Samuel,* 4-8.

[32] McCarthy, "II Samuel," 138; Cross, *Canaanite Myth,* 285-87; McCarter, *II Samuel,* 220.

[33] For a survey of the discussion of the historicity of the tabernacle at Gibeon, see H. G. M. Williamson, *1 and 2 Chronicles* (NCBC; Grand Rapids: Eerdmans, 1982) 130-31.

access to the Mosaic tabernacle, but when he sacrificed at Ornan's threshing floor in Jerusalem, fire descended from heaven as it had done at the tabernacle in the wilderness, indicating that Jerusalem would become the center of Israel's worship (21:26–22:1; cf. Lev 9:24).[34]

The privilege of actually building the temple was granted to Solomon in 1 Chronicles 17 as in 2 Samuel 7. But the Chronicler describes David's preparatory work for the temple in ways that suggest parallels between Moses and David,[35] and the tabernacle and temple. Like Moses, David received a God-given pattern (תבנית) for the sanctuary (Exod 25:9, 40; 1 Chron 28:11, 19). Like the tabernacle, the temple would have two courts separated by a veil of blue, purple, scarlet, and linen material (Exod 26:31; 2 Chron 3:14), and the holy of holies would contain the mercy seat as well as the ark and cherubim (Exod 25:17; 1 Chron 28:11).[36] Since construction of the temple would mean that the Levites would no longer need to carry the tabernacle, David assigned them to new tasks as singers and attendants in "the tabernacle of the house of God" (1 Chron 6:32 [17]; 6:48 [33]; 23:25–26, 32).

When Solomon began to reign, he went to the tabernacle at Gibeon, where he offered sacrifices and obtained the wisdom necessary to build the temple (2 Chron 1:3–13). When the temple was completed, the tent of meeting was brought up and a cloud of divine glory appeared, as in 1 Kings 8 (cf. 2 Chron 5:5, 13–14). The Chronicler adds that fire from heaven consumed Solomon's offerings, confirming that the temple had become the divinely approved heir to the Mosaic sanctuary (7:1–2; Lev 9:23–24). Then "all the children of Israel" gave thanks to God by singing "his steadfast love endures forever," a song that was once chanted at David's tent and the Mosaic tabernacle (2 Chron 7:3; 1 Chron 16:34, 41). Eventually the tax that Moses once levied for the tent of meeting was collected for the temple (2 Chron 24:6) and the temple itself was called "the tabernacle of the Lord" (29:6).

The present form of the Chronicler's work was produced in Judea, probably in the Persian period.[37] Although the circumstances that occasioned

---

[34] G. von Rad (*Das Geschichtsbild des Chronistischen Werkes* [BWANT 3; Stuttgart: Kohlhammmer, 1930] 101) and Williamson (*Chronicles,* 151) maintain that in this text Jerusalem becomes the cult site for Israel. R. Mosis, however, points out that Jerusalem does not yet have the same dignity as the Mosaic tabernacle (*Untersuchungen zur Theologie des chronistischen Geschichtswerkes* [Freiburger theologische Studien 92; Freiburg: Herder, 1973] 116–20]. Cf. W. Rudolph, *Chronikbücher* (HAT 21; Tübingen: Mohr/Siebeck, 1955) 197.

[35] Noted by von Rad, *Theology,* 1.351.

[36] See the comparative charts included in the discussion of the Temple Scroll under III.B below.

[37] Although 1 and 2 Chronicles have sometimes been dated in the Hellenistic period, a

the work are unclear, the author seemed to be aware that the cultic institutions of his own day differed from those of earlier periods. It also seems likely that there were tensions between groups within Israel that identified themselves with different lines of tradition.[38] In response, the Chronicler stressed the unity provided by the Jerusalem temple. His account describes how the ark and tabernacle existed separately for a time, but were united by their incorporation into the temple. The narrative combines elements of the Deuteronomistic history and priestly legislation, and it affirms the importance of the Aaronic priesthood while granting an expanded role to the Levites.[39]

Like other biblical writers, the Chronicler depicts the tabernacle as a place of revelation (1 Chron 21:30; 2 Chron 1:7-13) and sacrifice (1 Chron 16:39-40; 2 Chron 1:3-6). But he stresses that the tabernacle manifests the *continuity* in God's faithfulness toward Israel and in Israel's worship of God.[40] God brought Israel out of Egypt and continued to move "with all Israel" in a tent or tabernacle (1 Chron 17:5). Israel's worship was rooted in God's law (16:40) and conducted at the Mosaic sanctuary and David's tent until God himself provided plans for a new sanctuary, which incorporated the Mosaic heritage and became the legitimate successor to the tent sanctuaries.

C. The Tabernacle in the Psalms and Prophets

God's tent or tabernacle is mentioned only a few times in the Psalms and once in Ezekiel. Despite their differences in historical setting and purpose, both sources associate God's tabernacle with a temple, and can, therefore, be discussed together.

Psalms

The Psalms do not mention the tent of the wilderness period and refer to the tabernacle at Shiloh only once, in a passage that recalls its destruction

---

date in the Persian period seems more likely. See, e.g., D. N. Freedman, "The Chronicler's Purpose," *CBQ* 23 (1961) 436-42, esp. 441-42; J. M. Myers, *1 Chronicles* (AB 12; Garden City: Doubleday, 1965) LXXXVII-LXXXIX; F. M. Cross, "A Reconstruction of the Judean Restoration," *JBL* 94 (1975) 4-18; Williamson, *Chronicles*, 15-17; M. A. Throntveit, *When Kings Speak: Royal Speech and Royal Prayer in Chronicles* (SBLDS 93; Atlanta: Scholars, 1987) 97-107.

[38] On the historical context see Williamson, *Chronicles*, 30, 222.

[39] P. R. Ackroyd, "History and Theology in the Writings of the Chronicler," *CTM* 38 (1967) 501-15; idem, "The Theology of the Chronicler," *Lexington Theological Quarterly* 8 (1973) 101-16, esp. 110-16; R. North, "Theology of the Chronicler," *JBL* 82 (1963) 369-81, esp. 375; Throntveit, *When Kings Speak*, 109-25; cf. von Rad, *Geschichtsbild*, 57.

[40] On the importance of continuity see de Vaux, *Ancient Israel*, 2.297; Mosis, *Untersuchungen*, 130; Williamson, *Chronicles*, 28, 151, 182.

(Ps 78:60). The tent that David erected for the ark figures in Psalm 132, which recounts how David vowed not to enter his own "tent" (v. 3) until he found a "tabernacle" (מִשְׁכָּנוֹת) for God (v. 5; cf. v. 7).[41] The remainder of the Psalm traces the movement of the ark from David's tent to the temple on Mt. Zion, which became its "resting place" (vv. 8, 13-14).

Elsewhere in the Psalms, the terms "tent" (15:1; 27:4-6) and "tabernacle" (26:8; 43:3; 74:7; 84:1 [2]) are poetic descriptions for the temple or Mt. Zion, and Ps 46:4 [5] may speak of Jerusalem itself as "the holy tabernacle of the Most High." In these passages the word "tabernacle" is essentially a nominal form of the verb שָׁכַן, and, apart from Ps 78:60, it does not refer to Israel's tent sanctuaries. The term "tent" depicts the temple as a place of divine protection (cf. Ps 61:4), recalling the ancient function of sacred areas — including the tent sanctuaries — as places of asylum (e.g., 1 Kgs 1:50; 2:28).[42]

Many, if not all, of these texts probably originated prior to the exile. Most were probably used in connection with temple worship and some were almost certainly temple liturgies.[43] The terms "tent" and "tabernacle" did not become major metaphors in the Psalms. The occasional references to God's tent, however, do suggest that the temple was understood to be the successor to the ancient tent sanctuaries, and that the memory of Israel's tent sanctuaries was kept alive in part through liturgical activity in the temple.[44]

EZEKIEL

Like the psalms, the prophet Ezekiel envisioned God's tabernacle as a temple. The prophet knew a form of the Holiness Code (cf. Leviticus 17-26) which promised that God would establish his tabernacle in Israel as a mark of divine blessing (cf. Lev 26:11). Ezekiel's version of the promise appears in a vision of the future, when the northern and southern kingdoms would be reunited and the people would dwell in the land under God's covenant and Davidic leadership forever. God promised that at that time,

> My tabernacle shall be with them, and I will be their God and they shall be my people. Then the nations will know that I the Lord sanctify Israel, when my sanctuary is in the midst of them for evermore (Ezek 37:27-28).

----

[41] On the tabernacle in Psalm 132 see T. Fretheim, "Psalm 132: A Form Critical Study," *JBL* 86 (1967) 289-300; Cross, *Canaanite Myth,* 94-95, 233, 244-45.

[42] See H.-J. Kraus, *Psalmen* (BKAT 15; 5th ed.; Neukirchen-Vluyn: Neukirchener, 1978) 1.255, 360, 367; Koch, *TDOT* 1.127.

[43] The exceptions to the preexilic dating are Psalm 74 (exilic) and Psalm 78 (possibly postexilic). On the dates and connections to the temple see the sections on "Ort" for each psalm in Kraus, *Psalmen.*

[44] Kraus, *Psalmen,* 1.255, 367; Koch, *TDOT* 1.127.

The sanctuary that Ezekiel later described was not a small, mobile shrine, as in the priestly material, but a massive temple complex which resembled a city (40:2). Nevertheless, this sanctuary could be called a "tabernacle" (מִשְׁכָּן) because in it God would dwell (שָׁכַן) with Israel forever (43:7).[45]

In the first part of his book, the prophet described how Israel had fallen prey to idolatry and how, in response, God removed his glory from the temple (chaps. 8–11). The final chapters, however, offer hope that with the appearance of the tabernacle-temple, God would reverse his judgment and dwell with his people forever out of faithfulness to his own promises (20:40–44; 37:26–27; 43:7).[46] Through this new sanctuary, the nations would recognize that God himself sanctifies Israel, that they might be his holy people.

Ezekiel was a priest who had been exiled to Babylonia. His visions concerning the restored tabernacle-temple come from the period after the destruction of the first temple.[47] His work is roughly contemporary with that of the priestly writer, who also knew a form of the Holiness Code. The promise that God would reverse his judgment by placing Israel permanently in the land and that he himself would forever tabernacle with them would give hope to the exiles. The vision of the new sanctuary in chaps. 40–48 does translate the promise into a detailed program of restoration.[48] Yet Ezekiel expected God himself to be the agent of restoration, and there is little evidence that any group within Israel attempted to put Ezekiel's vision into practice. The impact of the tabernacle imagery is in its ability to inspire hope in the faithfulness of God.[49]

D. The Tabernacle in the LXX

The translation of the Bible into Greek, beginning in the third century B.C., opened up new ways of interpreting the tabernacle material.[50] The description of the tabernacle remained essentially the same as in the MT,

---

[45] The MT text calls a portion of the nave of the temple a "tent" (41:1). This reading does not appear in the LXX and initially may have been a scribal error. The reading gained currency, however, and the translators of the Vulgate, Peshitta, and *Tg. Jonathan* rendered it "tabernacle," perhaps implying that Ezekiel's temple was the successor to the Mosaic tabernacle. See W. Zimmerli, *Ezekiel 2* (Hermeneia; Philadelphia: Fortress, 1983) 342.

[46] W. Zimmerli, *Ezekiel 2,* 276–77, 327–28; W. Eichrodt, *Ezekiel: A Commentary* (OTL; Philadelphia: Westminster, 1970) 514–15; Clements, *God and Temple,* 104–7.

[47] On the date of 37:27 see Zimmerli, *Ezekiel 2,* 272.

[48] On Ezekiel 40–48 as a program of restoration see Clements, *God and Temple,* 106; and M. Greenberg, "The Design and Themes of Ezekiel's Program of Restoration," *Int* 38 (1984) 181–208.

[49] See Zimmerli, *Ezekiel 2,* 327–28.

[50] On σκηνή in the LXX see Michaelis, *TDNT* 7.369–73.

although the LXX sometimes discusses the furnishings in a different order, omits items in some passages, abbreviates material, and occasionally adds details that are not in the MT.[51] But more important for our purposes, the LXX used the term σκηνή for the tent of meeting (e.g., Exod 40:22; Lev 1:1; Num 1:1) and the tabernacle (e.g., Exod 40:5, 22; Num 1:50), as well as for "booth" (סֻכָּה), as in the "booth of David" (Amos 9:11) and "Sikkuth" (סִכּוּת), which was the name of an idol (5:26). Thus σκηνή provided potential connections between passages that were not possible in Hebrew, but would become important for the author of Acts. The Psalms call God's tabernacle a σκηνή (Ps 26:5–6) and a σκήνωμα (14:1; 25:8; 42:3; 60:5; 73:7; 83:2; 131:5, 7). Since σκήνωμα came to designate the human body,[52] it would enable the Fourth Evangelist to use tabernacle imagery for the incarnate logos. Finally, the LXX identified the tent of meeting in Exod 33:7 as Moses' own tent, which explained how a tent of meeting could exist since the tabernacle had not yet been constructed. This interpretation would appear in Philo's exegesis and would be adopted by many later interpreters.

E. CONCLUSION

The OT portrait of the tabernacle is a variegated one, comprised of texts and traditions that stem from different contexts and exhibit varying theological interests. Several characteristics, however, do appear in the present form of most narratives. (1) The tabernacle was a place of revelation, where God appeared in a cloud or by sacred lot at the tent door (Exod 33:9; Josh 19:51), in a voice from above the ark in the holy of holies (Exod 25:22), or in a dream (2 Chron 1:6–13). (2) Sacrifices were offered at the tabernacle, securing atonement and making it possible for Israel to live in holiness (e.g., Exod 29:38–46; Leviticus 16; Josh 22:19–29; 1 Chron 16:1). Sacrifices were also made at the tent David erected for the ark (2 Sam 6:17; 1 Chron 16:39–40), and are mentioned in connection with the tent imagery in the Psalms (Ps 27:6). (3) God's presence in the tabernacle shows his faithfulness to his covenant promises (e.g., Exod 25:8; Lev 26:11; Ezek 37:27; cf. Josh 18:1; 2 Sam 7:6; 1 Chron 17:5).

Distinctive theological emphases appear in individual blocks of material. In the oldest Pentateuchal traditions, the theophany at the tent of meeting reproduced the Sinai theophany. The priestly material indicated that through the tabernacle, Israel worshiped the God who created the world and

---

[51] See the detailed discussion in D. W. Gooding, *The Account of the Tabernacle: Translation and Textual Problems of the Greek Exodus* (Texts and Studies 6; Cambridge: University, 1959).

[52] On σκήνωμα as the body see, e.g., 2 Pet 1:13–14; *Par. Jer.* 6:6–7. The use of σκήνωμα for the temple also appears in 1 Esdr 1:48 and Jdt 9:8.

the sabbath, and who was not confined to one location. The present form of the pentateuchal narrative depicts the construction of the tabernacle as the counterpart to the apostasy Israel committed by fabricating the golden calf. In the present form of the DtH, the tabernacle foreshadows the construction of the house for God's name, which would be built when Israel had been given rest from its enemies, and Nathan's oracle ensured that the temple would be an expression of the divine will, not human presumption. According to the Chronicler, the actual Mosaic tabernacle existed until the temple was built, manifesting the continuity in Israel's worship. The Psalms sometimes use the word "tent" to designate the temple as a place of asylum. For Ezekiel, the establishment of God's tabernacle would be the counterpart to Israel's apostasy, as in the Pentateuch, and would be accompanied by Israel's restoration in the land forever.

The temple is regarded as the legitimate successor to the tabernacle throughout the present form of the OT. 1 Kings 8 and 2 Chronicles 5 say that the tent of meeting was brought to the temple at the time of dedication, and the Chronicler, Psalms, and Ezekiel use the terms "tent" or "tabernacle" for a temple. Traces of anti-temple sentiment appear in Nathan's oracle, but according to the present form of the material, the proscription against the temple was temporary and Solomon's temple was the legitimate successor to the tent sanctuaries. The priestly writer may have attempted to correct certain ideas associated with the temple, since he describes a sanctuary that was designed by God and built by free will offerings, unlike Solomon's temple which was a royal project that utilized forced labor, and he indicates that God "met" with Israel at the tent, but was not confined there. Yet the priestly account does anticipate the reconstruction of the temple by insisting that Israel have a central sanctuary, which would include features of the temple, and in which God would dwell permanently.

These texts and traditions were shaped in various contexts from the wilderness period until after the exile. Nevertheless, traditions concerning Israel's tent sanctuaries did play similar roles in different settings. First, God's tabernacle was associated with programs of restoration in the priestly material and Ezekiel, which stem from the exilic period. Neither program was fully carried out, but certain features of the priestly tabernacle — such as the veil between the holy of holies and forecourt, and the single lampstand — were incorporated into the postexilic temple, and some of the priestly material was utilized by the Chronicler.

Second, the tabernacle provided continuity with the past during times of transition. In the earliest tradition, which probably stems from the wilderness period, the tent of meeting provided the means by which God continued to speak to Israel after the departure from Sinai. When David established Jerusalem as a new center of worship, he constructed a tent there, showing the continuity between the new site and Israel's ancient sanctuary traditions. After the destruction of the first temple and the deportation of many of the people, the priestly writer drew on the ancient tent tradition to provide assurance that Israel's worship was not confined to one locale. The references to the tabernacle in the present form of the DtH may stem from the same period, and they demonstrate the continuity in Israel's worship during major periods of change: the beginnings of settled life in the land (Josh 18:1) and the construction of the first temple (2 Samuel 7; 1 Kgs 8:4). After the exile, the Chronicler drew on the tabernacle tradition to demonstrate the continuity between Israel's ancient sanctuaries and the Jerusalem temple, which was the sanctuary of his own time, and whose worship differed from that of earlier periods.

Third, references to the tabernacle also were intended to foster unity in Israel. In the priestly material, the tabernacle stood at the very center of the Israelite camp. The DtH says that the tabernacle was first set up in Canaan by "the whole congregation of the people of Israel" (Josh 18:1) and that it was to be Israel's sole sanctuary (22:19–29). David established a tent shrine in Jerusalem in order to secure public support for the city as a center of worship as well as political administration (2 Sam 6:17), and Nathan's oracle recalled how God had moved about "with all the people of Israel" by means of the tent sanctuaries (2 Sam 7:6–7). The Chronicler described how the tabernacle and the Levites who once carried it were incorporated into the temple, in order to demonstrate the unifying character of the sanctuary in Jerusalem (1 Chron 6:32–48; 23:25–32; 2 Chron 5:5; cf. 7:3). Finally, the hope for unity is turned toward the future in Ezekiel, who associates the reappearance of God's tabernacle with the reunification of the northern and southern kingdoms (Ezek 37:15–28).

III

JEWISH LITERATURE
200 B.C.-A.D. 150

During the period between the latest OT texts and the NT, the tabernacle continued to appear in Jewish writings. Many of these texts develop views of the tabernacle that were already present in the OT, and some introduce new perspectives. A survey of this literature in its own right helps to establish a context for the interpretation of the NT by sketching out the diverse ways in which the tabernacle was perceived during this period.

A. Pre-Maccabean Sources

By 200 B.C. the ancient tent of meeting had long ceased to exist. Nevertheless, the scriptures kept the memory of the tabernacle alive and provided basic information about it for people of the period. The authors of Tobit and Sirach drew their tabernacle imagery from different portions of the scriptures and developed it in light of the dominant Jewish institutions of their own time: the temple and the Mosaic law.

Tobit

Tobit is a Jewish tale that is set during the Babylonian exile, but probably reached its present form in the late third to early second century B.C.[1] In 13:10 Tobit urges readers to,

> Praise the King of the Ages, that his tabernacle may be raised for you again with joy.

---

[1] On dating see G. W. E. Nickelsburg, *Jewish Literature Between the Bible and the Mishnah* (Philadelphia: Fortress, 1981) 93; E. Schürer, G. Vermes, and M. Black, *The History of the Jewish People in the Age of Jesus Christ* (rev. ed.; Edinburgh: Clark, 1973–1987) 3.223–24.

The context is Tobit's prayer of rejoicing, a hymn that anticipates a return from exile (13:1-8) and the rebuilding of Jerusalem (13:9-18). Like other prayers of this type, Tobit 13 is a mosaic of biblical passages and conveys an attitude of dependence on God's power.[2] The prayer may have originated independently of the rest of Tobit. Unlike the book's other prayers,[3] chap. 13 makes no reference to specific events or characters in the story. The first twelve chapters emphasize God's mercy toward individuals (11:15), but chap. 13 envisions the deliverance of all Israel. The themes of return from exile and the rebuilding of Jerusalem are prominent in chap. 13, but receive little treatment in chaps. 1-12. Nevertheless, the prayer has been well integrated into its present context. The exhortations to "confess" God's power in 12:6-7, 20, 22 anticipate chap. 13. The themes of return, rebuilding Jerusalem and its temple, and the conversion of the Gentiles bind chap. 13 to 14:5-7 and suggest that the two passages should be read together.[4]

The glowing description of the tabernacle and new Jerusalem in chap. 13 anticipates the erection of the glorious "house of God," which would be built (οἰκοδομέω, 13:11; 14:5) "when the times of the age are completed," as the prophets foretold (14:5b). The book shows disappointment over the quality of the postexilic temple (14:5a) and viewed almsgiving as virtually equivalent to sacrifice (4:11; 12:9; 14:10-11). Yet the temple remained an integral part of the future hopes expressed in this passage. The Psalms sometimes called the Jerusalem temple God's "tent" or "tabernacle" (e.g., Ps 26:8; 27:4-6). Tobit recast this imagery in anticipation of the establishment of a new sanctuary in a new era.

SIRACH

Ben Sira (ca. 180 B.C.) uses tabernacle imagery in a poem in praise of wisdom (Sirach 24). After a brief introduction (24:1-2), personified wisdom speaks in the first person,[5] recounting her search for a resting place. Her account weaves together motifs from the biblical narratives of creation and the wilderness wanderings. In v. 3, wisdom says that she "came forth from the mouth of the Most High and covered the earth like a mist," echoing Gen

---

[2] Tob 13:2//Deut 32:39; Tob 13:4//Isa 63:16 and 64:8; Tob 13:5-6//Deut 30:2-3; Tob 13:14//Ps 122:6; Tob 13:16-18//Isa 54:11-12. A similar prayer appears in Judith 16. On the characteristics of these prayers see R. E. Brown, *The Birth of the Messiah: A Commentary on the Infancy Narratives in Matthew and Luke* (Garden City: Doubleday, 1979) 349.

[3] Tob 3:2-6, 11-15; 8:5-7, 15-17; 11:14-15; cf. Jdt 16:2-17.

[4] Since fragments of chaps. 13 and 14 were found among the Dead Sea Scrolls, both must have been included in the book from an early period. See Schürer et al., *History*, 3.224-25.

[5] Cf. Proverbs 8-9.

1:2; 2:6.[6] Then in v. 4 she says, "I pitched my tent" or "encamped" (κατεσκήνωσα) in the heights, recalling Israel's sojourn in the desert.[7] Next she says that her throne was in "a pillar of cloud," an expression which consistently refers to the wilderness period.[8] Wisdom journeyed through heaven and earth until the Creator "brought her tent to rest" (κατέπαυσεν τὴν σκηνήν, v. 8) and commanded her to "pitch her tent" (κατασκήνωσον) in Jacob. There, in Zion, the wisdom which traversed the entire universe (vv. 5–6) and which endures forever (v. 9) served as a priestess (ἐλειτούργησα) in the holy tabernacle (v. 10).

Once established in Zion, wisdom takes root and bears abundant fruit reminiscent of Eden (vv. 13–17) in a land watered by the four rivers of paradise (vv. 25–27; Gen 2:11–14) as well as by the Jordan and the Nile.[9] Among the fruits in wisdom's garden are the fragrances used for the tabernacle's incense: myrrh, cassia, galbanum, onycha, stacte, and frankincense (Exod 30:23–24, 34). Wisdom appears as both the priest and the incense that is offered "in the tabernacle" (Sir 24:15b).[10] Ben Sira does not depict the original Eden, but a paradise that stems from wisdom's residence and ministry in Jerusalem's tabernacle. Wisdom's waters also resemble the rivers which, according to prophetic visions of the new age, would gush from the temple (Ezek 47:1; Joel 3:18b; cf. Zech 14:8; Ps 46:4).

Yet for Ben Sira, wisdom's tabernacle was primarily the Mosaic law, rather than the present or future temple, and therefore he expected wisdom's waters to be poured out through instruction (24:33). After describing wisdom's activity he said, "All this is the book of the covenant of the Most High God, the law which Moses commanded us" (24:23). He patterned chap. 24 after the law, beginning with Genesis 1–2 (Sir 24:3) and concluding with Deut 33:4 (Sir 24:23). Ben Sira respected the temple cult (7:29–31) and even sought wisdom there (51:13–14). But he supported the cult because it was mandated by the *law* (35:5), which was becoming an equivalent to the cult for him (3:3, 30; 35:1–3; cf. Tob 4:11).

Ben Sira wrote at a time when Hellenism was becoming felt in Palestine.

---

[6] On the imagery see esp. G. T. Sheppard, *Wisdom as a Hermeneutical Construct: A Study in the Sapientializing of the Old Testament* (BZAW 151; Berlin: de Gruyter, 1980) 21–26.

[7] The verb probably translates either the Hebrew חנה (Exod 13:20; 15:27; 19:2; Num 33:5–49) or נטה אהל (Exod 33:7). See Sheppard's reconstruction of the original Hebrew text (*Wisdom*, 27–30).

[8] Cf. Exod 13:21; 33:9–10; Num 12:5; 14:14; Deut 31:15; Ps 99:7.

[9] The Greek has φῶς (light). The translator probably read אור (light) for יאור (Nile). See the comments by G. H. Box and W. O. E. Oesterley in *APOT* 1.399.

[10] The words "in the tabernacle" appear in the Greek, but not in the Syriac or Latin. Sheppard provides a detailed comparison of Sir 24:15 with Exod 30:23, 34 (*Wisdom*, 57–58).

Although his work has sometimes been considered to be an attack on Hellenism, George Nickelsburg has rightly observed that "the book is striking for its lack of specific, pointed, and explicit polemics against Hellenism."[11] Ben Sira recognized that wisdom had gained a possession among every people and nation (Sir 24:6), but he insisted that universal wisdom should be *sought* in the law of Moses. It was the person trained in the law who could discern the good and evil that existed outside Israel (39:4). Accordingly, the book could help diaspora Jews live according to the law and present the tradition to "outsiders" (prologue to Sirach).

SUMMARY

The tabernacle imagery in Tobit and Sirach has roots in different portions of scripture. The Psalms, like Tobit, sometimes call the temple a tabernacle or tent; Ben Sira's imagery stems from the "Book of the Covenant" or Pentateuch. Each author interpreted the tabernacle in terms of the dominant Jewish institutions of his own time. Tobit called the temple of the new age a tabernacle and Ben Sira used tabernacle imagery to describe wisdom's presence in the Mosaic law. In each passage the tabernacle imagery helps to convey a vision of renewal for God's people.

B. THE DEAD SEA SCROLLS

The Dead Sea scrolls include texts of diverse origins. Some texts, like the fragments of Tobit and Sirach, originated outside the Dead Sea sect, but were copied by members of the group. Other works, like the Community Rule and War Rule, were probably composed by members of the Dead Sea sect. In this section we will discuss texts that are preserved only in the Dead Sea library, recognizing that not all of these texts may have been composed within the Qumran community. Although none of the published scrolls mentions the Israelite tent of meeting, several do refer to God's tabernacle or tent, or mention tabernacle furnishings like the ark and veil.

THE TEMPLE SCROLL

One of the most intriguing sources of tabernacle imagery within the Dead Sea library is the Temple Scroll (11QTem).[12] This scroll describes a

---

[11] *Jewish Literature,* 64. On the interpretation of Sirach as a polemic, see M. Hengel, *Judaism and Hellenism: Studies in their Encounter in Palestine during the Early Hellenistic Period* (Philadelphia: Fortress, 1974) 1.138.

[12] Y. Yadin, the editor of the scroll, believed that the scroll was composed during the reign of John Hyrcanus (134–104 B.C.), but older, unpublished fragments of the same document or one of its sources now push the date of composition back to at least 150 B.C. See B. Z.

sanctuary in which God would make his name or glory to dwell (שׁכן)[13] prior to the "Day of Blessing," when God himself would create a temple for all times (xxix 8–10).

Although this sanctuary is never called a tabernacle, Yigael Yadin has argued that the biblical prescriptions for the tabernacle provided a model for both the content and the style of the Temple Scroll.[14] In Exod 25:9, for example, God uses the first person singular to give prescriptions for the tabernacle: "According to all that *I* show you . . . so you shall make it." The author of the Temple Scroll imitated the same first person style.[15] Some of the scroll's sanctuary furnishings do correspond to those of the tabernacle, but many of its features have no biblical precedent. The chart on the following pages compares the sanctuary in 11QTem with other Jewish temples.[16]

The furnishings of the Temple Scroll's sanctuary seem to include those of the tabernacle and the postexilic temple. All three sanctuaries have a single lampstand, incense altar, table, and probably a veil and screen. The Temple Scroll and the tabernacle have the ark, mercy seat, cherubim, bronze altar, and laver, while the Temple Scroll and the postexilic temple have the twenty by twenty cubit stone altar and a sanctuary that is sixty cubits high. The furnishings in the Temple Scroll parallel those of Solomon's temple only when both correspond to the tabernacle. The scroll has no apparent connection with the furnishings of Ezekiel's temple.

The architecture of the sanctuary does not resemble that of the tabernacle and has only indirect affinities with other biblical sanctuaries. Extant descriptions of the postexilic temple are too sketchy to permit comparison

---

Wacholder, *The Dawn of Qumran: The Sectarian Torah and the Teacher of Righteousness* (Cincinnati: Hebrew Union College, 1983) 205–6. M. Hengel, J. H. Charlesworth, and D. Mendels ("The Polemical Character of 'On Kingship' in the Temple Scroll: An Attempt at Dating 11QTemple," *JJS* 37 [1987] 28–38) argue that the section on kingship must be dated between 103 and 88 B.C., but they acknowledge that large portions of the scroll may be older, perhaps from the mid-second century B.C.

[13] 11QTem xxix 3, 7–8; xlv 12–14; xlvii 4; liii 9–10; lvi 5.

[14] *The Temple Scroll* (Jerusalem: Israel Exploration Society, 1983) 1.178.

[15] *Temple Scroll,* 1.71–73. This phenomenon appears consistently throughout the prescriptions for the sanctuary. See A. M. Wilson and L. Wills, "Literary Sources of the Temple Scroll," *HTR* 75 (1982) 275–88.

[16] Abbreviations in the chart include Chr for Chronicles, *Ap.* for Josephus's *Against Apion,* and cu. for cubit. Only one biblical citation is given for each item, even though an item is mentioned in several passages. On the veil and screen: 1 Macc 4:51 refers to the temple καταπετάσματα suggesting that the postexilic temple had both an inner veil and outer screen. On the altar: Yadin suggests a 20 x 20 cu. measurement for the altar by restoring רים . . . to עשרים, but does not include the word "twenty" in his translation (*Temple Scroll,* 2.48). On the dimensions of the courts in 11QTem, see Yadin, *Temple Scroll,* 1.204, 242, 251. On the structures in the inner court see Yadin, *Temple Scroll,* 1.210–41.

CHART 1

Furnishings	Temple Scroll	Tabernacle in Exodus	Solomon's Temple in 1 Kings	Solomon's Temple in Chronicles	Ezekiel	Postexilic Temple
ark	vii 12 (iii 8–9)	25:10	6:19	1 Chr 28:18		
mercy seat	iii 8; vii 9	25:17		1 Chr 28:11		
cherubim	vii 10	25:18	6:23	1 Chr 28:18		
lampstand	one iii 13 (ix 3, 11, 12)	one 25:31	ten 7:38	ten 2 Chr 4:7	(cf. 41:17–20)	one Ap. 1.198; 1 Macc 1:21; 4:49
table	one iii 10 (viii 10–14)	one 25:23	one 7:48	ten 2 Chr 4:8	(cf. 41:22 table = altar of wood)	one 1 Macc 1:22;
golden incense altar	viii 11 (iii 10)	30:1–3	7:48	1 Chr 28:18		1 Macc 1:21; 4:49; Ap. 1.198
veil	vii 13–14 golden	26:31 blue, purple, scarlet, linen		2 Chr 3:14 blue, purple, scarlet, linen		1 Macc 1:22; 4:51; Sir 50:5
screen	(x 10–14) red, scarlet, purple (cf. blue, purple, iii 2)	26:36 blue, purple, scarlet, linen				Ep. Arist. 86 (1 Macc 4:51)
bronze altar	iii 14–15	27:1–2	8:64		(cf. 9:2)	
laver	one xxxi 10	one 30:18	ten 7:38 (cf. 2 Kgs 16:10–14)	ten 2 Chr 4:6	(cf. 43:13–17)	1 Macc 4:47
stone altar—	xii 11					
20 x 20 cu.	xii 9					Ap. 1.198

CHART 1 (continued)

	Temple Scroll	Tabernacle in Exodus	Solomon's Temple in 1 Kings	Solomon's Temple in Chronicles	Ezekiel	Postexilic Temple
Dimensions	iv 9–10	26:15–25	6:2–3	2 Chr 3:3–4		Ezra 6:3
height	(60 cu.)	10 cu.	30 cu.	120 cu.		60 cu.
width		10 cu.	20 cu.	20 cu.		60 cu.
length		30 cu.	60 cu.	60 cu.		
vestibule depth	(10 cu.)		10 cu.	10 cu.		
Architecture						
vestibule/אולם	iv 8		6:3 (cf. 6:5, 10, יציע)	2 Chr 3:4	40:7–9	
protrusions/ מוצאים	iv 2					
terraces/ דרכם	iv 4		(cf 6:8)			
upper story/ עלייה	single vi 6; cf. xxxi 6			multiple 1 Chr 28:11		

CHART 1 (continued)

	Temple Scroll	Tabernacle in Exodus	Solomon's Temple in 1 Kings	Solomon's Temple in Chronicles	Ezekiel	Postexilic Temple
Courts		27:9–13	7:12	2 Chr 4:9	40:47; 42:20	
number	3	1	2	2	2	
shape	square	rectangular			square	
dimensions						
inner court	280 x 280 cu.	50 x 100 cu.			100 x 100 cu.	
middle court	480 x 480 cu.					
outer court	1600 x 1600 cu.				500 x 500	
Structures in Inner Court						
slaughterhouse with 12 pillars	xxxv 15	(cf. Exod 24:4)				
house for laver	xxxi 10					
house for utensils	xxxiii 8					
house for staircase	xxx 3–xxxi 9					
Stoa/פרבר	xxxv 10–15			(cf. פרבר) 1 Chr 26:18	(cf. 46:19–20)	

with the architecture of the Temple Scroll's sanctuary. The Temple Scroll and the biblical sanctuaries include a vestibule, but only 11QTem has רובדים ("terraces"). There may be an indirect connection between the פרבר (meaning uncertain) in 1 Chron 26:18 and the scroll's פרור ("stoa"), and between the Chronicler's multiple עליית ("upper stories") and the scroll's single עליה.[17] There is at most an indirect link between the arrangement, dimensions, and structures of the scroll's courts, and biblical precedents. Although the author created an ideal inner sanctuary by combining features of the tabernacle and the postexilic temple, the court system is his own design.

Yadin discerns a more intricate relationship between the Temple Scroll's sanctuary and biblical precedents than that suggested above. He finds instances where the author "relied on descriptions of the tabernacle for most of his data, adjusting them to the descriptions of Solomon's temple, whose dimensions were different."[18] For example, the scroll's fragmentary fourth column gives a measurement of "twenty cubits square" (iv 13), which could correspond to the dimensions of Solomon's holy of holies (1 Kgs 6:20). Col. vii apparently discusses items found in the holy of holies and mentions שמנים לו . . . (vii 5), which Yadin restores as "eighty boards" (לוחות). Yadin combines iv 13 and vii 5, contending that the scroll described a twenty by twenty cubit holy of holies, like that of Solomon's temple, which was paneled with eighty or eighty-two boards, each ten cubits long and one and a half cubits wide, like those of the tabernacle (Exod 26:16).[19]

Yet Yadin's proposal seems implausible for several reasons. (1) There is no reason to assume that the author intricately tried to correlate data from the tabernacle and Solomon's temple, since the author frequently departed from biblical precedents, as noted above. (2) If the author had tried to harmonize the tabernacle and first temple, we would expect him to use the term קרשים (Exod 26:15–29) or צלעות (1 Kgs 6:15–16), not לוחות.[20] (3) The most natural restoration of לוחות הע . . . (11QTem vii 3) is לוחות העדות,

---

[17] Yadin believed that 1 Chronicles 28 provided a pattern for architecture in 11QTem (*Temple Scroll*, 1.82–83). Both do mention the אולם (vestibule), various בתים (houses), and חצרות (courts). But 11QTem does not mention the אצרות קדשים (storehouses for the dedicated gifts), אצרות בית האלהים (storehouses of the house of God), גנוכים (treasuries), מרכבה (chariot), or the לשכות (chambers), all of which appear in 1 Chron 28:11–19. There is not a close correlation between these two texts.

[18] *Temple Scroll*, 1.180.

[19] Detailed discussion in *Temple Scroll*, 2.28–29.

[20] לוחות refers to boards in Exod 27:8; 38:7; 1 Kgs 7:36; Cant 8:9, and Ezek 27:5. In the other twenty-five biblical occurrences it indicates a writing surface, especially the tablets of the law. Rabbinic sources most frequently use לוחות for the tables of the law and occasionally for a writing surface (e.g., *m. Šabb.* 12:4). When referring to the boards of the tabernacle, rabbinic texts use קרשים (*b. Šabb.* 102b; *Exod. Rab.* 52; *m. Šabb.* 12:3).

"tablets of the testimony," as Yadin points out.[21] Yet he rejects this reading, insisting that the ark and its tablets are not discussed here. But since the ark is used as a reference point in vii 12 and probably in vii 9, we can assume that the ark and perhaps its tablets *are* mentioned in our passage. If 11QTem vii 5 does refer to eighty לוחות, their function is unknown; they do not establish a link between the tabernacle and Solomon's holy of holies.[22]

Yadin also maintains that the pattern of the Temple Scroll's sanctuary and courts "is based on the design of the camp of Israel, set around the Tabernacle in the wilderness according to the tribes and Levitical families."[23] The arrangement of the priestly families around the sanctuary does seem to follow the order in Numbers 3, as Yadin suggests, with Kohath located at the south (11QTem xliv 14; Num 3:29). Yet the arrangement of the tribes does not follow any biblical precedent.[24]

	Num 2	*Ezek 48*	*11QTem*
East			
	Judah	Joseph	Simeon
	Issachar	Benjamin	Levi
	Zebulun	Dan	Judah
South			
	Reuben	Simeon	Reuben
	Simeon	Issachar	Joseph
	Gad	Zebulun	Benjamin
West			
	Ephraim	Gad	Issachar
	Manasseh	Asher	Zebulun
	Benjamin	Naphtali	Gad
North			
	Dan	Reuben	Dan
	Asher	Judah	Naphtali
	Naphtali	Levi	Asher

---

[21] *Temple Scroll*, 2.25.

[22] Elsewhere Yadin suggests that the stone altar in the Temple Scroll was patterned after Ezekiel's altar, and that the author connected it to the tabernacle altar by using the term יסוד ("base," Lev 4:25) instead of גבול ("rim," Ezek 43:20). *Temple Scroll*, 1.240. But given the major differences between the sanctuaries of Ezekiel and the Temple Scroll, it seems implausible that the author would try to harmonize features from the tabernacle's altar and Ezekiel's altar by a word substitution.

[23] *Temple Scroll*, 1.189.

[24] Yadin discerns ideological factors in this arrangement and also notes that names are arranged by matrilineal relationships (*Temple Scroll*, 1.256, 408–9).

Yadin has rightly shown that 11QTem does apply the *laws* of the wilderness camp to the city of Jerusalem,[25] but the scroll does not adhere to the plans for the tabernacle or to the arrangment of tribes that is found in the Pentateuch.

The author of the Temple Scroll did not intend to recreate the tabernacle or any other biblical sanctuary. The dimensions and furnishings of the inner sanctuary are essentially those of the postexilic temple together with those of the tabernacle, while the design of the outer courts and their furnishings has little biblical precedent. By including the tabernacle furnishings in the sanctuary and by adopting the first person style of the tabernacle prescriptions in Exodus, the author indicated that the sanctuary was to be the legitimate *successor* of the Mosaic tabernacle.

The reasons why this sanctuary was designed remain unclear. Some scholars interpret the text as an Essene polemic against the condition of the Jerusalem temple, since the scroll contains regulations similar to statutes of the Dead Sea sect, and the sanctuary's system of outer courts would serve the sect's interest in ritual purity.[26] Others insist that the evidence is inconclusive and that the scroll should not be considered an Essene composition.[27] If the text is polemical, its attacks are implicit; the opponents are never mentioned, as they are in the Community Rule and Habakkuk Commentary. Moreover, the scroll's design for the temple's outer courts would have served sectarian interests in purity, but they also would have worked admirably for defense, which was a concern of the Hasmonean rulers who periodically *did* fortify the temple's outer courts (1 Macc 4:57–60; 10:11; 13:52). Therefore the scroll may attempt to accommodate at least some of the concerns of the Hasmonean rulers, while advocating reforms in temple practices that would accord with statutes similar to those of the Dead Sea sect.[28]

WORDS OF THE HEAVENLY LIGHTS (4QDibHam)

A reference to God's "tabernacle" appears in a fragment of a liturgical work known as the "Words of the Heavenly Lights." Maurice Baillet, the

[25] *Temple Scroll,* 1.277–320.

[26] E.g., Yadin, *Temple Scroll,* 1.386–99 and 2.4, 7–8, 32–33, 64, 163, 192, 201; J. Milgrom, "Studies in the Temple Scroll," *JBL* 97 (1978) 501–23, esp. 503, 510–11.

[27] E.g., B. A. Levine, "The Temple Scroll: Aspects of its Historical Provenance and Literary Character," *BASOR* 232 (1978) 5–23; L. H. Schiffman, "The Temple Scroll in Literary and Philological Perspective," *Approaches to Ancient Judaism II* (ed. W. S. Green; Chico: Scholars, 1980) 143–58.

[28] One of the innovations envisioned by the scroll, namely a special system of slaughtering, actually was instituted in the temple during the reign of John Hyrcanus. Yadin posits that Hyrcanus's action was prompted by the scroll or the sect which produced it (*Temple Scroll,* 1.388), which suggests that other aspects of the sanctuary may have been designed with the Hasmoneans as well as a sectarian group in mind.

editor of the text, dates extant copies to the mid-second century B.C.[29] The
context of the reference is an idealized description of Jerusalem under the
Davidic monarchy (4QDibHam[a] 1–2 iv 2–12).[30]

> (2) Your tabernacle . . .
> a resting place (3) in Jerusalem,
> the city which you have chosen from all the earth
> (4) that your name might be there forever.

> For you loved (5) Israel above all peoples,
> and you have chosen the tribe of (6) Judah;
> and you have established your covenant with David
> that he might be (7) as a princely shepherd over your people
> and sit upon the throne of Israel before you (8) always.

> All the nations saw your glory,
> (9) who sanctified yourself in the midst of your people Israel
> and to your great name (10) they brought their offering:
> silver and gold and precious stones
> (11) with all the treasures of their lands,
> to glorify your people, and (12) Zion your
> holy city, and your majestic house.

Although the interpetation of the reference to God's tabernacle in line
two is hampered by lacunae in the text, attention to the work's form and use
of the OT can help to elucidate the passage.[31] The work is a prayer that
begins after "Amen, Amen" in i 7 and concludes with the same formula in
vii 2. The poetic parallelism within the text makes it virtually certain that the
word "tabernacle" corresponds to "resting place" (מנוחה) and that both
terms refer to God's presence in Jerusalem.[32] The imagery is well-suited to
the context, which recalls God's election of Jerusalem (iv 2–4a), of Israel and
Judah (iv 4b–6a), and of David (iv 6b–8a).[33]

The only OT passage where משכן and מנוחה are collocated is Psalm
132, which is a liturgical composition, like 4QDibHam. The Psalm recounts

[29] "Un recueil liturgique de Qumrân, Grotte 4: Les paroles des luminaires," *RB* 68 (1961)
195–250; esp. 235–47 on dating.

[30] The English translation is the author's, based on the Hebrew text edited by Baillet in
DJD 7, #504. An English translation of the entire fragment appears in G. Vermes, *The Dead
Sea Scrolls in English* (2d ed.; Middlesex: Penguin, 1975) 202–5.

[31] On the pervasive use of the OT in the work see Baillet, "Un recueil," 247, and his
comments on individual texts on pp. 214–35; cf. DJD 7, pp. 140–51.

[32] Baillet, "Un recueil," 220.

[33] O. H. Steck, *Israel und das gewaltsame Geschick der Propheten: Untersuchung zur
Überlieferung des deuteronomistischen Geschichtsbildes im Alten Testament, Spätjudentum
und Urchristentum* (WMANT 23; Neukirchen-Vluyn: Neukirchener, 1967) 117.

how David brought the ark to its "tabernacle" in Jerusalem, and declares that "the Lord has chosen Zion," which is his "resting place forever" (132:5, 7, 13-14).[34] The designation of Jerusalem as the place for God's name (4QDibHam 1-2 iv 4) was associated with the presence of the temple in the city. According to Chronicles, David wanted to build "a house of rest" (מנוחה) for the ark, but God did not permit him to build "a house for his name" (1 Chron 28:2-3). That privilege was given to Solomon, whose temple did become the place for God's name (1 Kgs 8:16, 44; 2 Chron 6:5-6, 34). Therefore in 4QDibHam, God's choice of Jerusalem for his tabernacle probably anticipates the building of the temple or "majestic house" (1-2 iv 12), although the lacunae make it difficult to determine whether or not the word "tabernacle" actually designated the temple proper.

4QDibHam perceived God's choice of Jerusalem for his tabernacle, together with his election of Israel and his covenant with David, as a mark of divine favor. Throughout the work, the memories of God's past graciousness to Israel provide a basis for petitions for help in the present and the hope of future deliverance.[35]

The prayer was used by the Dead Sea sect, but it contains no elements peculiar to the sect, and it probably originated prior to the founding of the Qumran community.[36] The piece refers to Israel's sin and distress in terms general enough to fit many situations. Significantly, the material closely resembles prayers found in Dan 9:4-19, Bar 1:15-3:8, and other sources. By comparing the common elements in these prayers, Odil Steck has shown that 4QDibHam was part of a living liturgical tradition.[37] Steck's claim that the tradition was part of a covenant renewal ceremony conducted by Levitical groups has been challenged,[38] but his observations, together with those of Baillet, suggest that 4QDibHam may have been known outside the Dead Sea community.

Damascus Document (CD)

An apparent reference to God's "tent" appears in the Damascus Document (CD) vii 12b-20.[39]

---

[34] See Baillet, DJD 7, p. 144.

[35] Steck, *Israel,* 117-18.

[36] Baillet, "Un recueil," 250; cf. K. G. Kuhn, "Nachträge zur *Konkordanz zu den Qumrantexten,*" *RevQ* 4 (1963) 163-234, esp. 168-69.

[37] Steck, *Israel,* 110-36. Cf. M. R. Lehmann ("A Re-interpretation of 4 Q Dibrê Hamme'oroth," *RevQ* 5 [1964] 106-10), who notes similarities between these prayers and the *Tahanun* prayers known from rabbinic sources.

[38] J. J. Collins, *The Apocalyptic Vision of the Book of Daniel* (HSM 16; Missoula: Scholars, 1977) 185-87.

[39] The English translation is the author's, based on the Hebrew text of CD; see C. Rabin,

(12) . . . When the two houses of Israel were divided, (13) Ephraim departed from Judah. And all the apostates were given over to the sword, but those who held fast (14) escaped to the land of the north, as he said, "I will exile the *sikkuth* of your king (15) and the *kiyyun* of your images from my tent [to] Damascus." The books of the Torah are the "booth (16) of the king," as he said, "I will raise up the booth of David which has fallen." The "king" (17) is the community, and the "*kiyyun* of your images" are the books of the prophets (18) whose words Israel despised. The "star" is the interpreter of the Torah (19) who shall come to Damascus, as it is written, "A star shall come forth from Jacob and a sceptre shall rise (20) from Israel." The "sceptre" is the prince of the whole community, and when he comes "he shall smite all the children of Seth."

The passage cites Amos 5:26–27, which, according to the MT, reads "You shall take up Sikkuth your king and Kaiwan your star-god, your images which you made for yourselves. Therefore I will take you into exile beyond Damascus." In CD vii 15, however, the Hebrew expression "from beyond" (מהלאה) becomes "from my tent" (מאהלי) and the name Sikkuth (סכות) is understood as "booth" (סוכת). Thus the CD text reads, "I will exile the booth of your king and the *kiyyun* of your images from my tent [to] Damascus."

In the lines that follow, the author interprets the Amos text, equating the "booth" with the books of the law, the "king" with the congregation, and the "*kiyyun*" with the books of the prophets. He also interprets the word "star" — which appears in the MT of Amos 5:26 but not in the Amos citation found in CD vii — as "the interpreter of the law." The reference to the "star" indicates that the author knew a form of Amos 5:26 like that found in the MT, and suggests that CD vii 15 is the author's own paraphrase of the text. The expression "my tent" is not explicitly interpreted, but was probably understood to be the Jerusalem temple, from which the law had been exiled according to the views of the author of CD.[40]

This brief commentary on Amos appears in ms A of the CD document (CD vii 10–20), but not in ms B. Studies suggest that the Amos passage and

---

The Zadokite Documents (Oxford: Clarendon, 1954). The translation "my tent" was suggested by Rabin (ibid., 28) and was subsequently adopted by most scholars. The expression was taken as a construct form by L. Ginzberg, who translated it "those who tent in Damascus" (*An Unknown Jewish Sect* [New York: Jewish Theological Seminary of America, 1970] 196) and by E. Lohse, who translated it "tents of Damascus" (*Die Texte aus Qumran: Hebräisch und Deutsch* [München: Kösel, 1971] 80–81).

[40] A. S. van der Woude, *Die messianischen Vorstellungen der Gemeinde von Qumrân* (Studia Semitica Neerlandica 3; Assen: van Gorcum, 1957) 50; P. R. Davies, "The Ideology of the Temple in the Damascus Document," *JJS* 33 (1982) 287–301; idem, *The Damascus Covenant: An Interpretation of the Damascus Document* (JSOT Supplement 25; Sheffield: JSOT, 1982) 148.

commentary were added to an earlier form of the document.[41] The material may have been included to reaffirm the conviction that the law and its correct interpretation were preserved by the author's community, not by the temple authorities in Jerusalem. The text may have originated in a Jewish group that was closely related to the Qumran sect and that boycotted the temple,[42] or it may stem from a group that existed prior to the founding of Qumran and that continued to use the temple according to its own interpretation of the law.[43]

Songs of the Sabbath Sacrifice (4QShirShabb)

Two references to a celestial tabernacle appear in a fragmentary work known as the "Songs of the Sabbath Sacrifice" (4QShirShabb). The text has thirteen sections, one for each of the first thirteen sabbaths of the year. The date of its composition is unknown; the oldest extant fragments come from 75–50 B.C.[44]

One of the references to the heavenly tabernacle appears in the fragment 4Q405 20 ii–21–22 7–8.[45]

(7) . . . and exalt Him . . .
the Glory in the tabern[acle of the God of] knowledge.
The cherubim fall before him and bless.
As they rise, the sound of divine stillness (8) [is heard],
and there is a tumult of jubilation as their wings lift up,
the sound of divine [stillnes]s.
The image of the chariot throne do they bless
(which is) above the firmament of the cherubim.

The tabernacle seems to be the place of God, his glory, and his throne-chariot. It is situated above the firmament of the cherubim. The word תבנית refers to the form of the throne chariot as in 1 Chron 28:18, rather than to the pattern of the tabernacle as in Exod 25:9. Elsewhere the תבנית indicates the form of the uppermost heaven (4Q403 1 i 43–44), of the chiefs of the realm spirits (4Q403 1 ii 3), and of breastplates (11QShirShabb 8–7 4). None of these items appears to have an earthly copy.

---

[41] See the summary of the discussion in Davies, *Damascus Covenant,* 145–48.
[42] J. Murphy-O'Connor, "A Literary Analysis of Damascus Document VI,2–VIII,3," *RB* 78 (1971) 210–32; idem, "The Original Text of CD 7:9–8:2 and 19:5–14," *HTR* 64 (1971) 379–86.
[43] Davies, "Ideology," 299–301; idem, *Damascus Covenant,* 148.
[44] C. Newsom, *Songs of the Sabbath Sacrifice: A Critical Edition* (HSS 27; Atlanta: Scholars, 1985) 1–21; J. Strugnell, "The Angelic Liturgy at Qumrân. 4Q Serek Sîrôt 'Ôlat Haššhabāt," *VTSup* 7 (1959) 318–45, esp. 318.
[45] The translation is from Newsom, *Songs,* 306.

The other reference to the tabernacle is found in 4Q403 1 ii 10–16.[46]

(10) . . . And the tabernacle of highest loftiness,
the glory of His kingdom, the debir [. . .]
(11) And He/they consecrate/s the seven lofty holy places.
And there is a voice of blessing from
        the chiefs of His debir [. . .]
(12) And the voice of blessing is glorious in the hearing of
the godlike beings and the councils of
        [. . . (13) voice of] blessing.
And all the crafted furnishings of the debir hasten (to join)
with wondrous psalms in the debi[r . . .] (14) of wonder,
debir to debir with the sound of holy multitudes.
And all their crafted furnishings [. . .]
(15) And the chariots of His debir give praise together,
and their cherubim and thei[r] ophanim bless wondrously
(16) [. . .] the chiefs of the divine structure.
And they praise Him in His holy debir.

If the imagery of this passage is consistent with the previous one, the "highest loftiness" should refer to the uppermost region of heaven, above the firmament of the cherubim. The "tabernacle of highest loftiness" would be a sanctuary in the highest realm of heaven. The words "the glory of his kingdom" seem to stand in apposition to "the tabernacle of highest loftiness"[47] and to characterize this heavenly tabernacle. Since the "kingdom" includes all the heavens (4Q400 2 4) and numerous sanctuaries (4Q405 23 ii 11), the tabernacle seems to be a special locus of divine glory within the heavenly realms, as in 4Q405 20 ii-21-22.

The *debir* also seems to be in apposition to "the tabernacle of highest loftiness." In biblical Hebrew the *debir* is the inner sanctuary or holy of holies in the temple (e.g., 1 Kgs 6:19–23; 2 Chron 5:7, 9). 4QShirShabb depicts the *debir* as a region behind the inner veil, which is the region of the divine presence, the throne chariot, and other "furnishings" (4Q403 1 ii 11–16; 4Q405 15 ii-16 4). Since both the tabernacle and the *debir* contained the throne chariot, (4Q405 20 ii-21-22 7–8), the two terms must be synonyms for the heavenly sanctuary's holy of holies.

The structure of the heavenly sanctuary of 4QShirShabb is difficult to envision, because the text frequently interchanges singular and plural nouns. Lines 10, 11, 13, 15, and 16 of 4Q403 1 ii refer to a single *debir,* but line 11 mentions seven lofty holy places and line 14 speaks of moving from *debir* to

---

    [46] The translation is from Newsom, *Songs,* 229. The expression "is heard" is deleted from line 12, as indicated by the ancient scribe.
    [47] Newsom, *Songs,* 235.

debir, which suggests that there were multiple *debirim.*[48] The author may have envisioned seven heavenly sanctuaries with God's own dwelling place occupying the uppermost position. But in 4QShirShabb we may find "plurals of majesty and even intentional violations of ordinary syntax and meaning in a text which is attempting to communicate the elusive transcendence of heavenly reality."[49]

Despite these difficulties, two things emerge. First, the heavenly tabernacle does not follow the biblical prescriptions for the tabernacle. The heavenly tabernacle seems to be the divine throne room or holy of holies, rather than a sanctuary that included both the holy of holies and its forecourt as in Exodus. The Israelite tabernacle included an ark, lampstand, table and altar, but none of these items is mentioned in extant fragments of the Songs.[50] The heavenly sanctuary did have a curtain or פרכת, as did the Mosaic tabernacle (Exod 26:31) and the temple described in Chronicles (2 Chron 3:14), but the author apparently was interested in it because it was adorned with cherubim, not because it was part of the Mosaic sanctuary.[51]

Second, the heavenly sanctuary was not the model for an earthly shrine. According to Exod 25:9, Moses was to make the tabernacle according to the תבנית that God showed him. But in 4QShirShabb, the word תבנית does not refer to the heavenly pattern of an earthly sanctuary. The "tabernacle" designated God's heavenly dwelling place and was synonymous with the *debir.* The closest biblical usage appears in the canonical Psalms which sometimes refer to the temple as a "tabernacle" or "tent" (Ps 26:8; 27:4–6; 74:7; 84:1[2]).

The Songs were apparently intended to create a sense of being present at worship in the heavenly sanctuary, but the occasion for their composition is unclear. Scholars generally consider the Songs to be products of the Dead Sea sect. John Strugnell has suggested that they were intended to be models for an earthly liturgy that the sect conducted as a replacement for liturgies of the Jerusalem temple.[52] Carol Newsom, however, maintains that this was not the case. She suggests that the Songs produced an experience of being present in the heavenly sanctuary that confirmed the legitimacy of the priesthood at Qumran. Yet she remains uncertain about the actual setting in which the Songs were used.[53]

---

[48] Newsom, *Songs,* 48–51.
[49] Newsom, *Songs,* 49.
[50] See the concordance in Newsom, *Songs,* 389–466.
[51] Newsom, *Songs,* 54.
[52] Strugnell, "Angelic Liturgy," 320.
[53] Newsom, *Songs,* 59, 71–72.

Thanksgiving Hymns

A possible reference to God's "tent" is found in the Thanksgiving Hymns (1QH).[54] A translation of xii 2–3a, based on the *editio princeps,* edited by E. L. Sukenik, reads,

> 2. [I will dwell] safely in the dwelling
>   [in quiet]ness and peace
> 3. . . . his tent . . . . and salvation.

The words "tent" (אהל) and "dwelling" (מעון) seem to be parallel and refer to God's dwelling place. The context establishes no clear connection between God's "tent" and Jerusalem, the temple, or God's heavenly dwelling place. But God's tent is associated with safety, quietness, peace, and salvation. Therefore "dwelling in God's tent" may be a poetic way of referring to life under God's protection. Similar imagery appears in Ps 61:4, "Let me sojourn in your tent forever, let me seek refuge under the shelter of your wings."

A number of interpreters, however, take the final *waw* of אהלו as a *yod.*[55] The reading אהלי could be "my tent," referring to the tent of the author,[56] or it could be a construct plural, referring to "tents of [safety]."[57] In either case the passage would not refer to God's tent. The fragmentary character of the passage makes a firm decision difficult.

Summary

The non-biblical Dead Sea texts published thus far do not use the terms "tent" and "tabernacle" for the Israelite sanctuary of the wilderness period. Instead, they generally understand "tabernacle" in terms of a temple. The Temple Scroll incorporated the tabernacle furnishings into its idealized remodeling of the postexilic temple, which would be the legitimate successor of the Mosaic sanctuary. The Words of the Heavenly Lights used "tabernacle" for the Jerusalem of the monarchic period, which was the site of the

---

[54] The hymns are a collection of works, probably written at different times by different authors, with the extant collection completed by the first century A.D. The Hebrew text printed above is from E. L. Sukenik, ed., *The Dead Sea Scrolls of the Hebrew University* (Jerusalem: Magnes, 1955).

[55] The similarity between *yod* and *waw* is readily apparent in the photograph of 1QH xii (Sukenik, *Dead Sea Scrolls,* pl. 46).

[56] So A. Dupont-Sommer, "Le Livre des Hymnes decouvert près de la mer Morte (1QH)," *Sem* 7 (1957) 1–120, esp. 82; and M. Delcor, *Les Hymnes de Qumran (Hodayot),* (Paris: Letouzey et Ané, 1962) 245.

[57] So J. Licht, מגילת ההודיות (Jerusalem: Bialik, 1957) 172; M. Mansoor, *The Thanksgiving Hymns* (STJD 3; Grand Rapids: Eerdmans, 1961) 172; J. Carmignac and P. Guilbert, *Les Textes de Qumran Traduits et Annotés* (Paris: Letouzey et Ané, 1961) 1.262–63. Cf. Ps 118:15 which refers to the "tents of the righteous."

temple. The word "tabernacle" appears together with references to God's election, and the memories of divine favor provide a basis for petitions for help and the hope of future deliverance. The Damascus Document spoke of the temple as God's "tent." In the Songs of the Sabbath Sacrifice, the word "tabernacle," like the word *debir* used in temple terminology, designated the throne room within the heavenly sanctuary. The Thanksgiving Hymns used the word "tent" somewhat differently, as a poetic expression for divine protection. The tabernacle furnishings mentioned in the Temple Scroll appear in the Pentateuch; precedents for the use of "tabernacle" and "tent" for Jerusalem, a temple, and divine protection appear in the Psalms.[58]

C. Accounts of Israel's History

The Mosaic tabernacle appears in several works that recount portions of Israel's history. These texts draw on similar material from the Pentateuch and Joshua through Kings, but present it in different literary forms: the "Dream Visions" and *Jubilees* purport to be revelations given to Enoch or Moses; the *Testament of Moses* is presented as Moses' last words to Joshua; the *Biblical Antiquities* and the fragment from Eupolemos are apocryphal accounts of events from Israel's past. The dates of composition also vary: the "Dream Visions," *Jubilees,* and the Eupolemos fragment stem from the second century B.C.; the present form of the *Testament of Moses* dates from the early first century A.D.; the *Biblical Antiquities* were written later in the first century. Nevertheless, these texts can be conveniently treated together, since they all survey periods of Israel's history and deal to some extent with the relationship between the tabernacle and the temple.

1 Enoch 83-90: The Dream Visions

1 Enoch is a composite work that includes materials of diverse origin and date. The erection of the tabernacle is mentioned in the "Dream Visions" (chaps. 83-90), which were probably written ca. 164-161 B.C.[59] The entire text has been preserved only in Ethiopic, although some Aramaic fragments

---

[58] The words שכן and אהל are rarely used in connection with God elsewhere in the scrolls. A collection of fragments which Baillet calls the "Prières pour les Fêtes (ii)" (DJD 7, #508) says, "you have dwelt in our midst" (שכנתה בתוכנו, ii 1), referring to God. Baillet suggests that the context is the conclusion of a prayer for the new year and the beginning of a day of atonement liturgy which seems to follow. If this is correct, then ii 1 refers to the dedication of the temple which occurred on the first day of the seventh month, when God appeared in the tabernacle (cf. DJD 7, p. 178). The subject of the verb שכן in "The Ages of Creation" ii 1 (DJD 5, #180) and of "in your tent" in the "Lamentations" ii 3 (DJD 5, #179) is unclear.

[59] Charles, *APOT* 2.170-71; J. T. Milik, *The Books of Enoch: Aramaic Fragments of Qumrân Cave 4* (Oxford: Clarendon, 1976) 44; Nickelsburg, *Jewish Literature,* 93.

have been found among the Dead Sea Scrolls. The second "Dream Vision" (chaps. 85–90) allegorically recounts the history of the world, from Adam and Eve to the end times. The people of Israel appear as sheep and the Gentiles are portrayed as predatory animals and birds.

In 89:32–33, Moses, who is depicted as a sheep, ascends Mt. Sinai. The rest of the sheep become blind and stray from the path, an act which represents the building of the golden calf. God becomes angry and Moses rallies some of the sheep who slay some of the apostate sheep (cf. Exod 32:26–29). The rest of the sheep return to their folds. Then in 89:36, the sheep that represents Moses "became a man and built a house for the Lord of the sheep, and made all the sheep stand in that house."[60] The "house" is the tabernacle, and the context suggests that the tabernacle was, to some extent, a corrective to Israel's apostasy.[61]

Later, the tabernacle or "house" is brought into the promised land (89:40). But the sheep again become blind, are punished by predators, and are finally delivered (89:41–49). Then the "house," which is presumably the tabernacle, "became large and broad, and for those sheep a high tower was built on that house for the Lord of the sheep . . . and the Lord of the sheep stood on that tower, and they spread a full table before him" (89:50). Throughout the rest of the vision the "house" is Jerusalem, the "tower" is the temple, and the "table" is the altar. By playing on the word "house," the Ethiopic version suggests that the "house" of the tabernacle became the "house" of Jerusalem, which in turn was the foundation for the temple. Later, the sheep forsake the house and the tower, and are punished by predators (89:54–55). In time the tower and the house are destroyed, which alludes to the Babylonian conquest (89:66). After the exile, the house and tower are rebuilt, but all the bread that is offered there is unclean, and the sheep that rebuild the tower are blind (89:73–74). Although the author esteemed the first temple, he considered the second temple to be polluted from its inception.

A turning point comes with the Maccabean revolt which immediately preceded the composition of the "Dream Visions." The Maccabean victories usher in the end times, when the Lord of the sheep judges the wicked, "folds up" the "house" of Jerusalem and produces a new house, that is, a new Jerusalem (90:28–29). The Lord is in the midst of the new house (90:29) and

---

[60] English translations are from M. A. Knibb, *The Ethiopic Book of Enoch: A New Edition in the Light of the Aramaic Dead Sea Fragments* (Oxford: Clarendon, 1978) vol. 2. The Ethiopic word for "house" is *beta*. Part of the Aramaic text has been preserved in 4QEn[c] 4, which appears in Milik, *Enoch*, pl. XIV. Part of what may be an initial *mem* is visible in the photograph. Milik restores the text [משכ]מ עבד, "he built a tabernacle" (ibid., 352).

[61] Cf. R. H. Charles, *The Book of Enoch or 1 Enoch* (Oxford: Clarendon, 1912) 194.

the faithful sheep assemble there (90:33–36), but there is no mention of a new temple or "tower" in the city. The author apparently did not expect the resumption of the temple cult in the new age.

Themes of apostasy, punishment, and deliverance run throughout the work.[62] The tabernacle and the new Jerusalem function similarly within this schema. The building of the golden calf and the decadence of the postexilic period were instances of apostasy which God punished by having the faithful slay the apostates (89:32–35; 89:73–90:19). The tabernacle and new Jerusalem were "houses" in which those who remained were gathered (89:36; 90:29–36). Thus the tabernacle is an example of divine favor that provides hope for future deliverance.

JUBILEES

The book of *Jubilees* (mid-second century B.C.)[63] recounts the history of Israel from the creation to the revelation on Mt. Sinai. The work is written on two levels. It is presented as a revelation to Moses, but the message is intended to instruct later generations (1:5). Therefore each time the author mentions the tabernacle, he also mentions the temple or "sanctuary," which would have been the central cultic institution in his own time. In 1:10 God warns that many in Israel will forsake the tabernacle *and* the sanctuary. The work indicates that Israel will never lack a central shrine, since the tabernacle will stand until the temple is erected (49:18). Therefore all generations of Israel are commanded to observe the Passover "before the tabernacle of the Lord or before his house in which his name dwells" (49:21).

The author depicts a firm continuity between the tabernacle and the temple in order to stress that the law is binding upon all generations. The narrative shows that even Adam and Eve, Cain and Abel, Noah and Abraham —all of whom lived before Moses—stood under the law. The author's insistence on the law's abiding authority was occasioned by some Jews adopting Gentile practices like nudity and uncircumcision (3:31; 15:33–34). The apocalypse in chap. 23 indicated that a return to the law would bring in a period of bliss. Although this apocalypse does not mention the sanctuary, the first chapter of *Jubilees* does mention a new creation in which Israel will be obedient, and the building of a new sanctuary in which God will dwell forever (1:24–29). The term "tabernacle" is not used for the future sanctuary; it is reserved for the shrine of the Mosaic period.

---

[62] Cf. Nickelsburg, *Jewish Literature,* 92–93.

[63] On dating see esp. J. C. VanderKam, *Textual and Historical Studies in the Book of Jubilees* (HSM 14; Missoula: Scholars, 1977) 207–85. Cf. Schürer et al., *History,* 3.311–13; Nickelsburg, *Jewish Literature,* 78–79; and O. S. Wintermute in *OTP,* 2.43–44.

EUPOLEMOS

Eupolemos was a Greek-speaking Jewish historian of the mid-second century B.C. The tabernacle and ark appear in two extant fragments of his work,[64] one describing the erection of Solomon's temple and the other recounting the fall of Jerusalem. Eupolemos derived some of his material from Samuel and Kings, but he altered certain details and added extra-biblical material. Two aspects of his work are significant for our purposes.

First, like the book of *Jubilees,* Eupolemos stresses the continuity between the tabernacle and Solomon's temple. Before the temple was built, the tabernacle stood at Shiloh (*P.E.* 9.30.1). Eupolemos anachronistically claims that when David transferred royal authority to Solomon, he did so "in the presence of Eli the high priest" who had served at the Shiloh taber-nacle several generations earlier (9.30.8; cf. 1 Samuel 1-4). The temple that Solomon built bore little resemblance to the tabernacle and its furnishings. But even though Solomon constructed ten sacred lampstands, rather than only one, Eupolemos insists that "he took as his model the lampstand placed by Moses in the tent of meeting" (*P.E.* 9.34.5). When Solomon dedicated the temple he again went to Shiloh and offered sacrifices. Then he "took the tent and the altar of sacrifice and the vessels which Moses had made, and brought them into Jerusalem and placed them in the house. He also placed there the ark and the golden altar and the lampstand and the other vessels . . ." (9.34.12-13).[65] When the temple was destroyed, Jeremiah saved the ark and its tablets, which suggests that these items would provide continuity between the former sanctuaries and a future place of worship.

Second, Eupolemos depicts both the tabernacle and the temple as insti-tutions prescribed by prophetic authority. Moses, Joshua, and Samuel — the predecessors of the monarchy — were all prophets (9.30.1). The prophet Joshua pitched the tabernacle at Shiloh. Eupolemos says that the prophet Nathan[66] commanded David to entrust the building of the temple to Solomon, as in 2 Samuel 7, but he adds that Nathan also prescribed the

---

[64] Both of these fragments were preserved in Eusebius's *Preparation for the Gospel* (*P.E.*). On Eupolemos' life and works see B. Z. Wacholder, *Eupolemos: A Study of Judaeo-Greek Literature* (Cincinnati: Hebrew Union College, 1974) 1-26.

[65] Wacholder argues that only the first group of vessels were of Mosaic origin and that the others were made by Solomon (*Eupolemos,* 212). Yet Wacholder's interpretation is implaus-ible, since the single menorah mentioned in 9.34.13 was made by Moses, not Solomon. J. Freudenthal (*Alexander Polyhistor und die von ihm erhaltenen Reste jüdische und samari-tanischer Geschichtswerke* [Breslau: Skutsch, 1875] 112) pointed out that Eupolemos alluded to two separate movements, since according to scripture the ark and tabernacle were located in two different places (2 Sam 6:2; 1 Kgs 8:3-4).

[66] The text refers to an angel named Διαναθάν, which is probably an error for διὰ Ναθάν. See Freudenthal, *Alexander Polyhistor,* 120-21.

dimensions of the temple (9.34.2). At the dedication, Solomon brought the tabernacle vessels to the temple "as the prophet commanded him" (9.34.13). When the temple was destroyed, the prophet Jeremiah saved the ark and the tablets from Babylonian capture (9.39.5).

Eupolemos's work as a whole mirrors conditions in the second century B.C. and the interests of the Maccabees, for whom Eupolemos probably served as an emissary (1 Macc 8:17; 2 Macc 4:11).[67] His description of the temple probably reflects enthusiasm for the cult in this period; his anachronistic reference to Eli may have been an intentional slight to the priests who had supported the Hellenizing innovations that led to the Maccabean revolt.[68] Eupolemos may have stressed the continuity between the tabernacle and Solomon's temple in order to demonstrate the ancient origins, and therefore the legitimacy, of the Jewish cult.[69] The emphasis on prophetic authority in matters of cult reflects beliefs accommodated by the Maccabees. The wall of the pre-Maccabean sanctuary's inner court was believed to be "the work of the prophets" (1 Macc 9:54) and Maccabean innovations were considered interim measures instituted only until a prophet should appear (4:46; 14:41).

THE TESTAMENT OF MOSES (ASSUMPTION OF MOSES)

The *Testament of Moses* (early first century A.D.)[70] expands on the prophecy of Israel's future apostasy, which was made to Moses in the tent of meeting (Deut 31:14–21; *T. Mos.* 1:5). As the *Testament* begins, Moses appoints Joshua as his successor and as a minister "in the tent of testimony" (*scena testimonii*) with all its holy things" (1:7). Joshua would lead Israel into the land to fulfill the promise that God had made "in the tent" (1:9; 2:1).

Later, the tent of testimony would be moved to Jerusalem. There God would make "a court for his tent and a tower for his sanctuary" (2:4). The Latin is difficult,[71] but the author seems to depict the tabernacle as the

---

[67] On the Maccabean interests in Eupolemos, see M. Hengel, *Judaism and Hellenism*, 1.93–94; and the notes by F. Fallon in *OTP*, 2.866–67.

[68] Wacholder, *Eupolemos*, 151–55.

[69] Elsewhere Eupolemos attempts to show the antiquity of Mosaic teachings and the Jewish people (Eusebius, *H.E.* 6.13.7; *P.E.* 9.25.4).

[70] The extant form dates from the early first century. J. Licht and G. W. E. Nickelsburg argue that an earlier form originated in the second century B.C. See the debates in G. W. E. Nickelsburg, ed., *Studies on the Testament of Moses* (SCS 4; Cambridge: SBL, 1973) 17–30, 33–37. Cf. the discussion in Schürer et. al., *History*, 3.281–83; J. Priest, in *OTP*, 1.920–21.

[71] The MS reads "deus caelestis fecit palam scenae suae et ferrum sanctuarii." The translation above follows R. H. Charles, who emends "palam" to "aulam" and "ferrum" to "turrem." See his *The Assumption of Moses* (London: Black, 1897) 62. His emendation is also adopted by E.-M. Laperrousaz, "Le Testament de Moise," *Sem* 19 (1970) 1–137.

nucleus of the temple cult. Sacrifices would be offered in the sanctuary throughout the time of the monarchy, but during certain periods idols would be set up in the "tent" (*scena*) and in the "house of the Lord" (*domus domini,* 2:8–9). A king from the east would burn the city and the holy temple (*aedes,* 3:2), and carry away the sacred vessels. The *Testament* does not suggest that the vessels would be restored.

The author accepted the validity of both the tabernacle and the first temple, until the temple cult became idolatrous, but he considered the second temple to be wrong from the beginning. He insisted that after the exile the faithful would still lament, "because they will not be able to offer sacrifices to the Lord of their fathers" (4:8).[72] The second temple would be repeatedly polluted by idolatry (5:3) and by leaders who were not true priests (5:5; 6:1). When part of the temple was burned (6:9), time would quickly come to an end.[73] The vision of salvation in *T. Mos.* 10 does not mention a restored cult.

The extant form of the *Testament* was produced by an opponent of the Hasmonean priesthood, shortly after the Romans burned part of the temple and crucified a number of Jewish rebels in 4 B.C. (6:9). The author hoped to encourage those who suffered for their commitment to the Mosaic law by assuring them of future divine help (chaps. 8–10). He depicts the temple as a place of apostasy, but associates the tabernacle with God's covenant promises (1:7–9). These promises were fulfilled under Joshua and provide assurance of divine help in the end times (2:1; 12:13), as do the eschatological secrets that were revealed in the tent of meeting and preserved in the *Testament of Moses* itself.

Pseudo-Philo: The Biblical Antiquities

The *Biblical Antiquities* (first century A.D.)[74] recounts Israel's history from Adam through Saul. The tabernacle is first mentioned as something prescribed by divine command. The author tells how God showed Moses the "likeness" (*similitudo*) and the "pattern" (*exemplar*) of the tabernacle (11:15). Then, when Moses had completed the work, God revealed the prescriptions for the cult from within the tabernacle (13:1–2). The author recounts how Aaron's rod budded within the tabernacle (17:1) and how Joshua took the tabernacle from Gilgal (21:7–8) to Shiloh (22:8–9). The prescribed sacrifices continued to be offered in Shiloh[75] until the Jerusalem

---

[72] See the comments of R. H. Charles (*Assumption,* 15), and those of J. J. Collins and J. A. Goldstein (Nickelsburg, ed., *Studies,* 31, 49–50). Laperrousaz suggests that the verse laments only the poor quality of the second temple ceremonies ("Testament," 117).

[73] He describes events of 4 B.C. See Josephus *J.W.* 2.3.3 #49 and *Ant.* 17.10.2 #261–62.

[74] On dating see D. J. Harrington, *OTP,* 2.299; and Schürer et al., *History,* 3.328–29.

[75] The text says that sacrifices were still offered in Gilgal, which is apparently a mistake,

temple was built and "even unto this day" (22:8–9), which indicates clear continuity between the cults of the tabernacle and the first and second temples.

The *Biblical Antiquities* also includes a unique version of the hidden vessels tradition, which will be discussed more fully below. The tradition appears in an apocryphal story about Kenaz, the father of a judge about whom little is known (Jud 3:9). Kenaz examined each of the tribes to discern its sin.[76] The members of the tribe of Asher confessed that they had taken seven golden idols and jewels from the Amorites, and hidden them on Mt. Shechem (*Bib. Ant.* 25:10). An angel took the seven stones and cast them into the sea. Another angel replaced them with twelve stones of equal brilliance, which were inscribed with the names of the twelve tribes (26:8–11).

Then God commanded Kenaz to place the twelve stones in the ark, where they were to remain until the first temple was built. Then they would be placed upon the two cherubim before God. At the time of the temple's destruction, God would take the stones, along with the tablets of the law and the stones that were on the high priest's breastplate, and store them "in the place from which they were taken in the beginning" (26:13).[77] God was to reveal these and other stones when he visited the earth. Then the stones would provide such brilliant light for the righteous that they would no longer need sun or moon.

This story contains an anti-Samaritan polemic. The reference to the idols that were buried on "Mt. Shechem" (25:10) implicitly counters Samaritan traditions, which claimed that the vessels of the tabernacle were buried on Mt. Gerizim (Jos. *Ant.* 18.4.1 #86–87). The Samaritan tradition will be discussed in detail below. While the *Biblical Antiquities* cannot be taken as a consistently anti-Samaritan work, this story clearly does attack Samaritan claims.[78]

---

since the passage recounts how the cult was established at Shiloh. See C. Perrot and P.-M. Bogaert, *Pseudo-Philon: Les Antiquities Bibliques* (SC 230; Paris: Cerf, 1976) 2.144.

[76] There is an incidental mention of the tabernacle when the tribe of Levi confessed a desire to test the tent of meeting to see "whether or not it is holy" (25:9).

[77] If 26:13 refers to the place from which the *stones* were taken, then the place would be Havilah (25:11), which was associated with Eden (Gen 2:11–12; cf. *2 Bar* 4:6). If the text refers to the place from which the *tablets* of the law were taken, then perhaps Sinai is meant. The reference to a place "where eye has not seen nor has ear heard" (26:13; Isa 64:4) suggests that the exact location is unknown.

[78] See the discussion of the evidence for anti-Samaritan polemics in L. H. Feldman, "Prolegomenon," in M. R. James, *The Biblical Antiquities of Philo* (New York: Ktav, 1971) xxxiv–xxxv.

Summary

Each of the accounts in this section discerned continuity between the tabernacle and the Solomonic temple, but they differed markedly in their perceptions of the second temple. *1 Enoch's* "Dream Visions" recalls the building of the golden calf as an instance of apostasy to which God responded by having the apostates slain and the survivors gathered into his tabernacle or "house." The tabernacle was later transformed into Jerusalem, the site of the temple. The first temple in time became associated with apostasy and the second temple was polluted from its inception. God again responded to the apostasy by having the apostates slain by the Maccabees, and the author expected God again to gather the survivors into his "house," that is, the new Jerusalem. In contrast, the author of *Jubilees* saw clear continuity between the tabernacle and the temple cult of his own day, because the law that prescribed Israel's worship was binding on all generations. Eupolemos also stressed the continuity in Israel's cult, but his concern was to demonstrate the legitimacy of the temple of his own day by showing that it had ancient origins and authorization by the prophets. The views of the *Testament of Moses* resemble those of the "Dream Visions," since the author associated the temple with apostasy and the tabernacle with God's promises, which provided hope for deliverance in the end times. Pseudo-Philo, however, stresses the continuity between the cult of the tabernacle — which was prescribed by the law — and those of the first and second temples.

D. The Hidden Tabernacle and Vessels

The stories of the hidden tabernacle vessels, which appeared in Eupolemos and the *Testament of Moses,* belong to a tradition found in a number of ancient works.[79] Because many of the same elements recur in multiple sources, the common elements are presented in the chart on the next page. All recount how the tabernacle or its vessels were hidden in a cave, rock, or the earth, where they will remain until the end times. Three texts also ascribe a key role to Jeremiah.

Some scholars have posited the literary dependence of the *Paralipomena Jeremiou* on *2 Baruch*[80] and of the *Life of Jeremiah* on 2 Macca-

---

[79] The story has little basis in scripture. Jer 3:16 alludes to the destruction of the ark of the covenant and says that the ark will not be remembered or made again in the future. Jer 27:19-22 indicates that some of the sacred vessels remained in Jerusalem after the Babylonian conquest, but Jeremiah expected them to be taken to Babylon until God restored them to Jerusalem. The scriptures do not suggest that Jeremiah hid the tabernacle or any of its vessels.

[80] E.g., P. Bogaert, *Apocalypse de Baruch* (SC 144; Paris: Cerf, 1969) 1.177–221; M. E. Stone, "Baruch, Rest of the Words of," *EJ* 4 (1971) 276–77; A.-M. Denis, *Introduction aux Pseudepigraphes grecs d'Ancien Testament* (SVTP 1; Leiden: Brill, 1970) 75.

CHART 2

2 Maccabees 2:4–8	Life of Jeremiah 11–19	2 Baruch 6:5–9	Paralipomena of Jeremiah 3:1–9	Pseudo-Philo 26:12–15	Samaritan Tradition Jos *Ant.* 18.85–88
oracle gives command		Baruch watches	Jeremiah asks about the vessels / God gives command	God speaks to Kenaz	
Jeremiah takes the	Jeremiah takes the	angel take the	Jeremiah takes the	God takes the	Moses takes the
tabernacle / ark / incense altar	ark and things in it	mercy seat & tablets / incense altar / 48 stones / priests' clothing / veil and ephod / all the vessels of the tabernacle	the holy vessels of the worship-service	ark, tablets, stones / 12 stones (in ark)	sacred vessels
hides them in cave / which he seals	makes them be to be swallowed in a rock / which he seals with God's name	commits them to earth / earth swallows them	commits them to earth / earth swallows them	stores them	buries them
on Mt. Nebo / in an unknown place	between Mts. Nebo and Hor / in an unknown place			in the place from which they were taken (Havilah?); in an unknown place	on Mt. Gerizim
God will disclose them / after ingathering / (at Jerusalem temple) / Cloud and glory then appear	Aaron and Moses will bring them out / after resurrection and ingathering of refugees / at Mt. Sinai / Cloud and glory now appear over the place	earth will restore them / in the last times	at the ingathering	God will disclose them / when God visits the earth / stones will give light to the just	(prophet like Moses will disclose them / at the ingathering of refugees at Mt. Gerizim)

bees.[81] But differences between these versions make direct literary dependence unlikely. George Nickelsburg observed that (1) an angel hid the vessels according to *2 Baruch,* but Jeremiah did so in the other texts; (2) Jeremiah hid the vessels in response to an oracle in 2 Maccabees and in the *Paralipomena,* but not in the *Life of Jeremiah;* (3) *2 Baruch* does not mention the ingathering as do the other three texts; (4) 2 Maccabees mentions the tabernacle and its furnishings, the *Paralipomena* mentions the vessels, and *2 Baruch* mentions both the furnishings and vessels. The texts probably depended on a common tradition.[82]

The tradition apparently circulated in both written and oral forms. Besides the documents noted already, 2 Macc 2:1, 4 mentions a writing which included a version of the story of the hidden vessels and material similar to that in the Epistle of Jeremiah (2 Macc 2:2; Ep Jer 4–7); 2 Macc 2:13 says that the same stories are included in the Memoirs of Nehemiah, a source that is no longer extant.

2 MACCABEES

The story of Jeremiah and the tabernacle vessels appears in the second of two letters that preface the history of the Maccabean conflict. Both letters purport to have been sent from Jews in Jerusalem to Jews in Egypt, urging them to celebrate the Maccabean purification of the temple on the 25th of Chislev. The date of the second epistle (1:10–2:18) is debated. If original, the letter would have been sent in 164 or possibly 163 B.C.,[83] but many scholars consider it to be a pseudepigraph from the late second or first century B.C.[84]

A marked eschatological tone pervades the epistle.[85] The prayer ascribed to Nehemiah's time (1:24–29) includes petitions for the ingathering of Israel to the "holy place" or temple and for deliverance from the Gentiles. The letter concludes with the hope that God "will soon have mercy upon us and will gather us from everywhere under heaven into his holy place, for he has rescued us from great evils and has purified the place" (2:18). The victory over Antiochus IV and the purification of the temple were understood by the

---

[81] J. A. Goldstein, *II Maccabees* (AB 41A; Garden City: Doubleday, 1983) 183.

[82] G. W. E. Nickelsburg, "Narrative Traditions in the Paralipomena of Jeremiah and 2 Baruch," *CBQ* 35 (1973) 60–68.

[83] B. Z. Wacholder ("The Letter from Judah Maccabee to Aristobulus: Is 2 Maccabees 1:10b–2:18 Authentic?" *HUCA* 49 [1978] 89–133) argues for a date in 163 B.C.

[84] Cf. the discussion in Goldstein, *II Maccabees,* 157–67; and C. Habicht, *2 Makkabäerbuch* (JSHRZ 1/3; Gütersloh: Mohn, 1976) 199–200.

[85] The importance of the epistle's eschatology is stressed by Wacholder, "The Letter," 130; and by R. Doran, *Temple Propaganda: The Purpose and Character of 2 Maccabees* (CBQMS 12; Washington: CBA, 1981) 10.

author as signs that the time of ingathering was near (1:11, 17; 2:18).

He envisioned the restored community as a cultic community. Israel was to be gathered in the purified temple. The author reminded his Egyptian readers that God "saved all his people and restored to all the inheritance and the kingdom and the consecration, as he promised through the law" (2:17-18a). His words recall Exod 19:6, which describe Israel as "a kingdom of priests and a holy nation."

The story of the hidden vessels strengthened the author's hopes for a restored cultic community at the time of ingathering. Solomon had placed the tabernacle and its furnishings in the first temple. The temple had been destroyed, but Jeremiah had preserved the tabernacle, ark, and incense altar. These were "sealed"[86] in a cave on Mt. Nebo, the site of Moses' grave, and would be revealed after the ingathering. When Moses first completed the tabernacle and when Solomon placed the tabernacle in the first temple, a cloud and divine glory appeared (2 Macc 2:8; Exod 40:34-35; 1 Kgs 8:4, 10-11). Therefore the author expected that the glory and cloud would appear again when the tabernacle was revealed to those who gathered in the temple (2 Macc 2:8).

The author included the story in the letter in order to strengthen ties with Egyptian Jews who would expect to be included in the ingathering. The author wanted to convince them to celebrate the Maccabean purification of the temple, which had set the stage for the ingathering and reappearance of the tabernacle. When the tabernacle reappeared, God's glory would again be manifested, as it had been at dedications of previous sanctuaries.[87]

THE LIVES OF THE PROPHETS

The tradition appears again in the *Life of Jeremiah* (*Vit. Jer.*), which is part of a collection of stories known as the *Lives of the Prophets*.[88] Much of the material in the collection probably stems from Palestine, although the *Life of Jeremiah* also includes Egyptian material.[89] Many scholars date the material to the first century A.D., because of the interest in the burial sites of the prophets (cf. Luke 11:47), detailed references to Palestinian geography, and parallels with other first century traditions about the

---

[86] The word "seal" (ἐμφράσσω) has eschatological overtones. See the Greek translation of Dan 12:4, 9; cf. 8:26.

[87] Note that the epistle says that the Maccabees "purified" rather than "dedicated" the temple (2 Macc 1:18; 2:16). The dedication would occur when the tabernacle and vessels were revealed. See Goldstein, *II Maccabees*, 171.

[88] The collection exists in a number of versions which are available in T. Schermann, ed., *Prophetarum vitae fabulosae* (Leipzig: Teubner, 1907).

[89] See C. C. Torrey, *The Lives of the Prophets* (Philadelphia: SBL, 1946) 10.

prophets (cf. Heb 11:32–38).[90] But since a reference to Rome's destruction of the temple appears elsewhere in the collection (*Vit. Hab.* 12), we cannot assume that the present form of the material dates from before A.D. 70.

In its present form, the *Life of Jeremiah* is a Christian work. The author says that the Lord will come "when all the Gentiles worship a piece of wood" (v. 13). The passage probably alludes to Gentile reverence for the cross and expresses hope for the Lord's return when the full number of Gentiles has been converted.[91]

Yet the story of the hidden vessels gives the Mosaic law a central place. The author refers to "the ark of the law," rather than to the ark of the covenant (v. 11), and also says that Jeremiah hid the ark between the graves of Aaron and Moses, who was the lawgiver. While 2 Maccabees expects God's glory to appear only when the ark is revealed in the future, *Vit. Jer.* 18 says that even now there is a fiery cloud over the site of the hidden ark, "for the glory of God will never cease from his law."

The *Life of Jeremiah* ascribes a key eschatological role to Moses and Aaron. 2 Maccabees said that God would reveal the vessels, but *Vit. Jer.* 14 insists that Aaron will reveal the ark and that Moses, "God's chosen one," will disclose the tablets of the law. The term "God's chosen one" has messianic overtones (cf. Luke 23:35). Therefore Hare suggests that the *Life of Jeremiah* represents an eschatology which expected a Mosaic deliverer.[92]

The *Life of Jeremiah* does not explicitly refer to the restoration of the cult, nor does it exclude such a restoration. The author did expect Aaron the priest, as well as Moses the lawgiver to appear in the end times. Moreover, he mentions a tradition that was associated with the temple. *Vit. Jer.* 15 says that the saints will be gathered at Mt. Sinai as they flee from the enemy who wishes to destroy them. The same tradition probably lies behind *Vit. Hab.* 12–13 which says that the saints who flee will receive light from the temple curtain and from the capitals of two of the temple's pillars, which angels carried from Jerusalem to the wilderness "where the tent of witness was at first." The site is presumably Mt. Sinai, as in *Vit. Jer.* 15. Nevertheless, neither the *Life of Jeremiah* nor the *Life of Habakkuk* suggests that the temple would be rebuilt at Sinai. Israel's cultic heritage would be preserved by a community in which the law would occupy a central place.

2 BARUCH

The opening chapters of *2 Baruch* (ca. A.D. 100)[93] describe the fall of

---

[90] Denis, *Introduction,* 89: D. R. A. Hare, *OTP,* 2.380–81.

[91] Hare, *OTP,* 2.388 n. q.

[92] *OTP,* 2.383.

[93] On dating see the summaries in Schürer et al., *History,* 3.752–53; and A. F. J. Klijn in *OTP,* 1.616–17.

Jerusalem and prepare the reader for reflections concerning these events. In chap. 1 God tells Baruch that the fall of Jerusalem is imminent. When Baruch questions God's intention (chap. 3), God replies that the destruction and exile are only a temporary chastisement (4:1). Then God reassures Baruch with two eschatological traditions.

First, the true Jerusalem, the one "carved on God's palms" (Isa 49:16), is hidden with God and will not be destroyed.[94] Adam had seen the true Jerusalem and Paradise, but both were taken away when he sinned. God revealed the city to Abraham and again to Moses, when he showed Moses the pattern of the tabernacle (*maškanā'*, *2 Bar.* 4:5).[95] The city will be revealed again in the future, along with God himself (4:3a). According to this passage there is no earthly continuity between the city to be destroyed and the city to be revealed.

But a second tradition indicates that the tabernacle vessels will provide continuity between the present and future Jerusalem. Four angels appear, ready to demolish the walls of Jerusalem so that the Babylonian army can claim no credit for the victory. But a fifth angel commands them to wait until he has removed the tabernacle vessels from the holy of holies. The angel commits the vessels to the ground until the end times, when both the tabernacle vessels and the city will be restored (6:7-9).

On the basis of the opening chapters we would expect *2 Baruch* to provide a vision of the future, including images of the new Jerusalem, the restored cultus, and Paradise. But the book does not contain such a vision. There is a brief mention of a future Paradise in 51:8, 11 (cf. chap. 29) and of the rebuilding of Zion in 32:2-4,[96] but there is no mention of a restored cultus. A. F. J. Klijn points out that when the author recounts the events of chaps. 4-6 again in 80:1-3, he simply says that the vessels were hidden "lest

---

[94] For theological discussion of this section, see W. Harnisch, *Verhängnis und Verheissung der Geschichte: Untersuchungen zum Zeit- und Geschichtsverständnis im 4. Buch Esra und in der syr. Baruchapokalypse* (FRLANT 97; Göttingen: Vandenhoeck & Ruprecht, 1969) 110-12.

[95] As in the Peshitta of Exod 25:9, 40.

[96] R. H. Charles (*APOT* 2.499) takes 32:2-4 as an intrusion into the text. A. F. J. Klijn ("The Sources and the Redaction of the Syriac Apocalypse of Baruch," *JSJ* 1 [1970] 70) agrees, calling it an independent prophecy about the temple. He maintains that the first destruction refers to 587 B.C. and the second destruction to A.D. 70 (*OTP*, 1.616). P. Bogaert argues that the first destruction refers simultaneously to the destruction of the first and second temples; the second destruction will occur at the close of the messianic age (*Apocalypse de Baruch*, 1.422-25), but his view is unlikely since the author does not mention a temple in connection with the messianic age. F. J. Murphy (*The Structure and Meaning of Second Baruch* [SBLDS 78; Atlanta: Scholars, 1985] 104-5) suggests that 32:2-4 does refer to a renewed temple in order to bolster hope for the future, even though this idea does contradict the author's expectation of the world's passing away.

they be polluted by the enemies;" he does not indicate that either the vessels or Zion will be restored.[97] Instead, he reminds his readers that what they do have is God and his law (85:3).

The author did not provide his readers — who lived after the destruction of Jerusalem in A.D. 70 — with a consistent picture of the future. He apparently included the hidden vessels tradition in order to emphasize that the destruction of Jerusalem was God's doing and not an enemy victory. He also may have wanted to acknowledge that the tradition was a source of hope for some readers. But the book as a whole moves readers away from the hope for a restored earthly cult.[98]

THE PARALIPOMENA JEREMIOU (4 BARUCH)

A similar version of the hidden vessels tradition is found in the *Paralipomena Jeremiou,* which is probably a Jewish work with Christian interpolations (e.g., 9:14–32).[99] The work is dated between A.D. 70 and 136.[100] The story begins on the eve of Jerusalem's destruction and concludes after the exiles return to Jerusalem. Before the city is destroyed, four angels approach to demolish the city walls, as in *2 Baruch.* But instead of angelic intervention, Jeremiah himself asks God what should be done with the sacred vessels. God commands him to commit them to the earth until "the ingathering of the beloved" (συνέλευσις τοῦ ἠγαπημένου, 3:11). This Greek expression is awkward. S. E. Robinson translates it "until the coming of the beloved one,"[101] which would anticipate the coming of Jesus mentioned in 9:14, 20–21. Christian readers would probably have taken the expression this way. But since the word συνέλευσις literally means "coming together," and since Israel is called "the beloved people" (ὁ ἠγαπημένος λαός) in 4:7, the pre-Christian tradition probably referred to the ingathering of Israel, as in 2 Maccabees and the *Life of Jeremiah.*[102]

---

[97] "Sources," 71; *OTP,* 1.617.

[98] Murphy, *Structure,* 104, 113–14; Klijn, "Sources," 67–72.

[99] So G. Delling, *Jüdische Lehre und Frömmigkeit in den Paralipomena Jeremiae* (BZAW 100; Berlin: Töpelman, 1967) 68–74; M. E. Stone, "Baruch," 276–77; Nickelsburg, *Jewish Literature,* 315–16; S. E. Robinson, *OTP,* 2.415. For the arguments that the work is pre-Christian composition, see J. R. Harris, *The Rest of the Words of Baruch* (London: Clay, 1889) 13–17; and Bogaert, *Apocalypse,* 1.216–21.

[100] Harris dated it to A.D. 136 (*The Rest,* 33–34). Bogaert (*Apocalypse,* 220) and Nickelsburg (*Jewish Literature,* 315) follow this dating. Delling (*Jüdische Lehre,* 2–3) and Robinson (*OTP,* 2.414) date it to the first third of the second century. Denis (*Introduction,* 75) and Stone ("Baruch," 276–77) date it between 70–130.

[101] *OTP,* 2.419.

[102] See Nickelsburg, "Narrative Traditions," 64; idem, *Jewish Literature,* 315.

After Jeremiah commits the vessels to the earth, Jerusalem is captured and the people taken into exile. At the end of the story, people return to Jerusalem and celebrate by offering sacrifices. The sacred vessels are not mentioned again; their role in the restored community is unclear. Nevertheless, since the work concludes with a return to Jerusalem and a resumption of sacrifice, the author probably envisioned the reestablishment of the temple cult, as in *2 Baruch,* without the reappearance of the tabernacle. Before sacrifices were resumed in Jerusalem, however, Jews were exhorted to renounce Gentile practices and mixed marriages (7:37–8:3). Therefore the Jewish version of this work may have been intended to foster more rigorous adherence to the Jewish law in anticipation of a restoration of the cult.[103]

SAMARITAN TRADITIONS

Important evidence for a first-century Samaritan tradition about the hidden tabernacle vessels is found in Josephus *Ant.* 18.4.1 #85–88. Josephus recounts events which occurred toward the end of Pontius Pilate's reign (A.D. 35–36).

> The Samaritan nation also was not free from disturbance. For a man assembled them, and, since he regarded deceit as a small matter and contrived all things according to the desire of the multitude, he commanded them to come with him to Mt. Gerizim, which they suppose is the most holy of mountains. He insisted that he would show those who were present the sacred vessels which were buried there, for Moses had made a deposit of them there. Now they were armed, since they considered the story credible, and stationing themselves in a certain village —Tirathana it is called—they began receiving there those who were gathering, since they planned to make the ascent to the mountain as a great throng.

After describing how Pilate attacked this group with cavalry and infantry Josephus continues,

> After the disturbance had subsided, the council of the Samaritans went to Vitellius, a man of consular rank who held the governorship of Syria, and began to charge Pilate with the slaughter of those who had died, for it was not in rebellion against the Romans, but in flight from Pilate that they had come to Tirathana.

Vitellius thereupon removed Pilate from his post, ordering him to return to Rome to give an account of the matter.

This narrative reveals several things about the Samaritan hidden vessels tradition. First, the Samaritans apparently knew of the tradition before A.D.

---

[103] Cf. Nickelsburg, *Jewish Literature,* 316; Delling, *Jüdische Lehre,* 42–53; Robinson, *OTP,* 2.414–16. On the possible use of the Christianized form of the work as a tract intended for Jews or Jewish Christians, see Harris, *Rest,* 13–17; and Bogaert, *Apocalypse,* 1.216–21.

36. The man in the story assumed that people knew that Moses had buried the tabernacle vessels on Mt. Gerizim and that the vessels would one day reappear. He simply claimed that he was the one who would reveal the vessels.

Second, the tradition said that it was Moses who had hidden the vessels. Other versions attributed the concealment to Jeremiah, an angel, or God. Wayne Meeks has argued that the Samaritan tradition included a hope that "someone associated with Moses, in a way no longer clear, would recover the hidden cult implements. . . ."[104] Marilyn Collins goes further, identifying the man in the Josephus story with the eschatological prophet like Moses.[105] Collins notes that other first-century sources such as Philo's *Spec.* 1.65; 1QS ix 11; and John 1:45 convey the hope for an eschatological prophet like Moses (Deut 18:18). John 4:19, 25 may reflect a similar Samaritan expectation.[106]

Third, the Samaritans expected the vessels to be revealed to those who gathered together on Mt. Gerizim. They waited for many to assemble and planned to ascend the mountain in a group. The procedure resembled a pilgrimage and probably reflected the hope of eschatological ingathering.

Fourth, although Pilate interpreted the incident as a revolt, the Samaritan council insisted that the group consisted of fugitives, not rebels. The Roman governor found their case convincing enough to remove Pilate from office. The Samaritan explanation is plausible, since Pilate was known for brutal tactics in Judea (*Ant.* 18.3.2 #60–62). Some of the Samaritans were armed, but Josephus does not state that the group intended to revolt.[107] If we accept the Samaritan explanation, then those who assembled may have expected the ingathering and the disclosure of the vessels to occur at a time of persecution.

The Samaritans probably hoped for the reappearance of the tabernacle as well as the vessels. Forms of the tradition that expected the return of the vessels also anticipated the restoration of the cult. Since the Samaritans expected someone like Moses to restore the vessels, they probably expected

---

[104] *The Prophet-King: Moses Traditions and the Johannine Christology* (NovTSup 14; Leiden: Brill, 1967) 250.

[105] "The Hidden Vessels in Samaritan Traditions," *JSJ* 3 (1972) 97–116, esp. 110.

[106] G. Kippenberg (*Garizim und Synagoge: Untersuchungen zur samaritanischen Religion in der aramäischen Periode* [RGVV 30; Berlin: de Gruyter, 1971] 250) calls the man a "Moses redivivus," but does not identify him with the prophet like Moses.

[107] *Ant.* 18.4.1 #86 says that some of those who assembled were armed. It does not say that they armed themselves for the purpose of ascending the mountain. Neither Kippenberg (*Garizim,* 114) nor Schürer et al. (*History,* 1.386–87) detect a revolutionary motive in the incident. When the Samaritans did do battle with the Romans at Gerizim ca. A.D. 67, Josephus explicitly says that they assembled on the mountain in a warlike stance (*J.W.* 3.7.32 #307–15).

the restoration of the Mosaic tabernacle cult on Gerizim.

Fourth century Samaritan sources bear out this interpretation. Several references to the concealment and restoration of the tabernacle occur in the important Aramaic work known as the *Memar Marqah* (*MM*). Marqah was an influential Samaritan leader of the fourth century. He linked Mt. Gerizim with the time when "what is hidden there will be revealed" (*MM* III.4; 62,9; ET 97).[108] He also said that Moses erected the tabernacle (משכנה) and "All who sought the Lord would gather at it (Exod 33:7). So in the Day of Vengeance the great prophet Moses will do and he will deliver the beloved and destroy all the enemies" (*MM* IV.3; 89,2–3; ET 143). This passage refers to the future coming of Moses, the reestablishment of the tabernacle, the gathering of the faithful, and deliverance from oppression.[109]

The appearance of the tabernacle is associated with the return of glory and divine favor (רחותה), and its concealment is tied to a time of apostasy (פנווה), when "the Favour will be hidden away and evils will be multiplied the more, and the tabernacle of God will be concealed and Mount Gerizim defiled; apostasy will be found in every place and there will be none zealous for God" (*MM* V.2; 120,1–2; ET 197). The return of the tabernacle would mean the end of apostasy and the return of divine favor.[110]

The major instance of apostasy, according to Samaritan views, was the establishment of a shrine at Shiloh by Eli. But the hidden tabernacle tradition may have been closely tied to the destruction of the Gerizim temple by John Hyrcanus in 128 B.C. Hans Kippenberg notes a text which says, "My tabernacle[111] they have defiled, my holiness they have profaned . . . my house they have destroyed; from the True One they have turned away; my Favour they have concealed" (*MM* IV.12; 110,17–18; ET 184). The "house" may be the Gerizim temple.

Kippenberg and Collins argue that the destruction of the Gerizim temple would not have occasioned this tradition.[112] But Kippenberg acknowledges that in the years following the destruction of the Gerizim temple, the hidden

---

[108] Citations of the *Memar Marqah* are given as follows: First, the book number appears in Roman numerals, then the section number. After a semi-colon the page and line numbers of J. Macdonald's Aramaic text are given (*Memar Marqah: The Teaching of Marqah* [BZAW 84; Berlin: Töpelmann, 1963]). The page in Macdonald's English translation (ET) is also provided. Modified versions of Macdonald's translation are cited above.

[109] In the first century, hopes for a restored tabernacle were not necessarily linked with the Day of Vengeance idea. Kippenberg points out that many references to the Day of Vengeance make no mention of the tabernacle (*Garizim*, 241 n. 57).

[110] Kippenberg, *Garizim*, 249–50.

[111] The text reads לשכני, which is apparently an error for משכני. See Macdonald's translation and Kippenberg, *Garizim*, 244 n. 73.

[112] Kippenberg, *Garizim*, 249–50; Collins, "Hidden Vessels," 109.

tabernacle tradition would have fostered hopes for a new age of favor. According to Josephus' account, the tradition was popular with a large group of Samaritans in the first century and received at least tacit support from the Samaritan Council. Fourth-century Samaritan sources indicate that the tradition remained an important part of Samaritan theology in the first centuries A.D.

SUMMARY

Stories of the hidden tabernacle and vessels helped to assure readers that there would be some continuity between Israel's sanctuaries of the past and life in the future. The reappearance of the tabernacle or its vessels would provide a focal point for the ingathered community. The Samaritan version of the story probably anticipated the resumption of the Mosaic tabernacle cult. Some Jewish versions associated the tradition with a renewal of temple worship, but in other accounts, the connection with the temple is less clear. 2 Macc 2:4-8 anticipated the reappearance of the tabernacle, ark, and incense altar, together with God's glory, after the purification of the temple; the author definitely expected the temple cult to continue. The *Lives of the Prophets* do give Aaron and the temple's curtain and capitals an eschatological role, but do not suggest that the temple itself would be rebuilt. *2 Baruch* seems to suggest that the tabernacle vessels would provide continuity between the temple that was destroyed and a restored Jerusalem, but the work does not develop the idea of a restored cult. Instead, the law seems to be more important. The *Paralipomena Jeremiou* does conclude with a resumption of sacrifice, but does not make an explicit connection between these sacrifices and the reappearance of the vessels. The Eupolemos fragments that were noted in the previous section do not speak of a restoration of the temple, but given Eupolemos's enthusiasm for the second temple he presumably associated the tradition with an ongoing cult. Yet the *Biblical Antiquities,* also mentioned in the previous section, do not make a connection between the tradition and an eschatological temple cult.

E. THE WISDOM OF SOLOMON,
PHILO, AND JOSEPHUS

The Wisdom of Solomon (ca. 30 B.C. — A.D. 40)[113] and the works of

---

[113] D. Winston (*The Wisdom of Solomon* [AB 43; Garden City: Doubleday, 1979] 20–25), followed by Nickelsburg (*Jewish Literature,* 184) argues for a date during Caligula's reign (A.D. 37–41). C. Larcher (*Le Livre de la Sagesse ou la Sagesse de Salomon* [EBib; Paris: Lecoffre, 1983–85] 1.141–61) favors a date in the last third of the first century B.C. Cf. M. Gilbert, in *Jewish Writings of the Second Temple Period* (ed. M. E. Stone; CRINT 2; Assen

Philo (ca. 10 B.C.—A.D. 45) were written in Egypt; Josephus (ca. A.D. 37-100) spent much of his life in Palestine and wrote his *Antiquities* in Rome. Despite certain differences in setting, however, these sources contain interpretations of the tabernacle that are often closely related.

THE COSMOLOGICAL INTERPRETATION

Philo and Josephus interpret the tabernacle as a symbol of the cosmos and occasionally apply a similar interpretation to the Jerusalem temple.[114] The chart shows that several of the tabernacle furnishings were interpreted consistently by both authors. The seven lamps of the menorah always represent the seven planets[115] and the tabernacle curtains always stand for the four elements; Josephus interprets the temple menorah and curtains in these same ways. Philo consistently says that the tabernacle's incense altar represents thanksgiving for various substances, although the details vary slightly in each passage,[116] but Josephus ascribes the same significance to the temple's incense altar. He also says that the twelve loaves in both the tabernacle and the temple stood for the twelve months, an interpretation that Philo associates only with the temple.

These similarities reveal a clear link between explanations of temple and tabernacle furnishings. Jewish exegetes could have understood the tabernacle cosmologically and gradually applied these views to the temple.[117] But a more probable view is that interpretations first given to the temple's furnishings were gradually applied to those of the tabernacle. Josephus says that the temple's lampstand, table, and incense altar were "known to all people" (*J. W.* 5.5.5 #216). He then relates the cosmological significance of each item. Pilgrims to Jerusalem could have learned the cosmological

---

and Philadelphia: van Gorcum and Fortress, 1984) 312. Despite the evidence for a date in the Roman period, D. Georgi (*Weisheit Salomons* [JSHRZ 3/4; Gütersloh: Mohn, 1980] 395-97) argues for the late second century B.C.

[114] Wis 18:24 refers to the cosmological significance of the high priest's robes, a tradition which appears together with the cosmological interpretation of the tabernacle in Philo and Josephus. Therefore the tabernacle's cosmological significance also may have been known to the author of the Wisdom of Solomon.

[115] Sun, Moon, Mercury, Venus, Mars, Saturn, and Jupiter.

[116] *Mos.* 2.101 mentions earth and water; *Her.* 226 lists all four elements.

[117] J. Blenkinsopp ("The Structure of P," *CBQ* 38 [1976] 275-92) points out parallels between the priestly accounts of creation and the building of the tabernacle. He holds that the cosmological interpretation to which Josephus attests derived from the Bible's priestly source. The difficulty is that the parallels between creation and tabernacle become clear only when the priestly material is extracted from its present canonical context. There is no record of such a cosmological exegesis between the time of the priestly writer and the first century A.D.

CHART 3

	Philo	Josephus
Tabernacle as a copy	of immaterial archetypes *Mos.* 2.74	of universal nature (φύσις τῶν ὅλων) *Ant.* 3.123
Holy of holies	intelligible world *Q.E.* 2.68–69	heaven *Ant.* 3.123,181
Forecourt	heaven, earth, and sea *Her.* 221–229 perceptible world *Q.E.* 2.83 part of the intelligible world *Mos.* 2.82	earth and sea *Ant.* 3.123,181
Outer court	perceptible world *Ebr.* 134 sublunar region *Q.E.* 2.83	
Lampstand Tabernacle	seven planets *Mos.* 2.102–103; *Q.E.* 2.73–81; *Her.* 221	seven planets *Ant.* 3.182
Temple		*J.W.* 5.217
Table and twelve loaves Tabernacle	twelve months	twelve months *Ant.* 3.182
Temple	*Spec.* 1.172	*J.W.* 5.217
Incense altar Tabernacle	thankfulness for elements *Mos.* 2.101; *Her.* 226	all things are from God
Temple		*J.W.* 5.218
Curtains βύσσος – earth πορφύρα – sea/water ὑάκινθος – air κόκκινος/φοῖνιξ – fire Tabernacle	*Mos.* 2.88; *Q.E.* 2.85; *Cong.* 116–117	*Ant.* 3.183
Temple		*J.W.* 5.213

meaning of the temple furnishings and then applied these explanations to the tabernacle.[118]

The description of the tabernacle as a "portable temple" gives additional support to this hypothesis. Philo and Josephus use different terms for "portable temple"[119] and only Philo explains that the Israelites erected a tent rather than a temple for God, because they were in the desert rather than in a city. Therefore the idea probably reflects a common tradition. What is striking is that both Philo and Josephus assume that the tabernacle can be explained by comparison with the temple and both even call the tabernacle a ἱερόν (*Mos.* 2.71, 88; *Ant.* 3.9.3 #231) and a ναός (*Mos.* 2.89; *Ant.* 3.6.4 #125; 3.10.3 #242–43). These tendencies suggest that the cosmological interpretation originated with the temple furnishings and was only later applied to the tabernacle.

Philo and Josephus also interpret courts of the tabernacle in similar ways. For both, the holy of holies corresponds to the highest realm in the universe and the outer courts to lower regions. Philo sometimes makes the Platonic distinctions between the noetic and perceptible realms, while Josephus does not. In a study of Philo, Ursula Früchtel argues that the non-Platonic interpretation of Josephus was probably older than Philo's Platonized version,[120] which is plausible. But Philo does not Platonize the tradition as consistently as Früchtel suggests.

In *Ebr.* 134 the entire tabernacle is associated with the incorporeal realm and the altar in the outer court with the realm of perception. The same is true in *Mos.* 2.81, where Philo says that the five pillars separating the tabernacle's forecourt from the outer court symbolically distinguish the realms of mind and sense. But in *Mos.* 2.101–108, the furnishings of the forecourt correspond to heaven, earth, and sea, which are presumably in the realm of sense.[121] In *Her.* 225 the menorah is called a copy of heaven's archetype, but

---

[118] Philo's knowledge of the temple probably came from his own pilgrimage. Cf. *Prov.* 2.64; *Spec.* 1.69–75. On first-century pilgrimage to Jerusalem see S. Safrai, "Relations between the Diaspora and the Land of Israel," *The Jewish People in the First Century* (CRINT 1/1; ed. S. Safrai and M. Stern; Assen: Van Gorcum, 1974) 184–215.

[119] φορητὸν ἱερόν, *Mos.* 2.73 *Q.E.* 2.49, 83. μεταφερομένος καὶ συμπερινοστῶν ναός, *Ant.* 3.6.1 #103.

[120] *Die kosmologischen Vorstellungen bei Philo von Alexandrien: Ein Beitrag zur Geschichte der Genesisexegese* (ALGHJ 2; Leiden: Brill, 1968) 98.

[121] Früchtel's diagram of the tabernacle is misleading (*Kosmologischen Vorstellungen,* 77). In his *Vita Mosis* Philo uses the singular ἄδυτον for the holy of holies (2.87, 95), rather than the plural ἄδυτα as in the diagram. The plural indicates the holy of holies and the forecourt together (2.82, 152, 154). The five pillars separate the outer court from the forecourt, not the forecourt from the holy of holies.

neither the menorah nor the other furnishings are given specific, Platonic locations in the tabernacle. Only in the *Questions on Exodus* does Philo consistently divide the tabernacle into Platonic regions with the holy of holies as the intelligible realm, the forecourt as the supralunar region of the perceptible realm, and the outer court as the sublunar region (*Q.E.* 2.69, 83, 94).

Therefore, since Philo did not identify the regions of the tabernacle with Platonic regions in a consistent manner, the Platonic interpretation of the tabernacle was probably not fixed during Philo's lifetime. The more prevalent tradition probably resembled that of Josephus. Like the interpretation of the furnishings, the interpretation of the tabernacle's courts may also have originated with the Jerusalem temple. For example, Josephus says that the holy of holies of both the temple and the tabernacle was a region "inaccessible" to human beings.[122]

The cosmological interpretation of the tabernacle played a significant role in Jewish apologetics. Philo included it in his *Vita Mosis,* which was probably intended for non-Jews and for Jews on the edge of the Jewish community. Philo alludes to non-Jews in 2.44 when he says, "I believe that each nation would abandon its peculiar ways, and, throwing overboard their ancestral customs, turn to honoring our laws alone." In 1.31 he refers to Jews on the edge of the community, who, in a time of economic hardship would "look down on their relations and friends and set at naught the laws under which they were born and bred, and subvert the ancestral customs . . . adopting different modes of life, and, in their contentment with the present, lose all memory of the past."[123]

The *Vita Mosis* addressed these readers on the edge of Judaism by insisting that the Jewish law and cult conformed to nature. The Mosaic law was given by the Creator and its statutes were in accord with nature (2.48). The stories of the flood and Sodom and Gomorrah show that nature itself punishes those who rebel against God's law (2.52–65), indicating that the law should be obeyed by all. The tabernacle corresponds to the cosmos and one who participates in Israel's cult with right intention receives immortality, "sharing the eternal life of the sun and moon and the whole universe" (2.108).[124]

---

[122] ἄβατον, *J.W.* 5.5.5 #219; *Ant.* 3.6.4 #123; cf. ἀνεπίβατον, 3.7.7 #181.

[123] On the intended readership of *De Vita Mosis* see P. Borgen, "Philo of Alexandria. A critical and synthetical survey of research since World War II," *ANRW* 2.21/1 (1983) 94–154, esp. 118.

[124] E. R. Goodenough emphasized that through this cosmic cult worshipers rose to join in the hymn of the universe to its maker without transcending the cosmos. But Goodenough insisted that Philo did not envision Gentiles participating in this cult through observance of Jewish law (*By Light, Light: The Mystic Gospel of Hellenistic Judaism* [New Haven: Yale, 1935] 111, 115). Yet in *Mos.* 2.17–36, Philo tries to show that non-Jews do observe some Jewish

Josephus also used the cosmological interpretation apologetically. In *Ant.* 3.7.7 #179–180 he says,

> But one may well be astonished at the hatred which men have for us and which they have so persistently maintained, from an idea that we slight the divinity which they themselves profess to venerate. For if one reflects on the construction of the tabernacle . . . he will discover that our lawgiver was a man of God and that these blasphemous charges brought against us by the rest of men are idle. In fact, every one of these objects is intended to recall and represent the nature of the universe.

Josephus wrote this passage a generation after the Jerusalem temple was destroyed. He used the cosmological interpretation to defend the worship of Jews who did not actually have a temple, but who did adhere to the Mosaic law (cf. *Ant.* Proem 1.3 #14) Philo wrote before the destruction of the temple, but indicated that sacrifices were not necessary for true worship. Even though the tabernacle and temple shared the same cosmological symbolism, these authors used the cosmological interpetation of the tabernacle to commend a form of worship that was prescribed by the law, but could be conducted without an actual temple.

THE HEAVENLY TABERNACLE AND DIVINE WISDOM

The Wisdom of Solomon and several of Philo's works speak of a heavenly tabernacle that is associated with divine wisdom. One of these references appears in Wis 9:8 in Solomon's prayer for wisdom.

> (9:8) You told (me) to build a temple on your holy mountain
> and an altar in the city where you tabernacle (κατασκήνωσις),
> a copy of the holy tabernacle (σκηνή)
> which you prepared from the beginning.
> (9) With you is wisdom, who knows your works,
> and was present when you made the world,
> and who understands what is pleasing in your eyes,
> and what accords with your commandments.
> (10) Send her forth from the holy heavens,
> and from the throne of your glory send her,
> that she might be present with me and labor,
> and that I may know what is well-pleasing to you.

---

practices like the sabbath and Day of Atonement fast. His statement in 2.44, quoted above, indicates that those who want to live in harmony with the universe should do so by following Mosaic practices. See V. Tcherikover, *Corpus Papyrorum Judaicarum* (Cambridge: Harvard, 1957) 1.77; Borgen, "Survey of Research," 111–13.

The author understood the "pattern" of the tabernacle, mentioned in Exod 25:9, to be an actual heavenly tabernacle that had been erected by God. His framework of thought is Platonic.[125] The author refers to the earthly "copy" (μίμημα) of the tabernacle in v. 8b implying that there was also a heavenly archetype. Interestingly, the earthly copy is Solomon's temple, rather than the Mosaic tabernacle. Other ancient sources that mention the pattern of the tabernacle recognize that the tabernacle differed from the temple.[126] The views conveyed by Wis 9:8 may represent a harmonization of Exod 25:9 with 1 Chron 28:11, which said that the Solomonic temple, like the tabernacle, was built according to a divinely revealed "pattern" (תבנית/ παράδειγμα).

The focus of attention in Wisdom 9 is divine wisdom, not the tabernacle or temple. Wisdom is portrayed as a figure who sits by God's throne, who was present when God made the world, and who was presumably there when God constructed the heavenly tabernacle (9:4, 8–9). Therefore Solomon asks God to send him wisdom, in order that he might build an earthly copy of the heavenly sanctuary as God commanded. His prayer is an example for others to follow (cf. 6:1). Elsewhere the author shows almost no interest in the temple or sacrifice[127] and does not suggest that one finds wisdom by going to the temple. He does say, however, that one encounters wisdom by obeying her laws, which accord with God's laws, and are represented in the Mosaic law that is intended for all people (6:18; 9:10; 18:4).

Philo too associates wisdom with a heavenly tabernacle that is depicted in Platonic categories. In *Cong.* 116 he observes that the tabernacle had ten curtains (αὐλαία) and that ten is a perfect number, therefore heavenly wisdom becomes the court (αὐλή) and palace of God. Philo notes that God's dwelling could be perceived only by the mind, yet the tabernacle did provide a connection with the realm of the senses, since its curtains symbolized the four elements of the world. *Her.* 112–113 says that the tabernacle was also the earthly copy of heavenly wisdom. When God chose to send down the image of divine virtue (ἀρετή) from heaven to earth, he constructed the tabernacle as a representation and copy of wisdom (σοφία). In this passage Philo uses "wisdom" and "virtue" interchangeably.[128]

---

[125] Other traces of Platonism appear in 9:15 where the author contrasts the realm of the body and earth with that of soul and mind.

[126] Cf. *Bibl. Ant.* 11:15 and *2 Bar.* 4:5. Rabbinic sources mention heavenly and earthly temples (cf. Winston, *Wisdom*, 204–5), but do not suggest that they were patterned after the tabernacle.

[127] The author makes passing reference to the temple in Wis 3:14 and to sacrifices in 3:6 and 18:9.

[128] See also *L.A.* 3.46, 48; *Cong.* 114. On the close relationship between wisdom and virtue in Philo see E. Brehier, *Les idées philosophiques et religieuses de Philon d'Alexandrie*

Just as the tabernacle could represent heavenly or earthly wisdom, it could also signify heavenly or earthly virtue. In *Det*. 160, which quotes Exod 33:7, the tent of testimony is God's actual dwelling place and it corresponds to divine virtue. Its earthly copy is Moses' tent, which represents human virtue. According to *Ebr*. 134, the tabernacle itself is incorporeal virtue, while the altar is virtue's perceptible image.

A different interpretation is found in *L.A*. 3.46, which calls the tabernacle a dwelling for the wise man. The passage is based on Exod 33:7 (LXX), which says that Moses pitched "his tent" outside the camp. Each time Philo quotes Exod 33:7 he equates the camp with the realm of the body.[129] Philo insists that a person must flee the camp of the body and take up residence in "wisdom, in which the wise man tabernacles and dwells."

Philo invoked these interpretations to encourage his readers to pursue the wisdom and virtue that led one to God. Like the author of the Wisdom of Solomon, Philo assumed that wisdom was reflected in the Mosaic law, although the two were not identical.[130] Philo probably derived his wisdom interpretations of the tabernacle from traditions circulating in Alexandrian schools. Sirach, which was translated into Greek for use in Egypt by the late second century B.C., alludes to wisdom's heavenly tabernacle (24:4), her earthly tabernacle (24:8, 10), and to the wise man who pitches his tent near wisdom (14:25). The Wisdom of Solomon and Philo develop these ideas within a Platonic framework.

THE TABERNACLE AS THE SOUL

Philo identifies the tabernacle and its furnishings with the soul several times. The soul can be a sanctuary in which God manifests himself (*Q.E*. 2.51) and the rational virtues of the soul are incorruptible, like the ark's undecaying wood (2.53). The gold of the ark resembles the soul, whose virtues adorn the body (2.54) and the "wreathed wave" around the ark resembles the corruption of soul and body (2.55). The equation of the soul with the tabernacle is Philo's own interpretation, as he explicitly says in *Q.E*.

(Paris: Philosophique, 1925) 119; P. Borgen, *Bread from Heaven: An Exegetical Study of the Concept of Manna in the Gospel of John and the Writings of Philo* (NovTSup 10; Leiden: Brill, 1965) 102.

[129] See *L.A*. 2.54; 3.46; *Det*. 160; *Gig*. 54; *Ebr*. 100, all of which interpret Exod 33:7. See also the other references to the camp in *Ebr*. 96, 99, 124. The only exception to this pattern is *L.A*. 3.151, where the camp equals virtue.

[130] On the connection between wisdom and the law in Philo, see D. Winston, *Philo of Alexandria: The Contemplative Life, the Giants, and Selections* (Classics of Western Spirituality; New York: Paulist, 1981) 24–26 and 310 n. 72. Cf. S. Sandmel, *Philo of Alexandria: An Introduction* (Oxford: University, 1979) 98–99.

2.53, and all of the passages noted above mention the soul only after other views have been given.

Philo's other references to the tabernacle as the soul also suggest that the interpretation is his own. In *L.A.* 2.53–55 Philo comments on Exod 33:7. He initially equates the soul with the tabernacle by saying that just as Moses pitched (πήγνυμι) the *tent* outside the camp, the *soul* which flees the body gains a fixed (πῆξις) settlement in virtue. Yet by referring to a settlement *in virtue* Philo reflects the impact of the wisdom interpretations noted earlier. In *L.A.* 3.95 Philo calls Bezalel "the craftsman of all the works of the tabernacle, that is of the soul." But the idea is not developed in the context and seems to be a digression. *Her.* 225 relates the menorah to the soul, but again, the idea is not developed.

Philo's views may reflect an attitude toward the cult shared by "other allegorists" who say that "every soul desirous of moral excellence is a libation" (*Q.E.* 2.71).[131] But since Philo does not consistently identify the soul with the tabernacle, since he explicitly says that the interpretation is his own, and since these interpretations are not attested outside of Philo, the equation of soul and tabernacle was probably not a fixed exegetical tradition during Philo's lifetime.

"LITERAL" INTERPRETATIONS

Philo gives two "literal" interpretations of the tabernacle which provide examples for personal conduct. In *Ebr.* 130, he comments on the command that Aaron consume no wine or strong drink before entering the tabernacle (Lev 10:8–10). Philo equates entering the tabernacle with attending "prayers and holy services," commenting that those who attend public worship should not do so in a state of drunkenness. In *Q.E.* 2.54 he observes that Moses overlaid the ark with pure gold inside and outside (Exod 25:11), unlike others "who falsify the external appearance with deceit." These interpretations are not attested outside of Philo.

But a third "literal" interpretation has some affinity with other Jewish traditions. Philo explains that the ark was made of "undecaying wood" since the Law which was kept in the ark was incorruptible, and that "the sanctuary and all the order of things arranged in it were ordained not for a limited time, but for an infinite age" (*Q.E.* 2.53; cf. 41 and 57). The traditions of the hidden tabernacle and vessels imply the abiding significance of the tabernacle, since its vessels will be revealed in the future, and 2 Macc 2:2–3 and

---

[131] The translation "other allegorists" is Goodenough's ("The Menorah among the Jews of the Roman World," *HUCA* 23 [1950–51] 468). For a synopsis of Philo's references to other allegorists, see D. M. Hay, "Philo's References to Other Allegorists," *Studia Philonica* 6 (1979–80) 41–75.

Vit. Jer. 18 also mention the abiding value of the law. A later tradition, attested both in the targums and in rabbinic literature, says that while Mt. Sinai was consecrated for only an hour, the tent of meeting received an eternal consecration.[132] Therefore this interpretation may reflect wider Jewish tradition.

The final type of "literal" interpretation is Platonic. Philo comments on the verse, "You shall make for me a sanctuary and I shall appear among you" (Exod 25:8) by saying, "Clear indeed is the literal meaning, for the shrine is spoken of (as) the archetype of a sort of shrine, (namely as) the tent." The text is difficult and may be corrupt,[133] but Philo seems to be alluding to the heavenly tabernacle. Wis 9:8 also called the heavenly tabernacle an archetype, suggesting that others understood Exod 25:8–9 Platonically. Implicit evidence appears in Philo's own comment "clear indeed is the literal meaning," suggesting that the interpretation was well known to readers.

SUMMARY

The cosmological interpretation of the tabernacle is strongly attested in Philo and Josephus, and it may have been known to the author of the Wisdom of Solomon. The cosmological symbolism was used for both the tabernacle and the temple. Nevertheless, the cosmological interpretation of the tabernacle was used to commend forms of Jewish worship that did entail observance of the law, but did not necessarily involve the Jerusalem temple. Philo and the Wisdom of Solomon speak of a heavenly tabernacle in Platonic categories. This tabernacle is God's dwelling place and is associated with divine wisdom. The interpretation of the tabernacle as the soul is Philo's own, but his reference to the tabernacle's eternal ordination is attested in other sources, and Philo associated it with the abiding character of the Mosaic law.

F. LATER JEWISH SOURCES

Extant sources of rabbinic traditions were compiled long after most of the NT was written, but they preserve sayings ascribed to individuals who lived in the late first and early second centuries. Apart from a few Dead Sea fragments, extant targums are also later than NT writings. But if used with care, the targums and collections of rabbinic materials may provide information useful for NT study.

---

[132] See below under "Targumic Traditions."
[133] See Marcus, *Philo* suppl. II, 97 n. f.

RABBINIC TRADITIONS

Individual rabbinic traditions are often difficult to date. We will use the following principles for selecting early material. First, traditions found in older collections are more likely to be reliable than those found in more recent collections. Jacob Neusner suggests that the general order of reliability is (1) Mishna and Tosepta, (2) Tannaitic Midrashim (Mekilta, Sipra, Siprei), (3) *baraitot* in the Palestinian Talmud, (4) *baraitot* in the Babylonian Talmud, (5) later midrashim.[134] Second, sayings ascribed to rabbis living after A.D. 70 are considered to be generally reliable. Third, anonymous *baraitot* may have originated during the middle or late second century, but we cannot assume they stem from an earlier period.

A full treatment of early rabbinic traditions is beyond the scope of this study. But an examination of references to the משכן and אהל מועד in the Mishna, Tosepta, Mekilta, Sipra, Siprei, and Talmuds does reveal how the rabbis understood the relationship of the tabernacle to the temple and to the Mosaic law.[135]

Rabbinic sources, like Eupolemos, the *Testament of Moses,* and Pseudo-Philo, trace the movement of the cult from the tabernacle to the Jerusalem temple. According to rabbinic sources, the sequence was: the desert tabernacle, Gilgal, Shiloh, Nob and Gibeon, and finally the Jerusalem temple, which the Tosepta calls the "eternal house" (בית עולמים).[136] None of the earlier sources included Nob and Gibeon in the sequence. The rabbinic order derived Nob and Gibeon from scripture (2 Chron 1:3; 1 Sam 21:6, 9). In contrast to the pseudepigraphical sources, the Mishna calls the Shiloh sanctuary a "house of stone" rather than the "tent of meeting" or "tabernacle" (*m. Zebaḥ*. 14:6). The Mishna again seems to follow scripture, since 1 Sam 1:24 calls the Shiloh sanctuary a "house."

Eupolemos said that the ten lampstands in Solomon's temple were patterned after the single lampstand which Moses had made. The Tosepta

---

[134] *Eliezer Ben Hyrcanus: The Tradition and the Man* (SJLA 3–4; Leiden: Brill, 1973) 2.226.

[135] Passages were collected using the concordances of C. J. Kasowski, B. Kosovsky, and M. Kosovsky, which are listed in the bibliography. At the time of this study, the volume listing references to the משכן in the Jerusalem Talmud had not yet appeared. Only representative citations are given in this section, with preference given to the earliest references. The tannaitic midrash "Baraita d'Meleket ha-Mishkan" contains detailed discussion of the design and construction of the tabernacle and its furnishings, but says little about the significance of the tabernacle for the tannaim. Chaps. 13–14 contain haggadic material, but are often considered later additions. See L. Ginzberg, "Baraita on the Erection of the Tabernacle," *Jewish Encyclopedia* 2 (1902) 517. For an English translation of the work see J. Barclay, *The Talmud* (London: John Murray, 1878) 334–58.

[136] *t. Zebaḥ*. 13:2–6; *m. Zebaḥ*. 14:4–8.

goes further, claiming that the table and the lampstand which Moses made were actually used in the first temple (*t. Soṭa* 13:1).

The book of *Jubilees* insisted on continuity in legal observances from the tabernacle to the temple. Rabbinic sources describe a more complex relationship. Once the tabernacle was erected, the "Most Holy Things" (קדשי קדשים) were always eaten in the sanctuary up through the time of the temple. But regulations pertaining to the "Lesser Holy Things" (קדשים קלים, *m. Zebaḥ*. 14:4–8) and to the high places varied as the cult moved from place to place. Again, the rabbinic sources seem to mirror complexities found in scripture. For example, the high places seem to have been acceptable in certain periods and unacceptable in others (1 Sam 9:12-25; 1 Kgs 3:2; 11:7).

The most important connection between the tabernacle and the law is the sabbath commandments. The rabbis delineated the types of work prohibited on the sabbath according to the types of work done in the tabernacle. This view rests on a solid biblical basis, since the book of Exodus uses sabbath commands to conclude the initial prescriptions for the tabernacle (Exod 31:12-17) and to introduce the story of its construction (35:1-3). Sidney Hoenig notes that *Jubilees* 2 connects the labors forbidden on the sabbath with the labors of God at the creation, as does Exod 20:11.[137] The earliest evidence for the rabbinic tradition is a statement ascribed to R. Aqiba in a discussion about writing on the sabbath. "R. Aqiba said, they declared that [one who writes] even two letters is liable for making a mark, for thus they used to put marks upon the boards of the tabernacle, in order to tell which belonged together."[138] The Mishna ascribes similar views to R. Jose (*m. Šabb.* 12:3) and similar references appear elsewhere in rabbinic sources.[139] Hoenig suggests that the interpretation may predate R. Aqiba, but concludes that its importance was established only in the second century A.D.[140]

Rabbinic sources also include a form of the hidden vessels tradition. In the period of the first temple, King Josiah is said to have hidden away the tabernacle and the ark, together with the jar of manna, the bottle of anointing oil, Aaron's rod which budded, and the chest in which the Philistines placed wood for God. All these were stored in the holy of holies so that they would not be taken into exile (*t. Soṭa* 13:1). The rabbinic story is part of the same tradition reflected in Eupolemos, 2 Macc 2:4-8, the *Life of Jeremiah, 2 Baruch,* and the *Paralipomena Jeremiou.* But unlike the other versions

---

[137] "The Designated Number of Kinds of Labor Prohibited on the Sabbath," *JQR* 68 (1978) 193-217.

[138] *t. Šabb.* 11:6, following Lieberman's text. Zuckermandel's text ascribes the saying to R. Jose.

[139] E.g., *b. Šabb.* 31b, 49b, 73b-74a, 102b.

[140] "Designated Number," 195, 205.

of the tradition, the rabbinic story is based on 2 Chron 35:3, where Josiah commanded the Levites to put the ark in the temple.[141]

TARGUMIC TRADITIONS

The targums, or Aramaic translations of the Bible, are another source of ancient Jewish traditions. Fragmentary targums were found among the Dead Sea Scrolls, but the date of other targums and the value of targumic traditions for NT study has been vigorously debated. Some scholars argue that targumic traditions often stem from the first century and that some may be pre-Christian.[142] But others are more cautious in their dating of targumic materials, since extant targums date from the second century A.D. or later.[143] While they recognize that targums may contain traditions stemming from the first century, they rightly insist that each tradition must be traced individually. One cannot *assume* that traditions found in extant targums were known in the first century.

One targumic tradition about the tabernacle that may stem from the first century is found in *Tg. Neofiti* and the *Fragment Targums* to Lev 1:1.[144]

> And when Moses had completed erecting the tent and had anointed it, and consecrated it and all its vessels, and the altar and all its utensils, Moses thought in his heart and said, I did not ascend Mount Sinai, whose consecration was but the consecration of one hour and whose anointing was but the anointing of one hour, until the time that it was spoken with me from before the Lord. It is just that I should not enter within *the tent of meeting, whose consecration is an eternal consecration and whose anointing is an eternal anointing,* until the time it is spoken with me from before the Lord.

---

[141] For additional discussion of the rabbinic version of the tradition, see M. F. Collins, "Hidden Vessels," 104–6.

[142] A. Diez Macho, "The Recently Discovered Palestinian Targum: Its antiquity and relationship with other targums," VTSup 7 (1959) 222–45; idem, *Neophyti I: Targum Palestinese ms. de la Biblioteca Vaticana* (Madrid: Consejo Superior de Investigaciones Científicas, 1968) 1.57–95; M. MacNamara, *The New Testament and the Palestinian Targum to the Pentateuch* (AnBib 27; Rome: Biblical Institute, 1966) esp. 64–66, and *Targum and Testament. Aramaic Paraphrases of the Hebrew Bible: A Light on the New Testament* (Shannon: Irish University, 1972) esp. 86–89; and M. Black, *An Aramaic Approach to the Gospels and Acts* (3d ed.; Oxford: Clarendon, 1967) esp. 22–23.

[143] J. A. Fitzmyer, "The Languages of Palestine in the First Century A.D.," CBQ 32 (1970) 501–31, esp. 524–26; A. D. York, "The Dating of Targumic Literature," JSJ 5 (1974) 49–62; A. Shinan "The 'Palestinian' Targums — Repetitions, Internal Unity, Contradictions," JJS 36 (1985) 72–87; S. A. Kaufman, "On Methodology in the Study of the Targums and their Chronology," JSNT 23 (1985) 117–24.

[144] Translated by M. MacNamara, *Neophyti 1* (ed. Diez Macho) 1.317. Nearly identical passages appear in the Paris and Vatican MSS of the Fragment Targums. See M. Klein, *The Fragment Targums of the Pentateuch According to their Extant Sources* (AnBib 76; Rome: Biblical Institute, 1980). See also *Exod. Rab.* 19:3; 46:2; *'Abot R. Nat.* 2.

The last several lines resemble Philo's comment that "the sanctuary and the order of things arranged in it were ordained not for a limited time but for an infinite age" (*Q.E.* 2.53). The parallel suggests that the targumic tradition originated in the first century.

Yet the targumic reference is peculiar, since elsewhere the targums consider the temple (בית קודשא or בית מוקדשא) to be the most important sanctuary. For example, the targumic rendering of Jacob's blessings foretells that the temple will be built in the territory of Benjamin, and Issachar sees the temple as a resting place.[145] The targums also refer to "the language of the temple," which was probably Hebrew.[146] The targumic tradition apparently assumed that the "eternal consecration" applied not only to the tabernacle, but also to the temple.

The Tosepta provides some confirmation for this interpretation. *T. Zebaḥ.* 13:8 first delineates where offerings were to be made when the cult was in the wilderness, at Shiloh, and at Nob and Gibeon. Then, when Israel arrives at Jerusalem, "the eternal tabernacle" (משכן עולמים) is erected and they make offerings in "the eternal house" (בית עולמים). Here the eternal tabernacle and the eternal temple are one and the same.

SHEKINAH

Both the targums and rabbinic sources use the expression "Shekinah" (שכינה). Like the word משכן, or "tabernacle," it comes from the root שכן, "to dwell." Scholars have understood the Shekinah as an intermediary figure between God and the world, as a circumlocution for the divine name, or as God's mode of existing in the world.[147]

The Shekinah is mentioned only in the targums and in rabbinic literature; the term is not attested in first-century sources. The targums that refer to the Shekinah probably date from the second century A.D. or later. The Mishna mentions the Shekinah only three times; the references are attributed to the late second-generation tanna[148] R. Hananiah b. Teradion (ca. A.D. 110–135; *m. 'Abot* 3:2), possibly to the third-generation tanna R. Meir (ca. A.D. 130–160; *m. Sanh.* 6:5), and to the fourth-generation tanna R. Halafta b. Dosa (*m. 'Abot* 3:6). The Tosepta mentions the Shekinah

---

[145] *Frg. Tg.* and *Tg. Neof.* to Gen 49:15, 27.

[146] E.g., *Frg. Tg.* Gen 22:11; 35:18; 42:23, and *Tg. Neof.* Gen 31:47; 45:12.

[147] See the summary of research in A. M. Goldberg, *Untersuchungen über die Vorstellung von der Schekhinah in der frühen rabbinischen Literatur* (SJ 6; Berlin: de Gruyter, 1969) 1–12, and his own views on 531–38.

[148] Dates for the rabbis are taken from H. L. Strack, *Introduction to the Talmud and Midrash* (New York: Jewish Publication Society, 1931). Some MSS lack the reference to the Shekinah in *m. Sanh.* 6:5.

fourteen times; thirteen references are anonymous, one is attributed to R. Meir (*t. Menaḥ.* 7:8).

The term occurs more frequently in the tannaitic midrashim. The Mekilta mentions the term thirty-six times; three of the sayings are attributed to the late second-generation tannaim R. Ishmael and R. Aqiba, and two others to the third-generation tannaim R. Jose and R. Meir.[149] The Sipra uses the term twenty-two times; one appears in the opening *baraitot* that are ascribed to R. Ishmael, the rest are anonymous. The Siprei include the term sixty-two times; forty-six times in the book on Numbers and sixteen times in the book on Deuteronomy. None of the sayings is attributed to second-generation tannaim and only seven to third-generation tannaim.[150]

This survey of references indicates that we cannot assume that the term "Shekinah" was commonly used until well into the second century. Arnold Goldberg acknowledges the lack of first-century evidence for the term, but maintains that the lack of data is inconclusive for dating. He suggests that references to the Shekinah in exile or to the Shekinah within the community probably stem from the period after A.D. 70, but that the expression "the camp of the Shekinah" may have originated earlier.[151] Goldberg's suggestion is possible, but, as he acknowledges, has not been demonstrated. Therefore we cannot assume that the term was widely known until at least the time of R. Ishmael and R. Aqiba, ca. A.D. 110–135.

SUMMARY

Like earlier sources, rabbinic traditions stress the continuity between the tabernacle and the temple, and trace the movement of the cult from the wilderness to Jerusalem. Unlike earlier texts, the rabbinic sources include Nob and Gibeon among the locations of the tabernacle, and state that legal practices varied at different cult sites. The perception of continuity between tabernacle and temple may lie behind the targumic tradition that the tabernacle received an eternal anointing. An important connection between the tabernacle and the Mosaic law is the sabbath commandments. Rabbinic sources key the types of work prohibited on the sabbath to the types of work

---

[149] References to tractate and section appear first; after the semi-colon, the volume and page number in Lauterbach's edition is given. R. Ishmael (*Šabbata* 1; 3.198), R. Aqiba (*Pisḥa* 14; 1.114–15 and *Širata* 3; 2.27). R. Jose (*Baḥodeš* 3; 2.215) and R. Meir (*Bešallaḥ* 6; 1.233) were Aqiba's pupils.

[150] The section numbers are given. R. Josiah (*Sipre Num* 1), R. Jonathan (*Sipre Num* 1), R. Meir (*Sipre Num* 115), R. Simeon b. Yohai (*Sipre Num* 82; *Sipre Deut* 47, 255), R. Eleazer (*Sipre Deut* 173).

[151] *Schekhinah*, 443. Cf. D. Muñoz Leon, *Gloria de la Shekinah en los targumim del Pentatuco* (Madrid: Consejo Superior de Investigaciones Cientificas, 1977) 294.

done in the tabernacle, in contrast to *Jubilees* which keyed sabbath prohibitions to God's acts at creation. Rabbinic sources also include a version of the hidden vessels tradition, which claims that King Josiah hid the tabernacle, ark, and other items; earlier traditions typically linked the concealment to Jeremiah. The rabbinic traditions frequently differ from earlier sources because of a different or more extensive use of scripture.

C. Conclusion

Our survey of Jewish texts shows that the tabernacle was understood in diverse ways in the period from 200 B.C. to A.D. 150. Nevertheless, the characteristics of the tabernacle which were found in the OT continued to appear in many of the texts from the intertestamental period. (1) The tabernacle's role as a place of revelation was mentioned in Pseudo-Philo, was depicted as the place of apocalyptic vision in the *Testament of Moses,* and was associated with the wisdom and virtue that bring one closer to heavenly realities in Philo's works. (2) The tabernacle was remembered as a place of sacrifice by most authors, although Philo noted that sacrifices were not *essential* to the worship represented by the tabernacle. (3) The tabernacle also reminded readers how God acted faithfully toward Israel, by correcting Israel's apostasy during the wilderness period (*1 Enoch*), by promising and giving Israel the land (*T. Mos.*), and by choosing Jerusalem (4QDibHam). Such faithfulness provided a basis for hope that God would redeem his people in the future, as in the hidden tabernacle traditions.

Like the OT writings, intertestamental texts understood *Solomon's* temple to be the legitimate successor to the tabernacle, although their attitudes toward the *second* temple varied. Tobit was disappointed in the second temple, viewed almsgiving as virtually equivalent to sacrifice, and used the word "tabernacle" for the temple of the future. Ben Sira supported temple worship and used tabernacle imagery for wisdom's presence in the law, which was becoming equivalent to the cult for him, as for Tobit.

Tabernacle furnishings were included in the Temple Scroll's idealized remodeling of the second temple; the term "tabernacle" was used for a site in Jerusalem in 4QDibHam, a text that was favorable toward the first temple, and for the heavenly temple's holy of holies in 4QShirShabb, a text whose attitude toward the Jerusalem temple is unclear. The author of CD used the word "tent" for the temple, but considered the temple to be defiled.

The accounts of Israel's history, rabbinic texts, and targums perceived continuity in Israel's worship from the tabernacle to Solomon's temple. Some of these accounts also perceived continuity between the first and second temples (*Jub.,* Eupolemos, Pseudo-Philo, rabbinic sources, targums), but others disparaged the second temple (*1 Enoch, T. Mos.*).

According to Jewish hidden tabernacle traditions, the tabernacle, ark, and vessels were stored in the temple, then concealed when the temple was destroyed. Early forms of the tradition associated the reappearance of these items with the rededication of the second temple (2 Macc, cf. Eupolemos). Some versions that stem from the period after A.D. 70 anticipated a resumption of temple worship (*Par. Jer.*), but others were vague about the temple's restoration (*Lives of the Prophets, 2 Bar.,* cf. Pseudo-Philo).

Philo and Josephus revered the second temple, called the tabernacle a "portable temple," and used the same cosmological symbolism for both the tabernacle and temple. Yet the tabernacle represented a kind of worship that did not necessarily involve sacrifice, according to Philo, and continued to exist after the temple was destroyed, according to Josephus. The tabernacle and temple were related, but not identical.

The basic account of Israel's ancient tabernacle appeared in the book of Exodus, and later Jewish texts continued to perceive a close connection between the tabernacle and Mosaic law. Ben Sira used tabernacle imagery for wisdom's presence in the Mosaic law, and *Jubilees* stressed the continuity between tabernacle and temple because the author insisted that the laws of sacrifice were binding on all generations. The hidden tabernacle tradition indicated that the tent, ark, or vessels would be at the center of a law-observant community in the future. Philo associated the tabernacle with the abiding character of the law, and with the wisdom and virtue expressed in the law (cf. Wisdom 9). Like Josephus, he also used the cosmological interpretation of the tabernacle to commend observance of Jewish practices. Rabbinic texts delineated the sabbath regulations according to the tasks performed in the construction of the tabernacle.

The texts discussed in this chapter were composed in varied settings which cannot always be reconstructed with certainty, but memories of the tabernacle apparently continued to function as they had during the OT period. First, the tabernacle was sometimes associated with hopes for restoration or renewal in Israel. In the pre-Maccabean period, tabernacle imagery was used to express Tobit's expectations for a renewal of temple worship and for Ben Sira's hopes for a new outpouring of instruction. Traditions about the hidden tabernacle flourished after the Syrian desecration of the Jerusalem temple (167–164 B.C.), the destruction of the Samaritan temple in 128 B.C., and the destruction of the Jerusalem temple in A.D. 70, helping to foster hopes for a restoration of Israel's worship.

Second, references to the tabernacle provided continuity with the past for people in periods of transition. After the Maccabean purification of the temple, 2 Macc 2:4–8 conveyed expectations for the appearance of the tabernacle, which would confirm the continuity between the Maccabean temple and earlier sanctuaries. Eupolemos traced the continuity from tabernacle to temple to demonstrate the ancient origins of the cult of his own time. After the destruction of the Samaritan temple in 128 B.C. and the Jerusalem temple in A.D. 70, the hidden tabernacle tradition indicated that the tabernacle, ark, or vessels would provide continuity between the cult that was destroyed and worship of the future.

Third, remembering the tabernacle helped to foster unity in Israel. In the Hasmonean period, 2 Macc 2:4–8 was written to secure support for the Maccabees from Egyptian Jews and Eupolemos may have tried to accommodate the views of some Jews who expected worship to be directed by prophetic authority. *1 Enoch's* "Dream Visions" depicted the tabernacle as the place where God gathered the faithful after Israel's apostasy, which provided hope that the faithful would again be gathered together in a new Jerusalem, after the apostasy of the author's own time. The *Lives of the Prophets* and Samaritan tradition associated the reappearance of the tabernacle, ark, or vessels with the ingathering of God's people in time of persecution, and the Samaritan tradition actually precipitated such a gathering. Philo and Ben Sira used the tabernacle and tabernacle imagery to show the universal significance of the Jewish tradition in ways that would help draw Jews attracted by Hellenistic culture into the Jewish community.

The spectrum of texts discussed above shows how traditions concerning the tabernacle continued to develop in the changing circumstances of Jewish circles during the period 200 B.C. to A.D. 150. The authors of the NT were distinguished from the authors of these Jewish texts by the conviction that Jesus was the messiah. Yet we will see how early Christians drew on the OT and contemporary Jewish traditions, and transformed them in ways suitable for conveying Christian theology.

IV

THE BOOK OF ACTS

The tabernacle and tent of David appear at two key points in Acts: in the speech by Stephen before the Sanhedrin (Acts 7) and in the speech by James at the Jerusalem Council (Acts 15). Of these texts, the tabernacle's role in Stephen's speech is the more vigorously disputed. Marcel Simon has remarked that Stephen is apparently "an isolated figure in the history of the early Church"; in comparison to other forms of primitive Christian thought, his speech is "almost completely aberrant."[1] The speech is distinguished from most other early Christian writings by its hostility toward the Jerusalem temple. But what is even more puzzling is that, despite its antipathy toward the temple, the speech is favorable toward the tabernacle. Attention to these contrasting attitudes toward Israel's sanctuaries can help to clarify important aspects of the speech's theology. The role of the tabernacle in James's speech has received less attention, but the speech does occur at a pivotal juncture in the book and further develops the significance of the tabernacle in Acts.

A. The Tabernacle in Acts

Since the tabernacle appears in two different speeches, it may be useful to discuss the character of the speeches in Acts before dealing with each text individually.

On the Composition of Acts

Following the influential studies of Martin Dibelius,[2] scholars have often interpreted the speeches in Acts as literary compositions by the author of Luke-Acts rather than as transcripts of actual speeches. The Lucan authorship of the speech by James in Acts 15:13–21 seems clear. The main point, that God "visited the Gentiles to take out of them a people for his

---

[1] "Saint Stephen and the Jerusalem Temple," *JEH* 2 (1951) 127–42, esp. 127.

[2] "The Speeches of Acts and Ancient Historiography," *Studies in the Acts of the Apostles* (London: SCM, 1956) 138–85.

name," is based on the Greek version of Amos 9:12, not on the Hebrew text which reads quite differently. James himself almost certainly would have cited the Hebrew text at a council in Jerusalem, while the author of Luke-Acts regularly used the Greek version of the OT.[3]

The character of Stephen's speech has been more difficult to determine. The speech has been interpreted as a pre-Lucan composition, as a pre-Lucan work that has been edited, and as a composition by the author of Luke-Acts.[4] The view adopted here is that Luke derived his material from a source, but did not preserve his source verbatim. This interpretation is based on a number of factors.

First, the vocabulary of the speech is typical of that found elsewhere in Luke-Acts. Its style resembles the Greek of the LXX and the Lucan infancy narratives, and it is similar to the Greek of the surrounding narrative.[5] Therefore Acts 7 probably does not preserve a pre-Lucan source verbatim.

Second, the form of the speech differs from the other speeches in Acts. Eduard Schweizer has noted that speeches in Acts often begin by pointing out a misunderstanding among the hearers and include a proclamation of salvation. Speeches made to Jewish audiences regularly have a christological kerygma as well. These elements are missing from Stephen's speech.[6] The differences do not suggest that Luke composed a different type of speech that would be more appropriate for Stephen. Acts 7 is not a typical "martyr's apology," since it does not focus on the approaching death.[7] Although both the speech of Stephen and the one by Paul in Acts 13:16b–25 recapitulate Israel's history, Stephen's speech is many times longer than Paul's, even

---

[3] The MT text reads, "that they may possess the remnant of Edom." On the speech as a Lucan composition see, e.g., Dibelius, "Speeches," 178–79; E. Haenchen, *The Acts of the Apostles* (Philadelphia: Westminster, 1971) 448; G. Krodel, *Acts* (Augsburg Commentary on the NT; Minneapolis: Augsburg, 1986) 281.

[4] See the summary in E. Richard, *Acts 6:1–8:4: The Author's Method of Composition* (SBLDS 41; Missoula: Scholars, 1978) 26. Cf. H. Conzelmann, *Acts of the Apostles* (Hermeneia; Philadelphia: Fortress, 1987) 57–58.

[5] See B. W. Bacon, "Stephen's Speech: Its Argument and Doctrinal Relationship," *Biblical and Semitic Studies* (Yale Bicentennial Publications; New York: Scribners, 1901) 230–36; W. Mundle, "Die Stephanusrede Apg. 7: Eine Märterapologie," *ZNW* 20 (1921) 133–47, esp. 135; J. Bihler, *Die Stephanusgeschichte im Zumsammenhang der Apostelgeschichte* (Münchener theologische Studien I/16; Munich: Hueber, 1963) 81–86; Richard, *Acts,* 233–38.

[6] "Concerning the Speeches in Acts," *Studies in Luke-Acts* (ed. L. E. Keck and J. L. Martyn; Philadelphia: Fortress, 1980) 208–16. Cf. U. Wilckens, *Die Missionsreden der Apostelgeschichte: Form- und traditionsgeschichtliche Untersuchungen* (WMANT 5; 3d ed.; Neukirchen-Vluyn: Neukirchener, 1974) 30 n. 5.

[7] Mundle, "Stephanusrede." For critiques, see H.-W. Surkau, *Martyrien in jüdischer und frühchristlicher Zeit* (FRLANT 36: Göttingen: Vandenhoeck & Ruprecht, 1938) 109; Dibelius, *Studies,* 169.

though both recount approximately the same period of history.[8] Moreover, Stephen's speech is partially based on an OT text-type like that of the Samaritan Pentateuch, which is not found elsewhere in Acts.[9]

Third, the speech fits awkwardly in its context, since Stephen does not respond directly to the accusations made against him.[10] Witnesses charged that Stephen,

> never ceases speaking words against this holy place and the law; for we have heard him saying that this Jesus of Nazareth will destroy this place and will change the customs which Moses delivered to us (6:13–14).

Stephen did speak against the temple, but only after a lengthy rehearsal of Israel's history. More importantly, he did not *explicitly* link his anti-temple stance to Jesus as his opponents had charged and never responded to the charge that he had spoken against the law. On the contrary, he apparently accepted the "covenant of circumcision" (7:8), called the law God's "living words" (7:38), and charged that his opponents were the "uncircumcised in heart and ears," who had failed to keep the law (7:51, 53). Elsewhere in Acts, Peter and Paul respond much more directly to the charges made against them.[11] Since Stephen's response to charges is not typical Lucan style, Luke probably did not compose the speech to fit the narrative.

Fourth, Stephen's hostility toward the temple differs markedly from the more positive perception of the temple elsewhere in Luke-Acts. The gospel of Luke begins in the temple with the announcement of John the Baptist's birth and ends in the temple with the disciples blessing God. In Acts 1–5 the disciples continue to frequent the temple, and in 21:26 Paul enters the temple after performing the proper purifications.[12] Since the author of Luke-Acts was not hostile toward the temple, he probably would not have composed the sharp, anti-temple polemic that appears in Acts 7. Reasons why Luke included it will be explored below.

A number of scholars who have noted the non-Lucan elements in the speech have attributed the references to the tabernacle to a pre-Lucan source and ascribed the polemical portions, including the attack on the temple, to

[8] Similar recitations of past events are found in Josh 24, Pss 78 and 104, Neh 9, and Dan 9. See N. Dahl, "The Story of Abraham in Luke-Acts," *Studies in Luke-Acts,* 142; D. Juel, *Luke-Acts: The Promise of History* (Atlanta: Knox, 1983) 71.

[9] See R. Scroggs, "The Earliest Hellenistic Christianity," *Religions in Antiquity: Essays in Memory of Erwin Ramsdell Goodenough* (ed. J. Neusner; Studies in the History of Religions [Supplements to *Numen*] 14; Leiden: Brill, 1968) 193.

[10] On the history of the problem see J. Kilgallen, *The Stephen Speech* (AnBib 67; Rome: Biblical Institute, 1976) 6–10.

[11] Cf. Acts 4:7–12; 5:27–32; 11:1–18; 21:28/22:1–28.

[12] Cf. Acts 22:17; 24:18; 25:8.

Lucan redaction.[13] Yet attempts to divide the speech into polemical and non-polemical sections have been unsuccessful, since even the "neutral" portions of the speech have a polemical character. Stephen describes the jealousy of the patriarchs toward Joseph (7:9), in contrast to other summaries of Israel's history which omit the reference to jealousy or pass over the incident entirely (Ps 105:17; Josh 24:4; Neh 9:7-9; Jdt 5:10).[14] He also says that the patriarchs were buried at Shechem in Samaria, rather than at Hebron in Judea (Gen 25:10), which would be offensive to Jewish listeners. The reference to Moses' rejection in 7:35 is often treated as an addition, but the incident itself was recounted in detail in the "neutral" section 7:23-29. Many of the verses that are considered to be redactional are thoroughly integrated into their present context by the repetition of "this" Moses (7:35-38), and σκηνή and τύπος (7:43, 44). The accusation that Israel failed to keep the law (7:53) is not typical of Luke and does not clearly reveal Lucan editing. Therefore, since the speech cannot be neatly divided into a non-polemical source and polemical additions, we will read it as a unit.

ACTS 7:44-50: TABERNACLE VS. TEMPLE

According to the book of Acts, Stephen was brought before the Sanhedrin and charged with blaspheming the temple and the Mosaic law. He responded with a speech in which he recounted Israel's history. At the culmination of the speech he said,

> (7:44) Our fathers had the tent of witness (ἡ σκηνὴ τοῦ μαρτυρίου) in the desert, just as the one who spoke with Moses commanded him to make it according to the type that he had seen; (45) which our fathers in turn brought in with Joshua, at the dispossession of the nations, whom God drove out before our fathers, until the days of David, (46) who found favor before God, and asked to find a tabernacle (σκήνωμα) for the house of Jacob.
>
> (47) Yet Solomon built him a house. (48) But the Most High does not dwell in houses made with hands, as the prophet says, (49) "Heaven is my throne and earth is the footstool for my feet; what kind of house will you build for me, says the Lord, or what is the place of my rest? (50) Did not my hand make all these things?"

Acts 7:44-46 is comprised of a single sentence that favorably recounts the history of the tabernacle, from its beginning in the time of Moses to the

---

[13] Possible redactional elements include 7:35, 37, 39-40, 48-53. See Dibelius, *Studies,* 167-70; and esp. Haenchen, *Acts,* 288-89. M.-E. Boismard ("L'martyre d'Etienne. Actes 6,8-8,2," *RSR* 69 [1981] 181-94) attributes the polemical portions to the original speech and the non-polemical additions to Luke.

[14] See E. Richard, "The polemical Character of the Joseph Episode in Acts 7," *JBL* 98 (1979) 255-67.

establishment of a tent sanctuary in Jerusalem in the time of David. The language recalls the LXX. The tabernacle is called the σκηνὴ τοῦ μαρτυρίου and its pattern a τύπος.[15] Acts 7:46 says that when David found favor with God, he asked to find "a tabernacle for the house of Jacob." This verse cites a modified form of Ps 131:5 (LXX), which recalls how David brought the ark to Jerusalem and placed it in a tent (cf. 2 Sam 6:17).[16] The passage indicates that the construction of the tabernacle and the establishment of David's tent sanctuary in Jerusalem were in accordance with God's will.

Stephen's attitude toward the temple is quite different. He abruptly condemns Solomon's temple, calling it a house "made with hands" (χειροποίητος), an expression that often connoted idolatry.[17] Then he quotes Isa 66:1-2, which warns that human hands cannot build a house for God, since God's "hand" made heaven and earth for his throne and footstool.

Both the tabernacle and the temple were, of course, built by human beings. But the tabernacle was erected according to divine command, while Stephen considered the temple to be a purely human undertaking. Moses built the tabernacle because he was commanded to do so and David established a tent-shrine in Jerusalem because God was favorable toward the idea. But Stephen implies that the temple was solely Solomon's doing; he mentions no divine authorization for the project.

Most interpreters agree that Stephen sharply contrasted the tabernacle

---

[15] The LXX translates the Hebrew תבנית by τύπος in Exod 25:40 and by παράδειγμα in 25:9. On the complex relationship of Stephen's speech to OT texts see Richard, *Acts,* 38–155. See pp. 126–128 on Acts 7:44.

[16] The text of 7:46 is uncertain, but our interpretation can accommodate either of the main variants. Many MSS read "for the God of Jacob" instead of "for the house of Jacob." The "house" reading is preferable because it has better textual support and is a more difficult reading. The reading "God of Jacob" is probably a harmonization of Acts 7:46 with Ps 131:5; the author of Acts 7 may have changed "God of Jacob" to "house of Jacob" to make clear that the tent-sanctuaries were places of worship for Israel, not dwellings for God. Cf. B. Metzger, *A Textual Commentary on the Greek New Testament* (London: United Bible Societies, 1971) 351–53; A. F. J. Klijn, "Stephen's Speech – Acts VII.2-53," *NTS* 4 (1957–58) 25–31, esp. 29–30; G. Schneider, *Die Apostelgeschichte* (HTKNT 5; Freiburg: Herder, 1980) 1.466. If we accept "house of Jacob," then 7:44 and 46b are roughly parallel; "our fathers" had a tent in the wilderness and "the house of Jacob" had a tabernacle in Jerusalem. Accordingly, v. 47 is awkward, but intelligible; Solomon build a house "for him," that is, for Israel or the house of Jacob. Some scholars argue that "house of Jacob" is too difficult and prefer "God of Jacob." See Haenchen, *Acts,* 285; Wilckens, *Missionsreden,* 212; Richard, *Acts,* 131–32. Accordingly, the transition from v. 46 to v. 47 is much smoother, since the words "for him" now refer to God. According to both readings the tent sanctuaries were acceptable to God and the "house" or temple was not.

[17] Lev 26:1, 30; Isa 2:18; 10:11; 19:1; 21:9; 31:7; 46:6; Dan 5:4, 23; 6:27[28]; Jdt 8:18; Wis 14:8; Bel 5 (Theod.). In Isa 16:12 the term simply refers to a sanctuary.

and the temple, but a few exceptions should be noted. A. F. J. Klijn suggests that the "house of Jacob" was a select group or "house" within Israel which functioned as a sanctuary and replaced sacrifices.[18] Abram Spiro thinks that the "tabernacle" for the house of Jacob means the establishment of a secular capitol in Jerusalem,[19] and Rainer Storch maintains that the "tabernacle" indicates the temple as a house for *Israel* rather than as a house for God.[20] Similarly, Dennis Sylva argues that the tabernacle David sought must be the temple, since God did view his desire for a temple favorably (1 Kgs 8:18) and since Solomon himself said that God did not actually dwell in the temple (8:27). Accordingly, Stephen simply reasserted that "the Most High" transcended all sanctuaries "made with hands," without attacking the temple as such.[21]

Yet these interpretations contain difficulties. David never allotted a place to a special group within Israel who served as a sanctuary, nor did Stephen think that the sacrificial cult should be replaced by a sanctuary of human beings, as will be shown below. The word σκήνωμα, or "tabernacle" probably does not refer to a secular capitol, since elsewhere in the speech the cognate word σκηνή refers to a sanctuary. The "tabernacle" that David sought scarcely could be the temple since Stephen considered the temple to be Solomon's doing (Acts 7:47).[22] The structure of the speech, which will be discussed below, presents Solomon's temple in ways similar to the idolatrous tent of Molech, indicating that Stephen opposed the temple itself, not just the notion that God dwelt there.

Nils Dahl agrees that 7:44–46 refers to the tabernacle, but questions whether the speech sharply contrasts the tabernacle with the temple. He argues that since the rest of Luke-Acts shows a positive attitude toward the temple, Luke would not have included a harsh attack against the temple in Stephen's speech.[23] Nevertheless, the polemic tone of Acts 7:47–50 seems clear. Despite Luke's favorable attitude toward the temple elsewhere, the speech's hostility toward the temple is compatible with his interests, as will be shown below.

[18] "Stephen's Speech," 30.

[19] "Stephen's Samaritan Background," *The Acts of the Apostles* (J. Munck, et al.; AB 31; Garden City: Doubleday, 1967) 287.

[20] "Die Stephanusrede Apg 7.2–52" (Ph.D. diss., Göttingen, 1967) 96–97. See the summary in Wilckens, *Missionsreden,* 213.

[21] "The Function and Meaning of Acts 7:46–50," *JBL* 106 (1987) 261–75. See also E. Franklin, *Christ the Lord: A Study in the Purpose and Theology of Luke-Acts* (Philadelphia: Westminster, 1975) 105–7.

[22] See Wilckens' critique of Storch in *Missionsreden,* 213.

[23] "Abraham,"144.

THE TABERNACLE IN STEPHEN'S SPEECH

The movement of thought within the speech provides clues to the interpretation of 7:44-50. The speech recounts the fulfillment of the promises that God made to Abraham. The promises are drawn chiefly from Genesis 15 and 17, and are listed at the beginning of the speech.[24] God promised to give Abraham land as a possession (κατάσχεσις, 7:5; cf. Gen 17:8), which means possession of Canaan, and he also said that Abraham's descendants would be enslaved in Egypt and then freed (Acts 7:6-7a; cf. Gen 15:13-14). Finally, God promised that Israel would worship him "in this place" (Acts 7:7b). This final promise actually recalls a promise God made to Moses that after leaving Egypt, Israel would worship God "on this mountain," which was Sinai (Exod 3:12). Stephen's speech, however, transfers this promise from Moses to Abraham and changes the word "mountain" to "place." The word "place" refers to "the land in which you are now living" (Acts 7:4). Since the speech is addressed to people in Jerusalem, we must assume that worship in "this place" means worship in Canaan, or, more specifically, in the Jerusalem area.[25]

The body of the speech traces the fulfillment of these promises. In 7:8b Abraham receives a child as an initial step toward the fulillment of the land promise. Later, Abraham's descendents moved to Egypt, as God had foretold (vv. 9-15). When "the time of the promise drew near" (v. 17), Moses was born (v. 20) and later led the people out of Egypt (v. 36), thereby fulfilling the promise of deliverance. Joshua led the people into the land which they received for a possession (κατάσχεσις, v. 45), as God had promised (v. 5). When David established a tenting-place for God in Jerusalem, he fulfilled the final promise of worship in Jerusalem, showing that God was utterly faithful to his word.

One additional promise is introduced in 7:37, where Moses says, "God will raise up for you a prophet like me from among your brethren" (cf. Deut 18:15). Later, in 7:52 Stephen refers to "those who announced beforehand the coming of the righteous one," which alludes back to 7:37 and indicates that the advent of Christ fulfills the last promise mentioned in the speech.[26]

Stephen contrasts God's faithfulness to his promises with Israel's unfaithfulness.[27] He begins subtly by recalling how Joseph was sold into slavery and how God delivered him from affliction (7:9-10). Then he recounts

[24] Stressed by Dahl, "Abraham," 144; and Bihler, *Stephanusgeschichte,* 44-46. On the relationship of Acts 7:5-7 to the OT see Richard, *Acts,* 45-54.
[25] Cf. Haenchen, *Acts,* 279. Since the promise is addressed to Abraham, the "place" cannot be the temple, as in 6:13-14.
[26] Jesus is both the "Righteous One" and the prophet like Moses in Acts 3:14, 22.
[27] See Dahl, "Abraham," 147.

that Moses attempted to bring "deliverance" to an Israelite by killing an Egyptian, and that the Israelite later rebuked Moses by saying, "Who made you a ruler and a judge over us?" (7:27).

The next scenes are closely bound together by repeated expressions. Stephen introduces the account of the exodus by repeating the rebuke that an Israelite had made against Moses (7:27, 35). Then he extols Moses' greatness in a series of parallel statements.

> THIS MOSES—whom they refused, saying, "who made you a ruler and a judge?"—
> THIS one God sent both as ruler and deliverer by the hand of the angel which appeared to him in the bush.
> THIS one led them out, having done wonders and signs in the land of Egypt and at the Red Sea and in the wilderness for forty years.
> THIS is the Moses who said to the children of Israel, "God will raise up for you a prophet like me from among your brethren as he raised me up."
> THIS is the one who was in the congregation in the wilderness with the angel who spoke to him at Mt. Sinai and with our fathers; who received living words to give to us (7:35-38).

The words "this Moses" occur again in v. 40, providing a sharp contrast between the panegyric on Moses and Israel's apostasy. The people said to Aaron,

> Make for us gods which shall go before us,
> for THIS MOSES, who led us out of Egypt,
> we do not know what has happened to him.
> (Acts 7:40; Exod 32:1)

The expressions σκηνή, τύπος, and "made with hands" in 7:41-50 join the description of Israel's idolatry to the accounts of the building of the tabernacle and Solomon's temple.[28] At Sinai the Israelites offered sacrifices to "the works of their hands" (v. 41). Stephen described their actions in the words of Amos, who said that Israel took up "the tent (σκηνή) of Moloch and the star of the god Repham," which were figures or τύποι that they worshiped (7:42-43; Amos 5:25-27). Then Moses established a legitimate σκηνή according to the τύπος which he saw on Sinai (Acts 7:44). But Solomon later built a temple which was "made with hands" (7:48), like an idol.

The speech culminates by charging that Israel had consistently rejected God's law and prophets. Stephen refers to the prophets who "announced beforehand the coming of the righteous one" (7:52), which recalls the promise of a prophet like Moses (Acts 7:37). The coming of the prophet like

---

[28] See E. Richard, "The Creative Use of Amos by the Author of Acts," *NovT* 24 (1982) 37-53, esp. 43. On the use of σκηνή in Amos see chap. II above.

Moses was foretold by the law itself (Deut 18:15). Stephen believed that Jesus was the one whom the law and the prophets foretold. Therefore, those who rejected Jesus rejected God's law and prophet as Israel had done at Sinai.[29]

The emphasis on Israel's rejection of God's law and prophets is fundamental for the interpretation of Acts 7:44-50. Before describing the building of the tabernacle, Stephen recalls the apostasy at Sinai, when Israel rejected the prophet Moses and refused to obey the law, worshiping idols "made with hands."

Then he introduces the tabernacle as a sanctuary that was prescribed by the law. The angel who spoke to Moses on Sinai (ὁ λαλῶν, 7:38, 44) commanded him to make it and revealed the pattern. Then Moses, who was a prophet, constructed it. The law never mentions a temple, and the prophet Isaiah makes it clear that the silence of the law was no oversight; God did not want a "house"[30] (Isa 66:1-2; Acts 7:49-50). By building the temple, Solomon rejected what the law prescribed and what the prophet Moses had built. Therefore Solomon's action paralleled the apostasy at Sinai, when Israel rejected Moses and refused to obey the law.

Stephen's understanding of the tabernacle is twofold. First, the tabernacle stands for worship that is in accordance with God's law and prophets. Since the temple was not prescribed by law or established by a prophet, it was not a legitimate sanctuary. Christian worship is legitimate, however, because Jesus is the one foretold by the prophet Moses in the law.

Second, the tabernacle recalls the faithfulness of God. Even though Israel rejected Moses and the law, God provided them with a legitimate sanctuary, in order that they could worship in the land, as he had promised. By depicting the tabernacle as a direct contrast to the idolatrous "tabernacle of Moloch," Stephen presents the tabernacle as God's gracious response to Israel's idolatry.[31]

Other interpretations of Stephen's tabernacle theology do not fit the structure of the speech as well. According to William Manson, Stephen announced that it was time for Christians to move beyond Jewish institutions. "The mobile sanctuary of the early days corresponds with the idea of the ever-onward call of God to His people, the static temple does not."[32]

---

[29] Haenchen, *Acts,* 289; Franklin, *Christ the Lord,* 103-4.

[30] Stephen ignores the prophet Nathan, who approved the construction of Solomon's temple (2 Sam 7:3).

[31] The contrast between the golden calf incident and the construction of the temple is found in the present form of the Pentateuch. See chap. II above.

[32] *The Epistle to the Hebrews: An Historical and Theological Reconsideration* (Baird Lecture 1949; London: Hodder & Stoughten, 1951) 35. Cf. F. F. Bruce, *Commentary on the Book of Acts* (NICNT; Grand Rapids: Eerdmans, 1954) 157.

Similarly, other scholars maintain that the speech shows that God is not bound to a place. God revealed himself in Mesopotamia, Egypt, and the wilderness; his presence is not limited to one location. Therefore a mobile sanctuary is suitable for God, while a stationary temple is not.[33]

But Stephen reminded his listeners that God brought Israel into the land and provided the tabernacle as a means of true worship *in that place,* as he promised to Abraham. The mobile character of the tabernacle was not central for Stephen. Moreover, Stephen had not moved beyond all Jewish institutions, since he still considered the covenant of circumcision to be binding (7:8, 51-53).

Some scholars suggest that the speech's rejection of the temple included a rejection of sacrifices. Simon rightly points out that Stephen mentions sacrifices only in connection with idols (7:41-42) and suggests that the words "Did you offer to me slain beasts and sacrifices" (7:42) mean that God did not want sacrifices.[34] Martin Scharlemann says that by calling the tabernacle "the tent of witness," Stephen depicts it as the place where God spoke to Moses (e.g., Exod 33:7-11), rather than as a place of sacrifice.[35] Although only Isa 66:1-2a is quoted in the speech attributed to Stephen, Isa 66:3 does include a polemic against sacrifice.

Yet the speech does not necessarily oppose sacrifice. The question, "Did you offer to me sacrifices?" may mean that Israel offered sacrifices to idols when it should have offered them to God. Moreover, the OT commonly does identify the tent of meeting as a place of sacrifice,[36] and Stephen's indictment of temple worship does not mention sacrifices. He opposed the temple, but not necessarily the sacrificial cult.

ACTS 15:13-21: DAVID'S TENT REBUILT

After Stephen's death, the Christian mission was extended to Samaritans (chap. 8) and Gentiles (chaps. 10-14). The presence of Gentiles in the church sparked a debate concerning Gentile observance of the Mosaic law, which made it necessary to convene a council in Jerusalem to deal with the issue (chap. 15). Some conservative Jewish Christians insisted that circumcision and full observance of the Mosaic law were essential for Gentile Christians, but Peter argued that Jews and Gentiles alike were saved by grace

[33] B. Reicke, *Glaube und Leben der Urgemeinde: Bemerkungen zu Apg. 1-7* (ATANT 32; Zurich, 1957) 134; W. D. Davies, *The Gospel and the Land: Early Christianity and Jewish Territorial Doctrine* (Berkeley: University of California, 1974) 271.

[34] "Saint Stephen," 134; L. W. Barnard, "Stephen and Early Alexandrian Christianity," *NTS* 7 (1960-61) 31-45.

[35] *Stephen: A Singular Saint* (AnBib 34; Rome: Biblical Institute, 1968) 49.

[36] E.g., Exod 29:4, 10, 11, 32, 42; Lev 1:3, 5; 3:2, 8.

through the gift of the Holy Spirit and faith. Therefore, since the law was not essential for salvation, circumcision was not mandatory for Gentiles. After Barnabas and Paul spoke, James addressed the assembly.

> (15:13b) Brethren, listen to me. (14) Symeon has related how God first visited the Gentiles, to take out of them a people for his name. (15) And with this the words of the prophets agree, as it is written, (16) "After this I will return, and I will rebuild the tent (σκηνή) of David which has fallen; and I will rebuild its ruins, and I will restore it, (17) that the rest of humankind may seek the Lord, and all the Gentiles who are called by my name, (18) says the Lord, who does these things, which were known from of old." (19) Therefore, my judgment is that we should not trouble those of the Gentiles who turn to God, (20) but should write to them to abstain from the pollutions of idols, from unchastity, from what is strangled, and from blood. (21) For from early generations Moses has had in every city those who preach him, for he is read every sabbath in the synagogues.

The testimony of Peter, like that of Barnabas and Paul, was based on his experience in mission to the Gentiles. James confirmed this testimony by giving it a *scriptural* warrant.[37] His text was the Greek version of Amos 9:11-12, which spoke of the Gentiles — presumably uncircumcised Gentiles — who were called by God's name. Accordingly, James could maintain that Gentiles who had received the Holy Spirit could be counted as members of God's people even without circumcision.

The portion of Amos quoted by James presented the inclusion of Gentiles as a consequence of the rebuilding of "David's tent." This has sometimes been correlated with Jesus' resurrection,[38] since Luke presents Jesus as a descendant of David (Luke 1:32; 2:4) and indicates that Jesus' resurrection fulfilled the promise God made to David in the scriptures (Acts 2:25-36; 13:34-37). Nevertheless, a christological interpretation is highly unlikely, since Luke omitted *both* occurrences of the word "raise" (ἀνίστημι) from the Greek version of Amos 9:11-12, although the word would have provided a ready connection to Jesus' resurrection.[39]

Instead, the rebuilding of David's tent almost certainly refers to the establishment of the Jewish Christian church.[40] Elsewhere in Acts, Luke

---

[37] Krodel, *Acts,* 279; J. Jervell, *Luke and the People of God: A New Look at Luke-Acts* (Minneapolis: Augsburg, 1972) 189-91.

[38] Haenchen, *Acts,* 448.

[39] Noted by Krodel, *Acts,* 282.

[40] J. Munck, *Paul and the Salvation of Mankind* (Richmond: Knox, 1959) 112, 235; Franklin, *Christ the Lord,* 125, 128: Jervell, *Luke,* 143-44, 190; D. L. Tiede, *Prophecy and History in Luke-Acts* (Philadelphia: Fortress, 1980) 90-91. The Dead Sea scrolls contain varied interpretations of "the booth of David" mentioned in Amos 9:11. According to 4QFlor i 12-13,

presents David as a father of Israel (2:29; 4:25) and uses the term "build" (οἰκοδομέω) for the upbuilding of the church (9:31; 20:32). In Stephen's speech σκηνή and σκήνωμα designated the places of Israel's worship, culminating with David's establishment of a tent sanctuary in Jerusalem. Although Solomon built an idolatrous temple, God sent Jesus, the "Righteous One," and the implication was that true worship took place among those who accepted Jesus, as it had formerly taken place at David's tent. James makes this explicit, by identifying the Jewish Christian community as the restored tent of David.[41] Peter insisted that both Jewish and Gentile Christians depended on God's grace; James demonstrated that both represented the fulfillment of the words of the prophets.

The second part of the speech establishes a scriptural basis for table fellowship that did not require Jewish Christians to give up the law or Gentile Christians to observe it in its entirety.[42] By asking that Gentile Christians abstain from "the pollutions of idols and from unchastity and from what is strangled and from blood" (15:20), he was affirming what Moses had already said concerning sojourners in Leviticus 17–18, in the law that is "read every sabbath in the synagogues" (Acts 15:21). His plan would permit table fellowship within a church of Jews and Gentiles, while maintaining the church's continuity with its Mosaic heritage.

THE TABERNACLE IN ACTS

The book of Acts began with the programmatic statement by Jesus, "You shall receive power when the Holy Spirit has come upon you, and you shall be my witnesses in Jerusalem and in all Judea and Samaria and to the end of the earth" (1:8). At each stage of Christian expansion the author is concerned to show how the church maintained its continuity with the traditions of Israel.[43] The references to Israel's tent sanctuaries serve his purposes

---

"the fallen booth of David is the one who shall arise to save Israel," that is, the booth is a Davidic messiah. In CD vii 15–16, however, the booth is equated with the books of the law.

[41] Possible connections between Acts 7:44–46 and 15:16–17 have been noted by Dahl, "Abraham," 146; Juel, *Luke-Acts,* 75; and Richard, "Creative Use," 49. On the basis of this connection, Dahl argues that the promise to Abraham in Acts 7:7 was not fulfilled by either the tabernacle or the temple, but only by the early Christian community. But since *all* the other promises to Abraham were fulfilled in Acts 7, the tabernacle must be the fulfillment of worship "in this place." The early Christian community is the *rebuilding* of David's tent and the restoration of true worship in Jerusalem.

[42] A full discussion of the decree is beyond our study. For more extensive treatment see, e.g., Haenchen, *Acts,* 455–72; Conzelmann, *Acts,* 118–22; Krodel, *Acts,* 283–87.

[43] See, e.g., Jervell, *Luke,* 187–93; Tiede, *Prophecy,* 7–11; Juel, *Luke-Acts,* 101–12; R. J. Karris, "Missionary Communities: A New Paradigm for the Study of Luke-Acts," *CBQ* 41 (1979) 80–97.

well, since the tabernacle was an institution prescribed by law and established by the prophet Moses.

Stephen's address comes just before the Christian mission is extended to Samaria. The speech reaffirms the importance of "the covenant of circumcision" for Jewish Christians and indicates that those who accepted Jesus followed the will of God as made known through the law and the prophets, like those who worshiped in the tabernacle of old. In contrast, those who rejected Jesus were resisting God, like those who committed idolatry at Sinai and who built the first temple. Thus the speech establishes that Christian worship stood in continuity with the worship of ancient Israel, yet was independent of the Jerusalem temple. At the same time, the speech prepares for the extension of the Christian mission to the Samaritans, who followed the law but rejected the Jerusalem temple, and shows how such expansion was consistent with Israel's heritage.

Stephen's speech manifests a hostility toward the temple that differs from the more positive view of the temple elsewhere in Acts. Nevertheless, Luke could include this material because it was *compatible* with his interests. Acts was written after A.D. 70, when the temple had already been destroyed. Luke tried to show that the church continued the story of Israel but was not dependent on the continued existence of the temple. At first Christians frequented the temple, but Stephen's speech demonstrated that the touchstone for true worship was acceptance of Jesus, not loyalty to the temple. After Stephen's death Christians scattered, and some conducted a mission among the Samaritans, who observed the law but opposed the Jerusalem temple. Later, Paul was arrested in the temple, which initiated his journey to Rome. In his defense speech, Paul said that once he had approved of Stephen's death, but later, while he prayed in the temple, God sent him as a missionary to the Gentiles (22:20–21). Beginning with the story of Stephen, Luke described how Christians moved beyond the temple,[44] while remaining true to the tradition of the law and the prophets represented by Israel's tent sanctuaries.

The speech by James occurs at another key juncture in Acts—the Jerusalem Council's approval of the circumcision-free mission to Gentiles—and demonstrates that such a mission accords with the law and the prophets. Scriptural warrant appears in Amos 9:11–12, which refers to the rebuilding of the tent of David and the Gentiles called by God's name. James could tacitly identify David's tent with the Jewish Christian community since a similar connection was implicit in Stephen's speech, and he argued that if Gentiles could be called by God's name *as Gentiles,* then Gentile Christians

---

[44] See J. C. O'Neill, *The Theology of Acts in its Historical Setting* (2d ed.; London: SPCK, 1970) 81.

need not become circumcised. Instead, he proposed that Gentile Christians simply should follow several injunctions that the law itself prescribed for non-Jewish sojourners, while assuming that Jewish Christians would continue to observe the law. Thus the speech indicates that the circumcision-free mission to Gentiles was consistent with what was said in the law and the prophets.[45]

B. ANTECEDENTS FOR THE TABERNACLE IMAGERY IN ACTS

The speech of James is apparently a Lucan composition, and its interpretation of the "tent of David" as the Jewish Christian community was probably inspired by Stephen's speech. The speech attributed to Stephen, however, is probably comprised of pre-Lucan material that was adapted to its present context. Its message is Christian, but the antithesis between the tabernacle and temple is grounded in Israel's history, not in the advent of Jesus. Therefore it may be fruitful to explore pre-Christian sources for the roots of Stephen's attitude toward Israel's sanctuaries.

NATHAN'S PROPHECY

Marcel Simon has suggested that the speech reflects tensions between the tabernacle and temple that are already apparent in the OT.[46] He points out that in 2 Sam 7:5-6, God commanded Nathan to tell David,

> Would you build me a *house* to dwell in?
> I have not dwelt in a house since the day
> I brought up the people of Israel from Egypt to this day,
> but I have been moving about in a *tent* for my *tabernacle.*

The text contrasts the tent or tabernacle, which was God's chosen dwelling, with the house that David wanted to build. Simon interprets the text as radical opposition to the idea of a temple. In 2 Sam 7:13a God promised that Solomon *would* build a house for him, but Simon argues that the reference is an interpolation.[47]

---

[45] On the character of Paul's ministry in Acts see Jervell, *Luke,* 153–207; Krodel, *Acts,* 287.

[46] "Saint Stephen," 129–31 and "La prophétie de Nathan et le Temple," *RHPhR* 32 (1952) 41–58. His work builds on that of H.-J. Schoeps, *Theologie und Geschichte des Judenchristentums* (Tübingen: Mohr/Siebeck, 1949) 233–36. Cf. Bihler, *Stephanusgeschichte,* 72–73.

[47] "Saint Stephen," 130.

Simon rightly points out OT tensions between the tabernacle and the temple, but several difficulties make it unlikely that Nathan's prophecy was a major source for Stephen's views. (1) Even if 2 Sam 7:13a was *originally* an interpolation, the passage was known to the Chronicler (1 Chron 17:12), to the translator of the Greek version of Samuel, and to Eupolemos (*P.E.* 9.30.5-6). Therefore the verse was probably included in the text available to the author of Acts 7. (2) Nathan's initial response to the idea of a "house" was positive. He told David, "Go, do all that is in your heart for the Lord is with you" (2 Sam 7:3). (3) All the accounts of Israel's history noted in chap. III.C above were based in part on the OT, and all perceived continuity between the tabernacle and Solomon's temple. The extant form of 2 Samuel 7 eases earlier tensions between the tabernacle and the temple, and probably contributed little to the sharp contrast between the two sanctuaries presented in Acts 7:44-50.

SAMARITAN TRADITIONS

A number of scholars hold that Samaritan thought provides better precedents for Stephen's ideas. Abram Spiro observes that Samaritan sources reject the Jerusalem temple and call the Samaritan sanctuary a tabernacle, which was not of purely human construction, since it followed a heavenly pattern.[48] Martin Scharlemann adds that the Samaritans considered the period of Joshua and the tabernacle to be an age of "favor."[49]

The Samaritan interpretation is bolstered by various types of supporting evidence. (1) A tradition found in a 14th century work by Abul Fath indicates that Stephen was a Samaritan. (2) Acts 7:4, 5, 32, 37 diverge from the MT and LXX, but agree with the Samaritan Pentateuch. (3) Stephen alters biblical passages to reflect a Samaritan view of history. He changes the location of true worship from a "mountain" (Exod 3:12) to a "place," which was what Samaritans frequently called their sanctuary, says that Abraham was buried at Shechem (Acts 7:16) rather than at Hebron (Gen 25:10), and alters Amos's oracle from an attack on the northern kingdom to an attack on the southern kingdom by substituting the word "Babylon" for "Damascus" (Acts 7:43; Amos 5:27). (4) The speech has affinities with Samaritan theology, which ascribed a central role to Moses and the prophet like Moses (Acts 7:37), and opposed the Jerusalem temple. (5) After Stephen's death, members of Stephen's circle were active in Samaria (8:5).[50]

---

[48] "Samaritan Background," 286-87.

[49] *Stephen,* 50.

[50] Evidence for the Samaritan interpretation appears in Spiro, "Samaritan Background"; C. H. Scobie, "The Origins and Development of Samaritan Christianity," *NTS* 19 (1972-73) 390-414, esp. 391-400; Scharlemann, *Stephen,* 45-51; Scroggs, "Earliest," 189-97; Cullmann,

Yet there are a number of problems with this supporting evidence. (1) Most Samaritan sources are of late or uncertain date. We cannot assume that the tradition found in Abul Fath stems from the first century or that theological positions found in later sources reflect first-century beliefs.

(2) Recent investigations into the history of the OT text indicate that a number of OT text types were used in the first century. The Samaritan Pentateuch represents a type of "popular" text which circulated among various groups; examples of a similar text type have been found at Qumran. Therefore agreements between Stephen's speech and the Samaritan Pentateuch do not demonstrate connections with Samaria.[51]

(3) The claim that Abraham was buried at Shechem (Acts 7:16) probably does reflect a Samaritan tradition, which is also attested in material derived from Julius Africanus (third century A.D.).[52] The other changes however do not convey a distinctly Samaritan perspective. The author of Acts 7 cited Amos 5:25-27 (cf. Acts 7:42-43) because it refers to the wilderness period, and contains the words σκηνή and τύπος, which anticipate the discussion of the tabernacle. He changed "Babylon" to "Damascus," in order to indict the Judeans, but did not indicate that the Samaritans were guiltless.[53] A Samaritan author would not need to change the word "mountain" to "place," since the Samaritan sanctuary was located on Gerizim, which was a mountain. Moreover, the word "place" was used for various sanctuaries, including the Jerusalem temple.[54]

(4) Samaritan theology did ascribe a central role to Moses and included expectations for a prophet like Moses, but such ideas were not unique to them. Expectations of a prophet like Moses also appear in Philo (*Spec.* 1.65), the Dead Sea Scrolls (4QTest i 1-8; 1QS ix 11), and in Peter's speech in Acts

---

Johannine Circle, 46-50; Gaston, *No Stone,* 159-61; J. Bowman, *The Samaritan Problem: Studies in the Relationship of Samaritanism, Judaism, and Early Christianity* (Delitzsch Lectures 1959; Pittsburgh: Pickwick, 1975) 83-86.

[51] Cf. Scroggs, "Earliest," 192-93; R. Pummer, "The Samaritan Pentateuch and the New Testament," *NTS* 22 (1975-76) 441-43; E. Richard, "Acts 7: An Investigation of the Samaritan Evidence," *CBQ* 39 (1977) 190-208; C. H. H. Scobie, "The Use of Source Material in the Speeches of Acts III and VII," *NTS* 25 (1978-79) 399-421, esp. 402-5; W. H. Mare, "Acts 7: Jewish or Samaritan in Character?" *WJT* 34 (1971) 1-21, esp. 9. Mare cites instances where Stephen agrees with the LXX against the MT and Samaritan Pentateuch.

[52] The tradition attributed to Julius Africanus is attested by Syncellas (PG 10.72A) and Pseudo-Eustathius (PG 18.777D-780A). See Kippenberg, *Garizim,* 111-12. G. Stemberger ("Die Stephanusrede [Apg 7] und die jüdische Tradition," *Jesus in der Verkündigung der Kirche* [ed. A. Fuchs; Friestadt: Ploechl, 1976] 164-65) disagrees, since the tradition is not attested in Samaritan sources.

[53] Schneider, *Apostelgeschichte,* 1. 451-52. Cf. Bowman, *Samaritan Problem,* 84.

[54] BAGD, τόπος, 1b.

3:22. Both the Samaritans and the author of Stephen's speech opposed the Jerusalem temple, but they did so for different reasons. The Samaritans believed that Mt. Gerizim was the place that God had chosen for his sanctuary and that the era of God's favor ended when Eli established a rival sanctuary at Shiloh.[55] But Stephen says that David did find favor with God and established a legitimate sanctuary in Jerusalem, and he never advocates Gerizim as a place of worship. The Samaritans considered Eli to be apostate because he changed the *location* of the sanctuary; Stephen considered Solomon to be apostate because he changed the *character* of the sanctuary, from the tent which God desired, to a house of human making.

Apart from the tradition concerning the burial of the patriarchs, none of the evidence suggested thus far suggests that the speech is Samaritan *in origin*. Yet the speech does contain certain features that are *compatible* with Samaritan theology. The interpretation that best explains the character of the speech is that it was composed by Jewish Christians who did mission work in Samaria.[56] This hypothesis accords well with Acts 8:5, which says that Philip, who was Stephen's associate, initiated a ministry in Samaria. Moreover, the author of the speech may have learned of the Samaritan tradition concerning Abraham's tomb while engaged in the Samaritan mission. This interpretation falls short of proof, but it accounts for the presence of a Samaritan tradition in the speech better than any other hypothesis presented thus far.

DEAD SEA SCROLLS

In addition to Samaritan sources, scholars have proposed various Jewish antecedents for Stephen's theology. Oscar Cullmann has argued that Stephen's views were anticipated by the Qumran sect's opposition to the temple, and A. F. J. Klijn has suggested that Stephen's group was actually related to the Qumran sect.[57] A major difficulty with these proposals is that the Qumran community opposed the Hasmonean priesthood, not the temple itself, as did Stephen's speech.[58] Moreover, the extra-biblical Dead Sea Scrolls do not mention the Israelite tabernacle. The word "tabernacle" is used for Jerusalem as the place of the temple in the Words of the Heavenly Lights and for the heavenly throne room in the Songs of the Sabbath Sacrifice. The word "tent" was used for the temple in the Damascus Document and as a poetic description of God's protection in the Thanksgiving

---

[55] On Eli's apostasy see J. Macdonald, *The Theology of the Samaritans* (London: SCM, 1964) 17.

[56] See Scroggs, "Earliest," 200; Scobie, "The Use," 415.

[57] Cullmann, "L'opposition," 164–66; Klijn, "Stephen's Speech," 28–31.

[58] Haenchen, *Acts,* 260–61 n. 3.

Hymns. The Temple Scroll incorporated tabernacle furnishings into its plan for an ideal temple. But none of these passages resembles Stephen's speech.

DIASPORA JUDAISM

Some scholars have suggested that Stephen's views reflect the attitudes of Greek speaking diaspora Jews, who criticized the Jerusalem temple as philosphers criticized pagan temples. Simon notes that according to Justin's *Dialog with Trypho* 117.2, some Jews insisted that God desired prayers, not the sacrifices that were offered in Jerusalem. The *Sibylline Oracles* 4:8–11, 27–30 provide an even stronger critique by renouncing all temples and animal sacrifice.[59]

Possible parallels between Stephen's speech and *Sib.Or.* 4 are attractive, since both texts seem categorically to reject temple worship as idolatrous. *Sib.Or.* 4:2 also claims to be spoken by a prophet, which could echo the tension between the temple and prophetic authority that appears in the speech. Yet these texts also differ significantly. *Sib.Or.* 4:27–30 expressly rejects temples, altars, and animal sacrifices. Stephen opposed the Jerusalem temple, but esteemed the tabernacle, a sanctuary which included an altar on which animal sacrifices were made. Stephen's attitude toward sacrifices is ambiguous; he never overtly opposed the practice.

THE "DREAM VISIONS" AND TESTAMENT OF MOSES

1 Enoch's "Dream Visions" (second century B.C.) and the *Testament of Moses* (early first century B.C.) resemble Stephen's views more closely than any of the sources noted thus far.[60] Like Stephen, both of these works view the tabernacle favorably. The "Dream Visions" present the tabernacle as a response to Israel's idolatry at Sinai. The tabernacle in turn became the foundation for the first temple, but the temple was repeatedly polluted and was finally destroyed. The second temple was defiled from the beginning. In the end times, God would remove Jerusalem and the temple, and establish a new Jerusalem, where God's people would be gathered together as they once were at the tabernacle. The vision makes no mention of a restoration of the cult.

The *Testament of Moses* describes how the prophet Moses appointed Joshua as a leader for the people and a minister in the tent of witness (1:6–9). Like Stephen, the *Testament* is favorable toward the establishment of the tabernacle in Jerusalem (2:4) and grants that acceptable sacrifices were offered in Jerusalem during certain periods of the monarchy. Nevertheless, the author recalls that during the monarchy idols were set up in the sanctuary

---

[59] "Saint Stephen," 132, 136–37. Cf. Bihler, *Stephanusgeschichte,* 144–48.
[60] On these texts see sec. III.C above.

and the first temple became defiled. After the exile a second temple was built, but acceptable sacrifices were never offered in it (4:8). During the Hasmonean and Herodian periods the temple was constantly polluted (5:3) and many who offered sacrifices there could not be considered true priests (5:5; 6:2). When the Romans burned a portion of the temple in 4 B.C., the author of the *Testament* believed that time was nearing an end. His hope for salvation was rooted in God's faithfulness to the promises that he made in the tabernacle (1:6–9: 12:13), but his vision of the future did not mention a restored temple.

The "Dream Visions" and *Testament of Moses* esteemed the tabernacle, but insisted that the first temple became idolatrous during the monarchy and that the second temple was defiled from its inception. Stephen's speech may represent a further development of these views. The speech still views the tabernacle favorably, but argues that true worship was never possible in the Jerusalem temple, even in Solomon's time.

Possible connections between Stephen's speech and the *Testament of Moses* are bolstered by two passages that contain nearly identical wording. Note especially the last four lines: "in the land of Egypt, and at the Red Sea, and in the desert forty years."

CHART 4

T. Mos. 3:11	*Acts 7:36*
Moyses . . .	[Μωϋσῆς . . .]
qui multa passus est	ποιήσας τέρατα καὶ σημεῖα
in aegypto	ἐν γῇ Αἰγύπτῳ
et in mari rubro	καὶ ἐν ἐρυθρᾷ θαλάσσῃ
et in heremo	καὶ ἐν τῇ ἐρήμῳ
annis xl.	ἔτη τεσσεράκοντα

Moreover, the first part of *T. Mos.* 3:11 depicts Moses as a suffering prophet, a theme which is compatible with Stephen's description of Moses the rejected prophet. Additional similarities include the emphasis on Moses as prophet (1:5; 3:11; 11:16) and mediator of the law (1:14; 3:12), and on the covenant of circumcision (8:1).

There are also significant differences between these works, which make it unlikely that Acts 7 depended directly on the *Testament of Moses*. Both have messianic hopes, but Stephen's speech mentions the prophet like Moses and "the righteous one," while the *Testament* refers to a priestly messenger or angel (10:2). The *Testament* frequently depicts Moses as an intercessor (11:11, 14, 17; 12:6) and mediator of apocalyptic secrets, but these ideas are not found in Acts 7.

Despite these differences, the speech and the *Testament* view the tabernacle and temple in similar ways, have verbal parallels, and share similar views of Moses. Therefore they may have originated in a similar milieu. Like the "Dream Visions," the *Testament* almost certainly was composed in Palestine, which suggests that Stephen's speech also stems from Palestine. Unfortunately, the *Testament* cannot readily be identified with any known Jewish group. Attempts to attribute it to the Dead Sea sect or to the Samaritans have not been successful, since the *Testament* has not been found at Qumran, mentions no sectarian community, and contains no distinctly Samaritan beliefs, like the sanctity of Gerizim. Therefore, the interrelationship between the circles which produced the *Testament* and Stephen's speech remains unclear.

THE PSEUDO-CLEMENTINE RECOGNITIONS

Similarities between Stephen's speech and portions of the Pseudo-Clementine *Recognitions* have often been noted,[61] and a brief comparison of the texts provides indirect evidence that the theology of the speech was associated with Jewish Christians living in or near Palestine. In its present form, the *Recognitions* dates from the third or fourth century A.D. But Georg Strecker has plausibly argued that chaps. 33–71 preserve an older source, known as the *Ascents of James,* which circulated among law-observant Christians in Transjordan.[62] The most important similarities between Stephen's speech and the *Ascents* are as follows:

	Recog. Book I	Acts
Moses works miracles	34.4–7; 41.1	7:36
Moses receives the law	35.2	7:38
Israel's apostasy	35.5	7:39–40
God appoints a "place" of sacrifice	36.1	7:44 (tabernacle)
Moses foretells true prophet	36.2	7:37
King impiously erects temple at the "place"	38.5	7:47–50
True prophet rejected	40.2	7:52
Law remains binding for Christians	43.2	7:8, 53

[61] Bacon, "Stephen's Speech," 259–60; Schoeps, *Theologie,* 240, 440–44; Simon, "Saint Stephen," 139–40.

[62] *Das Judenchristentum in den Pseudoclementinen* (TU 70; 2d ed.; Berlin: Akademie, 1981) 221–54.

Both works depict the tabernacle or "place" as God's response to Israel's idolatry and the first temple as an act of impiety, describe the rejection of Moses, and indicate that the law was binding for Christians. Since both works contain a very similar theology, there may be a connection between them.

The similarities simply may reflect the literary dependence of the *Ascents* on Acts 7. The author of the *Ascents* did know the canonical book of Acts and *Recog.* I.33–41 runs roughly parallel to Stephen's speech.[63] Therefore *Recog.* I.33–41 could be a reworking of Acts 7. But the *Ascents* may also convey elements of a tradition similar to Stephen's speech, which circulated outside canonical Acts. The *Ascents* explicitly calls the tabernacle a place of sacrifice and a place of prayer (*Recog.* I.37.1; 38.5) and insists that the tabernacle was only instituted for a limited period of time (37.2; 39.1). These elements are not readily apparent in Acts 7 and probably stem from other sources. Therefore, the *Recognitions may* provide evidence that theology similar to that of Stephen's speech circulated among Jewish Christians in and around Palestine into the second century.

SYNTHESIS

On the basis of the preceding investigation we can attempt to place Stephen's speech within theological currents from the Maccabean period to the second century A.D. We recall that Stephen revered the tabernacle because it was mandated by the law and established by a prophet. He rejected the temple because it met neither criterion.

During the Maccabean period, certain groups insisted that cultic matters were to be governed by prophetic authority (e.g., 1 Macc 4:46). Eupolemos, a Maccabean supporter, accommodated these beliefs.[64] Before describing Solomon's temple, he mentioned the prophets Moses, Joshua, and Samuel, who were associated with the tabernacle in the wilderness and at Shiloh. Then Eupolemos described how the prophet Nathan approved of Solomon's temple and even provided its dimensions, which accorded with those of the postexilic temple (*P.E.* 9.34.2). The temple's lampstands were patterned after the lampstand in the Mosaic tabernacle (9.34.5) and at the dedication, Solomon placed the tabernacle in the temple "as the prophet commanded him" (9.34.13). Later, Simon Maccabeus became high priest in perpetuity, "until a trustworthy prophet should arise" (1 Macc 14:41).

---

[63] Strecker, *Judenchristentum,* 224; J. L. Martyn, *The Gospel of John in Christian History: Essays for Interpreters* (New York: Paulist, 1978) 59, 63–64. On the text and transmission of this material see my article "The Origin and Significance of the Flight to Pella Tradition," *CBQ* 51 (1989) 90–106, esp. 97–103.

[64] On Eupolemos see chap. III.C above.

Jonathan Goldstein points out that the proviso about the prophet probably reflects a concession made to certain Jewish parties at the time of Simon's accession.[65]

Others tried to overcome the discrepency between the actual shape of the second temple and the Mosaic law's prescriptions for the tabernacle. The Chronicler had dealt with the difficulty by claiming that *David* received plans for the first temple "in writing from the hand of the Lord" (1 Chron 28:19). In the second century B.C. the Temple Scroll went further, purporting to give the temple plans which *Moses* received from God. Yet the actual second temple did not follow the plans of this new Torah.

In subsequent years, the second temple and its priesthood came under repeated attacks from various groups. The Qumran community charged that the Hasmonean priests had defiled the sanctuary (1QpHab xii 8-9). One of the Pharisees asked Simon's successor John Hyrcanus to relinquish the high priesthood (*Ant.* 13.10.5 #291). In the first century B.C. the *Psalms of Solomon* charged that Pompey's invasion of the temple was due to the sins of temple leaders, whose "lawless actions surpassed those of the gentiles before them; they completely profaned the sanctuary of the Lord" (1:8; 2:3; 8:13).

Some of the more extreme critics rejected the second temple entirely. The "Dream Visions" and the *Testament of Moses* traced the history of the cult from its legitimate beginnings under Moses to the establishment of a sanctuary in Jerusalem. But idolatry polluted the first temple during the period of the monarchy, and the second temple was defiled from its inception. Neither the "Dream Visions" nor the *Testament* expected a restoration of the temple cult in the end times.

Similar views reappear in Stephen's speech. The author of the speech still acknowledged the legitimacy of the tabernacle because it was prescribed by law and had been established by the prophet Moses, but his condemnation of the temple was more sweeping than that of his predecessors. He insisted that the first temple was idolatrous from the beginning. For him true worship was Christian in character, because Jesus was the one who had been foretold by the prophet Moses in the law.

In the late first century, after the destruction of the temple, the views represented in Stephen's speech were incorporated into the book of Acts. During this period Christianity was becoming increasingly distinct from Judaism, but the author of Acts insisted that the church maintained its continuity with Israel's heritage. Stephen's speech acknowledged that true worship accorded with the law and the prophets and was represented by the tabernacle, but it insisted that such worship occurred in the church, not in

---

[65] *I Maccabees* (AB 41: Garden City: Doubleday, 1976) 508.

the temple. After the speech, Luke recounted the expansion of Christianity to the Samaritans, a group that observed the law but rejected the temple. Luke developed Stephen's tabernacle theology further in the speech attributed to James, where the growth of the Jewish Christian community was depicted as the restoration of David's tent, which laid the foundation for a circumcision-free mission to Gentiles, as promised in Amos 9.

C. Conclusion

Stephen's speech presents a twofold interpretation of the tabernacle. First, the tabernacle stands for worship that is in accordance with God's law and prophets. The author of the speech rejected the temple because it was not prescribed by the law or established by a prophet. Christian worship was legitimate, however, because Jesus was the one foretold by the law and the prophets. Therefore the church followed the will of God, like those who worshiped in the tabernacle of old.

Second, the tabernacle represents God's faithfulness despite Israel's unfaithfulness. The patriarchs sold Joseph into slavery, but God delivered him. An Israelite rejected Moses as "ruler and judge"; yet God sent "this Moses," who had been rejected as "ruler and judge," to free Israel. The people rejected "this Moses" and took up an idolatrous σκηνή and τύποι, but God's angel revealed the τύπος of a legitimate σκηνή, so that Israel could worship in the land as God had promised. Solomon rejected the tabernacle and built a temple, but God later sent the Righteous One. Many in Israel rejected him, and there the speech concludes. Stephen did not say what God would do next. Luke provided his own answer in the account of the Samaritan mission.

Stephen's affirmation of the covenant of circumcision and his antipathy toward the temple introduced Luke's account of the extension of Christianity to the Samaritans, a group that did observe the law but did not accept the Jerusalem temple. The speech by James in turn gave scriptural warrant for the circumcision-free mission to Gentiles. James cited Amos 9:11-12 and tacitly equated the rebuilt tent of David mentioned there with the Jewish Christian community. Since Amos indicated that the rebuilding of David's tent would mean the inclusion of Gentiles in God's people, James concluded that that circumcision could not be required of Gentile Christians.

The OT texts that lie behind Stephen's speech include Exodus 25-40, which describes the construction of the tabernacle, and Psalm 132 which recalls David's desire to establish a tent sanctuary in Jerusalem. The speech of James cites Amos 9:11-12, as noted above. The intertestamental sources with views of the tabernacle and temple closest to those found in Acts include *1 Enoch's* "Dream Visions" and the *Testament of Moses.* Both of these texts depict the tabernacle favorably, indicate that the first temple began well but became idolatrous, and insisted that the second temple was unfit from its inception. Stephen's speech may represent a further development of these views, which insisted that even the first temple was idolatrous from its beginning.

V

JOHN'S GOSPEL

John's gospel includes one allusion to the tabernacle: "The Word became flesh and tabernacled among us, and we beheld his glory" (1:14). This verse is often considered to be the climax of the prologue, and considerable attention has been given to the significance of "flesh" and "glory" for John's christology.[1] The tabernacle imagery has attracted much less attention, but it may provide an alternative approach to the interpretation of John 1:14 and to its significance for the theology of the Fourth Gospel.

A. The Tabernacle in John's Gospel

In order to interpret John's tabernacle imagery, we will first examine the composition of the prologue, then discuss 1:14 and its role within the prologue, and finally explore the significance of 1:14 for the gospel as a whole.

On the Composition of the Prologue

John's allusion to the tabernacle is sometimes interpreted as part of a pre-Johannine source to which editorial comments have been added, and sometimes as part of a unified composition by the evangelist. Those who follow the source and redaction approach usually maintain that 1:14 was a line of a logos-hymn that formed the nucleus of John's prologue. There are several reasons for this view.[2] (1) Parts of the prologue are highly poetic,

---

[1] R. Bultmann considered the reference to "flesh" to be a frontal attack on docetic christology (*The Gospel of John: A Commentary* [Philadelphia: Westminster, 1971] 63). E. Käsemann has argued that flesh is primarily a means for the revelation of the divine *glory* that dominates John's christology and actually reflects unconscious docetic tendencies ("The Structure and Purpose of the Prologue to John's Gospel," *New Testament Questions of Today* [Philadelphia: Fortress, 1969] 138–67, esp. 158–59; idem, *The Testament of Jesus According to John 17* [Philadelphia: Fortress, 1968] 26).

[2] The main issues and opinions are succinctly presented in R. E. Brown, *The Gospel According to John* (AB 29–29A; Garden City: Doubleday, 1966–1970) 1.18–23; R. Schnackenburg, *The Gospel According to St John* (New York: Herder & Herder, 1968) 1.221–29. An extensive comparison of proposals and additional bibliography are provided by G. Rochais, "La formation du prologue (Jn 1,1–18)," *ScEs* 37 (1985) 5–44.

while others seem to be written in prose. Climatic parallelism and a rhythmic pattern are most evident in 1:1–5, but also seem to be present in 1:14 and 16. Passages like 1:6–8 and 15 do not seem to have the same poetic character. (2) Certain verses, like the passages on John the Baptist (1:6–8, 15), disrupt the movement of thought. (3) John 1:14 contains key words and concepts that do not appear in the body of the gospel, including σκηνόω ("to tabernacle"), πλήρης ("full"), and χάρις ("grace"), and the use of λόγος ("word") as a christological title. Those who favor the logos-hymn hypothesis ascribe lines that are written in prose, interrupt the movement of thought, and contain typical Johannine vocabulary to the redactor. The other lines, including 1:14, are attributed to the logos-hymn.

Other scholars argue that the prologue can best be understood as a unified composition.[3] (1) A sharp distinction between prose and poetry is difficult to maintain; the entire prologue is written in "rhythmical prose." (2) The sections that appear to be interpolations give symmetry to the prologue. Comments on Jesus' relationship to God, on his coming into the world, and on John the Baptist occur twice: once in the first half of the prologue and again in inverse order in the second half (1:1/18; 1:6–8/15; 1:9/14). (3) Although 1:14 contains key words not found in the body of the gospel, the verse also includes μονογενής ("only-begotten") and δόξα ("glory"), which are important in the body of the gospel. Moreover, those who advocate the logos-hymn hypothesis do agree that the present form of the prologue is firmly wedded to the gospel by themes like light, life, glory, truth, and acceptance and rejection.[4] Therefore even though the evangelist may have used a logos-hymn as a source, the present form of the prologue can be treated as a unified composition and an integral part of the gospel.

The evangelist unified the prologue by repeating key words. This technique is most highly developed in 1:1–5, where the words λόγος ("word"), θεός ("God"), ἀρχή ("beginning"), γίνομαι ("to become"), ζωή ("life"), φῶς ("light"), and σκοτία ("darkness") bind the section tightly together. The word φῶς ("light") in 1:6–8 connects the comments on John the Baptist with 1:4–5 and 1:9. References to κόσμος ("world") in 1:9–10 join the story of the Word's rejection to the story of creation (1:9–10). Παραλαμβάνω and λαμβάνω ("to receive") connect the comments on those who did and those who did not receive the Word (1:11–12).

---

[3] C. K. Barrett, *The Gospel According to St. John* (2d ed.; Philadelphia: Westminster, 1978) 150; P. Borgen, "Logos was the True Light," *NovT* 14 (1972) 115–30, esp. 116–17; R. A. Culpepper, "The Pivot of John's Prologue," *NTS* 27 (1980–81) 1–31, esp. 1–2. See also E. Haenchen ("Probleme des johanneischen Prologs," *ZTK* 60 [1963] 305–34, esp. 309) who acknowledges that the whole prologue is written in hymnic prose, although he does attempt to distinguish the logos hymn from redactional elements.

[4] E.g., Bultmann, *John*, 13; Brown, *John*, 1:19; Schnackenburg, *John*, 1.221.

The same technique links 1:14 to 1:1–13, and especially to 1:15–18. The word σάρξ ("flesh") joins 1:13 and 1:14, and the word λόγος ("word") ties the thought of 1:14 to 1:1. The words πλήρης / πλήρωμα ("full"/"fulness"), χάρις ("grace"), and ἀλήθεια ("truth") join 1:14 to 1:16–17, and the word μονογενής ("only-begotten") joins 1:14 and 1:18. Therefore 1:14 must be interpreted in light of the verses that precede and follow it.

JOHN 1:14—THE WORD TABERNACLED AMONG US

The whole of John 1:14 reads:

The Word became flesh
and tabernacled (ἐσκήνωσεν) among us,
and we beheld his glory,
glory as of the only Son from the Father,
full of grace and truth.

Σκηνόω describes the significance of the incarnate Word for human beings. The verb is a play on words that embraces both "flesh" and "glory." The verb resembles the noun σκῆνος, which can be connected with the idea of "flesh" because it often refers to the tabernacle of the human body (Wis 9:15; 2 Cor 5:1,4: *Par. Jer.* 6:6–7), as does the term σκήνωμα (2 Pet 1:13–14). The verb σκηνόω can also be connected with the idea of glory, for it resembles the noun σκηνή, which the LXX uses for the Israelite tabernacle. The tabernacle was the place where God *spoke* with Moses (Exod 33:9) and where he manifested his *glory* (Exod 40:34). Therefore tabernacle imagery is uniquely able to portray the person of Jesus as the locus of God's Word and glory among humankind.[5]

THE TABERNACLE IN THE PROLOGUE[6]

John 1:1–13 describes the activity of the Word, from his role at creation to his acceptance and rejection among humankind. John 1:1–5 portrays the Word as God's agent of creation, the source of life, and a light that shines

---

[5] Similar word plays occur elsewhere in the gospel. For example, ἄνωθεν in 3:3 and 7 means both "a second time" and "from above." The verb ὑψόω in 3:14; 8:28; and 12:32 and 34 connotes both death and exaltation.

[6] Numerous detailed outlines of the prologue have been proposed. For a survey see A. Feuillet, *Le prologue du quatrième évangile* (Paris: Desclée de Brouwer, 1968) 137–77. Many scholars maintain that the prologue's symmetrical elements form a chiastic pattern. But in a chiasm one would expect the key word λόγος to appear in 1:1 and 18, rather than in 1:1 and 14. Moreover, proponents of this thesis find it difficult to fit vv. 11–13 into a chiastic structure. See the convenient summary of proposed chiastic outlines for the prologue in Culpepper, "Pivot," 2–6.

in darkness. The language recalls the creation account of Gen 1:1–2:4. John 1:6–8 clarifies John the Baptist's relationship to Jesus, the Word, and 1:9–13 recounts the Word's entry into the world and Jesus' earthly ministry.[7] The scope gradually narrows from the presence of the Word in the entire created "world" (1:9–10b) to the rejection of the Word by the human "world" (1:10c). The section concludes by recounting how the Word was rejected by his own people, the Jewish people (1:11),[8] and how he was accepted by others, who became children of God.

John 1:14–18 conveys the significance of the Word for those who received him. The first person plurals in 1:14, 16 mark the witness of the believing community: the Word "tabernacled among *us*"; "*we* beheld his glory"; "*we* have received grace upon grace."[9] The community's testimony continues through 1:18, since there is no apparent change in speaker, and it includes a number of elements: (1) testimony to Jesus' glory and divine origin (1:14), (2) acceptance of John the Baptist's witness to Jesus' origin (1:15), (3) confession that grace and truth came through Jesus Christ (1:16–17), (4) acknowledgment that the law was given through Moses (1:17), and (5) insistence that no one has ever seen God; Jesus has made him known (1:18).

---

[7] Some scholars insist that the account of Jesus' earthly ministry begins in 1:5, which should be read with 1:6–13 (e.g., Bultmann, *John,* 45–60; Käsemann, "Prologue," 143; E. C. Hoskyns, *The Fourth Gospel* [2d ed.; London: Faber, 1947] 143). But the consistent use of creation imagery in 1:1–5 and the comments on John the Baptist in 1:6, indicate that 1:1–5 should be read as a unit that describes the pre-incarnate activity of the Word. Cf. Brown, *John,* 1.26. Some interpreters insist that the earthly ministry of Jesus begins only in 1:14, where the incarnation is specifically mentioned, and that John 1:9–13 deals with the pre-incarnate logos, which functions as divine wisdom. See esp. E. Haenchen, "Probleme," 306; idem, *John 1* (Hermeneia; Philadelphia: Fortress, 1984) 115–19; and Schnackenburg, *John,* 1.256–66. See also M.-E. Boismard, *St. John's Prologue* (London: Aquin, 1957) 35; B. F. Westcott, *The Gospel According to St. John* (London: John Murray, 1889) 12. But the references to becoming God's children who are born of God rather than of the flesh in 1:12–13 must refer to the incarnate ministry of Jesus as in 3:1–8. See Brown, *John,* 1.29.

[8] Bultmann (*John,* 56), Käsemann ("Prologue," 144), and others argue that "his own" are all human beings, since οἱ ἴδιοι in 1:11 is parallel to κόσμος in 1:10. But most scholars take οἱ ἴδιοι as the Jewish people; e.g., Brown, *John,* 1.10; Barrett, *John,* 163; J. L. Martyn, *Gospel of John,* 106 n. 169. See also the earlier works noted by Käsemann, "Prologue," 143 n. 34.

[9] The first person plurals have sometimes been taken as evidence that the speaker was an eyewitness, but the reception of grace would not be limited to eyewitnesses. The first person plural probably represents a community that perceived itself as the heir of an eyewitness tradition. See Bultmann, *John,* 70; Käsemann, "Prologue," 165; D. N. Smith, "Johannine Christianity: Some Reflections on Its Character and Delineation," *NTS* 21 (1974–75) 222–48, esp. 224; Barrett, *John,* 143; R. E. Brown, *The Community of the Beloved Disciple* (New York: Paulist, 1979) 32.

The community's testimony to Jesus' glory and divine origin distinguishes its members from Jews who rejected Jesus (1:11), and it reflects both
continuity and discontinuity with the Jewish heritage. Continuity is provided
by the use of imagery reminiscent of the Sinai theophany.[10] John 1:14 recalls
that when the tabernacle was completed it was filled with God's glory (Exod
40:34). The expression "full of grace and truth" (1:14, 17) echoes Exod 34:6,
where God announced that he was "great in steadfast love and truth" or
"faithfulness" (רב חסד ואמת).[11] John 1:17 states that the law was given
through Moses, recalling Exod 34:32, where Moses gave Israel the law with
his face still radiant from his encounter with God. John 1:18 reminds readers
that no one had seen God, and in Exod 33:17-23 Moses was not permitted
to see God's face.

Nevertheless, the community's testimony also reflects discontinuity with
the past. John 1:14-18 does not simply present Jesus as a new Moses and his
arrival as a second Sinai.[12] Jesus was not a new Moses, but the tabernacle
in which God's glory was manifested. Moses did not see God; Jesus made
him known. "Grace and truth" or חסד ואמת were announced at Sinai and
"occurred" (ἐγένετο) in Jesus.[13] In the prologue ἐγένετο signals a new condition, perhaps echoing the creation story (Gen 1:3, 6, 9, 11, etc.). The term
means coming into being (John 1:3, 10), becoming flesh (1:14), or appearing
on the scene (1:6). The advent of Jesus meant a new occurrence of "grace and
truth."

The element of newness in 1:14-18 suggests that the verb σκηνόω may
also echo passages from the prophets,[14] where God promises, "Sing and
rejoice O daughter of Zion, for behold, I will tabernacle (κατασκηνώσω) in
your midst" (Zech 2:14[10]); "So you shall know that I am the Lord your
God, who tabernacles (κατασκηνῶν) in Zion" (Joel 3:17); and "My taber-
nacling-place (κατασκήνωσις) shall be among you (Ezek 37:27; cf. Lev 26:11
MT). The promise of God's tabernacling presence was realized when the
Word became flesh.

In summary, John 1:14 continues 1:1-13 by announcing that the Word
of God, who was present at creation, was present in the person of Jesus. The

---

[10] On the allusions to Sinai see esp. Boismard, *Prologue*, 135-45.

[11] The expression רב חסד ואמת occurs only in Exod 34:6, although the word pair
חסד ואמת is found elsewhere in the OT (2 Sam 2:6; 15:20; Ps 25:10; 61:8[7]; 85:11[10]). The
LXX usually translates חסד as ἔλεος, rather than as χάρις. But John is alluding to OT passages,
rather than providing literal translations.

[12] Stressed especially by Meeks, *Prophet-King*, 319; Schnackenburg, *John*, 1.281.

[13] Some MSS sharpen the contrast between Jesus and the law by adding the word δέ in 1:17.
But the best evidence indicates that the δέ is an addition.

[14] Noted by Boismard, *Prologue*, 49; Brown, *John*, 1.49.

allusion to the tabernacle also introduces the believing community's corporate testimony to Jesus' glory and divine origin (1:14–18). Such testimony
distinguishes the members of the community from non-Christian Jews. The
community's testimony uses Sinaitic imagery which establishes continuity
with Israel's past, yet it also depicts the advent of Jesus as a new event, which
the evangelist may have understood as the fulfillment of OT promises.

THE TABERNACLE IN THE GOSPEL

The tabernacle is one of several sanctuaries that play a role in John's
gospel. The temple is mentioned in 2:19, where Jesus says, "Destroy this
temple and in three days I will raise it up." John explains that the temple is
Jesus' body (2:21). The Jerusalem temple and the Samaritan holy place at
Gerizim appear in Jesus' conversation with the Samaritan woman. Jesus
says, "the hour is coming when neither on this mountain nor in Jerusalem
will you worship the Father," for true worship occurs "in spirit and in truth"
(4:21–23). In 1:51 Jesus promises, "you will see angels ascending and descending on the Son of Man," which alludes to Jacob's dream at Bethel (Gen
28:10–22), and may be an implicit reference to the Bethel sanctuary.

A number of scholars have suggested that the tabernacle is the first of
several sanctuaries which Jesus replaced during his earthly ministry.[15] They
note that the tabernacle, Jerusalem temple, and possibly Bethel are replaced
by the person of Jesus. Since the tabernacle was a portable sanctuary, it may
represent worship that is not bound to a place, as in 4:21-23.

Connections between the passages on the tabernacle and the temple are
strongest, since the tabernacle is associated with Jesus' flesh and the temple
with his body. The relationship of 1:14 to 1:51 is less clear. In 1:51 Jesus is
presented as the link between heaven and earth, but not necessarily as the
replacement for the Bethel sanctuary.[16] Both 1:14 and 4:21-23 do deal with
worship sites, but the other themes of the passages differ. The spirit plays a
key role in 4:21-23, but not in the prologue. John 1:14 says that the Word
tabernacled among human beings, but does not mention the tabernacle's
mobile character. Most importantly, the theme of Jesus' glory and divine
origin is prominent in 1:14, but is not explicitly mentioned in connection with
the other sanctuaries.

Some interpreters suggest that the Shekinah concept provides an implicit link between the glory motif in 1:14 and Jesus' replacement of the

[15] See esp. the discussion in Cullmann, "L'opposition," 169–71; idem, *Johannine Circle*,
44–45; Brown, *John*, 1.32-33, 90–91, 125; idem, *Community*, 49; Davies, *Gospel and the Land*,
295–96. See also Hoskyns, *Fourth Gospel*, 148–49; A. Schlatter, *Der Evangelist Johannes: Wie
er spricht, denkt und glaubt. Ein Kommentar zum vierten Evangelien* (Stuttgart: Calwer, 1930)
28, 81, 122.

[16] For a survey of possible interpretations see Brown, *John*, 1.88-91.

temple.[17] Like σκηνόω in 1:14, the word Shekinah contains the root letters *skn,* indicates God's presence among his people (e.g., *m.* *'Abot* 3:2), and is associated with God's glory (e.g., *Tg. Neof.* Lev 26:11). Moreover, John 1:14 may recall OT passages that anticipated the time when God would tabernacle among his people. The LXX translates these passages with κατασκηνόω and the targums with "I will cause my Shekinah to dwell" (אשרי שכינתי).[18] The Shekinah was thought to be present in the Jerusalem temple. Therefore by replacing the Shekinah in 1:14, Jesus takes the first step toward replacing the temple in 2:19–21.

Yet there are two difficulties in using the Shekinah idea as background for John 1:14. First is the problem of date. The Shekinah is mentioned occasionally in sayings attributed to rabbis who lived in the early second century and more frequently in sayings attributed to later rabbis. The term also appears in targums that date from the late second or third centuries. The Shekinah idea was probably beginning to develop in the late first century, but is not well-attested until later. Therefore it may not have been known to the Fourth Evangelist.

Second, and more important, the evangelist probably expected his readers to detect a word play on the Greek root σκην-, which connoted both the tabernacle (σκῆνος) of the body and the Israelite tabernacle (σκηνή). But he probably did not expect them to make a connection between the Greek word σκηνόω and the Semitic שכינה. In the body of the gospel the evangelist provides the Greek equivalents for common Hebrew and Aramaic words like "rabbi," "messiah," and "rabboni" (1:38, 41; 20:16), and for the names Cephas and Siloam (1:42; 9:7). Since he did not expect his readers to understand the word "rabbi," it is unlikely that he would expect them to catch a veiled reference to the Shekinah in 1:14.

An alternative approach is to determine how the theme of Jesus' glory and divine origin functions in the gospel, then to ask why the evangelist introduced this theme by alluding to the tabernacle. The prologue presents Jesus' glory and divine origin as a central element in the believing community's testimony to Jesus (1:14–18). Other passages confirm that Jesus' glory is seen only by those who believe (2:11), and that those who see his glory also discern his divine origin (11:40–42; 17:20–25). Testimony to Jesus' glory and origin provided a point of unity among believers. In 1:14 the community corporately confesses, "*we* beheld his glory" and in 17:20–25 Jesus' glory and

---

[17] E.g., Schlatter, *Der Evangelist,* 23; Hoskyns, *Fourth Gospel,* 148–49; Cullmann, *Johannine Circle,* 44. Cf. Brown, *John,* 1.33–34.

[18] See *Tgs. Neofiti* and *Onqelos* to Lev 26:12, and *Tg. Jonathan* to Joel 4:17 [3:17]; Zech 2:14; and Ezek 37:27.

knowledge of his divine origin are explicitly linked to unity among Christians.

The prologue indicates that testimony to Jesus' glory and divine origin distinguished members of the believing community from non-Christian Jews (1:11). Elsewhere in the gospel most of the elements of the community's testimony appear in disputes between Jesus and his Jewish opponents. In chap. 5 Jesus insists that he does not receive glory of human origin (5:41; 1:14); he cites the testimony of John the Baptist and Moses (5:33-35, 45-47; 1:15, 17), and insists that his opponents have never seen God (5:37; 1:18). In chap. 7, Jesus says that he seeks the glory of the one who sent him, which proves that he is true (7:18; 1:14). He charges that his opponents do not observe the law of Moses (7:19; 1:17), and they respond that he has a demon. Again in chap. 8, Jesus insists that his glory comes from God and that his Jewish opponents do not know God (8:50, 54-55; 1:14, 18). His listeners charge that he is a Samaritan and has a demon.

These disputes may provide clues to the evangelist's reasons for introducing the theme of Jesus' glory and origin with an allusion to the tabernacle. Several recent studies plausibly suggest that the debates between Jesus and his opponents reflect disputes between Jews and Johannine Christians.[19] Accordingly, the charges made against Jesus may reflect accusations made against the Johannine church. Many Johannine Christians probably were of Jewish origin, but the charge that Jesus was a Samaritan (8:48) suggests that the group also included some Samaritans. Jesus rejected the charge of demon possession, but not the accusation that he was a Samaritan. Moreover, in contrast to the Synoptics, John says that Jesus made converts in Samaria (4:39-42) and he names places that may lie in the region of Samaria (3:23; 11:54).[20]

---

[19] See J. L. Martyn, *History and Theology in the Fourth Gospel* (2d ed.; Nashville: Abingdon, 1979) 18-30; Brown, *Community,* 17-19; K. Wengst, *Bedrängte Gemeinde und verherrlichter Christus: Der historische Ort des Johannesevangeliums als Schlüssel zu seiner Interpretation* (Biblisch-theologische Studien 5; 2d ed.; Neukirchen-Vluyn: Neukirchener, 1983) 29-36.

[20] On the Samaritan element in Johannine Christianity see J. Bowman, "The Fourth Gospel and the Samaritans," *BJRL* 40 (1958) 298-308; Meeks, *Prophet-King,* 318; Scobie, "The Origin," 401-8; E. D. Freed, "Samaritan Influence in the Gospel of John," *CBQ* 30 (1968) 580-87; idem, "Did John Write His Gospel Partly to Win Samaritan Converts?" *NovT* 12 (1970) 241-56; J. D. Purvis, "The Fourth Gospel and the Samaritans," *NovT* 17 (1975) 161-98; Cullmann, *Johannine Circle,* 37-38, 46-51; Brown, *Community,* 36-40. G. W. Buchanan ("The Samaritan Origin of the Gospel of John" [*Religions in Antiquity* (ed. J. Neusner)] 149-75) overstates the importance of the Samaritan element, while M. Pamment tries to minimize it ("Is There Convincing Evidence of Samaritan Influence on the Fourth Gospel?" *ZNW* 73 [1982] 221-30).

The tabernacle would have been a positive symbol for Christians of Jewish and of Samaritan origin. Although Jews rejected Gerizim and Samaritans opposed the Jerusalem temple, the tabernacle was respected by both groups. It had been the sanctuary of all Israel, before the split into northern and southern kingdoms, and it recalled a common Mosaic heritage. Moreover, Ezekiel prophesied that the two kingdoms would be reunited when God established his tabernacle among his people (Ezek 37:15-28). Therefore the tabernacle was a suitable image with which to introduce the testimony to Jesus' glory and divine origin that united Christians of Jewish and Samaritan origin within the Johannine community.

In the first century neither Jews nor Samaritans worshiped in a tabernacle. By portraying Jesus as the tabernacle, the evangelist may have wanted to show that the Christian community had a center that was distinct from the Jerusalem temple and from Gerizim, yet had continuity with Israel's cultic heritage. Again the image would have been an appropriate introduction to the Johannine community's testimony to Jesus, since its testimony distinguished its members from non-Christian Jews.

If this last suggestion is correct, then the allusion to the tabernacle functions like the "replacement" pattern noted earlier. Jesus announced the end of true worship at Jerusalem and Gerizim (4:21-23), and took the place of the Jerusalem temple, which was destroyed before the gospel reached its final form (2:19-21). Jesus even replaced the Sabbath, Passover, Feast of Booths, and Feast of Dedication.[21] Christian worship was centered in Jesus, not in contemporary religious practices, although references to such practices could be used to convey the significance of Jesus.

B. Antecedents for John's Tabernacle Imagery

Much of the imagery in John 1:1-18 is derived from the OT, but extra-biblical traditions also may have contributed to the present shape of the prologue. A study of possible antecedents, in light of the preceding analysis, may enhance our understanding of the prologue's origin and theology.

Wisdom Traditions

The importance of wisdom traditions for the interpretation of John's tabernacle imagery has been widely recognized.[22] Although the prologue

---

[21] On Jesus' replacement of festivals see Brown, *John,* 1.201-4; *Community,* 49.

[22] Extensive treatments of wisdom traditions and the prologue appear in J. R. Harris, *The Origin of the Prologue of St. John's Gospel* (Cambridge: University, 1917); R. Bultmann, "Der religionsgeschichtliche Hintergrund des Prologs zum Johannesevangelium," *Eucharisterion: Studien zur Religion und Literatur des Alten und Neuen Testaments: Hermann Gunkel*

uses the term "logos" rather than "wisdom," the logos functions like the personified wisdom figure of Proverbs 8 and Sirach 24 and has many of the traits that Wisdom 7:22–8:1 ascribes to wisdom. Like the logos, wisdom was:

present at the beginning	Prov 8:22	John 1:1–2
an agent of creation	Prov 8:30	John 1:3
a source of life	Prov 8:35	John 1:4
rejected by some	Prov 8:36	John 1:10–11
came from the mouth of God	Sir 24:3	(1:1)
an agent of creation	Sir 24:3	1:3
gained a possession among every people/		
as many as received him	Sir 24:6	1:12
tabernacles in Israel/among us	Sir 24:8	1:14
an agent of creation	Wis 7:22	1:3
a reflection of light	Wis 7:26	1:4–9
not overcome by evil/darkness	Wis 7:29–30	1:5
an emanation of glory	Wis 7:25	1:14
present in the world	Wis 8:1	1:10, 14
creates friends/children of God	Wis 7:27	1:12–13

Numerous other passages from wisdom writings convey similar ideas, including wisdom as present with God (Sir 1:1), as an agent of creation (Wis 9:2), a source of life (Bar 4:1), a figure that appeared among humankind (Bar 3:37), and something that people rejected (Sir 15:7; Bar 3:12; *1 Enoch* 42:2).

The prologue's tabernacle imagery is strikingly similar to that of Sir 24:8. Both passages recount how a wisdom figure, who was present at creation, established a tabernacle among God's people. The similarities probably reflect a common tradition rather than the literary dependence of the Fourth Gospel on Sirach. Neither Sirach nor any of the other texts noted above includes all of the prologue's wisdom elements, and each has material that is not found in the prologue. For example Sir 24:13–29 compares wisdom to various trees and rivers, and Wis 7:25–26 uses words like ἀπόρροια ("emanation"), ἀπαύγασμα ("radiance"), and εἰκών ("image"), which are not typical of John's Greek style.[23]

---

zum 60. Geburtstage (ed. H. Schmidt: FRLANT 36.2; Göttingen: Vandenhoeck & Ruprecht, 1923) 1–26; idem, *John,* 22–23; C. Spicq, "Le Siriacide et la structure littéraire du Prologue de saint Jean," *Mémorial Lagrange* (Paris: Gabalda, 1940) 183–95. More recent discussion appears in Brown *John,* 1.33, 521–23; Schnackenburg, *John,* 1.231, 269; Barrett, *John,* 153, 165–66; Boismard, *Prologue,* 49, 73–76; Haenchen, *John 1,* 135–40. See the lists of parallels in C. H. Dodd, *The Interpretation of the Fourth Gospel* (Cambridge: University, 1953) 274–77.

[23] Philo was familiar with similar wisdom traditions, but develops them in a manner

Ben Sira associated wisdom's dwelling in the tabernacle with her presence in the Mosaic law (Sir 24:23). A similar view appears in Bar 3:37–4:1, without the tabernacle imagery. In the prologue, the Fourth Evangelist acknowledged that the law was given through Moses, presumably by God, and he used Sinaitic imagery to convey the significance of Jesus. Yet he also indicated that Jesus brought a new occurrence of grace and truth and made God known in a way that was not even granted to Moses. In 5:39–47 he presented the law as a witness to Jesus; in the prologue he used a wisdom tradition that was closely associated with the law as a positive way to portray Jesus, and, at the same time, implicitly asserted Jesus' superiority to the law.

Given the many similarities between John's prologue and wisdom traditions, it is surprising that these traditions apparently did not provide the imagery for John 1:14b–18.[24] Although the wisdom traditions noted above do associate personified wisdom with the Mosaic law, they do not use Sinaitic imagery, as does John 1:14–18. Sir 24:16–17 compares wisdom to a tree with branches of "glory and grace," which bears fruit of "glory and abundance," but these words are not theophanic or connected with Sinai. Wis 7:25 does call wisdom an "emanation of glory," but the word "emanation" is foreign to John's gospel, and Wisdom 7 makes no allusion to Sinai. Therefore John 1:14 marks a transition point; it completes a series of images that closely resemble wisdom traditions, and introduces allusions to Sinai, which derive from other sources.

ODES OF SOLOMON

The distinctive character of the prologue's Sinaitic imagery can be highlighted by comparing it with *Ode. Sol.* 12, which represents a later development of wisdom traditions like those known to the Fourth Evangelist.[25] Like

---

different from John. Instead of referring to the earthly tabernacle of a personified wisdom figure Philo perceives the tabernacle as the earthly copy of noetic wisdom or virtue (*Her.* 112–13; *Det.* 160). See sec. III.E above. Like the Fourth Evangelist, Philo ascribes some of wisdom's characteristics to a "logos" figure, but the logos is not said to "tabernacle" on earth. For discussion of the logos in Philo and in John, see Dodd, *Interpretation,* 276–79; Brown, *John,* 1.LXVII–LXVIII, 521–22; Schnackenburg, *John,* 1.485–87.

[24] Noted by S. Schulz, *Komposition und Herkunft der johanneischen Reden* (BWANT 5/1; Stuttgart: Kohlhammer, 1960) 42; Schnackenburg, *John,* 1.228; Haenchen, *John 1,* 119, 139.

[25] The Odes are Christian hymns that were probably written in the early second century A.D. They are difficult to date because they lack references to specific events. Reasons for a date in the early second century include similarities to some of the Dead Sea Scrolls, the writings of Ignatius, and John's gospel. For a summary of opinions on the date see Charlesworth, *OTP,* 2.726–27; Schürer et al., *History,* 3.787–88. Many interpreters maintain that the *Odes* are literarily dependent on John. Others argue that there is no relationship of literary dependence

John's prologue, *Ode* 12 extols God's "word" (*petgamā'*) in language that often parallels references to wisdom in Sirach 24 and Wisdom 7. Nevertheless, the odist and Fourth Evangelist knew these traditions independently of each other and drew different elements from them, as can be seen in the chart below.[26] The Word or wisdom:

	Sirach	*Ode.Sol.*	*John*
is or is from God's "mouth"	24:3	12:3, 11	
is an agent of creation	24:3		1:3
tabernacles	24:8	12:12	1:14
bears fruit	24:17	12:2b	
flows like water	24:25-33	12:2a	
	Wis.Sol.		
is sharp	7:22	12:5	
is subtle	7:22-23	12:5	
is swift	7:24	12:5	
manifests divine glory	7:25		1:14
is light	7:26	12:3, 7	1:4-5
is given to generations/worlds	7:27	12:4	1:9-10

John's prologue and *Ode* 12 develop these wisdom traditions in very similar ways. *Ode* 12:12 says, "The tabernacle of the Word is man," or literally, "a son of man" (*maškanā' ger dăpetgāmā' bar 'našā' hû*). The expression "son of man" may have messianic significance,[27] or it may mean "human being." Either way, the passage is strikingly similar to John 1:14.[28] The other important verse is *Ode* 12:11, which says, "the mouth of the Most High spoke to them and his interpretation (*măpašqanûtā'*) prospered

---

between them; both stem from a common milieu. See the summary of positions in J. H. Charlesworth and R. A. Culpepper, "The Odes of Solomon and the Gospel of John," *CBQ* 35 (1973) 298-322. The following comparison of the *Odes* and John's prologue indicates that the second view is more probable, although it does not support the view that both writings stem from the same community.

[26] Versification follows Charlesworth, *The Odes of Solomon* (Chico: Scholars, 1977); idem, "Odes of Solomon," *OTP*, 2.735-71.

[27] Elsewhere in the *Odes*, "son of man" occurs only in 36:3, where it may have messianic significance.

[28] R. Harris suggests that *Ode* 12:12 refers to the Word's indwelling within humanity as a whole (*The Odes and Psalms of Solomon* [Cambridge: University, 1909] 106). But J. H. Bernard sees no significant difference between the thought of *Ode* 12:12 and John 1:14 (*The Odes of Solomon* [Cambridge: University, 1912] 76.)

through him." God's "mouth" is the Word, and the idea that the Word "interprets" God is also found in John 1:18, where the only Son interprets God or makes him known (ἐξηγέομαι).

Despite these similarities, numerous differences indicate that the odist did not derive these ideas from John's prologue.[29] *Ode* 12:12b mentions "truth," but does not use the expression "grace and truth" as in John 1:14 and 16. The theme of love (*Ode* 12:12) is prominent in John, and the emphasis on concord (12:9–10) may resemble John's interest in the unity of believers (John 17:22). But neither love nor concord is mentioned in the prologue.

Other *Odes* also include images similar to those of John's prologue, but these images are not collocated in any one passage and are developed in a manner different from the prologue. *Ode* 16:19 depicts the Word (*meltā'*) as an agent of creation and *Ode* 41:14–15 refers to the Word's preexistence and light. *Ode* 18:6 says, "Let not light be conquered by darkness, nor let truth flee from falsehood," which resembles John 1:5. But since similar imagery appears in 1QS iii 13–iv 26 and *Jos. As.* 8:10, John and the odist may have derived the imagery from a common tradition.[30] *Ode* 7:12 says "He has allowed him to appear to them that are His own, in order that they may recognize Him that made them . . ." (cf. 7:4). The language resembles "he came to his own" in John 1:11, but shows no trace of the rejection motif that dominates John 1:10–11. Therefore the odist probably derived these images independently of the Fourth Gospel.

Because John and the odist use many of the same traditions independently of each other, a comparison of the two helps us to identify distinctive elements in John's prologue. Like *Ode* 12, the prologue uses the language of wisdom traditions to depict the tabernacling presence of God's Word in a human being who was God's interpreter, but it differs from *Ode* 12 in two significant ways. (1) John uses the tabernacle image to introduce the corporate confession of a believing community; the odist does not. (2) Only John uses the allusion to the tabernacle as a bridge from wisdom to Sinaitic imagery. These distinctive elements suggest that the connection between the tabernacle and the allusions to Sinai were of special importance to the Johannine community, and that the Sinaitic imagery was not derived from wisdom traditions.

THE HIDDEN TABERNACLE TRADITION

The story of the hidden tabernacle may provide clues to the significance of the prologue's Sinaitic imagery. This story circulated in a number of

---

[29] An extensive list of parallels appears in Charlesworth and Culpepper, "Odes," 321–22.
[30] Parallels noted by Charlesworth, *Odes,* 80.

forms, but the versions found in 2 Maccabees, the *Lives of the Prophets,* and Samaritan tradition are especially important for our study.[31]

2 Macc 2:4-8 says that the tabernacle, ark, and incense altar were concealed on Mt. Nebo by Jeremiah. They were to be restored when God's people were gathered together. When the tabernacle and vessels appeared, mercy would occur, and God's glory would be manifested as it had been at the dedication of the tabernacle in the time of Moses.

According to the *Lives of the Prophets,* Jeremiah concealed the ark near Mt. Nebo and the location of the ark was marked by God's glory (*Vit. Jer.* 11-19). The ark would reappear when God's people were gathered together at Mt. Sinai during a time of persecution. The tradition expected Moses, who bore the messianic title "God's chosen one," to appear with Aaron at that time. A related tradition linked the ingathering of God's fugitive people to the place where the tent of meeting once stood, and said that God would be made known there (*Vit. Hab.* 12-13).

The Samaritans believed that Moses had hidden the tabernacle vessels on Mt. Gerizim and that the vessels and tabernacle would be restored at the time of ingathering. Like the *Lives of the Prophets,* the Samaritan tradition expected the ingathering to occur during a time of persecution and to involve a Mosaic eschatological figure. The Samaritans believed that when the tabernacle was restored, God's favor would return to his people.

These traditions contain a number of similarities to the latter part of John's prologue. (1) The *Lives of the Prophets* and the Samaritan tradition expected God's people to be gathered together during a time of persecution. John 1:11-13 recounts how a new community of faith was created despite opposition to Jesus. (2) *Vit. Jer.* 14-19 and 2 Macc 2:4-8 associated the tabernacle or ark with God's glory and expected the tabernacle or ark to stand at the center of the ingathered people. According to John 1:14, God's glory was present in Jesus, the tabernacle. Testimony to his glory formed the center of the community's corporate confession. (3) The Samaritans believed that the appearance of the tabernacle would bring Favor (רחותה) to God's people and 2 Macc 2:7 said that mercy would occur (γίνομαι). According to John 1:16-17 the tabernacling Word bestowed "favor upon favor" (χάρις ἀντὶ χάριτος) and that "grace and truth occurred" (ἐγένετο) through him. (4) *Vit. Jer.* 14 and the Samaritan tradition expected a Mosaic messiah to appear at the ingathering. John 1:17 acknowledges the importance of Moses, yet indicates that Jesus was more than a Moses. (5) *Vit. Hab.* 13 said that God would be known at the place where the tent of meeting stood. John 1:18 says that God was known through the only Son, who was the tabernacling Word.

---

[31] On the hidden tabernacle traditions see chap. III.D above.

If the evangelist did know hidden tabernacle traditions, *he used them in the same way that he used wisdom traditions.* Both types of tradition circulated in various forms, and the evangelist drew elements from these diverse traditions without closely adhering to individual sources. No extant source includes all the elements of the wisdom or hidden tabernacle traditions that appear in the prologue, and all extant sources contain elements that the prologue does not have. Therefore just as John 1:1-14 almost certainly recalls wisdom traditions, 1:14-18 may echo hidden tabernacle traditions.

SYNTHESIS

The wisdom and hidden tabernacle traditions are not collocated in ancient sources outside the Fourth Gospel. But both types of tradition were popular in the first century and are well-attested in various Jewish writings that stem from Palestine and Egypt. Neither type of tradition was peculiar to a single Jewish group and both were known to Christians at an early period.

Forms of the wisdom tradition appear in Proverbs, Sirach, Baruch, the Wisdom of Solomon, and *1 Enoch,* all of which were composed before the middle of the first century. Proverbs circulated widely; Sirach, Baruch, and *1 Enoch* stem from Palestine, and the Wisdom of Solomon and the Greek translation of Sirach originated in Egypt. Early Christians used language from these wisdom traditions in order to convey the cosmic significance of Christ's activity (e.g., Heb 1:1-3; Col 1:15-17), but John's prologue is the earliest extant work to apply the wisdom tradition's tabernacle imagery to Christ. The *Odes of Solomon* show that, in the early second century, other Christians interpreted the same wisdom traditions christologically.

The hidden tabernacle tradition is first attested in the second century B.C. (Eupolemos, 2 Maccabees) and seems to have been quite popular among Jews in the late first century, after the destruction of the Jerusalem temple (Pseudo-Philo, *2 Baruch, Lives of the Prophets, Paralipomena Jeremiou*). All of these sources were either composed or read in Palestine, and 2 Macc 2:4-8 and the traditions in the *Life of Jeremiah* were probably known in Egypt. The Samaritan version was popular enough to precipitate a gathering of Samaritans who expected to witness the reappearance of the tabernacle vessels in A.D. 35-36 (*Ant.* 18.4.1 #85-88). The tradition received at least tacit approval from the Samaritan council and is well-attested in later Samaritan sources. Extant forms of the *Life of Jeremiah* and the *Paralipomena Jeremiou* include Christian elements, which indicates that the tradition was known among Christians at a very early period.

Jews sometimes used the hidden tabernacle tradition polemically against Samaritans (*Bib.Ant.* 25:10). Nevertheless, the tradition also provided a potential point of unity for Christians from both groups. The main elements of their traditions were similar and focused on the tabernacle or its furnishings, which both groups respected.

C. CONCLUSION

The tabernacle imagery in John 1:14 conveys the significance of the incarnate Word for the community of faith. The Israelite σκηνή or tabernacle was the place where God spoke and manifested his glory. The cognate words σκῆνος and σκήνωμα were often used for the tabernacle of the human body. Therefore tabernacle imagery was uniquely able to capture the idea that people encountered God's Word and glory in the person of Jesus.

The allusion to the tabernacle introduces the Johannine community's testimony to Jesus. The group probably included members from Jewish and Samaritan backgrounds, who jointly bore witness to Jesus' glory and divine origin. Although Jews rejected Gerizim and Samaritans opposed the Jerusalem temple, both groups respected the tabernacle. Therefore the tabernacle was an appropriate image with which to introduce the testimony that united persons from both groups in a new community of faith.

The Johannine community's testimony to Jesus distinguished its members from non-Christian Jews and resulted in conflict between the two groups. Nevertheless, the community did not abandon its Jewish heritage, but appropriated and transformed it into a vehicle suitable for Christian theology. The prologue insists that Jesus brought about a new occurrence of grace and truth, and made God known in a way that had not been granted even to Moses. Yet the imagery recalls the tabernacle, Sinai theophany, and perhaps other OT passages that spoke of God's tabernacling presence among his people.

The prologue's tabernacle imagery is based in part on Exodus and perhaps passages from the prophets, like Ezek 37:27, Joel 3:17, and Zech 2:10. Moreover, it almost certainly recalls a wisdom tradition like that found in Sirach 24, and it may echo Jewish and Samaritan forms of the hidden tabernacle tradition. The wisdom tradition recounts how a wisdom figure, who was present at creation, established a tabernacle among God's people. The hidden tabernacle tradition associated the tabernacle's reappearance with the ingathering of God's people and manifestations of divine glory and favor or mercy. Taken together, these traditions provided language with which to announce that God's word and glory are encountered in the person of Jesus.

VI

THE BOOK OF REVELATION

Tabernacle imagery plays a varied and sometimes puzzling role in the book of Revelation. The book culminates in a vision of the new Jerusalem and the proclamation, "Behold the tabernacle of God with men!" (21:3); yet the new Jerusalem would contain no temple (21:22). Rev 15:5 refers to "the temple of the tent of witness in heaven," which R. H. Charles found exceedingly peculiar, since apocalyptic visions were regularly set in temples, not in the tabernacle.[1] Rev 7:15 clearly alludes to Ezek 37:27/Lev 26:11, which refers to God's tabernacling presence among his people. But the expression "those who tabernacle in heaven" (12:12; 13:6) has no clear biblical precedent.

A. The Tabernacle in Revelation

Since tabernacle imagery appears in a number of places in Revelation, we will first note several characteristics of the book as a whole, then discuss each occurrence of tabernacle imagery individually, and finally note how the tabernacle functions within the entire composition.

On the Composition of Revelation

Revelation's tabernacle imagery is derived from diverse biblical and extra-biblical sources, many of which are listed on the charts at the end of this chapter. Allusions to OT texts have often been noted and are especially important for our study because they enable us to see how the author consciously or unconsciously used traditional materials. The charts show that the author frequently alluded to the OT, but did not quote OT texts verbatim.[2] He sometimes reordered a sequence of verses or even parts of a single

---

[1] *A Critical and Exegetical Commentary on the Revelation of St. John* (ICC; Edinburgh: Clark, 1920) 2.37.

[2] See the extensive analysis in Charles, *Revelation,* 1.lxv–lxxxii.

verse.[3] He also wove two or more texts together and alluded to several OT texts at the same time.[4] Often he wove several images from an entire block of material into his text. The charts also suggest that he used non-biblical materials in these same ways.

The method of composition resembles that of a musical composer who used traditional melodies. A composer can vary a theme to achieve different effects, combine elements from two or more melodies into a single theme, or play two melodies at the same time. The author of Revelation did the same with traditions.[5]

REV 7:15: GOD TABERNACLES OVER THE FAITHFUL

In 7:9–12 the author sees a white-robed multitude, comprised of people from every nation. They stand before God's throne with palm branches in their hands and give praises to God and the Lamb. The heavenly angels, elders, and creatures prostrate themselves before the throne and add their own acclamations. One of the elders explains that the multitude has "come out of the great tribulation," which is the final tribulation at the end of time (Rev 3:10; Dan 12:1; Mark 13:19). These people have "washed their robes and made them white in the blood of the Lamb," and they "worship day and night in the temple" (7:13–15a).

Some interpreters have argued that the great multitude represents the full company of martyrs, since martyrs received white robes (6:11) and were empowered to lay down their lives by the blood of the Lamb (12:11). The present tense of "those who come (οἱ ἐρχόμενοι) from the great tribulation" could imply that the tribulation is still in progress and that the end has not yet come. The passage may assume that ordinary Christians would be glorified only at the end of time and that martyrs would be glorified at the time of death.[6]

But it is more likely that the scene depicts all the redeemed at the end of time, not just the martyrs. Both 7:9–17 and 5:9–10 picture a multitude from every tribe, tongue, people, and nation, who were ransomed by the Lamb's blood, but neither passage mentions martyrdom (cf. 1:5). The thematic connections between 7:15–17 and chap. 21, which are given below,

---

[3] E.g., Ps 86:9 and Jer 10:6b–7 in Rev 15:3b–4; Isa 25:8 and 65:17, 19 in Rev 21:4.

[4] E.g., the sources for Rev 7:17; 15:3–4, 8; 21:19–21, 25–26.

[5] On the impact of Revelation on hearers see E. Schüssler Fiorenza, "Composition and Structure of the Book of Revelation," *CBQ* 39 (1977) 344–66, esp. 345; reprinted in her book *The Book of Revelation: Justice and Judgment* (Philadelphia: Fortress, 1985). J. L. Martyn used a similar musical analogy for John's gospel in his *History and Theology in the Fourth Gospel,* 19.

[6] Cf. Charles, *Revelation,* 1.201–2; W. Bousset, *Die Offenbarung Johannis* (MeyerK 16; 6th ed.; Göttingen: Vandenhoeck & Ruprecht, 1906) 286.

suggest that 7:9–17 is a proleptic vision of the end time. Therefore the great multitude probably includes all the redeemed.[7]

The promise of God's tabernacling presence is one of several promises that describe the final blessedness of the redeemed (7:15c–17). This section is a tapestry of allusions to disparate OT texts. The reference to God's tabernacling presence comes from Ezek 37:27. Other important sources for the passage are given in chart 6 at the end of this chapter.

Revelation 21 takes up most of the themes in this passage, including God tabernacling with the faithful (7:15/21:3), an end to thirst (7:16/21:6), no sun (7:16/21:23), springs of living water (7:17/21:6), and wiping away tears (7:17/21:4). Therefore the significance of God's tabernacling presence will be disussed later, in the section on Rev 21:3.

Rev 12:12 & 13:6: Heaven and the Heavenly Host

Both 12:12 and 13:6 refer to "those who tabernacle in heaven." According to the context of Rev 12:7–12 these beings are apparently the angels who cast Satan down from heaven and the glorified martyrs (12:11). Rev 12:12 appears to conflate passages from the Psalms, which are noted in chart 7 at the end of this chapter. The term σκηνόω may be a translation of יֹשֵׁב (Ps 98:7b), which in Rev 12:12 refers to the host of heaven, rather than those who dwell on earth, as in the Psalm.

The expression "those who tabernacle in heaven" appears again in Rev 13:6–7. The passage describes the beast from the sea,

> which opened its mouth in blasphemies toward God, to blaspheme his name and his tabernacle, those who tabernacle in heaven.
> And it was permitted to make war on the saints and to conquer them.

The expression "those who tabernacle in heaven" stands in apposition to "his tabernacle" and indicates that the blasphemy was directed against the inhabitants of the σκηνή, rather than at the σκηνή itself. Therefore the σκηνή probably refers to heaven and "those who tabernacle in heaven" to angels and perhaps to the glorified martyrs as in 12:12.[8] This interpretation fits the larger context well. The beast from the sea is Satan's viceroy (13:2). The beast defiantly curses the angels and martyrs in the heavenly tabernacle who

---

[7] H. B. Swete, *The Apocalypse of St John* (3d ed.; London: Macmillan, 1911) 102–3; I. T. Beckwith, *The Apocalypse of John* (New York: Macmillan, 1922) 539–40; E. Schüssler Fiorenza, *Priester für Gott: Studien zum Herrschafts- und Priestermotiv in der Apokalypse* (NTAbh 7; Münster: Aschendorff, 1972) 392–97.

[8] Beckwith, *Apocalypse,* 637; P.E.-B. Allo, *Saint Jean: L'Apocalypse* (EBib; 3d ed.; Paris: Gabalda, 1933) 208; Bousset, *Offenbarung,* 363; Charles, *Revelation,* 1.352. Some mss insert a καί between "his tabernacle" and "those who tabernacle in heaven," which eases the strained syntax (Bousset, ibid.). Cf. E. Lohmeyer, *Die Offenbarung Johannes* (HNT 16; 2d ed.;

conquered his master Satan. The imagery of 13:6-7 comes from Daniel 7-8. Specific passages appear in chart 8 at the end of this chapter. The expression "those who tabernacle in heaven" does not occur in Daniel, but may recall the host of heaven of Dan 8:10.

The reference to heaven as God's tent does not have strong OT precedents. Isa 40:22 says that God spread out the heavens "like a tent to dwell in" and Deut 26:15 calls heaven God's "dwelling" (מעון/οἶκος). 1QH xii 2-3 places אהל parallel to מעון, which suggests that the terms could be used as synonyms. The σκηνή of Rev 13:6 may reflect a similar tendency to call heaven God's tent.

Therefore, the words σκηνόω and σκηνή in 12:12 and 13:6 seem to be equivalent to ישב and מעון, respectively. Both passages echo portions of the OT, but neither has any clear connection with the Israelite tabernacle.

REV 15:5: THE TEMPLE OF THE TENT OF WITNESS IN HEAVEN

Revelation 15 weaves together two visions: a vision of seven angels with the seven last plagues (15:1, 5-8), into which the author inserted a vision of the faithful standing beside a glassy sea (15:2-4). The combination of the two visions is not a sign of redactional activity, but a literary device which indicates that the two visions should be read together. The device also appears elsewhere in Revelation (8:1-6) and in other early Christian literature (e.g., Mark 11:12-26).[9]

The author has already called heaven God's "tabernacle" in 13:6. In 15:5 he identifies the "tent of witness" with the heavenly temple or ναός, which is the predominant term for the celestial sanctuary elsewhere in this chapter (15:6, 8) and in the rest of Revelation. The heavenly temple houses an altar (6:9; 8:3, 5; 9:13; 11:1; 14:18; 16:7), the ark of the covenant (11:19) and God's throne (e.g., 16:17); before the throne are seven lamps and a glassy sea (4:5-6). The plan of the heavenly temple differs markedly from that of the tent of witness, which lacks a throne and glassy sea.[10]

Nevertheless, the author identifies the heavenly sanctuary with the "tent of meeting" to sustain a series of images from the story of the Exodus and

---

Tübingen: Mohr/Siebeck, 1953) 112; H. Kraft, *Die Offenbarung Johannes* (HNT 16A; Tübingen: Mohr/Siebeck, 1974) 174). But the reading without καί is preferable, since it is more difficult and better attested.

[9] Schüssler Fiorenza, "Composition," 360-61. R. H. Charles took the combination of visions as a sign of redactional activity (*Revelation,* 2.30-31).

[10] *1 Enoch* 14:11 and *T.Levi* 2:7; 3:2 refer to waters in connection with the heavenly temple.

wilderness wanderings. Chap. 15 refers to plagues, victors beside the sea, the song of Moses, the tent of witness, figures dressed like Aaronic priests, and to a manifestation of divine glory that barred entry to the sanctuary, as at the tabernacle's dedication. Specific sources of imagery are given in chart 9 at the end of this chapter.

Revelation 15 also recalls important elements from Deuteronomy 31–32. Similarities include the "song of Moses," two allusions to the words of the song (Rev 15:3–4; Deut 32:4), and the "last plagues," which recall the evils that would strike the disobedient in "the latter days" (אחרית הימים, Deut 31:29). The author could readily combine imagery from Exodus and Deuteronomy because both included similar elements: plagues, the song of Moses, and the tent of witness. Together, these images depict the eschatological judgment of the ungodly and the salvation of the faithful.

REV 21:3: THE TABERNACLE-CITY

After the seer witnesses the last plagues and final judgment, he sees a vision of a new heaven, a new earth, and a new Jerusalem descending from heaven, "prepared as a bride adorned for her husband."[11] When the city descends, a voice proclaims, "Behold the tabernacle of God with men!" (21:3). By juxtaposing this proclamation with the descent of the city, the author indicates that the city is God's tabernacle.[12]

The connection between city and tabernacle appears even more clearly when the main elements of 21:1–5a are presented chiastically. The main items of each column in the chart on the following page correspond to each other in form and content.[13] Heaven and earth include "all things," the

---

[11] Although some scholars argue that 21:1–8 and 21:9–22:5 present two distinct visions of the new Jerusalem (e.g., Charles, *Revelation*, 2.144–54; Kraft, *Offenbarung*, 262), the entire section can be read as a unit. Both passages are written in the same distinctive Greek style and treat similar themes: the new Jerusalem (21:2/21:9–11), God's presence with his people (21:3/21:22–23; 22:3), the water of life (21:6/22:1), the blessedness of the faithful (21:7/22:4) and the banishment of the profane (21:8/21:27; 22:3). The second vision seems to explicate the first one. Cf. D. Georgi, "Die Visionen vom himmlischen Jerusalem in Apk 21 und 22," in *Kirche: Festschrift für Günther Bornkamm zum 75. Geburtstag* (ed. D. Lührmann and G. Strecker; Tübingen: Mohr/Siebeck, 1980) 351–72, esp. 355; J. Comblin, "La liturgie de la nouvelle Jérusalem (Apoc XXI,1–XX11,5)," *ETL* 29 (1953) 5–40, esp. 5–6; P. Prigent, "Le temps et le Royaume dans l'Apocalypse," *L'Apocalypse johannique et l'Apocalyptique dans le Nouveau Testament* (ed. J. Lambrecht; Paris-Gembloux: Duculot and Leuven University, 1980) 231–45, esp. 232–33.

[12] Cf. Schüssler Fiorenza, *Priester,* 352.

[13] Some interpreters distinguish 21:4 from 22:5–8 since the words "And he who sat upon the throne said . . ." (v. 5a) seem to introduce a new section. But v. 5a should be included with the preceding section because it completes the chiasm, and vv. 4–5 allude to Isa 43:18–19. Scholars who join v. 5a with the preceding section include Bousset (*Offenbarung,* 444), Lohmeyer (*Offenbarung,* 166), and Kraft (*Offenbarung,* 262).

CHART 5

οὐρανὸς καινὸς καὶ γῆ καινή	1a		5a	καινὰ ποιῶ πάντα
ὁ πρῶτος οὐρανὸς / γῆ ἀπῆλθαν	1b		4b	τὰ πρῶτα ἀπῆλθαν
ἡ θάλασσα οὐκ ἔστιν ἔτι	1c		4a	ὁ θάνατος . . . οὐκ ἔσται ἔτι
Ἰερουσαλῆμ καινή	2		3	ἡ σκηνὴ τοῦ θεοῦ

"former heaven" and "former earth" are parallel to the "former things," the sea is the realm of the dead (20:12) and an ancient source of fear,[14] and the city is God's "tabernacle."

The tabernacle-city is the Christian community in the new age. The foundations of the city bear the names of the twelve apostles and its gates are named for the twelve tribes of Israel. The number twelve is constitutive for both the city and the people of God: 12,000 from each tribe were sealed for God (7:5-8) and the walls of the city were 12,000 stadia long (21:16); the total number of the sealed is 144,000 (7:4; 14:1) and the city walls are 144 angelic cubits high (21:17).[15]

The tabernacle-city has characteristics of a sanctuary. Like the holy of holies, the new Jerusalem is a cube (21:16) in which the glory of God appears (21:11) and in which the faithful serve with God's name on their foreheads like high priests.[16]

Many of these same motifs appear in Rev 3:12, which refers to the Christian community as a temple and anticipates chap. 21.

> He who conquers, I will make him a pillar in the temple of my God; he shall never go out of it. And I will write on him the name of my God, and the name of the city of my God, the new Jerusalem which comes down from my God out of heaven, and my own new name.

The tabernacle-city is, in part, the temple in which faithful Christians are the pillars. The motif is not consistently sustained, since the author says that God and the Lamb are the temple of the new Jerusalem (21:22). Nevertheless, images of the tabernacle and the Christian community as a temple do contribute significantly to the picture of the new Jerusalem in Rev 21:1-22:5.

---

[14] See Charles, *Revelation*, 2.204-5.

[15] M. Rissi, *The Future of the World: An Exegetical Study of Rev 19.11-22.15* (London: SCM, 1972) 61-64; Schüssler Fiorenza, *Priester*, 357-58. Georgi agrees, but is skeptical of the connection between the 144,000 and the height of the walls ("Die Visionen," 356 n. 17). Cf. J. Comblin, *Théologie de la ville* (Paris: Universitaires, 1968) 200.

[16] Schüssler Fiorenza, *Priester*, 407; Rissi, *Future*, 61-64; A. Yarbro Collins, *The Apocalypse* (NTM 22; Wilmington: Glazier, 1979) 149; Comblin, *Théologie*, 206.

The author of Revelation derived his imagery from numerous parts of the OT. The main sources appear in chart 10 at the end of this chapter. The image of Jerusalem as a tabernacle stems in part from the book of Ezekiel. In Ezek 37:27-28 God promised, "My tabernacle shall be with them and I will be their God and they shall be my people . . . when my sanctuary is in their midst forevermore." The sanctuary that Ezekiel saw looked like a city (40:2), part of which was called a "tent" according to the MT (41:1). Ps 46:4 refers to God's city as his "tabernacle" and Tobit 13 calls Israel's future sanctuary in a restored Jerusalem a "tabernacle."

The promise that God will tabernacle among his people appears in several OT passages: Ezek 37:27, Lev 26:11-12, and Zech 2:10-11. According to Ezekiel and Leviticus, God's tabernacling presence means a renewed relationship with Israel; according to Zechariah it means that many nations become part of the people of God. Rev 21:3 combines the two perspectives by paraphrasing Ezek 37:27 and Lev 26:12 to say, "they shall be his peoples."[17]

The author of Revelation did not create his vision of the new Jerusalem from isolated OT verses. He wove together allusions from entire sections of Ezekiel, Zechariah, Tobit, Psalm 46 and other sources. Key passages from Ezekiel include:

	Rev	*Ezek*
Vision of a city/sanctuary	21:2, 10	40:2
God's tabernacle among his people	21:3	37:27
Manifestation of God's glory	21:11	43:4
Measuring the square city/sanctuary	21:15	40:3
12 gates with names of 12 tribes	21:12	48:30-34
River of water	22:1	47:1
Trees bearing fruit each month		
with leaves for healing	22:2	47:12

Psalm 46 calls God's city a "tabernacle" that contains God's presence and a river (Rev 22:1, 3). Zechariah includes the motifs of measuring the city, continuous day, collecting the wealth of the nations and living waters flowing out of Jerusalem. Tobit refers to the future tabernacle, a Jerusalem built with gems, and nations bringing their wealth to it.

By fulfilling a catena of biblical promises, the tabernacle-city manifests divine faithfulness. The descent of the city shows God's fidelity to his word. Interpreters have sometimes understood the city as the climax of human

---

[17] Many MSS have the singular, "his people," but the plural form seems to have slightly better attestation, and the singular may be a harmonization with OT passages that refer to one people of God, including Ezek 37:27; Zech 2:11; 8:8.

aspirations,[18] but the pervasive use of biblical imagery indicates that author himself wanted to present the city as a manifestation of God's faithfulness to his purposes.

THE TABERNACLE IN REVELATION

Rev 7:15 anticipates the time when God will tabernacle with his people, as promised in Ezek 37:27 and Lev 26:11, but before the promise is fulfilled, the forces of Satan must be overcome. The angels and martyrs who "tabernacle" in heaven vanquish Satan (12:12), but the power of evil appears again in the beast from the sea, who blasphemes the inhabitants of the heavenly tabernacle who had cast Satan out (13:6). The tent of witness in heaven opens and seven angels emerge with bowls full of the seven last plagues (15:5). The final plague drenches "Babylon," the harlot city that sat upon the beast from the sea. The harlot is replaced by the bride — New Jerusalem. As the city descends from heaven a voice proclaims, "Behold the tabernacle of God with men" (21:3). The descent of the city fulfills the vision of Rev 7:15 and a catena of biblical promises, indicating that it manifests God's faithfulness.

The tabernacle-city is the church in the new age. Its foundations are the twelve apostles, its gates are the twelve sons of Israel, and its dimensions recall the number of the elect (21:12-17). There, in the church, God's glory is manifested as in the holy of holies (21:23) and like high priests, God's servants bear the divine name on their foreheads (22:4). They see God's face, worship, and reign as servants of the Almighty God and the conquering Lamb, whose kingdom endures forever (22:5).

The imagery of the New Jerusalem also fulfills promises made in the letters to the seven churches of Asia Minor (chaps. 2-3), who were the intended recipients of the apocalypse. The members of these churches apparently considered themselves to be Jewish, although their belief in Jesus distinguished them from non-Christian Jews. Two of the churches experienced conflict with "those who say they are Jews and are not but are a synagogue of Satan" (2:9; 3:9), who were probably denouncing Christians before the Roman authorities.[19] In two of the other churches there were teachers who were open to Gentile culture and taught that Christians could eat meat offered to idols (2:14, 20).

The author of Revelation insisted that true Jews were those who accepted Jesus and who abstained from Gentile practices. In the face of

[18] E.g., G. R. Beasley-Murray, *The Book of Revelation* (NCB; London: Oliphants, 1974) 311. Cf. A. Yarbro Collins, *The Combat Myth in the Book of Revelation* (HDR 9; Missoula: Scholars, 1976) 3.

[19] On the setting in which Revelation was written see esp. A. Yarbro Collins, *Crisis and Catharsis: The Power of the Apocalypse* (Philadelphia: Fortress, 1984) 84-110.

emerging conflict with Jews and Roman authorities, together with the more subtle attractiveness of pagan culture, the author made pervasive use of biblical images like that of the tabernacle in order to urge his readers to remain firm in their Christian convictions and to maintain their identity as a people set apart from the surrounding culture.

B. ANTECEDENTS FOR
REVELATION'S TABERNACLE IMAGERY

The author of Revelation drew on extra-biblical as well as biblical sources. A study of extra-biblical antecedents for Revelation's tabernacle imagery, in light of the preceding analysis, may contribute to our understanding of the character and origins of Revelation's theology.

THE SHEKINAH

Many scholars maintain that the terms σκηνή and σκηνόω in Revelation recall the Shekinah concept. The words σκηνή / σκηνόω and Shekinah share the root letters *skn,* are associated with God's glory (Rev 21:3, 11) and his throne, and indicate God's presence among his people (7:15; 21:3). Both 7:15 and 21:3 allude to Lev 26:11, which the targums render, "I will set the Shekinah of my glory among you."[20]

But there are a number of problems with this view. (1) The author of Revelation equated the σκηνή with the city of Jerusalem; rabbinic texts speak of the Shekinah *in* Jerusalem, but not *as* Jerusalem.[21] (2) The term "glory" appears in 7:12a and 21:11; σκηνή / σκηνόω occurs in 7:15c and 21:3. There is not a close connection between the σκηνή and glory in these passages. (3) The targums to Lev 26:11 consistently refer to "the Shekinah *of my glory.*" Since Revelation never refers to the σκηνή *of glory,* the author probably did not rely on targumic traditions here. (4) The term Shekinah is found in sayings attributed to rabbis of the early to mid-second century and in targums that date from the mid-second century or later. But the term does not appear in first-century apocalyptic literature and apparently did not stem from apocalyptic circles. Therefore the Shekinah idea probably did not contribute significantly to Revelation's tabernacle imagery.

---

[20] See Swete, *Apocalypse,* 104, 278; Charles, *Revelation,* 2.206; G. B. Caird, *A Commentary on the Revelation of St. John the Divine* (HNTC; New York: Harper & Row, 1966) 166–67, 263–64; Lohmeyer, *Offenbarung,* 166; G. R. Beasley-Murray, *Revelation,* 311; Schüssler Fiorenza, *Priester,* 351; Georgi, "Die Visionen," 356.

[21] See the collection of texts in Goldberg, *Schekhinah,* 103–9. Discussion of the Shekinah also appears under "Shekinah" in chap. III.F above and under "The Tabernacle in John's Gospel" in chap. V.

THE HEAVENLY TABERNACLE

Similarities between Revelation's heavenly sanctuary and celestial temples like those of of *1 Enoch* 14–16 and *T.Levi* 3–4 have often been noted.[22] These sources also refer to the angels who "dwell" in heaven (*1 Enoch* 12:2; 15:7–10; 47:2) or who minister there (*T.Levi* 3:5–7), but do not call heaven or the heavenly sanctuary a "tabernacle" as in Rev 13:6 and 15:5.

The Dead Sea "Songs of the Sabbath Sacrifice" (4QShirShabb) do describe a heavenly throne room which is called a "tabernacle" (משכן) and which is part of a larger "temple" (היכל).[23] Like Revelation, the 4QShirShabb envision angelic minsters in the heavenly temple/tabernacle (Rev 15:5–8; 4Q403 1 ii; 4Q405 20–21–22 ii). But the specific characteristics of Revelation's heavenly sanctuary differ significantly from the 4QShirShabb. Revelation's sanctuary includes an altar (6:9), the ark of the covenant (11:19), seven lamps (4:5), and a glassy sea (4:6). Extant fragments of the 4QShirShabb mention none of these items and do not say that the angels "tabernacle" (שכן) in heaven.[24]

2 Bar 4:5 and *Bib. Ant.* 11:15 refer to the "pattern" of the tabernacle, and Wis 9:8 mentions a heavenly tabernacle. But these sources do not refer to angels within the heavenly tabernacle, as in Rev 15:5–8. All of the sources named above may reflect currents that contributed to Revelation's tabernacle imagery, but none of them seems to have had a direct influence on the book.

THE WORDS OF THE HEAVENLY LIGHTS

A more promising antecedent for Revelation's tabernacle imagery appears in a Dead Sea text known as the "Words of the Heavenly Lights" (4QDibHam),[25] part of which describes a utopian Jerusalem under the Davidic monarchy. According to 4QDibHam[a] 1–2 iv 2, God's "tabernacle" is in this ideal Jerusalem; according to Rev 21:3, the tabernacle is the new Jerusalem. Moreover, both texts associate the tabernacle with divine faithfulness: in 4QDibHam the tabernacle is included with references to divine election which provide a basis for continued hope for God's favor, and in Revelation 21 the descent of the tabernacle fulfills numerous OT promises.

4QDibHam also includes numerous other images that appear in Rev 21:1–22:5.

---

[22] E.g., Charles, *Revelation,* 1.111–18; Beckwith, *Apocalypse,* 499–500; Kraft, *Offenbarung,* 96.

[23] The משכן is mentioned in 4Q403 1 ii 10 and 4Q405 ii–21–22 7. The היכל appears in 4Q400 1 i 13 and 11QShirShabb 2–1–9 7. For more detailed discussion of the heavenly sanctuary in the 4QShirShabb see chap. III.C above and Newsom, *Songs,* 39–58.

[24] A concordance to 4QShirShabb is included in Newsom, *Songs,* 389–466.

[25] See chap. III.B above for additional discussion of 4QDibHam.

	Rev	*4QDibHam[a] 1-2*
Jerusalem as holy city	21:2, 10	iv 12
No crying, pain/misfortune	21:4	iv 11–12
Water of life/living water	21:6; 22:1	v 2
God's people as God's "son"	21:7	iii 6–7
Nations bring gifts	21:24–26	iv 8–10
Those who are written in the Book of Life are brought to the city and worship God	21:27; 22:3	vi 13–15
God's name upon his people	22:4	ii 12

Many of these images are found in disparate parts of the OT. What is striking is that they are *combined* in both 4QDibHam and in Rev 21:1–22:5.

According to both Revelation and 4QDibHam, the ideal Jerusalem is not only the place of God's tabernacle; it is also the counterpart to the plagues of the end times. In Deut 31:29 Moses warned, "In the latter days evil will befall you, because you will do what is evil in the sight of the Lord." The author of 4QDibHam believed that he was experiencing these plagues, "of which Moses wrote . . . that [God] would send evil against us in the latter days" (1–2 iii 12–13). The next column contains the description of the ideal Jerusalem. Similarly, the author of Revelation introduced the "last plagues" (Rev 15:1–8) by alluding to Deuteronomy 31–32.[26] Later he contrasted the new Jerusalem with the last plagues by including "one of the seven angels who had the seven bowls full of the seven last plagues" in his vision of the new Jerusalem (Rev 21:9).[27]

Echoes of 4QDibHam may appear in Rev 7:15–17 and 15:1–8. Similarities include:

	Rev	*4QDibHam[a] 1-2*
God's tabernacle	7:15	iv 2
No hunger & thirst/misfortune	7:16	iv 11–12
The one on the throne shepherds God's people	7:17	iv 7
Plagues in the last days	15:1–8	iii 12–13
Moses the servant of God	15:3	v 14
God as holy	15:4	iv 9
Nations see God's judgments/glory	15:4	iv 8

The similarities between 4QDibHam and Rev 7:15–17; 15:1–8; and 21:1–22:5 suggest that there is some relationship between these two works.

---

[26] More detailed discussion of 15:5 is found under part "A" above.

[27] Rev 21:9 also recalls 17:1, where one of the seven angels shows the seer a vision of Babylon the harlot. There is an intentional contrast between Babylon the harlot and Jerusalem the bride.

The author of Revelation probably did not use 4QDibHam as a literary source, since the texts do differ in details. 4QDibHam speaks of an idealized Jersualem of the past and Revelation 21 refers to the new Jerusalem. The "living water" of Rev 22:1 echoes Zech 14:8, while 4QDibHam v 2 recalls Jer 2:13. Rev 21:7 derived the image of Israel as God's "son" from 2 Sam 7:14, while 4QDibHam alludes to Exod 4:22.

But the author of Revelation may have known a tradition very similar to 4QDibHam. 4QDibHam is a liturgical composition that contains prayers for each day of the week. The text was apparently composed prior to the founding of the Qumran community and may therefore have been known outside the sect. The penitential parts of the work have formal parallels in Dan 9:4-19 and Bar 1:15-3:8. Therefore 4QDibHam was probably part of a wider liturgical tradition.

Liturgical elements in Revelation have often been noted.[28] The visions came to the seer on "the Lord's Day" (1:10), which was probably a time for corporate worship. The seer expected his work to be read aloud (1:3; 22:18), presumably in a liturgical setting, and he concluded the book with several liturgical sayings (22:17-21). Revelation's doxologies, acclamations, and expressions like "Amen" and "hallelujah" indicate that the author was thoroughly familiar with liturgical traditions. One of these traditions was apparently quite similar to 4QDibHam.

If the author did know a tradition similar to 4QDibHam, he used it as he used biblical materials. Earlier we noted that he incorporated elements from entire sections of Ezekiel, Zechariah, Tobit, Psalm 46, and other texts into his vision of the new Jerusalem, without quoting a single biblical text verbatim. Similarly, he may have woven elements of the ideal Jerusalem, eschatological plagues, and other parts of the 4QDibHam tradition into his composition, without following the exact wording or sequence of the tradition.

2 CORINTHIANS 6:14-7:1

The new Jerusalem of Revelation 21 is also the Christian community and temple in which God tabernacles. Similarly, 2 Cor 6:16 also speaks of God's tabernacling presence within the temple of the Christian community. The reference is part of a fragment of material (6:14-7:1) that many scholars

---

[28] On Revelation's liturgical character see G. Delling, "Zum gottesdienstlichen Stil der Johannesapokalypse," *NovT* 3 (1959) 107-37; M. Shepherd, *The Pascal Liturgy and the Apocalypse* (Ecumenical Studies in Worship 6; Richmond: Knox, 1960); L. Thompson, "Cult and Eschatology in the Apocalypse of John," *JR* 49 (1969) 330-50; K.-P. Jörns, *Das hymnische Evangelium: Untersuchungen zu Aufbau, Funktion und Herkunft der hymnischen Stücke in der Johannesoffenbarung* (SNT 5; Gütersloh: Mohn, 1971); A. Yarbro Collins, *Combat Myth*, 5-8, 234; E. Schüssler Fiorenza, "Composition," 351-55; P. Prigent, "Un trace de liturgie judéo-chrétienne dans le chapitre XXI de l'Apocalypse de Jean," *RSR* 60 (1972) 165-72.

believe to be non-Pauline, because it radically interrupts the epistle's progression of thought, seems to be a self-contained unit, and contains six words that do not occur elsewhere in the NT.[29]

God's tabernacling presence is mentioned in 6:16:

> What agreement has the temple of God with idols?
> For we are the temple of the living God; as God said,
> "I will dwell (ἐνοικήσω) and move among them,
> and I will be their God and they shall be my people."

The second part of the verse paraphrases Ezek 37:27/Lev 26:11–12, which also appears in Rev 21:3. The difference is that 2 Cor 6:16 uses the word ἐνοικέω rather than σκηνόω, as in Rev 21:3. Yet neither 2 Cor 6:16 nor Rev 21:3 follows the LXX, which reads "I will put my covenant among them." Therefore both are probably independent translations of a similar Hebrew text.

2 Cor 6:14–7:1 paraphrases a number of other OT texts, nearly all of which appear in Revelation 21.

	Rev	*2 Cor*
Ezek 37:27/Lev 26:11–12	21:3	6:16b
Isa 52:11	18:4; cf. 21:8, 27	6:17a
2 Sam 7:14	21:7	6:18a
2 Sam 7:8? (παντοκράτωρ)	21:22	6:18b

The title παντοκράτωρ ("almighty") appears only in Revelation and 2 Cor 6:18 in the NT. Both passages also apply the words, "I shall be your father and you shall be my son" (2 Sam 7:14) to the faithful, rather than to Jesus as in Heb 1:5. Only the reference to Ezek 20:34 in 2 Cor 6:17b does not appear in Revelation.

The image of the Christian community as a temple is not unique to 2 Cor 6:14–7:1 and Revelation, but only these two texts associate the temple imagery with the promise of God's tabernacling presence (Lev 26:11/Ezek 37:27). Paul calls the Christian community a temple because it is the dwelling place of the Holy Spirit (1 Cor 3:16–17).[30] According to Mark 14:58, Jesus promised to build a temple "not made with hands"; the temple that Jesus was to build may be the church.[31] But neither Revelation 21 nor 2 Cor 6:16 depicts the Christian community as the temple that Jesus built or as a temple

---

[29] Cf. J. A. Fitzmyer, "Qumran and the Interpolated Paragraph in 2 Cor 6,14–7,1," *CBQ* 23 (1961) 271–80; V. P. Furnish, *II Corinthians* (AB 32A; Garden City: Doubleday, 1984) 371–83.

[30] He calls the body of an individual Christian a "temple" of the Holy Spirit in 1 Cor 6:19.

[31] E. Schweizer, *The Good News According to Mark* (Atlanta: Knox, 1970) 329; Klinzing, *Umdeutung,* 203; Juel, *Messiah and Temple,* 135–36.

of the Holy Spirit. Both consider the church to be the temple where God tabernacles or dwells, as he promised in Lev 26:11/Ezek 37:27.[32]

Revelation and 2 Cor 6:14-7:1 share a dualistic perspective. Both sharply distinguish those inside the community from those outside it and associate belief with purity and unbelief with idolatry (2 Cor 6:15-16; 7:1; Rev 21:8,27). Taken together, the common elements mentioned above suggest the possibility of a relationship between these two texts.[33]

The author of Revelation did not use 2 Cor 6:14-7:1 as a literary source, since the two texts translate Ezek 37:27/Lev 26:11-12 differently and call the devil "Satan" and "Beliar," respectively. Instead, the similarities suggest that the author of Revelation was familiar with a type of Christianity like that which produced 2 Cor 6:1-7:1.

SYNTHESIS

Revelation 21 referred to Jerusalem as God's tabernacle and to God's tabernacling presence in the temple of the Christian community. This imagery may reflect the confluence of two types of tradition: 4QDibHam preserves a liturgical tradition that locates God's tabernacle in an ideal Jerusalem, and 2 Cor 6:14-7:1 refers to God's tabernacling presence within the temple of the Christian community. Both types of tradition have affinities with the theology of the Dead Sea sect.

In its present form 2 Cor 6:14-7:1 is a Christian text, but its theology resembles that of the Dead Sea sect in many ways. The passage sharply distinguishes between uprightness and iniquity, light and darkness, Christ and Beliar; it opposes idolatry, conceives of the community as a temple, urges separation from impurity, and includes a concatenation of OT texts.[34] The fragment appears to have been written or edited by a Christian with roots in a form of Judaism similar to that of the Dead Sea Sect. Since the author of Revelation has a similar dualistic outlook, a similar view of the

---

[32] Eph 2:21-22 refers to the church as a temple that grows together in Christ for a dwelling place of God in the Spirit. Lev 26:11/Ezek 37:27 is not mentioned.

[33] Schüssler Fiorenza (*Priester,* 406-10) recognizes the many similarities between Revelation and 2 Cor 6:14-7:1, including the idea of the community as a temple. But she argues that the author of Revelation radically reinterpreted the temple motif by applying it only to the community of the future, rather than to the community of the present as in 2 Cor 6:16. Yet many scholars maintain that Rev 11:1-2 does allude to the present Christian community as a temple. These verses originally spoke of the preservation of the Jerusalem temple, but since the author knew that the temple had been destroyed, he must have interpreted the oracle symbolically. He may have thought of the Christian community as the "temple" that was preserved from destruction. Cf. Swete, *Apocalypse,* 132-33; Charles, *Revelation,* 1.276-77; A. Feuillet, *Johannine Studies* (New York: Alba, 1965) 235-40.

[34] Fitzmyer, "Qumran," 273.

community as a temple, and includes nearly identical OT texts, he was probably familiar with a Christian circle like that which composed 2 Cor 6:14–7:1.

4QDibHam was composed prior to the founding of the Qumran community and may have been known outside the sect. Similar liturgical forms appear in Daniel, Baruch, and other works, but only the Dead Sea version includes the description of the ideal Jerusalem. The tradition used by the author of Revelation seems to have been closer to the Qumran text than to any other extant version.

Taken together, the similarities between Revelation, 2 Cor 6:14–7:1, and 4QDibHam suggest that the author of Revelation either came from or was very familiar with a type of Christianity that had roots in a form of Judaism like that of the Dead Sea sect. The evidence does not suggest, however, that the author came from the Qumran community itself, since Revelation does not mention such things as the "pesher" method of biblical interpretation, the "Teacher of Righteousness" or the "Wicked Priest," which are peculiar to Qumran.[35]

The fusion of elements from sources similar to 4QDibHam and 2 Cor 6:14–7:1 may have been occasioned by the circumstances of the author. He wrote to seven churches in Asia Minor in order to warn them of a coming persecution and to urge them to remain steadfast in their faith (Rev 2:10; 3:10). A tradition like that found in 4QDibHam would have served his purposes well, since it depicted an ideal Jerusalem as the place of God's tabernacle in a way that offered hope to those who thought they were experiencing the plagues of the end times. The author also wanted to warn against contact with idolatry and against eating meat offered to idols (2:14, 20). Material like that found in 2 Cor 6:14–7:1 would help to address the issue because it depicts the Christian community as the place where God dwells and it urges Christians to remain separate from all uncleanness.

C. Conclusion

Rev 7:15 envisions a time when God will tabernacle with the redeemed, as promised in Ezek 37:27 and Lev 26:11. But before the promise is fulfilled, the armies of God must conquer the forces of Satan. The angels and martyrs who "tabernacle" in heaven vanquish Satan and rejoice (12:12). But Satan's power reappears in the beast from the sea, who defiantly blasphemes the

---

[35] A number of scholars have noted other similarities between Revelation and the Dead Sea sect. A striking parallel is that Rev 21:12–21 and 4QpIsa[d] interpret the description of Jerusalem in Isa 54:11–12 in terms of the eschatological community. See J. M. Baumgarten, "The Duodecimal Courts of Qumran, Revelation, and the Sanhedrin," *JBL* 95 (1976) 59–78; Rissi, *Future,* 48–50. See also Yarbro Collins, *Crisis,* 129–31.

inhabitants of the heavenly tabernacle who had cast Satan out (13:6). The tabernacle in heaven opens, and seven angels emerge with bowls full of the seven last plagues (15:5). The final plague drenches "Babylon," the harlot city that sat upon the beast from the sea.

The harlot is replaced by the bride—New Jerusalem. As the city descends from heaven a voice proclaims, "Behold the tabernacle of God with men" (21:3). God's tabernacle is not his Shekinah; the city itself is his tabernacling place. The descent of the tabernacle-city fulfills the vision of Rev 7:15 and a catena of promises from Ezekiel, Leviticus, Zechariah, and the Psalms, indicating that it is a manifestation of divine faithfulness.

The tabernacle-city is the church in the new age. Its foundations are the apostles, its gates are the twelve sons of Israel, and its dimensions recall the number of the elect (21:12-17). In the church, God is present for all peoples (21:3, 22-23). Those who are inscribed in the Lamb's Book of Life come from every nation, bringing homage to God and to the Lamb who are enthroned in the church (21:24-22:3). There, within the church, God's glory is manifested as in the holy of holies (21:23) and like high priests, God's servants bear the divine name on their foreheads (22:4). They see God's face, worship, and reign as servants of the Almighty God and the conquering Lamb, whose kingdom endures forever (22:5).[36]

The seer's description of the tabernacle-city is a unique creation, which weaves together OT pericopes and later Jewish and Christian traditions. His sources include sections from Ezekiel, Zechariah, Psalm 46, and Tobit 13, together with a liturgical tradition like that of 4QDibHam and the tradition of God's tabernacling presence within the temple of the Christian community. The author combined these traditions into a picture of the church as God's tabernacle in the new age.

The vision of the tabernacle-city was initially addressed to Christians in Asia Minor who considered themselves to be Jews, but who were distinguished from non-Christian Jews by their belief in Jesus. The author's use of biblical imagery would have helped to confirm the identity of Christians as the true people of God and the heirs to God's promises. Since the church would be God's tabernacling place in the new age, Christians must remain faithful to their convictions despite emerging conflict with non-Christian Jews and Roman authorities, while remaining a people set apart from the surrounding Gentile culture and its idolatry.

---

[36] Schüssler Fiorenza (*Priester,* 351) and Georgi ("Die Visionen," 356) rightly observe that the New Jerusalem includes more than the present Christian community. But following R. Schnackenburg, Schüssler Fiorenza notes that in the new age the "Church" and the "Kingdom of God" do coincide (*Priester,* 353).

CHART 6

	Rev 7:15c-17	Ezekiel	Isaiah	Psalm 23	Other	4QDibHam
15c	He who sits upon the throne will tabernacle upon them.	My tabernacle shall be upon them (37:27).			I will make my tabernacle among you (Lev 26:11)	...your tabernacle... in Jerusalem (iv 2)
16	They shall not hunger anymore or thirst anymore; neither sun nor any scorching heat shall fall upon them.		They shall not hunger or thirst, neither scorching wind nor sun shall smite them;			There was no misfortune...they are and were satisfied (iv 13–14)
17	for the Lamb who is in the midst of the throne will shepherd them, and he will lead them to springs of living water and God will wipe away every tear from their eyes.	I will set up over them one shepherd...David, and he shall feed them (34:23)	for he who has pity on them will lead them... by springs of water (49:10) Lord God will wipe away tears from all faces (25:8).	The Lord is my shepherd...he leads me beside still waters (23:1-2)	(they have forsaken me) the fountain of living waters (Jer 2:13) Keep...your eyes from tears (Jer 31:16)	(David to sit) before you on the throne... as a princely shepherd (iv 6b,a) fount of living waters (v 2)

CHART 7

Rev 12:12	Ps 96:11	Ps 98:7
Rejoice O heavens and those who dwell in them	Let the heavens be glad and let the earth rejoice; let the sea roar and all that fills it.	Let the sea roar and all that fills it, the world and those who dwell in it

CHART 8

Rev 13:6-7a	Dan 7:20-21	Dan 7:25	Dan 8:9-10
And (the beast) opened its mouth in blasphemies toward God, blaspheming his name and his tabernacle, those who tabernacle in heaven. And it was permitted to make war on the saints and to conquer them.	(The beast had a horn with) a mouth that spoke great things . . . this horn made war with the saints and prevailed over them.	(The fourth beast) shall speak words against the Most High and shall wear out the saints	A little horn . . . grew great even to the host of heaven.

CHART 9

	Revelation	Exodus	Deuteronomy	Psalms	Other	4QDibHam
1	And I saw another sign in heaven, great and wonderful, 7 angels with 7 plagues which are the last, for with them the wrath of God is completed.	10 plagues/signs (7–12)	In the latter days evil will befall you (31:29)		I will bring more plagues upon you, 7 times as many as your sins (Lev 26:21)	You caused the (plagues) to cleave to us, of which Moses wrote....that you would send against is in the latter days (iii 11–14)
2	And I saw something like a sea of glass mixed with fire, and those who were victorious over the beast and its image and the number of its name, standing beside the sea of glass holding harps of God,	(God) triumphed gloriously (15:1) Israel went into the midst of the sea on dry ground (14:22)		Sing praises to the Lord with the lyre (98:5)		

CHART 9 (continued)

	Revelation	Exodus	Deuteronomy	Psalms	Other	4QDibHam
3	and they sing the song of Moses the servant of God, and the song of the Lamb, saying, Great and wonderful are your works, O Lord God, the the Almighty Just and true are your ways, O King of the nations.	Moses...sang this song (15:1) (Lord's) servant Moses (14:31)	Moses spoke...this song (31:30) Moses the servant of the Lord (34:5) His work is perfect for all his ways are justice (32:4a)	Sing to the Lord a new song.... for he has done marvelous things (98:1) Great are the works of the Lord (111:2) Wonderful are your works (139:14) The Lord is just in all his ways (145:17)	Moses the servant of the Lord (Josh 1:1,2,7) Lord God Almighty! (Amos 3:13; 4:13 LXX) King of the nations...	Moses your servant (v 14)

CHART 9 (continued)

	Revelation	Exodus	Deuteronomy	Psalms	Other	4QDibHam
4	Who shall not fear, O Lord, and glorify your name? For you only are holy, for all the nations shall come and worship before you, for your judgments have been revealed.		Just and holy is the Lord (32:4b LXX)	...shall glorify your name... (86:9c) ...all the nations... shall come and bow down before you (86:9a,b) In the sight of the nations he has revealed his vindication (98:2)	who would not fear you? ...your name is great in might (Jer 10:7b,a,6b)	You made yourself holy... and all the nations... brought their offering to your great name (iv 8–10)
5	And after these things I looked and the temple of the tent of witness in heaven was opened	pattern of the tabernacle (25:9)	Lord appeared in the tent of meeting (31:15)			

CHART 9 (continued)

	Revelation	Exodus	Deuteronomy	Psalms	Other	4QDibHam
6	And out of the temple came the 7 angels with the 7 plagues, clothed in pure, bright linen, and girded about their breasts with golden girdles.					
7	And one of the 4 creatures gave the 7 angels 7 golden bowls full of the wrath of God, who lives forever and ever.					
8	And the temple was filled with smoke from the glory of God and from his power, and no one was able to enter the temple until the 7 plagues of the 7 angels were completed.	The cloud covered the tent of meeting, and the glory of the Lord filled the tabernacle. And Moses was not able to enter the tent of meeting… (40:34–35)	A pillar of cloud stood by the door of the tent… and the Lord appeared (31:15b, a)		A cloud filled the house of the Lord so that the priests could not stand to minister…for the glory of the Lord filled the house of the Lord (1 Kgs 8:10b–11)	

	Revelation 21	Isaiah	Ezekiel	Zechariah
1	And I saw a new heaven and a new earth, for the former heaven and the former earth had passed away and the sea was no more.	Behold I create new heavens and a new earth and the former things shall not be remembered... (65:17)		
2	And I saw the holy city, new Jerusalem, coming down out of heaven from God, prepared as a bride adorned for her husband.	Jerusalem the holy city (52:1). I create a Jerusalem rejoicing (65:18). as a bride adorns herself with her jewels (61:10).		
3	And I heard a loud voice from the throne saying, "Behold the tabernacle of God with men. He will tabernacle with them, and they shall be his peoples and God himself will be with them.		My tabernacle shall be upon them. and I will be their God and they shall be my people. (37:27)	I will tabernacle in your midst, and many nations shall...be my people (2:10–11) They shall be my people and I will be their God. (8:8)
4	He will wipe away every tear from their eyes, and death shall be more, neither shall there be mourning, nor crying, nor pain anymore, for the former things have passed away."	God will wipe away tears from all faces... he will swallow up death forever (25:8b,a) (In Jerusalem no...) weeping... The former things shall not be remembered (65:19,17)		

10

Other	4QDibHam	Tobit 13	Pseudo-Philo
There is a city...the holy tabernacle of the Most High (Ps 46:4)	Zion, your holy city (iv 12)	O Jerusalem, the holy city (13:9)	
I will make my tabernacle among you...and I will be your God and you shall be my people (Lev 26:11-12). I will be their God and they shall be my people...	...your tabernacle... a resting place in Jerusalem (iv 2)	...that his tabernacle may be raised for you again (13:10)	
Keep...your eyes from tears (Jer 31:33,16) (Ransomed ...come to Zion...) and sorrow and sighing shall flee (Isa 51:11; cf. 35:10) Remember not the former things...	There was neither adversary nor misfortune (iv 12-13)		

	Revelation 21	Isaiah	Ezekiel	Zechariah
5	And he who sat upon the throne said, "Behold I make all things new." Also he said "Write this, for these words are trustworthy and true."			
6	And he said to me, "It is done. I am the Alpha and the Omega, the beginning and the end. To the thirsty I will give from the fountain of the water of life without payment.	Let everyone who thirsts come to the waters; and he who has no money, come (55:1).		
7	The one who conquers shall have this heritage, and I will be his God and he shall be my son.			
8	But as for the cowardly, the faithless, the polluted, murderers, fornicators, sorcerers, idolators, and all liars, their lot shall be in the lake that burns with fire and sulphur, which is the second death.			

Other	4QDibHam	Tobit 13	Pseudo-Philo
Behold I am doing a new thing (Isa 43:18–19)			
(They have forsaken me) the fountain of living waters (Jer 2:13)	...the fountain of living waters (v 2)		
I will be his father and he shall be my son (2 Sam 7:14)	You have named Israel 'My son, my firstborn' (iii 6)		

	Revelation 21	Isaiah	Ezekiel	Zechariah
9	Then came one of the 7 angels who had the 7 bowls full of the 7 last plagues, and spoke to me saying, "Come, I will show you the bride, the wife of the Lamb."		the hand of the Lord...	
10	And in the Spirit he carried me away to a great high mountain, and showed me the holy city Jerusalem, coming down out of heaven from God.	Jerusalem the holy city (52:1)	brought me in the visions of God... and set me down upon a very high mountain, on which was a structure like a city (40:1–2)	
11	having the glory of God, its radiance like a most rare jewel, like jasper, clear as crystal.		the glory of the Lord filled the temple (43:5)	
12	It had a great, high wall with 12 gates, and at the gates the 12 angels, and on gates the names of the 12 tribes of the sons of Israel were inscribed.	Upon your walls O Jerusalem I have set watchmen (62:6)		
13	on the east 3 gates, on the north 3 gates, on the south 3 gates, and on the west 3 gates.		On the north... 3 gates... On the east... 3 gates... On the south... 3 gates... On the west... 3 gates... (48:30–34)	

Other	4QDibHam	Tobit 13	Pseudo-Philo
	Zion, your holy city (iv 12)		
There shall be 12 stones with their names according to the names of the sons of Israel. (Exod 28:21)			(Description of the 12 stones bearing the names of the 12 sons of Israel (26:9–11)

	Revelation 21	Isaiah	Ezekiel	Zechariah
14	And the wall of the city has 12 foundations, and on them the 12 names of the 12 apostles of the Lamb.			
15	And he who spoke with me had a measuring reed of gold to measure the city and its gates and its walls.		There was a man... with...a measuring reed in his hand (40:3)	Behold a man with a measuring line in his hand...to measure Jerusalem, to see what is its breadth and what is its length (2:1-2)
16	The city lies foursquare, its length the same as its breadth. And he measured the city with his rod, 12,000 stadia; its length and breadth and height are equal.		(The city was 4500 cubits square 48:16; the temple was 500 cubits square, 42:20)	
17	He also measured its wall, 144 cubits by a man's measure, that is, an angel's.			
18	The construction of its wall was jasper and the city was pure gold, like pure glass.			

Other	4QDibHam	Tobit 13	Pseudo-Philo
You shall make a breastplate ...it shall be square... (Exod 28:15–16)			

	Revelation 21	Isaiah	Ezekiel	Zechariah
19	The foundations of the wall of the city were adorned with every jewel. The first foundation was jasper, the second sapphire, the third agate, the fourth emerald.	I will set your stones in antimony and lay your foundation with sapphires, I will make your pinnacles of agate.	(To King of Tyre:) Every precious stone was your covering: carnelian, topaz, jasper, chrysolite, beryl,	
20	the fifth onyx, the sixth carnelian, the seventh chrysolite, the eighth beryl, the ninth topaz, the tenth chrysoprase, the eleventh jacinth, the twelfth amethyst.		onyx, sapphire carbuncle, and emerald.	
21	The 12 gates were 12 pearls, each of the gates made of a single pearl, and the street of the city was pure gold, like clear glass.	your gates of carbuncles, and all your wall of precious stones (54:11–12)	and wrought in gold were your settings (28:13)	
22	And I saw no temple in the city, for its temple is the Lord God Almighty and the Lamb.			

Other	4QDibHam	Tobit 13	Pseudo-Philo
(The stones in the high priest's breastplate:)		Jerusalem will be built with sapphires and emeralds, her walls with precious stones, and her towers and	(The stones bearing the names of the 12 tribes:
sardius, topaz, carbuncle, emerald,			sardius topaz emerald carbuncle
sapphire, diamond, jacinth, agate, amethyst, beryl, onyx, jasper,		battlements with pure gold. The streets of Jerusalem will be paved with beryl and ruby and stones of Ophir ... (13:16–17)	sapphire jasper ligure amethyst agate chrysolite beryl onyx) (26:9–11)
they shall be set in gold filigree (Exod 28:17–20)			

	Revelation 21	Isaiah	Ezekiel	Zechariah
23	And the city has no need of sun or moon to shine upon it, for the glory of God is its light and its lamp is the Lamb.	The sun shall no more be your light by day nor...shall the moon give you light by night, but the Lord will be your everlasting light and your God will be your glory...		
24	By its light shall the nations walk, and the kings of the the earth shall bring their glory into it.	Nations shall come to your light and kings to the brightness of your rising (60:19,3)		
25	and its gates shall never be shut by day and there shall be no night there;	Your gates shall be open continually; day and night they shall not be shut;		There shall be continuous day not day and not night (14:7)
26	they shall bring into it the glory and honor of the nations.	that men may bring to you the wealth of the nations (60:11)		The wealth of all the nations...shall be collected (14:14)
27	But nothing unclean shall enter it, nor anyone who practices abomination or falsehood, but only those who are written in the Lamb's book of life.	O Jerusalem...there shall no more come into you the uncircumcised and the unclean (52:1)... they will be called holy, everyone who has been recorded for life in Jerusalem (4:3)		

Other	4QDibHam	Tobit 13	Pseudo-Philo
			And the just will not lack the brilliance of the sun or the moon, for the light of these precious stones will be their light (26:13)
	All the nations have seen your glory...		
	they brought their gifts of silver and gold and precious stones, with		
	all the treasures of their lands, that they might glorify	Many nations will come...bearing gifts ...for the King	
	...your holy city (iv 8-12) Deliver your people...everyone who is inscribed in the book of life (vi 12-14)	of heaven (13:11)	

	Revelation 22	Isaiah	Ezekiel	Zechariah
1	And he showed me the river of the water of life, bright as crystal, flowing from the throne of God and the Lamb.		Behold, water was issuing from below the threshold of the temple	On that day living waters shall flow out from Jerusalem, half of them
2	In the middle of the street of the city and on both sides of the river the tree of life with its 12 kinds of fruit, bearing its fruit each month, and the leaves of the tree were for the healing of the nations.		toward the east (47:1) And on the banks on both sides of the river there will grow all kinds of trees for food...they will bear fresh fruit each month...and their leaves will be for healing. (47:12)	to the eastern sea and half of them to the western sea (14:8)
3	There shall no more be anything accursed, but the throne of God and the Lamb shall be in it and his servants shall worship him;		The name of the city...shall be, "The Lord is there." (48:35)	There shall be no more curse; Jerusalem shall dwell in security (14:11)
4	they shall see his face and his name shall be on their foreheads.			
5	And night shall be no more; they need no light of lamp or sun, for the Lord God will be their light and they shall reign for ever and ever.	The sun shall no more be your light by day...but the Lord will be your everlasting light (60:19)		

Other	4QDibHam	Tobit 13	Pseudo-Philo
There is a river whose streams make glad the city of God, the holy tabernacle of the Most High (Ps 46:4)			
A river flowed out of Eden...the tree of life in the midst of the garden... (Gen 2:10,9)			
At that time Jerusalem shall be called the throne of the Lord (Jer 3:17)	(David) a princely shepherd...to sit before you on the throne (iv 6)		
When shall I...see	To serve you and give thanks (vi 15)		
the face of God? (Ps 42:2) "Holy to the Lord" (shall be on Aaron's forehead) (Exod 28:36–38)	We were called by your name (ii 12)		
The saints of the Most High...shall possess the kingdom for ever, for ever and ever (Dan 7:18)			

VII

THE EPISTLE TO THE HEBREWS

The Israelite tabernacle plays an important, yet enigmatic, role in the Epistle to the Hebrews. Two aspects of the tabernacle have proved to be especially elusive for interpreters. The first concerns the relationship of the tabernacle to the Jerusalem temple. Several chapters of Hebrews discuss Israel's cult, but the temple — which was the central cultic institution for Jews in the first century — is never mentioned. The discussion centers on the tabernacle cult, which had been defunct for many centuries. Yet if Hebrews was written before A.D. 70 and the temple was still standing, why was it never mentioned? If Hebrews was written after A.D. 70, why didn't the author refer to the temple's destruction as evidence that the time of its cult had ended?

Some interpreters understand the tabernacle as a cipher for the Jerusalem temple.[1] They note that the epistle speaks as if sacrifices were still being offered (Heb 8:4-5; 9:6-7; 10:1-2, 11) and maintain that the epistle's arguments would make most sense if the temple cult were still functioning. Others note that Josephus (*Ag. Ap.* 2.6 77) and *1 Clem* 40:4-5 speak as if the Jerusalem temple were still functioning, even though both wrote after A.D. 70. They suggest that the focus on the tabernacle gives the argument a timeless character that would fit well in the period after the temple was destroyed.[2]

The second problem concerns the background of the tabernacle imagery in Hebrews. At points the author identifies parts of the tabernacle with higher and lower realms of being (9:9b; 10:20). Therefore many scholars

---

[1] E.g., C. Spicq, *L'Epître aux Hébreux* (EBib; Paris: Gabalda, 1952–53) 1.253–61; F. F. Bruce, *The Epistle to the Hebrews* (NICNT; Grand Rapids: Eerdmans, 1964) xlii–xliv; D. Guthrie, *New Testament Introduction* (Downer's Grove: Inter-Varsity, 1970) 716–18; G. W. Buchanan, *Hebrews* (AB 36; Garden City: Doubleday, 1972) 256–63; J. A. T. Robinson, *Redating the New Testament* (Philadelphia: Westminster, 1976) 200–20.

[2] E.g., W. G. Kümmel, *Introduction to the New Testament* (Nashville: Abingdon, 1975) 403; O. Michel, *Der Brief an die Hebräer* (MeyerK 13; Göttingen: Vandenhoeck & Ruprecht, 1975) 56–58; Brown, *Antioch and Rome,* 150. See also the list of scholars in Robinson, *Redating,* 200.

have argued that the tabernacle imagery stems from a "Hellenistic" milieu, similar to that of Philo and early gnosticism.[3] Others note that the parts of the tabernacle are equated with periods of time that reflect an "apocalyptic" background (9:9a).[4] Although many interpreters acknowledge that Hebrews combines spatial and temporal categories, the interrelationships of these two modes of thought and the milieu in which such interrelationships are likely to have been affirmed have been difficult to determine. Our study of the tabernacle in Hebrews will attempt to address these issues.

A. THE TABERNACLE IN HEBREWS

Since the tabernacle appears in a number of passages of Hebrews, we will first note several characteristics of the book as a whole, then discuss individual references to the tabernacle, and finally note how the tabernacle functions within the entire work.

ON THE COMPOSITION OF HEBREWS

The Epistle to the Hebrews is a "word of exhortation" (13:22) that is intended to admonish and encourage its readers.[5] Accordingly, the author framed his lengthy discussion of Christ and the Levitical cult with exhortations to "hold fast our confession" (4:14; 10:23) and to "draw near" to Christ's throne of grace (4:16; 10:22), and he constructed an argument that tries to move readers beyond "the elementary doctrine of Christ" to maturity (6:1). The argument itself presupposes that the author and readers shared certain convictions, which provided a basis for introducing new ideas. Our grasp of the argument will be enhanced by attempting to distinguish between the views presupposed by the author and those for which he argues.

One of the author's important assumptions is that his readers would be Christians who would be familiar with certain christological concepts.[6] For

---

[3] On Philo see esp. Spicq, *Hébreux*, 1.72–76. The Gnostic hypothesis is developed by E. Käsemann, *The Wandering People of God: An Investigation of the Letter to the Hebrews* (Minneapolis: Augsburg, 1984) 223–26.

[4] E.g., C. K. Barrett, "The Eschatology of the Epistle to the Hebrews," *The Background of the New Testament and its Eschatology* (Studies in Honor of C. H. Dodd; ed. W. D. Davies and D. Daube; Cambridge: University, 1956) 363–93, esp. 383–90.

[5] On the paraenetic character of Hebrews see Michel, *Hebräer*, 26–27; W. Nauck, "Zum Aufbau des Hebräerbriefes," *Judentum, Urchristentum, Kirche: Festschrift für Joachim Jeremias* (ed. W. Eltester; BZNW 26; Berlin: Töpelmann, 1960) 199–206; J. W. Thompson, "The Underlying Unity of Hebrews," *ResQ* 18 (1975) 129–36; idem, *The Beginnings of Christian Philosophy* (CBQMS 13; Washington: CBA, 1982) 155–56.

[6] Scholars generally agree that the intended recipients of the epistle were Christians, although they disagree whether they were of Jewish or Gentile origin. The author warns against falling away (3:12; 6:6), but does not indicate that readers were in danger of giving up all faith

example, he presupposed that Jesus could be presented without explanation as the Christ, the Son of God, and as a figure similar to the personified wisdom depicted in Jewish literature. He also assumed that readers would grant that Jesus had died a sacrificial death and had been exalted to eternal life in heaven, although he did not think that they grasped the implications of these events.

A second presupposition is that the biblical prescriptions for the priesthood, tabernacle, and sacrifices were an integral part of the Mosaic covenant. In the book of Exodus, the prescriptions for the tabernacle were given immediately after the covenant was first ratified (Exodus 24–31), and the tabernacle was constructed as soon as the covenant was renewed, after the golden calf incident (Exodus 34–40). Accordingly, the epistle to the Hebrews includes all its references to the law (νόμος), its commandments (ἐντολαί), and the Mosaic covenant (διαθήκη) in its discussion of the Israelite cult.[7] The author made no distinction between "moral" and "ritual" law. Certain views of the tabernacle were also presupposed by the author. Our task will be to discern what the author assumed that the tabernacle meant and how these views figure in his argument.

HEB 8:1-6: HEAVENLY AND EARTHLY TABERNACLES

The first explicit reference to the tabernacle appears in Hebrews 8.

(8:1) The main point in what we are saying is that we have such a high priest, who sat down at the right hand of the throne of majesty in the heavens, (2) a minister of the sanctuary (τὰ ἅγια) and the true tent (ἡ σκηνή) which the Lord, not a human being, erected. (3) For every high priest is appointed to offer gifts and sacrifices; therefore this one too must have something to offer. (4) Now if he were on earth he would not be a priest, because there are [priests] who offer gifts according to the law, (5) who serve a representation and a shadow of the heavenly [sanctuary], just as Moses was divinely admonished when he was about to construct the tabernacle, for [God] said, "See that you make everything according to the type that was shown to you on the mountain." (6) But now, [Jesus] has received a ministry that is superior [to theirs] to the same extent as he is also mediator of a better covenant, which has been enacted on better promises.

---

in Christ. See P. Andriessen, "La communauté des 'Hébreux': Etait-elle tombee dans le relachement?" *NRT* 96 (1974) 1054–66; J. Dahms, "The First Readers of Hebrews," *JETS* 20 (1977) 365–75. On the christological basis of the argument see also H. Koester, " 'Outside the Camp': Hebrews 13:9–14," *HTR* 55 (1962) 299–315; Michel, *Hebräer,* 70–75.

[7] The "covenant" in 12:24 and 13:20 is the new covenant, not the Mosaic covenant.

This section develops the conclusions and pattern of argument found in the preceding discussion of Jesus' high priesthood. In chap. 7 the author pointed out that the scriptures refer to not one but *two* types of priesthood. One was established by the Mosaic law, which required that priests be descendants of Levi. The other was mentioned in Psalm 110, which spoke of a priest "after the order of Melchizedek," who would hold office "forever." The author acknowledged that Jesus was not a priest by Mosaic standards, but was singularly qualified for the eternal Melchizedek priesthood since he had been exalted to eternal life in heaven. The argument shows that temporally, the Mosaic law and its priesthood obtained only for a limited period of time, while Jesus' priesthood endures forever (7:12, 18). Spatially, the law and its priesthood belong to a realm marked by death and weakness, while the priesthood of Jesus belongs to the realm of everlasting life and perfection (7:23–28).

Chap. 8 begins by restating that Jesus serves as high priest in heaven, using imagery that echoes Psalm 110 and Heb 1:1–3, which portrays Jesus as a figure similar to the personified wisdom found in Jewish tradition.[8] Then the author observes that the Mosaic law spoke of not one but *two* sanctuaries. One was the earthly sanctuary erected by Moses. The other was the heavenly "pattern" for the tabernacle, which the author understood to be an actual heavenly sanctuary (Heb 8:5; Exod 25:9, 40). He located the ministry of the exalted Christ in the heavenly sanctuary and tied the service of priests appointed under the Mosaic law to the earthly tabernacle.

The heavenly tabernacle is called "the sanctuary (τὰ ἅγια) and the true tent (ἡ σκηνή)" in 8:2. Some interpreters argue that this verse depicts a bipartite heavenly sanctuary, with τὰ ἅγια referring only to the holy of holies and ἡ σκηνή designating either the outer court or the sanctuary as a whole. Reasons for this view include (1) that passages like Heb 9:8 and 11 seem to posit a distinction between τὰ ἅγια and ἡ σκηνή, and (2) that the biblical account of the day of atonement ritual, which informs the author of Hebrews, uses τὸ ἅγιον for the holy of holies and σκηνή for the entire tent (e.g., Lev 16:16).[9]

Nevertheless, there are stronger reasons to think τὰ ἅγια and ἡ σκηνή in 8:2 are synonyms, connected by an explicative καί.[10] (1) The complex

---

[8] See the section on the wisdom tradition in sec. B below.

[9] O. Hofius, *Der Vorhang vor dem Thron Gottes: Eine exegetisch- religionsgeschichtliche Untersuchung zu Hebräer 6,19f. und 10,19f.* (WUNT 14; Tübingen: Mohr/Siebeck, 1972) 59–60. Cf. A. Vanhoye, " 'Par la tent plus grand et plus parfait . . .' (Heb 9,11)," *Bib* 46 (1965) 1–28, esp. 4; P. Andriessen, "Das grössere und vollkommenere Zelt," *BZ* 15 (1971) 76–92, esp. 87; M. Rissi, *Die Theologie des Hebräerbriefs: Ihre Verankerung in der Situation des Verfassers und seiner Leser* (WUNT 41; Tübingen: Mohr/Siebeck, 1987) 37–41.

[10] See esp. H. Braun, *An die Hebräer* (HNT 14; Tübingen: Mohr/Siebeck, 1984) 228. Cf.

imagery in Hebrews 9 will be discussed below, but here we simply note that the author is flexible in his use of terms. For example, the term τὸ ἅγιον, which the LXX used for the holy of holies in Leviticus 16, designates the entire earthly sanctuary in Heb 9:1; ἅγια without the article refers to the outer court in 9:2, and σκηνή is used for each of the tabernacle's two courts in 9:2-3. (2) The LXX itself does not use terms in a consistent manner. For example, τὸ ἅγιον can designate the holy of holies (Lev 16:16) or the sanctuary as a whole (Num 3:38); τὰ ἅγια can refer to the whole sanctuary (Lev 10:4; Num 3:28) and can be virtually synonymous with σκηνή (Exod 29:30). (3) In Heb 8:5 the author contrasts τὰ ἐπουράνια with the earthly σκηνή. Although τὰ ἐπουράνια could refer to "heavenly realities" in 8:5a (*JB;* cf. *KJV*), the parallel use of σκηνή in 8:5b makes it probable that τὰ ἐπουράνια is the heavenly sanctuary (τὰ ἐπουράνια ἅγια; *RSV, NIV, NAB, NEB*), giving added support to the view that the terms τὰ ἅγια and ἡ σκηνή in 8:2 are simply synonyms.

The main contrast is between the heavenly sanctuary and the earthly one, which is called a "representation" (ὑπόδειγμα) and a "shadow" (σκιά). These terms can be used for both temporal and spatial contrasts. In 8:5 ὑπόδειγμα refers to the earthly representation of the heavenly tabernacle, but in 4:11 it is used for an example of past disobedience that encourages perseverance in the present and future.[11] Σκιά characterizes the earthly tabernacle in contrast to its heavenly counterpart in 8:5, but in 10:1 the word distinguishes past from future realities.[12]

In chap. 8, the author implies that the heavenly tabernacle is superior to the earthly one without pressing the point as he will later. The heavenly tabernacle was erected by God, not by a human being, which suggests that it was a sanctuary of the highest order, but the earthly tabernacle is not disparaged as a shrine "made with hands" (χειροποίητος, cf. 9:24), which sometimes connoted idolatry. The contrast between a heavenly "type" and

---

J. Moffatt, *A Critical and Exegetical Commentary on the Epistle to the Hebrews* (ICC; Edinburgh: Clark, 1924) 103-5; Spicq, *Hébreux,* 2.234; Michel, *Hebräer,* 288; O. Kuss, *Der Brief an die Hebräer* (RNT 8/1; Regensburg: Pustet, 1966) 197.

[11] The term ὑπόδειγμα usually means "example" (2 Pet 2:6; Jas 5:10; John 13:15; Sir 44:16; 2 Macc 6:28; 4 Macc 17:23; Josephus *J.W.* 2.11.2 #208; 2.16.4 #397; 6.2.1 #103, 106; Philo *Conf.* 64; *Her.* 256; *Som.* 2.3). It also refers to the shape of the heavenly temple in Ezek 42:15 LXX and to idolatrous representations of creatures in Aquila's translation of Deut 4:17 and Ezek 8:10. Philo calls the fat of animal sacrifices a representation (ὑπόδειγμα) of a soul fattened by wisdom (*Post.* 122). Although the RSV and NEB translate the word as "copy," this meaning is not well-attested in ancient sources. See L. D. Hurst, "How 'Platonic' are Heb viii.5 and ix.23f?" *JTS* 34 (1983) 156-68.

[12] The term ἀντίτυπος in 9:24 is similar to ὑπόδειγμα and σκιά. The author of Hebrews uses ἀντίτυπος only once, to contrast the earthly sanctuary and the true, heavenly one (9:24). But 1 Pet 3:21 uses ἀντίτυπος for past, as opposed to present realities.

its earthly "representation" is not overtly pejorative in 8:5; other ancient authors referred to the "pattern" of the tabernacle to give dignity to the earthly shrine, not to disparage it,[13] and by recalling that God commanded Moses to make an earthly sanctuary according to the type revealed at Sinai, the author acknowledges that the earthly tabernacle was the divinely ordained representation of the heavenly sanctuary. Only the word "shadow" points to the inferior, transitory nature of the earthly shrine.

The brunt of the argument comes in the contrast between the covenants with which these sanctuaries were associated, not in the differences between the sanctuaries themselves. The two covenants differed first in quality. The covenant on which the earthly tabernacle was based was imperfect, like the Levitical priesthood, but Christ's ministry in the heavenly tabernacle is part of a superior covenant that is based on better promises. There is also a temporal contrast between the first (πρώτη) covenant and the second (δεύτερα) or "new" covenant. The author described the earthly tabernacle cult in a μέν clause in 8:4–5, then contrasted it with Jesus' ministry under the new covenant by using the words νυνὶ δέ in 8:6, which make a sharp, temporal distinction.[14] The Mosaic covenant and its cult were valid in the past, *but now* Christ's superior covenant and ministry supersede it. By quoting Jer 31:31–34 (Heb 8:8–12) the author reinforces his claim that the new covenant has made the old covenant obsolete (8:13).

Heb 9:1-10: First and Second Tents

The close connection between the tabernacle and the Mosaic covenant is sustained in chap. 9, where the tabernacle is presented as one of the regulations of the first covenant.

(9:1) Now the first [covenant] did have regulations for priestly service and an earthly sanctuary (τὸ ἅγιον). (2) For the first tent (σκηνή) was prepared, in which were the lampstand and the table and the presentation of the loaves, which is called the "holy place." (3) Behind the second curtain was the tent called the "holy of holies," (4) containing the golden incense altar and the ark of the covenant covered all over with gold, in which were a golden jar containing the manna, the rod of Aaron that had budded, and the tablets of the covenant; (5) and

---

[13] Acts 7:44; *Bib.Ant.* 11:15. Cf. A. Cody, *Heavenly Sanctuary and Liturgy in the Epistle to the Hebrews* (St. Meinrad: Grail, 1960) 20–21. A possible exception may be *2 Bar* 4:5. See Murphy, *Structure,* 87–88.

[14] The words νυνὶ δέ or νῦν δέ can convey a logical, rather than a temporal, distinction as in 11:16 (Spicq, *Hébreux,* 2.238), but since the author explains that Jesus' ministry inaugurates a *new* covenant, the words should be interpreted temporally (cf. 9:26). See also D. Peterson, *Hebrews and Perfection: An Examination of the Concept of Perfection in the Epistle to the Hebrews* (SNTSMS 47; Cambridge: University, 1982) 131.

above it were the cherubim of glory overshadowing the mercy seat. Concerning these things we cannot now speak in detail.

(6) Now with these things prepared in this way, the priests enter regularly into the first tent (σκηνή) to conduct their priestly service, (7) but into the second [tent] only the high priest goes only once a year, and not without blood, which he offers for himself and for the people's sins of ignorance. (8) By this the Holy Spirit makes clear that the way into the sanctuary (τὰ ἅγια) has not yet been manifested while the first tent (σκηνή) is still standing; (9) which is a symbol for the present time, according to which gifts and sacrifices are offered which are not able to perfect the conscience of the worshiper, (10) but only concern food and drink and various ablutions, regulations of the flesh instituted until the time of correction.

The words "first" (πρώτη) and "second" (δεύτερα), which were used to describe the two covenants, continue to play a key role in the description of the Israelite tabernacle. The tabernacle's forecourt is called the "first tent" (9:2, 6, 8) and the holy of holies is the "second tent" (9:3, 7) or "sanctuary" (τὰ ἅγια, 9:8). The terminology is peculiar because the scriptures depict the tabernacle as a single tent with two parts, not as a sanctuary comprised of two tents. Yet by using these words the author was able to associate the first and second parts of the tabernacle with the first and second covenants (cf. 9:15-22).

The terms "first" and "second" were also useful because they could be used both temporally and spatially. In 8:13 the temporal sense of "first" is prominent. The "first" covenant was the first in a series of two covenants and had now been made obsolete. When the author referred to the sanctuary of the "first" covenant (9:1), readers would assume that it too had become obsolete. Readers would also assume that the "first tent" of 9:2a was the entire tabernacle prescribed by the Mosaic covenant. Only in 9:2b-3a would they realize that the author had begun to use the term "first" spatially, to denote the tabernacle's forecourt. The spatial force of "first" and "second" remains dominant in 9:6-7, where the author describes priestly duties in the tabernacle's forecourt and holy of holies.

In 9:8-10 the temporal force of "first" reappears. The author says that the "first tent" symbolized "the present time," which was thought to be evil (cf. Gal 1:4) and which would end at the "time of correction" (Heb 9:10). By identifying the "first tent" with "the present time" the author suggests that the "second tent" is "the age to come" (cf. 6:5). While the first tent/present age still stands, the way into the second tent/age to come is still blocked. Therefore entry into the second tent/new age signals the end of the first tent/present age.

A spatial contrast is also present in 9:8-10. The first tent corresponds to the realm of the flesh (σάρξ, 9:10), and its regulations concern only food, drink, and ablutions, which do not lead to perfection. The second tent corresponds to the realm of the conscience (συνείδησις, 9:9) within which perfection can be attained. Thus in 9:8-10 the first tent represents both the present age and the realm of the flesh, and the second tent is both the age to come and the realm of conscience.[15]

The section concludes as it began, by reaffirming the connection between the first tent and the entire Mosaic covenant. The first tent included not only "gifts and offerings," but regulations for "food, drink, and various ablutions" (9:9-10). The terms used for food (βρῶμα/βρῶσις) and drink (πόμα/πόσις) were sometimes used in connection with sacrifices (Lev 7:14 [24]; 19:7; Ep. Arist. 158), but consistently referred to the portions of sacrifices eaten by worshipers rather than to the priestly portions. Moreover, the same words often referred to clean and unclean food and drink without any mention of sacrifices.[16] Since the food and drink pertain to all worshipers, the "various ablutions" probably include all washings prescribed by the Mosaic law, not just the priestly ablutions.[17] Thus Heb 9:9-10 identifies the tabernacle with the Mosaic purity regulations that were incumbent on all Jewish worshipers, and relegates them to the realm of the flesh and the period before the "time of correction."

HEB 9:11-12: THE GREATER AND MORE PERFECT TENT

The author now contrasts the Israelite tabernacle and priestly ministry that were described in 9:1-10 with the work of Christ.[18]

9:11   Χριστὸς δὲ παραγενόμενος ἀρχιερεὺς
τῶν γενομένων ἀγαθῶν,
διὰ τῆς μείζονος καὶ τελειοτέρας σκηνῆς,
οὐ χειροποιήτου, τοῦτ᾽ ἔστιν οὐ ταύτης τῆς κτίσεως,
9:12   οὐδὲ δι᾽ αἵματος τράγων καὶ μόσχων,
διὰ δὲ τοῦ ἰδίου αἵματος
εἰσῆλθεν ἐφάπαξ εἰς τὰ ἅγια,
αἰωνίαν λύτρωσιν εὑράμενος

[15] F. J. Schierse, *Verheissung und Vollendung: Zur theologischen Grundfrage des Hebräerbriefs* (Münchener theologische Studien 1/9; Munich: Zink, 1955) 38-40; Cody, *Heavenly Sanctuary*, 149-50; Thompson, *Beginnings*, 108-9.

[16] Lev 11:34; *Ep.Arist.* 128, 142. Cf. Col 2:16; Rom 14:17; 1 Cor 10:2-4.

[17] E.g., Lev 11:25, 40; 14:7; 15:5; 16:4. Spicq, *Hébreux*, 2.255.

[18] Instead of γενομένων some texts read μελλόντων. But γενομένων is attested in a greater variety of ancient witnesses, and μελλόντων is probably a harmonization with 10:1. Therefore γενομένων is the preferred reading. Cf. Cody, *Heavenly Sanctuary*, 138-40; Metzger, *Textual Commentary*, 668.

The passage is a single sentence that contains a complex series of images in which Christ is said to go into the sanctuary (τὰ ἅγια) through the greater and more perfect tent (σκηνή). The "sanctuary" is clearly the heavenly holy of holies, but the significance of "the greater and more perfect tent" is disputed.

A number of interpreters have argued that "the greater and more perfect tent" is Christ's body. The structure of the passage includes several balanced positive and negative statements beginning with διά and οὐ or οὐδέ respectively, as shown by the indented lines above. The "greater and more prefect tent" is therefore structurally parallel to "his own blood."[19] Additional support for this view is found in 10:19-20 where Jesus' flesh is equated with the tabernacle curtain that stood at the entry to the holy of holies. This interpretation also fits well with the syntax, allowing all three instances of διά with the genitive to be taken instrumentally: Christ entered the sanctuary by means of his body or "tent," and by means of his own blood, not animal blood.[20]

Nevertheless, the interpretation of the "tent" as Jesus' body is implausible. The lines of the passage are parallel in form but not in content. In the lines beginning with οὐ and οὐδέ, the expression "made with hands" (χειρο-ποίητος) is hardly an apt description for "the blood of goats and bulls," and we therefore cannot assume that "tent" should be taken together with "blood" in the lines beginning with διά. Rather, the tent "not made with hands" must be a location, since it should be equated with the tent "that the Lord erected" of 8:2, and in the immediate context the word "tent" consistently refers to a location in time or space (9:1-10, 26-28). Other scholars suggest that "the greater and more perfect tent" is a heavenly region in front of the holy of holies, like the forecourt of the earthly tabernacle. According to this view, Christ moved through (διά) this region and into (εἰς) the sanctuary or holy of holies as the earthly high priest moved though the tabernacle's forecourt and into the holy of holies. Additional support for this view is found in 4:14, which says that Jesus is a high priest who has "passed through the heavens."[21]

---

[19] On the structure of 9:11-12 see A. Vanhoye, *La structure littéraire de l'Epître aux Hébreux* (2d ed.; Paris: Desclée de Brouwer, 1976) 149; O. Hofius, *Vorhang,* 66.

[20] Vanhoye (*La structure,* 149, 157, 267-68; idem, " 'Par la tent plus grande et plus parfaite . . .' [Heb 9,11]," *Bib* 46 [1965] 1-28) refers to Christ's resurrected body; J. Swetnam (" 'The Greater and More Perfect Tent': A Contribution to the Discussion of Hebrews 9,11," *Bib* 47 [1966] 91-106) refers to Christ's eucharistic body; Cody (*Heavenly Sanctuary,* 161-62) and Schierse (*Verheissung,* 57) refer to Christ's whole humanity; B. F. Westcott (*The Epistle to the Hebrews* [2d ed.; London: Macmillan, 1892] 256-58), who develops patristic interpretations, sees an allusion to the church as Christ's body.

[21] Moffatt, *Hebrews,* 120; Spicq, *Hébreux,* 2.256; Michel, *Hebräer,* 310-11; Andriessen, "Das grössere," 76-82; Michaelis, *TDNT* 7.377; Peterson, *Hebrews,* 143-44.

Yet there are also problems with this interpretation. It does demand that the word διά be taken locally in the first instance but instrumentally in the second and third instances. But more importantly, the words "tent" and "sanctuary" in 8:2 apparently refer to a location *in* heaven, not beyond it, and in 9:24 Christ is said to have gone *into* heaven itself, not through it. The fluidity of the author's language makes interpretation difficult.[22]

Therefore, a useful way to approach this passage is to recall how the description of the sanctuary *develops* throughout chaps. 8 and 9. In 8:2 the terms "tent" and "sanctuary" are apparently synonyms for the locus of Jesus' high-priestly ministry in heaven. In 9:1-10 the author describes the earthly sanctuary as a shrine comprised of two "tents," which begin to appear as two ages and two realms rather than as two parts of the same sanctuary (9:8-10). By 9:11 the author is thinking of the "first tent" as the earthly tent and the "second tent" as the heavenly sanctuary. The words χριστὸς δέ in 9:11 correspond to μὲν οὖν καὶ ἡ πρώτη in 9:1 and set Christ's heavenly ministry over against the entire earthly cult.[23]

The author is far more interested in the redemptive effect of Christ's sacrifice than in the physical structure of the heavenly tabernacle. The description of Christ's entry into the sanctuary in 9:11-12 is framed by references to the effects of various types of offerings (9:9-10, 13-14) and his interest in the effects of Christ's ministry provides a clue to the interpretation of the tent. Strictly speaking, the three phrases beginning with διά modify the main clause, εἰσῆλθεν ἐφάπαξ εἰς τὰ ἅγια, not the participial clause αἰωνίαν λύτρωσιν εὑράμενος. Nevertheless, the author understood entry into the tabernacle and making atonement as part of the same action. Therefore the phrases beginning with διά clarify the entire redemptive action of Christ. The sense of the passage is as follows:

> When Christ appeared as high priest of the new age, he entered once into the holy of holies and obtained the eternal redemption that purifies the conscience — not by means of a tabernacle that was fabricated by human beings in this

---

[22] See H. Montefiore, *A Commentary on the Epistle to the Hebrews* (Black's NT Commentaries; London: Black, 1964) 152-53. On the grammar see O. Hofius, "Inkarnation und Opfertod Jesu nach Hebr. X,19f.," *Der Ruf Jesu und die Antwort der Gemeinde: Exegetische Untersuchungen für Joachim Jeremias zum 70. Geburtstag* (ed. E. Lohse, C. Burchard, and B. Schaller; Göttingen: Vandenhoeck & Ruprecht, 1970) 132-41, esp. 136-37. On the fluidity of the description of the sanctuary see Käsemann, *Wandering People,* 223; U. Luck, "Himmlisches und irdisches Geschehen im Hebräerbrief," *NovT* 6 (1963) 192-215, esp. 199, 204; Kuss, *Hebräer,* 118; Thompson, *Beginnings,* 105-6.

[23] Cf. Vanhoye, *La structure,* 149-51; Michel, *Hebräer,* 309; Thompson, *Beginnings,* 105. Ten verses separate the μέν from the δέ, which include another μέν-δέ construction, but similar phenomena occur in other writers of the period; e.g., Epictetus *Disc.* 1.9.12-16 and Philo *Op.* 10.

world, or by means of the blood of goats and bulls, but by means of the heavenly tabernacle and his own blood.

The interplay between temporal and spatial categories that appeared earlier in the chapter is also apparent in this passage. Spatially, the effects of animal sacrifices are limited to the realm of the flesh (9:13), but Christ's ministry is carried out by means of a tent in the higher realm of perfection, and its effects purify the conscience. Temporally, Christ appeared as high priest of "the good things that have occurred," which means that "the good things to come" (10:1) are now present. The time of correction has arrived. Christ's entry into the heavenly tabernacle marks the end of "the present time" and with it the end of the Mosaic purity statutes.

HEB 9:19-24: PURIFYING THE TABERNACLE

After describing Jesus' entry into the heavenly sanctuary, the author returns to the first and second covenants. In connection with this theme he recounts the purification of the tabernacle.

> (9:19) For when every commandment of the law had been declared by Moses to all the people, he took the blood of calves and goats with water, scarlet wool, and hyssop, and sprinkled both the book itself and all the people, (20) saying, "This is the blood of the covenant which God commanded you." (21) And in the same way he sprinkled the tabernacle (ἡ σκηνή) and all the vessels for worship with blood. (22) Indeed, according to the law, practically everything is purified with blood, and without an outpouring of blood there is no forgiveness.
>
> (23) Therefore it was necessary that the representations of the heavenly things be purified with these [sacrifices], but the heavenly things themselves with better sacrifices than these. (24) For Christ did not enter into a sanctuary (ἄγια) made with hands, an antitype of the true one, but into heaven itself, now to appear in the presence of God on our behalf.

The connection between the tabernacle and the entire Mosaic law is very clear in this passage. In the preceding verses, the author stated that Jesus' death established the new covenant, just as animal blood was used to ratify the first, Mosaic covenant (9:15-18). Here he summarizes Exod 24:6-8, a text which originally said that Moses sprinkled *the altar* and the people with blood. Yet the author substituted the word "book" for "altar," so that Moses sprinkled "*the book* itself and the people" with blood. Then in nearly identical language he says that Moses sprinkled the tabernacle and all the vessels for worship. The result is that the items that were sprinkled included the law with all its commandments (9:19a), the people, and the tabernacle and its vessels.

In 9:23-24 the author relegated the Mosaic cultus to an inferior earthly realm, in contrast to its heavenly counterpart. He calls the earthly tabernacle a "representation" (cf. 8:5) and an "antitype" of the heavenly sanctuary, using terms that are not necessarily pejorative, but adds that the earthly tabernacle was a shrine "made with hands," which sometimes connoted idolatry. The heavenly sanctuary is the true one, which required *better* sacrifices than those offered in the earthly cult.

A sharp temporal contrast also appears in the discussion of the tabernacle. Jesus has "now" entered into the heavenly sanctuary (9:24), which means "now, once, at the close of the age" (9:26). The Mosaic tabernacle belongs to a time that has passed; the sanctuary of the new age is the heavenly one in which Jesus ministers.

The status of the tabernacle is inseparable from the status of the Mosaic law. The tabernacle and the law were part of an earthly realm and were purified with animal blood, in contrast to the heavenly sanctuary where Christ's superior sacrifice was offered. Like the tabernacle, the law was a "shadow of the good things to come" in the new age (10:1), but has now been replaced through the work of Christ.

HEB 6:19–20: INSIDE THE VEIL

The same perception of the tabernacle is reflected in two passages that refer to the veil (καταπέτασμα) which separated the tabernacle's forecourt from the holy of holies. A spatial argument is prominent in 6:19–20, which speaks of a hope,

> (6:19) which we have as a sure and steadfast (βέβαια) anchor of the soul, which enters into the inner region of the veil, (20) where Jesus has gone as a forerunner on our behalf, having become a priest forever, according to the order of Melchizedek.

The expression "the inner-region of the veil" appears in Lev 16:2, 12, 15, a passage that describes the entry of the high priest into the holy of holies on the day of atonement.

The scriptures never refer to atonement as an anchor or as a steadfast hope; these images reflect rhetorical forms of the Greco-Roman period. The image of the anchor was well-known throughout the Mediterranean region.[24] The other images in Heb 6:19–20 appear in 4 Maccabees, a Jewish work which draws heavily on Hellenistic philosophy. The author of Hebrews equated the holy of holies or the "inner region of the veil" with heaven. Both Hebrews and 4 Maccabees associate heaven with firmness and speak of a "firm hope" in God or Jesus (Heb 6:19; 4:14; 4 Macc 17:4–5). By calling Jesus a "forerunner," the author of Hebrews implies that the faithful will

---

[24] Moffatt, *Hebrews*, 89; Spicq, *Hébreux*, 2.164.

eventually follow him into heaven, where Jesus now sits beside the throne
(Heb 6:20; 8:1-2); 4 Macc 17:18 also envisions the faithful before the throne
in heaven.[25] Thus Heb 6:19-20, like Hebrews 9, equates the holy of holies
with heaven.

Jesus entered the region behind the veil as a priest "after the order of
Melchizedek," not as a Levitical priest. This passage anticipates the discussion in Hebrews 7, which makes clear that Jesus' priesthood sets aside the
Mosaic provisions for an imperfect, earthly priesthood (7:17-19). When he
entered the heavenly holy of holies, Jesus moved beyond the realm of the
Mosaic law, and, as a "forerunner," anticipated that his followers would do
the same.

Heb 10:19-20: The Veil of Jesus' Flesh

Similar perspectives appear in 10:19-20, which mentions the tabernacle
veil and introduces the exhortations that conclude the discussion of Jesus'
high priestly ministry.

> (10:19) Therefore brethren, since we have boldness for a way into the sanctuary
> (τὴν εἴσοδον τῶν ἁγίων) by the blood of Jesus, a new (πρόσφατον) and living way
> (ὁδόν), (20) which he made new (ἐνεκαίνισεν) for us through the veil, that is
> through his flesh . . . (22) let us draw near with a true heart. . . .

Only in this passage does the author equate the tabernacle veil with Jesus'
flesh. Because the image is unusual and becomes unintelligible when pressed
into a full typology, some interpreters have argued that the words "through
his flesh" actually refer to the "way" or to the whole of v. 20a, not to the
veil.[26] James Moffatt, however, has rightly called the reference to Jesus' flesh
a "daring poetic touch" which should not be taken as a full typology.
Moreover, the word order, and the parallel use of genitive case for
καταπέτασμα and σάρξ indicates that "through his flesh" does refer to the
curtain rather than to the way, a conclusion which is consistent with the
appositional use of τοῦτ' ἔστιν elsewhere in the epistle (2:14; 7:5; 9:11; 13:15;
cf. 10:20).[27]

By identifying Jesus' flesh with the veil, the author recalls the spatial
interpretation of the tabernacle that appeared in chap. 9. There the author

---

[25] For other similarities between Hebrews and 4 Maccabees, see L. K. K. Dey, *The Intermediary World and Patterns of Perfection in Philo and Hebrews* (SBLDS 25; Missoula:
Scholars, 1975) 50-51, 58, 62, 78-79, 152, 222-26; Thompson, *Beginnings,* 63-64. Thompson
also notes differences between the two works (ibid., 42).

[26] Westcott, *Hebrews,* 319-21; Spicq, *Hébreux,* 2.316; Hofius, *Vorhang,* 81.

[27] Moffatt, *Hebrews;* cf. Michel, *Hebräer,* 345; Bruce, *Hebrews,* 247-48; Braun,
Hebräer, 307. On the grammar see esp. N. H. Young, "τοῦτ' ἔστιν τῆς σαρκὸς αὐτοῦ (Heb. x.20):
Apposition, Dependent or Explicative?" *NTS* 20 (1973-74) 100-4.

identified the forecourt of the tabernacle with the realm of the flesh, and the holy of holies with the realm of the conscience or heaven (9:9–10, 24). The veil of the tabernacle separated the two regions. At the time of his death,[28] Jesus left the realm of the flesh and entered the heavenly realm, where he offered the sacrifice that purifies the conscience (9:14; 10:22).[29]

The emphasis on the newness of the way also recalls the temporal contrasts of Hebrews 9, where the tabernacle's forecourt was "the present time" and the holy of holies was the new age (9:9, 11, 26). The author stresses that Jesus "made new" (ἐνεκαίνισεν) a "new" (πρόσφατον) way into the sanctuary, since his high priestly ministry marked the beginning of a new age.

In chap. 9, the lower realm and the present age were associated with Mosaic statutes (9:9–10). The verses surrounding 10:19–20 also relegate the Mosaic law to a time that has passed and an inferior realm. The law prescribed various offerings for sin, but Christ abolished them and instituted a new covenant, so that there is *no longer* any offering for sin (10:8, 16–18). The new covenant, unlike the Mosaic covenant, is inscribed on the heart and mind, which, like the conscience, is associated with a higher realm of being (10:22). By his sacrificial death, Jesus moved beyond the realm of the Mosaic law, making it possible for his followers to do the same.

Heb 13:9–14: Those Who Serve in the Tabernacle

The final reference to the tabernacle appears in an enigmatic comment near the close of the epistle.

(13:9) Do not be led astray by diverse and strange teachings, for it is good that the heart be made firm (βεβαιοῦσθαι) by grace and not by foods (βρώματα), which have not benefited those who walk in them. (10) We have an altar from which those who serve in the tabernacle (ἡ σκηνή) have no authority to eat. (11) For the bodies of those animals, whose blood is brought into the sanctuary (τὰ ἅγια) by the high priest as a sacrifice for sin, are burned outside the camp. (12) So too Jesus, in order to sanctify the people by means of his own blood, suffered outside the gate. (13) Therefore let us go forth to him outside the camp, bearing his disgrace. (14) For here we have no abiding city, but we seek the one that is to come.

The passage is complex and contains several images that appear nowhere else in Hebrews, including the "diverse and strange teachings," the Christian "altar," and the area "outside the camp." But many of the other images do

---

[28] Hofius's attempt to argue that Jesus' flesh refers primarily to the incarnation ("Inkarnation," 139–41) is unsuccessful. See Young, "τοῦτ' ἔστιν," 102–4.

[29] Dey, *Intermediary World,* 160–61.

occur elsewhere in Hebrews, which suggests that 13:9–14 should be interpreted in light of the rest of the epistle.

In previous passages the author distinguished the higher realms of
heaven and conscience from the lower realms of earth and flesh. In 13:9–14
he makes similar contrasts. The heart (10:22a), grace (4:16), and firmness
(6:19) are associated with the upper realm, while "foods" (9:10) are part of
the lower realm. The offering of Jesus' blood pertains to the higher realm and
the offering of animal blood to the lower realm (9:13–14). According to this
pattern, the Christian altar corresponds to the higher realm (9:24) and the
"tent" to the lower realm.[30]

Similarly, Jesus' suffering "outside the gate" is closely tied to his sacrifice
at the heavenly altar, since it is the counterpart to the burning of animal
bodies outside the earthly "camp." James Thompson also observes that the
summons to go "outside the camp" in 13:13 echoes earlier exhortations to
"strive to enter that rest" (4:11), to "draw near with boldness to the throne
of grace" (4:16), to "draw near with a true heart" (10:22), and to "run with
perseverance" (12:1), all of which urge Christians to move towards a heavenly reality. The reference to Jesus' death "outside the gate" does allude to
Golgatha, but elsewhere the author consistently brings together Jesus' death
and exaltation to heaven (1:3; 5:8–9; 12:1–2).[31]

A temporal distinction most clearly emerges in 13:14, where the author
contrasts the city that does not abide with the city "that is to come," which
is part of the "age to come" (6:5; cf. 2:5; 9:11; 10:1). Yet temporal contrasts
actually do appear throughout 13:9–14. The main verb in 13:9b is in aorist
tense and that in 13:10a is in present tense. The passage can be translated,

> For it is good that the heart be made firm by grace and not by foods, by which
> those who used to walk in them did not profit. For we (now) have an altar from
> which those who are (now) serving in the tabernacle have no right to eat.

The "foods" belong to the past and the Christian altar to the present. In 9:10,
the author indicated that the first covenant's regulations pertaining to
"foods" were to last only until the time of correction. In 13:9 he assumes that
the time of correction has come and that the "foods" belong to the past.
Likewise, the first tabernacle corresponded to the present age, not to the age
to come. Therefore those who continue to serve in the tabernacle are serving
an obsolete institution.

The next verse (13:11) describes a sequence of events. According to
Leviticus 16, the high priest first takes blood into the sanctuary (16:14–15),
then, after atonement has been made, other people take the bodies of the

---

[30] Cf. Schierse, *Verheissung,* 191; Thompson, *Beginnings,* 146–49.
[31] *Beginnings,* 147–49.

goat and bull outside the camp to burn them (16:27).[32] Therefore since Jesus' atoning death has already occurred, the time has come for the faithful to leave the camp. Animal sacrifices were part of the present age according to Heb 9:9; the sacrifice of Jesus inaugurated the age to come (9:11–12, 26). The summons to leave the camp is a call to enter a new age.

The temporal dynamics in the passage become explicit in the image of the two cities in 13:14. Like the tabernacle and the camp, the city that does not abide corresponds to the present age. Like the Christian altar and the area outside the camp, the city that is to come corresponds to the new age. As in earlier sections, temporal and spatial distinctions are closely interwoven throughout the passage.

With the preceding analysis in mind we can try to determine more precisely what it means to "serve in the tabernacle" (13:10). The meaning of the expression has been widely debated, but several things seem clear. (1) The expression must be interpreted in light of the contrasts within the passage: foods vs. grace, the tabernacle vs. the altar, animal sacrifices vs. Christ's sacrifice, the city that does not abide vs. the city to come. (2) The βρώματα of 13:9 are the same as those of 9:10, where "drink and various ablutions" are also mentioned. Therefore 13:9–14 should be read in light of chap. 9. (3) The issue in this passage is a debate within Christianity, not a conflict between Christians and non-Christian Jews. The author assumes that he can argue on a christological basis. Jesus' messiahship is not disputed; the issue involves the implications of his sacrifice.[33]

"Serving in the tabernacle" probably means observing Jewish laws of purity, especially with regard to foods. According to 9:10, the βρώματα were included among the regulations of the "first" or Mosaic covenant. Other ancient sources use the terms βρώμα / βρώσις in connection with the "covenant" (1 Macc 1:63) and with "sabbath" and "circumcision," which clearly refer to Jewish practices.[34] The reference to "walking" in accordance with foods (Heb 13:9) uses a common expression for observance of the Jewish law.[35]

Some scholars argue that the Jewish laws would not be called "various and strange teachings" and that Jewish legal observances were not considered

---

[32] The LXX of 16:27 reads, "And the bull for the sin offering and the goat for the sin offering, whose blood was brought in to make atonement in the sanctuary, *they* shall take them outside the camp and *they* shall burn them with fire. . . ." The MT mixes the singular and plural verbs: "*he* shall take outside the camp and *they* shall burn. . . ."

[33] On point two see H. Koester, "Outside," 299–315; G. Theissen, *Untersuchungen zum Hebräerbrief* (SNT 2; Gütersloh: Mohn, 1969) 76. On point three see Schierse, *Verheissung,* 188; Koester, "Outside," 304.

[34] Col 2:16; *Diogn.* 4:1; *Barn.* chaps. 7–12, esp. 10:9. See Koester, "Outside," 306.

[35] E.g., Bar 1:18; 2:10; Tob 3:5; and the rabbinic term "halakah." On this interpretation see Spicq, *Hébreux,* 2.424; Manson, *Hebrews,* 150.

a means to "make firm the heart" (13:9).[36] But the term "various" is often used in arguments where an author does not precisely describe what he opposes (e.g., 2 Tim 3:6; Titus 3:3), and therefore we cannot assume that "foreign" is an exact characterization of the views which are disputed.[37] Moreover, according to Wis 6:18, one's firm assurance (βεβαίωσις) of immortality does come through the observance of wisdom's laws. Although Hebrews does not speak of immortality, the author does understand firmness (βεβαιόω) and benefit (ὠφελέω) in terms of ultimate salvation.[38] Moreover, Philo says that a soul finds firmness (βεβαίωσις) in the ordinances of virtue, *which he equates with the tent of meeting* (*L.A.* 2.55). Heb 13:9 apparently presupposes similar views.

Other interpretations of "serving in the tabernacle" do not fit the context as well. James Moffatt suggested that the issue may have involved Christian participation in pagan sacrificial meals, as in 1 Corinthians 10.[39] But the author makes no explicit reference to idolatry, as Paul does, and paganism does not appear to be a problem elsewhere in the epistle. Otto Michel suggested that the dispute involved ascetic dietary practices, like those mentioned in 1 Tim 4:3 and Rom 14:2, 21.[40] But ascetic regulations stressed what should *not* be eaten; Heb 13:9-10 suggests that one is strengthened by what *is* eaten, which is a different issue.[41]

A number of scholars perceive allusions to the Lord's Supper in this passage. Paul Andriessen and Albert Vanhoye maintain that the Christian altar mediates the work of Christ and clearly refers to the Eucharist, just as Paul associates the altar with the Eucharist in 1 Cor 10:18.[42] Franz Schierse notes that Heb 13:9-17 presupposes a connection between eating and grace, the altar, the cross, and Christian worship. He suggests that the author opposes a misunderstanding of the sacrament which undermines Christian discipleship and worship (13:13, 16-17).[43] Others insist that the author

---

[36] Moffatt, *Hebrews,* 233; Michel, *Hebräer,* 495-96; Theissen, *Untersuchungen,* 76.

[37] Cf. Thompson, *Beginnings,* 144.

[38] On βέβαιος see 3:14; 6:19. On ὠφελέω see 4:2 and Theissen, *Untersuchungen,* 77. D. Winston notes that Wis 6:18 could refer to the statutes of natural law (*Wisdom,* 42), but the Wisdom of Solomon assumes that "law" is God's law (2:12-13; 6:4; 16:6; 18:4, 9) and that the Mosaic law was intended for all the world (18:4). Harmony with natural law therefore means acceptance of the Mosaic law.

[39] *Hebrews,* 233.

[40] *Hebräer,* 495.

[41] See the critiques by Koester, "Outside," 304; and Theissen, *Untersuchungen,* 76.

[42] P. Andriessen, "L'Eucharistie dans l'Epître aux Hébreux," *NRT* 94 (1972) 269-77; A. Vanhoye, *Old Testament Priests and the New Priest According to the New Testament* (Studies in Scripture; Petersham: St. Bede's, 1986) 228-29.

[43] *Verheissung,* 184-95.

opposes all sacramental interpretations of the Lord's Supper. Moffatt observes that sacrifices made on the day of atonement were burned, not eaten; therefore Jesus' death has no connection with any meal.[44] Helmut Koester argues that the area "outside the camp" was profane, rather than sacred; therefore Jesus' death has no connection with sacred rituals like the Eucharist.[45] Gerd Theissen notes that the church fathers spoke of the power of the Eucharist to "make one firm"; 13:9–10 denies the power of the sacrament to guarantee salvation.[46]

The problem with all attempts to see an allusion to the Lord's Supper in this passage is that there is no explicit reference to the sacrament elsewhere in the epistle. Moreover, the author assumes a connection between the βρώματα and the Mosaic covenant in 9:10, grants that the βρώματα were instituted for a limited period of time, and insists that they had now become outmoded by Christ's death. Such a temporal argument would not apply to a dispute about the sacrament.

James Thompson maintains that Heb 13:9–14 does not address any specific dispute. The references to the tabernacle and Levitical customs are a foil for the author's contrast between earthly and heavenly securities.[47] Thompson's view draws heavily on the spatial contrasts implicit in the passage, but does not account for the temporal dimension of the argument. The contrast is not only between the heavenly and the earthly, but also between the old and the new. Moreover, Thompson too quickly passes over the probable connections between "foods" and the Mosaic law.

Therefore, Heb 13:9–14 reflects a debate over the need for Christians to continue observing the statutes of the Mosaic covenant. "Serving in the tabernacle" refers to observance of Jewish practices, especially with regard to foods. In chaps. 8–9 the author argued that the Mosaic law was concerned with matters of the flesh, had been instituted for a limited time, and had now been superseded by Jesus' heavenly self-sacrifice which inaugurated a new age. Those who remain within the tabernacle and the camp continue to live in the realm of the flesh and in the old age.[48]

THE TABERNACLE IN HEBREWS

The author of Hebrews interpreted the tabernacle both temporally and spatially, and associated it with observance of the Mosaic law. In 8:1-6 he

---

[44] Moffatt, *Hebrews*, 233–34; Cf. O. Holtzmann, "Der Hebräerbrief und das Abendmahl," *ZNW* 10 (1909) 251–60.

[45] "Outside," 315.

[46] *Untersuchungen*, 77. Cf. Braun, *Hebräer*, 462.

[47] *Beginnings*, 150–51.

[48] See Brown, *Antioch and Rome*, 151–58; Dahms, "First Readers," 374.

contrasted the high priestly ministry of Jesus in the heavenly tabernacle with the priestly service and earthly tabernacle prescribed by Mosaic law. God himself made the heavenly sanctuary and commanded Moses to build an earthly representation of the celestial shrine. But this earthly tabernacle was part of a covenant that obtained for a limited period of time and had been superseded by a second, superior covenant that was inscribed on the human heart and mind.

In 9:1–10 he described the tabernacle as a sanctuary that had two "tents." The "first tent," like the "first covenant," was associated with daily priestly ministry, Mosaic regulations, the realm of the flesh, and the present time. The "second" tent was the place of high priestly ministry and was associated with the realm of the conscience and the age to come, like the "second" covenant. By 9:11, the author envisioned only the heavenly tent of the new age and the earthly tent of the present time. Christ's entry into the heavenly sanctuary marks the beginning of the new age, provides cleansing in the realm of conscience, makes the Levitical cult and Mosaic regulations obsolete, and inaugurates the second or new covenant.

Similar views are reflected elsewhere in the epistle. In 6:19–20 the region behind the veil was the heavenly realm that Jesus entered as a priest "after the order of Melchizedek," whose ministry superseded that established by Mosaic law. In 10:20, the author identified the curtain with Jesus' flesh. At his death, Jesus moved beyond the flesh, opened a new way to the heavenly realm, abolished the need for sacrifices, and inaugurated a covenant inscribed on the heart and mind. 13:10 speaks of "those who serve in the tabernacle," who are Christians who continue to observe the Mosaic law. The author associates such practices with the flesh and insists that the time has come to leave them behind.

B. Antecedents for
Hebrews' Tabernacle Imagery

Proposed backgrounds for the interpretation of the tabernacle in the epistle to the Hebrews span a wide range of ancient literature. A brief survey of several important, but problematic proposals will help to introduce discussion of antecedents that are more viable.

Gnosticism

A gnostic background for the epistle to the Hebrews has been proposed by Ernst Käsemann. He noted that the tabernacle veil separates the realm of flesh or matter from the heavenly realm and bars access into the heavenly sanctuary (Heb 10:20). Entry into the heavenly regions requires that one leave the realm of the flesh. Such ideas are typical of gnostic thought.[49] Problems with the gnostic hypothesis include the late date of most gnostic sources, the tendency to reconstruct first-century gnostic thought from disparate later sources, and the fact that a dualistic distinction between material and spiritual realms is not distinctively gnostic.[50]

RABBINIC SOURCES

Rabbinic parallels have been explored by a number of scholars. For example, an unattributed saying says that there is a temple (בית המקדש) in the heavenly Jerusalem in which Michael serves at the altar (b. Ḥag. 12b). A saying attributed to R. Simeon b. Yohai says that the heavenly temple (בית המקדש) is eighteen miles higher than the earthly one (Gen. Rab. 69:7; cf. 55:7). R. Nathan is supposed to have said that the sanctuary (מקדש) above lies directly over the sanctuary (מקדש) below (Midr. Tanhuma ויקהל 124a).[51]

These parallels are of dubious value because the sayings are taken from late collections which do not necessarily preserve early material. Some sayings are attributed to rabbis who lived in the second century, but their views were not necessarily current in the first century. Moreover, these rabbinic sources refer to a heavenly temple (בית המקדש) or sanctuary (מקדש), but not to a heavenly tabernacle as in Hebrews.

MERKABAH MYSTICISM

Merkabah mysticism has been suggested by several scholars as a backdrop for Hebrews. Important sources include 3 Enoch, the Pirqe d'Rabbi Eliezer, and some references in rabbinic collections. Similarities between this type of thought and Hebrews include an interest in the divine throne which is separated from lower regions by a cosmic veil, an interest in angels, and the idea of a pilgrimage to the divine realm. Moreover the mystic sources sometimes call the heavenly sanctuary a "tabernacle" (e.g., Num. Rab. 12:12).[52]

---

[49] Wandering People, 223–26.

[50] See the discussion in Theissen, Untersuchungen, 115–52; Hofius, Vorhang, 28–48; Thompson, Beginnings, 2–5.

[51] Str-B 3.700–701; H. Bietenhard, Die himmlische Welt im Urchristentum und Spätjudentum (WUNT 2; Tübingen: Mohr/Siebeck, 1951) 123–29; Hofius, Vorhang, 19–27. Cf. Cody (Heavenly Sanctuary, 23–26) and Schierse (Verheissung, 17–18) who discuss rabbinic parallels, but hesitate to make connections with Hebrews.

[52] The note on the "tabernacle" appears in L. H. Schiffmann, "Merkavah Speculation at Qumran: The 4 Q Serek Shirot 'Olat ha-Shabbat," Mystics, Philosophers, and Politicians: Essays in Jewish Intellectual History in Honor of Alexander Altmann (ed. M. Reinharz and D.

A major difficulty with this view is that the texts are of late or uncertain date: *3 Enoch* cannot plausibly be dated prior to the end of the third century and the *Pirqe d'Rabbi Eliezer* is probably even later. Some mystic traditions may stem from the second century, but we cannot assume that late texts preserve first-century material.

Advocates of the mystic background note that the "Songs of the Sabbath Sacrifice" (4QShirShabb) from Qumran do provide evidence of Merkabah speculation from the first century B.C. These texts refer to the divine throne within a heavenly holy of holies or "tabernacle" (4Q403 1 ii 10; 4Q405 20 ii-21-22 7). The divine throne is separated from the lower regions by a veil (4Q405 15 ii-16 3). But the veil divided regions of heaven, not heaven and earth as in Hebrews. Moreover, the heavenly tabernacle does not seem to have an earthly counterpart, nor does it have the structure or furnishings of the Israelite tabernacle. These mystic texts have few affinities with Hebrews.[53]

DEAD SEA SCROLLS

The Dead Sea Scrolls are sometimes cited as background for the epistle to the Hebrews. Hans Kosmala argues that Hebrews was written by a member of the Qumran sect who converted to Christianity. Kosmala assumes that the author considered the biblical "tent of meeting" (אהל מועד) to be primarily a place where Israel met God and the biblical "tabernacle" (משכן) to be a place of sacrifice. The sectarians met in a "house of meeting" (בית מועד; 1QM iii 4) which Kosmala thinks is the counterpart to the tent of meeting, but they opposed the temple cult which carried on the sacrificial tradition of the "tabernacle." Kosmala argues that Heb 9:1-10 conveys a negative attitude toward the "tabernacle," and that 9:11 and 12:22 view the "tent" positively as Israel's gathering place.[54] Yigael Yadin interpreted

---

Swetschinski; Durham: Duke, 1982) 36. The other evidence appears in Hofius, *Vorhang*, 4-19; H.-M. Schenke, "Erwägungen zum Rätsel des Hebräerbriefes," *Neues Testament und christliches Existenz: Festschrift für Herbert Braun zum 70. Geburtstag* (ed. H. D. Betz and L. Schottroff; Tübingen: Mohr/Siebeck, 1973) 421-37; R. Williamson, "The Background of the Epistle to the Hebrews," *ExpT* 87 (1976) 232-37.

[53] For more detailed discussion of 4QShirShabb see chap. III.B above. Schenke cited 11QMelch as evidence for a form of first-century mysticism presupposed by Hebrews. Yet detailed comparisons of Hebrews and 11QMelch reveal few similarities between the two texts. See F. L. Horton, *The Melchizedek Tradition: A Critical Examination of the Sources to the Fifth Century A.D. and in the Epistle to the Hebrews* (SNTSMS 30; Cambridge: University, 1976) 167-70; P. J. Kobelski, *Melchizedek and Melchireša'* (CBQMS 10; Washington: CBA, 1981) 127-28.

[54] *Hebräer — Essener — Christen: Studien zur Vorgeschichte der frühchristlichen Verkündigung* (SPB 1; Leiden: Brill, 1959) 378-86.

Hebrews as a polemic against Christians with roots in the Qumran community. They expected a restoration of the temple cult in accordance with the Mosaic law (1QM ii 1-6), organized their community according to the model of the tribes in the wilderness, and took the measurements for shields and weapons from the measurements of the tabernacle.[55] F. F. Bruce finds parallels to the idea of a heavenly pattern and earthly copy in the "New Jerusalem" texts.[56]

One problem with Kosmala's view is that it rests on the unlikely assumption that the sectarians would have distinguished between the "tabernacle" and the "tent"; the two expressions are used almost interchangeably in the Bible. But the major problem confronting all these suggestions is that the extra-biblical Dead Sea Scrolls published thus far do not mention the Israelite tabernacle. 4QShirShabb mentions a heavenly tabernacle that has no earthly copy, 4QDibHam speaks of God's "tabernacle" in Zion, and CD refers to God's "tent," but none of the published scrolls refer to the Israelite "tabernacle" or "tent of meeting."[57]

APOCALYPTIC SOURCES

Apocalyptic sources sometimes refer to a heavenly sanctuary. In *1 Enoch* the seer was taken to heaven in a vision and he "drew near to a great house which was built of white marble . . . and there was nothing inside it." He also saw "a second house . . . and inside it a lofty throne" (14:10, 13, 15, 18). Similarly, the *Testament of Levi* refers to a heavenly temple (ναός, 5:1) which contained the divine throne and the archangels who offer bloodless sacrifices on behalf of the righteous (3:4-6).[58] But these texts refer to a heavenly house or temple, not to a tabernacle, and neither text calls the heavenly sanctuary a pattern for the earthly shrine. The *Apocalypse of Baruch* makes passing mention of the pattern of the tabernacle (*2 Bar.* 4:5), but shows no further interest in either a heavenly or earthly tabernacle. Therefore these apocalyptic texts do not account for the prominence of the tabernacle motif in the epistle to the Hebrews.

---

[55] "The Dead Sea Scrolls and the Epistle to the Hebrews," *Scripta Hierosolymitana* 4 (1958) 36-55.

[56] " 'To the Hebrews' or 'To the Essenes'?" *NTS* (1962-63) 217-32, esp. 230.

[57] For additional discussion of relationships between Hebrews and Qumran see C. Spicq, "L'Epître aux Hébreux, Apollos, Jean-Baptiste, les Hellénistes et Qumrân," *RevQ* 1 (1959) 365-90; J. Coppens, "Les affinités qumraniennes de l'Epître aux Hébreux," *NRT* 94 (1962) 128-41, 257-82; F. C. Fensham, "Hebrews and Qumran," *Neot* 5 (1971) 9-21.

[58] Cody, *Heavenly Sanctuary*, 21-23; Schierse, *Verheissung*, 17; Barrett, "Eschatology," 383-89; Bruce, "To the Hebrews," 230; G. W. MacRae, "Heavenly Temple and Eschatology in the Letter to the Hebrews," *Semeia* 12 (1978) 179-99, esp. 183; Michel, *Hebräer*, 62.

THE COSMOLOGICAL INTERPRETATION

A more promising antecedent is the cosmological interpretation of the tabernacle that appears in the writings of Philo and Josephus.[59] According to this tradition, the structure of the tabernacle corresponds to the parts of the universe. Josephus equated the holy of holies with heaven and the forecourt with earth and sea (*Ant.* 3.7.7 #181). Philo sometimes followed this interpretation (*Mos.* 2.81), but occasionally recast it in Platonic categories, equating the holy of holies with the noetic realm and the forecourt with either the realm of the senses (*Q.E.* 2.69) or the noetic realm (*Mos.* 2.81).

Like Philo, the author of Hebrews identified the holy of holies with heaven (Heb 9:24) and equated the parts of the tabernacle with realms of being. The author of Hebrews spoke of the realms of flesh and conscience, and Philo distinguished the realm of sense perception from that of the mind or soul. Since Philo associated sense perception with the flesh or body (e.g., *Q.E.* 2.69) and considered the soul to be the seat of the conscience (*Op.* 128), his views resemble those of the author of Hebrews quite closely.[60]

Philo and Josephus used the cosmological interpretation of the tabernacle to commend observance of the Mosaic law. Philo included his most extensive discussion of the tabernacle's cosmological significance in a section of his *Vita Mosis* which demonstrated that people who want to live in harmony with the universe should do so by following the Mosaic law. Josephus discussed the cosmological significance of the tabernacle in the hope of gaining greater tolerance for Judaism and perhaps persuading some to adopt Jewish practices.

The author of Hebrews referred to the tabernacle's cosmological significance for the opposite reason. While Philo, and to some extent Josephus, tried to show that the tabernacle and Mosaic law were of *universal* value and joined people to the world, the author of Hebrews insisted that the "first tent" or "tabernacle" and the Mosaic law were of *limited* value, since both pertained to the realm of the flesh.

When Philo and Josephus discussed the tabernacle's cosmological significance, they were vague about the relationship of the tabernacle to the Jerusalem temple. Both men respected the temple's legitimacy and knew that the same cosmological symbolism was used for the tabernacle and the temple. Yet Philo insisted that the worship associated with the tabernacle did not require one to offer animal sacrifices at an altar, and Josephus assumed that the tabernacle continued to represent Jewish worship even a full generation

---

[59] On the cosmological interpretation see chap. III.E above.

[60] Philo and Josephus also interpreted the furnishings within the tabernacle cosmologically. Knowledge of this tradition could lie behind Heb 9:5b, where the author declines to discuss the furnishings individually, for lack of time.

after the destruction of the temple. Similarly, the author of Hebrews left the relationship of the tabernacle to the temple unspecified.

Knowledge of these traditions would help explain why the author of Hebrews identifies the parts of the tabernacle with the parts of the universe and realms of being, closely associates the tabernacle with Mosaic statutes, and leaves the relationship of the tabernacle to the temple rather vague. Nevertheless there are several aspects of the tabernacle in Hebrews that do not appear in the cosmological interpretation. (1) The author of Hebrews interprets the tabernacle temporally as well as spatially; the two "tents" correspond to two ages. (2) He claims that the second "tent," or holy of holies, contained the ark of the covenant *and* the incense altar (9:3-4). But the OT, Philo, and Josephus say that the incense altar stood in the tabernacle's forecourt. Moreover, the author's claim contradicts his own argument, since he says that daily priestly ministry — which involved the incense altar — took place in the forecourt, *not* in the holy of holies (9:6-7).[61] (3) He says that the ark contained a jar of manna, Aaron's rod, and the tablets of the law (9:4). The OT, Philo, and Josephus insist that the ark contained *only* the tablets. The jar of manna and Aaron's rod were kept in front of the ark.[62]

HIDDEN TABERNACLE TRADITIONS

These peculiarities suggest that the author knew a form of the tradition about the hidden tabernacle and its vessels similar to that found in 2 Macc 2:4-8 and the *Life of Jeremiah*.[63] (1) These traditions are eschatological in character. They say that Jeremiah hid the tabernacle or ark and that these items will remain hidden until the time of the ingathering, when they will reappear. (2) According to 2 Macc 2:5, Jeremiah hid three items: the tent, the incense altar, and the ark. All three were to reappear at the time of ingathering. The tent, incense altar, and ark are also mentioned in Heb 9:3-4 and comprise the "second tent" which the author associates with the age to come. (3) Forms of this tradition indicate that the ark of the covenant contained more than the tablets of the law. *Vit. Jer.* 11 refers to the ark and "the things in it" (τὰ ἐν αὐτῇ) which apparently included more than just the tablets (αἱ πλάκες, v. 14). Pseudo-Philo says that the ark contained twelve stones (*Bib. Ant.* 26:12-15). Rabbinic traditions say that the jar of manna, Aaron's

---

[61] Philo, *Mos.* 2.101; Josephus, *Ant.* 3.6.8 #147. The position of the incense altar in Exod 30:1, 6 is ambiguous, but 30:7 says that incense was to be burned on it each day; therefore it could not be in the holy of holies, which the high priest entered only once a year. Cf. Michel, *Hebräer,* 300 n. 1.

[62] 1 Kgs 8:9; 2 Chron 5:10; Num 17:10 [25]; Exod 16:33-34; Philo, *Mos.* 2.97; Josephus, *Ant.* 3.6.5. #138; 8.4.1 #104.

[63] Michel, *Hebräer,* 301; Murphy, *Structure,* 96. On the hidden tabernacle tradition, see chap. III.D above.

rod, and other items were hidden away with the ark, although not inside it (*t. Soṭa* 13:1). The author of Hebrews may have known a form of the hidden vessels tradition that located the jar of manna and Aaron's rod inside the ark, rather than in front of it.

Other features of Hebrews support the likelihood that the author knew one or more forms of the hidden tabernacle tradition. The tradition typically associated the hiding of the tabernacle vessels or furnishings with Jeremiah, and the author of Hebrews quoted Jeremiah at length (Heb 8:8–12; Jer 31:31–34) before listing the furnishings of the tabernacle. The tradition also depicted the end time in imagery that recalled the Sinai theophany; *Vit. Jer.* 15 expected the theophany and ingathering to occur at Sinai itself, while 2 Macc 2:4–8 assumed that Jerusalem would be the location. The author of Hebrews also used imagery of Sinai and the ingathering for the end time (12:18–24), and insists that the events pertain to Jerusalem and not to Sinai, which suggests that he knew both forms of the tradition.[64] Moreover, the tradition was included in collections of apocryphal stories about prophets, and the author of Hebrews was familiar with such collections (Heb 11:35; cf. *Vit. Jer.* 1; *Vit. Isa.* 1).

Traditions concerning the hidden tabernacle stressed the abiding value of the Mosaic law. The account in 2 Maccabees is prefaced by exhortations not to forget the law or to let the law depart from one's heart (2 Macc 2:1–3). The author expected the tabernacle to reappear soon because through the Maccabees God had restored Israel's inheritance, kingship, priesthood, and consecration, "as he promised through the law" (2:17–18). The *Life of Jeremiah* expected the tablets of the law to be revealed in the end times and maintained that prior to that time a fiery cloud would hover over the ark, "for the glory of God will never cease from his law" (*Vit. Jer.* 14, 18).

The author of Hebrews argues in the opposite direction. He grants the close connection between the tabernacle and the Mosaic law, then identifies them with the "first tent" and insists that they have a place only in "the present time," not in the age to come. The tabernacle of the new age is the heavenly one in which Christ ministers. Christ entered the heavenly tabernacle as the mediator of a new covenant and his actions marked the end of the "first tent" and the "first" or Mosaic covenant.

The hidden tabernacle traditions do not depict the relationship between the tabernacle and the temple in a uniform way. 2 Macc 2:4–8 was written while the temple was still standing. The author recalled that God's glory had appeared in the same way at the dedications of the tabernacle and Solomon's temple. He expected God's glory and the tabernacle to reappear at the

---

[64] Thompson (*Beginnings,* 41–52) argues that Heb 12:18–29 reflects philosophical interests, but he acknowledges that eschatological traditions lie behind the passage.

ingathering which would center on the purified temple of the Maccabean period (2:7, 18). The *Life of Jeremiah* was probably written after the destruction of the temple in A.D. 70, but the author did not mention hopes for the temple's restoration, and he expected the ingathering to occur at Sinai, rather than at Jerusalem where the temple was located. The forms of the tradition found in other sources also vary in their views of the relationship between the tabernacle and the temple. Therefore we cannot be sure whether or not the forms of the tradition known to the author of Hebrews posited a strong connection between the tabernacle and the temple.

WISDOM TRADITIONS

Another promising antecedent appears in the Wisdom of Solomon, which calls Solomon's temple "a copy (μίμημα) of the holy tent that [God] prepared from the beginning" (9:8).[65] Exod 25:9 simply refers to the "pattern" of the tabernacle that Moses built, but Wis 9:8 and Heb 8:2 conceive of it as an actual heavenly sanctuary that was erected by God. Wis 9:8 and Heb 8:5 also indicate that the heavenly tabernacle had an earthly copy, which they call a μίμημα and σκιά respectively. Both words were common in Platonic philosophy.

Both Wisdom and Hebrews link the heavenly tabernacle with a wisdom figure. Like wisdom, Jesus is God's agent of creation, who renews or upholds all things, and who bears God's "radiance" or ἀπαύγασμα (Heb 1:2-3; Wis 7:24-27; 9:9). Like wisdom, Jesus sits by God's throne and is associated with the heavenly tabernacle (Heb 8:1-2; Wis 9:4, 8-9). The Wisdom of Solomon does not depict wisdom as a priest, but Sir 24:10, which is part of the same wisdom tradition, does portray wisdom as a priestess in the tabernacle.

Wis 9:8 differs from Hebrews and other ancient sources in that it calls Solomon's *temple* a copy of the heavenly tabernacle. The author may have done so because both the Mosaic tabernacle and Solomon's temple were built according to a heavenly "pattern" (Exod 25:9; 1 Chron 28:11). Nevertheless, the author of Wisdom shows almost no interest in the temple elsewhere and never suggests that the temple was the place where one encountered divine wisdom on earth. He does say, however, that one gains wisdom by keeping her laws, which are inseparable from the Mosaic law that is intended for all people (6:18; 18:4). The author did not recount the story of Solomon because the temple was so important. He did so because Solomon was an example of someone who prayed for the wisdom necessary to do what God enjoined, for wisdom "understands what is right according to God's commandments" (9:9).

---

[65] See "The Heavenly Tabernacle and Divine Wisdom" in chap. III.E above.

THE TABERNACLE'S ETERNAL CONSECRATION

Philo, as well as some later Jewish sources, contains one other tradition that may have contributed to the view of the tabernacle presupposed by the author of Hebrews.[66] According to this tradition, the tabernacle was consecrated forever, not for a limited period of time. Philo mentions the tradition to help explain why the ark of the covenant was made of undecaying wood (*Q.E.* 2.53). He observes that the law is incorruptible and that the sanctuary and its furnishings "were ordained not for a limited time but for an infinite age." Since the ark housed the law that stood in the sanctuary, it was made of undecaying wood. Like Philo, the author of Hebrews closely associates the time of the law and the time of the tabernacle (Heb 9:8–10). But where Philo says that the law and the tabernacle are abiding institutions, the author of Hebrews insists that the law and the tabernacle were instituted only until "the time of correction."

SYNTHESIS

Four types of extra-biblical material have important affinities to the view of the tabernacle in the Epistle to the Hebrews. (1) Philo presents a cosmological interpretation of the tabernacle that equates the parts of the tabernacle with the regions of the universe and with realms of being, as in Heb 9:8–10 and 24. (2) The hidden tabernacle tradition associates a tent, incense altar, and ark of the covenant with the age to come, as in Heb 9:3–4 and 8–10. (3) Wis 9:8 speaks of a heavenly tabernacle that was erected by God, has an earthly copy, and is associated with a wisdom figure, as in Heb 8:1–5. (4) Philo says that the law and the tabernacle are abiding institutions; Heb 9:8–10 says that both were instituted for a limited period of time.

Some of these traditions interpret the tabernacle temporally, and some interpret it spatially, yet taken together they account for the temporal and spatial characteristics of the tabernacle in Hebrews. Moreover, all of these traditions posit a close relationship between the tabernacle and the Mosaic law, as does the author of Hebrews. Despite certain differences, these traditions can plausibly be related to each other and help to establish a context for the interpretation of the tabernacle motif in Hebrews.

The author of Hebrews apparently knew the forms of these traditions that circulated in Egypt. Especially important are the epistle's affinities with Philo and the Wisdom of Solomon, both of which stem from Egypt.[67] First,

---

[66] See "Targumic traditions" under chap. III.F above.

[67] C. Spicq discerned so many parallels between Hebrews and Philo that he considered the author of Hebrews to be a Philonist converted to Christianity (*Hébreux*, 1.39–91). R. Williamson (*Philo and the Epistle to the Hebrews* [ALGHJ 4; Leiden: Brill, 1970]) has shown

all three sources discern a connection between the tabernacle and divine wisdom. Wis 9:4 and Heb 8:1-5 associate the tabernacle that God erected with a wisdom figure who sits beside the divine throne; Philo links the heavenly tabernacle with a less personal form of wisdom or virtue (e.g., *Cong.* 116; *Ebr.* 134).

Second, Philo, Josephus, and the author of Hebrews identify the parts of the tabernacle with regions of the universe, but only Philo and Hebrews equate these regions with the conscience or soul and flesh or sense perception. The author of Hebrews also equates the higher realm that lies inside the inner curtain with the region "outside the camp" as does Philo (Heb 13:9-14; *Gig.* 53-54).[68]

Third, Hebrews, Wisdom, and Philo all refer to a heavenly sanctuary and its earthly counterpart in language that has affinities with Platonism. Philo uses the terms παράδειγμα ("pattern") and ἀρχέτυπος ("archetype"), μίμημα ("copy") and σκιά ("shadow," *Mos.* 2.74; *L.A.* 3.96); Wis 9:8 uses μίμημα, and Heb 8:5 mentions σκιά.

Fourth, all three sources also know the idea that "fixity" (βεβαιόω/ βεβαίωσις) comes through observance of the regulations that are reflected in the Mosaic law, and Philo and the author of Hebrews perceive a connection between this notion and the tent of meeting (Heb 13:9; Wis 6:18; *L.A.* 2.55). Josephus also associated the tabernacle with the law, but indicated that it provided "well-being" (εὐδαιμονία) rather than "fixity" (*Ant.* 3.5.8 #99; cf. Proem 1.3 #14).

Fifth, references to the tabernacle's eternal consecration appear in Philo, several targums, and rabbinic sources, but only Philo and Hebrews stress that the law and the tabernacle were ordained for the same period of time. Philo indicates that both were established forever, while Hebrews insists that both were valid only until "the time of correction." The close connection between the time of the law and that of the tabernacle is absent from the targumic and rabbinic forms of the tradition.

The forms of the hidden tabernacle tradition that may have been known to the author of Hebrews also have strong ties to Egypt.[69] The tent, incense altar, and ark (Heb 9:3-4), and the hope of ingathering at Jerusalem (12:22)

---

that Hebrews is not literarily dependent on Philo, yet acknowledges that Hebrews and Philo reflect a common milieu (pp. 492-93). The numerous affinities among the Wisdom of Solomon, Philo, and Hebrews, which have been noted by Dey (*Intermediary World*) and Thompson (*Beginnings*), also suggest that these texts stem from a similar milieu.

[68] Noted by Dey, *Intermediary World*, 159. Wis 9:15 makes similar distinctions between realms of body and soul without applying them directly to the parts of the tabernacle.

[69] On 2 Macc 2:4-8 and the *Life of Jeremiah* see chap. III.D above.

resemble 2 Macc 2:4-8, which was written in Jerusalem for Jews in Egypt. The mention of several items inside the ark (Heb 9:4), the hope of an ingathering at Sinai (12:18-21), and the interest in Moses and Aaron (3:2; 5:4) may echo a tradition found in the *Life of Jeremiah,* which is comprised largely of Egyptian material.

These traditions not only circulated in the same geographical area, they also functioned in a similar way. Each tradition associated the tabernacle with the universal or abiding significance of the Mosaic law. The tabernacle did not necessarily represent a strong commitment to blood sacrifice or — after A.D. 70 — to the reestablishment of the sacrificial cult in Jerusalem.

Philo noted the connection between the tabernacle and sacrifices, but said that worship with correct intentions leads to immortality even without sacrifices. The tabernacle was prescribed by the Mosaic law, which was intended for all people, and it represents the universe and universal worship. Therefore those who wished to live in harmony with the universe should adopt Mosaic practices (*Mos* 2.25-44, 108). Philo indicated that the tabernacle was ordained for an "infinite age," not for a limited time, and the law which was housed within it was also an enduring institution (*Q.E.* 2.53). Thus Philo could even equate the tent of meeting with the statutes of virtue, which were conveyed by the Mosaic law (*L.A.* 2.55).

The Wisdom of Solomon said that God commanded Solomon to build the temple as a copy of the heavenly tabernacle. The author associated wisdom itself with the heavenly tabernacle, but did not suggest that wisdom could be found in the earthly temple. Instead, one found wisdom by keeping her laws, which were inseparable from the Mosaic law that was intended for all people (Wis 6:18; 18:4). The book shows little interest in the temple or sacrifices apart from this passage. The author recalled Solomon's construction of the temple as an example of one who prayed for the wisdom to do what God commanded (9:9).

The hidden tabernacle traditions in 2 Maccabees and the *Life of Jeremiah* depict the community of the new age as the law-observant heirs of Israel's cultic heritage, but do not exhibit a consistent view of the temple. The version found in 2 Macc 2:4-8 was written in the second century B.C., after the Maccabees had purified the temple, and the author expected the temple cult to continue. The passage is prefaced by exhortations to keep the law. In the *Life of Jeremiah,* which may have been written after the destruction of the temple in A.D. 70, the temple seems much less important. The author expected the ingathering to occur at Sinai and stressed the central and abiding importance of the Mosaic law, but does not give the temple a role in the eschatological events.

In a study of the sanctuary motif in Hebrews, George MacRae suggested that the "Philonic" characteristics of the tabernacle convey the author's own philosphical perspective, while the eschatological events reflect the apocalyptic outlook of the intended readers.[70] It seems more likely, however, that both the temporal and spatial or "Philonic" aspects of the tabernacle circulated within *the same* Christian group.[71] The author of Hebrews did not use spatial or philosophical categories to bolster an eschatological interpretation of the tabernacle. Instead, he used both temporal and spatial categories to show that the tabernacle and Mosaic law have been superseded by Christ's entry into the heavenly tabernacle at the dawn of a new age.

Scholars have long debated whether the Christians addressed by this epistle were of Jewish or Gentile origin.[72] Since the tabernacle traditions noted above circulated in Jewish circles, it seems probable that the intended readers were Jewish Christians. Yet it is also significant that Philo included the cosmological interpretation in his *Vita Mosis,* which addressed Gentiles as well as Hellenized Jews. Moreover, the Wisdom of Solomon refers to the heavenly tabernacle in connection with Solomon, who is presented as an example not only for Jews, but for rulers everywhere (Wis 6:1–3). Therefore the author of Hebrews may have intended his work for Christians of Jewish or Gentile origin, who associated the tabernacle with the universal and abiding significance of the Mosaic law.

C. CONCLUSION

The Epistle to the Hebrews was written by a Christian author for Christian readers, but the discussion of the tabernacle presupposes a knowledge of first-century Jewish traditions, especially in their Egyptian forms. Some of these traditions interpret the tabernacle temporally and some interpret it spatially, yet they all associate the tabernacle with the abiding or universal value of the Mosaic law. The author of Hebrews used these traditions, together with the OT, to convey the significance of Christ's heavenly ministry, which inaugurated a new age, in which observance of Mosaic statutes was no longer necessary. His discussion of the cult can be understood as an explication of the programmatic statements he made at the beginning of the epistle, where he said that God spoke "of old" by the

---

[70] "Heavenly Temple," 196.

[71] The vivid eschatological expectation of 2 Macc 2:4–8 and the *Life of Jeremiah* is absent from Philo and the Wisdom of Solomon, but Wisdom, Philo, 2 Maccabees, and Hebrews do share other key concepts, such as the notion of suffering as *paideia* unto perfection (Wis 11:9–10; 12:22; *Her.* 73; 2 Macc 6:12–31; Heb 5:8–9; 12:5–11; cf. Dey, *Intermediary World,* 222–25). The viewpoints of these texts were not mutually exclusive.

[72] On a Jewish Christian readership see, e.g., Spicq, *Hébreux,* 1.220–52; Michel, *Hebräer,* 41–56; Bruce, *Hebrews,* xxx; Rissi, *Theologie,* 23–25. On a Gentile Christian readership see, e.g., Moffatt, *Hebrews,* xvi; Kümmel, *Introduction,* 399–400; Braun, *Hebräer,* 2.

prophets, but "in these last days" he spoke through his son, who now is seated "on high" (1:1-4).

Accordingly, the author acknowledges that the heavenly tabernacle is the locus of divine wisdom, as in wisdom traditions (Wis 9:4-10; *Cong.* 116; cf. Sir 24:10). Wisdom literature indicates that divine wisdom was present in the Mosaic law, but the author of Hebrews argues that all wisdom's traits belong to Jesus, who occupies an exclusive place in the heavenly tabernacle, beside God's throne (Heb 1:1-3; 8:1-2).

The author agrees that the heavenly tabernacle had an earthly counter-part that was authorized by God in the Mosaic covenant (8:3-5; Wis 9:8), but he insists that the earthly tabernacle was only ordained for a limited period of time. Christ's ministry inaugurated the new covenant that had been promised through Jeremiah, making the prescriptions of the Mosaic cove-nant obsolete (Heb 8:6-13).

The author acknowledges that the parts of the tabernacle correspond to the parts of the universe and to the realms of flesh and conscience, as in the cosmological interpretation (Philo *Mos.* 2.76-108; Josephus *Ant.* 3.7.7 #179-183). The cosmological interpretation was used to convey the *universal* value of the law, but the author of Hebrews insisted that its regulations pertained only to food, drink, and ablutions, which were *limited* to the realm of the flesh. In contrast, Christ's ministry is performed in heaven, and he moved beyond the realm of the flesh and its regulations in order to perform his priestly task. Therefore those who follow Christ must do the same (Heb 9:19-20; 9:11-14; 10:19-20; 13:9-14).

The author grants the tabernacle a role in the worship of the new age, as in the hidden tabernacle tradition (2 Macc 2:4-8). But the tabernacle of the new age is the heavenly one, in which Christ ministers, not an earthly tent (Heb 9:11-12). The hidden tabernacle tradition depicted the community of the new age as the law-observant heirs of Israel's heritage. But the author of Hebrews insists that the new age marks the end of the old age and that Jesus' ministry in the heavenly tabernacle signals the end of the earthly tabernacle and its regulations. Those who continue to observe the practices associated with the first tabernacle serve an obsolete institution.

EXCURSUS: TABERNACLE TRADITIONS
AND THE DATE OF HEBREWS

The cosmological interpretation and hidden vessels tradition were popular both before and after the destruction of the temple in A.D. 70. Philo included the cosmological interpretation in his *Vita Mosis,* which was com-posed before A.D. 45, the approximate date of Philo's death. Josephus included the same tradition in his *Antiquities,* which was written about A.D.

94, a generation after the temple was destroyed. The hidden vessels tradition appears in 2 Macc 2:4-8, which probably was written in the second century B.C., and in the *Life of Jeremiah,* which seems to stem from the late first century A.D. Therefore the analysis of the tabernacle motif permits a date either before or after 70 for the composition of Hebrews.

At the same time, the preceding analysis does weaken arguments for a pre-70 date of composition. Advocates of a pre-70 date insist that the discussion of the tabernacle pertains primarily to temple worship and that the present tense verbs indicate that the temple was still standing. But for both Philo and Josephus the tabernacle represented forms of law-observant Jewish worship that did not require a temple. Philo insisted that one could worship without sacrifices; Josephus understood the tabernacle as a symbol of Jewish worship a generation after the temple's destruction. The discussion of the tabernacle in Hebrews probably addresses such an understanding of the tabernacle, rather than the Jerusalem temple cult. Therefore its argument would be quite relevant after 70.

The references to hearing the gospel secondhand (Heb 2:3), to the history of a Christian community (10:32), and to the death of a number of Christian leaders (13:7) would best apply to the last three decades of the century. Therefore a date after 70 is preferable.[73]

---

[73] On the date and circumstances of composition see also Michel, *Hebräer,* 48–58; and Brown, *Antioch and Rome,* 151–56.

VIII

CONCLUSION

The NT texts considered here were written by and for Christians in the late first century, most probably after the destruction of the second temple, when Jews were coming to terms with the loss of their cultic center. During the same period, Christianity was becoming increasingly distinct from Judaism. Belief in Jesus set Christians apart from non-Christian Jews and formed the focal point of a community of faith that came to include people of Jewish, Samaritan, and Greek origin.

The growing separation between Christianity and Judaism is reflected in the texts discussed here. Stephen's speech in Acts 7 is presented as a response to charges that he was claiming that "Jesus of Nazareth will destroy this place and change the customs which Moses delivered to us" (Acts 6:14). His speech associated the tabernacle, tent of David, and advent of Jesus with the promises of God, and depicted the golden calf, temple of Solomon, and rejection of Jesus as instances of apostasy. The speech showed that the faithful in Israel were to be found in the Jewish Christian community, not among non-Christian Jews, and it introduced the story of the Christian mission to Samaria. Later, conservative Jewish Christians insisted that it was necessary that Gentile Christians be circumcised and keep the law of Moses (15:5), but James responded with scriptural warrant for including uncircumcised Gentiles in the community of faith (15:13-21).

The prologue of John's gospel recalled that Jesus was rejected by many of his own people, the Jewish people, and the author insisted that it was those who received Jesus who were children of God. John 1:14-18 introduces the believing community's testimony to Jesus' glory and divine origin in language that echoes disputes between Jesus and his Jewish opponents later in the gospel. Yet the allusions to the tabernacle and to Sinai in 1:14-18 would have had positive connotations for Christians of Jewish and Samaritan origin, while the logos imagery in 1:1-14 would have been appealing to Christians from various backgrounds in the Greco-Roman world.

The author of Revelation attacked "those who say they are Jews but are not" (Rev 2:9; 3:9), since the true Jews were those who believed in Jesus. He

184

also warned readers to abstain from Gentile practices, including the consumption of meat offered to idols (2:14, 20). In the face of emerging conflict with Jews and Roman authorities, the author used numerous biblical images, like that of the tabernacle, to urge his readers to remain firm in their Christian convictions and to maintain their identity as a people set apart. Although the epistle to the Hebrews does not reveal open conflict between Christians and non-Christian Jews, its does seem to reflect a debate over the need for Christians to continue observing Mosaic statutes. The traditions presupposed by the author associated the tabernacle with the abiding or universal value of the Mosaic law. The author, however, relegated the Mosaic tabernacle and Jewish purity regulations to a time that had passed and the realm of the flesh, urging readers to move beyond them. He insisted that God spoke "of old" by the prophets, but "in these last days" he spoke by a son (Heb 1:2).

In a setting where the differences between Christianity and Judaism were becoming increasingly clear, tabernacle imagery helped to establish continuity between Christianity and Israel's cultic heritage. The author of Acts made a connection between the Jewish Christian church and the worship associated with the tabernacle and David's tent before describing the extension of Christianity into Samaria and the approval of the circumcision-free mission to Gentiles. Although the Fourth Evangelist perceived the incarnation of the Word and formation of the Christian community as new events, he portrayed their significance by alluding to the ancient tabernacle and Sinai theophany. The author of Revelation used tabernacle imagery for the church of the new age in a way that could maintain the church's identity as the people of God who were set apart from the idolatry of the surrounding culture. While the author of Hebrews wanted to move his readers beyond the Jewish practices associated with the tabernacle, he preserved Christianity's continuity with Israel's heritage by portraying Christ as a priest in the heavenly tabernacle.

The tabernacle's role in providing continuity during a period of change was not new; it had functioned similarly in the OT and later Jewish writings, as noted in chaps. 2–3 above. Like earlier writers, some NT authors also associated the tabernacle with hopes for a restoration and unity in Israel. According to Acts the growth of the Jewish Christian community marked the restoration of David's tent, and in Revelation the church of the new age appears as the tabernacle-city where God and the Lamb will be worshiped and idolatry will be banished. John's prologue speaks of a new worshiping community that is centered on the tabernacling Word. The tabernacle imagery also may have fostered unity between Christians of Jewish and Samaritan origin within the Johannine community, since the tabernacle was a sanctuary respected by both groups.

The tabernacle was theologically attractive to early Christians because it recalled God's faithfulness to his covenant promises. The author of Acts viewed the construction of the tabernacle as God's response to Israel's idolatry, the establishment of a tent sanctuary in Jerusalem as the fulfillment of God's promise to Abraham, and the growth of the Jewish Christian church as the rebuilding of David's tent that was promised in Amos 9:11. According to John's prologue, the abundant grace and truth that were announced when God made the covenant at Sinai occurred with the advent of Jesus, the tabernacling Word. In the book of Revelation, the descent of the new Jerusalem as God's tabernacle-city was accompanied by the announcement of God's covenant relationship with people and the fulfillment of a catena of biblical promises. The author of Hebrews assumed that the tabernacle was inseparable from the covenant, but argued that the Mosaic tabernacle and first covenant had been superseded by Jesus' ministry in the heavenly tabernacle, which was part of a new covenant and a new age.

The tabernacle is also depicted as a place of revelation and sacrifice, but to a lesser extent than in earlier writings. John's prologue used tabernacle imagery to announce that God's word and glory were present in the person of Jesus, and the book of Revelation used tabernacle imagery for God's presence in the new Jerusalem. The Epistle to the Hebrews, like the Gospel of John, depicted Jesus as the one in whom God is revealed (Heb 1:3), but associated Jesus with the heavenly rather than the earthly tent. Hebrews was the only NT writing in which the connection between the tabernacle and sacrifice was prominent, and the author of the work tried to show that the sacrifices offered in the earthly tent had been superseded by Jesus' own self-sacrifice.

In her study of cultic language in the NT, E. Schüssler Fiorenza remarked that the authors of the NT "do not so much re-interpret cultic institutions and terminology but express a new reality in cultic language."[1] Her observation is correct. None of the NT writers composed a commentary on the biblical tabernacle texts; their starting point was the person of Jesus, whose significance they sought to convey in language taken from the scriptures and Jewish traditions. The advent of Jesus was a recent event, and belief in Jesus set Christians apart from non-Christian Jews. But the use of traditional images — like that of the tabernacle — helped to establish the identity of Christians as heirs of Israel's rich and ancient heritage. Moreover, in a time of division and controversy, the tabernacle imagery provided a way to speak about the fidelity of God, who remained committed to his promises.

---

[1] "Cultic Language," 162 n. 12, which was noted in chap. 1 above. See also Juel, *Messianic Exegesis,* 14–15.

BIBLIOGRAPHY

I. Primary Texts

"Apocalypse of Baruch." *The Old Testament in Syriac According to the Peshitta Version.* 4/3. Edited by S. Dedering. Leiden: Brill, 1973.

The Apocrypha and Pseudepigrapha of the Old Testament. 2 vols. Edited by R. H. Charles. Oxford: Clarendon, 1913.

The Assumption of Moses. Edited and trans. by R. H. Charles. London: Black, 1897.

Baraita d'Meleket ha-Mishkan. "The Tabernacle." In *The Talmud,* trans. by J. Barclay. London: John Murray, 1878.

The Babylonian Talmud. 35 vols. Edited by I. Epstein. London: Soncino, 1935–52.

Biblia hebraica stuttgartensia. Edited by K. Elliger and W. Rudolph. Stuttgart: Deutsche Bibelstiftung, 1967–77.

The Book of Enoch or 1 Enoch. Edited and trans. by R. H. Charles. Oxford: Clarendon, 1912.

The Books of Enoch: Aramaic Fragments of Qumrân Cave 4. Edited and trans. by J. T. Milik. Oxford: Clarendon, 1976.

The Dead Sea Scrolls in English. Trans. by G. Vermes. 2d ed. Middlesex: Penguin, 1975.

The Dead Sea Scrolls of Hebrew University. Edited by E. L. Sukenik. Jerusalem: Magnes, 1955.

Discoveries in the Judean Desert of Jordan V. Qumran Cave 4 I (4Q148– 4Q186). Edited by J. M. Allegro. Oxford: Clarendon, 1968.

Discoveries in the Judean Desert VII. Qumrân Grotte 4 III. Edited by M. Baillet. Oxford: Clarendon, 1982.

Ecclesiastico: Testo ebraico con apparato critico e versioni greca, latina e siriaca. Edited by F. Vattioni. Naples: Instituto Orientale, 1968.

The Ethiopic Book of Enoch: A New Edition in Light of the Aramaic Dead Sea Fragments. Vol. 2, *Introduction, Translation, and Commentary.* Edited and trans. by M. A. Knibb. Oxford: Clarendon, 1978.

187

Eupolemos. Fragments in Eusebius, *Die Preparatio Evangelica I–X*. Edited by K. Mras. GCS 43/1. Berlin: Akademie, 1954.

The Fragment Targums of the Pentateuch According to their Extant Sources. 2 vols. Edited by M. Klein. AnBib 76. Rome: Biblical Institute, 1980.

Josephus with an English Translation. 10 vols. Edited and trans. by H. S. J. Thackeray, R. Marcus, and L. H. Feldman. LCL. Cambridge: Harvard, 1926–65.

Memar Marqah: The Teaching of Marqah. 2 vols. Edited and trans. by J. Macdonald. BZAW 84. Berlin: Töpelmann, 1963.

Mekilta de-Rabbi Ishmael. 3 vols. Edited and trans. by J. Z. Lauterbach. Philadelphia: Jewish Publication Society, 1933–35.

Midrash Rabbah. מדרש רבה על חמשה חומשי תורה וחמש מגלות. 2 vols. Wilna, 1878.

Midrash Rabbah. 10 vols. Edited and trans. by H. Freedman and M. Simon. London: Soncino, 1939.

Midrash Tanḥuma: מדרש תנחומא. Vienna, 1863.

Mishnah. ששה סדרי משנה. 6 vols. Edited by C. Albeck. Jerusalem: Bialik, 1952–59.

The Mishnah. Trans. by H. Danby. Oxford: Clarendon, 1933.

Neophyti 1. Palestinese MS de la Biblioteca Vaticana. 6 vols. Edited by A. Diez Macho. Madrid: Consejo Superior de Investigaciones Cientificas, 1968–79.

Novum Testamentum Graece. 26th ed. Edited by E. Nestle and K. Aland. Stuttgart: Deutsche Bibelstiftung, 1979.

The Odes of Solomon. Edited and trans. by J. H. Charlesworth. Texts and Translations 13, Pseudepigrapha Series 7. Chico: Scholars, 1977.

The Old Testament in Syriac According to the Peshitta Version. Edited by the Peshitta Institute. Leiden: Brill, 1972–

The Old Testament Pseudepigrapha. 2 vols. Edited by J. H. Charlesworth. Garden City: Doubleday, 1983–1985.

Paralipomena Jeremiou. Edited and trans. by R. A. Kraft and A.-E. Purintun. Missoula: SBL, 1972.

Philo with an English Translation. 10 vols. and 2 suppl. vols. Edited and trans. by F. H. Colson, R. Marcus, et al. LCL. Cambridge: Harvard, 1929–64.

Prophetarum vitae fabulosae. Edited by T. Schermann. Leipzig: Teubner, 1907.

Pseudo-Philon. Les Antiquities Bibliques. Vol. 1. Edited and trans. by D. J. Harrington and J. Cazeaux. SC 229. Paris: Cerf, 1976.

Septuaginta: Vetus Testamentum graeca. Edited by Auctoritate Societatis Göttingensis. Göttingen: Vandenhoeck & Ruprecht, 1931–

Septuaginta. 2 vols. Edited by A. Rahlfs. Stuttgart: Württembergische Bibelanstalt, 1935.

Sifra. Commentar zu Leviticus aus dem Anfange des III. Jahrhunderts. ספרא דבי רב הוא ספר תורת כהנים. Edited by I. H. Weiss. Vienna: Schlossberg, 1862.

Siphre ad Deuteronomium. ספרי על ספר דברים. Edited by L. Finkelstein. Berlin: Jüdischer Kulturbund in Deutschland, 1939. Reprinted as *Sifre on Deuteronomy.* New York: Jewish Theological Seminary, 1969.

Siphre d'be Rab, fasciculus primus: Siphre ad Numeros adjecto Siphre zutta. ספרי דבי רב, מחברת ראשונות: ספרי על ספר במדבר וספרי זוטא. Edited by H. S. Horovitz. Leipzig: Gustav Fock, 1917. Reprint. Jerusalem: Wahrmann, 1966.

The Songs of the Sabbath Sacrifice: A Critical Edition. Edited and trans. by C. A. Newsom. HSS 27. Atlanta: Scholars, 1985.

Der tannaitische Midrasch Sifre Deuteronomium. Trans. by H. Bietenhard. Judica et Christiania 8. Bern: Peter Lang, 1983.

Der tannaitische Midrasch Sifre zu Numeri. Trans. by K. G. Kuhn. Stuttgart: Kohlhammer, 1959.

Talmud Bavli. תלמוד בבלי. Wilna, 1886. Reprint. Jerusalem. n.d.

Talmud Yerushalmi. תלמוד ירושלמי. Krotoshin, 1866. Reprint. Jerusalem, 1969.

The Temple Scroll. 3 vols. Edited and trans. by Y. Yadin. Jerusalem: Israel Exploration Society, 1983.

The Testaments of the Twelve Patriarchs: A Critical Edition of the Greek Text. Edited by M. de Jonge. PVTG 1/2. Leiden: Brill, 1978.

The Tosefta. תוספתא. 4 vols. Edited by S. Lieberman. New York: Jewish Theological Seminary of America, 1955–73.

Tosefta. תוספתא. Edited by M. S. Zuckermandel. Pasewalk, 1880. Reprint. Jerusalem: Wahrmann, 1970.

The Tosefta Translated from the Hebrew. 5 vols. Trans. by J. Neusner. New York: Ktav, 1977–81.

The Zadokite Documents. Edited and trans. by C. Rabin. Oxford: Clarendon, 1954.

II. Concordances

Aland, K. *Vollständige Konkordanz zum griechischen neuen Testament unter zugrundelegung aller modernen Textausgaben und des Textus Receptus.* 3 vols. Berlin: de Gruyter, 1983.

Barthélemy, D., and O. Rickenbacher. *Konkordanz zum hebräischen Sirach.* Göttingen: Vandenhoeck & Ruprecht, 1973.

Goodspeed, E. J. *Index patristicus sive clavis natrum apostolicorum operum.* Leipzig: Hinrichs, 1907. Reprint. Naperville: Allenson, 1960.

———. *Index apologeticus sive clavis Iustini Martyris operum aliorumque apologetarum pristinorum.* Leipzig: Hinrichs, 1912.

Hatch, E., and H. A. Redpath. *A Concordance to the Septuagint and the Other Greek Versions of the Old Testament (Including the Apocrypha).* Oxford: Clarendon, 1897. Reprint. Graz: Akademische, 1975.

Kasowski, C. J. אוצר לשון המשנה: ספר המתאימות-קונקורדנציה לששה סדרי משנה/*Thesaurus Mishnae. Concordantiae verborum quae in sex Mishnae ordinibus reperiuntur.* 4 vols. Tel Aviv: Massadah, 1967.

———. אוצר לשון התוספתא: ספר המתאימות (קונקורדאנציא) לששה סדרי התוספתא/*Thesaurus Thosephthae. Concordantiae verborum quae in sex Thosephthae ordinibus reperiuntur.* 6 vols. Jerusalem: Jewish Theological Seminary of America, 1932–61.

———. אוצר לשון התלמוד: ספר המתאימות (קונקורדנציא) לתלמוד בבלי/*Thesaurus Talmudis. Concordantiae verborum quae in Talmude Babylonico reperiuntur.* 41 vols. Jerusalem: Jewish Theological Seminary of America and Ministry of Education and Culture (Government of Israel), 1954–82.

———. אוצר לשון התנאים: ספר המתאימות (קונקורדנציא) למכילתא דרבי ישמעאל/*Otzar Leshon Hatannai'im. Concordantiae Verborum quae in Mechilta d'Rabbi Ismael reperiunter.* 4 vols. Jerusalem: Jewish Theological Seminary of America, 1965.

———. אוצר לצון התנאים: ספר המתאימות (קונקורדנציא) לספרא-תורת כהנים/*Otzar Leshon Hatanna'im. Concordantiae verborum quae in Sifra aut Torat Kohanim reperiuntur.* 5 vols. Jerusalem: Jewish Theological Seminary of America, 1967–69.

———. אוצר לשון התנאים: ספר המתאימות (קונקורדנציא) לספרי (במדבר, דברים)/*Otzar Leshon Hatanna'im. Thesaurus "Sifrei." Concordantiae verborum quae in "Sifrei" Numeri et Deuteronomium reperiuntur.* 4 vols. Jerusalem: Jewish Theological Seminary of America, 1970.

Kosovsky, M. אוצר לשון תלמוד ירושלמי/*Concordance to the Talmud Yerushalmi.* Jerusalem: Israel Academy of Sciences and Humanities, and Jewish Theological Seminary of America, 1979–

Kuhn, K. G. *Konkordanz zu den Qumrantexten.* Göttingen: Vandenhoeck & Ruprecht, 1960.

———. "Nachträge zur *Konkordanz zu den Qumrantexten.*" *RevQ* 4 (1963) 163–234.

Mandelkern, S. ספר היכל הקדש הלא הוא קונקורדנציא עבריח וארמית/ *Veteris Testamenti concordantiae hebraicae et chaldaicae.* Leipzig: Veit, 1896. Reprint. Israel, n.d.

Mayer, G. *Index Philoneus.* Berlin: de Gruyter, 1974.

Rengstorf, K. H. *A Complete Concordance to Flavius Josephus.* 4 vols. Leiden: Brill, 1973–83.

III. Secondary Sources Cited

Ackroyd, P. R. "History and Theology in the Writings of the Chronicler." *CTM* 38 (1967) 501–15.

———. "The Theology of the Chronicler." *Lexington Theological Monthly* 8 (1973) 101–16.

Allo, P. E.-B. *Saint Jean: L'Apocalypse.* EBib. 3d ed. Paris: Gabalda, 1933.

Andriessen, P. "Das grössere und vollkommenere Zelt." *BZ* 15 (1971) 76–92.

———. "L'Eucharistie dans l'Epître aux Hébreux." *NRT* 94 (1972) 269–77.

———. "La communauté des 'Hébreux': Etait-elle tombee dans le relachement?" *NRT* 96 (1974) 1054–66.

Bacon, B. W. "Stephen's Speech: Its Argument and Doctrinal Relationship." *Biblical and Semitic Studies.* Yale Bicentennial Publications. New York: Scribners, 1901.

Baillet, M. "Un receil liturgique de Qumrân, Grotte 4: Les Paroles des Luminaires." *RB* 68 (1961) 195–250.

Baltzer, K. "The Meaning of the Temple in the Lukan Writings." *HTR* 58 (1965) 263–77.

Barnard, L. W. "Stephen and Early Alexandrian Christianity." *NTS* 7 (1960–61) 31–45.

Barrett, C. K. "The Eschatology of the Epistle to the Hebrews." In *The Background of the New Testament and Its Eschatology,* Studies in Honor of C. H. Dodd, edited by W. D. Davies and D. Daube, Cambridge: University, 1956.

———. *The Gospel According to St. John.* 2d ed. Philadelphia: Westminster, 1978.

Baumgarten, J. M. "The Duodecimal Courts of Qumran, Revelation, and the Sanhedrin." *JBL* 95 (1976) 59–78.

Beasley-Murray, G. R. *The Book of Revelation.* NCB. London: Oliphants, 1974.

Beckwith, I. T. *The Apocalypse of John.* New York: Macmillan, 1922

Bernard, J. H. *The Odes of Solomon.* Cambridge: University, 1912.

Beyerlin, W. *Origins and History of the Oldest Sinaitic Traditions.* Oxford: Blackwell, 1965.

Bietenhard, H. *Die himmlische Welt in Urchristentum und Spätjudentum.* WUNT 2. Tübingen: Mohr/Siebeck, 1951.

Bihler, J. *Die Stephanusgeschichte im zusammenhang der Apostelgeschichte.* Münchener theologische Studien 1.30; Munich: Hueber, 1963.

Black, M. *An Aramaic Approach to the Gospels and Acts.* 3d ed. Oxford: Clarendon, 1967.

Blenkinsopp, J. "The Structure of P." *CBQ* 38 (1976) 275-92.

Bogaert, P. *Apocalypse de Baruch.* 2 vols. SC 144. Paris: Cerf, 1969.

Boismard, M.-E. *St. John's Prologue.* Westminster: Newman, 1957.

———. "L'martyre d'Etienne. Acts 6,8-8,2." *RSR* 69 (1981) 181-94.

Borgen, P. *Bread from Heaven: An Exegetical Study of the Concept of Manna in the Gospel of John and the Writings of Philo.* NovTSup 10. Leiden: Brill, 1965.

———. "Philo of Alexandria: A critical and synthetical survey of research." *ANRW* 2.21/1 (1983) 98-154.

———. "Logos was the True Light." *NovT* 14 (1972) 115-30.

Bousset, W. *Die Offenbarung Johannis.* MeyerK 16; 6th ed. Göttingen: Vandenhoeck & Ruprecht, 1906.

Bowman, J. "The Fourth Gospel and the Samaritans." *BJRL* 40 (1958) 298-308.

———. *The Samaritan Problem: Studies in the Relationships of Samaritanism, Judaism, and Early Christianity.* Franz Delitzsch Lectures 1959. Pittsburgh: Pickwick, 1975.

Braun, H. *An die Hebräer.* HNT 14. Tübingen: Mohr/Siebeck, 1984.

Brehier, E. *Les Idées Philosophiques et Religieuses de Philon d'Alexandrie.* Paris: Librairie philosophique, 1925.

Brown. R. E. *The Gospel According to John.* 2 vols. AB 29-29A. Garden City: Doubleday, 1966, 1970.

———. *The Birth of the Messiah: A Commentary on the Infancy Narratives in Matthew and Luke.* Garden City: Doubleday, 1979.

———. *The Community of the Beloved Disciple.* New York: Paulist, 1979.

——. "Not Jewish Christianity or Gentile Christianity, but Types of Jewish/Gentile Christianity." *CBQ* 45 (1983) 74–79.

——, and J. P. Meier. *Antioch and Rome: New Testament Cradles of Catholic Christianity.* New York: Paulist, 1983.

Bruce, F. F. *Commentary on the Book of Acts.* NICNT. Grand Rapids: Eerdmans, 1954.

——. " 'To the Hebrews' or 'To the Essenes'?" *NTS* 9 (1962–63) 217–32.

——. *The Epistle to the Hebrews.* NICNT. Grand Rapids: Eerdmans, 1964.

Buchanan, G. W. "The Samaritan Origin of the Gospel of John." In *Religions in Antiquity: Essays in Memory of Erwin Ramsdell Goodenough,* edited by J. Neusner. Studies in the History of Religions (Supplements to *Numen*). Leiden: Brill, 1968.

——. *Hebrews.* AB 36. Garden City: Doubleday, 1972.

Bultmann, R. "Der religionsgeschichtliche Hintergrund des Prologs zum Johannesevangelium." In *Eucharisterion: Studien zur Religion und Literatur des Alten und Neuen Testaments. Hermann Gunkel zum 60. Geburtstage,* edited by H. Schmidt. FRLANT 36.2. Göttingen: Vandenhoeck & Ruprecht, 1923.

——. *The Gospel of John: A Commentary.* Philadelphia: Westminster, 1971.

Caird, G. B. *A Commentary on the Revelation of St. John the Divine.* HNTC. New York: Harper & Row, 1966.

Carmignac, J., and P. Guilbert. *Les Texts de Qumran Traduits et Annotés.* Vol. 1. Paris: Letouzey et Ané, 1961.

Charles, R. H. *A Critical and Exegetical Commentary on the Revelation of St. John.* 2 vols. ICC. Edinburgh: Clark, 1920.

Charlesworth, J. H., and R. A. Culpepper. "The Odes of Solomon and the Gospel of John." *CBQ* 35 (1973) 298–322.

Childs, B. S. *The Book of Exodus: A Critical, Theological Commentary.* OTL. Philadelphia: Westminster, 1974.

Clements, R. E. *God and Temple.* Philadelphia: Fortress, 1965.

Cody, A. *Heavenly Sanctuary and Liturgy in the Epistle to the Hebrews.* St Meinrad: Grail, 1960.

Collins, A. Yarbro. *The Combat Myth in the Book of Revelation.* HDR 9. Missoula: Scholars, 1976.

——. *The Apocalypse.* NTM 22. Wilmington: Glazier, 1979.

——. *Crisis and Catharsis: The Power of the Apocalypse.* Philadelphia: Westminster, 1984.

Collins, J. J. *The Apocalyptic Vision of the Book of Daniel.* HSM 16. Missoula: Scholars, 1977.

Collins, M. F. "The Hidden Vessels in Samaritan Traditions." *JSJ* 3 (1972) 97–116.

Comblin, J. "La liturgie de la Nouvelle Jérusalem." *ETL* 29 (1953) 5–40.

———. *Théologie de la ville.* Paris: Universitaires, 1968.

Conzelmann, H. *Acts of the Apostles.* Hermeneia. Philadelphia: Fortress, 1987.

Coppens, J. "Les affinités qumrâniennes de l'Epître aux Hébreux." *NRT* 94 (1962) 128–41, 257–82.

Cross, F. M. "The Tabernacle." *BA* 10 (1947) 45–68.

———. *Canaanite Myth and Hebrew Epic: Essays in the History of the Religion of Israel.* Cambridge: Harvard, 1973.

———. "A Reconstruction of the Judean Restoration." *JBL* 94 (1975) 4–18.

Cullmann, O. "L'opposition contre le temple de Jerusalem, motif commun de la theologie johannique et du monde ambiant." *NTS* 5 (1958–59) 157–73.

———. *The Johannine Circle: Its Place in Judaism, Among the Disciples of Jesus, and in Early Christianity.* London: SCM, 1975.

Culpepper, R. A. "The Pivot of John's Prologue." *NTS* 27 (1980–81) 1–31.

Dahl, N. A. "The Story of Abraham in Luke-Acts." In *Studies in Luke-Acts,* edited by L. E. Keck and J. L. Martyn. Philadelphia: Fortress, 1980.

Dahms, J. V. "The First Readers of Hebrews." *JETS* 20 (1977) 365–75.

Davies, G. H. "Tabernacle." *IDB* 4 (1962) 498–506.

Davies, P. R. "The Ideology of the Temple in the Damascus Document." *JJS* 33 (1982) 287–301.

———. *The Damascus Covenant: An Interpretation of the "Damascus Document."* JSOTSup 25. Sheffield: JSOT, 1982.

Davies, W. D. *The Gospel and the Land: Early Christianity and Jewish Territorial Doctrine.* Berkeley: University of California, 1974.

Delcor, M. *Les Hymnes de Qumran (Hodayot).* Paris: Letouzey et Ané, 1962.

Delling, G. "Zum gottesdienstlichen Stil der Johannesapokalypse." *NovT* 3 (1959) 107–37.

———. *Jüdische Lehre und Frömmigkeit in den Paralipomena Jeremiae.* BZAW 100. Berlin: Töpelmann, 1967.

Denis, A.-M. *Introduction aux Pseudepigraphes grecs d'Ancien Testament.* SVTP 1. Leiden: Brill, 1970.

de Vaux, R. *Ancient Israel.* 2 vols. New York: McGraw-Hill, 1965.

——. *The Bible and the Ancient Near East.* Garden City: Doubleday, 1971.

Dey, L. K. K. *The Intermediary World and Patterns of Perfection in Philo and Hebrews.* SBLDS 25. Missoula: Scholars, 1975.

Dibelius, M. *Studies in the Acts of the Apostles.* London: SCM, 1956.

Diez Macho, A. "The Recently Discovered Palestinian Targum: Its Antiquity and Relationship with the Other Targums." VTSup 7 (1959) 222–45.

Dodd, C. H. *The Interpretation of the Fourth Gospel.* Cambridge: University, 1953.

Doran, R. *Temple Propaganda: The Purpose and Character of 2 Maccabees.* CBQMS 12. Washington: CBA, 1981.

Dupont-Sommer, A. "Le Livre des Hymnes decouvert près de la mer Morte (1QH)." *Sem* 7 (1957) 1–120.

Eichrodt, W. *Ezekiel: A Commentary.* OTL. Philadelphia: Westminster, 1970.

Feldman, L. "Prolegomenon." In *The Biblical Antiquities of Philo,* edited and trans. by M. R. James. New York: Ktav, 1971.

Fensham, F. C. "Hebrews and Qumran." *Neot* 5 (1971) 9–21.

Feuillet, A. *Johannine Studies.* New York: Alba, 1965.

——. *The Apocalypse.* New York: Alba, 1965.

——. *Le prologue de quatrième évangile.* Paris: Desclée de Brouwer, 1968.

Fitzmyer, J. A. "Qumran and the Interpolated Paragraph in 2 Cor 6,14–7,1." *CBQ* 23 (1961) 271–80.

——. "The Languages of Palestine in the First Century A.D." *CBQ* 32 (1970) 501–31.

Franklin, E. *Christ the Lord: A Study in the Purpose and Theology of Luke-Acts.* Philadelphia: Westminster. 1975.

Freed, E. D. "Samaritan Influence in the Gospel of John." *CBQ* 30 (1968) 580–87.

Freedman, D. N. "The Chronicler's Purpose." *CBQ* 23 (1961) 436–42.

Fretheim, T. E. "Psalm 132: A Form-Critical Study." *JBL* 86 (1967) 289–300.

——. "The Priestly Document: Anti-Temple?" *VT* 18 (1968) 313–29.

Freudenthal, J. *Alexander Polyhistor und die von ihm erhaltenen Reste jüdischer und samaritanischer Geschichtswerke.* Breslau: Skutsch, 1875.

Fritz, V. *Tempel und Zelt. Studien zum Tempelbau in Israel und zu dem Zeltheiligtum der Priesterschrift.* WMANT 47. Neukirchen Vluyn: Neukirchener, 1977.

Früchtel, U. *Die kosmologischen Vorstellungen bei Philo von Alexandrien: Ein Beitrag zur Geschichte der Genesisexegese.* ALGHL 2. Leiden: Brill, 1968.

Furnish, V. P. *II Corinthians.* AB 32A. Garden City: Doubleday, 1984.

Gärtner, B. *The Temple and the Community in Qumran and the New Testament.* SNTSMS 1. Cambridge: University, 1965.

Gaston, L. *No Stone on Another: Studies in the Significance of the Fall of Jerusalem in the Synoptic Gospels.* NovTSup 23. Leiden: Brill, 1970.

Georgi, D. "Die Visionen vom himmlischen Jerusalem in Apk 21 und 22." In *Kirche: Festschrift für Günther Bornkamm zum 75. Geburtstag.* Edited by D. Lührmann and G. Strecker. Tübingen: Mohr/Siebeck, 1980.

——. *Weisheit Salomons.* JSHRZ 3/4. Gütersloh: Mohn, 1980.

Gese, H. "Der Davidsbund und die Zionserwählung." *ZTK* 61 (1964) 10–26.

Ginzberg, L. "Baraita on the Erection of the Tabernacle." *Jewish Encyclopedia* 2 (1906) 517.

——. *An Unknown Jewish Sect.* New York: Jewish Theological Seminary of America, 1970.

Goldberg, A. M. *Untersuchungen über die Vorstellung von der Schekhinah in der frühen rabbinischen Literatur.* SJ 6. Berlin: de Gruyter, 1969.

Goldstein, J. A. *I Maccabees.* AB 41. Garden City: Doubleday, 1976.

——. *II Maccabees.* AB 41A. Garden City: Doubleday, 1983.

Goodenough, E. R. *By Light, Light: The Mystic Gospel of Hellenistic Judaism.* New Haven: Yale University, 1935.

——. "The Menorah among the Jews of the Roman World." *HUCA* 23 (1950–51) 449–92.

Gooding, D. W. *The Account of the Tabernacle: Translation and Textual Problems of the Greek Exodus.* Texts and Studies 6. Cambridge: University, 1959.

Görg, M. *Das Zelt der Begegnung. Untersuchung zur Gestalt der sakralen Zelttraditionen Altisraels.* BBB 27. Bonn: Hanstein, 1967.

Gray, J. *I and II Kings: A Commentary.* OTL. Philadelphia: Westminster, 1963.

Greenberg, M. "The Design and Themes of Ezekiel's Program of Restoration." *Int* 38 (1984) 181–208.

Guthrie, D. *New Testament Introduction.* Downer's Grove: Inter-Varsity, 1970.

Habicht, C. *2 Makkabäerbuch.* JSHRZ 1/3. Gütersloh: Mohn, 1976.

Haenchen, E. "Probleme des johanneischen Prologs." *ZTK* 60 (1963) 305-34.

——. *The Acts of the Apostles.* Philadelphia: Westminster, 1971.

——. *John 1.* Hermeneia. Philadelphia: Fortress, 1984.

Haran, M. "The Nature of the ''Ohel Mo'ed' in Pentateuchal Sources." *JSS* 5 (1960) 50-65.

——. "Shiloh and Jerusalem: The Origin of the Priestly Tradition in the Pentateuch." *JBL* 81 (1962) 14-24.

——. "The Priestly Image of the Tabernacle." *HUCA* 36 (1965) 191-226.

——. *Temples and Temple Service in Ancient Israel: An Inquiry into the Character of Cult Phenomena and the Historical Setting of the Priestly School.* Oxford: Clarendon, 1978.

——. "Behind the Scenes of History: Determining the Date of the Priestly Source." *JBL* 100 (1981) 321-33.

Harnisch, W. *Verhängnis und Verheissung der Geschichte: Untersuchungen zum Zeit- und Geschichtsverständnis im 4. Buch Esra und in der syr. Baruchapokalypse.* FRLANT 97. Göttingen: Vandenhoeck & Ruprecht, 1969.

Harris, J. R. *The Rest of the Words of Baruch.* London: Clay, 1889.

——. *The Odes and Psalms of Solomon.* Cambridge: University, 1909.

——. *The Origin of the Prologue of St. John's Gospel.* Cambridge: University, 1917.

Hartmann, L. "Zelt und Lade." *ZAW* 37 (1917-18) 209-44.

Hay, D. M. "Philo's References to Other Allegorists." *Studia Philonica* 6 (1979-80) 41-75.

Hengel, M. *Judaism and Hellenism: Studies in their Encounter in Palestine during the Early Hellenistic Period.* Philadelphia: Fortress, 1974.

——, J. H. Charlesworth, and D. Mendels. "The Polemical Character of 'On Kingship' in the Temple Scroll: An Attempt at Dating 11QTemple." *JJS* 37 (1987) 28-38.

Hoenig, S. B. "The Designated Number of Kinds of Labor Prohibited on the Sabbath." *JQR* 68 (1978) 193-217.

Hofius, O. "Inkarnation und Opfertod Jesu nach Hebr. X,19f." In *Der Ruf Jesu und die Antwort der Gemeinde: Exegetische Untersuchungen für Joachim Jeremias zum 70. Geburtstag,* edited by E. Lohse, C. Burchard, and B. Schaller. Göttingen: Vandenhoeck & Ruprecht, 1970.

——. *Der Vorhang vor dem Thron Gottes: Eine exegetisch- religionsgeschichtliche Untersuchung zu Hebräer 6,19f. und 10,19f.* WUNT 14. Tübingen: Mohr/Siebeck, 1972.

Holtzmann, O. "Der Hebräerbrief und das Abendmahl." *ZNW* 10 (1909) 251–60.

Horton, F. L. *The Melchizedek Tradition: A Critical Examination of the Sources to the Fifth Century A.D. and in the Epistle to the Hebrews.* SNTSMS 30. Cambridge: University, 1976.

Hoskyns, E. C. *The Fourth Gospel.* Edited by F. N. Davey. 2d ed. London: Faber, 1947.

Hurst, L. D. "How 'Platonic' are Heb viii.5 and ix.23f?" *JTS* 34 (1983) 156–68.

Jervell, J. *Luke and the People of God: A New Look at Luke-Acts.* Minneapolis: Augsburg, 1972.

Jörns, K.-P. *Das hymnische Evangelium: Untersuchungen zu Aufbau, Funktion, und Herkunft der hymnischen Stücke in der Johannesoffenbarung.* SNT 5. Gütersloh: Mohn, 1971.

Juel, D. *Messiah and Temple: The Trial of Jesus in the Gospel of Mark.* SBLDS 31. Missoula: Scholars, 1977.

———. *Luke-Acts: The Promise of History.* Atlanta: Knox, 1983.

———. *Messianic Exegesis: Christological Interpretation of the Old Testament in Early Christianity.* Philadelphia: Fortress, 1988.

Karris, R. J. "Missionary Communities: A New Paradigm for the Study of Luke-Acts." *CBQ* 41 (1979) 80–97.

Käsemann, E. *The Wandering People of God: An Investigation of the Letter to the Hebrews.* Minneapolis: Augsburg, 1984.

———. *The Testament of Jesus According to John 17.* Philadelphia: Fortress, 1968.

———. "The Structure and Purpose of the Prologue to John's Gospel." In *New Testament Questions of Today.* Philadelphia: Fortress, 1969.

Kaufman, S. A. "On Methodology in the Study of the Targums and their Chronology." *JSNT* 23 (1985) 117–24.

Kennedy, A. R. S. "Tabernacle." *Hastings Dictionary of the Bible* 4 (1911) 653–68.

Kilgallen, J. *The Stephen Speech: A Literary and Redactional Study of Acts 7,2–53.* AnBib 67. Rome: Biblical Institute, 1976.

Kippenberg, H. G. *Garizim und Synagoge: Traditionsgeschichtliche Untersuchungen zur samaritanischen Religion in der aramäischen Periode.* RGVV 30. Berlin: de Gruyter, 1971.

Klijn, A. F. J. "Stephen's Speech: Acts VII, 2–53." *NTS* 4 (1957–58) 25–31.

———. "The Sources and Redaction of the Syriac Apocalypse of Baruch." *JSJ* 1 (1970) 65–76.

Klinzing, G. *Die Umdeutung des Kultes in der Qumrangemeinde und im Neuen Testament.* SUNT 7. Göttingen: Vandenhoeck & Ruprecht, 1971.

Kobelski, P. J. *Melchizedek and Melchireša'.* CBQMS 10. Washington: CBA, 1981.

Koch, K. "'ōhel." *TDOT* 1 (1974) 118-30.

Koester, C. "The Origin and Significance of the Flight to Pella Tradition." *CBQ* 51 (1989) 90-106.

Koester, H. " 'Outside the Camp': Hebrews 13:9-14." *HTR* 299-315.

Kosmala, H. *Hebräer — Essener — Christen: Studien zur Vorgeschichte der frühchristlichen Verkündigung.* SPB 1. Leiden: Brill, 1959.

Kraft, H. *Die Offenbarung Johannes.* HNT 16A. Tübingen: Mohr/Siebeck, 1974.

Kraus, H.-J. *Psalmen.* 2 vols. BKAT 15. 5th ed. Neukirchen-Vluyn: Neukirchener, 1978.

Krodel, G. *Acts.* ACNT. Minneapolis: Augsburg, 1986.

Kümmel, W. G. *Introduction to the New Testament.* Nashville: Abingdon, 1975.

Kuss, O. *Der Brief an die Hebräer.* RNT 8/1. Regensburg: Pustet, 1966.

Lambrecht, J., ed. *L'Apocalypse johannique et l'apocalyptique dans le Noveau Testament.* BETL 53. Gembloux: Duculot and Leuven University, 1980.

Laperrousaz, E.-M. "Le Testament de Moise." *Sem* 19 (1970) 1-137.

Larcher, C. *Le Livre de la Sagesse ou la Sagesse de Salomon.* 3 vols. EBib. Paris: Lecoffre, 1983-85.

Lehmann, M. R. "A Re-interpretation of 4 Q Dibrê Ham-me'oroth." *RevQ* 5 (1964) 106-10.

Levine, B. A. "The Temple Scroll: Aspects of its Historical Provenance and Literary Character." *BASOR* 232 (1978) 5-23.

Licht, J. מגילת ההודיות. Jerusalem: Bialik, 1957.

Lindars, B. *The Gospel of John.* NCB. Grand Rapids: Eerdmans, 1972.

Lohmeyer, E. *Die Offenbarung Johannes.* 2d ed. HNT 16. Tübingen: Mohr/Siebeck, 1953.

Lohse, E. *Die Texte aus Qumran: Hebräisch und Deutsch.* München: Kösel, 1971.

Luck, U. "Himmlisches und irdisches Geschehen im Hebräerbrief." *NovT* 6 (1963) 192-215.

McCarter, P. K. *I Samuel.* AB 8. Garden City: Doubleday, 1980.

——. *II Samuel.* AB 9. Garden City: Doubleday, 1984.

McCarthy, D. J. "II Samuel and the Structure of the Deuteronomic History." *JBL* 84 (1965) 131–38.

Macdonald, J. *The Theology of the Samaritans.* London: SCM, 1964.

McKelvey, J. *The New Temple: The Church in the New Testament.* Oxford Theological Monographs. Oxford: University, 1969.

MacNamara, M. *The New Testament and the Palestinian Targum to the Pentateuch.* AnBib 27. Rome: Biblical Institute, 1966.

———. *Targum and Testament. Aramaic Paraphrases of the Hebrew Bible: A Light on the New Testament.* Shannon: Irish University. 1972.

MacRae, G. W. "Heavenly Temple and Eschatology in the Letter to the Hebrews." *Semeia* 12 (1978) 179–99.

Manson, W. *The Epistle to the Hebrews: An Historical and Theological Reconsideration.* Baird Lectures 1949. London: Hodder & Stoughten, 1951.

Mansoor, M. *The Thanksgiving Hymns.* STJD 3. Grand Rapids: Eerdmans, 1961.

Mare, W. H. "Acts 7. Jewish or Samaritan in Character?" *WTJ* 34 (1971–72) 1–21.

Martyn, J. L. *History and Theology in the Fourth Gospel.* 2d ed. Nashville: Abingdon, 1979.

———. *The Gospel of John in Christian History: Essays for Interpreters.* New York: Paulist, 1978.

Meeks, W. A. *The Prophet-King: Moses Traditions and the Johannine Christology.* NovTSup 14. Leiden: Brill, 1967.

Metzger, B. M. *A Textual Commentary on the Greek New Testament.* London: United Bible Societies, 1971.

Michel, O. *Der Brief an die Hebräer.* MeyerK 13. Göttingen: Vandenhoeck & Ruprecht, 1975.

Michaelis, W. *"skēnē, ktl."* *TDNT* 7 (1971) 368–94.

Moberly. R. W. L. *At the Mountain of God: Story and Theology in Exodus 32–34.* JSOT Supplement 22. Sheffield, 1983.

Moffatt, J. *A Critical and Exegetical Commentary on the Epistle to the Hebrews.* ICC. Edinburgh: Clark, 1924.

Montefiore, H. W. *The Epistle to the Hebrews.* Black's New Testament Commentaries. London: Black, 1964.

Mosis, R. *Untersuchungen zur Theologie des chronistischen Geschichtswerkes.* Freiburger theologische Studien 92. Freiburg: Herder, 1973.

Munck, J. *Paul and the Salvation of Mankind.* Richmond: Knox, 1959.

Mundle, W. "Die Stephanusrede Apg 7: eine Märtyrerapologie." *ZNW* 20 (1921) 133–47.

Muñoz Leon, D. *Gloria de la Shekinah en los targumim del Pentatuco.* Madrid: Consejo Superior de Investigaciones Cientificas, 1977.

Murphy, F. J. *The Structure and Meaning of Second Baruch.* SBLDS 78. Atlanta: Scholars, 1985.

Murphy-O'Connor, J. "A Literary Analysis of Damascus Document VI,2–V111,3." *RB* 78 (1971) 210–32.

——. "The Original Text of CD 7:9–8:2." *HTR* 64 (1971) 379–86.

Myers, J. M. *I Chronicles.* AB 12. Garden City: Doubleday, 1965.

Nauck, W. "Zum Aufbau des Hebräerbriefes." In *Judentum, Urchristentum, Kirche: Festschrift für Joachim Jeremias,* edited by W. Eltester. BZNW 26 Berlin: Töpelmann, 1960.

Neusner, J. *Eliezer Ben Hyrcanus: The Tradition and the Man.* SJLA 3–4. Leiden: Brill, 1973.

Newman, M. L. *The People of the Covenant.* Nashville: Abingdon, 1962.

Nickelsburg, G. W. E. "Narrative Traditions in the Paralipomena of Jeremiah and 2 Baruch." *CBQ* 35 (1973) 60–68.

——. *Jewish Literature Between the Bible and the Mishnah.* Philadelphia: Fortress, 1981.

——, ed. *Studies on the Testament of Moses.* SCS 4. Cambridge: SBL, 1973.

North, R. "Theology of the Chronicler." *JBL* 82 (1963) 369–81.

Noth, M. *A History of Pentateuchal Traditions.* Englewood Cliffs: Prentice-Hall, 1972.

——. *Das Buch Josua.* HAT 7. 2d ed. Tübingen: Mohr/Siebeck, 1953.

——. *Exodus: A Commentary.* OTL. Philadelphia: Westminster, 1962.

——. "David and Israel in II Samuel 7." In *The Laws of the Pentateuch and Other Studies.* Philadelphia: Fortress, 1967.

O'Neill, J. C. *The Theology of Acts in Its Historical Setting.* 2d ed.; London: SPCK. 1970.

Pamment, M. "Is There Convincing Evidence of Samaritan Influence on the Fourth Gospel?" *ZNTW* 73 (1982) 221–30.

Perrot, C., and P.-M. Bogaert. *Pseudo-Philon: The Biblical Antiquities.* Vol. 2. SC 230. Paris: Cerf, 1976.

Peterson, D. *Hebrews and Perfection: An Examination of the Concept of Perfection in the Epistle to the Hebrews.* SNTSMS 47. Cambridge: University, 1982.

Prigent, P. "Une trace de liturgie judéo-chrétienne dans le chapitre XXI de l'Apocalypse de Jean." *RSR* 60 (1972) 165–72.

Pummer, R. "The Samaritan Pentateuch and the New Testament." *NTS* 22 (1975–76) 441–43.

Purvis, J. D. "The Fourth Gospel and the Samaritans." *NovT* 17 (1975) 161–98.

Rad, G. von. *Das Geschichtsbild des chronistischen Werkes.* BWANT 3. Stuttgart: Kohlhammer, 1930.

――――. *Studies in Deuteronomy.* SBT 9. London: SCM, 1953.

――――. *Old Testament Theology.* 2 vols. New York: Harper & Row, 1962–65.

――――. "The Tent and the Ark." In *The Problem of the Hexateuch and Other Essays.* Edinburgh: Oliver and Boyd, 1966.

Reicke, B. *Glaube und Leben der Urgemeinde: Bemerkungen zu Apg. 1–7.* ATANT 32. Zürich: Zwingli, 1957.

Richard, E. "Acts 7: An Investigation of the Samaritan Evidence." *CBQ* 39 (1977) 190–208.

――――. *Acts 6:1–8:4. The Author's Method of Composition.* SBLDS 41. Missoula: Scholars, 1978.

――――. "The Polemical Character of the Joseph Episode in Acts 7." *JBL* 98 (1979) 255–67.

――――. "The Creative Use of Amos by the Author of Acts." *NovT* 24 (1982) 37–53.

Rissi, M. *The Future of the World: An Exegetical Study of Revelation 19:11–22:5.* London: SCM, 1972.

――――. *Die Theologie des Hebräerbriefs: Ihre Verankerung in der Situation des Verfassers und seiner Leser.* WUNT 41. Tübingen: Mohr/Siebeck, 1987.

Robinson, J. A. T. *Redating the New Testament.* Philadelphia: Westminster, 1976.

Rochais, G. "La formation du prologue (Jn 1,1–18)." *ScEs* 37 (1985) 5–44.

Rudolph, W. *Chronikbücher.* HAT 21. Tübingen: Mohr/Siebeck, 1955.

Safrai, S., and M. Stern, eds. *The Jewish People in the First Century.* CRINT 1/1. Assen: Van Gorcum, 1974.

Sandmel, S. *Philo of Alexandria: An Introduction.* Oxford: University, 1979.

Scharlemann, M. H. *Stephen: A Singular Saint.* AnBib 34. Rome: Biblical Institute, 1968.

Schenke, H.-M. "Erwägungen zum Rätsel des Hebräerbriefes." In *Neues Testament und christliches Existenz: Festschrift für Herbert Braun zum 70. Geburtstag,* edited by H. D. Betz and L. Schottroff. Tübingen: Mohr/ Siebeck, 1973.

Schierse, F. J. *Verheissung und Vollendung: Zur theologischen Grundfrage des Hebräerbriefes.* Münchener theologische Studien 1.9. Munich: Zink, 1955.

Schiffman, L. H. "Merkavah Speculation at Qumran: The 4 Q Serek Shirot 'Olat ha-Shabbat." In *Mystics, Philosophers, and Politicians: Essays in Jewish Intellectual History in Honor of Alexander Altmann,* edited by J. Reinharz and D. Swetschinski. Durham: Duke University, 1982.

Schlatter, D. A. *Der Evangelist Johannes: Wie er spricht, denkt und glaubt. Ein Kommentar zum vierten Evangelien.* Stuttgart: Calver, 1930.

Schmitt, R. *Zelt und Lade als Thema alttestamentlicher Wissenschaft: Eine kritische forschungsgeschichtliche Darstellung.* Gütersloh: Gerd Mohn, 1972.

Schnackenburg, R. *The Gospel According to St John.* Vol. 1. New York: Herder & Herder, 1968.

Schneider, G. *Die Apostelgeschichte.* 2 vols. HTKNT 5. Freiburg: Herder, 1980.

Schoeps, H.-J. *Theologie und Geschichte des Judenchristentums.* Tübingen: Mohr/Siebeck, 1949.

Schulz, *Komposition und Herkunft der johanneischen Reden.* BWANT 5/1. Stuttgart: Kohlhammer, 1960.

Schürer, E., G. Vermes, F. Millar, and M. Black. *The History of the Jewish People in the Age of Jesus Christ.* 3 vols. Revised ed. Edinburgh: Clark, 1973–87.

Schüssler Fiorenza, E. *Priester für Gott: Studien zum Herrschafts- und Priestermotiv in der Apokalypse.* NTAbh 7. Münster: Aschendorff, 1972.

———. "Cultic Language in Qumran and in the NT." *CBQ* 38 (1976) 159–77.

———. "Composition and Structure of the Book of Revelation." *CBQ* 39 (1977) 344–66.

———. *The Book of Revelation: Justice and Judgment.* Philadelphia: Fortress, 1985.

Schweizer, E. *The Good News According to Mark.* Atlanta: Knox, 1970.

———. "Concerning the Speeches in Acts." In *Studies in Luke-Acts,* edited by L. E. Keck and J. L. Martyn. Philadelphia: Fortress, 1980.

Scobie, C. H. H. "The Origins and Development of Samaritan Christianity." *NTS* 19 (1972–73) 390–414.

——. "The Use of Source Material in the Speeches of Acts III and VII." *NTS* 25 (1979–80) 399–421.

Scroggs, R. "The Earliest Hellenistic Christianity." In *Religions in Antiquity: Essays in Memory of Erwin Ramsdell Goodenough,* edited by J. Neusner. Studies in the History of Religions (Supplements to *Numen*). Leiden: Brill, 1968.

Shepherd, M. *The Pascal Liturgy and the Apocalypse.* Ecumenical Studies in Worship 6. Richmond: Knox, 1960.

Sheppard, G. T. *Wisdom as a Hermeneutical Construct: A Study in the Sapientializing of the Old Testament.* Berlin: de Gruyter, 1980.

Shinan. A. "The Palestinian Targums—Repetitions, Internal Unity, Contradictions." *JJS* 36 (1985) 72–87.

Simon, M. "Saint Stephen and the Jerusalem Temple." *JEH* 2 (1951) 127–42.

——. "La prophétie de Nathan et le Temple." *RHPR* 32 (1952) 41–58

Smith, D. M. "Johannine Christianity: Some Reflections on Its Character and Delineation." *NTS* 21 (1974–75) 222–48.

Soggin, J. A. *Joshua: A Commentary.* OTL. London: SCM, 1972.

Spicq, C. "Le Siracide et la structure littéraire du Prologue de Saint Jean." In *Mémorial Lagrange.* Paris: Gabalda, 1940.

——. *L'Epître aux Hébreux.* 2 vols. EBib. Paris: Gabalda, 1952–53.

—— "L'Epître aux Hébreux, Apollos, Jean-Baptiste, les Hellénistes et Qumrân." *RevQ* 1 (1959) 365–90.

Spiro, A. "Stephen's Samaritan Background." In *Acts,* by J. Munck. AB 31. Garden City: Doubleday, 1967.

Steck, O. H. *Israel und das gewaltsame Geschick der Propheten: Untersuchung zur Überlieferung des deuteronomistischen Geschichtsbildes im Alten Testament, Spätjudentum und Urchristentum.* WMANT 23. Neukirchen-Vluyn, Neukirchener, 1967.

Stemberger, G. "Die Stephanusrede (Apg 7) und die jüdische Tradition." In *Jesus in der Verkündigung der Kirche,* edited by A. Fuchs. SNTU 1. Friestadt, Austria: Ploechl, 1976.

Stone, M. E. "Baruch, Rest of the Words of." *EncJud* 4 (1971) 276–77.

——, ed. *Jewish Writings of the Second Temple Period.* CRINT 2. Assen and Philadelphia: Van Gorcum and Fortress, 1984.

Strack, H. L. *Introduction to the Talmud and Midrash.* New York: Jewish Publication Society, 1931.

Strecker, G. *Das Judenchristentum in den Pseudoclementinen.* TU 70. 2d ed. Berlin: Akademie, 1981.

Strugnell, J. "The Angelic Liturgy at Qumrân: 4 Q Serek Šîrôt 'Ôlat Haššabāt." VTSup 7 (1959) 318–45.

Surkau, H.-W. *Martyrien in jüdischer und frühchristlicher Zeit.* FRLANT 36. Göttingen: Vandenhoeck & Ruprecht, 1938.

Swete, H. B. *The Apocalypse of St John.* 3d ed. London: Macmillan, 1911.

Swetnam, J. " 'The Greater and More Perfect Tent.' A Contribution to the Discussion of Hebrews 9,11." *Bib* 47 (1966) 91–106.

Sylva, D. D. "The Function and Meaning of Acts 7:46–50." *JBL* 106 (1987) 261–75.

Tcherikover, V. A., and A. Fuks. eds. *Corpus Papyrorum Judaicarum.* Vol. 1. Cambridge: Harvard, 1957.

Theissen, G. *Untersuchungen zum Hebräerbrief.* SNT 2. Gütersloh: Mohn, 1969.

Thompson, J. W. *The Beginnings of Christian Philosophy: The Epistle to the Hebrews.* CBQMS 13. Washington: CBA, 1982

Thompson, L. "Cult and Eschatology in the Apocalypse of John." *JR* 49 (1969) 330–50.

Throntveit, M. A. *When Kings Speak: Royal Speech and Royal Prayer in Chronicles.* SBLDS 93. Atlanta: Scholars, 1987.

Tiede, D. L. *Prophecy and History in Luke-Acts.* Philadelphia: Fortress, 1980.

Torrey, C. C. *The Lives of the Prophets.* Philadelphia: SBL, 1946.

VanderKam, J. C. *Textual and Historical Studies in the Book of Jublilees.* HSM 14. Missoula: Scholars, 1977.

Vanhoye. A. " 'Par la tente plus grand et plus parfaite . . .' (He 9,11)." *Bib* 46 (1965) 1–28.

———. *La structure littéraire de l'Epître aux Hébreux.* 2d ed. Paris: Desclée de Brouwer, 1976.

———. *Old Testament Priests and the New Priest According to the New Testament.* Studies in Scripture. Petersham: St. Bede's, 1986.

Wacholder, B. Z. *Eupolemos: A Study of Judaeo-Greek Literature.* Cincinnati: Hebrew Union College, 1974.

———. "The Letter from Judah Maccabee to Aristobulus: Is 2 Maccabees 1:10b–2:18 Authentic?" *HUCA* 49 (1978) 89–133.

———. *The Dawn of Qumran: The Sectarian Torah and the Teacher of Righteousness.* Cincinnati: Hebrew Union College, 1983.

Wellhausen, J. *Prolegomena to the History of Israel.* Edinburgh: Black, 1885.

Wengst, K. *Bedrängte Gemeinde und verherrlichter Christus: Der histo-rische Ort des Johannesevangeliums als Schlüssel zu seiner Interpretation.* Biblisch-theologische Studien 5. 2d ed. Neukirchen-Vluyn: Neukirchener, 1983.

Wenschkewitz, H. "Die Spiritualizierung der Kultusbegriffe Temple, Priester und Opfer im Neuen Testament." *Angelos* 4 (1932) 70–230.

Westcott, B. F. *The Gospel According to St. John.* London: Murray, 1889.

———. *The Epistle to the Hebrews.* 2d ed. London: Macmillan, 1892.

Wilckens, U. *Die Missionsreden der Apostelgeschichte: Form- und tradi-tionsgeschichtliche Untersuchungen.* WMANT 32. 3d ed. Neukirchen-Vluyn: Neukirchener, 1974.

Williamson, H. G. M. *1 and 2 Chronicles.* NCBC. Grand Rapids: Eerd-mans, 1982.

Williamson, R. *Philo and the Epistle to the Hebrews.* WLGHJ 4. Leiden: Brill, 1970.

———. "The Background of the Epistle to the Hebrews." *ExpT* 87 (1976) 232–37.

Wilson, A. M. and L. Wills. "Literary Sources of the Temple Scroll." *HTR* 75 (1982) 275–88.

Winston, D. *The Wisdom of Solomon.* AB 43. Garden City: Doubleday, 1979.

———. *Philo of Alexandria: The Contemplative Life, the Giants, and Selec-tions.* Classics of Western Spirituality. New York: Paulist, 1981.

Woude, A. S. van der. *Die messianischen Vorstellungen der Gemeinde von Qumrân.* Studia Semitica Neerlandica 3. Assen: van Gorcum, 1957.

Yadin, Y. "The Dead Sea Scrolls and the Epistle to the Hebrews." *Scripta Hierosolymitana* 4 (1958) 36–55.

York, A. D. "The Dating of Targumic Literature." *JSJ* 5 (1974) 49–62.

Young, N. H. "τοῦτ᾽ ἔστιν τῆς σαρκὸς αὐτοῦ (Heb. x.20): Apposition, Depen-dent or Explicative?" *NTS* 20 (1973–74) 100–4.

Zimmerli, W. *Ezekiel 2.* Hermeneia. Philadelphia: Fortress, 1983.

INDEX

(Italicized numbers indicate reference to chart or table)

OLD TESTAMENT

207

NEW TESTAMENT

PSEUDEPIGRAPHA

DEAD SEA SCROLLS

PHILO

LATER JEWISH AND SAMARITAN SOURCES

OTHER EARLY CHRISTIAN LITERATURE

Politics in the
Postwar American West

Edited by Richard Lowitt

UNIVERSITY OF OKLAHOMA PRESS : NORMAN AND LONDON

Library of Congress Cataloging-in-Publication Data

Politics in the postwar American West / edited by Richard Lowitt.
     p.   cm.
    Includes bibliographical references (p.   ) and index.
    ISBN 0-8061-2711-2 (alk. paper)
    1. West (U.S.) — Politics and government. I. Lowitt, Richard, 1922–
F595.2.P65 1995
978'.033 — dc20   94-43095
                                                    CIP

Book design by Bill Cason

The paper in this book meets the guidelines for permanence and durability of the Committee on Production Guidelines for Book Longevity of the Council on Library Resources, Inc. ∞

1 2 3 4 5 6 7 8 9 10

Contents

Maps

Preface

The essays in this volume examining aspects of western state politics in the latter half of this century follow no prescribed form. The authors were free to scrutinize their states in any way they chose. Consequently the range of the chapters varies widely. Some authors made an interpretative survey of the political framework of their state. Others focused on a specific issue, such as an election, incident, or piece of legislation that aroused controversy among state citizens or, as in the case of Alaska, with the federal government. As would be expected in a volume examining western politics, the environment has to be taken into account. Utilization of water resources and Native Americans' claims to the land merit significant attention. Although no state is examined comprehensively, in toto, the chapters present a fairly complete portrait of causes and concerns affecting politics in the American West in the last decades of this century.

Two definitions are in order: What is the scope of the American West? And what constitutes politics? For the purpose of this volume, the American West comprises all of the plains states, from the Dakotas to Texas, and extends westward to the Pacific coast and beyond to include Alaska and Hawaii—nineteen states in all. Politics is also broadly defined. According to political scientist Harold Lasswell, politics is who gets what, when, and how; the study of politics is a study of influence and the influential. These definitions are generally appropriate to the essays in this volume. Electoral politics, the most obvious form of the struggle for power, is the subject of several chapters, but political culture in the West is also considered in a broader context. Besides partisan politics, conflicts over the control and use of available resources (in large part with the federal government), mediation of state authority through local agencies or groups seeking control, efforts at modernization, and concern about the impact of outside interests within a state are included within this broader framework.

Not all of the authors are historians, but all have considered their states within a historical context, ranging from largely narrative to deliberately interpretive. The overall design is to achieve a composite portrait that is more than the sum of its nineteen parts. What emerges is an American West that, while it relates to the mainstream, is still very much a distinctive part of the United States.

Finally, I wish to express my appreciation to the eighteen authors, who worked hard to meet the assigned deadlines and took all criticisms with good grace (though several of the essays needed no revision). And no one could find a better editor than John Drayton, who took seriously my off-hand suggestion of a volume of this type and thereafter, along with Sarah Nestor, offered guidance that helped to make the project more pleasurable than I had anticipated.

RICHARD LOWITT

POLITICS IN THE POSTWAR AMERICAN WEST

CHAPTER 1

The Crude and the Pure: Oil and Environmental Politics in Alaska

PETER COATES

Overlooking Prince William Sound at the Trans-Alaska Pipeline Terminal, a thirteen-foot bronze monument commemorates the "larger-than-life qualities demanded of the pipeline planners and builders—bravery, strength, tenacity, confidence, and imagination." A brochure explains how this assemblage of five figures is dedicated to these "Twentieth Century pioneers." The sculptor, who (according to the brochure) specializes in depicting "heroic" Americans, describes The Surveyor who faces the massive wall of the coastal range: "Looking toward those mountains . . . he has a feeling of awe, watching the ingenuity of man complete an almost impossible task." The Teamster is hailed as "a unique woman. . . . a woman who wanted to be a pioneer, to build something in possibly the last frontier in the world." Besides including women, the official corporate portrait of twentieth-century pioneering in Alaska is unblemished by aboriginal victims. A third figure, The Workman, a Native Alaskan, is introduced as "a man from another culture, who came together with many other people and did his part."

Yet the most striking feature of Alyeska's celebration of this quintessence of twentieth-century pioneering is its attempt to embrace nature as well as nonwhites and women. Time-honored frontier-busting rhetoric is absent. A subtle distinction is made between the desire to conquer the last frontier and the desire to build something *in* it. The oil industry's public relations euphemisms present the pipeline as simply part of the frontier's fabric. This curious new pioneering without conquest suggests a novel mixture of traditional pride and unfrontierlike humility.

Author's note: The following acronyms occur frequently in the text: ANILCA (Alaska National Interest Lands Conservation Act); ANWR (Arctic National Wildlife Range/ Refuge); APIC (Alaska Public Interest Coalition); EIS (environmental impact statement); NEPA (National Environmental Policy Act); TAPS (Trans-Alaska Pipeline System, refers to both the pipeline project and the consortium that proposed it).

Leaving aside the question of how convincingly Alyeska managed to blend old and new images of pioneering (and whether or not the pipeline project was truly a showpiece of corporate ecological enlightenment), this authorized portrait encourages a belief in the persistence of the Alaskan frontier as a place and a spirit and of pioneering as a process. The oil men are not alone in stoking the fires of frontier mythology in the northland. Ever since the United States acquired "Walrussia" in 1867, its boosters have kept faith in Alaska's role as a northern extension of the West— America's unfinished frontier business. Many of the conservationists and environmentalists with whom these promoters have clashed repeatedly since 1945 also approach Alaska as an integral part (more accurately, a pure reincarnation) of the American West. Although the former express their affection by seeking to avoid rather than repeat the western historical pattern—loving the frontier for what it is, not for what it might become— both camps revere the western frontier and the qualities attributed to it by Frederick Jackson Turner. Contemporary western historians may have renounced their founding father, but these opponents in Alaskan history have been his lay disciples, even if they have never read his work or heard of him.

In 1968 the largest oil field in North America was found in the Alaskan Arctic. That discovery, and the rush to exploit it, underscored the vibrancy of the frontier process. Since the Progressive conservation era, conflict over the disposition of natural resources, generated by clashes between unreconstructed and postfrontier values, has been a staple of western politics and public discourse. Such disputes have been inter- twined with the older struggle between localities and the federal center and further complicated by the fact that Native peoples have not "van- ished." Alaska is no exception.

Western natural politics are increasingly dictated by energy issues. The bitterest controversy in Alaska since statehood (1959) was the furor over the proposed Trans-Alaska Pipeline System (TAPS). TAPS was the most ambitious construction scheme in U.S. history and the most expensive private undertaking in world history. As such, the enterprise prompted irresistible comparisons with earlier feats of frontier engineering such as the transcontinental railroads. The project to transport arctic oil to Valdez spawned a four-year debate (1969–73). TAPS became a cause célèbre, the prime testing ground for the nation's nascent environmental awareness.

By the time statehood was achieved, the oil industry had assumed the lead in the effort to "open up" Alaska, which became an oil state within ten years of entering the Union. In 1958 there was no oil production, but by 1963, oil and gas accounted for 77 percent of Alaska's mineral output.[1] By 1965, largely due to brisk offshore oil and gas production from Cook Inlet, Alaska's income from all forms of natural resource extraction exceeded that from federal military expenditures for the first time in Alaskan history.[2] Oil displaced fisheries as the leading single source of state income in 1967.[3] The first measure of real independence from Washington (and the narrow, tottering economic pillars of fur, salmon, and gold) had been attained, but only through a growing dependence on corporate capitalism.

The thrust of oil exploration had since moved much further north than Cook Inlet. In 1961 the Sinclair Oil Corporation (an American firm that had acquired the first federal leases on the North Slope region) ran a widely distributed advertisement that showed two "restless" petroleum geologists alighting from a helicopter onto the snowy tundra. The caption, "Go and look behind the Ranges," was a quotation from Rudyard Kipling's "The Explorer":

> Something hidden. Go and find it. Go
> and look behind the Ranges—
> Something lost behind the Ranges.
> Lost and waiting for you. Go!

Here were the pathfinders for the new imperialists, who took up the modern oil consumer's burden. Sinclair explained how the nation's "insatiable demand for energy" was pushing its "roving" oil seekers into far-flung and inhospitable corners of the globe—such as the Alaskan Arctic. Others soon followed. After difficulties in Iran, its major source for almost half a century, British Petroleum, eager to diversify operations, acquired Alaskan leases in 1959.

The first state leases were sold in 1964. In common with other western states entering the Union, Alaska was entitled to select a portion of the territory's unappropriated public domain. Alaska's "birthday present" of 102.5 million acres—27 percent of the state—was particularly generous. This amount exceeded that received by all other western states combined. Among the state of Alaska's first selections was 2 million acres of potentially oil-rich terrain along the arctic coast—lands that the state insisted were free of Native use and occupancy.

Two years later, Walter Hickel ("Alaska's Number One Young Businessman")[4] was elected Republican governor on an aggressively prodevelopment platform. A real estate and construction magnate, Hickel had been in the vanguard of the Anchorage-based statehood movement, which believed that what stood between Alaska and progress were artificial barriers such as federal ownership (99.8 percent of Alaska prior to 1959) and conservation policies, not harsh climate and physical environment. On assuming public office (his first), propriety dictated he resign as chairman of the Anchorage Natural Gas Company and as a director of the Anchorage Pipeline Company—both Texas subsidiaries. The latter owned a franchise to supply the city with oil and gas from the nearby Kenai Peninsula, where gas had been discovered following Alaska's first commercial oil strike (1957). Hickel approved the upcoming sale of oil leases on 37,000 acres of the North (Arctic) Slope, which his less ebullient Democratic predecessor had postponed after Native protest.

So far, Native Alaskans had retained comparatively undisturbed possession of their ancestral land base. Native land rights had been guaranteed by the original treaty of purchase from Russia (1867) and those acts establishing the machinery of territorial government (1884 and 1912). The statehood act had also reiterated these rights, but they were jeopardized as soon as the state of Alaska began making its land selections under the terms of statehood. In December 1966, to protect Native interests, the Secretary of the Interior, Stewart Udall, imposed a moratorium on applications for title to unappropriated public domain in Alaska. This so-called "land freeze" was to remain in force until Congress reached a comprehensive settlement of outstanding Native claims. Hickel and other development-minded Alaskans denounced Udall's action as a violation of the letter and spirit of the statehood act. Adamant that nothing should hinder oil development and interfere with the state's selection of lands (a process far from complete), Hickel filed suit in federal district court in February 1967 in a bid (unsuccessful as it turned out) to nullify Udall's freeze.

Atlantic Richfield made the first commercial strike on the state-leased lands in January 1968. Hickel acted impulsively to force an overland connection with the arctic oilfields. For the benefit of the local trucking industry, state bulldozers blazed a four-hundred-mile winter road north from the point at which public roads ended. Of questionable legality in view of the freeze (since extended to cover all public land transactions), the road was an economic disaster and an environmental fiasco, deteriorating into a ditch once the unprotected permafrost was exposed to the spring thaw. Hickel's subsequent nomination as secretary of the interior in the incoming Nixon administration provoked an outcry matched only by the reaction against James Watt in 1981. Discussion of Hickel's oil interests dominated his confirmation hearings.

In early 1969 the Trans-Alaska Pipeline System (TAPS), a loose consortium of oil companies, announced plans to construct a 798-mile, subsurface, hot oil pipeline from Prudhoe Bay south to Valdez, the northernmost ice-free port in the United States. Some three-quarters of the route traversed public domain, so TAPS applied to the Department of the Interior (DOI) in June for a pipeline right-of-way and transportation corridor to allow construction of a parallel road. Approval by the end of the month was desired, so that construction could begin in September. That approval was considered a formality is suggested by the contracts already signed with Japanese steel companies for the pipe.

The federal task force set up to monitor the project expressed concern over the impact of Alaska's climate and physical environment on the engineering, and vice versa. Specific issues were the impact on fish of removing large quantities of gravel needed for construction; the potential disruption of wildlife activities north of the Yukon, especially caribou migration, by human and mechanical intrusion into a hitherto largely undisturbed area; the need for revegetation of disturbed tundra; and, of overriding importance for federal geologists, the impact of conventional burial, on the permafrost underlying much of the proposed route. TAPS's ignorance of Alaskan conditions and Alaskan engineering history astonished and alarmed federal scientists. As Henry W. Coulter of the U.S. Geological Survey recalled (1981), "TAPS simply planned to dig a ditch from one end of Alaska to the other and bury the pipeline in it."[5] Permafrost had caused major headaches for all road and railroad enterprises in Alaska, not least the Alaska Highway and its related Canol military oil pipeline during World War II. The Soviet Union had already encountered similar difficulties while laying gas pipelines in Siberian permafrost. The American steel industry (no doubt miffed at being snubbed by TAPS) stressed that wary conservationists were by no means alarmist.[6] Much of the pipe would need to be raised. Further problems the task force emphasized were the dangers of pollution from land spills; oil discharge into Prince William Sound at the pipeline's southern terminus and during the tanker leg of delivery to refineries on the West Coast of the "lower forty-eight"; seismic dangers—the southern third of the route traversed a prime earthquake zone; and finally, and certainly not least, the unerasable element of Native claims.[7]

The state of Alaska was already growing restless and anxious, its initial euphoria dampened by recognition of the federal government's authority over the pipeline proposal and by the lukewarm popular reaction. The first public hearings on the project in the fall, though required primarily by Udall's freeze, were dominated by environmental impact concerns. (Hickel, as a condition of his confirmation as secretary of the interior, had promised to consult the Senate Interior Committee before modifying Udall's action.) Environmentalists regarded the freeze as the only defense against a wholesale alienation of public lands. Many witnesses worried most about the impact on the Brooks Range, now commonly identified as America's last great wilderness frontier. In his best-selling, prizewinning book *Arctic Dreams* (1986), Barry Lopez, the nature writer, remarks on the uncaring attitude of the vast majority who work at Prudhoe Bay. "A supervisor at an isolated drilling rig smiled sardonically when I asked him if men ever walked away from the buildings in their off-hours. 'You can count the people who care about what's out there on the fingers of one hand.' "[8] But the uproar over the proposed pipeline indicated that large numbers of other Americans did care about the fate of what had customarily been dismissed as a featureless wasteland of ice and snow with no intrinsic value.

Already by the 1950s an advance guard of conservationists (mostly directly acquainted with the country) were rejecting the belief shared by boosters and an earlier generation of conservationists that a combination of remoteness, inhospitability, and worthlessness would always provide informal protection for Alaska (and especially its arctic region). Stimulating this reappraisal of Alaska's vulnerability were the influx of people during and after the war, the impact of new roads and, especially, of the airplane. Since the campaign to protect part of the Arctic got underway in the early 1950s, leading to the establishment of the Arctic National Wildlife Range (ANWR) in 1960, stress had been laid on the area's significance as a living embodiment, a reprise, of the nineteenth-century western frontier. Here in northeastern Alaska was "America's last chance to preserve an adequate sample of the pioneer frontier."[9]

Conservationists involved in postwar Alaskan affairs have frequently agonized, as Frederick Jackson Turner did, over the future of a frontierless United States. Time and again we encounter expositions of the frontier thesis with a conservationist bent. One supporter of ANWR, who had lived in Alaska almost twenty years, warned in 1959, "The American wilderness, to a great extent, made Americans what they are, with an outlook different from that in the older countries, not cramped and crowded. Destroy all wilderness, and you will have changed Americans. Let us Alaskans pass on the secret of Americanism to future generations."[10] ANWR proponents were intent on preserving a cultural setting for vicarious, recreational pioneering and eager to protect an unblemished ecosystem. Conservationists sought to derive the historical benefits for nation and individual of confronting wild nature without inflicting damage on the land itself. Opponents of the range and proponents of TAPS rejected surrogate pioneering for the real thing: the unhindered use of public land and the exploitation of natural resources. Many Alaskans supported the range proposal largely because they assumed that the region offered little of economic value. For example, the Fairbanks Chamber of Commerce backed it, but on the condition that nothing would interfere with the exploitation of valuable minerals, should any be located.[11]

The new value assigned to the Arctic that surfaced in 1969 came as a nasty shock to the oil men and their Alaskan allies. Aesthetic preference for the visually stunning and geologically spectacular had traditionally determined the tastes of preservationism and dictated the choice of landscapes deemed worthy of protection. The Brooks Range certainly invited comparison with the Rocky Mountains prior to the intrusion of the transcontinental railroads a century earlier. What had enchanted Bob Marshall, one of the founders of the Wilderness Society, during his visits to the region in the late 1920s and 1930s were dramatic canyons and peaks overshadowing those of Yellowstone and Yosemite. He never visited or raved about the arctic prairie. The North Slope is waterlogged and flat, dominated by cotton grass tussocks, mosquito-infested pools of water, and shallow lakes. Devoid of any dramatic topography, it is, in short, not a pleasant place to camp, hike, or picnic. But the region was ecologically intact. That this unlikely locale was now prized indicates the emerging ecological perspective that would increasingly inform preservationism and natural resource politics.

And perhaps even more pertinent was the cultural significance the Arctic had acquired. Conservationists and the interested public (the majority of whom had never been to Alaska) were disposed to perceive the region as a recreation of the expanses across which settlers voyaged westward in their prairie schooners. The seductive image of the Alaskan Arctic as an untouched land, offering a chastened nation a rare chance to atone for the past with a gentler and more thoughtful relationship with the American earth suffused the politics of redemption pursued by environmentalists during the TAPS controversy. In 1974 the radical and recent nature of the shift in attitude toward wilderness in general and arctic wilderness in particular struck Bil Gilbert, a jouralist on pipeline assign-ment. Huddled in a tent in the Brooks Range during a blizzard, he reflected, "History is a record of people trying to get out of places like this . . . trying to come in from the cold, get out of caves and tents. . . . [Wilderness] is what has been snapping at our heels like a wolf at a caribou."[12]

Impatient Alaskan boosters interpreted delay as further agonizing evidence of a conspiracy to retard Alaskan development. Alaska and its future had suddenly become tremendously important to other Americans, unfortunately not in a way that served the boosters' cause. They had hoped Hickel's accession to national power would give them a friend at the top and felt betrayed. In fact, Hickel was doing all he could to clear the way for the project. In December 1969, the relevant congressional committees approved his modification of Udall's freeze to allow construction to begin on the haul road, and in March 1970 he announced his intention to issue the permit. The National Environmental Policy Act (NEPA) that had just come into effect required a public statement of the environmental impact of any project that was federally financed or that involved public lands, so the DOI produced an eight-page token document identifying no environ-mental dangers. Hickel was poised to issue the permit when the entire project was paralyzed by a lawsuit filed by five Native villages. A few weeks later, the Wilderness Society, Friends of the Earth, and the Environmental Defense Fund brought their own suit against Hickel, claiming that TAPS violated the maximum width provisions of the Mineral Leasing Act of 1920 and citing the section of NEPA that required the study of alternatives. The judge issued a restraining order forbidding the issue of a road construction permit for the 19.8 miles of the route traversing lands claimed by the Natives of Stevens Village, one of the five communities filing suit. He also ruled that an environmental impact statement (EIS) covering the entire project was needed before all or any part of it could be approved.

Many who regretted the delay as much as the state of Alaska blamed Big Oil's failure to demonstrate technological competence and total inexperience in the field of arctic engineering. Even oil industry allies such as Hickel, sobered (if temporarily) by his elevation to national office, realized they had to go by the book. He reminded fellow Alaskans that a comparable project in any other public land state would be facing similar requirements. In August 1970, the TAPS consortium was replaced by Alyeska Pipeline Service Company, a formal corporate entity that finally acknowledged the supreme importance of settling the Native claims issue, which had the oil men over the proverbial barrel. The Alaska Native Claims Settlement Act of December 1971 extinguished further Native land claims but in return gave Native Alaskans outright ownership of 44 million acres (12 percent of the state) and a cash settlement of almost $1 billion. The act specified that if the secretary of the interior wanted to set aside a pipeline corridor, neither the state of Alaska nor Natives could select lands within it. Half the cash settlement was to be paid from royalties on oil production. This gave the Native community an immediate interest in the project's rapid authorization. That removed one legal obstacle. NEPA and the Mineral Leasing Act remained to be surmounted.

Alyeska tried to improve the oil industry's environmental credibility. Examples of environmental "vandalism," dating back to naval explorations in the 1940s, were suddenly the object of public outrage. Scarification of the tundra ("arctic graffiti") inflicted by the tracks of exploratory "cat" (caterpillar tractor) trains received a lurid high profile in conservation journals. Indignation also ran high over piles of trash, notably the fifty-five-gallon fuel drum. Rates of biodegradation in the Arctic—whose lack of precipitation qualifies it for desert status—are as slow as in the Grand Canyon. It had become a commonplace observation that no natural environment, with the possible exception of the hot deserts, was as poorly equipped to withstand and conceal the traces of industrial humankind and its technology as the arctic cold desert. As the federal task force overseeing the project noted, "Orange peelings last months, paper lasts years, wood scraps last decades and metal and plastic are almost immortal."[13] Many of the rusting barrels the oil industry was obliged to move in 1970 were from wartime naval explorations and construction of the Distant Early Warning Line (1953–57).

The now-flourishing corporate use of "ecocredentials" in advertising can be traced to the early years of the TAPS controversy. At pains to replace the industry's hit-and-run image with a caring one, British Petroleum (which owned a majority share in Alyeska) ran an advertisement borrowing its caption from a play by Eugene O'Neill. "Ah, Wilderness!" featured a discarded oil drum dominating an otherwise featureless white desert, solemnly calling it "one of man's most enduring monuments." Clean-up crews ("the Neighborhood Improvement Association") were painstakingly collecting drums and flying them out at great expense because "when B.P. Alaska touches the wilderness, we try to touch it gently."[14] To collect drums and other refuse, a vehicle called the "roll-igon" was devised. Instead of tires or cleated tracks it traveled on inflated rubber bags, so it could be used in summer without damaging the vegetation protecting the permafrost. Advertisements for this gentle giant showed a man lying happily between balloon tires and tundra. This contrasted with the traditional advertising symbols and slogans invoked by Alaskan construction firms and contractors, in which the relentless image of a merciless wilderness survived intact. ERA Helicopters spoke proudly of providing the "hard-working men and machines to help tame Alaska's wilderness."[15]

In January 1971, DOI released its draft EIS. The rather glib 246-page document curtly dismissed the feasibility of other forms of transit (ice-breaking supertanker, jumbo jet, nuclear submarine, railroad) and alter-native pipeline routes (notably via Canada's Mackenzie Valley). Its authors accepted the industry's premise that the TAPS route was the most economically advantageous method of transporting arctic oil and the least ecologically disadvantageous. They freely acknowledged, however, the irreversible effect on the environment: "No stipulation can alter the fundamental change that development would bring . . . for those to whom unbroken wilderness is most important, the entire project is adverse . . . because the original character of this corridor area in northern Alaska would be lost forever."[16]

The statement was disowned by Hickel's successor, Rogers C. B. Morton, an easterner with no oil links. Public hearings in Washington, D.C., and Anchorage exposed the extent of opposition at both federal and private levels. The complete record amounted to thirty-seven volumes. The gist of objection was that a feckless DOI study had been governed by a predetermined conclusion and so had failed to study all aspects of the transportation system (a blatant omission being the marine leg) and to consider all alternatives in good faith—including the possibility of no action. Much criticism from private citizens had little to do with tangible environmental or prosaic engineering issues. For some, the pipeline was a symptom of a society and culture hopelessly addicted to supertechnology and built precariously on a profligate and dirty economy powered by nonrenewable fossil fuels. The project served as a springboard for diatribes against many manifestations of a chronic malaise in American life, from electric toothbrushes and smog to the Vietnam war, becoming a highly visible target for the countercultural assault on "technocratic chauvinism."[17]

Advocates stressed the modest, even innocuous nature of the undertaking in terms of the scale of Alaska itself. One Alaskan booster (omitting the area consumed by the oilfields) emphasized that the pipeline corridor would only occupy 60 square miles — one-hundredth of 1 percent of the total area of Alaska. Vide Bartlett, a native-born white Alaskan and widow of a senator, came up with this image of the pipeline's relative insignificance: "If you took a daily newspaper, laid it out to one full double page and stretched across it a piece of ordinary black thread, you'd have some idea of just how much the pipeline is going to take."[18] For preservationists, though, statistics were irrelevant, as the project — in itself evil or benign — was alien in principle to their image of northern Alaska. The potential impact on specific aspects of the natural environment and its biota were largely identifiable, to some extent quantifiable, and with careful planning and construction, mitigable in part. What could not be measured and what was not amenable to redress was the inscrutable yet fatal injury perpetrated by *any* pipeline, which was profane in essence. The authors of the impact statement had recognized this; and as one exasperated oil man remarked, there was nothing anyone could do "if a pipeline five miles away, something he can't see or hear or smell or otherwise sense, is going to ruin a man's experience."[19]

Foremost among interested federal agencies that signaled their dissatisfaction were the Environmental Protection Agency, the Department of Transportation's Office of Pipeline Safety, and to some surprise, the U.S. Army Corps of Engineers. Their reports accepted the need for arctic oil development and repeated the economic and security arguments for Alyeska's pipeline but believed the draft EIS paid insufficient attention to the threat of pollution in Prince William Sound, with its implications for Alaska's biggest employer (if not biggest earner), the fishing industry. Many Americans, including prominent federal experts, remained unconvinced that Alyeska could build a pipeline that could withstand Alaska's environmental hazards and would not hurt the environment unduly. To this must be added the harder stance of those who felt the wrong pipeline route had been chosen and that of the rigid core who wanted the oil left in the ground.

In the spring of 1989, as thousands of outraged Americans were cutting up their Exxon credit cards and mailing the bits to the company's chief executive, the cuddly, charismatic, and now oil-soaked otter became the symbol of Alaska's lost innocence and purity. During the pipeline controversy, the caribou had provided a similar symbolic focus for public anxiety and emotion. The oil industry was under pressure to ensure that pipe raised to avoid permafrost would not impede caribou movement. In view of the short and unpredictable arctic summer season, and the imperative to calve before mosquitoes and other insects became too abundant, the timing of arrival at the coastal calving grounds was crucial. Cows arrived emaciated and exhausted after their long trek from winter ranges in the mountains to the south. There was little margin for error. Almost reflexive references to the transcontinental railroads and the memory of the buffalo were ubiquitous during the pipeline debate. Native Alaskans and white sympathizers pointed out that the indigenous way of life in northern Alaska depended as heavily on caribou as Plains Indian cultures had on the buffalo.

In Alaska in the 1970s, state game laws and oil company regulations precluded anything comparable to the near-extermination of the buffalo on the plains after the coming of the railroads. Slaughter aside, their ultimate fate was obviously linked to habitat usurpation by railroad-facilitated colonization and livestock grazing. There was clearly no danger of the Arctic being settled in this way, but concerns did focus on the project's impact on their breeding and migration patterns. Still, when pipeline opponents looked at caribou, they usually saw buffalo. For these animals (unimpressive as individuals but majestic en masse) were of more than biological significance. In 1971, Kenneth Brower, the son of the former executive director of the Sierra Club, described a three-man trek through the Alaskan Arctic in the summer of 1967. He referred to the "Lewis and Clark Syndrome" of one member of the expedition. "We were a lot like Lewis and Clark, he said as he contemplated the Okpilak River bluffs, which reminded him of the bluffs Lewis and Clark saw on the Missouri. We had seen the same grizzlies and the same great plains, he said, except that here the plains were tundra instead of buffalo grass and the herds were caribou instead of buffalo."[20]

After the hearings in early 1971, the opposition crystallized and formed the Alaska Public Interest Coalition (APIC) to coordinate and intensify the campaign. Shoulder-to-shoulder with established groups such as the Sierra Club, the Wilderness Society, and the Izaak Walton League stood groups representing the new environmentalist generation, such as Friends of the Earth and the Environmental Defense Fund, both litigants in the antipipeline suit. A number of members had no direct or previous interest in Alaska. For the Consumer Federation of America, representing 30 million and involved in campaigns to ensure the safe packaging of hazardous household materials and reduce auto exhaust emissions, the pipeline raised general questions about corporate behavior and government accountability. Although APIC's backbone was the large population centers of the lower forty-eight, it was reinforced by an Alaskan dimension. For many Alaskans the greatest dangers were those associated with the marine leg of the delivery system. The Cordova District Fisheries Union (CDFU), at the center of the dispute over a Valdez terminal, filed its own legal action in April 1971. In Cordova, whose population was one thousand, fishing and fish processing accounted directly for half of the town's employment. Most of the other jobs were in related services.

Any harm to the fishing industry would have tremendous economic consequences for Cordova. The draft EIS had devoted only two pages to this threat. From historical experience, Cordovans were wary of the boom-and-bust cycle associated with the activities of outside resource exploiters such as the fish trusts and mining corporations. Cordova was the port from which copper mined at Chitina by Kennecott, a leading mining corporation, was moved south. In 1938 the mines closed when copper prices collapsed. Fisheries, by contrast, offered a renewable resource if managed on a long-term, sustained-yield basis in pollution-free waters. National environmental organizations accepted the fishers as both ecologists and allies. Yet most Cordovans had more parochial concerns. In an early expression of the not-in-my-backyard (nimby) syndrome, what local residents opposed was not the development of arctic oil or its transportation by pipeline as such, but the location of the terminal at nearby Valdez.[21] Indeed, their conviction that the marine dangers surpassed those associated with the project's overland section was often accompanied by indifference and downright insensitivity to the ecological value and integrity of the Arctic. Calls for the preservation of the last great wilderness were not persuasive among Cordovans. According to an air taxi operator, "Tundra ain't good for much anyway. But why ruin this?"[22]

The deadline for the final EIS was repeatedly pushed back due to Alyeska's tardiness in providing a comprehensive project description. Once received, the DOI task force proceeded on the assumption that NEPA did not require discussion of anything beyond what Alyeska had submitted. In January 1972 the U.S. circuit court of appeals ruled that NEPA required consideration of alternatives. The final EIS, released in March 1972, amounted to a weighty tome of 3,500 pages. Though replete with warnings about the potential environmental damage and stressing the extent to which information was still inadequate, it restated the general approval given from the start. The authors reemphasized that the national interest in reducing dependence on foreign oil demanded a pipeline across Alaska as soon as possible and one wholly under American control. The plaintiffs in the legal action submitted a 1,300-page rebuttal claiming that DOI had been subservient to the oil industry since the original permit application in June 1969; that there was still no proper discussion of alternative energy sources; that superior transportation alternatives existed—specifically, an oil and gas corridor through Canada; and that the economic and national security data were specious and distorted. Many opinions expressed in the body of the statement did not uphold the official conclusion concerning national security. Certain federal officials denied that arctic oil would significantly reduce dependence on imports, dismissed the contention that Canadian involvement was a security threat, and conceded the environmental advantages of a Canadian route. In the wake of Pearl Harbor, the vulnerability of American sea lanes had been the primary justification for choosing an interior route for a highway to geopolitically strategic yet exposed Alaska. Thirty years later, DOI argued that national security considerations dictated a tanker route down the West Coast, the views of the secretary of state and Department of Defense notwithstanding.[23]

In May 1972 Morton announced his decision to issue the permits. Some who had objected to the project since 1969 were now satisfied, won over by federally stipulated design modifications: installation of automatic leak detection and valve shut-off systems, underpasses and ramps to allow big game to cross elevated sections of pipe, and contingency measures to contain oil spills at Valdez. Others remained unsatisfied, and the opponents gained fresh recruits that summer when the Canadian Wildlife Federation and its British Columbian affiliate, fearing oil spillage along the British Columbian coast, filed their own suits against Alyeska and DOI. In August, the injunction against the pipeline based on noncompliance with NEPA was dissolved. In October, however, the federal appeals court in Washington, D.C., decided that approval must await congressional amendment of the Mineral Leasing Act's width provisions. In February 1973, the same court ruled conclusively that the permits Morton was about to issue violated the act. It judiciously declined to rule on the adequacy of the environmental impact statement. This left unresolved the fundamental issue of whether or not NEPA's EIS provision was primarily a procedural matter, requiring only that environmental impact—adverse or benign—be formally considered.

Alaskan advocates were fond of recalling the free hand enjoyed by the military builders of the Alaska Highway thirty years before the advent of popular environmentalism and the demands of NEPA. They observed that conservationist sensibilities would have been brushed aside and the current intricate debate over the sensitivity of the engineering abruptly terminated in the event of a wartime situation or comparable emergency.[24] That critical event turned out to be the energy crisis. Sen. Frank Moss (a Democrat from Utah) judged that interest in caribou was a full-gas-tank phenomenon: "I cannot get overly upset about observing the ritual of the mating season for Alaskan caribou when in the city of Denver last weekend it was almost impossible to find gas."[25] By the spring of 1973 many of the unreconciled had adopted (if reluctantly) the so-called Canadian alternative as the most effective way to fight the pipeline project in Congress, the new arena for the conflict as proponents worked at amending the Mineral Leasing Act. The "leave-it-in-the-ground" strategy was impractical. Brock Evans, APIC's chair, offered malcontented environmentalists (many of them Canadian) a hard-headed justification for this considerable shift in policy. Conceding that most environmentalists in their hearts wanted to scuttle arctic oil development altogether, he explained to a Canadian skeptic, "We could not last thirty seconds in any Senator's office by talking about just leaving the oil in the ground—not when the oil companies are shutting down gas stations everywhere."[26]

A Canadian route attracted considerable public and congressional support from easterners and midwesterners for economic as well as environmental reasons, those regions being more dependent on oil imports than was the West. Minnesota and Indiana Senators Walter Mondale and Birch Bayh sponsored a bill to remove the final decision on the pipeline from DOI and allow the National Academy of Sciences to study all aspects of alternative routes, leaving the final decision up to Congress. Mondale (like many project opponents) was convinced that Alyeska wanted oil delivered to the West Coast so that it could export a significant quantity to Japan.[27] Mondale charged the Nixon administration with deliberately misrepresenting the position of the Canadian government, producing documents purporting to show its receptivity to transporting Alaskan oil.[28]

Many Canadian environmentalists, however, were outraged by the American support for a pipeline through Canada. There is no ecological frontier (using "frontier" in the old European sense) between the American and Canadian Arctic. As Friends of the Earth emphasized, "Tundra and caribou have no nationality."[29] APIC's policy subordinated ecological principles not only to political exigencies but also to nationalistic requirements. APIC's yardstick was not the amount of northern wilderness affected. It was the quantity of *American* wilderness. Whatever its other ecological advantages, a pipeline down the Mackenzie River being considerably longer than the Alyeska route to the Pacific would affect far more wilderness. American environmentalists, their Canadian counterparts charged, were quite happy to sacrifice Canada's own pristine North.

The crucial breakthrough for the pipeline project (if not the formal victory) came on 17 July 1973, when the Senate narrowly passed Alaska Sen. Mike Gravel's amendment to the official bill sponsored by Washington State Senator Henry M. Jackson, which sought to release the project from further legal delay by declaring that DOI had fulfilled all of NEPA's requirements. Vice-President Spiro Agnew used his tie-breaking power to cast the decisive vote. (Many who supported the project, not least Senator Jackson, who had been NEPA's sponsor, deplored the way the project was advanced at NEPA's expense.) Despite powerful backing from DOI, the Nixon administration, organized labor, and the state of Alaska, only the energy panic had secured widespread congressional and popular support. Few Americans had been moved by Alaskan boosters' emphasis on the value of oil development to the state's economy. Leading DOI officials conceded that the "vast majority" of the huge quantity of mail received opposed the pipeline.[30] Senator Gravel also acknowledged this, on and off the record. If a national referendum was held, he told the Alaskan press in the spring of 1973, the project "would probably be defeated."[31] In the throes of the energy squeeze, environmentalism (and the integrity of NEPA) seemed a luxury to project advocates and politicians. The American way of life and the United States' status in the world depended on that pipeline. As Representative Craig Hosmer (a Republican from California) put it, "To preserve the 7,680 acres that would be occupied by the pipeline seems an inordinate price to pay for fuel rationing, cold homes, cold schools, and blackmail by the Arab world."[32] On 6 October 1973, Egypt and Syria invaded Israel and, in retaliation for U.S. military aid to the latter, the Arab members of the Organization of Petroleum Exporting Countries (OPEC) imposed an embargo on oil exports to the United States. The pipeline became the flagship of Nixon's Project Independence to enhance national energy autonomy. Only five senators and fourteen members of the House voted against the final authorization bill in November 1973. Alaska's congressional delegation of three rejoiced that their state's value as a natural resource storehouse had at last been recognized.

Those who had battled the pipeline project did, however, derive considerable consolation from the Alaska National Interest Lands Conservation Act (ANILCA) of 1980, which placed 104 million acres under some sort of federal protection. Over half of the allocation was within the wilderness area system. Despite the glaring fact of the pipeline, the conceit of Alaska as a New World reborn was spectacularly revived for the ANILCA campaign. The division of control over Alaska's land and natural resources that began with statehood and was accelerated by oil discovery in 1968 might have seemed a complete process. The state of Alaska, Native Alaska, the oil industry, and the conservationist community (private groups and federal agencies) had all, in turn, received their shares. Yet the degree of resolution was deceptive. Conflict has persisted as parties have sought to defend or enlarge their gains.

Production from Prudhoe Bay has passed its high point, and the last drops of crude from it and the neighboring Kuparuk field are expected to flow through the pipeline early next century. Alaska's boosters and congressional delegation, their eyes on the oil within the Arctic National Wildlife Refuge (ANWR, the former wildlife range, renamed and extended in 1980), still consider the "dangers of dependency on foreign supplies" their winning card. Opening the coastal plain of the refuge to drilling was the centerpiece of the Bush energy policy. Iraq's invasion of Kuwait in 1990 appeared to have ended the breathing space opponents gained from the Exxon spill of April 1989, but in November 1991, Senate opponents successfully filibustered an administration-backed bill that would have opened the refuge. Environmentalists, encouraged by the advent of the Clinton-Gore administration, now aim to secure permanent protection for the coastal plain through wilderness designation.

Native Alaska is split over drilling in ANWR. The seven-thousand strong Gwitch'in Nation—consisting of caribou-dependent villages scattered across northeast Alaska and northwest Canada—leads the opposition. Coastal Inupiat organizations, having enjoyed oil royalties, favor drilling (with safeguards, of course). This reflects a larger division within Native Alaska that the Alaska Native Claims Settlement Act of 1971 enshrined rather than resolved. The act granted Natives a piece of the state equal to 12 percent of its total area, but within a Euro-American, capitalist framework and on corporate terms. The 40 million acres are controlled by Native corporations, in which all Alaska Natives hold shares. ANCSA's provision that individual shares could be sold on the open market as of 1992 has been forestalled by measures such as "Native preference" (whereby the corporation has the first right of refusal). Should a Native corporation go bankrupt or be taken over, however, Native lands may sooner or later serve as a conduit for outside influence. Hundreds of thousands of acres within national parks, forests, and wildlife refuges are owned by Native corporations that need to generate revenue for their shareholders. If environmentalists cannot find the means to buy these holdings, Native corporations may be forced into leasing their lands to the logging industry. Alaska's current governor, a proudly unreconstructed Walter Hickel, is fundamentally hostile to the public purchase of private lands and is fighting efforts to use Exxon oil spill settlement funds to buy holdings in southeast and southcentral Alaska. Entering the 1990 race on a platform resurrected from 1966, he won on the votes of Anchorage and Alaska's other major urban center, Fairbanks. Perhaps most fanciful of the grand schemes he has aired is his plan for an underwater pipeline to carry Alaskan water to parched California.

Just as it is too early to assess the long-term ecological damage from the Exxon spill (1989), it is too soon to measure the long-term impact on the oil industry's relationship with the state of Alaska. The state's casual attitude to regulation during the 1980s was as culpable as Alyeska's shoddy approach to safety. The Department of Environmental Conservation, supposedly the official watchdog, served instead as Alyeska's poodle. Even at the height of confusion and corporate ineptitude, as the spill spread unchecked during perfect weather and placid seas, there was never any chance that the state would apply its ultimate sanction and shut down the pipeline. That would have been a self-inflicted wound for a state that raked in on average $1.5 billion a year in oil-related income between 1969 and 1987. Alaska, dependent for 80 percent of its revenue on oil taxes and royalties (from which each Alaskan annually receives circa $900), may lack the will to tighten the screws on its benefactor.[33]

Arctic oil cannot be exported to Japan (or anywhere else), but Alaska, like the rest of the American West, has been drawn increasingly into the orbit of the Pacific Rim. Alaska and its natural resource developers have always looked west to Asia, from the Chinese markets for otter pelts that attracted the first Russians in the 1740s to the Japanese fishing fleet in the North Pacific that served as a prime customer for Cook Inlet oil in the 1960s. Today, old growth sitka (peddled by the U.S. Forest Service at a heavily subsidized price) are pulped in the mills of the Japanese-owned

Alaska Pulp Corporation and converted into rayon in Japan, which is then made into clothing in Korea and exported to the United States. The Native economy, too, is becoming integrated with Asia (perhaps reverting to the original historical relationship). Salmon roe from the Yukon, for example, is exported en bloc to satisfy Japanese demand for the delicacy. Alaska may never succeed in transcending its colonial extractive economy or in shaking off the shackles of dependence on the American East or the Pacific East. Perhaps, as Bernard DeVoto suspected of the booming West in the late 1940s, in Alaska today "resentment of its Eastern enslavement has always tended to be less a dislike of the enslavement than the belief that it could be made to pay."[34]

CHAPTER 2

The Cultural Politics of Water in Arizona

PETER IVERSON

Sixteen years ago on a warm Arizona January afternoon, an old man told me stories about his youth. We sat in two chairs outside the front door of his small home on the Fort McDowell Reservation. He remembered the subject of my research, a cantankerous fellow from the Yavapai named Wassaja, or Carlos Montezuma. In another time Montezuma had helped his people avoid eviction from their home; then, in the late 1970s, another threat appeared to the Yavapais because of a proposed dam. If completed, Orme Dam would flood most of the reservation.

In both instances, the old man related, the problem involved water. The Verde River flowed through the small reserve, and thus outsiders coveted Fort McDowell. In some ways the situation had changed dramatically over the past century, for Fort McDowell no longer could claim physical separation from the sprawl of greater metropolitan Phoenix. The relatively new community of Fountain Hills, perched on the reservation doorstep, demonstrated the proximity of outsiders. Yet early or late in the twentieth century, the basic issue remained the same: water.

Those who drive from Phoenix to Fort McDowell must pass Fountain Hills, named as one would guess for a towering fountain created by its developer. That creation symbolized the character of this community, every bit as the quiet Verde did Fort McDowell. In Fountain Hills and Fort McDowell, then, one could see symbols of different values and different hopes. In a larger sense, the political history of modern Arizona may be seen in part in the choices that have been made about water.

One can make too much of these differences. The two worlds of

Author's note: Some of the ideas expressed in this chapter were presented originally at the W. K. Kellogg Foundation National Fellows' Forum in December 1989 in Battle Creek, Michigan, and at "Water in the 20th Century West," a conference held at the Heard Museum in Phoenix, Arizona, in March 1990.

Fountain Hills and Fort McDowell overlap, to be sure. In both communities the kids play basketball; the adults share common anxieties about health care and other matters. Yavapai kids may go to school in Fountain Hills; the grown-ups from Fountain Hills are more than welcome to lose their money in the Fort McDowell Gaming Center. Nonetheless, it is safe to say the Yavapais would never fashion a fountain such as the one they watch spew forth nearby. They have never been much for golf. They are desert people, rooted to the land. They do not use much water. The Yavapais have claimed Fort McDowell as home since the turn of the century; they have claimed the region as home for hundreds of years.

Not far away during the balmy winter months live elderly retirees known locally as snowbirds. The Salt River Valley is one of many destinations for such migratory folks; in Arizona, these temporary residents have made the eastern part of the valley a kind of midwestern aluminum San Juan Capistrano. They return with Nordic steadfastness to golf and gabble in a land blessed with warmth and with water delivered from afar. They are not desert people. They want Saginaw without snow, Ypsilanti without ice.

The snowbirds share much in common with many year-round residents who came to Arizona from the Midwest and other woodlands environments. But while winter visitors began to stream into Phoenix and Tucson generations ago, only a trickle of people accepted the challenge of July. However, as California began to fill up and as air conditioning became widespread, the Arizona alternative became somewhat more feasible. There is an old folk saying in the state that with refrigeration came Republicans. It is probably true.

Even if they came, the visitors did not necessarily like what they saw: the land marked usually by few trees but by sun and wind, heat, insects, and railroads. To employ Mary Austin's phrase for the neighboring Mojave desert Paiute country, they encountered "a land of little rain."[1] As Edward Abbey reminded us in one of his timeless essays, "The BLOB Comes to Arizona," "Ninety per cent of my state is an appalling burn-out wasteland, a hideous Sahara with few oases, a grim bleak harsh overheated sun-blasted God-damned and God-forgotten inferno."[2] "Arizona," he continued cheerfully, "is the native haunt of the scorpion, the solpugid, the sidewinder, the tarantula, the vampire bat, the cosenose kissing bug, the vinegarroon, the centipede, and three species of poisonous lizard: namely the Gila monster, the land speculator and the real estate broker. . . . The water table is falling and during a heavy wind you can see the sand dunes form on Central Avenue in Phoenix." The sheer contrary nature of nature had captivated this particular migrant. "I am describing the place I love," Abbey concluded. "Arizona is my natural native home. Nobody in his right mind would want to live here."[3]

On 26 June 1990, it reached 122 degrees in Phoenix; Coolidge, Arizona, hit a mere 121 three years later on the very same date. But the people keep coming. Rather than a new England, they have appeared determined to create here a new Ohio. This story is part of a larger saga. The tale of the westward expansion of the American people is as much the chronicle of emulation as that of innovation. Crossing the Mississippi River did not cause one to forsake one's religion, one's architecture, or a variety of other cultural forms.

We generally term those belongings "cultural baggage." As Robert Berkhofer suggested thirty years ago in "Space, Time, Culture, and the New Frontier," culture influenced what we wanted to do with the land.[4] People who hailed from a land of lawns and bushes and trees without thorns, from lands of more than a little rain, wanted to recreate that world. They planted certain flowers; they wanted the shade of certain trees. Such replication eased their adjustment to alien terrain. They relied on readily available water to carry out the task. And if the city of Phoenix threatened to prevent them from planting grass in their front yards, as the city contemplated a few years ago for new residents, these folks have proven likely to respond in the irate words of one furious constituent, who spluttered, "It's . . . it's unconstitutional!"

Not only did it appear unconstitutional, it might have seemed unnecessary. The steady progression of American technology inspired in Arizona and elsewhere an almost unshakable faith that the environment can indeed be overcome. It is a tribute to Indian intransigence and a truly arid landscape that so little of Arizona could be occupied by outsiders for so long. Without adequate amounts of water delivered to the land, only limited urban and rural development could take place.

Following the repeated failure of local, state, and private enterprise, the federal government accepted the challenge of the arid West and passed the Reclamation Act of 1902, or the Newlands Act, named after its aptly named congressional sponsor Francis Newlands of Nevada. The movement for irrigation largely was inspired less by a new era than by the old. Irrigation would allow for family farms and homesteads. That irrepressible optimist William Smythe rejoiced, "The green fruit has ripened on the bough of time in the sunshine of events." Smythe's book and chapter titles mirror the gospel he preached. The so-called bible of the irrigation-ists, *The Conquest of Arid America*, included "The Budding Civilization of Arizona."[5]

It would be a new method accompanying an old model. Smythe and others pictured the new federal involvement lending "an element of certainty, of stability, which was sadly lacking in the past." Three years after the passage of the Reclamation Act, Smythe predicted with utmost confidence, "When Uncle Sam puts his hand to a task, we know it will be done. Not even the hysteria of hard times can frighten him away from the work. When he waves his hand toward the desert and says, 'Let there be water!' we know that the stream will obey the command."[6]

The cynical observer may be tempted to mutter at this point, "Ah, those were the days," but it cannot be denied that the twentieth century has witnessed prodigious achievements in the name of progress, accompanied by the wave of Uncle Sam's hand. Not only farmers but urban promoters and speculators quickly benefited from the new efforts in reclamation. The Salt River Project in Arizona is an important regional example of early rural and urban growth spurred by such federal involvement.

The Salt River Valley had suffered the usual failures of private interests to make good on the development of irrigation works. Territorial legisla-tor William ("Bucky") O'Neill had had enough. Observing that the federal government had invested enormous sums in the economies of the East and the South, he argued that it could do the same for Arizona. As Karen Smith noted in *The Magnificent Experiment: Building the Salt River Reclamation Project, 1890–1917*, "The concept of social overhead—that some improvements are worthwhile to society despite their failure to earn a fair return on the capital invested in them—underlay much of the government's efforts in financing internal improvement projects."[7] None-theless, the federal government did little prior to the passage of the Reclamation Act to encourage local boosters. With passage of the act, landowners in the valley had to alter thinking and their way of doing business to fit in with the legislation's terms. They promptly established the Salt River Valley Water Users' Association, with the articles of incorporation seeking "to reconcile reclamation law with territorial vested rights."[8] A month after incorporation, the association received word that the Salt River Project would be among the first big projects to be undertaken. The construction of Roosevelt Dam, completed in 1911, assured the valley of a reliable and sufficient source of water. This engineering achievement, Smith concludes, "was probably the most important turning point in the rise of Phoenix as a major southwestern city."[9]

The very success of the Salt River Project encouraged leaders in later generations to see it in some ways as a model. Jack Williams, former governor of Arizona, in the late 1970s wrote in a small volume published by the Salt River Project, *The Taming of the Salt,* that in a century the people of the area had gone from being "the prisoners of nature" to enjoying "the successful conquest of our physical environment." Even given contemporary environmental problems, Williams concluded, "The evils and dangers of the present day are, I reckon, no greater, no more unconquerable, no more reason for despair than were the hardships and difficulties of a hundred years ago."[10] Williams spoke for most Arizonans. They saw nature as an entity to be conquered and technology as a servant of the people. Despite their frequent bashing of the federal government, they recognized its utility in sponsoring ambitious and far-reaching endeavors well beyond the meager confines of the state budget. When they traveled to Hoover Dam, just over the state boundary, they did not remember the suffering of the laborers who constructed it, nor the gigantic profits of the Six Companies who combined to help create it. When they journeyed to Glen Canyon Dam or lumbered into the inland sea of Lake Powell, they did not rue the submergence of the magnificent sandstone canyons that constituted the land that no one then knew. They saw Roosevelt and Hoover and Glen Canyon dams as monuments to American ingenuity, imagination, and yes, pride.[11]

Such a heritage contributed to the political and cultural environment that prompted the Central Arizona Project (CAP)—the largest of all such technological manipulations. Before discussing that project, which is today under a considerable cloud, it is useful to remember that technology should not bear all of the blame for contemporary problems. It is convenient to lay the blame at the door of technology, but that door has opened because of social, political, and economic priorities. Neither gods nor gremlins built Hoover Dam or Glen Canyon Dam. If a water crisis exists today in Arizona, it exists because people have made choices through the years about this resource. And those choices have been influenced by the cultural baggage brought in from beyond the desert.

Arizona represents a particularly fascinating laboratory in which to study the results of such choices, in part because of the nature of the land and in part because of what a new state it truly is. Established in 1912 as the forty-eight state in the Union, Arizona remained a large state with a small population until after the Second World War. The war ushered in a new age. New air bases, new electronics companies, air conditioning, and the growth of modern transportation networks not only linked Arizona with the rest of the country but also showed other Americans that life in the desert could be not merely managed but desirable. The 1950s brought a previously unimaginable number of immigrants. Abbey recoiled: "The growth figures would shock even a banker. Tucson has grown from a population 45,000 (counting dogs) in 1950" to over 300,000 in the 1970s. Phoenix quadrupled in size from 106,000 in 1950 to 439,000 in 1960.[12] Some of that increase came from annexation as well as in-migration, but the overall result suggested a future of boundless promise. Sure, there were possible problems with the air quality and traffic—but water? History had taught us that one way or another, water would not only be there but would be cheap as well.

That availability and price encouraged enterprises that may seem questionable today but seemed perfectly appropriate at the time. Suburban communities sometimes included artificial lakes. Residents in central Tempe could purchase new homes in the late 1970s with waterfront property; their home addresses of Commodore Place, Whalers Way, and Steamboat Bend Drive attested to their maritime moorings. Other developments in metropolitan Phoenix offered similar vistas. The movement even spread to Casa Grande, which became home to Casa Grande Lakes. Any everywhere you looked you could spot a golf course.

As do other westerners, Arizonans appropriate Indian names for subdivisions, peaks, and freeways, but golf courses usually carry an Anglo-Saxon name. Of course, golf is not exactly indigenous. In Scottsdale, Paradise Valley, and even Tucson, however, golf courses receive a stunning amount of water to produce greens and fairways that are the envy of Ireland. Such decisions are dictated not merely by the pursuit of pleasure but by that cult of individualism that is a guiding force in Arizona politics and may even be perceived as a religion. In a state with so many new people, it is not surprising that individuals often do not feel very responsible for the accumulated impact of choices that contribute to decreasing water quantity or water quality. Personal freedom in building, farming, in the way I want, planting, what I want in and so forth is given top priority, regardless of the ecological cost.

It is easy to batter metropolitan Phoenix on a lot of these matters. However, water use to an important extent is as much a rural as an urban problem. As is generally the case in the arid West, a significant amount of

Arizona's water goes to agriculture rather than to its cities. A recent study estimated that about 85 percent of the water supply goes to agriculture. Municipalities and industry use 8 percent. Mining operations consume 3 percent, and the remaining 3 percent goes to other uses, such as recreation, fish and wildlife, and power generation.[13]

It may be far more satisfying to criticize Phoenix; indeed it is a ritual learned from birth by residents of Pima County. But it is crucial to include rural people in our examination of the politics of water. In Arizona the rural water issue involves both quality and quantity. Nitrates, agricultural chemicals, synthetic organic chemicals, agricultural drainage wells, leading lagoons, sanitary landfills, hazardous waste sites, abandoned dumps, land application, chemical and fuel handling and storage, and the construction, maintenance, and abandonment of wells are all problem areas.[14] Such a list, somehow, does not pop up in cinematic conversations between Ray Kinsella and the ghost of Shoeless Joe Jackson; we would rather our fields be made up of other dreams. We are tempted to see modern agriculture through a lens fashioned a century ago.

The consequences of modern agriculture in Arizona also include salinity. Salinity in the Colorado River and elsewhere is caused by nature and by people, but irrigation is the major culprit in the increasing salinity of such rivers. Increasing salinity means lower crop yields and greater expenses for farmers. Some crops are more tolerant than others, but as Philip Fradkin points out in his book about his journey down the Colorado, *A River No More,* such crops tend to be less valuable. More water and more fertilizer are tempting alternatives.[15]

Most Arizonans believed the advent of the Central Arizona Project would solve any lingering problems with water in the state. Passage of congressional legislation authorizing the project represented a goal pursued arduously and zealously for many years by the state's few representatives in the House of Representatives and the Senate. Arizona's suspicion about the motives of other Colorado River basin states, particularly California, led it to withhold approval of the Colorado River Compact of 1922 until February 1944. Negotiation of the treaty with Mexico over the river, finally completed in 1944, prompted Arizona to conclude its contract with the secretary of the interior over delivery of the state's share of Colorado River water.[16] Approval in Washington, of course, did not actually provide water. State legislators toyed with the idea of using Arizona funds to build the CAP—without any federal assistance. Not surprisingly, the expense of such an expression of the pioneer spirit quickly dampened enthusiasm for the venture. Returning to the more feasible, even traditional, option of federal investment did not automatically loosen purse strings on the Potomac. It would take another generation before the dream became reality.

The executive director of the Central Arizona Project Association, Rich Johnson, later penned a history of the fight to pass the project. Johnson's account is understandably sympathetic to the goal, but even his insider's perspective admits to confusion and compromise in the protracted process. Nonetheless, the CAP came to so symbolize Arizona's own rise and potential that public opposition to it within the state appeared almost nonexistent (except for queries from Indian communities, who were perceived as outside of the workings of state politics at the time, anyway). When President Lyndon B. Johnson signed Senate Bill 1004 into Public Law 90-537 on 30 September 1968, it seemed that at last Arizona's maturity as a state could not be denied. Rich Johnson observed that through the decades of effort on behalf of the project, "Arizona had changed from a struggling frontier state with a vast but largely untapped resources potential, to an aspiring and dynamic society intent upon taking its rightful place of importance in the nation and the world."[17]

Such rhetoric reminds one of that devil to the West, California. Given the history of California and its insatiable thirst, one might have expected Arizona's neighbor to be not entirely neighborly about a fledgling state acquiring something as big as the CAP. One would be absolutely correct. John Saylor, of Pennsylvania—the senior Republican member of the House Interior Committee—was sympathetic to the pleas of his five California colleagues on the committee. He helped block the project until California was paid a ransom for acquiescence. Regardless of drought and overallocation of the Colorado River, California was guaranteed its full entitlement of 4.4 million acre-feet of water every year. If California ever received less, it could demand that the CAP be turned off. Arizona's congressional delegation consented.[18]

The CAP had been promoted so much and for so long that any possible shortcomings in it could not be acknowledged publicly. Former congressman Sam Steiger remembered, "Of course I was for it. Any Arizona politician who wanted any kind of political future had to be for it. Besides, I was on the Interior Committee, which authorized the thing—one of two Arizonans versus five Californians on the committee. If I had voted against it, I would probably have been shot."[19]

Steiger did gain lasting notoriety in Arizona politics and folklore by once shooting one of his burros; he might have been tempted to threaten William Martin, too. An economist at the University of Arizona, Martin had coauthored with Robert Young a volume that actually dared to question the need for the CAP. *Water Supplies and Economic Growth in an Arid Environment* considered what might happen if the project were never constructed. Martin and Young concluded that farmers would continue to contribute to a falling water table, pumping costs would escalate, and some farmers might lose their farms. However, higher costs might spur conservation, and thus there might not be a flood of farmers needing to find other work. For the CAP to make fiscal as well as political sense, it had to deliver water at a lower rate than the cost of depleting the water table. Environmentalist Marc Reisner summarized Martin and Young's findings: "The farmers would make *more* money if they continued pumping groundwater than if they bought water from the CAP. In fact, if the price of distribution systems—which the farmers would presumably have to build themselves—was as high as it promised to be, buying CAP water might be a ticket to bankruptcy."[20]

Even with a decision in 1984 by the Congress to make interest-free loans available to area farmers to reduce their immediate costs of building such systems, the farmers appeared by the 1980s to be confronting a more uncertain future. Yet given the history of inexpensive water, the possibility of CAP escalating water costs seemed implausible to many who would be affected—if, indeed, they bothered to consider the matter at all. In the state, few town dwellers realized how much of Arizona's water already was going to agriculture or the declining contribution of farming to the overall economy. Older residents recalled the "Four Cs" of cattle, cotton, copper, and citrus as the mainstays of that economy, but Arizona in the postwar years had become an entity driven by urban interests. In 1940, agriculture accounted for only 13 percent of personal income in Arizona. The 1940s brought a temporary upturn—to 16 percent in 1950— and then the decline began: to 7 percent in 1960, 3 percent in 1970, and 2 percent in 1980. In addition, almost two-thirds of agricultural land in 1980 was devoted to cotton (47 percent) and alfalfa (16 percent)—hardly the stuff of the old midwestern family farm cherished nostalgically by migrants from that region. With but 4 percent of Arizona cropland in vegetable production and a mere 3 percent in citrus, farmers could hardly claim substantial credit for feeding Arizonans. Ironically, given the availability of inexpensive water prior to the CAP, in a time of urbanization, farmers actually increased their overall acreage in the state. Particularly in Maricopa county, farmers lost lands to burgeoning suburban developments; but they compensated for such reductions by expansion elsewhere.[21]

In the meantime, a new political debate surfaced that drew attention away from agricultural claims on the state's water supply and highlighted one of the CAP's weaknesses. The controversy involved a proposed dam to be built at the site where the Verde and Salt rivers come together. Proponents argued that Orme Dam could store CAP water during the summer months, when demand for it was greatest, and would reduce the chances of flooding in the area below the dam, where the Phoenix metropolitan area was located. At one point in Arizona's political history, opposing a dam would have constituted heresy; opposition to Orme— which emerged from three separate sectors—indicated that times had changed. By the mid-1970s, "tubing" on the Salt River had become a favorite pastime for many Arizonans, and the dam threatened to deny the pleasure of floating down the river on an inner tube on a slightly warm summer afternoon. Environmentalists worried about the flooding of bald eagle habitat. Yavapai residents of the Fort McDowell Reservation faced the prospect of having most of their community inundated.[22]

Non-Indian environmentalists and Indians have not always shared common political ground in modern Arizona, but in the fight over Orme Dam they discovered that their interests overlapped. The eagle habitat was on Yavapai land; environmentalists recognized that others in the general public sympathized with the small Indian reserve seemingly being bullied by federal and state officials. The collapse of the Teton Dam also inspired distrust of the Orme Dam, expected to be a comparable high-earth structure. Hearings on Orme Dam in the summer of 1976 allowed critics to raise publicly many concerns. Supporters' statements only served to heighten opposition. To their surprise, the Yavapais heard utility executive Keith Turley compare Fort McDowell to a barrio that ought to be vacated. They were flabbergasted also by the suggestion that they would actually gain from having their lands flooded, for they "would have a chance to own and operate businesses supplying food, beverages, and recreation equipment"; thus "the reservoir and its periphery would constitute a valuable economic resource base for the tribe, providing an opportunity for tribal income and employment."[23]

By the time the Fort McDowell community voted on the dam, the people could not be swayed by the prospect of sudden wealth. If they had approved the dam, each individual would receive thousands of dollars,

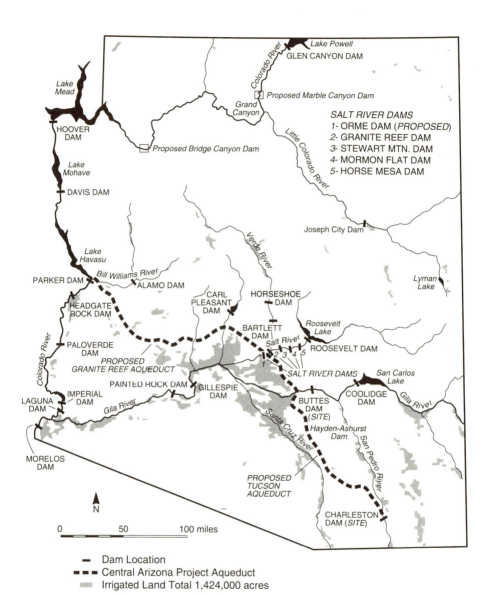

Irrigated Land and Major Dams in Arizona

Colorado River
Lake Powell
GLEN CANYON DAM
Proposed Marble Canyon Dam

Lake Mead

Grand Canyon

Little Colorado River

HOOVER DAM

SALT RIVER DAMS
1- ORME DAM (*PROPOSED*)
2- GRANITE REEF DAM
3- STEWART MTN. DAM
4- MORMON FLAT DAM
5- HORSE MESA DAM

Proposed Bridge Canyon Dam

Lake Mohave

DAVIS DAM

Joseph City Dam

Verde River

Lake Havasu

Bill Williams River

PARKER DAM

ALAMO DAM

Lyman Lake

CARL PLEASANT DAM

HORSESHOE DAM

HEADGATE ROCK DAM

BARTLETT DAM

Roosevelt Lake

Salt River

PALOVERDE DAM

PROPOSED GRANITE REEF AQUEDUCT

ROOSEVELT DAM

2 3 4 5

SALT RIVER DAMS

San Carlos Lake

Colorado River

PAINTED ROCK DAM

GILLESPIE DAM

BUTTES DAM (*SITE*)

COOLIDGE DAM

Gila River

LAGUNA DAM

IMPERIAL DAM

Gila River

Santa Cruz River

Hayden-Ashurst Dam

San Pedro River

MORELOS DAM

PROPOSED TUCSON AQUEDUCT

CHARLESTON DAM (*SITE*)

N

0   50   100 miles

— Dam Location
▬▬▬ Central Arizona Project Aqueduct
▒ Irrigated Land Total 1,424,000 acres

Irrigated Land and Major Dams in Arizona

and the reservation economy might have tempted some to accept such an offer. However, tribal leader Hiawatha Hood's straightforward sentiments spoke for most residents: "We don't want the dam. We want our land. We want our culture. We want our way of life." The 25 September 1976 vote was against Orme, 144 to 57, with some of the support clearly derived from Yavapais who were enrolled as members of the Fort McDowell community but who did not actually reside on the reservation.[24] This kind of determined resistance would have pleased an earlier advocate of Yavapai land rights, Dr. Carlos Montezuma. A Yavapai, he had traveled from his home in Chicago during the first two decades of the twentieth century to help rally his people against efforts to move them from the reservation and other threats to their well-being. Ill with tuberculosis and diabetes, he returned home to die at Fort McDowell in 1923. Montezuma was buried in the tribal cemetery. In 1978, Yavapai elder John Williams mentioned Montezuma in describing community opposition to Orme: "I don't want to see the land where Montezuma is buried covered by water."[25]

The Yavapais' unwillingness to be coerced into supporting the project can be traced in part to their affection for their homeland. Their ability to mount an effective campaign against the reservoir can be credited to no small degree to a Mexican-American ally. Married to an engineer and a resident of prosperous northern Scottsdale, Carolina Castillo Butler at first glance might have seemed an unlikely crusader. But when asked by the tribal chairman, Robert Doka, for assistance, she assented. Her willingness to serve as a cultural mediator—explaining, clarifying, and reassuring—eventually earned the kind of accolade Indians seldom pay outsiders. "If it wasn't for her," said Dixie Davis, a Yavapai from Fort McDowell, "we would have lost."[26] Buoyed by this experience, Butler has continued as a community activist in other campaigns involving the use of water in the state.

Another factor further complicated the debate over the dam. Those who had advocated the construction of Orme because of the need for flood control found new evidence to buttress their argument. Three years in a row (1978, 1979, and 1980) the Phoenix area experienced record rains, causing floods and attendant problems. The flood of February 1980 limited motorists to two places to cross the Salt River, which produced major traffic jams. Commuting had never been pleasant in Phoenix, freeways having been delayed by the odd notion that they would encourage even more people to come to the area; but collapsed bridges funneled traffic into interminable waits, and political pressure naturally swelled because of the inconvenience. Lorenzo ("Pat") Murphy, editor-in-chief of the Phoenix morning newspaper, the *Arizona Republic,* helped lead the chorus:

> I'm mad . . . about being stranded in flood waters for the umpteenth time in the last couple of years . . . about sitting in traffic for hours trying to get to work because flood waters have again washed out all but two major bridges . . . about 1.5 million people in the Phoenix area who have been asking for help, and waiting for help, and hoping for help—but not getting any help. . . . And I'm mad—mad as Hell—that high and dry Washington bureaucrats have been dilly-dallying for at least 10 years over approval of the Orme Dam, worrying more about nesting bald eagles than the lives and property and jobs of the people of Phoenix who must endure floods. Now dammit, give us our dam![27]

Although many people subscribed to Murphy's sentiments, not all were persuaded. Bob Gessner wrote his own letter to the editor, noting that for the cost of the proposed dam—$300 million dollars—"sensible alternatives" could be created that would provide more "than a dam and some mud flats." He added, "If we give the Salt River a channel to flow through, well built and properly engineered bridges to flow under and improve the dams we already have we will save money, Indian people, flood damage and bald eagles." As the rains dissipated and the flood waters subsided, so, too, did the simple notion that Orme offered the only answer. With the construction of new bridges, designed to survive more significant flows of water, the movement for Orme Dam continued to lose steam. When, of all people, Secretary of the Interior James Watt ventured by helicopter to Fort McDowell in September 1981, he seemed sympathetic to the Yavapai position. A "Trail of Tears" march later that month by seventy Yavapais from Fort McDowell to the state capitol in Phoenix yielded much positive publicity. By October the state engineer, Wes Steiner, admitted it was time to retreat from an Orme Dam. On 22 October 1981, Senators Barry Goldwater and Dennis DeConcini and Congressman John Rhodes echoed this sentiment. Watt's adoption of a plan in the following month that omitted Orme made it all official, at least for the time being.[28]

The Yavapai victory gained particular recognition in the popular press because of the nature of the Orme Dam proposal, but other Indian communities were waging less-noticed water battles of their own. In such instances, they generally sought not to deny additional water but to acquire it. Given the reservations' location and resources, an inadequate water supply hindered economic development and social welfare as much as anywhere else in Arizona. The example of the Ak-Chin Reservation serves as a useful illustration of the contemporary efforts of a number of Arizona Indian nations. It reminds us once again that we need to remember the cultural expectations as well as the economic implications for the appropriation and use of water.

In an age where many others emphasize the commodity value rather than community value of water, rural peoples such as those at Ak-Chin see water as the key to their cultural as well as their economic survival. Ak-Chin is a reservation created in 1912 by executive order of Pres. William Howard Taft. Although the people had historically been farmers, limited water supplies severely restricted farming. Compounding the situation, the Bureau of Indian Affairs often promoted the leasing of Ak-Chin land to outsiders. The residents of Ak-Chin were primarily Tohono O'odham (or Papago) in their language and culture, but the power of community and family heritage made them wish to remain rather than to retreat to the large Tohono O'odham Reservation to the south. Slightly smaller than Fort McDowell at 21,840 acres, Ak-Chin was the home of several hundred people.

At the time it established Ak-Chin, the federal government had promised water. As at the Fort Belknap reservation in northern Montana, the subject of the U.S. Supreme Court's famous *Winters v. United States* decision in 1908, outsiders had attempted to divert water away from the Ak-Chin community. In all likelihood, the example of the so-called Winters Doctrine, that Indian reservations were entitled to an amount of water sufficient for their needs as a community, prompted such solicitude. However, again as elsewhere, a promise was one thing and delivery of water another. Even with their history as farmers, Ak-Chin residents remained stymied until well after the Second World War.[29]

Tribal leader Leona Kakar remembered the 1940s and 1950s as grim years, when the land was leased out and the people had to work for non-Indians: "The only beef we ate we stole. Every couple of years or so a stray cow would wander into town from some non-Indian ranch. The men would hide under the mesquite trees, and on a dark and rainy night when nobody was up and about they would slaughter it. The next day you would see beef jerky hanging on the clotheslines." Hunting quail and jackrabbit, growing small amounts of pomegranates, apricots, figs, and grapes, the people struggled to get by, with little reason to harbor much hope for the future.[30]

Leona Kakar's brother, Richard Carlyle, took the lead in trying to alter the dismal situation. In 1961 Ak-Chin established its first constitution,

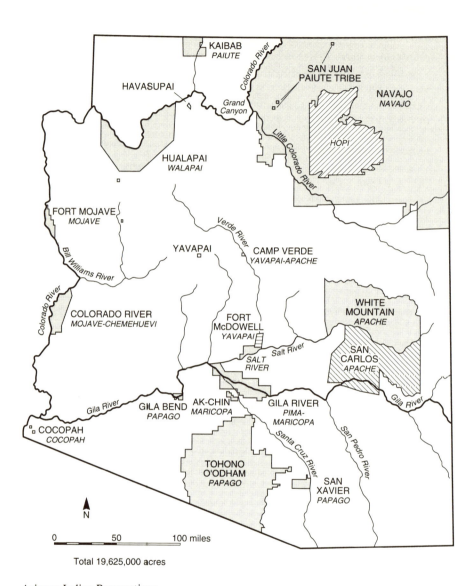

KAIBAB
PAIUTE

HAVASUPAI

SAN JUAN
PAIUTE TRIBE

Colorado River

Grand
Canyon

Little Colorado River

NAVAJO
NAVAJO

HOPI

HUALAPAI
WALAPAI

FORT MOJAVE
MOJAVE

Bill Williams River

Verde River

YAVAPAI

CAMP VERDE
YAVAPAI-APACHE

WHITE
MOUNTAIN
APACHE

Colorado River

COLORADO RIVER
MOJAVE-CHEMEHUEVI

FORT
McDOWELL
YAVAPAI

SALT
RIVER

Salt River

SAN
CARLOS
APACHE

Gila River

Gila River

GILA BEND
PAPAGO

AK-CHIN
MARICOPA

GILA RIVER
*PIMA-
MARICOPA*

COCOPAH
COCOPAH

TOHONO
O'ODHAM
PAPAGO

Santa Cruz River

San Pedro River

SAN
XAVIER
PAPAGO

N

0   50   100 miles

Total 19,625,000 acres

Arizona Indian Reservations

and Carlyle gained additional authority as tribal chairman. If the Bureau of Indian Affairs would not act as trustee, then the people themselves would. He began to terminate leases and not renew others. Carlyle turned to Wayne Sprawls, a white farmer who had been a friend of Carlyle's father's, to help in the creation of Ak-Chin Farms, a community-based effort to take back the land and farm it for the benefit of all. By 1964, nearly 5,000 acres were being farmed, and Ak-Chin Farms had already realized a profit of $21,000.[31]

It seemed too good to be true. When Carlyle died in the following year in an automobile accident, it would have been easy for the community to let their grief over the tragedy lead to the collapse of Ak-Chin Farms. Leona Kakar took over as leader, though, and by the late 1960s Ak-Chin netted a million dollars per year from the enterprise. The tribal council put half of it into capital and maintenance and invested the remainder in housing and other community improvements. The concrete, visible results deflated any real movement toward per capita distribution of the funds. Any person at Ak-Chin who wanted to work could do so on the farms. Almost all did. The federal government provided aid to less than 2 percent of the population.[32]

Once again it seemed too good to be true, and again a crisis developed—this time a plummeting water table. Area farmers were mining their available water through pumping and suddenly the Ak-Chin groundwater became endangered. Aided by Blackfeet consultant Forrest Gerrard, the people decided to try Congress rather than the courts to find redress for their grievances. From the Ak-Chin perspective, this course had two potential advantages: less cost and more immediate results. Senator DeConcini introduced Senate Bill 1582 in May 1977, with the cosponsorship of Senator Goldwater; Congressman Morris Udall offered the bill in the House. The bill became Public Law 95-328 on 27 July 1978, with Pres. Jimmy Carter's signature.[33]

The combined support of DeConcini, Goldwater, and Udall may be traced to their willingness to see Ak-Chin receive an appropriate amount of water. As politicians their lives were made considerably easier by making water delivery a federal responsibility while not threatening neighboring farmers who were equally dependent on the precious resource. In other words, the government vowed somehow to find the water without reducing the amount others could use, and local irrigators, as anthropologist Thomas McGuire put it, "incurred neither blame nor expense for depleting the aquifer under the reservation."[34]

Rising costs, disputes over water rights and the amount of groundwater quickly necessitated the alteration of the agreement. Uncertainty over the role of the CAP in diverting water to Ak-Chin may also have prompted the creation and passage in 1984 of Public Law 98-350, the conclusion of the drama. PL 98-350 guaranteed 75,000 acre-feet of water to be delivered to Ak-Chin starting no later than 1 January 1988 and provided additional funds to help Ak-Chin Farms use the water effectively.[35]

To date the arrangement seems to have worked. It is CAP water, via a four-mile extension to an aqueduct, that comes to Ak-Chin. Through the law, CAP water is also available to the white farmers in the Maricopa-Stanfield Water District. Of course the water comes at a price; but for Ak-Chin, the settlement indeed represented cause for celebration. In fact, every January the community holds a gathering to do just that. Leona Kakar has called the settlement "the most important thing that will ever happen on this reservation." "It is vital now," she said, "and will be just as important to our people 100,000 years from now. The water assures our future and the future of all our children."[36]

In the years since passage of PL 98-350, Ak-Chin Farms has continued to prosper. Fields are leveled through the use of laser technology, and the profits from farming have helped Ak-Chin to live up to its claim that "the community has already reached a level of independence that is unparalleled in Indian country." A new "ecomuseum" has been completed to house and display elements of the Ak-Chin past, present, and future. Designed by a member of the Arizona State University faculty, architect Kristine Woolsey, the handsome building incorporates elements of traditional design and symbolizes a bright future.[37]

The future is more cloudy, however, for other Arizona farmers and users of CAP water. Writing for the *Casa Grande Dispatch*, Susan Edmond reminded her readers, "For those who grew up in Arizona in the 1950s and 1960s, the Central Arizona Project was a dream that would solve the state's water problems." "Today," she noted, "the CAP is in trouble—big trouble." Edmond sums up the dilemma:

> The project cost more to build than was expected. Farmers who were supposed to buy CAP water until the cities and industries were ready for it were earning 1960s prices in the 1990s. When farmers no longer could afford the water and the assessments for the ditches they built to bring the CAP water to their fields, the banks stopped financing them. Thousands of acres of farmland began to lay idle, and the financial burden of those repayments shifted to the remaining farmers in the CAP irrigation districts.[38]

In other words, economist Martin has basically been proven correct. The high costs of using CAP water combined with all the problems of the contemporary economy for farmers have created a situation almost unimaginable to state politicians a generation ago. The CAP is funneling more water into the state than the state can afford and, thus, use. As reporter Tony Davis phrased it somewhat crudely, "The project is sucking financial wind and remedies are sour. CAP could mean a huge financial burden to the people of Arizona, the loss of water to some other state, or loan defaults to match Charlie Keating's savings and loan larceny."[39]

As noted previously, cotton farmers play a major role in the workings of Arizona agriculture. Slated to use a major portion of CAP water in the initial stage of the project before ballooning metropolitan areas needed a larger percentage, these farmers are not able to play their expected role. Cotton prices are too low, CAP water prices are too high, and property taxes have been increased to build the necessary distribution canals. If the farmers do not pay for the water, the federal government and the rest of Arizona must pick up the tab. Either the cities start using more of the water sooner than anticipated, and with correspondingly higher water bills, or Arizona may have to forfeit some of its allocated portion of the Colorado River to ever-thirsty California and Nevada. Neither higher water bills nor loss of water appeals to politicians. Not surprisingly, soon after his election in 1990, Gov. Fife Symington named a task force to investigate the matter; by 1993 his CAP advisory committee was racing to find answers before 1 October, when "take or pay" provisions take effect, requiring districts to contribute operating, maintenance, and replacement costs for all CAP water not used by city, industrial, or Indian users, even if—and here is the real catch—the farmers do not use all of this water.[40] Arizona's Groundwater Management Act (passed after considerable debate in 1980 through the influence of then Gov. Bruce Babbitt and the requirements of the terms of the CAP) controls city water use. The law not only limits pumping but dictates that there must be a century-long supply of water for new urban developments. The only way to be able to build, then, is to say you will purchase water from the one sure source: the CAP.[41]

To say the least, times have changed. Now secretary of the interior, Bruce Babbitt knows as well as any politician that the CAP's debt repayment clauses did not haunt public officials in the 1960s, when the gospel of economic development promoted growth. He remembered, "It was just sort of an article of faith that we'd do whatever is necessary to get and use the water. The premise of reclamation was that you sign now and worry about economics later."[42] Obviously, "later" arrived in the 1990s.

Although Arizona contains only two counties with cities over 100,000 people, state politics now are driven by urban votes. The Phoenix and Tucson metropolitan areas constitute the majority of the population, and conventional wisdom dictates that one wins or loses a statewide election in the cities rather than in the country. At the same time, the contemporary problems of the CAP clearly demonstrate that the fate of urban Arizona is linked to that of rural Arizona. Even if most residents of urban Maricopa County could not find neighboring rural Pinal County on a map, they cannot avoid the consequences of economic castastrophe nearby. Within Pinal County the threat of urban-driven solutions has brought together constituencies that do not always talk, let alone communicate effectively, with each other. In June 1993 members of the Pinal County Government Alliance brought together town residents, farmers, land developers, economic development specialists, educators, politicians, water company executives as well as representatives of towns, mines, financing institutions, chemical companies, implement dealers, and other farm businesses to try to draft a proposal more in keeping with county interests. In other words, they got together just about everybody in the county to try to reach a consensus. Their draft plan calls for irrigation districts to be permitted to sell some of their CAP water in the state in order to meet debts for their irrigation systems, to recharge or save extra water in wet years, and to sell some water out of state. Of course, what makes sense to Pinal may not be equally convincing to other counties or other interests in Arizona.[43]

Environmentalists hope that the crisis may yield policies more conducive to saving rivers such as the San Pedro and may force an overall reassessment of how water is used in the state. They see sweet irony in the problems facing the CAP. Perhaps Arizonans, at last, will have to reconsider what they choose to do with their water.[44] There are signs that such a reconsideration is already underway. Despite the support of the *Arizona Republic* and other major civic boosters for the Rio Salado Project, voters in Maricopa County turned down the effort to transform a stretch of the usually dry Salt River into an urban lake. However, it is probably too late to stop the movement toward more and better golf courses in Arizona; if Santa Fe and Missoula cannot halt the trend toward more fairways, prohibition is unlikely to take root in Paradise Valley.[45] Yet one can observe some tentative signs, especially among those citizens who have resided in the state for some time or who have grown up there, that more attention is being devoted to water as a finite and expensive resource. Tucson has, for the most part, accepted the idea that Arizona is a desert. There are encouraging signs of less grass and more desert vegetation in newer sections of metropolitan Phoenix. However, there are no checkpoints at the state borders for cultural baggage, and politicians know that the sacrifice of resources, rather than personal sacrifice, has characterized Arizona. The forthcoming decisions about the CAP and the general use of water will tell us a good deal about the evolving cultural politics of America's forty-eighth state.

A Half-Century of Conflict: The Rise and Fall of Liberalism in California Politics, 1943–1993

JACKSON K. PUTNAM

When Earl Warren took office as California's governor on 4 January 1943, he took over a political system that was made-to-order for his talents, and he was quick to use it. Sometimes referred to as "neoprogressivism," the system had grown out of the efforts of Hiram Johnson and his successors to institutionalize nonpartisanship. But in addition to their deliberate efforts to weaken the political party, the neoprogressives came to emphasize political pragmatism over ideology, moderation over extremism, and governmental activism over laissez faire.[1] By Warren's time, and especially under the influence of the New Deal, this general approach to politics had been rebaptized as "liberalism," and under Warren's leadership liberalism gained a new lease on life in California.

Although he had spent most of his political life in law enforcement (serving as Alameda County deputy district attorney and district attorney and California attorney general), Warren had identified himself with the progressive wing of the Republican party in California since the days of Hiram Johnson's governorship (1911–17). As governor he found the liberal traditions of nonpartisanship, pragmatism, moderation, and activism well suited to his ends. Although a lifelong Republican, he wore his party label loosely. He followed the old Johnson tradition of emphasizing "the man, not the party"; in addition, in Warren's time the Republicans had become the minority party, so to gain and hold power he constantly depended on Democrats. That he was elected to the governorship for an unprecedented three terms and that under his leadership his party, though in the minority, dominated the legislature, the state constitutional offices, and the state's congressional delegation and continued to do so for five years after he left office are testimonials to his effective use of the nonpartisan approach to politics.[2]

More important, of course, than his political finesse in gaining and holding power was what Warren did with it. Here his sustained liberalism was most in evidence. A congenital pragmatist, Warren was also a moderate compromiser in dealing with a legislature that was often more conservative than he. Keenly aware of the formidable problems of massive population growth in his state, he was a supreme political activist in devising solutions to deal with those problems.[3] While World War II was still in progress, he secured funding increases for state services of all kinds; and although a large increase in tax receipts enabled him to sign a bill for temporary tax reduction, he insisted on saving much of the revenue surplus as a "rainy day fund" to ease the state's transition to a peacetime economy in the postwar period.[4]

Beginning in 1945, Warren embarked on a major program of social reform. It started with a massive upgrading of state installations and institutions—higher education, public hospitals, workers' compensation, and state highways (the latter requiring a head-to-head conflict with the powerful oil lobby over an increase in gasoline taxes). Next, Warren established a new mental health system and proposed a highly controversial program of comprehensive health care modeled on the federal Social Security system. In the latter he went down to ringing defeat at the hands of the California Medical Association, which had hired the campaign firm of Whittaker and Baxter (ironically, the same company that had run Warren's gubernatorial campaign and that would go on to defeat Pres. Harry S Truman's health insurance program) to use the dread charge of "socialized medicine" to beat the measure.[5] In retrospect this defeat seems to demonstrate the breadth of Warren's political vision. He was obviously ahead of his time, and in light of the traumatic nature of today's health care crisis, it is interesting to speculate about what might have been if this measure had passed. Would it serve as a guide for dealing with the present problems?

Nor was this the only instance where Warren's defeats would prove as instructive as his victories. He was only partly successful, for example, in his support of public power agencies against the large power companies that are still dominant in California.[6] More revealing, however, was his unsuccessful foray into the field of race relations. Despite his expedient and unprincipled exploitation of the anti-Japanese hysteria during the war, he early became aware of the plight of racial minorities, especially African Americans, who were flocking into the state. In 1945, he astounded the public by calling for the establishment of a fair employment practices commission to protect minorities from discrimination by employers and unions.[7] Here again he was defeated first by the legislature and then by the voters, but this time his failure was only an opening battle in an eventually successful war waged by Warren himself on the U.S. Supreme Court and by a later governor, Edmund G. ("Pat") Brown, in California. Again Governor Warren was clearly ahead of his time.

On other issues his liberal activism proved timely. He made pioneering efforts against crime and lobbying excesses, and he generally ingratiated himself with the labor unions and secured the bulk of the labor vote by opposing a number of antiunion measures and supporting several pro-union ones.[8] Possibly his greatest achievement, however, was in damping and deflating the anticommunist hysteria in the state. McCarthyism, California style, was focused in three major areas.[9] In the legislature, Sen. Jack Tenney chaired the Joint Committee on Un-American Activities. He embarked on the same sorts of witch-hunts and issued the same types of smears for which McCarthy himself became infamous. The movie industry cravenly blacklisted its employees who refused to cooperate with such committees. And the University of California Board of Regents sought to fire faculty and staff members who refused to sign a special noncommunist oath of its own manufacture. Warren not only publicly opposed and condemned all three of these efforts, but by drawing upon his well-known anticommunist credentials (which protected him from the charge of being "soft on communism"),[10] he attacked extremists of both Right and Left, in the process defining a broad position in the middle of the road down which a vast majority of the California electorate followed him. Perhaps it is not too much to say that this isolation of political extremists enabled the California political system to focus on necessities rather than irrelevancies at a time when it needed to do so. When he left California for the Supreme Court in October 1953, Earl Warren left the state very much in his debt.

Warren had also shown how to gain wide popularity while governing effectively, and unsurprisingly his successors sought to mimic his methods and attract his followers. Former lieutenant governor Goodwin Knight, who completed the remainder of Warren's third term (1953–54), was the first to do so. Although he had been a voice for conservatism during the Warren administration, Knight moved adroitly toward the center-Left upon taking the governor's office. He proved particularly adept at picking up labor support by opposing a "right-to-work" law, and this, more than anything else, assured his election to the governorship for a full four-year term in 1954.[11]

Adopting a thoroughly unabashed liberal stance after his election, Knight expanded existing state programs and established new ones. He increased the budgets for higher education, old-age pensions, workers' compensation, unemployment insurance, and disability insurance, and presided over the birth of a new child care program, the widely admired Short-Doyle mental health act, and new programs in crime control and alcoholic beverage regulation.[12] Having so thoroughly adopted Warren's liberal mantle, which he assumed represented the Republican mainstream in the state, Knight looked forward confidently not only to reelection in 1958 but to a strong bid for the White House two years later. Unfortunately for him, California was on the verge of a vast political upheaval which would claim him as one of its first victims.

Many California Republican leaders and pundits had long resented Warren's liberalism and yearned to take the party back to conservative ways. Now, with Warren out of the way and Knight "betraying" traditional Republican principles, they made their move. Both of California's other Republican "big guns," Vice-President Richard Nixon and U.S. Senate Minority Leader William Knowland, were happy to give their service to this cause. They, too, coveted the presidency, and Knowland subscribed to the conventional wisdom of the time that the governor of a large state could make a more effective bid for the White House than could a U.S. senator. Thinking thusly, he made a decision that produced an immediate disaster but an ultimate triumph for conservative Republicanism.

In early 1957, Senator Knowland announced that he would not run for reelection, and later in the year he proclaimed his candidacy for governor instead. Taking a strong antilabor stand he easily attracted a host of conservative Republican financiers to his cause, and the hapless but highly electable Governor Knight angrily allowed himself to be talked into (by Nixon, among others) running for Knowland's vacated Senate seat instead. This ludicrous campaign, which various wags referred to as "the big switcheroo," the "musical chairs" contest, and an act of Republican "hara kiri," culminated in a Democratic clean sweep: the Democrats won the U.S. Senate seat, the governorship, a majority of the U.S. House of Representatives delegation, majorities in both branches of the state legislature, and control of all of the other state constitutional

offices except secretary of state.[13] With liberalism thus officially repudiated by the California's Republicans, liberals now relied on the Democrats
to preserve their philosophy and practices.

They did. Led by Attorney General Edmund G. ("Pat") Brown, the
state's Democrats had earlier begun a concerted move to break the
Republican hegemony in the mid-1950s which, as noted, paid off spectacularly in 1958. They succeeded in weakening (and ultimately repealing) the cross-filing law, which enabled them to regain control of the
nominating process in their party; they established an extralegal private
party organization, the California Democratic Council (CDC), which
allowed them to do the same things for their party that the Republicans
had long been doing with their California Republican Assembly (CRA);
and, led by their remarkable State Chair Elizabeth Snyder, they successfully mobilized thousands of women activists and incorporated them
into the party mainstream.[14] These actions produced steady increases in
the Democrats' polling strength, and their 1958 victory of about 60
percent of the votes reflected their registration advantage over the
Republicans—approximately the same sixty-to-forty ratio. Thus solidly
entrenched, the Democrats were expected by many observers to dominate
political life in California for at least as long as the Republicans had done
so up to that time, approximately sixty years.[15]

Although this prediction proved premature, Pat Brown made a major
effort to fulfill it and to govern California actively, pragmatically, and
effectively. He called his program "responsible liberalism" and made no
secret of the fact that he sought to don the political mantle of Earl Warren
(a personal friend whom he openly admired) that the Republicans had
deliberately discarded. The result was an administration that rivaled those
of Warren and Hiram Johnson in its numerous positive enactments.[16]
Marshaling the Democratic majorities in the legislature and enlisting the
aid of the powerful Jesse Unruh in the assembly (first, as chair of the Ways
and Means Committee and, after 1961, as Speaker), Brown pushed
through expansions of existing social services such as schools, higher
education, highways, workers' compensation, minimum wages, old-age
pensions, welfare, mental health, and public health (including the Medi-
Cal Act of 1965, which brought the state into the federal Medicaid
system). He also secured substantial tax increases (on incomes, inheri-
tances, banks, insurance companies, racetracks, beer, and cigarettes) to
finance these measures and doubled the state's budget during his eight-
year tenure—from about $2.5 billion to almost $5 billion.

Not content with being a tax-and-spend politician, constantly expanding the scope of traditional liberal programs, Brown became genuinely innovative in four main areas of public life: race relations, higher education, water policies, and governmental reorganization.[17] He put the state in the vanguard of the civil rights revolution already underway on the Warren Court by securing passage of a fair employment practices law, several public accommodations laws, and the highly controversial Rumford Fair Housing Act of 1963.[18] In higher education Brown supported the passage of the Fisher Act to upgrade the quality of public education by requiring teachers to have academic majors in college, but his most genuine claim to fame in this field is his leadership in the passage of the Donahoe Act, or Master Plan Act, of 1960.[19] This landmark law not only rationalized the state's higher education system by allocation of students, functions, and curriculum to its various components (the community colleges, the California State Universities, and the Universities of California) but came close to attaining its expressed ideal of making a college education affordable to everyone in the state who was academically eligible for one. For about a generation it aroused worldwide admiration.

In Brown's own estimation his most admirable achievement was the California Water Project.[20] Derived from California's anomalous twentieth-century demography, which placed the bulk of its population in the dry South rather than in the wet North, the California Water Project was designed to build dams, canals, pumping stations, siphons, and irrigation networks to bring the water to the people. The project was technically feasible, but politics had heretofore rendered it unattainable. Brown's task was to use his political talents to break down regional rivalries and rural-urban conflicts. Using compromise, conciliation, cajolery, and, where necessary, capitulation, he did. The result was the passage of the Burns-Porter Water Bonds Act of 1959. It financed the initial construction of the Oroville Dam and the beginning of the California Aqueduct, which eventually was able to shift some four million acre-feet of water annually from the "surplus" region of the North to the water-starved central and southern portions of the state. Although it is fashionable and reasonable to criticize the project nowadays on ecological grounds, it was nevertheless a political achievement of the highest magnitude.

Finally, Pat Brown and Jesse Unruh succeeded in reorganizing and streamlining California's giant governmental bureaucracy. A perennial problem for liberals, who tend to proliferate governmental agencies to deal with social problems, California's government had become huge and unwieldy since its last systematic reorganization in the 1920s.[21] Between 1961 and 1963, Brown and the legislature consolidated the functions of hundreds of state boards and commissions into ten large agencies and departments, by no means achieving administrative perfection but vastly improving the bureaucratic chaos that had existed.[22] More impressive were the efforts of Jesse Unruh in upgrading the quality of the legislature and the state constitution. Forced by Supreme Court decisions to democratize itself, the legislature, led mainly by Unruh in 1966, pushed through a state constitutional amendment that not only scrapped the state's "federal plan" (which had apportioned state senate seats grossly inequitably) but also eliminated hundreds of thousands of words of antiquated verbiage in the constitution and went on to modernize radically the legislature itself.[23] The legislature became a thoroughly professional body, meeting annually, with legislators receiving adequate compensation and greatly upgraded staffs. For a time at least, these improvements largely freed legislators from excessive influence of lobbyists, upon whom they had been habitually dependent not only for funding but for technical services and for information about the desirability and potential impact of proposed legislation. These attainments earned Unruh national prominence.[24]

By this time Brown's reelection and defeat of Richard Nixon in 1962 had given him a national reputation. One might conclude that the California liberal Democrats had indeed proven themselves capable of dominating the state government far into the foreseeable future, but this was emphatically not the case. By the early 1960s, the traumatic upheavals of the Vietnam war and the other massive discontents of that mad decade indicated that the Democrats' days were numbered in both nation and state. California Republicans clearly had a good chance at a return to power if they could only regain their focus and momentum.

And they did. The California Republican defeat in 1958 was a massive one, but that election also initiated a great right-wing resurgence. Although probably not qualifying as a "critical election" in the technical sense of the term,[25] the 1958 campaign acquired a large dedicated following, including a very activist female contingent; began the process of shifting the state party's political center of gravity sharply to the right; and, within a few years, purged all of its moderates from leadership positions.[26] Gathering in a host of energetic extremists including members of the John Birch Society, far-right Republicans took over the Republican volunteer organizations, the CRA, the United Republicans of

California (UROC, an already conservative group), and the Young Republicans. Then, in 1964, the far Right won the Republican presidential primary with the choice of Barry Goldwater over Nelson Rockefeller and triumphed in the election of George Murphy to the U.S. Senate.[27] Under the leadership of Party Chairman Gaylord Parkinson (famous for his "Eleventh Commandment" — "Thou shalt speak no evil of other Republicans"), the party maintained an aura of harmony while the Democrats were cutting themselves to pieces. All the Republicans needed at that point was an attractive, charismatic gubernatorial candidate to oppose Brown in his ill-advised bid for a third term in 1966. They found him in Ronald Reagan, and the era of Democratic dominance came quickly to an end.[28] Reagan won by almost a million votes. In addition, the Republicans swept all of the state constitutional offices except one and sliced the Democratic majorities in both houses of the legislature to razor-thin margins.[29]

The 1966 election thus brought defeat to the Democrats, but did it automatically kill off liberalism as well? Certainly at the rhetorical and symbolic levels the answer would seem to be yes, for everything about Reagan's public speaking and posturing during the campaign was explicitly antiliberal. The aforementioned major components of the old neo-progressive-liberal creed—nonpartisanship, pragmatism, activism, and moderation—were specifically spurned by Reagan, who enthusiastically embraced their opposites—partisanship, ideology, laissez faire, and extremism. In his oft-repeated speeches about the "creative society" that he hoped to develop in the state he specifically attacked liberals not only in the universities, where they were allegedly responsible for the turmoil on the campuses, but in the welfare state in general; and he repeatedly asserted that his primary political objective was to reduce the scope of government and especially to reduce its cost.[30] As soon as he took office, he appeared to act dramatically to implement his principles. He secured the dismissal of Clark Kerr, president of the University of California, and announced a 10 percent budget cut as the opening action in his avowed policy of "cut, squeeze, and trim." This was quickly followed by proposed slashes in allocations for higher education, welfare, and public health, especially mental health.[31]

Rhetoric was one thing, however, and reality was another. Reagan soon began to compromise his sacred principles in action, and the liberal state remained largely intact throughout his eight-year tenure as governor. This was especially true in the most fundamental conservative issue and the one closest to his heart, fiscal affairs. Instead of reducing the state's budget and taxes, he more than doubled the former (from under $5 billion to over $10 billion) and massively increased taxes no less than three separate times (in 1967, 1971, and 1972). In the process he allowed the institution of withholding taxes on incomes, a policy that he had fervently opposed on the principle that "taxes should hurt"; and on two occasions (in 1968 and 1972) he and the legislative leaders adamantly and successfully opposed property tax relief initiatives of the type later made famous in the Jarvis-Gann amendment (also known as Proposition 13) of 1978. Finally, in his seventh year in office, seemingly uneasy over his embarrassing fiscal record, he called a special election to pass a revenue and budget control measure in the form of an initiative constitutional amendment only to see it decisively defeated at the polls in an opposition campaign led by Robert Moretti, the liberal Speaker of the assembly.[32]

On the issue of campus uprisings, particularly "the mess at Berkeley," the governor made continuous verbal assaults on the state colleges and universities and at least two physical ones. For these he received widespread public acclaim; but he brought about no fundamental changes in these institutions, and their budgets after 1967 continued to climb at least proportionately with other state expenditures. He probably exulted in the dismissal of Clark Kerr, but he expressed no satisfaction with any of Kerr's successors, nor did they with him.[33]

On racial affairs Ronald Reagan's most significant action was probably inaction. He had promised to secure a repeal of the Rumford fair housing act on the ground that it interfered with private property rights. But he soon was apprised of the volatility of such a demand, and seemingly not wishing to see the outbreak of another Watts riot—this time on his watch rather than Pat Brown's—he prudently withdrew his support for repeal. The Rumford law remains on the books to this day.[34]

On ecology matters Reagan proved to be a pleasant surprise to many environmentalists. Expecting the worst after his famous offhand remark about the proposed enlargement of the Redwoods National Park ("A tree's a tree. How many do you need to look at?"), they expressed relief at his opposition to a couple of large dams sought especially by agribusiness. He also signed into law bills requiring stringent air and water quality standards as well as major legislation requiring the filing of environmental impact reports on public works projects. Many members of his political constituency in the business community railed against these "cumbersome," and "meddlesome" interferences with their "rights" and still do, but most environmentalists applauded, realizing that the Reagan administration had proved far more open to their concerns than they, at first, had any reason to expect.[35]

Quite surprisingly Reagan also turned out, in 1967 at least, to be a moderate on the abortion issue. Although it was not then the explosive topic that it later became, a liberalized abortion law was a controversial and vexing subject. When Anthony Beilenson, a liberal state senator, pushed one through the legislature in Reagan's first year in office, it caught the governor off-guard. He agonized indecisively and was buffeted by contradictory opinions from his advisers. Finally he signed the bill into law. As many predicted, it brought abortion-on-demand to California some six years before the Supreme Court's *Roe v. Wade* decision brought it to the nation at large, and it saddled the dithering governor with a discomfiting prochoice legacy that he later emphatically repudiated.[36]

Finally, the issue on which Reagan had probably directed his most vociferous attacks and in which he claimed the greatest amount of success also turned out to be a partial victory at best. This was the subject of welfare. Here, legend has it he slew the welfare monster—a haven for cheats, spongers, and "welfare queens" that threatened to drown the state in a sea of red ink. In reality, Reagan and Speaker of the Assembly Moretti made a sustained effort to reform the welfare laws by negotiation, and the result was very much a compromise by liberal and conservative bargainers. Reagan won tightened eligibility rules but lost on "closed-end" financing. Moretti agreed to greater antifraud measures but prevented across-the-board reduced grants. And so it went in all other aspects of the issue. Because the measure went into effect in 1972, just as the welfare case load began dropping, Reagan was able to claim the law as a great success. In fact, the decline in the number of welfare recipients was probably due more to the economic upturn that began about then and, ironically, to the liberalized abortion law that decreased the size of welfare families. At any rate, the law did not induce any long-range reduction in the number of people receiving welfare. In the mid-1970s the welfare budget began its inexorable upward climb, which bedevils the current administration. By that time, however, Reagan had gone on to greater things.[37]

There was, of course, nothing sinister or even unusual about the way Reagan conducted himself in office. There was a long tradition for California governors elected with extremist backgrounds (both far-right and far-left) to move toward the middle of the road upon taking office.[38] Taking extreme (if simplistic) positions on controversial issues often

tended to make them more electable, especially against moderate, pragmatic, "wishy-washy" incumbents (like Pat Brown), but the complex task
of governing effectively required negotiation, finesse, and compromise.
This movement toward moderation often enabled such governors to
broaden their following by picking up middle-of-the-road voters, but it
also created risks, the main one being the loss of their fervent, ideological, true-believer constituents. The latter thought such "sell-outs" had
betrayed the sacred cause and transferred their loyalties to new zealots.

The amazing thing about Ronald Reagan is that he moved toward the
middle without paying the price. Despite his many compromises on right-
wing issues and some outright abandonments of right-wing causes, he
maintained the image of a consistent, principled, noncompromising
right-wing leader who refused to engage in the maneuvers and trade-offs
of the professional politician. In the eyes of his followers, he remained an
unsullied "citizen politician" instead. This was unquestionably his greatest political achievement.[39]

How did he do it? Two answers come to mind. First, there is some truth
to Reagan's "nonpolitician" image. Despite his willingness to negotiate
and compromise, and even to cut a deal now and then, he tended to remain
aloof from the nitty-gritty of the political process and from most professional politicians as well. Like most ideological (as opposed to pragmatic)
political leaders, he did not immerse himself in the complex details of
political issues and socioeconomic processes and consequently shunned
the company of most hands-on politicians, except on formal or ceremonial
occasions. The opposite of today's "policy wonk," Reagan relied on a
coterie of close advisors to digest complex issues in policy statements and
legislative enactments into one-page "mini memos" for his perusal and
disposition.[40] This practice left him remarkably uninformed or only
superficially cognizant of many of the pressing issues of the day and
foreshadowed his failings in the presidency, when he would be condemned
by his critics for gross ignorance of basic matters and for his lack of
hands-on leadership.[41] In the governor's office, however, these tactics
seemed to serve him well and to preserve his image intact.

The other reason for the enduring triumph of Reagan's image was his
total mastery of the modern media. All the while he was compromising
and engaging in politics-as-usual, he was active before the television
screen and in broadcasting studios beguiling the public with success
stories of his "cut, squeeze, and trim" policies and continually asserting
his philosophical adherence to basic conservative values. Well aware that,

to a television audience, images are far more compelling than ideas and facts, he ceaselessly projected a calculated conservative image of himself. It worked perfectly. An anaesthetized and amnesiac television public quickly forgot his record and remembered his image; seemingly, many do so to this day.[42]

At the end of Reagan's second administration, liberalism was somewhat dormant but by no means dead, and its primary vehicle — the Democratic party — was still in a dominant position. One of Reagan's signal shortcomings was his failure to increase the strength of the Republican party, which, despite its promising showing into 1966, was able to win control of the legislature for only two of Reagan's eight years (1969–1970). The 1970 election was a personal triumph for Reagan, who was reelected over the surprisingly clumsy Jesse Unruh, but was a huge setback for Republicans in California. Reagan's close friend and ideological soulmate, U.S. Senator George Murphy, was defeated; Edmund G. ("Jerry") Brown, Jr. (who would be elected governor in 1974) won the office of secretary of state; and Democratic majorities were returned to both houses of the legislature, giving the party control of the crucial reapportionment process. The election of 1974, when Reagan chose not to run for a third term, was an even greater Republican debacle. The Democrats regained control of the governor's office and all of the other constitutional offices except that of attorney general and greatly increased their lead in both houses of the legislature.[43] Thus the liberal dragon against which Reagan and the Republicans had struggled and supposedly defeated was not in a position to come roaring back.

It did not. The greatest irony in "the strange death of liberal California" is that it began to come about when California was safely back in the control of the Democrats, liberalism's presumed caretakers, and at the hands of one who came to power "proud of his credentials as a liberal," Jerry Brown.[44] In light of Jerry Brown's political background, all observers of his actions as secretary of state and his 1974 gubernatorial campaign viewed him very much as the "old man's son" who would revive liberalism in the state.[45] To a certain extent he did. He steered through the legislature in 1975 the Agricultural Labor Relations Act, a pioneer enactment providing long-deferred collective bargaining rights to farm workers; he took strong stands on environmental issues, especially a consistent opposition to nuclear energy plants and endorsement of alternative energy sources; he championed the expansion of personal privacy rights such as the decriminalization of marijuana possession and a "consenting adults" law for sexual behavior; he consistently, though ineffectively, opposed the reimposition of the death penalty; and, of greatest importance, he appointed hundreds of racial minorities and women to positions of government service.[46]

Regarding the most fundamental components of California liberalism, however, Brown proved either indifferent or opposed. None of the traditional hallmarks of the neoprogressive-liberal tradition—nonpartisanship, pragmatism, activism, and moderation—seemed to make any impression on him. He could adopt or oppose any or all of them on any issue at any time, and expediency seemed always to be his ruling credo. At first this stance made him appear refreshing and original, but liberals gradually awakened to the fact that he was opposed to two of their most fundamental postulates: the need for an extended and activist government, and the companion need for adequate goverment finances. In the Watergate era, when Brown came to power, government and politicians incurred widespread disrespect as incompetent or corrupt or both; and Brown gained enormous public approbation by catering to these cynical and simplistic sentiments. He not only consistently criticized the government (which, after all, he headed) but went on to suggest that government in general was incapable of meeting society's needs. Instead he called on people to "lower their expectations" and accept an "era of limits" on government activity. In a dazzling display of the inconsistency characteristic of his administration, he insisted at the same time that he was bringing "a new spirit" to Sacramento and would soon vastly elevate his own "expectations" by attempting to bring this new spirit to Washington, D.C., as well.[47]

His personal life-style proved as captivating to the public as his rhetoric. He refused to live in the newly constructed governor's mansion but rented a modest apartment in which he reportedly slept on a mattress on the floor. He drove a state-owned blue Plymouth instead of a luxury automobile, which was preferred by most officials. He hosted the visiting Prince of Wales to an austere luncheon of two hamburgers and a coke. A bachelor, he maintained a relationship with popular singer Linda Ronstadt. He practiced theosophical contemplation at the San Francisco Zen Center and, announcing himself a convert to "Buddhist economics" as outlined by the British economist E. F. Schumaker, added the slogan Small Is Beautiful to the ever-lengthening list of mottoes associated with his name.[48] The public perception of him as an American original (which he skillfully nurtured with a media mastery almost as adept as Reagan's) served him well when he made a foray into national politics with his candidacy for the White House in 1976. He entered too late to stop Jimmy Carter, but he reaped a rich harvest of heady national publicity and apparently acquired an abiding thirst for the presidency that endures unslaked to this day.

He sought reelection in 1978 so as to be in a strong position for a second bid for the White House in 1980. Fervently wishing to avoid a tax increase, and in keeping with his general contempt for traditional activist governmental programs (which he referred to as "dollars chasing problems"), he kept governmental budgets consistently low and spent barely enough to keep pace with inflation, thus starving many state services. Inflation plus the economic upturn that took place in the latter 1970s brought huge revenue surpluses into the state treasury. This in turn provided a new rationale for property tax reductions because the consequent decreases in local revenues could be offset by increased state spending. When Howard Jarvis and Paul Gann crafted a state initiative (Proposition 13, or the Jarvis-Gann amendment) to implement this policy and secured its passage in June 1978, they worked a veritable revolution in modern California politics, a revolution that caught Brown napping.[49]

Recognizing many economic inequities in "Prop. 13," as it was called, Brown went on record as opposing it before realizing its enormous popularity. Faced with a Republican opponent (Attorney General Evelle Younger) who had mildly endorsed the proposition, Brown did a rapid about face, presided over the process of transferring the treasury surplus into local coffers, and conveyed the impression to the public that he was enthusiastically in favor of Jarvis-Gann. The electorate rewarded him by returning him to office by a landslide at the same time that it elected a number of ultra-right-wing "Prop. 13 babies" or "caveman" to the Republican ranks in the legislature. This in turn completed the process begun in 1958 of recasting the Republican party into an almost totally far-right organization and solidifying a pervasive and persistent antitax attitude in the public mind.[50]

Jerry Brown's response to this rightward shift was to capitulate to it and attempt to capitalize upon it. He adopted a strong probusiness rhetoric and began appointing business and agribusiness leaders to state offices. He fought with the liberal Democratic leadership in the legislature (especially Speaker of the Assembly Leo McCarthy) over funding for welfare and state employee salaries. He attacked the Carter administration for its alleged fiscal irresponsibility (which did not prevent him from demanding federal funds for various state projects), and he astounded many former followers when he endorsed a movement to pass a balanced budget amendment by the risky means of a national constitutional convention.[51]

Having performed these illiberal actions in order to wage a credible conservative campaign for the presidency in 1980, Brown then proceeded to do just the opposite. His campaigns in the presidential primaries of New Hampshire and several other states, especially Wisconsin, were throwbacks to the 1960s, with followers drawn from devotees of holistic medicine, health foods, spiritual movements, and new energy sources; sponsorship by a mysterious organization called the "Order of the Eye"; and the oft-repeated campaign slogan "Explore the Universe." The media, which Brown had previously exploited to his advantage, now became the instrument of his downfall, as they ceaselessly reiterated James Kilpatrick's description of him as a "topless intellectual" and Mike Royko's nickname for him, "Governor Moonbeam." When the chastened candidate dropped out of the race and attempted to rebuild his reputation through a more responsible governing of California in the latter two years of his term, he was repeatedly tripped up by a host of faux pas and intractable political problems. His unsuccessful race for the U.S. Senate against Republican Pete Wilson in 1982 has proved thus far his penultimate "hurrah."[52]

The fall of Jerry Brown, however, was not in any real sense a downfall of liberalism. As noted, he had already parted company with liberalism, and liberalism itself seemed still strong in the democratically dominated legislature and other state offices. The real test of its persistence came in the governor's race of 1982, and liberalism came within the proverbial "cat's whisker" of a revival. In the end, however, the liberal Democrat Thomas Bradley was defeated by the committed conservative George Deukmejian, dramatically disrupting California's liberal tradition to this day.[53]

Despite his campaign promises to bring a return of "common sense" to the governor's office, George Deukmejian had no intention to return to the pragmatic moderation of most of his predecessors. A conservative true believer whose twenty years in public life had seemingly strengthened his ideological approach to politics, he saw eye-to-eye with his fellow Republicans in the legislature who had by this time become nearly unanimously committed to equally rigid right-wing views. At the same time, the Democrats who controlled the legislature under the leadership of Speaker of the Assembly Willie Brown had become overwhelmingly liberal in their political persuasion, and the ability of both to settle issues by negotiation and compromise diminished accordingly.[54] A culture of partisanship thus became dominant after more than a half-century of neoprogressive nonpartisanship, and other reversals soon followed: ideology triumphed over pragmatism, extremism over moderation, and legislative activism challenged by the principles of laissez faire.

True to these principles, Deukmejian came into office with a very short agenda well calculated to exacerbate interparty antagonism: he pledged to be fiscally frugal and to "get tough" on crime. The former policy immediately provoked a protracted conflict with the Democratically controlled legislature that largely set the tone for the rest of his administration. With the Reagan recession underway when Deukmejian came into office in January 1983, the state budget was already out of balance, and the governor proposed to balance it not by a tax increase but by increased user fees (especially a highly controversial tuition charge at the community colleges) and a seemingly unconstitutional exercise in deficit finance.[55] The Democrats fought back with delaying tactics, propaganda barrages, and enlarged budget proposals, but the governor was armed with the ultimate weapon of the item veto and used it to prevail. The next five years saw an annual repetition of this confrontational process with, to the Democrats' angry discomfiture, the same basic result.

This annual partisan ritual was not completely fatal to California liberalism, however. When the recession turned into a protracted expansion in the mid- and late 1980s, revenues in the California treasury began to increase accordingly. Deukmejian on only one occasion insisted that these surpluses be returned to the taxpayers and instead allowed them to be used as increased expenditures for all of the usual state services, especially education. The result was that the state budget doubled (from about $25 billion to over $50 billion), just as it had under Ronald Reagan. So long as increased budgets did not require increased taxes, "the Duke" was content to leave the spending momentum largely undisturbed.[56]

The increased revenues came in especially handy for the governor's anticrime program. Long an advocate of capital punishmnt, increased penalties, and mandatory prison sentences, Deukmejian was gratified when Democratic as well as Republican legislators began initiating such legislation, which actually began in 1977 when the state, in effect, abandoned rehabilitation in favor of retribution as its primary approach to the crime problem. Numerous mandatory incarceration laws were passed, and the governor presided over a large-scale prison-building program. A fivefold increase in the prison population followed, as California's incarceration rate exceeded that of any country in the world (including the United States, South Africa, and the Soviet Union), with a prison-building budget of more than $3 billion per year. Despite the political popularity of this program, it was a social failure. The crime rate was not reduced; the prisons became heavily overcrowded (currently at about 180 percent of capacity), ironically with a greater proportion of nonviolent offenders and parole violators than violent offenders. The prison population became massively skewed toward African Americans and Latinos rather than whites, and the governor adamantly refused to consider other methods of dealing with the high recidivism rate such as education, drug counseling, and alternative sentencing procedures.[57]

The governor's preoccupation with crime brought him into a highly controversial dispute with the state supreme court, especially its chief justice, Rose Elizabeth Bird. Because Justice Bird was against the death penalty while Deukmejian supported it, he opposed her reelection in 1986, despite the disturbing implications of politicizing the judiciary in this way. In the eyes of most constitutional scholars Deukmejian then compounded his offense by also opposing the reelection of two other state supreme court justices appointed by Jerry Brown, suggesting that Deukmejian was trying to pack the court. Although since the reform law of 1934 no state supreme court justice had ever failed to be reelected (they had no electoral opponents and were seldom campaigned against, especially by political leaders), all three of these appointees (Bird, Joseph Grodin, and Cruz Reynoso) went down to defeat in the same election in which Deukmejian was returned to office by a wide popular majority.[58]

Deukmejian was a popular executive in part because of his anticrime and fiscal frugality stands and in part because of his carefully constructed media image of colorless competence. Although the Democratic legislature made him look bad on a number of environmental issues, defeated him in the agonizing reapportionment struggle, and blocked some of his more controversial appointments,[59] this may actually have redounded to his credit, because the legislature itself began to suffer, somewhat justifiably, a gigantic loss in public esteem. Already polarized by a vast increase in ideological partisanship, the legislature forfeited more public confidence when its members raised huge sums of money from special interest groups, which not only seemed to place them in the groups' debt but enabled the legislators to outspend their opponents in election campaigns and assure themselves a near-permanent hold on their offices. Furthermore, expensive, high-tech campaign tactics often debased the political process and seemingly contributed to a vast fall-off in voter participation. Legislators contributed further to public dissatisfaction in the late 1980s by allowing outright corruption to reappear in their ranks. Especially notable was a sensational FBI sting operation that sent three legislators to jail along with some convicted staff members and brought others under indictment in a still ongoing investigation. Finally, both the legislature and the governor seemed to evade rather than address the most serious social issues, and massive problems related to the environment, the economic infrastructure, transportation, education, health care, crime and homelessness grew steadily worse.[60]

These problems and many others were exacerbated after 1988, when the economic downturn brought the state budget out of balance. Although in the following year the governor and legislature got together on a few issues, the election year of 1990 brought a return to excessive partisanship and deadlock intensified by a deepening recession and revenue shortfalls. The frustrated chief executive who had once bragged that he had brought the state's finances from a condition of "IOU to A-OK" now saw his dream of fiscal solvency shattered, and his administration ended on a rather sour note.[61]

In such circumstances it is perhaps surprising that the election of 1990 proved fatal neither to the Republicans nor to liberalism. The Democrats retained their control over the legislature (and proved to be even more liberal than they had been),[62] and the Republicans elected a governor who was an avowed moderate and activist, Pete Wilson.[63] Fearful of losing the statehouse and with it any control over the crucial reapportionment process in the new decade, reluctant right-wing Republican leaders agreed to an uncontested nomination of the politically moderate U.S. Senator Wilson because of his proven vote-getting abilities. Waging a vigorous campaign against the Democrats' Diane Feinstein, Wilson endorsed the controversial but popular Proposition 140, placing term limits on all constitutional officers and legislators. Although the measure passed by a wide margin and probably played an important role in Wilson's election, his endorsement of it automatically made him a mortal enemy of the Democratic legislators, especially the formidable Speaker of the Assembly Willie Brown. This did not augur well for future cooperation between the executive and legislative branches, a necessary condition if the state would deal effectively with the many problems facing it.

The problems were truly daunting. In addition to the natural disasters that plagued the state in the early 1990s — drought, fires, earthquakes, and a killing frost — an economic downturn, more serious than in the nation at large, emerged and produced a massive deficit in the state budget. Although Wilson, unlike most of his Republican cohorts, was a "man with a plan" who made some creative proposals in his inaugural address,[64] he soon learned how enormously difficult it was to deal with these disasters through the political process. For one thing, the political atmosphere around Sacramento had changed enormously since he had served in the legislature in the 1960s. The old culture of compromise and relative nonpartisanship had given way to institutionalized partisan and ideological excess exacerbated by personal and factional feuds. Wilson's own party members seemed more prone to these extremes due to their frustrating sense of powerlessness derived from their minority status.[65] In addition, the budget continued to hemorrhage, reaching a deficit of more than $14 billion by the end of the fiscal year.

In these circumstances Wilson found it necessary to make a deal with Willie Brown and the Democrats, while the Republicans, fragmented and demoralized, confined themselves to collective inaction and shrill condemnations of any and all tax increases to cover the deficit.[66] In the end Wilson, the Democrats, and a minimal number of moderate Republicans "balanced" the budget by splitting the difference between tax increases and spending reductions. Levies were increased or broadened on retail sales, incomes, alcoholic beverages, and motor vehicle registrations. These amounted to the largest tax increase in the history of the state; and although state spending on welfare and salaries was sharply curtailed, and the master plan for higher education was virtually gutted, the governor was ceaselessly savaged by right-wing members of his own party for allowing any tax increases at all.[67] At the same time the governor infuriated the Democrats, and probably a few incumbent Republican legislators as well, by refusing to negotiate on any of their reapportionment formulas. He vetoed all the reapportionment bills, thus throwing the job of redistricting the state into the hands of the state supreme court. Finally, by supporting and then vetoing an antidiscrimination bill regarding homosexuals, he infuriated supporters of gay and lesbian rights but gained no support in the conservative community due to an angry reference to homophobic "bigots" in his veto message.[68]

By early 1992 Governor Wilson's ratings had slipped badly in the polls and he had to make an agonizing choice. He could continue to work with the Democratic majority in the legislature or he could adopt a confrontational stance with them to regain credibility in his own party. He chose the latter. The entire year was a sustained political donnybrook in which governor and legislature, and Democrats and Republicans, routinely insulted each other on practically every issue, with two particular controversies generating mutual invective of epic proportions.[69] These were the usual budget quarrel and an effort to bring about workers' compensation reform. The governor simply rejected all legislative budget proposals and did not even submit one of his own until mid-August, a month and a half after the constitutional deadline for its passage. With the state's treasury literally empty the government was forced to issue IOUs for most of its transactions; and when a budget was finally agreed upon, a record sixty-three days late, it contained the usual compromises over gubernatorial versus legislative demands, and the final budget total was some $500 million larger than the one offered to the governor in July. Wilson, however, declared a victory and signed it.[70]

The effort to reform the workers' compensation system ended in stalemate and complete failure. The system was costly to employers, but not very remunerative to workers; instead insurance companies, doctors, and lawyers seemed the chief gainers. The governor submitted his program to the legislature and ordered it to pass it without hearings or changes. Naturally, the legislature refused to comply, and when hearings revealed that the governor's proposal mainly benefitted doctors and insurance companies, Wilson promised to veto any altered version of his plan, thereby killing it.[71] Looking for reasons for the governor's strange behavior, one must remember that this was an election year, and he hoped for vindication in November.

He did not get it. Wilson took a risky stand on four electoral issues and did not prevail on a single one. He pledged to carry the state for Pres. George Bush; he personally sponsored John Seymour for the U.S. Senate against his own opponent of 1990, Diane Feinstein; he passionately backed Proposition 165 to make Draconian cuts in welfare allowances and vastly increase the fiscal powers of the governor; and he sought to capitalize on the new reapportionment law to bring the Republicans to dominance in the state legislature and congressional delegation. Instead, Bill Clinton and Feinstein carried the state; Proposition 165 lost decisively; and the Democrats gained seats in the U.S. House of Representatives and state assembly and held their lead in the state senate.[72] It seemed a sharp repudiation of the governor's leadership and forced him to reevaluate his policy of confrontation in the second half of his term.

In early 1993 the political pendulum began to swing sharply back toward political moderation and compromise.[73] Both Wilson and the Democrats in the legislature could easily see the need to appear once again as responsible political leaders after the disgraceful dogfights of 1992 that had caused their approval ratings to plunge toward single digits.[74] Furthermore, the governor had to prepare for his reelection campaign, while legislators continued to be embarrassed by malfeasance convictions of their colleagues.[75] Both Democratic liberals and the more flexible of the Republican conservatives moved toward the political center in order to deal more effectively with pressing political issues.

The unquestioned leader of this movement toward moderation and legislative activism was not Governor Wilson but Speaker of the Assembly Willie Brown. To the wonderment of seasoned political observers the agile parliamentarian not only secured the passage of the annual budget bill before the passage of the constitutional deadline (1 July) but pushed through a comprehensive reform of the nettlesome workers' compensation system, as well as a series of tax breaks and other benefits for business designed to fight the recession and improve the economy.[76] The $52 billion budget was a typical conservative-liberal compromise. For the second year in a row, it actually reduced total expenditures slightly; the governor succeeded in transferring $2.6 billion in property tax receipts to the general fund from the counties and localities to the latters' enormous chagrin; he also held firm against increased spending for education, again secured cuts in welfare grants, and suspended the income tax credit for low-income renters. In balance, though, the governor agreed to roll-over part of the deficit into the next fiscal year, extended the emergency sales tax increase for another six months, and vowed to place an indefinite extension of it on a special election ballot in November (it passed). He also agreed to a proposal to restore the renter's credit by ballot amendment in 1994 and to offset the severity of welfare cuts by granting increased allowances of earned income and property holdings for welfare recipients and providing cash grants and child care assistance to teenage mothers on welfare who were attempting to complete their high school education. Finally, by calling a special election for a right-wing educational voucher initiative and then opposing it as too costly, Wilson contributed to its overwhelming defeat in November and enhanced his image as a moderate at a time when extremist proposals seemed to be losing their popular appeal.[77]

As the 1994 election year approached, the governor sought to strengthen his standing as a moderate while holding onto support from the

Republican far Right. By seizing on the issues of violent crime and illegal immigration, he seemed to be making headway in his effort. Opinion polls showed him to be rising in public esteem, and right-wing Republicans agreed not to oppose him in the 1994 primary.[78] With the Democrats fragmenting themselves among three opposing gubernatorial candidates (Kathleen Brown, John Garamendi, and Tom Hayden), the governor's prospects seemed to be better than they had been since his election. If partisan Democrats viewed this situation with alarm, liberals in general could regard it with greater equanimity. Despite their partisan rhetoric, all candidates for governor (as well as those for many other state offices) seemed to be taking basically moderate positions on most issues, and the radical-right movement appeared to be nearing exhaustion.[79] The prospect for an at least modest rebirth of liberalism in California appeared a reasonable possibility.

Liberalism, a fundamental feature of California politics in the 1940s, '50s, and '60s, has found itself challenged and undermined but not destroyed in more recent decades. A competing culture of excessive partisanship, ideological extremism, and fiscal and legislative conservatism has emerged to oppose the liberal ideals of pragmatism, compromise, and governmental activism. Simultaneously, Californians have come to regard their government and politicians with contempt and view both as failing to address their problems effectively. Few seem to realize, however, that by demanding that politicians solve social problems they are making a plea for a return of liberalism to the state. Recently, Republican moderates such as Pete Wilson have demonstrated a grudging awareness of this fact, although such a realization is often masked by the partisan excesses of an election campaign. In these circumstances the antiliberal impulse may be in decline, and philosophically conservative average Californians may be coming to regard liberalism as necessary, even if undesirable. In that case the reputed death of California liberalism may prove to be like that of Mark Twain—greatly exaggerated.

Water Politics in Colorado: Change, or Business as Usual?

SANDRA K. DAVIS

As nineteenth-century western settlers struggled to establish communities that would thrive, the provision of domestic and irrigation water became essential for development of the arid West. Assorted laws and water distribution organizations were established and often found unsuitable for facilitating the development of western lands. In Colorado it was not until the late 1930s that a water organization structure and its alliance with federal agencies and congressional supporters provided a stable system to build and operate the essential water delivery systems. Select water storage and delivery projects will be used to illustrate water politics in Colorado since World War II. Factors explaining the establishment and success of the systems that built the projects will be examined; in turn, recent changes that have challenged the hegemony of the systems will be analyzed to determine the implications for the future.

THE RISE OF THE WATER PROVISION SYSTEM

In the early settlement of western lands, the government facilitated western expansion by providing land to settlers. Government, however, responded slowly to requests for affordable water. Although the government did little at first to regulate or deal with water development, citizens plunged ahead with irrigation projects and suffered the consequences of their inability to afford large irrigation projects because of dependence on private capital and, later, their forfeiture on repayment of Bureau of Reclamation project contracts. Through trial and error the state and federal governments successively developed water rights and water organizations that fostered western development.[1]

An important piece of the puzzle was created in response to northern Colorado water interests who wanted to stabilize agriculture by acquiring desperately needed water from a federally funded water project.[2] After three years of intrastate negotiations among water interests, an agreement was reached in 1937 that paved the way for local users to simultaneously lobby the U.S. Congress and state legislature for funding and a water district organizational structure that would allow them to realize their dream of a transmountain water diversion project—the Colorado–Big Thompson, or C-BT, project. Within a year they convinced the state legislature to pass a law permitting conservancy districts with taxing power; established their own district, the Northern Colorado Water Conservancy District; and persuaded Congress to authorize and fund the project.

The creation of this conservancy district and approval of the C-BT project challenge the traditional deemphasis of the government in western development because of individualism. In fact, the role of the government in making societal decisions such as water policy is an important one. Historian Donald Worster describes the state as an empire that is based on subsidized irrigation systems and run by a monolithic hierarchical elite that destroyed frontier democracy.[3] Certainly the elite that created and now operates the C-BT project used technical and political expertise to plan the system and to persuade legislators and administrators to approve it. Furthermore, Northern Colorado Water Conservancy District (NCWCD) board members are appointed by state judges and not accountable to district taxpayers. Although the district is a powerful institution lacking in accountability, it is popular with farm and municipal leaders who credit it with providing sufficient water to support a healthy agricultural sector and to attract additional residents and industries.[4]

Rather than assigning the hegemonic label to water institutions, sociologist John Walton suggests that state entities are an exercise in legitimation that depends on cultural justification.[5] The NCWCD, for example, is able to legitimate its activities and appointive board by relying on its contribution to the most critical of community values: it delivers water, promotes growth and development, and ultimately provides a prosperous economy. Its lack of accountability to the taxpayer is not considered much of a problem because few know of its existence and even fewer worry about the selection of its board. Of course, critics do periodically raise the accountability issue, but NCWCD supporters have always successfully argued that appointment keeps directors out of politics and free from campaign expenses.[6]

Walton also explores "incorporation theory," which argues that government tries and often succeeds in using its administrative capacity and

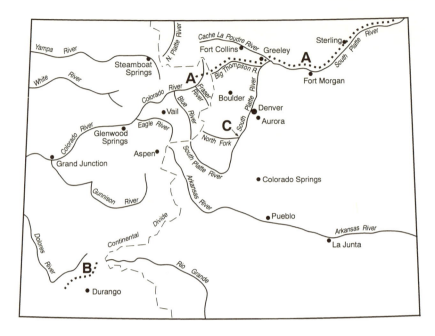

SELECT WATER PROJECTS IN COLORADO

A Colorado-Big Thompson Project
B Animas-LaPlata Project
C Proposed Two Forks Dam

coercive power to shift power away from individuals and local communities, bringing them under state dominion. The superior government tries to create a hierarchical relationship in which it supersedes parochial traditions and forms of authority.[7] In the C–BT project, however, the initiation to incorporate water users into the New Deal/Bureau of Reclamation orbit came from the bottom up, as astute local leaders realized the project's benefits. Thus, Northern Colorado leaders were swift to seize the opportunity for a massive federally funded water project that incorporated their local water interests into the superior domain of federal water projects. Local leaders have remained content with this relationship because it brought the economic prosperity they sought[8] while allowing them to establish their own control over water supplies that both state and federal agencies are reluctant to challenge.[9] They succeeded in the relationship with state and federal authority, at least in part, because they protected their own power by cloaking themselves in the mantle of "prior appropriation" water rights.[10]

Walton's reliance on political culture and incorporation theory takes a longer historical perspective on water politics that is oriented toward explaining change that occurs over decades. It does not, however, explain the alliances that underlie water policy decisions. The theory of iron triangles, however, while more static, does explain the decision-making process and the success of local water interests.

IRON TRIANGLES AND THE SUCCESS OF WATER PROVISION SYSTEMS

"Iron triangles theory" describes water politics in which local water organizations,[11] their elected representatives sitting on congressional committees that control water project funding, and federal agencies such as the Bureau of Reclamation or U.S. Army Corps of Engineers share the distributive policy goal of supporting water projects that will provide concentrated benefits to members and disperse the costs to all taxpayers. The traditional beneficiary, the agricultural community, was joined after World War II by powerful urban interests led by engineers and supported by political and business leaders who recognized the importance of water to development and growth.[12]

The decision process is typically closed to all but its narrow membership. Although formal congressional approval for the project must be obtained, a coalition of support is developed by promises of vote trading on similar projects that will benefit the constituents of other legislators. Most issues are low-conflict matters; any potential conflict is avoided through accommodation.

Triangle members prefer to discuss projects in nonpartisan, technical terms. The debate is nonpartisan as most of the benefits are delivered along geographic rather than partisan lines.[13] By emphasizing the technical nature of decisions, the triangle strives to justify the removal of the decisions from public scrutiny. In fact, the primary determinants of water decisions are political considerations rather than economic or technical issues.[14]

The closed water iron triangle successfully excluded demands from an Indian iron triangle that was unable to protect Indian water rights. In Congress the Indian triangle was based in the Committee on Indian Affairs that, incongruously for an iron triangle, had members who were hostile to Indian rights. The hostile members sought to serve the interests of their non-Indian constituents by providing them with Indian land and water resources. The other committee members were sympathetic to Indian rights on moral grounds but not necessarily effective in protecting them.[15]

In addition to schizophrenic congressional committees, the interest groups representing Indians comprised whites who lobbied for the so-called best interests of the Indians, which often meant programs requiring that Indians assimilate.[16] The final leg of the triangle was the Bureau of Indian Affairs (BIA), an agency that did not see its primary mission as the protection of Indian resources, was organizationally weak, and lacked the expertise to generate persuasive arguments in Congress.[17] Not surprisingly, it was difficult to develop the congressional support needed for Indian water projects. Instead, supporters developed the "Indian blanket" approach to deal with opposition to Indian projects: construction projects benefiting Indian and non-Indian recipients were combined into one bill that could be supported by Indian and anti-Indian factions in Congress.

While the iron triangle theory typically assumes that members pursue narrow economic interests, at least some individuals prize water control because it indicates that the community has organizational and political power.[18] Loss of water may result in the weakening of the community's tax base, infrastructure, and ability to support residents. Water is also a special resource with important symbolic and emotional value to poor rural communities and Indian tribes, where it is bound with culture and a way of life.[19]

By the late 1960s and early 1970s a series of challenges to the dominance of the water iron triangle began. Challenges came from Indians with water claims, environmentalists, and presidents concerned about the cost of water projects. The Animas–La Plata and Two Forks projects illustrate both the success of the water iron triangle under conditions of closed decision and the new forces that are making it increasingly difficult to build new projects.

The Animas–La Plata Project

Since 1938 local water users have sought the construction of the Animas–La Plata project to serve southwestern Colorado and northern New

Mexico. It is primarily an irrigation project that would divert surplus water from the Animas River to the larger area of potentially irrigatable land in the La Plata River basin.[20] Its supporters have primarily been Colorado farmers but also include New Mexico farmers and the Southern Ute and Ute Mountain Ute tribes. Water conservancy districts were established in both states as early as 1944 to promote it vigorously.[21] Sam Maynes, a local water attorney, has shepherded the project for decades. He and Leonard Burch, Southern Ute tribal chairman, have worked together since the 1960s to create a cooperative atmosphere among tribal and local governments, avoiding much of the racial tensions that plague Indian resource development in other areas.[22]

Typically, the impetus for the project was local, and the success of the project hinged upon the political muscle of legislators who had strong ties to the water users. This was true in Colorado, where Democratic Congressman Wayne Aspinall had political clout, strong ties to constituents, and a firm belief in the necessity of water projects for Western development. He was effective in holding the Central Arizona Project (CAP) hostage to five water storage facilities (including the Animas–La Plata project) that would protect Coloradans' right to divert water from the Colorado River.[23] Supporters of the CAP were willing to trade with Aspinall, but other obstacles existed.

Key problems included administrative delay and the lack of support from other institutional actors, notably the Bureau of the Budget. The Bureau of Reclamation was not even close to completing its planning reports on four of the projects and Bureau of the Budget clearance was necessary. The Budget Bureau initially refused, citing the problems with marginal irrigation projects (partly due to irrigation for Indian lands at the edges of the project) and minimal provision of municipal and industrial water. With encouragement from Secretary of the Interior Stewart Udall, the Bureau of Reclamation worked overtime to complete the reports and revise the Animas–La Plata Project to respond to Budget Bureau criticisms, including the removal of Indian irrigation to improve the cost-benefit ratio.[24]

Authorization of the CAP and five Colorado projects in 1968 illustrates the operations of the water iron triangle in the 1950s and 1960s.[25] The crucial determinant of the success of a project was political support from the dominant non-Indian water triangle, especially local water users. Local users focused their energies on Congress, their key access point, and won approval of the project when legislators chose to keep the decision-making system closed and to minimize conflict through mutual accommodation. Although an Indian triangle existed, it did not have the internal unity or political clout to affect decisions.

Despite the authorization of the Animas–La Plata project in 1968, the actual construction has languished. Animas–La Plata supporters have battled new opposition to keep the project afloat for the past twenty-five years. First, funding was a source of almost constant conflict. Although the 1968 bill planned to fund much of the project with revenues from power plants, pressure from the Carter and Reagan administrations made it obvious that state and local governments would have to negotiate a cost-sharing arrangement. State and local agencies finally agreed to pay 38 percent of the estimated cost for the first phase—the highest percentage of local cost sharing on record at the time of the agreement.[26] Despite the cost sharing, critics complain that only $1,272 of the $5,300 investment per water user will be repaid by local customers, leaving state and federal taxpayers to bear the brunt of the project costs.[27]

Second, local opposition (a factor from the start) has grown larger and more effective over time. Taxpayers for the Animas River (TAR) fought an almost single-handed war against the project for many years, complaining about its costs, environmental effects, and the inability of indebted farmers to afford it.[28] More recently TAR has created a coalition of regional groups that oppose the project on various grounds. The Four Corners Action Coalition includes river rafters, environmentalists, farmers, and some Southern Ute tribal members.

A local Indian rebellion is led by Ray Frost, tribal council member. Frost initially supported the project but now complains that it offers few of the benefits that Indians expect. He says that the cost-sharing agreement severely limits Indians' access to water from the project. That agreement divided the project into two phases. Water due according to tribal water rights will be stored in a reservoir created in the largely federally funded Phase I, but only 2,600 acre-feet out of the 58,900 acre-feet that belong to Indians will actually reach reservation cropland. Delivery systems are part of $154 million Phase II, which must be completely paid for by water users. Furthermore, Indians are prohibited from selling or leasing water off the reservation.[29]

Third, buoyed by the defeat of the Two Forks dam project, environmentalists began intervening. The 1990 U.S. Fish and Wildlife Service announcement that the project would violate the Endangered Species Act by threatening the Colorado squawfish[30] provided their window of opportunity. As soon as federal biologists agreed that a major reconfiguration of the project would sufficiently reduce harm to the fish, environmental groups filed a lawsuit to require that supplemental analysis be done to consider changes in data on endangered species, habitat, and new construction components of the project.[31] Since 1990 the Sierra Club Legal Defense Fund (with the support of its allies) have twice delayed project construction. Through four successful lawsuits they have established that the Bureau of Reclamation violated five separate federal laws. A court decision now requires the exploration of credible alternatives to the project. Ten state and national environmental groups have hired Jeris Danielson, former state water engineer, to suggest options for providing water without spending millions of dollars.[32]

Despite this impressive opposition, the project may ultimately survive because it represents the settlement of an Indian water rights conflict and, for this reason, has congressional backing. The Southern Utes and Ute Mountain Utes in southwestern Colorado sued for state court recognition of water rights with a priority date of 1868, which would make theirs the most senior water rights in the region. Although Indian irrigation projects were removed from the 1968 agreement to improve the cost-benefit ratio, an agreement has been made to provide 36 percent of the project's water to Indians. The construction would prevent white farmers from losing their existing water rights to the Indians, settle the Indian claim, and provide additional irrigation to white farmers.[33] This settlement is popular in Congress and strongly supported by Colorado's Democratic Sen. Ben Nighthorse Campbell, a Northern Cheyenne. Campbell argues that attempts to find alternatives to the Animas–La Plata project are just attempts to kill another federal treaty the government has made with Indians.

Two Forks Dam

To understand the Two Forks dam controversy it is necessary to explore the role of the Denver Water Board (DWB). In 1918 when Denver citizens voted to buy a private water company and create the Denver Water Department (DWD), a five-member appointed board was created to run the department. It was given the authority to be independent with the expectation that it would stay attuned to politics in the city and state. The DWB has performed the active political role that was envisioned, assertively filing for water rights across the continental divide and building the necessary storage and transfer facilities to bring water across the mountains and into the Denver region.[34] The board's style of operation was symbolized by its chief counsel, Glenn S. Saunders, who was known as an aggressive negotiator whose primary goal was to provide Denver with as much water as possible.[35]

Although the Denver city charter specifies that Denver customers must be provided with water service before the DWD can offer water service to suburban customers, the DWB has a long and somewhat erratic history of providing water to outlying municipalities. Various disputes, occasional limits on water service to suburbs, and the need to attract industry and retail centers that generate local government revenues produced conflict and mistrust between Denver and other local governments.[36]

For many years these tensions were of little concern to Denver because it ruled by edict. After World War II, Denver gradually began to compete with the suburbs, and by the 1970s, the city found itself in a political environment that had changed drastically. Environmentalists and no-growth advocates such as Gov. Richard Lamm believed that water provided a solution: stopping water development would limit growth and protect the environment. Suburban leaders concurred to the degree that they wanted to slow Denver's growth while procuring water that would support their own expansion.[37] As the decade proceeded, DWB's situation worsened. The board was short of treated water to offer suburban customers, but its proposal to construct the Foothills Treatment Plant and Two Forks Dam faced substantial obstacles: city residents did not want to pay for suburban services; new federal environmental constraints impeded the project; powerful suburban foes prevented Denver from expanding via annexation and thereby stripped away its perennial rationale for acquiring more water; and environmentalists used public participation provisions to fight the project.

Environmentalists became part of a broad coalition opposed to Denver growth that fought the Foothills Treatment Plant. The DWB jettisoned the Two Forks project and concentrated on the treatment facility. After a series of law suits, Congressman Tim Wirth (a Democrat from Colorado) negotiated a political settlement allowing the construction of the first stages of the Foothills Plant. In return, DWB made concessions: a strict conservation program, promises to provide minimum water levels for fish, and payment of part of the environmentalists' legal fees.[38]

By the early 1980s water shortages again appeared to be in the offing. As a result, the DWB began planning for Two Forks again. Environmentalists were as opposed as ever and complained that the DWB had failed to implement the promised conservation measures agreed to in the Foothills settlement. The environmentalists formed an alliance, the Environmental Caucus, which included national environmental organizations, local chapters of environmental groups, and government-oriented associations such as the League of Women Voters and homeowner associations. The goals of the caucus were to speak with a unified voice on water planning issues, promote metropolitan water planning, oppose the Two Forks project, and minimize the environmental impacts of water delivery.[39] They charged that DWB had pressured the U.S. Fish and Wildlife Service to recommend the dam. More important, they persuasively marshaled data to question the financial and technical soundness of the dam.[40]

This time Denver decided that it could make a stronger case for water development with the help of allies. Beginning in 1982 Denver created an uneasy alliance with more than forty suburban water providers (many of them municipalities and water districts) that resulted in a partnership to build Two Forks reservoir and dam. Denver and the suburban providers intended to provide all the financing of the project, removing the need for federal authorization and appropriations. They hoped that unified support for the project would overcome the objections of environmentalists and federal agencies such as the Environmental Protection Agency (EPA).

In the alliance, Denver was to pay 20 percent of the cost and receive 20 percent of the water but would use its expertise and experience to apply for permits and supervise construction. While the suburban providers would pay most of the cost and receive most of the water, they would have little control over the project.[41] Their incentive, of course, was acquisition of additional water in a situation hostile to water development. The wrangling over the project began in 1984, when the DWB and the providers announced they would seek the necessary permits from the U.S. Army Corps of Engineers. It continued in 1987, when the corps released a draft environmental impact statement (EIS) and the U.S. Fish and Wildlife Service announced its approval for the project (subject to a mitigation plan to protect animal habitat), and in 1988, when the final EIS was released. Criticism came from the EPA and environmental organizations, with environmental opposition being particularly effective because it challenged the project's technical merits.[42]

When Monte Pascoe, member and president of the DWB, used Denver water as a bargaining chip to promote metropolitan cooperation,[43] the partnership to build the water project became more than just an exercise in water development. For Governor Roy Romer, Denver mayor Federico Peña, and many local and state officials, it became an attempt to create a metropolitan water authority that would more efficiently provide and share water supplies. In return for water, the suburban governments were to finance central services such as indigent medical care and cultural facilities for suburban residents. Many were convinced that Denver water was the best glue to hold together metropolitan reform.[44] In this vein, Gov. Roy Romer recommended that a twenty-five-year dredge-and-fill permit be issued, but that construction begin only when it was demonstrated that the additional water was needed. The permit seemed destined to receive approval, but by 1990, the EPA vetoed it,[45] citing the loss of a scenic river that provided prize trout fishing, recreation opportunities, and an important aquatic habitat close to the Denver metropolitan area. Furthermore, the EPA noted, there were less-damaging alternative projects.[46]

POLITICAL CHANGES AFFECTING WATER POLITICS

By the late 1960s and early 1970s a series of challenges to the dominance of the water iron triangle began. Many of these are illustrated in the political disputes that characterized the Two Forks and Animas–La Plata projects.

The Challenge of Indian Water Rights

A more aggressive campaign to pursue reserved Indian water rights commenced. Although Indians have been guaranteed reserved water rights (sufficient water reserved for Indians to sustain human communities) by the Winters Doctrine since 1908, these rights were largely ignored because they were so threatening to those with prior appropriation water rights. If Indian rights were perfected, every acre-foot of water given to Indians could be taken from an existing water user.[47] Political leaders had no incentive to use the vague, open-ended Winters Doctrine to strip politically powerful water users of their existing water rights. As political scientist Daniel McCool notes, "For the most part water rights in the West have been determined not by abstract legal principles but by diversion, possession, and use."[48]

The modern era of Indian rights began as the alliance among the old

Indian triangle broke down, leaving two participants: more assertive Indian interest groups, and a BIA that is still ineffective in dealing with Congress. This uneasy partnership often places the rights and claims of Indians and non-Indians in direct opposition. This engenders conflict and fear that water decisions are a zero-sum game.

Many Indians increasingly resent attempts by environmentalists to derail water projects such as the Animas–La Plata in order to protect fish on the endangered species list. These Indians insist that the project will finally provide them with desperately needed water. Judy Knight Frank, the Mountain Utes' leader, noted that many Indians are forced to leave the reservation to seek employment. She complained:

> The environmentalists tell us: "Wait, this isn't the right project. There is something better for your people." But they have yet to tell us what the better thing is. For 100 years we did not have running water on this reservation. Where were the environmentalists then? They weren't hollering about the terrible conditions for our children. But now suddenly, the squawfish is so important. More important than the Indian people, apparently.[49]

Indian resentment mirrors the sentiment of many who make their living in rural communities, but it also suggests an element of class-based and racial conflict. Many environmentalists are white, prosperous newcomers to the area who do not appear to the Indians to understand how hard it is to make a living on remote and barren reservation land. Charles Wilkinson, the noted environmental law professor, suggests, "Environmentalists like to wrap themselves in the Indian blankets when they can. And there is some natural alliance. But that alliance comes into collision in the face of such terrible poverty in Indian country."[50] This antagonism between a poor racial minority, environmentalists, and the dominant class of water rights holders creates a redistributive issue that may keep Indians from entering the water iron triangle as major participants who can use mutual accommodation to accomplish their goals.[51]

Although more powerful than they used to be, Indians are still relegated to a secondary role. Because it is now harder to get water projects approved, Indian support can now be essential for water leaders trying to build a successful coalition, as Animas–La Plata supporters found out. But when the Indian blanket strategy is used by the dominant parties to procure their own interests, Indians do not end up with what they would have preferred, if their needs had been the driving force behind the project.[52] Thus, Indians are politically too weak to control the issue agenda and often have to choose from limited and less desirable options.[53]

The Challenge from Environmentalists

The role of environmentalists in the two projects is different but illustrates the opportunities and constraints under which they operate. Environmentalists came into the Animas–La Plata process rather late in the proceedings. The project had been approved in 1968, before regional and local organizations had enough resources to try to influence all large projects. The construction site was in a remote part of the state with limited population centers, so there was little to draw the attention of environmental groups. One of the environmentalists most active in fighting the Two Forks project, Dan Luecke of the Environmental Defense Fund, indicated that while his organization usually opposed dam projects, it shied away from the Animas–La Plata fight because he assumed it would be killed as the last of the "giant pork barrel projects."[54] Outside environmental groups have become active in just the last few years, forcing the Bureau of Reclamation to complete a supplemental EIS, which probably will not kill the project.[55] Animas–La Plata seems destined for construction, but environmentalists may be right when they predict that the final project will be a scaled-back version.[56]

Two Forks, however, is quite a different situation. The site of the project included 13½ miles of scenic river property that was heavily used for recreation because it was located so close to urban population centers such as Denver. The project was proposed by the DWB, which environmentalists and no-growth advocates love to hate because it has successfully and sometimes arrogantly built transmountain water diversion projects to fuel the growth of the Front Range.

Both the project and timing made this the perfect target for environmental groups. The timing was good because by the 1980s, when the project was again taken up, the environmentalists had become well organized and politically skilled. They opposed massive projects such as Two Forks to transfer, store, and treat water, complaining they were expensive and harmful to the environment when alternative management practices such as conservation could provide water without construction. Opposition from environmentalists and the EPA expanded the decision arena so that neither Denver nor the suburban water providers were able to control water development decisions.

It is difficult to generalize about the role that environmentalists play in specific project decisions. In some instances they hold life-and-death control over a project; in others they may be ineffective[57] or completely disengaged from policymaking. In the projects described here, environmental groups filed suits, critiqued environmental studies, and negotiated with water organizations. Without doubt they brought into the policymaking arena arguments about nonstructural alternatives and protection of resources that would not otherwise have been part of the negotiations. The bottom line, though, is that they face substantial hurdles because their goals are inconsistent with powerful water users' short-term interests.[58]

Environmentalists may have made their greatest contribution by elaborating symbols that stimulate people to act for or against projects. Furthermore, as national environmental organizations have promoted and shaped federal legislation, they have provided opportunities for participation via public comment periods and lawsuits that have opened up the old water triangles and helped local activists to devise strategies.

This expansion of the water triangles can be viewed as one more example of incorporation of local interests into the national domain. In the 1930s, the incorporation involved water users choosing to ally themselves with New Deal promotion of federally funded projects to stimulate the economy via irrigation projects. To be sure, these water users had disputes with federal agencies about the projects[59] and, furthermore, they succeeded in Colorado in maintaining the independence of their own community structures while participating in the development and operation of the resulting irrigation projects. They were incorporated in the sense that they shared a vision of economic prosperity that was fostered by federal irrigation projects. This vision prompted them to create statewide coalitions necessary to pass state legislation that established local structures such as water conservancy districts that could contract with federal agencies for the irrigation construction projects.[60]

The incorporation process continues in the 1980s and 1990s but, ironically, the water users who chose to be incorporated into the state's domain in the 1930s and 1940s are now finding it more difficult to maintain their autonomy in the face of national pressures such as environmental values, protective legislation, and opposition strategies to new projects. Lest this difficulty be overstated, it should be noted that while local water users and organizations no longer control the decision-making arena, they are still powerful participants armed with the potent weapon of prior appropriation water rights on which the federal government has chosen to tread lightly.

The Challenge from Presidential Administrations

The intrusion of presidential administrations, especially those intent upon controlling the budget, has made it harder for water triangles to accomplish their goals. Presidents Jimmy Carter and Ronald Reagan both sought to limit the authorization and funding of water projects, expecting state and local governments to make up the shortfall. Of the two, the Reagan administration, despite its professed support for water development, actually did more to control project funding. By 1986 Congress and the Reagan administration passed the Water Resources Development Act, which increased nonfederal cost shares for project construction and required more up-front financing by local organizations. Also, by the mid-1980s it appeared that water appropriations were more skewed toward operation and maintenance than was true in the past. This arrangement provides less money for new projects that reward additional iron triangle members.[61]

Although these changes proved burdensome, they have not devastated water interests. Despite rising budget deficits and threats to cut federal programs, funds for water projects have been fairly consistent, even when the Reagan administration convinced Congress to cut general domestic spending. Second, legislators are likely to continue to use pork barrel to win support from constituents. This political reality will limit presidential influence and support the water triangle.[62]

The Challenge from Urban Interests

In the past the primary conflict in Colorado over water has pitted western-slope interests against eastern-slope interests because the concentration of people and much of the agricultural production is across the continental divide from the primary water sources.[63] This competition still continues, but a new battle line has been superimposed: conflict between urban and rural interests. Like most western states, about 90 percent of water in Colorado is used to irrigate farmland. Post–World War II urban and industrial growth has increased demands for water. In recent years, Front Range communities have sought to transfer water to nonagricultural users through massive construction projects such as Two Forks, requests to pump huge amounts of groundwater from the San Luis Valley[64] and pipe it to urban communities, and city purchase of agricultural water rights.[65] All these attempts have been controversial, and many have met with staunch resistance, but it appears that Colorado will increasingly move to transfer water from agricultural to urban uses.

The urban-agricultural competition for water is exacerbated by urban-suburban rivalries that result in inefficient use and sharing of water within urban areas. Cities have spent millions of dollars to transfer water for hundreds of miles without considering the benefits to be derived from cooperation and pooling of resources. Most water experts agree that there would be enough water available for Front Range areas if existing resources were efficiently managed.

Many communities find urban-suburban cooperation difficult because of historical animosities. First, water users often feel they have a right not to share, especially when water is critically important to attract growth and wealth into their community.[66] Second, the Denver metropolitan area is served by a proliferation of water service agencies. Many of these were created as a reaction to the DWB's policy.[67] Denver failed to take the necessary political risks to promote a central water system, and the resulting fragmentation makes it difficult to respond to problems and crises.[68] During the 1980s Denver realistically assessed the hostile climate for the Two Forks dam and sought to promote both the dam and metropolitan cooperation by allying itself to forty-four suburban water providers. This could have provided the greatest incentive for integrated water management in the state's history,[69] but when the Two Forks project failed, so did any realistic chance for metropolitan cooperation on water. In fact, Denver resumed feuding with the suburban water providers and they, in turn, began scouring the state for likely water supplies, large or small.

CONCLUSION

The construction of water projects illustrates changes in water politics that have occurred since World War II. Local values, governmental structures, and water negotiation strategies have changed to reflect dominant national values. Local water users embraced these changes in the New Deal water project era (and when it appeared that Indian water demands might help them obtain the Animas–La Plata project). At other times they feared national forces as environmental values, national budget deficits, and Indian water claims that might limit their ability to develop their water resources.

Even though many changes have occurred, much remains the same. Agricultural interests remain important, although increasingly urban interests compete with them for water. Agricultural, industrial, and urban water users all remain committed project supporters who believe in water's ability to make their communities prosper.[70] Local and congressional political leadership is essential in lobbying for projects, although this leadership now responds to an expanded community including some Indian claims. Congress still remains important because of its ability to fund projects, but it is now more difficult to get project approval; critics strive to promote projects and federal agencies more attuned to conservation, water recycling, and nonstructural solutions. The previous losers, such as environmentalists, Indians, and poor rural people, are still fighting uphill battles even though they have more influence than before.[71] Although environmentalists can strategically position themselves to kill some projects, they are not active on all water issues and may not always succeed in their efforts. Political scientist Helen Ingram concludes that while projects today are not so objectionable as those of the past, they generally are not examples of environmentally sensitive water management.

The hallmark change is the expansion of the decision-making process to accommodate a larger number of group claims.[72] Today environmentalists, Indians, presidential administrations concerned about budget deficits, and urban water users are increasingly influential. Projects are no longer simply disputes about water supply: they often become debates about metropolitan cooperation in the provision of urban services, disagreements about growth policy, environmental management issues, and disputes over local control and life-style. Thus, water politics are characterized by more openness, less consensus, and a greater diversity of issues. Robert Gottlieb calls this "politics of the moment," in which there is no one alternative that is agreed upon.[73]

Water politics may be moving in the direction of the policy niches that have come to describe agricultural politics in which a diverse array of farmers, food processors, consumers, and environmentalists divide up to vie for influence in specific issue arenas.[74] The transformation in water policy is in progress and may never reflect every facet of agricultural policy niches, but the similarities exist. Politics remains the same in that there are still distinct issues or niches in which a few interests will be especially active. Participants in these niches can often win because they have advantages that others lack. Policy as a whole is not handled in a comprehensive fashion, and narrow interests continue to divide up the spoils.[75]

Yet this open system of policy niches is substantially different than iron triangles. Interest groups do not control policy even though some groups are more powerful than others.[76] Because interests are more diverse, the policy process is more complex and policy is unstable. Individual groups pursuing their own economic benefits cope with the complexity by creating short-term coalitions to collect information, negotiate agreements on policy, and devise strategies to support the policy.[77] Thus, there is no clear, concise lasting model of influence distribution.[78] Although many issues will involve distributive benefits, regulatory and redistributive policies will also be discussed.[79] Increasingly, when all water issues are viewed as a whole, there will be widely varying, conflicting representation of interests.[80]

CHAPTER 5

Labor and Ethnicity in Hawaiian Politics

H. BRETT MELENDY

Hawaii, the fiftieth state, is unique among the states given its Pacific Ocean island location. The Aloha State also differs from most mainland states because of its many ethnic populations, none of whom constitute a majority of island residents. This diverse ethnicity has had a major impact on state politics and social reform. For some two decades following World War II, the Japanese composed the largest minority, averaging about 33 percent of the total. From 1970 to 1990, Caucasians had 33 percent of the total, while the Japanese had 22 percent.

Other important ethnic groups in the 1990s, most of whom had been in the islands for much of the twentieth century, were Chinese (6 percent), Filipinos (15 percent), Koreans (2 percent), and Hawaiians. Native Hawaiians constituted less than 2 percent of the total, although through intermarriage, those people of Hawaiian or part-Hawaiian ancestry formed about 12.5 percent of the total population. To a lesser degree, Southeast Asians, Puerto Ricans, Samoans, African Americans, and American Indians have contributed to Hawaii's ethnic mix. Generally, harmony has existed among these various peoples, but from time to time, underlying tensions have exploded into violence.[1]

In 1990 there were 8,500 Hawaiians and about 17,500 part-Hawaiians in the state. Although stridency for self-determination has intensified in recent decades, Hawaiians remained the only indigenous people not recognized by the U.S. government. They demanded, to varying degrees, redress for the overthrow of the Hawaiian monarchy one hundred years ago. Their intense fervor has forced both business and political interests to pay close attention to their concerns. In response to Hawaiian demands, the state created the Hawaiian Affairs Office as an advocate for the islands' native population.[2]

The Hawaiian Islands have demonstrated clearly two lessons of history:

the desire by some people for continuity and the demand by others for change. As the Aloha State has moved toward the twenty-first century and confronted critical problems, the demand for change has been paramount. Some of Hawaii's problems were common to every state but others were unique. By the 1990s Hawaii faced (1) growing environmental problems throughout its islands and in the surrounding sea, (2) overpopulation with attending urban difficulties, (3) limited land and water resources, and (4) a fragile economy.

The six decades of territorial status made a lasting impact on the islands' social and economic structure and greatly determined the first thirty years of statehood. Unlike other Western states, Hawaii already had an autonomous government when it became an organized territory in 1900 that determined who would be in control. During the decades of territorial government, the sugar planter oligarchy, led by the Big Five sugar factors, successfully maintained its socioeconomic way of life by controlling island politics. Change first began to occur in the islands during New Deal years and World War II. In the postwar years, major shifts in society and politics developed as workers demanded an increasing share in the islands' economic benefits.

The Big Five, the islands' leading conservative force, were already well entrenched at the time of American annexation in 1898. These companies had gained control of most of the plantations and sugar mills. The Big Five consisted of three island-based corporations, one mainland firm, and one British company. Two of the island companies, Alexander & Baldwin's and Castle & Cooke's, evolved out of the nineteenth-century missionary companies sent to Hawaii by the American Board of Foreign Missions. The third island company, originally Hackfeld & Company of Bremen, Germany, was reorganized as American Factors by the Alien Property Custodian during World War I. The other two were C. Brewer of Philadelphia and Theo. Davies & Company of England. Coordinated control of the sugar industry was vested in the Hawaiian Sugar Planters Association (HSPA). U.S. Assistant Attorney General Seth Richardson's 1932 report on territorial governance revealed that numerous interlocking directorates enabled the Big Five to keep a stranglehold on the islands' economy. The Big Five usually controlled the governor's office, the legislature, and a coterie of friendly judges. Of the thirteen federally appointed territorial governors, eight were Republicans and five were Democrats.[3]

Sugar and pineapple plantation owners kept a strong check on their labor force, composed mostly of immigrants from the western Pacific.

When Native Hawaiians proved unenthusiastic plantation workers, plant-ers began overseas recruiting of Chinese, Japanese, and Filipinos, who provided the bulk of an inexpensive work force. During the first decade of the twentieth century, the planters had mixed success in recruiting Portuguese, Spanish, and Puerto Rican workers. Some Asian immigrants joined Hawaiians to work as longshoremen for dock and warehouse companies affiliated to varying degrees with the Big Five.

Plantation owners proved generally paternalistic toward their workers as long as they followed orders and did not participate in labor organiza-tions or politics. Under New Deal collective bargaining legislation, dockworkers started organizing with the International Longshoremen and Warehousemen Union (ILWU) as it began its rise to power.

Of the many threads forming Hawaii's postwar tapestry, none proved more dominant than that of labor, whose members came largely from the territory's nonwhite ethnic groups. An examination of this thread finds it intertwined closely, sometimes tightly knotted, with threads of the Big Five, territorial politics and governance, communism, and the drive for statehood. Following a series of struggles sometimes resembling sieges, island laborers gained a voice in their working conditions, made the Democratic party a viable political force, gained control of the territorial legislature, and dominated elected and appointed state offices from 1962 to the 1990s. What is more important, Hawaii's workers and their families, with a new measure of independence, improved their socio-economic status.

For several years following World War II, the ILWU demonstrated its economic and political clout. Economic warfare continued until manage-ment and labor reached a consensus regarding each other's role in the islands—the former wanting to keep the status quo and the latter opting for change.

In August 1945 the ILWU negotiated the first industry-wide sugar contract, covering all but one of the thirty-four plantations. The contract established a uniform wage system and increased wages seven cents per hour. Two years later, the ILWU signed an island-wide pineapple contract on 9 August 1947, that included a ten-cent pay raise retroactive to 16 July, the day workers ended the strike.[4]

With the expiration of the sugar contract in 1946, the ILWU called a strike involving 28,000 workers after negotiations broke down. This work stoppage, lasting seventy-nine days, brought an end to much of the plantation paternalism. Workers were no longer beholden to owners for plantation housing or plantation-run medical programs. They gained a wage increase, but the ILWU failed to gain a union shop or to reduce the workweek from forty-eight hours to forty.[5]

Eric Beecroft, chief of the Department of the Interior's Pacific Branch, Division of Territories and Island Possessions, felt in 1946 that island workers had stumbled unknowingly into an explosive situation, complicated by a potential loss of sugar cane ready for harvesting, racial tensions, a growing food shortage, and the HSPA's recent decision to recruit Filipino workers to augment the shrinking plantation work force.[6]

As the 1947 sugar strike continued, Hawaii also experienced a maritime strike that caused food shortages. These two strikes provoked the Honolulu Chamber of Commerce to assert that the ILWU sought to take over management functions and to control Hawaii's docks and plantations. Stanley White of the U.S. Conciliation Service, however, blamed the Hawaii Employers' Council for stalling strike negotiations "so that a war of attrition and public hysteria and starvation could be waged."[7] These years of intense feelings carried over into statehood as labor and management fought each other to gain the advantage.

A charge that communists had inspired the 1946 sugar strike led to a deep split between Hawaii's conservatives and liberals, a division affecting political life in the islands for years to come. As early as 1939, U.S. Army intelligence and the Federal Bureau of Investigation (FBI) reported that communists had been active in the islands. The army simplistically divided communists into two groups: "the usual middle-class intellectuals" and "labor organizers, agitators and their ilk."[8]

The ILWU's Political Action Committee, during the 1946 election, endorsed thirty-four candidates, twenty of whom won election. The 1947 session of the House of Representatives saw Democrats and Republicans evenly divided, fifteen each. The subsequent struggle to name a Speaker revealed the political clout of Jack Hall, the ILWU territorial chief. Conservative Democrats, led by Gov. Ingram Stainback, saw the territory's recurring labor strife as communist motivated. They believed that communists and fellow travelers were seeking control of the Democratic party.[9]

Harry Bridges, the ILWU's militant president, had been accused of being a communist, and it was common knowledge in Hawaii that Jack Hall had been a member of the Communist party. However, the extent of communism throughout the territory remained unknown. Sen. Guy Cordon, chairman of the Senate Subcommittee on Territory and Insular

Affairs, gathered testimony about the islands' fitness for statehood. His report noted that some mainland communist operatives were in Hawaii disguised as labor organizers. He felt confident that workers and the general public had resisted infiltration and that there was no danger of communists taking over Hawaii.[10]

Charges made in 1947 by Stainback and business leaders about the interrelationship of the ILWU, communists, and the Democratic party continued to surface at several congressional hearings concerned with statehood. Stainback believed that many Nisei (second-generation Japanese Americans), with college educations and improved standards of living, were "considerably embittered" about past discriminations against them and their Issei (Japanese immigrant) parents. They associated "the white race and its government with tyranny and oppression," making them, in Stainback's eyes, prime targets for communism.[11] The FBI reported that the plan of several island labor leaders who were directing the communist effort was to infiltrate several unions, particularly the ILWU. The FBI indicated that it had discovered forty-two known Communist party members and another thirty-one suspected of membership.[12]

Stainback's worry about the seizure of the Democratic party seemed realized in 1948 when the Oahu Democratic committee chairman deactivated Oahu's Democratic precinct clubs and ordered elections of new precinct officers and convention delegates for the 1 April island convention. Army intelligence and the FBI viewed this move as the long suspected drive for the communist takeover. The FBI reported that of the 500 convention members, 41 were members of the Communist party, 5 of whom were on the Communist party executive board. This Democratic convention saw a decrease in the political power of the old guard and an increase in Democratic control of the territorial legislature. The ILWU placed its favorites in key Democratic party positions but made no attempt to take complete control.[13]

Internal dissension rent the Democratic party over the next few years. Both liberal and moderate Democrats wanted Governor Stainback replaced with a governor who favored statehood. In 1951 Pres. Harry S Truman appointed Oren E. Long to succeed Stainback. Unlike Stainback, Long, a longtime island resident and moderate Democrat, favored statehood.

Anticipating that statehood would soon be realized, the territorial political parties elected delegates to the 1950 state constitutional convention that convened in April. Later that month, the Democrats held their island-wide convention. Before the election for constitutional convention delegates, the U.S. House Un-American Activities Committee (HUAC) issued warrants for the arrest of thirty-nine island residents. Known as the Reluctant 39, they received contempt citations for refusing to testify before the committee.

Fourteen of the Reluctant 39 were delegates and two were alternates to the Democratic territorial convention. Jack Kawano, president of Oahu's ILWU Local 136 and one of the thirty-nine on the HUAC list, charged that a motion offered early at the convention to unseat the fourteen was really an all-out attack on the ILWU. As it became clear that liberals controlled the convention and opposed ousting the challenged delegates, conservatives walked out, allowing new leaders and new directions to emerge. Out of this resulting chaos, John ("Jack") A. Burns, one of the "standpatters," emerged as the party's permanent chairman and remained the Democrats' top leader until illness forced his retirement as governor in 1974. Burns had earlier lobbied Democratic officials in Washington to gain Oren Long's appointment as governor. He extracted an agreement from Long that the new governor would not interfere with Burns's agenda for the Democratic party. In the late 1940s, he had forged an alliance with the Nisei and the ILWU.

Following the convention, the territorial central committee asked fifteen of the delegates and alternates whose seats had been contested to submit a notarized statement that they were not communists. Nine did so, five refused, and one resigned. The new Democratic leaders purged the party to such an extent that the FBI reported that no identified communist ran for any office in the 1950 primary election.[14]

Republican conservative senators and southern Dixiecrats in Washington, each of whom had a different agenda, kept the communist issue alive. Southerners did not want Hawaii with its ethnic mix admitted to the union because of the potential impact on the African Americans in their states. The Republican party's ultra-right wing, in concert with the spirit of McCarthyism, saw communists everywhere. Nebraska Sen. Hugh Butler used undercover investigations and hearings in Hawaii and in Washington to build up a fear of communism in Hawaii and to stall any statehood bill in the Senate.[15] Butler remained an implacable foe of Hawaiian statehood and served as a rallying figure until his death on 1 July 1954.[16]

The communist issue continued to plague the territory's drive for statehood. In August 1951 FBI agents arrested seven persons suspected of being communists for violating the 1940 Smith Act. After lengthy legal wranglings, a federal district court jury found the seven guilty. The circuit court overturned the convictions on appeal. At the time of the seven's arrest, the FBI, after years of submitting monthly reports, concluded that the territory's Communist party had a membership of only fifteen. Island conservatives, supported by Senator Butler and others in Washington, continued clamoring against a perceived communist threat. Oahu's conservatives, led by Republican Lawrence Judd, the former governor, organized the Hawaii Residents' Association, better known as IMUA, a Hawaiian word meaning "forward." IMUA moved from antiunion efforts to a continuing attack against communism. Mississippi Sen. James O. Eastland, chairman of the Senate Judiciary Committee, dispatched a subcommittee to Hawaii in 1956 to investigate again the penetration of communists into island unions. After a decade of turmoil, the controversy slowly faded away, but the issue made a lasting impact on island residents and the new state's political parties.[17]

Before World War II, there were several attempts to obtain statehood for Hawaii. In the postwar years, the combination of conservative forces in Washington, D.C., and in Hawaii stymied progress on a statehood bill although Presidents Harry Truman and Dwight Eisenhower came to favor statehood status for both Alaska and Hawaii. Anticipating quick action, the sixty-three delegates to Hawaii's April 1950 constitutional convention represented a middle-of-the-road outlook, with the majority of delegates being Republican. The ILWU elected only two of its fourteen candidates. Territorial voters ratified the proposed constitution, the basis for the one adopted in 1959.[18]

Democrat Jack Burns, whose first two attempts to be Hawaii's delegate in Congress failed, won election in 1956 and began his fight to gain statehood for the islands. Given the growing prowess of island Democrats, business leaders in the territory and Republican politicians in Washington, D.C., worried about their party's future in the islands, always considered a Republican stronghold. The prevailing Republican view in the 1950s was that statehood for Hawaii would bring three of their party to the halls of Congress, offsetting the anticipated three Democrats from Alaska. To strengthen the Republican party, a decision made in Washington to appoint younger men to leadership in Hawaii led to the replacement of Samuel King, the incumbent governor, then seventy-one years old, with William Quinn, at thirty-eight the youngest territorial governor. Quinn, a popular and able politician, defeated the Democratic party's leader, Jack Burns, at the first state election in 1959.[19]

However, with the defeat of Quinn's administration in the 1962 state election, the Democrats started their march to virtual control of state politics as Jack Burns led his ethnic coalition to power. His first lieutenant governor, William Richardson, was of Hawaiian ancestry. Republican Hiram Fong, a Chinese American, became the first person of Asian descent to serve in Congress. First elected in 1959, he remained in the U.S. Senate until 1983 because of a friendly alliance with the ILWU. Democrat Daniel Inouye became the first Japanese American to win election to the House of Representatives. In 1962, he gained Hawaii's second Senate seat, winning reelection five times, the last being in 1992. When Hawaii gained two seats in the House in 1962, Spark Matsunaga and Patsy Takemoto Mink, both Democrats, won election. In 1983, Fong was succeeded by Matsunaga as a U.S. senator until his death in April 1990. Republican Patricia Sakai and Democrat Daniel Akaka served in the House during the 1980s, and with Matsunaga's death, Akaka, a Hawaiian, joined Inouye in the Senate.[20]

After serving three terms as governor, Jack Burns was succeeded by George Ariyoshi, the first Japanese American to serve as a state governor. Ariyoshi had been Burns's last lieutenant governor. Ariyoshi's lieutenant governors were of Japanese, part-Hawaiian, and Hawaiian descent. John Waihee, his last lieutenant governor, followed Ariyoshi to the governor's chair in 1990. Waihee's lieutenant governor was Filipino Benjamin Cayetano. Indeed, Hawaii's voters have regularly elected candidates from the several ethnic groups. Members of these groups have also filled appointive offices in the governors' cabinets.

The state's judiciary and legislature reflected the strong power of the Democratic party. Ten years after statehood, the state senate had sixteen Democrats and nine Republicans and the house had thirty-nine Democrats and twelve Republicans. By 1992 the Republican party had become moribund. Of the seventy-six-member state legislature, only seventeen were Republicans. With such a margin, the Democratic leadership has had no great problems in accomplishing its legislative goals.[21] The Democrats launched many social and economic programs to improve the life of the islands' work force.

In a real sense, Honolulu, under Democrats and earlier under Republicans, resembles Paris more than an American city, with its highly centralized concentration of both private and public sectors. Honolulu is the state's business, banking, and government center. It serves as the islands' transportation hub—for both freight and passengers moving through Honolulu harbor and the international airport.

Hawaii's schools compose a single district with a statewide unified curriculum managed by the state department of education. An early legislative decision in the 1960s reversed the Big Five's idea that territorial schools were to offer vocational education to train future plantation workers. The Democratic legislature mandated that vocational education would not be part of the public school curriculum. Like parents everywhere, Hawaiians wanted their children to have an opportunity to have richer lives and to escape the plantations and docks. To offset the lack of vocational education, the legislature created a community college system that by the 1990s operated one college on each neighboring island and four on Oahu. These colleges had a two-track system, offering vocational education and a college transfer program. The state underwrote the upgrading of existing postsecondary campuses as well as construction of several new buildings and complete campuses. Higher education was centralized in the University of Hawaii's Board of Regents. By the 1990s, the regents oversaw the Manoa campus in Honolulu, with its professional colleges; a West Oahu College; the University of Hawaii at Hilo, a four-year campus; and the community colleges.

The university and the state library system provided contractors, usually Democratic party supporters, great opportunities during the Burns administration to erect new structures. This development repaid political obligations while providing jobs and services to the state's people. With scant concern for the islands' environment, Governor Burns encouraged developers to build public works, high-rise office buildings, and hotels. With Democrats in charge, however, many Republican general contractors were unable to win contracts for state-funded construction projects. Burns was willing to fund one-time capital improvements but proved reluctant, as in the case of libraries, to hire sufficient staff to operate the newly built libraries because of the on-going costs that staff incur.

He instituted a loyalty test of sorts to fill vacant positions and micromanaged the naming of all appointments. For example, when a gardener retired at Kauai Community College in the early 1970s, the governor decided who his replacement would be. Burns used that vacancy to reward a deserving Democrat. Such tactics, common in places like Chicago and other political realms, guaranteed a retinue of party faithful. The Democratic machine created by Jack Burns has continued into the 1990s, controlling most of the state and national positions and publicly funded programs. Island business and political leaders know that the machine can determine their economic and political futures.[22]

Indicative of pressing social concerns, Hawaii became a national leader in health care. A government official from Alaska has written, "It never ceases to amaze me, how the 'youngest' states to the Union are the first to provide quality human services to the citizens of our states, and the 'oldest' states are just beginning to examine the need for delivery and access for health care!"[23] Hawaii's outstanding health plan has been evolutionary, not revolutionary. In 1970, Hawaii became the first state to legalize abortions. Four years later, the Hawai'i Prepaid Health Care Act required all employers to provide health insurance to all employees working more than nineteen hours per week. Workers' contributions were limited to 1½ percent of monthly wages. Supplementing this law was the Medicaid program (sponsored by both the federal and state governments) for the "medically indigent who are 62.5% below the poverty level."[24] The 1989 legislature enacted the State Health Insurance Program (SHIP) "to provide access to primary preventative health care services to Hawaii's medically uninsured residents." To be eligible for SHIP programs, a person had to be a resident of Hawaii and be ineligible for another government-sponsored program or health insurance through an employer. An applicant to SHIP had to have a gross family income that was less than 300 percent of the federal poverty level adjusted by family size. Additionally, the applicant had to have been without health insurance for at least three months to be eligible.

SHIP became operative in mid-1990, and by December 1991 it had provided service to 22,990 island residents. According to Dr. John C. Lewin, state director of health, Hawaii is committed to 100 percent coverage. By March 1992, the state had "achieved about 98 percent coverage." Through the foresight of its citizens and their legislature, Hawaii in 1991 had, according to the Northwest National Life Insurance state health rankings, "one of the best and most comprehensive health programs state-by-state." The survey indicated that "Hawaii ranked as the all-around healthiest state in the nation." Hawaii compared favorably with the Canadian national health plan and offered a model for a national health plan.[25]

Hawaii's citizens have inherited ongoing social and economic problems that are related to the islands' scarce resources. The increase in the state's population has severely affected the quality of life, a situation encountered by many mainland states. Along with demographic changes, the fragile economy brought great concerns for state government leaders and economists who had to forecast trends.[26]

In 1946 the territory's population was 545,439. At the time of statehood in 1959, Hawaii had 622,087 people. Thirty years later, 1,108,229 people lived in the island paradise. About 75 percent of the state's population lived on the island of Oahu. In 1959, only two cities had an excess of 10,000 residents: Honolulu, with some 248,000; and Hilo, with about 22,000. By the 1990s, eight communities exceeded 29,000. By 1990 Hilo's population had increased by almost 16,000 while Honolulu had grown by about 117,000.[27] Urban crowding increased traffic congestion, while increases in crime and drug use have had unhappy consequences. In 1977 Governor Ariyoshi, concerned about these problems, advocated the barring of immigration to Hawaii as a new influx of immigrants arrived from Southeast Asia. These newcomers greatly strained the state budget and further complicated the state's urban concerns. The legislature enacted a one-year residency requirement for most county and state jobs.[28]

At the time of statehood in 1959 sugar and pineapple plantations provided the most jobs and the greatest income, with tourism occupying third place. In the following years, tourism and national defense alternated as the number-one industry. By 1980 tourism remained fixed in first place. In 1959, 243,216 tourists arrived in the islands as jet air travel made access to Hawaii very affordable. This number of visitors increased to 3,700,000 by 1979. A large number of these tourists came from Japan and made a major impact on island businesses. In 1988 Hawaii's income from tourism was $9.2 billion. Meanwhile sugar and pineapple fell to third and fourth place in generating state income. Sugar substitutes, increased mainland sugar production and local growing conditions in the islands, often climatic, reduced Hawaii's cane sugar production. With pineapple produced more cheaply in the Philippines, Indonesia, and Thailand, Hawaiian pineapple plantations abandoned their fields. The island of Lanai, devoted almost entirely to the growing of pineapple since the 1920s, closed its fields and by 1992 was building resort hotels. Actually, Hawaii's largest cash crop was marijuana, known as Maui Gold.[29]

On Oahu, Big Five companies converted plantation lands to suburbs of Honolulu. Mililani Town, with 29,359 residents in 1990, did not exist in 1970. Castle & Cooke's carved this development out of its plantation lands. In rural Oahu and on the neighboring islands, considerable agricultural lands changed to resort hotels and golf courses. The demand for resorts led to a significant influx of Japanese money to build or buy hotels and golf courses. This substantial concentration of Asian investment as wcll as tourists created something of a backlash as islanders saw their future residing in the hands of outsiders.

Tourism, essentially a service industry dependent on visitors, has had to rely completely on outside factors including national and international economic conditions. Tourism and other service industries, together with an expanding population, have intensified the islands' resource problems — using up available land and threatening scarce water resources. Additionally, tourism, expanding suburbs, and automobiles have exacerbated both air and water pollution — particularly befouling offshore waters with untreated sewage. All in all, the islands' environment has come under great stress.

Hawaii, the last organized territory to be admitted to the United States, has made great social strides since statehood. Ethnic plantation workers and dockworkers, once the pawns of the Big Five, have flourished in state and local politics and bettered their economic status. As with other states, the citizens of Hawaii must solve major crises as the "Loveliest Fleet of Islands that lies anchored in any ocean," according to Mark Twain,[30] sails into the twenty-first century.

CHAPTER 6

Harassment, Hate, and Human Rights in Idaho

STEPHEN SHAW

The last of the fifty states to be sighted by white, Anglo-European explorers (1805), Idaho "remains one of the least known and most puzzling of American states."[1] Idaho contains the largest wilderness area in the lower forty-eight states; the Frank Church River of No Return Wilderness Area, established in 1980 and named after the late, four-term (1957–81) Democratic U.S. Senator, is over two million acres in size. Hells Canyon, in the Hells Canyon National Recreation Area, is the deepest gorge in North America. Idaho ranks forty-second in population (just over one million residents, according to the 1990 census statistics), yet is thirteenth in area (83,557 acres). However, "if Idaho were flattened by a steam roller, its land mass would expand into the largest of all the lower forty-eight."[2]

Not surprisingly, the Gem State's political history varies as much as its terrain. Idaho's state seal is the only one designed by a woman (Emma Edwards Green). The first (and only) Jewish governor in the state, Moses Alexander, was the first Jewish governor in the country. In 1885, the Test Oath Act was adopted by the territorial legislature (Idaho joined the Union on 3 July 1890), which was designed to ban members of the Church of Jesus Christ of Latter-Day Saints (Mormons) from voting or holding office. Yet just a decade later, in 1896, Idaho urged the U.S. Congress to grant women the right to vote. Evidencing early the state's prominent and lingering sectionalism—it's the only state with three state fairs—the University of Idaho was located at Moscow in 1889 in northern Idaho allegedly in order to keep the North from seceding. Various parts of northern Idaho still threaten to carry out that late-nineteenth-century urge to join another state or to create a wholly new one—if for no other reason than to remind contemporary Idahoans, especially those in Ada County, home of the capital city of Boise, that they have not forgotten their history.

As late as 1983, several northern Idaho local governments passed resolutions to secede and form a new state.

Idaho last supported a Democrat for the White House in 1964, when Pres. Lyndon B. Johnson narrowly defeated Barry Goldwater of Arizona. More recently, Idaho has consistently been one of the most dependable states for the Republican presidential ticket. In 1980 and 1984, Idaho delivered a greater percentage of votes for Ronald Reagan than any other state except Utah. In 1992, however, Pres. George Bush barely edged out H. Ross Perot, the independent presidential candidate from Texas. The state prides itself (though not without some rather glaring exceptions) on a "live-and-let-live" philosophy of tolerance, yet until 1982, the Idaho Constitution (Article 6, sec. 3) prohibited from voting, holding office, or jury service anyone who, in essence, belonged to the Mormon church.

In the words of one writer, "Wedged between six states, in a region so remote settlers once viewed it as more of an obstacle than a destination, is the last frontier of the America that was."[3] Often depicted as pristine, uncorrupted, or some kind of Eden ("If God made anything prettier, He must have kept it for Himself"),[4] the fact remains that, with the exception of being one of the country's most homogenous states, Idaho "is one of the most varied of states," where "conflict is inherent. Idaho survives by settling conflict or suppressing it. And it seldom stays suppressed for long."[5] An excellent illustration of this particular thesis is the fact that "since 1975 the Gem State and its environs have become haven to a virulent strain of bigotry and racism."[6] Perhaps it would be more accurate to say, "almost-haven," for as surely as organized hate reared its ugly head in Idaho in the past two decades, a countermovement emerged to deny white supremacists the realization of their vision of a new political entity in Idaho and the Pacific Northwest.[7]

On 11 June 1993, the U.S. Supreme Court announced its long-awaited decision in the closely watched case *Wisconsin v. Mitchell*.[8] At issue in the case was a Wisconsin statute enacted in 1989 that enhances the maximum penalty for a crime, such as aggravated battery, whenever an individual "intentionally selects the person against whom the crime . . . is committed . . . because of the race, religion, color, disability, sexual orientation, national origin or ancestry of that person."[9] Such so-called penalty enhancement laws became commonplace in the 1980s: close to one-half of the states passed these statutes as part of their collective effort to address the increase in crimes based on religious and racial hatred.

Writing for a unanimous Court in *Mitchell,* Chief Justice William H.

Rehnquist upheld the Wisconsin statute against the primary claim that it violated the free speech clause of the First Amendment.[10] The Chief Justice acknowledged the fact that under the Wisconsin law the same criminal conduct may be more heavily punished if the victim is selected because of his race or other protected status than if no such motive existed.[11] However, rejecting the argument that the statute violates the First Amendment by punishing one's bigoted thoughts, Rehnquist noted that "motive plays the same role under the Wisconsin statute as it does under federal and state antidiscrimination laws, which we have previously upheld against constitutional challenge."[12] Moreover, Rehnquist argued that the Wisconsin statute was aimed properly at conduct (unlike speech or expression) that is not protected by the First Amendment. Thus, the Court, through Rehnquist's opinion, concluded that the Wisconsin penalty enhancement law, by virtue of being "a permissible content-neutral regulation of conduct"[13] and due to its existence as an expression of the state's concern about conduct thought to inflict great individual and social harm, was not an unconstitutional attempt to criminalize bigoted thought.

As noted, several other states have enacted penalty enhancement provisions similar to the one involved in *Wisconsin v. Mitchell,* such as the law enacted in Idaho in the early 1980s. The decision in *Mitchell,* therefore, was of interest not only to lawmakers and others in Wisconsin; rather, individuals and groups across the country were waiting anxiously for the Court's decision.[14] The state of Idaho was no exception.

Proclaiming "a new chapter in Idaho's history,"[15] Gov. John V. Evans signed into law the Malicious Harassment Act on 30 March 1983. The law, which went into effect on 1 July 1983, was the product of bipartisan effort in the Idaho legislature and especially between a Democratic governor and a Republican attorney general, Jim Jones. The law made it a felony "for any person, maliciously and with the specific intent to intimidate or harass another person because of that person's race, color, religion, ancestry or national origin" to cause "physical injury" to another individual, to "damage, destroy, or deface" the property of another person, or to threaten to commit such acts if there is reasonable cause to believe the threat will be carried out.[16]

The legal and constitutional status of the law was called into question almost a decade after its enactment when, on 28 October 1992, an Idaho district court judge citing, inter alia, *R.A.V. v. City of St. Paul,*[17] *State v. Wyant,*[18] and *State v. Mitchell,*[19] ruled that the Idaho law ran afoul of the First Amendment: "The statute is broad enough to extend to social protest of a nature that has previously been afforded First Amendment protection. . . . However the statute is approached, it goes beyond punishing a specific act and punishes for wrong thoughts."[20] Idaho Attorney General Larry EchoHawk announced the state would appeal the decision and seek to restore the 1983 act.[21] At the same time, the state joined twenty-eight other states as amici in the *Mitchell* case going before the Supreme Court. Awaiting that decision, the state requested and received a stay of the appeal of the district judge's decision in *State v. Sullivan*.

The Idaho law against malicious harassment primarily owes its existence to the Idaho Human Rights Commission. In an attempt to respond accurately and effectively to a perceived rise in racial hatred and religious bigotry in Idaho in the late 1970s and early 1980s, the Human Rights Commission convened a panel of public and private figures on 24 July 1982 for purposes of gathering information on the extent of racially and religiously inspired harassment in Idaho and finding ways to combat the threat to human rights and civil liberties.[22] In particular, the commission was interested in legislation drafted by a deputy attorney general assigned to the commission. In December 1982 the Human Rights Commission submitted its legislative proposal to the state legislature, motivated in large part by the perception of the commission's director that northern Idaho, especially the Coeur d'Alene–Hayden Lake region, was quickly becoming an area of "international white supremacist activity."[23] The bill was introduced in the next session of the state legislature by State Senator Norma Dobler of Moscow, and according to the coordinator of the Kootenai County Task Force on Human Relations, the proposed measure produced more mail from constituents to legislators than any other piece of legislation during the 1983 session.[24]

What led the Idaho Human Rights Commission, the Citizens Coalition Against Malicious Harassment, the Interstate Task Force on Human Relations, and numerous other organizations[25] to organize and campaign for the Malicious Harassment Act was the presence and activities primarily of one man and his organizational and ideological offspring.

Richard Girnt Butler moved to Idaho in 1973 from southern California, where he had worked for Lockheed Aircraft as an engineer in Lancaster. A native of Colorado, born into a Presbyterian family on 23 February 1918, Butler fell under the spell of the Reverend Wesley Swift,[26] whose church in Los Angeles—the Anglo-Saxon Christian Congregation, also known as the Church of Jesus Christ-Christian—Butler began attending in 1963. Swift, who died in 1970, was at one time "the top West Coast lieutenant of

Gerald L. K. Smith, the notorious anti-Semite and racist who led the Christian Nationalist Crusade for over 40 years and published its hate sheet, *The Cross and The Flag.*[27] Smith, a pivotal part of "the old Christian right,"[28] found in Swift, a onetime Ku Klux Klan organizer, one of his most loyal and zealous followers. Butler followed the Swift precedent of discipleship by becoming one of Swift's most trusted assistants. In speaking of Swift, Butler would later remark, "He had the answers I was trying to find."[29]

Those "answers" exist largely in the confines of what is known as "Christian Identity," "Kingdom Identity," or also "Anglo-Israelism." (Butler's church in Hayden Lake, Idaho, the Church of Jesus Christ-Christian, which he claims to be the direct successor to Swift's congregation in California, is an Identity church.)[30] According to one writer, "The deceptively mild-sounding Identity movement . . . is one of those phenomena that seem to occur only in the novels of Kurt Vonnegut."[31] There is nothing mild, however, about the tenets of Identity, which has given to Butler and others in the contemporary hate movement much of the moral and theological (or pseudo-theological) justification for their beliefs and conduct.

Christian Identity is most succinctly (and accurately) depicted as a theology of hate or a theology rooted in racism.[32] Primary among its doctrinal underpinnings are the beliefs that white Europeans and their descendants are the chosen, favorite people of God, and that they are the lost tribe of Israel; that Jews are the children of Satan (whom members believe impregnated Eve with Cain);[33] that blacks are subhuman and thus have no souls;[34] that the federal government is in the hands of an international Jewish conspiracy and thus is illegal (the federal government is disparagingly called the Zionist Occupation Government—ZOG); and that there is an impending, inevitable, and eagerly awaited racial Armageddon, the culmination of their apocalyptic vision.[35]

Central to Identity is the doctrine of the inherent superiority of the white race. Blacks and others from non-Aryan races, often referred to as "mud races,"[36] are on a spiritual par with animals. In essence, Wesley Swift "turn[ed] apocalyptic racial hatred into a religion."[37] Identity links biology and theology; one's virtue is found in one's skin color. By its very nature, it is "a violent doctrine because it presupposes an Armageddon-type battle between whites and minorities, and fighters in this war take on the status of holy warriors."[38] Identity essentially performs a dual role. It "provides religious unity for differing racist political groups and it brings religious people into contact with the racist movement."[39] In sum, Identity "is nothing but white supremacy with a religious veneer."[40]

According to one scholar, "The Anglo-Israel movement was already well established in the Pacific Northwest by 1970, and several Church of Jesus Christ Christians were themselves living in retirement near Coeur d'Alene."[41] The "mother church"[42] of the Identity movement was soon to be established by Richard Butler and his followers, who journeyed to northern Idaho in the early 1970s following the death of Wesley Swift. Joining Butler were Swift's daughter and her husband, each of whom would split from Butler's organization in less than a year.

Butler and his racial cosmology first found safe haven in Idaho in the Posse Comitatus ("power of the country"), to which he belonged from late 1974 to early 1976. He rose to the rank of county marshall of the Kootenai County Posse Comitatus, only to be evicted from the group in an internecine power struggle. In 1974, on the forty acres of land he had purchased near Hayden Lake, Idaho, Butler started what has become the religious arm of the Aryan Nations, the Church of Jesus Christ-Christian. The Identity pseudo-theology became his "reservoir of support"[43] at his compound, which he has referred to as "the world capital of the white race."[44]

Butler, however, was not content with merely a church in the wildwoods of northern Idaho. Envisaging something grander, in April 1980 at an Identity conference in Hays, Kansas, Butler "hoisted for the first time the Aryan Nations flag and proclaimed the founding of a racially clean homeland, bounded by the Rocky Mountains, the Mississippi River, the northern Canadian plains, and the Mexican border."[45] His proposed state within the United States would be "separated from all alien, mongrel people" and would, with its legal code and administrative structure, "provide for the common defense of our Racial Nation."[46] By mid-decade, however, Butler's plan had undergone a drastic, noticeable geographical shift. In 1985, Butler announced a new "racialist" nation prospect, calling for a northwest Aryan Republic; and in 1986 at the annual Aryan Nations World Congress at the Hayden Lake headquarters, the Northwest Territorial Imperative was revealed. It would consist of a new five-state (Washington, Oregon, Montana, Wyoming, and Idaho) Pacific Northwest Aryan Nation with Kootenai County, Idaho, as its provisional capital.[47] Butler's "10 percent solution," of course, to this date at least has not met with any clear degree of success.

Butler's Aryan Nations, and its religious arm, the Church of Jesus

Christ-Christian, never has had a large number of followers, at least in terms of persons who attend the church in Hayden Lake or are active participants in Aryan Nations and Aryan Nations–related activities.[48] Nonetheless, Butler and his loyal compatriots have had a measurable impact on Idaho politics throughout the 1980s, even into the 1990s.

According to one group that monitors the actions of groups such as the Aryan Nations, "In its Aryan Nations form, Identity has led to racist terror and violence."[49] Richard Butler, the self-described disciple of Jesus Christ, Thomas Jefferson, and Adolf Hitler,[50] complained in the early 1980s, "We, the white race, we have no state for our nation."[51] One of the favored slogans of the Aryan Nations is My Race Is My Nation. Butler proudly sits with a picture of Hitler at his desk. His office is ordained with the flags of the United States, the Aryan Nations (whose symbol Butler refers to as his "Resurrection swastika"), and a Third Reich battle flag. Butler proclaimed that fellow-believing, nonmongrelized whites, "a stateless people," would rise up in arms within five years.[52] Such a call to arms is key in Identity–Aryan Nations ideology, given the doctrinal belief in an eventual war between the races. Butler was not engaging in mere rhetoric; indeed, there were direct and immediate consequences entailed in his advocacy, to the extent that in late 1982, the U.S. Department of Justice commissioned a study of organized hate within Idaho.[53]

In 1979, at his headquarters near Hayden Lake, Butler sponsored and hosted the initial Aryan Nations World Congress (or Pacific States National Kingdom Identity Conference). With the exception of 1985 (due to the federal prosecution of the Order), this has become an annual gathering of Aryan Nation members and "fellow patriots," including in recent years neo-Nazi "skinheads."[54] Shortly thereafter, the Aryan Nations became more visible and aggressive both in Idaho and surrounding states, even into other parts of the country outside the Pacific Northwest. Posters began to appear on telephone poles and in post offices and other public venues in northern Idaho announcing "Runnin' Nigger Shoots"; in 1981, a "Summer Conference and Nigger Shoot," for which Butler later denied any responsibility or involvement, was advertised on Aryan Nations letterhead over Butler's signature. In the same year, an announcement appeared in several magazines, such as *Shotgun News*, proclaiming, "Aryan Brotherhood Welcome: Last White Stronghold in North America. Sell your goods, buy an M1A rifle and bring the family."[55] Butler himself was arrested, tried, and convicted for trespass in the spring of 1981 in Boise while on a southern Idaho speaking and recruiting trip.

However, these activities were only the relatively amateurish opening act for a well-planned and well-staged series of events over the next couple of years constituting a campaign of terrorism aimed at overthrowing the government and establishing a racialist state. Many of these right-wing terrorists, "perhaps the most violent in American history since the notorious Black Legion of the 1930s,"[56] came from the ranks of Butler's Aryan Nations. Calling themselves the White American Bastion, the Aryan Resistance Movement, or Bruders Schweigen ("Silent Brotherhood"), soon they were most well known simply as the Order.[57] Formed in October 1983, the Order's operations over the next eighteen months, according to one analysis, constituted "the first attempt by right-wing extremists in this century to launch a violent revolution against the American government."[58]

The Order, initially a group of twelve Aryan Warriors, began counterfeiting $50 bills at the Aryan Nations print shop in Kootenai County in November 1983 as the first step in amassing the financial war chest necessary to implement their goal of a whites-only republic. A month later a Seattle, Washington, bank was robbed; the lone gunman who escaped with over $25,000 was Robert Mathews.[59] In January 1984 a second bank was robbed, this time in Spokane, Washington; in March 1984 an armored car was held up in Seattle, and in April $500,000 was taken from another armored vehicle in Seattle. That same month the Embassy Theater (an adult movie theater) in Seattle was bombed, and one week later, a bomb was exploded at the Congregation Ahavath Israel Synagogue in Boise, the largest synagogue in the state. In June 1984, Alan Berg, a Denver radio talk show host, was murdered in his driveway by the Order. (The murder weapon was found at an Order member's home during a search of the residence following a tip from a Federal Bureau of Investigation informant.) The next month, the Order robbed an armored truck in California of $3.6 million; the terrorists met in Boise two days later to divide the proceeds.[60]

The ringleader of the Order, Robert Jay Mathews, would later die in a shootout with authorities in December 1984 on Whidbey Island in Puget Sound. A month before his death, the Order issued its Declaration of War: "We, from this day forward declare that we no longer consider the regime in Washington to be a valid and lawful representative of all Aryans who refuse to submit to the coercion and subtle tyranny placed upon us by Tel Aviv and their lackeys in Washington. . . . Let friend and foe alike be made aware. This is war!"[61] According to the declaration, any agent of the

Zionist Occupation Government of North America "will be considered our enemy."[62]

Following Mathews's death, the Order began to disintegrate. On 12 April 1985, a federal grand jury in Seattle returned a ninety-three-page indictment against twenty-three of its members, charging them with violations of the federal Racketeer Influence and Corrupt Organization (RICO) statute and other criminal acts, including murder.[63] After a three-month trial, those members of the Order who had not already pled guilty to the charges against them were found guilty and given prison sentences ranging from twenty-five to one hundred years. The successful prosecution (at a cost of over $1 million) involving the presentation of over 1,500 pieces of evidence and the testimony of close to three hundred witnesses, "is said to have involved one-quarter of the total manpower resources of the FBI, which followed a trail of sixty-seven separate crimes including robberies, arson, bombings, counterfeit schemes and murders throughout the country."[64]

The convictions of the terrorists in the Order, however, did not bring to an end other Aryan Nations activities in Idaho. Richard Butler stated, "I believe they jumped the gun. I still agree with them philosophically."[65] In September 1986 four bombs destroyed the relative tranquility of Coeur d'Alene, Idaho, one of them at the rectory of the Reverend Bill Wassmuth, a Roman Catholic priest.[66] In 1987 the Northwest Coalition Against Malicious Harassment was formed, becoming the first multistate public venture to fight bigotry and promote racial and religious tolerance in response to the white supremacist movement in the Pacific Northwest.[67]

In 1987 Butler, along with twelve other white supremacists, was indicted for "seditious conspiracy."[68] They were charged with conspiring between 1983 and 1985 to establish a white supremacist state and plotting to destabilize the government and foment a white supremacist revolution. In February 1988 Butler and his colleagues went on trial—the first trial since World War II involving white supremacists and sedition charges. On 7 April 1988, after seven weeks of testimony and twenty hours of jury deliberation, all thirteen individuals were acquitted of all charges.

At roughly this same time, in February 1988, federal indictments were brought against several individuals who had formed what came to be known as the Order II, some of whom were involved in the 1986 bombings in Coeur d'Alene. This so-called Bruders Schwcigen Strike Force II had established a hit list of federal judges, law enforcement officials, and Aryan Nations opponents, including Butler himself, who in the eyes of this band was moving too slowly along the infallible revolutionary trail. All of the individuals against whom charges were brought pled guilty in September 1988.[69]

In 1989 Butler and the Aryan Nations sponsored the first nationwide gathering of skinheads at the compound at Hayden Lake; and in September of that year Butler announced plans for a new Aryan Nations branch near Pulaski, Tennessee, the birthplace of the Ku Klux Klan in the nineteenth century.[70] In May 1990, three Aryan Nations members were indicted for plotting to bomb a gay bar, a Jewish synagogue, and several Korean businesses in Seattle.[71] They were all found guilty in the fall of 1990. And in 1991 the Aryan Nations annual World Congress again was held, along with an Aryan Nations Youth Congress in April to coincide with the birthday of Hitler. One of the games for children present was "Pin-the-Nose-on-the-Jew." At that same affair, one of the several pamphlets being circulated among the participants was "Understanding the Struggle, or Why We Have to Kill the Bastards," which recommended killing or deporting any known opponent of the drive for racial purity.[72]

According to the U.S. Commission on Civil Rights, "The phenomenon of racial and religious violence is a serious threat to the maintenance of a peaceful, democratic, and pluralistic society."[73] The events of the past two decades in Idaho and the Pacific Northwest evidence much more than the ideology of a misguided few: Richard Butler and the Aryan Nations acted on their so-called gospel righteous hatred and racial revenge. Exactly why they chose Idaho as their home base, from which to export their myopic vision of an Aryan republic, is more a matter of conjecture than certainty. Land in northern Idaho was cheap. Idaho is one of the most homogenous states in the country, with a small minority and Jewish population. (It was the last state to report a case of acquired immune deficiency syndrome — in 1985 — known to be disproportionately affecting gay men and nonwhites.) Idaho's remote mountain setting, politically conservative reputation, and tolerance of unusual beliefs,[74] so it is argued, were reasons why white supremacists set up shop and still practice their philosophy there today.[75]

In the words of one longtime observer of politics in the Gem State, "Occasionally Idaho gets national attention. Maybe because of an earthquake. Or a herd of Mud Lake farmers bashing jackrabbits."[76] Or perhaps due to a violent minority plotting the overthrow of the government and the establishment of apartheid. In the eyes of many individuals and groups, Idaho became the haven of hate during the past two decades.[77] Arguably, however, the primary effect of the Aryan Nations "was to make their neighbors more self-consciously tolerant."[78] Due to the tireless and creative efforts of the Northwest Coalition Against Malicious Harassment, the Interstate Task Force on Human Relations, the Kootenai County Task Force on Human Relations, the Citizens Coalition Against Malicious Harassment, and the Idaho Human Rights Commission, along with numerous other groups and individuals, a countermovement was established and maintained in Idaho to combat the efforts of Butler and his compatriots.[79]

However, the white supremacist movement still exists in Idaho.[80] According to Raymond L. Stone, the mayor of Coeur d'Alene, "The woods north of Hayden Lake . . . remain home to the Aryan Nation." He argues that in combatting the "vile philosophy" of white supremacy, the communities in northern Idaho have "won a victory of sorts, but we cannot pretend that the battle is over."[81] In recent years, attempting to exploit dire economic circumstances in some communities in the Pacific Northwest, white supremacists including members of the Aryan Nations have been courting unemployed loggers to make common cause with them in their opposition to environmentalists and the federal government.[82]

The latest chapter in Idaho's battle with white supremacists was the Ruby Ridge incident, a series of events that occurred over a three-year period. Randy Weaver, a former Green Beret, self-described white separatist, and acknowledged adherent of Christian Identity, had been arrested for selling two sawed-off shotguns to federal agents running an undercover operation and investigation by the U.S. Bureau of Alcohol, Tobacco and Firearms into illegal gun operations by white supremacists in northern Idaho. He was indicted in December 1990 and released on his own recognizance, but he failed to appear on his trial date in January 1991, apparently due to a mistake made by federal authorities in Weaver's trial date.

Weaver holed up with his wife and children and family friend Kevin Harris in a cabin he began building in 1984 out of plywood and particle board atop isolated Ruby Ridge in the Selkirk Mountains, less than one hour from the Canadian border. He was under surveillance from February 1991 until 21 August 1992, when an eleven-day siege began with a gun battle between U.S. marshals and Harris and one of Weaver's sons, who was killed, as was a deputy marshal. Weaver's wife was later killed by sniper fire. The siege ended when Weaver surrendered on 1 September 1992.

Weaver and Harris were put on trial for, among other things, conspiring against the federal government and killing the marshal. In a trial that lasted eight weeks, Weaver was represented by the noted criminal defense attorney Gerry Spence. Following a contentious trial in which the federal government was rebuked severely on several occasions by the presiding judge and in which the government admitted to tampering with evidence, a jury deliberated for nineteen days (the longest deliberation in any criminal trial in Idaho history) before acquitting Weaver and Harris on the most serious charge of murder.[83]

There was no evidence introduced at the trial linking Weaver, Harris, or other family members to any organized neo-Nazi operation.[84] In the eyes of many, Weaver, who earlier had refused to inform on the Aryan Nations, became a folk hero, particularly after his wife and fourteen-year-old son were shot and killed.[85] Others feared that according Weaver such status would breathe new life into the neo-Nazi, white supremacist ranks.[86]

There is no mistaking or denying that the White Christian Republic of which Richard Butler and others still dream is just that. Butler's numbers have dwindled and his supporters are few. Neither should it be overlooked that Idaho law and politics clearly register, and will for some time to come, the battles fought between the forces of exclusion and the forces of inclusion. It is a battle that our constitutional democracy has been fighting ever since its inception, with no apparent end in sight. Idaho, like virtually every other state in the country, may not be some political, functional equivalent of heaven on earth. Neither is it, however, the haven of hate and harassment that some imagined it could be.

CHAPTER 7

Kansas and Water:
Survival in the Heartland

JAMES E. SHEROW AND HOMER E. SOCOLOFSKY

Survival in Kansas, as in all western states, has depended on an available water supply. Since World War II, the growth of urbanization, consumerism, and agribusiness has given rise to mounting problems over water policies and development. Differences in Kansas have grown among and between interests involving farmers, the U.S. Army Corps of Engineers, the major cities in the state, environmental groups such as the Audubon Society (which has endeavored to protect Cheyenne Bottoms, a sizable wetland), and irrigators tapping aquifers such as the Equus Beds and the Ogallala Aquifer. The Kansas Water Act of 1945 paved the way for these conflicts by intentionally making water a distinct economic commodity, sensitive to shifting market and social trends in the post–World War II period. In short, water became a limited economic resource in Kansas subject to increasing demands.

Since 1945, rising tensions over water development have illustrated the changing nature of Kansas: a state with increasingly powerful urban interests overtaking farm concerns. Moreover, the sensitivities of a consumer-based middle class have made gains against the traditionally powerful voice of agribusiness. As Gerald Nash, a noted historian of the twentieth-century West, shows, the West has undergone a "social and cultural transformation" in the postwar period, and the water history of Kansas reflects this same change.[1]

At the end of World War II, for the first time Kansans developed an effective regulation of water within the state. Earlier laws and policies were a hodgepodge of conflicting interpretations regarding the application of riparian rights based on English common law and the prior appropriation system of water rights.[2] In 1944 the Kansas Supreme Court declared invalid any application of prior appropriation and left the riparian doctrine governing the state.[3]

In 1945 George Knapp, who had become the chief engineer in the state Division of Water Resources in 1919, labored to devise a system whereby people could develop the economic potential of water. He realized the need to eliminate the riparian doctrine and to reverse the effects of the 1944 decision if the state were to stimulate and encourage the economic development of water. In 1944 Knapp wrote that "unused water cannot widely be held in perpetuity for a common-law owner who may never have use for it, without resulting in underdevelopment, permitting the water to flow out of the state and on toward the ocean, as an economic waste and loss of a valuable natural resource."[4] For an engineer steeped in conservation ideology, the problem lay simply in devising an effective code ensuring the efficient economic use of water throughout the state. Gov. Andrew Schoeppel appointed Knapp chairman of a committee of ten that rewrote the Kansas water law. In April 1945 the legislature codified the committee's work in the Kansas Water Act, thereby giving the state a set of consistent water laws designed to stimulate the economic development of water.

The 1945 act made water amenable to economic development by establishing a prior appropriation system similar to those in other western states. The legislature declared all water within the state to be public property subject to regulation by the chief engineer of the Division of Water Resources, an agency within the Kansas State Board of Agriculture. Kansans filed their applications for a water right with the Chief Engineer, who then assigned an appropriation date to the right along with an amount of water the right carried. The act established a hierarchy of water uses: domestic, municipal, irrigation, industrial, recreational, and power production. However, an important part of the act read, "The date of priority of an appropriation right, and not the purpose of use, determines the right to divert and use water at any time when the supply is not sufficient to satisfy all water rights that attach to it."[5] Hypothetically, if during drouth[6] a stream failed, the holder of a recreational right dated 1946 could demand water at the expense of someone holding an agricultural right dated later, forcing a farmer to curtail water use. In this aspect the Kansas code differed from hierarchical uses in other western states. For example, Colorado law would allow an irrigator's right to take precedence over recreational, or instream flow, use.

Two other features of the 1945 law involved the protection of vested rights and the use of eminent domain. Prior to the 1945 legislation, Kansas water users perfected their rights under a medley of laws blending riparian and prior appropriation doctrines. The legislature clearly intended to protect any rights so developed, provided that water users applied these rights in beneficial pursuits. All water rights, however, were previously subject to condemnation through the use of eminent domain for municipal uses. The 1945 water act did not address the eminent domain aspects of water use, and this omission would lead to explosive situations in the next decade.

The most innovative feature of the 1945 act was the administration of groundwater under the prior appropriation doctrine. Only one other western state, New Mexico, had put groundwater under effective public administration. After 1945, Kansas groundwater, which the state courts had previously ruled "a part of the real property in which [the groundwater was] situated," became part of the state's public domain.[7] Knapp, and other like-minded Kansans, hoped that the 1945 act, along with revisions passed in 1957, would encourage the rapid economic development of all water resources in the state, including groundwater.

Knapp also worked to lure the federal government's aid in building water projects. However, constructing federal dams, like Tuttle Creek on the Blue River, often created conflict. Kansas's worst natural disaster, with little loss of life but tremendous loss of property, was the flood of 1951. Initial property damage estimates of $1 billion ballooned quickly to $2.5 billion, a figure so large that it was difficult to comprehend in a state with an annual government budget of about $200 million. The Kansas River, its tributaries, and many other rivers flooded at their highest level since 1844, ten years before white settlement. Plans emerged over many years for major flood control reservoirs in the eastern half of the state, but only two had been built—Kanopolis Lake on the Smoky Hill River, and Fall River Lake in southeast Kansas. As a consequence of the devastating 1951 flood, pressure for flood protection brought a series of political confrontations, pitting farmers against townspeople and downriver populous areas against upriver small towns. The most volatile was the Tuttle Creek controversy, which brought a highly visible presence of the Army Corps of Engineers into Kansas.

The stimulus to build Tuttle Creek was the huge 1927 Mississippi River flood. Economic losses along the great water course stimulated Congress to charge the Corps of Engineers with devising a plan for controlling floods on the "Mighty Miss." This entailed locating potential flood control structures on any tributary of the Mississippi.[8] Part of the corps's plans called for building levees along the Kansas River in Kansas City;

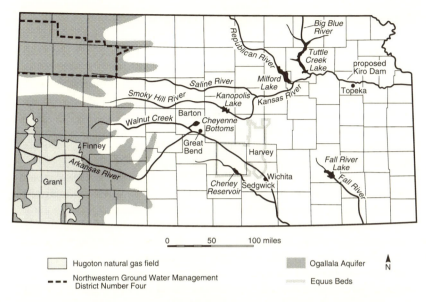

Kansas Water Resources and Management Based on map by Jennifer Sims.

however, vigorous complaints came from industrialists and railroad companies that could be materially affected by the corps's strategy. They formed the Flood Protection Planning Committee and hired F. H. Fowler, a consulting engineer who began surveying alternative sites for flood control structures in 1934. In 1937 he revealed his plan for upstream dams near Milford on the Republican River and near Tuttle Creek on the Blue River.[9]

Relief efforts of the Great Depression of the 1930s, however, veered away from his suggestions. The corps remained apathetic about Fowler's plan and, instead, contemplated a huge two-mile-long dam across the Kansas River at Kiro, just west of Topeka. Such a program would have employed thousands of people in need of work, but a Kiro dam would have also produced an enormous reservoir and have necessitated the relocation of many towns, hundreds of farms, many cemeteries, several railroads, and major highways. The Kiro dam idea encountered a fast political death.

Tuttle Creek, however, remained alive. The project became part of the Pick-Sloan Plan of 1944, a combined effort on the part of the corps and the

Bureau of Reclamation to merge flood control with multipurpose dams along the Missouri River and its tributaries.[10] However, other projects commanded the attention of the corps — until the flood of 1951. Knapp had always endorsed the corps's flood control projects, and he seized the opportunity the flood provided him to lure the corps to Kansas to build Tuttle Creek Dam.

Virtually no one in the Blue Valley had looked forward to the possible arrival of the corps. After World War II farmers from the proposed reservoir site organized the Tri-county Blue River Association. The Blue River Study Club followed; and finally after the 1951 flood, dam opponents from a large area formed the Blue Valley Study Association (BVSA). The BVSA, funded by volunteer contributions, campaigned against the dam. Late in 1951, BVSA joined with others opposing federal water projects and formed the Kansas Watersheds Association, Inc. It supported alternative proposals for watershed treatment through a series of hundreds of smaller, upland dams for water retention. Congress refused any appropriations for Tuttle Creek other than small planning funds until 1952. At that time, an initial $5 million was authorized for the corps on the recommendation of Pres. Harry Truman and Congressman Albert M. Cole, who represented the Blue Valley and northeastern Kansas.

Farmers in the valley were in the midst of a busy season for farm work, so their wives, the Blue Valley Belles, busily spread their message of opposition to "big dam foolishness." Downriver people who expected Tuttle Creek Dam to protect them from flooding regarded the farm and small-town populations of the Blue Valley as selfish obstructionists. An army colonel labeled Blue Valley folks "crackpots and nitpickers," whereas opponents of Tuttle Creek considered the army engineers arrogant, entrenched bureaucrats. The Blue Valley Belles received national media attention when they went to Kansas City to see President Truman and after a telephone call to General Eisenhower's presidential campaign headquarters in Denver opened the way for a sizable delegation to visit Ike. The BVSA sought to defeat Cole, whom they had previously supported, when he sought reelection to a fifth term. They successfully elected Howard S. Miller, who became the "dam congressman" from Kansas. Miller could do little, but no additional funds were appropriated for Tuttle Creek in 1953. Successful party primary candidates for the first congressional district in 1954 were Miller and William H. Avery, both opposed to big dam foolishness. Avery won the election but was unable to deter a congressional appropriation in 1955 and later for continuing construction of the dam, which was dedicated in 1963. The more than three thousand people who lost their homes to the dam did little celebrating.[11]

The Corps of Engineers won the battle and always contended that Tuttle Creek was the key dam for the entire Kansas Valley. Nowhere else, so goes the folklore around Manhattan, had the corps such difficulty in gaining its goal except on a project on the Feather River in California.[12] Nonetheless, the construction of Tuttle Creek provided the corps and the Bureau of Reclamation the opportunity to build many other flood-control projects throughout the state. More than twenty major federally funded dams and reservoirs would cover 120,000 surface acres by 1985.[13]

Knapp's vision for Kansas water and the economic development of it came to life in the western portion of the state, where occurred the exploitation of a seemingly abundant source of water. In the 1950s, drouth plagued the farmers in western Kansas, who encountered less precipitation for agriculture than they had during the dust bowl days of the 1930s.[14] Farmers of this era, unlike their counterparts in the depression years, possessed new implements, techniques, and institutions for combating the dry conditions. In addition, soil conservation methods, supported by the Soil Conservation Service, had shown productive results. Moreover, an increasing number of farmers in southwestern Kansas, like their counterparts in other states, were beginning to tap the Ogallala Aquifer through new pump technologies, which freed them from a reliance upon rainfall and gave them a sense of security (even though they were actually depleting their natural resource base). So, the drier 1950s never witnessed the immense dust storms that provided added publicity of the disaster of the dust bowl of Kansas and neighboring western states. The economic development of groundwater, however, would soon give rise to tensions over the uses of several aquifers.

The Ogallala Aquifer, a huge underground water basin encompassing 134,000 square miles, underlies the High Plains from South Dakota to Texas. The total "drainable" water measured 3.25 billion acre-feet in 1986, or enough water to fill Lake Huron, third largest of the Great Lakes. The saturated thickness of the aquifer varied so that some irrigators had very deep sources beneath their land while others did not. For example, "some farmers in north Finney County have no drainable water, but those in the southern portion of the county 25 miles away have more than 200 feet of saturated thickness, enough water to permit irrigation for over one hundred years at 1980s' depletion rates."[15]

After World War II, developments in pump irrigation technologies and the 1945 Kansas Water Act made the use of the aquifer for farming economically feasible on nearly any terrain. Elsewhere, irrigators still used an older style of flood irrigation on virtually level land. Frank Zybach's invention of the center pivot irrigation system, first patented in 1949, gave rise to the circular, dotlike green patterns of western Kansas and other western areas that are visible to airline passengers. These aluminum pipe megamachines mounted to A-frame towers riding on tandem wheels circle a center-post swivel where ground pipes tap the water, which is drawn to the surface by large pumps driven by diesel- or natural gas–powered engines. A 360-degree sweep of the frame can irrigate about 133 acres out of a 160-acre quarter section.[16]

The existence of pump technology and its rapid diffusion throughout western Kansas emphasized a geographically variable, rather than uniform, depletion of the aquifer. From the start of pumping in Kansas in the late 1800s to 1980, 166 million acre-feet of water were pumped.[17] Compared to the huge quantity underground this seems insignificant. Nevertheless, irrigators' pumps have failed in some areas where their operations overlie a shallow saturated thickness of the aquifer. Some farmers in the southern portions of Kansas, particularly in Grant County, have experienced significant declines in their water tables, while irrigators to the north have not. This differential posed problems in the formation of policy for water users in the area.

The Ogallala Aquifer contains water thousands of years old. Recharging has been nearly nonexistent in historic times. The irrigators who pump this aquifer are depleting a nonrenewable natural resource, and ultimately drawing water from this reservoir will no longer prove economically feasible for Kansas farmers. In the 1970s and 1980s, some irrigators realized their dilemma and wanted to forestall or slow the rate of depletion; others disregarded any planned depletion and demanded a right to pump for as long as they could. In response to tensions among farmers and with state bureaucrats and environmentalists, the Kansas legislature passed the Groundwater Management District Act of 1972 to provide irrigators with the legal machinery to regulate their own groundwater use.

The pattern developed by the Northwest Kansas Groundwater Management District Number Four illustrates how tensions can flare over planning. In February 1976, 1,058 irrigators voted two to one to organize District Number Four. When the district's board of directors began preparing groundwater use plans, discomfort and strains soon surfaced among the members. In the drouth of the late 1980s the district irrigators collectively pumped about three and one-half times the recharge rate of the aquifer. The board's response, led in large part by District Manager Wayne Bossert, called for "zero depletion," or pumping only the amount of groundwater replenished through normal recharge. Bossert estimated that only about 25 percent of the 1990 pumping level could continue under his plan.[18]

Many district members reacted coolly to zero depletion. In fact, family disputes arose over these policies. For example, the disagreement between Sharon Steele and her brother Ken Frahm centered on Bossert's proposed program. Steele, an advocate of zero depletion, believed "we can make much better use of the water if we refine how we use it." Her brother contended that his generation "made a huge investment in irrigation, so that we could be productive with it. We were assuming we would have time to get our mortgages paid off." Frahm also stated, "We all went into that investment knowing that the water wasn't going to last forever, maybe 30 years. We didn't go into it with ideas that we would face artificial constraints."[19] While the debate continued to split the members of the district, Bossert and the board feared a future of costly litigation.

Farmers were not the only interests encountering limits and mounting disagreements over the wholesale exploitation of groundwater. After World War II, the needs of the Wichita metropolitan area for additional water supplies led to serious conflicts. The war had transformed Wichita in many ways. Not only had it become the largest city in Kansas, but very quickly one in six Kansans lived in Wichita and Sedgwick County. These people went to work in growing industries, particularly in the aircraft plants. Expansion in Wichita's major manufacturing and wholesale plants provided an incentive to develop other services available in this largest market in Kansas.

To Robert H. Hess, the first director of the Wichita Water Department (formed in 1957), and like-minded Wichitans, planning for Wichita's growth meant the acquisition of additional water supplies. Hess came well prepared to lead the city in its pursuit of water. He had completed a master's degree in chemistry and physics and was working on a doctorate when he accepted a job in Wichita to analyze the city water supply. He soon became the city's chief chemist, and in 1957 he became the director of the city water department.[20]

Hess oversaw a department with a complex history. Beginning in 1938, the city switched from a reliance upon the Arkansas River and city wells to tapping a portion of the Equus Beds, a large groundwater aquifer in northwestern Sedgwick and western Harvey counties. A peculiar system operated whereby the city owned the wells and delivery system and a private company purified the water, delivered and metered water supplies, and administered billing. When the drouth of 1952 struck, the city began pumping its wells heavily. The groundwater level in the Equus Beds dropped precipitously, hurting scores of farmers. These irrigators banded together to oppose the city, and conflict raged in and out of court. The city extended its reach further into the Equus Beds after 1952, leading to a protracted legal battle over the constitutionality of the Water Act of 1945. Farmers in the affected region protested vigorously—someone even shot at city work crews installing pipes and pumps. The city employed the doctrine of eminent domain and shoved aside the contesting farmers, who retaliated by making a court challenge to the 1945 act.[21] In 1990, Evelyn Regier, who farmed with her husband near Burrton, remembered Wichita's attempt to "steal" their water, and of her own and the other nearby farmers' emotions. "There are still a lot of hard feelings and those feelings will not be gone until my generation is gone," she remarked.[22]

Clearly, in the 1950s the continued growth of Wichita and lawsuits over the Equus Beds revealed to Hess a need for an alternative water source. He, powerful business interests in Wichita, and Senators Andrew Schoeppel and Frank Carlson began lobbying for the construction of Cheney Reservoir. In September 1960 their efforts bore fruit when Pres. Dwight Eisenhower signed the bill approving the dam and reservoir. Five years later, the Bureau of Reclamation had completed building the dam and the Army Corps of Engineers began its administration.

By the mid-1970s, the Wichita city planners realized that continuing current consumption trends for projected population increases necessitated additional water resources. Two controversial proposals surfaced: the creation of a water market for water rights to the Equus Beds, and an intrastate transfer of water. In 1990, the city, reinforced with a $4 million allowance, placed ads in the *Wichita Eagle-Beacon* looking for individuals willing to sell their water rights. The city offered $400 per acre-foot, about one-fourth of what Colorado farmers could receive for water. The bid generated little enthusiasm among prospective sellers, many of whom remembered the ruckus of the 1950s.[23]

The other plan involved the transfer of water from Milford Lake in the northern portion of the state into a pipeline system underwritten by the joint efforts of Wichita and fourteen other central Kansas communities. In

October 1989, after ten years of discussions, the water officials of these cities and towns formed the Central Kansas Wholesale Water Supply District Number Ten (CKWWSD) to carry forward plans for a pipeline 199 miles long and capable of transporting 60 million gallons of water per day. The project carried a $212 million price tag when first conceived.[24]

The pipeline, however, faced many barriers. First, water officials and concerned citizens in the Kansas–Lower Republican watershed viewed the CKWWSD's project with skepticism and outright opposition. Anticipating a threat to their water supplies, these northeast Kansas interests formed the Kansas River Alliance (KRA) in 1982. KRA activists such as R. E. Pelton, who led the association in the early 1980s, kept a vigilant watch for signs of Wichita's water "stealing." Moreover, any pipeline project has to meet the provisions of the Kansas Water Transfer Act of 1983, which requires that the state consider the economic, environmental, and public health implications of any transfer of water.

Not surprisingly, the pipeline issue ended up in the state legislature. The KRA and CKWWSD represented about one-half of the state's population, so the issue gained high visibility in the Capitol. Legislators, realizing the high stakes involved, shifted the decision to the bureaucracy in the Kansas Water Authority. In the fall of 1992, the agency decided to hire engineers for a study that many thought would take years to complete.[25] In the meantime, the citizens of expanding Wichita continued to increase per capita water consumption and water options narrowed for Wichita planners. The Equus Beds showed serious contamination problems ranging from the incursion of salt water left over from sloppy oil drilling techniques to the influx of petrochemicals associated generally with agriculture.[26]

Wichitans, however, did not view their water problems single-mindedly. Among the many voices were those of urban environmentalists, whose sensibilities had been formed in large part by a consumer-based economy and who, worried about quality-of-life issues, demanded greater conservation efforts on the part of city officials. Slowly officials in the Wichita Water Department responded by considering new building codes requiring water-saving plumbing in new homes and buildings. Environmentalists replied that the city water planners had been acting too slowly to curb "shameless water gluttons." Some critics noted that many Wichitans consumed six times the water necessary to keep their lawns green; in fact, most of their water use was in keeping lawns green.[27]

The same changes in American sensibilities that gave rise to demands for urban conservation led to rising concerns for wetland preservation. The protection of Cheyenne Bottoms, one of the most important wetland areas in the nation, illustrates the point nicely. This wetland encompasses a sixty-four-square-mile depression in central Kansas and has provided a nesting and feeding area for migrating birds for nearly 100,000 years. During their migrations along the central flyway, 95 percent of five shorebird species exclusively use Cheyenne Bottoms, the only remaining great freshwater marsh in the interior states. In total, an estimated 45 percent of all shorebirds that migrate through the interior of the United States use this wetland.[28]

For nearly five decades before World War II many Kansans had worked to preserve Cheyenne Bottoms. Their efforts resulted in agreement between state and federal bureaus on a joint undertaking. As early as 1890, people in nearby Great Bend sought to manage the water level in Cheyenne Bottoms to promote tourism, but nothing came of their efforts. Later, the Kansas Forestry, Fish and Game Commission, formed in 1925, assumed responsibility for managing the bottoms, and the federal government supplemented the Kansas effort with funding provided through the Pittman-Robertson Act of 1937.[29]

Not until after World War II did officials in both Kansas and federal wildlife agencies worry about external environmental threats to Cheyenne Bottoms. They viewed with alarm the continuing depletion of flow in the Arkansas River and the increased groundwater pumping, both of which were reducing surface flows into Cheyenne Bottoms. In 1947, R. A. Schmidt, the regional director of the Federal Wildlife Service, unsuccessfully tried to introduce his concerns into the formation of the Arkansas River Compact, which divided the water impounded behind John Martin Dam between Kansas and Colorado water users.[30]

In 1949 the state, aided with federal funding, built canals, dikes, control structures, roads, and blinds in the bottoms. Water had to flow through the Arkansas River and Walnut Creek to make these systems work. The flows in the Arkansas River and Walnut Creek declined, however, and led to a dry Cheyenne Bottoms on numerous occasions—even after 1958 to the present, when precipitation remained higher than average. Farmers use of center-pivot irrigation since the mid-1970s had lowered groundwater tables, causing a sink into which surface creek and river flows drained.

Sportspeople and environmentalists took note of the profound changes to Cheyenne Bottoms and asked the Division of Water Resources to curtail pump irrigation in the Walnut Creek watershed. Since World War II, these groups have commanded increasing attention of the state's water officials. Moreover, the 1945 water act clearly recognized the economic worth of recreational uses of water, and these uses, especially the "nonconsumptive" uses of bird-watchers, mounted in importance. For example, in 1985, hunters contributed $128,000 to the economy of Barton County whereas bird-watchers spent an estimated $606,195. By the late twentieth century, the Audubon Society, Wildlife Federation, and the Kansas Ornithologist Society, representing many bird-watchers, eclipsed hunters as the main economic motivation for preserving the wetland. Together, all of the recreational groups made an effective publicity and lobbying effort to protect the bottoms.[31]

The public relations efforts of environmentalists and sportspeople led to a unique decision in western water use, one based on the Kansas Water Act of 1945. In 1992, David Pope, the chief engineer in the State of Kansas, curtailed irrigation pumping in the Walnut Creek watershed in order to protect the water rights of Cheyenne Bottoms. Pope decided the bottoms had not been receiving its full entitlement of water, 19,000 acre-feet per year, based on its 1947 water right on Walnut Creek. Consequently, users with groundwater rights postdated 1947 had to curtail their water pumping for five years to permit enough recharge to make viable the water rights of Cheyenne Bottoms. Environmentalists hailed Pope's decision as a victory for the new consciousness of their movement, but a closer examination of his decision reveals a rather different reasoning on the part of Pope.[32]

Pope claimed he had simply obeyed the mandate of the Kansas water code and had ultimately conserved the water supply in the interests of all Kansans regardless of their individual perspectives on his decision. Had he allowed irrigation to continue unabated, he said, then the farmers' "wells would have been sucking air." Pope simply enforced the principle of first in time the first in right, and in essence, he believed he had helped to save irrigators from themselves. "The thing that I guess a number of them may not have understood . . . was that a permit to appropriate water is not a guarantee that water will be available either physically or legally."[33] Pope's decision awakened those farmers with rights dating two decades after the 1945 water code to some grim realities.

Pope's actions sat poorly with pump irrigators, who construed his actions largely in the same light as had the environmentalists—favoring wildlife over farmers' interests. Fliers circulated in the region vilifying

"The Pope of Kansas Water." Bernard Juno, a farmer who had converted from dryland farming to pivot irrigation in the late 1960s became, in his own words, "a dryland farmer with wetland debt, so what's left to do—give up and get a minimum wage job in town?" Predictably, the entire matter headed to the courts. The counsel for the farmers, Mark Calcara, viewed Pope's decision as the beginning of a battle "my grandchildren may be fighting."[34]

If competition between water interests had not created enough tension, the growing complexity of institutional control over water in Kansas has certainly added to it. By 1990 eleven state agencies, overseeing more than seventy programs, have varying responsibilities for the uses, quality, and protection of water. Most of these bureaus came into being or gained significant obligations in Kansas water matters since World War II.

This widespread tangle of institutional duties for water development, competition among water interests, and water users' political influence in the legislature has hamstrung efforts to implement a statewide water plan. The 1963 state legislature enacted the first tentative water plan, followed with a more detailed one in 1965. In general, the plan allowed the state, through the Water Resources Board (in 1981 replaced by the Kansas Water Authority) to participate as a partner in federal projects in the state.

The high costs envisioned in the proposed plan put urban and environmental interests in conflict with agricultural interests, especially the Kansas Livestock Association and Kansas Farm Bureau, the largest farm groups in the state. Much of the funding for the Kansas water plan would have come from fees for the use of water and farm chemicals, supplemented by some general fund revenues. Powerful farm interests in the state rebelled over these funding provisions and through the early 1990s successfully lobbied the legislature to reject such assessments levied against agribusiness in the state.[35]

These conflicts stimulated urban critics to question the ability of the Division of Water Resources to guide water development for the common good, not just to advance the interests of farmers. This issue made its way into the legislature, where urban and agricultural interests clearly squared off over the funding of the state water plan. Since the mid-1960s, as a result of reapportionment, urban representatives formed the largest group in the Kansas legislature. The 1950 federal census showed for the first time in the history of the state that more than half of all Kansans lived in "an urban area" as defined by the U.S. Bureau of the Census. After this time, as the battle over funding the water plan reveals, the collective political power of urban voters began chipping away at the longtime dominance of rural and farm power.

Since War World II, Kansans have encountered mounting difficulties in their struggles to allocate and develop the state's available water supply. Tensions between various interest groups arose because of the same general social, political, economic, and environmental changes that affected the West as a region. Throughout the West, states made water a commodity; and the Kansas Water Act of 1945, with subsequent revisions, institutionalized water as a marketable resource. Urban interests, and those farmers tapping the Ogallala Aquifer, certainly predicated their decisions on the market value of water. The same consumer-based social concerns over environmental issues marking postwar U.S. society definitely influenced water decisions affecting Cheyenne Bottoms and the environmentalism around and in Wichita. The urbanization of the state gave city interests a greater voice in determining water uses through both the market and legislature. Kansans contended with the continuing presence of the federal government in developing water, as in the instances of Tuttle Creek, Cheney Dam and Reservoir, and Cheyenne Bottoms. In all cases, Kansas reflected the post–War World II history of the West.

In some ways, survival in the heartland became considerably more intricate after World War II. The water issues pitting Kansans against each other showed mounting tensions and increasing complexities. State-level institutional controls over water became more dispersed with little coordinated planning among the various bureaus other than through the effects of the market. The water issues in Kansas certainly highlighted the changing nature of a state passing from rural dominance to urban development. World War II, as the water issues in Kansas show, marked a turning point in the state's history, the start of a transformation still unfolding. Kansans were joining the West, both in their attitudes toward water and in their struggles for solutions.

CHAPTER 8

The Price of "Freedom": Montana in the Late and Post-Anaconda Era

DAVID EMMONS

Montanans have always known—and other Americans are lately becoming more aware than they may care to be—that Montana is a big and empty place. Different people have used so many comparative devices to make the point that another will not matter much: According to the 1990 census, the population of the state of Montana was 799,065, about 20,000 fewer people than live in metropolitan San Jose, California, and only 12,000 more than lived in Montana in 1980. As of February 1993, 24,000 more had left since the census numbers were published. The remaining 775,000 people or so occupy an area about the size of New York, New Jersey, Pennsylvania, and New England combined. The new United Germany is slightly smaller than the state of Montana; the whole of Japan slightly larger.[1]

To put it differently, Montana is like a medium-sized city with very long streets. Its towns and villages are its neighborhoods—distinct and segregated. Butte, for example, is a tougher, more lived-in part of "town" than Whitefish, which more nearly resembles the country club district; the neighborhood of Browning is racially and socially distinct from that of Miles City. There are a few rich parts of this geographically extended city, and many more that are poor. The state's farms, ranches, mountains, and forests are its parks and amusement centers—some more open to the public than others.[2]

Like the citizens of all established medium-sized cities that have not grown much in the last fifty years, Montanans have a well developed sense of themselves, their place, and their history. Well developed, however, does not mean accurate, particularly when it comes to their sense of their past. The popular version of Montana's history was written essentially by two men. Joseph Kinsey Howard said the place was high, wide, handsome—and a colony of eastern corporations. K. Ross Toole said it was an uncommon land, a state of extremes—and the plaything of reactionary capital. There was little subtlety to either man's analysis: from the fur traders of the nineteenth century to the coal barons of the twentieth, Montana gave up its material treasure as well as its political chastity to plunderers.[3]

Chief among these capitalist freebooters was the Anaconda Copper Mining Company (ACM). Known simply as the Company, ACM was a monstrous presence. The fifth largest corporation in the world, located in a politically immature and sparsely populated state, it used this imbalance of power to advance its own interests—which were not necessarily the same as those of the state. It also had sturdy and helpful friends: the Montana Cattlemen's Association, the State Chamber of Commerce, the Montana Farm Bureau, Peabody Coal, the Montana Power Company (with which it was once joined in an interlocking directorate), and the Great Northern, Northern Pacific, and Milwaukee railroads. There are diverse interests represented here; and for that reason, and because it was so clearly at the top of the economic food chain, the Company came to stand for all of them.[4]

It is the further point of the Howard-Toole thesis that these agents of Montana's pain behaved with uncommon rapacity. The extent of their offenses against the commonwealth was unique. The forces of liberalism, for example, whether small farmers or the more politicized members of the working class, were bought off, bullied, manipulated, or robbed blind. In some western states, progressive elements fought back; they did in Montana, too, but only in ineffectual bursts of rage followed by defeat, apathy, and sullen despair. If, then, Montana seems not to have realized its full potential, however defined and in whatever area, the iron grip of the Company bore the blame. Corporate satrapies are not accountable for their failings for the simple reason that they are the objects, not the agents, of history.[5]

For at least eighteen years, Michael Malone has been fighting a lonely battle against this whining and self-pitying interpretation of Montana's past. In 1975 he argued that "Montana never really was the exclusive property of the copper trust." This was hardly a ringing endorsement of state autonomy, particularly when Malone followed it by saying, "even though it seemed that way during the first quarter of this century." Still, it represented a significant revision of the notion that Montana was "America's largest feudal empire," its people having "surrendered their birthright and their treasure." It marked a considerable advance over Howard's

hyperbolic " 'The Company' controlled virtually every Montana legislature since it drove Heinze from Montana," or Toole's bitter judgment that
the state legislature wore "the stamp of subservience," that "the Company never let things get far out of hand. In all essential respects it controlled
the legislature, the press, and most facets of the economy."[6]

In 1985 and 1986 Malone strengthened his case. In two short essays he
told Montanans that although the Company had at times been heavy-
handed, so had other companies in other western states. He pointed out
the obvious fact that Montana was, and for some time had been, a part of a
world economy and that the state's failures owed less to the evil influence
of ACM and more to the inescapable realities of global economic change.
Montana's history, in other words, was not uncommon. Unfortunately, the
notion that it was and that what made it so must never be repeated, led the
state to adopt a strong anticorporate attitude that severely limited its
ability to adjust to changes in national and international markets. Malone
mentions in particular the state's aversion to a sales tax. In 1971 the matter
came up to a popular vote; the Republicans, ACM, and Montana Power
favored it, sufficient evidence to a people raised on conspiracy theories
that it should be rejected. As of 1993, Montana's tax system still punishes
industry and business and is still without a sales tax—all in order to get
even with the Company.[7]

There is little evidence that many in positions of political influence
were listening as Malone made his arguments for historial balance and
sanity. The myth of Montana as singularly beset lingered, in large part
because it allowed Montanans a chance at the ultimate self-indulgence:
the avoidance of all responsibility by the assignment of blame to sinister
outside forces. Thomas Power, a University of Montana economist, has
argued that the influence of large extractive industries that export their
goods not only upsets the political and environmental order but leaves
deep scars in a state's collective psyche; it enfeebles the people and leaves
them politically helpless. He suggests the substitution of an economy
based on consumption for the old Montana model, which emphasized
production. Power makes no reference to ACM but he seems to have
studied the Howard-Toole historical treatise. Albert Borgmann, a University of Montana philosopher, notes Power's comments with approval and
adds his own reproach: extractive industry was the "bane" of Montana.
Borgmann follows that with the statement that in Missoula at least "the
timber industry is declining," being replaced with "crafts . . . specialized
horticulture, and professional services." He offers this as good news.[8]

More difficult to explain than the mere survival of the myth of uncommonality is the fact that it outlived the Company, which gave it its force and meaning. Malone uses the wonderful analogy of the smile on the Cheshire cat in *Alice in Wonderland;* the cat left, the smile (or leer) remained. Corporate fiefdoms should not survive past the collapse of their corporate lords. The formula is simple: ACM kept Montana in thrall, preventing the full flowering of the state's potential. ACM vanished in 1977, as surely as slaveholders as a class disappeared with the Thirteenth Amendment. As a consequence of points one and two, Montana's social and economic recovery should have dated from 1977, the year of its manumission.[9] This argument is strengthened by the fact that the 1977 emancipation had been coming for a long time, at least since the end of World War II.

Although the Anaconda Company was never the only game in town, as both symbol and economic force, ACM dominates the historical discussion. It is, then, appropriate to tell its story, particularly where it intersects with that of the state and of the unions who represented its miners and smelters.

Marcus Daly formed what would become the Anaconda Company in 1876 and, although it was never the only game in town, as both symbol and economic force, ACM dominates the historical discussion. As early as 1913, when still a holding of Standard Oil's Amalgamated, Anaconda began to look for copper-mining properties overseas. Between 1916 and 1929 it bought huge mines in Chile and Mexico, among them the Chilean holdings of the Guggenheims, including Chuquicamata, with the world's largest known copper ore deposit. In 1922 ACM achieved a measure of vertical integration by buying the American Brass Company, with its seven fabricating plants in Connecticutt, Canada, and the Midwest. This was followed in 1929 by the formation of Anaconda Wire and Cable Company, with eight production plants located from Pawtucket, Rhode Island, to Orange, California. Anaconda, it would seem, was more important to Montana than Montana was to it.[10]

In 1946 ACM produced 3.7 million ounces of silver; 30,000 ounces of gold; 1.47 million pounds of molybdenum; 1.55 million pounds of cadmium; 4,883 tons of arsenic; 15.6 million pounds of lead; 1.5 million pounds of zinc; 111,397 tons of manganese; and 742 million pounds of copper. It was the largest and most diversified copper company among the big five and probably in the world. Not coincidentally, in 1948, per capita income in Montana was 16 percent higher than the national average, 14 percent higher than the average of the five Rocky Mountain States. The state's per capita income probably ranked first or second nationally. Flush times for Anaconda were not solely responsible for this, but neither were they inconsequential.[11]

In retrospect, this was Anaconda's—and Montana's—last hurrah. In 1955, Cornelius Kelley, the last of the old, home-grown Anaconda CEOs, stepped down. The previous year he had announced that the Company would begin open pit mining of the Butte Hill. Designed to tap the low-grade copper ores that were about all that was left of the "richest hill on earth," pit mining would replace the old techniques of underground shafts and drifts; it would also replace the old underground miners with truck drivers and heavy-equipment operators, halve the work force, and bury most of the old working-class neighborhoods of uptown Butte.

There were a lot of good reasons for this corporate decision. The Butte miners had been unrepresented by any union since the International Union of Mine, Mill, and Smelter Workers was expelled for alleged Communist sympathies from the Congress of Industrial Organizations (CIO) in 1950, so there would be no protest from organized labor. In addition, it was harder after the war to find workers willing to go underground, and the company was determined to reduce its dependence on an increasingly unstable work force. Finally, open pit mining made it easier to deal with a long strike should there be a new round of protracted negotiations. Open pits could be shut down and left untended unlike underground mines, which could fill with water or face the threat of fire during an extended shutdown.[12]

Most assumed there would be extended shutdowns. The Company was well used to them and well practiced in dealing with them. Toole, in particular, is hard pressed to decide whether the corruption of the state, the destruction of the environment, or the manhandling of labor unions was ACM's most egregious sin. In 1912, 1914, 1917–20, 1933–34, and 1967, the Company faced, and faced down, genuine labor-management crises. There is now reason to believe that it had plenty of help in its dirty work from job-conscious pragmatists and ethnic exclusionists in the various miners unions. There is even more reason to believe, however, that for sheer corporate brutality in dealing with labor, the Colorado Fuel and Iron Company and the Arizona-based Phelps-Dodge Corporation were far worse than Anaconda at its bloodiest.[13]

Open pit mines were thought to ease some of these tensions, but Butte's pit also rearranged the political calculus in the state and began the process of liberation. The Company now had fewer workers, a smaller payroll, and the diminished influence that went with both. It also had a new corporate image. Kelley was the last of a breed; Marcus Daly, William Scallon, John Ryan, and Kelley had run ACM for the first eighty years of its corporate life. Each had a distinct management style, but each had much in common. The next generation of leaders would lead ACM toward a more modern and civic-minded future.[14]

In 1959, befitting its new image, ACM sold all of its Montana newspapers. Since it controlled all but one of the major dailies in the state, this was a considerable concession to those who believed the Company's control was absolute. There were times during the Anaconda years when Montana's newspapers, particularly the Company's flagship *Anaconda Standard,* were among the best in the country; there were also times when the Company's press was less than dogged in its pursuit of truth. On balance, however, the sale of the papers represented a significant advance toward freedom, even if the new Lee newspapers did not represent much of an advance in journalistic competence.[15]

As important in its way as the sale of the newspapers was the formation in 1957—and with no significant ACM opposition—of a legislative council to keep track of bills as they passed through the legislature. Until then, legislators had no staff and no way to know what was going on, except as ACM provided them with both. Clearly, the Company was relaxing its hold. Just as clearly, the state was becoming less dependent on the Company. In the early 1960s, ACM broke its interlocking corporate ties with the Montana Power Company, ending the era of the Montana Twins. In 1967 Butte miners, represented now by the United States Steelworkers Union, went on strike. In past years a shutdown of that sort would have rattled the entire state; this one's effect was limited to Butte and ACM. In 1971, the Company closed down its watering holes in Helena. A part of political life in Montana for almost a century, the Company's open bars were a favorite gathering place for lobbyists and legislators. Their closure convinced even the most skeptical that a new age was dawning. Finally, in 1972, Montanans called a constitutional convention to modify and modernize their law and to permit more direct voter (as distinct from corporate lobbyist) influence. The Company and its allies had been well served by the old constitution. *Time* magazine reported, in fact, that they had "foisted" it on an unwilling people. The new one passed by the barest of margins, but it did pass, and with no overt opposition by the state's major corporations.[16]

Perhaps ACM was distracted. The same year that the Company closed its Helena hospitality centers, Salvador Allende and his leftists closed Anaconda's Chilean operation. The Montana legislature was obviously more tractable than Chilean despots. The nationalization of the Company's properties in Chile, something that had been threatened for years, set in motion a series of events that destroyed Anaconda and wobbled the state. The Company went through receivership and reorganization before being sold in 1977 to the Atlantic Richfield Corporation (ARCO). The new owners promised an anxious state that they would run the mines and smelters at full bore, that payrolls and investments would grow, and that they would be model corporate citizens and neighbors. Raised on exaggerated tales of ACM perfidy, the people of the state rejoiced. They were still beholden to corporate masters, but these new ones did not insist on mastery.[17]

Within two years of this promise ARCO shut down the smelters in Anaconda and Great Falls; in 1983, ARCO suspended operations in the Berkeley open pit in Butte, turned off the pumps, and watched that great hole in the ground fill with water. Unlike Anaconda's, these shutdowns would be permanent; ARCO was going to leave the state severely alone. The major activity in the Butte-Anaconda area now is that of the Environmental Protection Agency as it administers the largest, and arguably the slowest, Superfund clean-up operation in the United States. As for the population statistics from Butte and Anaconda, headquarter cities of the Company, they are exactly what one would expect. Silver Bow County (Butte) lost 20,000 people—more than 40 percent of its population—between the beginning of World War II and the census of 1990. In Deer Lodge County (Anaconda), the comparable figures were 7,000 and 41 percent.[18]

The destruction of the Company—however mixed a malediction it may have appeared at the time—had a disastrous effect on the Montana economy and on the state's ability to pay its bills and meet its legitimate social obligations. All of this should have been foreseen, particularly by those who argued that the Company's power for mischief was felt throughout the state. If ACM really could dictate state policy, then its destruction was bound to be felt statewide. Joseph Kinsey Howard, for example, wrote that Butte was Montana's "black heart." He was half right.[19]

The unlamented demise of Anaconda was not the only arrhythmia in the Montana economy. The postwar years were no kinder to other key components of the state's industrial mix. Economically, at least, freedom was coming to resemble free-fall. Merely to list some of the casualties is enough. In the early 1980s the Milwaukee Railroad, the most modern and in some — apparently irrelevant — respects the best-run line in the West, went bankrupt. Its depots became restaurants — also since failed; its roundhouses and repair shops were razed. Wheat and cattle prices were in steep decline. Between 1960 and 1970, thirty-nine of Montana's fifty-six counties lost population. Most of those thirty-nine were in the wheat and cattle country in the eastern part of the state. All told, the rural farm population of the state fell from 175,707 in 1940 to 88,460 in 1970 to under 80,000 in 1990. Ten eastern Montana counties are on Frank Popper and Deborah Popper's list of counties in "land use distress" and facing "near total desertion over the next generation." As such they are likely candidates for "deprivatization" by the federal government and inclusion in the Big Open section of the Buffalo Commons.[20]

State population figures are equally melancholy. The thirty-nine-county decline in the 1960s was followed by a decline in twenty-two counties in the 1970s and by thirty-six more in the 1980s. The bottom was reached in this last decade, when the state grew by only 12,000 people, to just under 800,000 — this in the face of 1984 population projections of 860,000 by 1990. Among the consequences was the loss of one of the state's two congressional seats. Montana had had two seats since 1912; it is now the largest single congressional district in the nation. The contest for that one seat assumed the proportions of a political epic — Pat Williams, liberal Democrat from the old western district, in a sudden-death runoff with Ron Marlenee, conservative Republican from the erstwhile eastern district. Williams won, proving mostly that western Montana added a few people and eastern Montana lost a lot.[21]

These losses were obviously not owing entirely to the demise of the Anaconda Company. In fact, in the early and mid 1970s, as ACM was playing out its last act, there was the belief that the Treasure State was about to yield another of its treasures, but this time in a fashion that would allow the state and its people to benefit as surely as the corporations. Eastern Montana has more subbituminous coal than any area of comparable size in the world. It also has the makings of a major oil and natural gas producer, and in the 1970s, a certain urgency attached to the extraction of each. The result was a classic Montana boom, followed by a classic Montana bust. The numbers are too sad to recount. Suffice it to say that for a time, there were jobs, the state and county coffers were full, roads were repaired, schools were built, the poor and marginalized of the state were treated with the dignity they deserved. (Midwestern consumers of Montana coal even paid the state the ultimate compliment: they referred to Montanans as "blue eyed Arabs.") The Montana Power Company and Peabody Coal did all right, too. By 1975 the boom began to sound choked and muffled; by 1980, the most attentive listener could not have discerned the trace of an echo.[22]

Something like this also happened in lumber and wood products. Cutting down trees was always an important element of the state's economy, particularly in western Montana, but it was not until after World War II that wood products assumed a dominant role. Old companies, often family owned, grew; new ones were formed. By 1979, there were almost 11,000 jobs in Montana's woods and mills; by 1982, there were only slightly more than 7,100. There were 330 sawmills in Montana in 1956. There were still 142 in 1981. Today, there are fewer than 80. Lumber production fell by 29 percent between 1979 and 1982, recovered slightly, and then fell by 14 percent between 1988 and 1991. It is likely that 6,500 western Montana timber workers will lose their jobs in the next decade. It is not likely that many of these 6,500 will find work in the huckleberry harvest.[23]

The result of all of this was a calamitous decline in natural resource industries—formerly the blessing as well as the curse of the state. In 1983, a good year only relative to what came later, natural resource industries accounted for 24 percent of total state revenues; in 1990, their contribution was down to 11 percent. Some of this was owing to tax cuts designed to stimulate production. The cuts did not work; most of the loss was from lower industrial yields. In other words, Montanans witnessed the near total collapse of the extractive industries that had provided their jobs and paid their bills. Montana historically has had one simple responsibility: give up treasures. It discharged that responsibility in a variety of ways. It grew wheat, raised cattle, mined ores, cut trees, milled raw lumber, dug coal, drilled for oil and natural gas, and dammed and put turbines on its rivers. Discovering that the world no longer needed what generations of Montanans had made had a far more chilling effect on the state's collective psyche than had any alleged subservience to ACM.[24]

To be sure, the state was also expected to entertain out-of-state visitors, show them a good time, and then show them the door. Ross Toole believed—and Tom Power seems still to believe—that the state's open space, once the chief impediment to economic stability, would prove its salvation. It has not worked out that way—at least not yet. Montana's quality of life is, in fact, enviable; but there is a very short line of employers waiting to share in it. Tourism does not require that the state's resources be plundered; neither does it pay very well. Ted Turner, now one of the state's largest landowners, does not tread heavily on the land; neither does he, or the other seasonal residents, pay the bills.[25]

All of these postwar economic blows occasioned considerable pain and political dislocation. Main Street suffered; shops closed; the tax base eroded. Medical care, except in the favored areas, deteriorated, and educational opportunities were stifled. Lives changed—for those who were able to hang on and for those who were pushed out. There is no colder statistic than per capita income; there is a ruthlessness even to the sound of it. But make what you can of the fact that in Montana it fell from 16 percent *above* the national average in 1948 to 83 percent *of* the national average by 1990. The state is now in thirty-ninth place nationally, and falling.[26]

Adding to the misery is the fact that other western states that went through the same kinds of economic and demographic changes are doing well, or at least better than Montana. Nebraska, Colorado, Utah, Arizona, Washington, even Idaho have far more robust economies than Montana's. These states' extractive industries are either terminal or gone; agriculture survives, but their rural counties are losing people. The difference is that migration out of their rural areas does not mean migration out of the state. There are no cities in Montana large enough or economically diversified enough to absorb the state's exiles. They go to the Twin Cities if from eastern Montana, Denver if from southern, Spokane or Seattle if from the west. Idaho can keep some of its economically superfluous sons and daughters; they can go to Boise and work in service, specialized production, or information-processing industries. They are lost to the farm but not to the state. It has been said—half jokingly—that more Montanans watch the University of Montana–Montana State University football game on big-screen television in Seattle bars than from the stands in Missoula or Bozeman.[27]

Some of Montana's towns and counties have dodged the full effects of these economic catastrophes, and they have become artful dodgers in the process. Red Lodge, once a coal-mining town with an ethnically varied work force, has become a major ski town, filled with contrived charm. So has Whitefish in the upper Flathead Valley. "Stump town," as the locals once called it, was a logging and railroad center with a small, local ski area. That ski area, the Big Mountain, has in the last decade become the playground for hundreds of thousands of skiers yearly; the area has become the seasonal home of movie stars and rock musicians, joined by a few relief pitchers, tight ends, and power forwards. New golf courses, some of them of championship caliber, have been built in places where forty years ago the game was all but unknown. Jack Nicklaus is designing another course to be constructed just outside Anaconda—at the Old Works, on top of toxic slag heaps left over from almost a century of the smelting of copper ores. Real estate is booming in these favored locales, but the state's general economy has been ravaged.[28]

In 1988 Ian Davidson, president of the Great Falls based D. A. Davidson Investment Company, offered his judgment on Montana's post-war economic nose dive. The problem with Montana, he said, is that it is a state with "an agricultural base and an industrial mentality" trying to make its way in "the information age." Montana is superfluous and irrelevant. Davidson's comment was both wise and humane. There is no recrimination in it. There is considerable pathos. It recognizes that the state must change, but it at least acknowledges that the changes will be difficult and that, in some important ways, will leave us poorer, whatever their economic effects.[29]

But Davidson's references to an agricultural state and an industrial mentality speak to more than just the economy. Montana's identity was fixed early. That is true of all the states; their citizens identify and legitimate themselves on the basis of what they *do for a living,* a phrase that should be read slowly and interpreted literally. "Miner" was not just a label for what the workers of Butte did; it was what they were. The same was true for rancher, farmer, logger, and for the communities these useful and honorable enterprises created. Montana took its collective identity, its sense of community in the face of immense distances and regional differences, from the work its people did, the usefulness of that work, and the skill and pride they took in doing it. It was this that connected the people to the state and to one another, in the process giving coherence to their towns and meaning to their sense of themselves as residents of a state. All of that has changed.

Other centripetal forces have not changed, or at least not as much. Montana remains surpassingly beautiful, and from one end of the state to the other, the people know this and acclaim what it means to them. It is still cold in the winter, and spring is still greeted with the same sense of renewal, relief, and self-congratulation in Baker as in Troy. The absence of any really large metropolitan area slows recovery but it eases the tensions between rural and urban by making "urban" in the usual sense meaning-less, if not comical. And of course, being broke together is its own unifying force. Still, there is no escaping the obvious. The work and the men and women who performed it, the principal defining elements of Montana, are disappearing, victims of the postindustrial blues. It is hard for people to learn that what they and their parents and grandparents did for a living is no longer relevant, that work once thought honorable is no longer seen as such, that they must give way to new and different occupations.

New people bring new values, political values included. Ross Toole's Montana, whatever its other faults, did capture the open and fractious politics of the place. The producing-class liberalism of Butte miners joined by the small farmers of the Farmers' Union cannot survive in the absence of miners and small farmers. The miners are gone, small farms have been consolidated into large ones. Montana's political progres-sives—still Democrats—are now to be found almost exclusively among deep thinkers in the urban areas of the western half of the state. The Constitution of 1972, for example, passed despite the fact that forty-four counties voted against it. Of the twelve counties that supported it, all were urban and nine were in the western district. The agenda of these new-style Democrats is different from that of the old; indeed many of the latter, including Marc Racicot, the present Republican governor, left the party—or were abandoned and left politically homeless by its new leaders. New Democrats favor postindustrial issues such as environmentalism and multiculturalism. Their tactics are different; they are more tendentious and confrontational. They are also more meticulous in their record keeping and much less likely to get out the cemetery vote. The old Democrats, however, sent James Murray, Mike Mansfield, and Lee Metcalf to the Senate. The new ones have yet to do as well.[30]

To a lesser extent, the state's Republicans have also been transformed. The distinctions are too simple, but if Democrats can be divided into labor liberals and intellectual liberals, then Republicans with equal fairness can be divided into farm/ranch conservatives and country club conservatives. As some of the larger farms and ranches come to resemble country clubs, this dividing line becomes fuzzy. As the Democratic base was forced to move, so was the Republican, and—with the possible exception of Racicot—with no better results.

Even these distinctions, however, are ephemeral. Politics in Montana once had meaning because the government once had the money to do something. The debate was over what to do. Those were the generous years because the state could afford to be generous—could afford six university units, fifty-six counties, more school districts than California, a workers' compensation law that was both solvent and compensatory. We still have six university units, fifty-six counties, and more school districts than California, but we cannot afford any of them; we are $225,000,000 in debt and our workers' compensation fund is bankrupt.

To say that political options are not as numerous as they once were is to state the obvious. But politics has always been more than a choice of policy options. In Montana it was both cause and effect of communal values. Politics formed communities and was formed by them. But as some of the state's towns deteriorate, this communal function loses both its power to create and the source of its creation. And the state loses some of its defining character. Its people become estranged from one another. The connecting cords begin to stretch and snap. There is an ethnic dimension to this as well, as there was to the former sense "neighborhoods." The state took its identity from this, too—from Irish and Cornish copper miners in Butte, Croatian smeltermen in Anaconda and stonemasons in Lewistown, French Canadian ranchers and farmers in Grass Valley, Italian coal miners in Sand Coulee or Stockett, Finnish coal miners in Red Lodge, Ukrainian farmers in Brockton, Norwegian farmers in Outlook, railroaders from Japan to Montenegro in Havre and Livingston.

There is a huge irony in much of this. Montana lately has experienced a literary renaissance dedicated in considerable measure to a celebration of the communal spirit of the place and to the preservation of that spirit. The works of Ivan Doig and Norman Maclean come first to mind. So does *The Last Best Place*, the giant anthology of Montana writing that has become a surprise best-seller. Also worthy of note is a recent publication that may seem not to belong on a list of Montana tales. Albert Borgmann's *Crossing the Postmodern Divide* is a plea for the construction of a new society. But Borgman not only lives in Missoula, Montana, he wraps the place around him; it is his refuge and his strength. He takes his examples from Missoula; he sees it and the state as what the world can be once it shakes off its dependence on the extraction of raw materials for export. Missoula has moved far toward the "focal realism" in the form of community celebrations that is at the core of Borgmann's definition of life beyond the postmodern divide.[31]

Those celebrations, however, to be truly celebratory and not simply contrived and self-conscious, must arise from some kind of "liturgical" calendar. In other words, they can center on seasons or on work, which in both instances means center on making a Montana living. There could be—indeed there once were—celebrations, often spontaneous, that focused on well-timed rain or snowstorms, planting and harvesting crops, branding calves, shearing sheep, watching and listening to the breakup of the big rivers that signaled the start of the log drives. Butte miners celebrated Miners Union Day with a parade and contests of skill between hammer and drill teams. These were commemorations of work and of the fact that the world still needed what Montanans made. Even the immigrant celebrations were as much occupational as ethnic, which is to say that what one did was as much a part of an evolving culture as who one was. In addition, every town, hamlet, village, and collection of houses, stores, and bars, proclaimed the secular faith on the Fourth of July, the anniversary of Jefferson's paean to Locke, two rationalist relics who will reach the postmodern promised land only with difficulty. But farming and ranching are moving from family to family corporation to agribusiness. The timber industry, Borgmann reminds us, is "in decline." Hard rock mining did not—by definition could not—cross the postindustrial divide. Ironically, what is left of ethnic enclaves, including Indian reservations, now find themselves the objects of contemporary approval, meaning that what is left of ethnic consciousness and community may now assimilate to a host society that affirms both. There is comfort in that, no doubt, but ethnic celebrations had more meaning (and were a lot more fun) when they were segregant and defiant. As for the villages, hamlets, and collections of bars and huts, as the new post-Anaconda demographics make clear, they will not make it over the top either.[32]

That being the case, what form can the new "focal reality" take? If there are no un-self-conscious celebrants, how can there be true celebrations? More specifically (and only half-seriously), if there is no Anaconda Company, how can Butte's miners celebrate their defiance of it? The new celebrations will be sterile affairs, unconnected and exclusive, the social fashion of a people no longer belayed to one another or to the place where they live. The manufactured gaiety will be limited to those who can afford it. The poor will be excluded, a problem which Borgmann anticipates and laments but cannot cure. These, too, are among the costs of Montana's new "freedom" from the grip of extractive industries and their demon allies.[33]

Montana will have to change; remaining economically irrelevant risks total stagnation. But the changes will be difficult to effect. The state is still a long way from major markets, its tax structure is still archaic, its university system is in disarray, and too many of its citizens still evince symptoms of historically (and historian-) induced paranoia. The changes will also come at some considerable social cost, and Montanans have not yet calculated the price of their soul. They are all diminished when Jordan loses another hundred people, or Butte another thousand, but by what extent remains uncertain. More certain is that the present generation of Montanans will have to reinvent the state and cast it in a new image. A great deal is riding on them. They can succeed only if they pay a proper attention and respect to the old ways of making a Montana living as they go about the task of finding new ways.

CHAPTER 9

Employer Offensive in Nebraska Politics, 1946–1949

WILLIAM C. PRATT

The historiographical image of Nebraska, like that of other Great Plains states, is overwhelmingly agrarian. While few observers would quarrel with this characterization, it should be recognized that Nebraska has had a labor history or a history of labor-management relations that also helps account for its political development in the twentieth century. Historians of the state have neglected this topic. With the exception of studies of Omaha, there is very little published scholarship on Nebraska labor history. In this chapter, I seek to show the utility of a labor-management relations approach to the study of state political history in the post–World War II era. Much of my attention is focused on efforts to make Nebraska a right-to-work state and other measures designed to weaken unions. Such episodes were part of a broader employer offensive against organized labor in the United States, and an examination of these topics in this particular state should add to our understanding of post–World War II domestic politics generally.

Nebraska has had a richer labor history than most observers have suspected. Craft unionists, railroad brotherhoods, and the Knights of Labor all had an early presence, and Omaha emerged as a center of labor ferment as early as the 1880s.[1] The Nebraska militia intervened in Omaha labor disputes several times, and building-trades unions have remained organized since the late nineteenth century.[2] In contrast, teamsters and packinghouse workers were not permanently organized until the late 1930s. Employer resistance led to a number of union defeats. In packing, for example, workers lost strikes in 1894, 1904, and 1921–22, and each time the union was ousted for a period of years. The most important antiunion effort was locally led and directed primarily against the building trades, printers, and teamsters. It was spearheaded by the Omaha Business Men's Association (OBMA), formed in 1903, and pretty much established Omaha as an open-shop town for a generation.[3] In the 1930s, the OBMA boasted that "Omaha is the best open shop city of its size in the United States."[4]

Nebraska labor history, of course, is not exclusively an Omaha story, and a number of other communities, including Lincoln, North Platte, Nebraska City, Grand Island, Fremont, and Plattsmouth, have also had a significant labor presence at times.[5] One study has uncovered as many as 150 different Knights of Labor assemblies in Nebraska in the late nineteenth century. Of that total, 30 units were based in Omaha and South Omaha, while the other 120 were scattered across the state.[6] Railroad workers, printers, and building-trades people often were organized then and later. Several communities in addition to Omaha and Lincoln had central labor bodies affiliated with the American Federation of Labor (AFL); in 1947, the state had eight such groups.[7]

Still, Omaha was the center of both organized labor and organized resistance to unions in Nebraska. In 1917, the OBMA refused to cooperate with the state's board of mediation during a building-trades strike and in 1921 orchestrated a legislative campaign, which resulted in a law that virtually abolished picketing. The following year, after the labor movement and the Nonpartisan League (NPL) forced a referendum vote on this legislation, it was overwhelmingly approved in the fall election.[8] Only four counties in the state voted against the measure, all of them districts where the NPL had a strong following.[9] Between 1918 and 1924, a concerted effort was undertaken to build a Farmer-Labor movement. Aside from a few episodes like the 1922 prolabor vote in NPL counties, however, Nebraska Farmer-Laborism met with little success.

One reason for its failure may have been George Norris. He had prolabor sympathies but was unwilling to back third-party causes.[10] He played a major role at the national level in implementing prolabor legislation, as testified by his sponsorship of the Norris-LaGuardia Act. It should be pointed out, however, that he was not very involved in such efforts at the state level. This observation is not intended to denigrate Norris's efforts on behalf of the labor movement. That he worked for national legislation at a time when organized labor was weak in his own state is noteworthy and explains why he attracted strong union backing. But perhaps there were times when unions back home could have used his help as well.[11]

Organized labor in Nebraska, as elsewhere, underwent a major revival in the depression years and also came to assume a more active role in politics. It took credit for dumping Democratic Sen. Edward Burke in the 1940 primary and strongly backed Norris both in 1936 and again in 1942, although labor's vote was not sufficient to ensure his reelection in 1942.[12]

The Nebraska labor movement may have been stronger in the World War II era than at any previous time in its history. The Omaha packing industry was then organized by the Congress of Industrial Organizations (CIO). Teamsters had spread across the state, along with a number of building-trades and craft unions and rubber workers in Lincoln and brewery workers in Omaha were unionized as well. While labor was divided between the AFL, CIO, and independents, its combined numbers by 1946 were greater than ever before, perhaps as high as 70,000 members.[13] Organized labor enjoyed similar gains in many parts of the country, but antiunion forces in Nebraska and elsewhere were not reconciled to the closed shop, big labor, or the New Deal–labor coalition. During World War II, they began a counteroffensive that culminated years later with a number of right-to-work laws at the state level and the Taft-Hartley Act.[14]

The phrase "right-to-work" is misleading, in that its proponents were not espousing the right to a job but rather the right not to join a union. They were primarily opposed to what they called "compulsory unionism" and used arguments about individual rights to weaken organized labor.[15] Traditionally, unionists had sought to establish what was called a closed shop, or an arrangement that required workers at a job site or in a plant to join the union before they obtained employment. To counteract this strategy, employers proposed the so-called open shop, wherein employees did not have to become union members at any time. Prior to the Wagner Act, many employers would not knowingly hire union members. The business agent of the Omaha Bricklayers Union approached the county board in 1929 with a request to hire some of his members to work on a building project. But the request was turned down, and one county commissioner was quoted as saying, "If we allow those men to be mixed it will only be a short time before they'll all be union. . . . Those union men will get on the job and try to influence the other workmen to join the union. I know how these union men work."[16]

Historically, the phrase "right-to-work" had been applied to different measures designed to restrict union activities. For example, backers of Nebraska's 1921 antipicketing law called it the "right to work" law.[17] More recently, however, the term is usually applied to legislation or constitutional amendments that prohibit contracts limiting employment to union members. Union representatives sometimes talk as though a right-to-work provision covers much more than a prohibition against a closed or union shop, but technically speaking, that is what it has entailed over the past forty years or so.[18]

During World War II, a rash of antiunion legislation was introduced at the state level. Right-to-work measures were only one of a number of items proposed to restrict or weaken organized labor. Florida and Arkansas became right-to-work states in 1944, and similar proposals were introduced in several other states in the war years. A number of restrictive laws were implemented, including limits and bans on picketing and registration and disclosure measures for unions.[19] One observer, writing in the *Iowa Law Review*, noted, "Many of the provisions of these statutes will inevitably be regarded by organized labor as a whole and not merely by its leaders as war legislation in a very sinister sense—legislative declarations of war against labor unions."[20]

A new picketing law was proposed in the Nebraska Unicameral in 1945. It was accompanied by two other restrictive labor measures, one of which called "for registration of all labor organizations with the department of labor, showing names of officers, lists of members, dues, salaries and other items." Although these bills were killed in committee, testimony was offered on all of them. Most of the proponents of the picketing and disclosure measures identified in the press were from Omaha. Among them was David Swarr, an attorney associated with the OBMA, which had sponsored the 1922 antipicketing law. Concerned that the earlier measure would not survive a court test in light of recent U.S. Supreme Court decisions, Swarr urged the adoption of the new bill, which, among other provisions, required that pickets must stand thirty feet back from any building that they picketed. Another advocate of the restrictive legislation was a Farm Bureau spokesman. AFL and CIO representatives were also present to denounce the measures.[21] Unlike their counterparts in some other states, including Kansas and South Dakota, Nebraska unionists escaped the wartime antiunion assault. They were not as fortunate, however, during the second phase of the employer assault, which followed in the immediate postwar years.

In March 1946 Lincoln and Omaha newspapers reported rumors of an effort to amend the Nebraska state constitution to ban the closed shop.[22] Then, after this report surfaced, the Nebraska Small Business Men's Association (NSBMA) was formed. All of its officers were Omaha businessmen.[23] The new group soon announced that it would launch a campaign to make Nebraska a right-to-work state.[24] Although people from other parts of Nebraska came to be identified with the NSBMA, it was viewed as an Omaha operation by the labor movement. Apparently, informal meetings among interested people had been held as early as 1945, but that was not revealed publicly until the fall of 1946.[25]

A key figure from the beginning was Lloyd Skinner, an executive of the Skinner Manufacturing Company, a family-owned macaroni business. Skinner was a thirty-two-year-old World War II veteran when he emerged as the secretary of the NSBMA.[26] His firm had its own labor troubles in the spring of 1946, as four unions were out on strike for seventeen weeks. The AFL central labor body boycotted Skinner products for the duration of the strike and publicized the dispute in its weekly paper, the *Unionist*.[27] (Later, Skinner suggested that the strike had allowed him to spend more time on the anti-closed-shop campaign.[28]) Among other open-shop influentials were J. A. Moran (NSBMA president), executive of a local printing firm; L. O. Schneiderwind (NSBMA vice-president), head of the Omaha Welding Company; and A. C. Scott (NSBMA treasurer), executive of the Scott Tent and Awning Company. Firms represented among the incorporators included a local laundry, a local furnace company, and a local hamburger stand chain.[29]

The NSBMA strategy was to use the state's initiative and referendum law to amend the state constitution. This effort required over 50,000 signatures to put the issue on the 1946 ballot. The labor movement denounced the effort from the time of the first press reports. It tried to discredit the campaign, stressing the labor-management harmony that had existed during World War II, denouncing the measure as unconstitutional, and attempting to portray the effort as part of a larger design of the National Association of Manufacturers.[30] One approach used was to discourage union members and their families from signing the petitions through advertisements in the *Unionist* and other papers.[31] But the anti-closed-shop campaign had little trouble attracting the requisite number of signatures. On 3 July 1946, Skinner and other NSBMA notables rented an armored car and dramatically delivered their petitions with more than 100,000 signatures to the state capitol.[32]

Both sides now sought to generate support among the electorate. Ultimately, the labor movement was able to line up the Democratic party and liberal groups, such as the American Veterans Committee and the Omaha Education Association, to back their effort against the right-to-work amendment.[33] The NSBMA, though, enjoyed the support of the

Farm Bureau, the Grange, and the Nebraska Stock Growers Association, among other organizations.[34] According to the Nebraska Farm Bureau president, "who has been attending all the District Meetings [of the group], . . . the sentiment against the $40.00 School Amendment and in favor of the Right-to-Work Amendment is almost unanimous among the farm bureau members in the state."[35] While the labor movement encouraged pheasant hunters to distribute their literature during hunting season, the NSBMA rented billboards with the message: "End Labor Boss Dictatorship. Vote 'X' Yes 302."[36] Opponents of the amendment attracted some newspaper support, but the press's attention to labor strife since war's end probably reinforced the antiunion sentiments of much of the conservative electorate.[37] Nebraska had voted Republican every year beginning in 1940. The GOP had captured every statewide contest, and also monopolized the congressional delegation since the defeat of Norris in 1942. It apparently did not take much of an effort in 1946 to convince a majority of the voters to outlaw the union shop through constitutional amendment.

The measure carried 212,443 to 142,701, winning all but four counties. Douglas and Lancaster counties, the sites of Omaha and Lincoln, voted against the measure, but in the case of Lancaster, the proposition lost by less than 50 votes.[38] Omaha employers had made Nebraska a right-to-work state by mobilizing rural and small town voters against the labor movement, which was concentrated in the two largest cities. Later, some questioned the effectiveness of the labor movement's campaign against the measure,[39] but the NSBMA did not have a hard time selling its position in Nebraska. Years later Skinner recalled that the group had raised $80,000 or $85,000 for the campaign but did not spend all of it.[40] A central Nebraska newspaper, the *Grand Island Daily Independent*, offered a reasonable explanation for what had happened:

> The anti-closed shop amendment could be interpreted as a protest vote. Work stoppages since the war ended, the interminable disputes in the large eastern industrial centers, the threatened coal strike, and other difficulties have tended to bring a surge of indignation against all labor organizations, good or bad, and this is unfortunate, because labor organizations in the main have benefited the man who works and have given him a dignity he would not otherwise have had. The Nebraska constitutional amendment which makes closed shop contracts unlawful will not solve a thing. It will merely complicate the union-management relationship and create new currents of indignation. But the people who voted it into the constitution saw a chance to give vent to their long-smoldering anger and they did it.[41]

The immediate response of the labor movement was to reiterate its belief that the amendment violated the U.S. Constitution. It announced it would not comply with the measure and supported a court challenge in early 1947 that eventually did work its way to the U.S. Supreme Court, where the Nebraska right-to-work provision was ruled constitutional in early January 1949.[42]

Part of the reason the NSBMA has opted for a constitutional amendment over a statute was simply because the Nebraska Unicameral did not meet in 1946. But the following year, when the legislature was in session, a number of restrictive labor bills were introduced. These included implementation legislation for the right-to-work amendment, a union disclosure measure, and prohibitions on strikes of government and public utilities workers. Another bill, designed to prevent teacher strikes, provided for the forfeiture of any accumulated pension contributions of a striking teacher. All but the last measure, which was killed in the education committee after the attorney general cast doubt on its constitutionality, were considered by the labor committee.[43] In contrast to these restrictive items, a bill was introduced to extend the right of collective bargaining to workers of publicly owned utilities.[44]

A number of people turned out to testify at the first hearing. The lineup on the measures was predictable. Organized labor testified on behalf of the collective bargaining measure and against the right-to-work and union disclosure bills, while the NSBMA was on the opposite side. This time, CIO representatives joined their AFL counterparts in denouncing the antilabor measures. Lloyd Skinner and David Swarr spoke on behalf of the right-to-work legislation, Skinner complaining that "'labor bosses are openly flaunting' the amendment banning the closed shop." The Farm Bureau was joined by the Nebraska Grange and the Farmers Union in its antiunion stance at the hearing;[45] apparently the conservative element now controlled the Nebraska Farmers Union, which nationally and in neighboring states was prolabor.

A telephone strike was underway at the time of the legislative hearing, and it ultimately provoked Gov. Val Peterson to call for legislation to ban government and public utility strikes.[46] His measure preempted a more far-reaching bill and was given special attention by the labor committee after testimony had been given on other labor bills. Like the earlier proposal, the governor's bill called for the establishment of an industrial court that would have powers of binding arbitration in labor disputes involving government and public utility employees. Prior to the hearing on the governor's bill, the labor committee killed LB 468, which would have made it legal for these employees to bargain collectively.[47] It was argued that unless the governor's measure was adopted, "we will be faced with an initative law written by the people, and it will carry." Earlier, business leaders had opposed the bill calling for an industrial court because it covered all labor disputes. Now, however, they supported the more narrowly drafted legislation. The attorney for the local telephone company spoke in its favor and one Lincoln businessman "urged that food be included in the list of public service industries."[48]

Most labor representatives, AFL and CIO alike, opposed the bill. One striking telephone worker asserted, "This bill would be the end of collective bargaining in Nebraska." But John J. Guenther, the AFL state president, did not denounce the measure, offering instead a series of amendments, and called for a labor-management conference to address the issue. The labor committee did not adopt his suggestions, but advanced the bill 7 to 2.[49] Soon after the hearing, the Omaha Central Labor Union called for Guenther's removal, as it was opposed to binding arbitration and Guenther had acted on his own in offering the amendments. Guenther was suspended briefly from his post, at least in part for his response to LB 537. It was apparent that AFL circles were divided over his leadership.[50]

Ultimately, the 1947 Unicameral passed three measures that related to organized labor. All were signed into law by the governor. One consisted of right-to-work legislation based on the constitutional amendment of the previous year, another allowed "unions to sue or be sued the same as any company or corporation"; and a third was the governor's anti strike bill, which also provided for an industrial court for disputes involving government or public utilities employees. Guenther, now back as state AFL president, asserted that "labor had fared extremely well in this term of the Legislature."[51] Considering the testimony of other labor leaders at earlier hearings and the Omaha Central Labor Union's response to Guenther's actions, his comment seems an exaggeration. But in the context of the antilabor atmosphere of 1947, he may have had a point.

That year, in addition to the Taft-Hartley Act being passed over Truman's veto at the national level, a number of state legislatures enacted right-to-work laws, antipicketing measures, or other restrictive labor legislation.[52] More states banned the union shop in 1947 than in any other year in American history, and *Business Week* noted, "Unions in more than half of the United States will operate this year under drasticallly tightened restrictions, no matter what happens in Washington. Many new state laws have already been written. Others are pending. At least half go well beyond the curbs provided in the Taft-Hartley measure."[53]

The formation of the NSBMA in 1946 provided Nebraska antiunion employers with a new vehicle to promote their agenda. Its utility proved itself again and again over the next few years. In 1948, Omaha was wracked by a major packinghouse strike. More than eight thousand workers walked off the job the first day, and most of them stayed out nine weeks. This episode was accompanied by massive picketing and repeated violence on the picket line and elsewhere. The strike was part of a national action conducted by the CIO's United Packinghouse Workers of America (UPWA) against the four largest packing companies, rather than local firms represented by the NSBMA.[54]

Certain developments in the course of the strike subsequently were exploited by the NSBMA, though. Henry Boesen, the acting police chief, proved to be a friend of the strikers during the strike. He spoke to at least one of their meetings and was photographed handing a check from the police union to the chairman of the union's strike committee.[55] The *Omaha World-Herald* editorialized indignantly about the episode, calling for Boesen's removal and a ban on local police membership in national unions.[56] Later, the NSBMA lobbied the city council to prohibit the affiliation of police and fire fighters with such organizations.[57]

Soon after the Boesen episode, ten Omaha businessmen and lawyers drove to Lincoln to urge Governor Peterson to call out the National Guard. The governor was noncommittal and ultimately declined to intervene in the dispute. Among those who personally urged National Guard involvement were Lloyd Skinner and L. O. Schneiderwind, then NSBMA president.[58]

The packinghouse strike itself ended in defeat for the UPWA, as the strikers returned to work for the same terms their employers had offered before the walkout.[59] Omaha workers, like their counterparts in many other parts of the country had suffered another setback. Although these were tough times for Nebraska unionists, they were able to enjoy a major political victory in 1948 and the packing strike may have played a role. The Omaha congressional seat had been held by Howard Buffett since 1943. He was a staunch conservative and had a strong antiunion record in the House. Though opposed to the 1946 railroad worker draft measure, Buffett, like the other members of Nebraska's congressional delegation, had supported the Taft-Hartley Act. The Democrats ran Eugene O'Sullivan, a prounion lawyer against the Republican incumbent. Resentment against the right-to-work campaign, Taft-Hartley, and the packinghouse defeat combined to mobilize the union vote in 1948, and O'Sullivan defeated Buffett by four percentage points, becoming "the first Democrat elected to a major office in Nebraska since 1940.[60] But the high hopes of unionists in Nebraska and elsewhere for repeal of Taft-Hartley and state antilabor legislation soon were dispelled.

Early in January 1949, the U.S. Supreme Court ruled that the Nebraska right-to-work amendment was constitutional, establishing the constitutionality of all state-level anti-union-shop bans.[61] As a result, the only course of action for unionists in right-to-work states was to mount a popular campaign to repeal the legislation or overturn the right-to-work amendment.

Over the next decade, the Nebraska labor movement sought unsuccessfully to repeal the measure or restrict its implementation legislatively. As a practical matter, it seems unlikely that it ever will be repealed.[62] Only one state, Indiana, has ever repealed its right-to-work law, and that occurred more than two decades ago.[63]

The Nebraska Unicameral met in 1949. One of the major pieces of legislation that year was a new antipicketing measure. It was reasonably clear that the 1922 law, which seemingly outlawed picketing in labor disputes, could not stand a constitutional challenge. Local authorities had not used it either in the 1947 telephone strike or the 1948 packinghouse strike. Rather, they had sought to work out compromises that allowed both picketing and access to buildings that were being picketed. But such arrangements had not met with great success during the 1948 Omaha strike.[64] LB 415, reputedly authored by David Swarr, was introduced early in the 1949 session.[65] It provided "that no more than two pickets may be within either fifty feet of any entrance to the struck plant or of any other pickets at any one time." Swarr, Skinner, and Schneiderwind all testified in favor of the measure. This time, they were joined by Yale Holland, an attorney who represented the major packers in court appearances during the 1948 strike. Holland, according to the *Lincoln Star*, "carried the ball for the proponents of the bill, and presented to the committee many pictures taken at the Omaha strike." In the course of his remarks on picketing, he referred to the incident in which the acting police chief made a donation to the strike fund.[66]

A number of labor representatives from across the state, including the Nebraska CIO director, the president of the state AFL, and the state AFL's attorney, argued in vain against the measure. It was carried by a five-to-two vote within the committee.[67] Though the bill was amended to "forbid interference with lawful picketing or intimidation of strikers by threatening loss of employment rights," efforts to weaken its provisions by prolabor senators failed. It was passed by a decisive vote and signed into law on 6 May 1949.[68]

The passage of the right-to-work measures and the new antipicketing law were serious setbacks for organized labor in Nebraska, and union members have lamented them for decades. Aside from O'Sullivan's 1948 congressional victory (and he was overwhelmed in a rematch with Buffett two years later), the local labor movement enjoyed few political victories in the immediate post–World War II era.[69] Perhaps more significant was the relative permanence of the antiunion innovations of the 1946–49 era. Nebraska remains a right-to-work state to this day, and the 1949 antipicketing law continued in effect until 1988, when most of its key provisions were ruled unconstitutional.[70]

But the practical consequences of these developments can be exaggerated. First, despite Nebraska's right-to-work status, the union shop was not entirely eliminated in the state, at least initially. The UPWA at the Armour plant and perhaps at others had a modified union shop for a number of years, and the 1951 National Railroad Act allowed this arrangement for railroad workers.[71]

Nebraska trade unionists often attribute the weakness of their labor movement to the state's right-to-work status. But studies on this general topic often suggest that right-to-work measures did not seriously interfere with union organizing efforts. Apparently, in the 1950s and 1960s, union membership in Nebraska and other right-to-work states grew at about the same rate as elsewhere. As a result, some authorities have concluded that a right-to-work campaign may be more a symbolic contest than one of substance.[72] But symbolism can be important too, and symbolic defeats are still defeats. That Nebraska became a right-to-work state reflected the power relationship between its organized workers and their employers. In states such as Montana, where the labor movement apparently was stronger vis-à-vis employers, attempts to ban the union shop did not succeed.

The story of the Nebraska employer offensive is similar to that of a number of other western states that opted for right-to-work measures. Much of the agitation dated to the World War II and immediate postwar eras; the proponents exploited antilabor sentiments encouraged by labor disputes outside the region. Antilabor forces were able to enlist rural voters in the struggle essentially against organized urban workers; and like Nebraska's, these states' right-to-work and other antiunion laws are still on the books today.

But the Nebraska experience is also different from that of plains and some other western states. The difference relates to the collective bargaining rights of state employees. Among the antiunion legislation of the 1946–49 period was a measure that created the Court of Industrial Relations (CIR). At the time, the labor movement opposed it, one unionist claiming, "This bill would be the end of collective bargaining in Nebraska."[73] Years later, however, in 1969, Nebraska lawmakers adopted legislation to provide for collective bargaining for public employees, and the CIR became a key mechanism in the process.[74] Today perhaps as many as thirteen thousand state employees and state and university professors are covered by collective bargaining agreements. This situation stands in contrast with the neighboring right-to-work states of South Dakota, North Dakota, and Wyoming, where relatively few state employees have bargaining rights. In South Dakota, to be sure, faculty at state colleges and universities can bargain, but the vast majority of state employees cannot. Neither faculty nor state workers have collective bargaining in North Dakota and Wyoming.[75]

Nebraska's employer offensive of the 1946–49 era helped reshape the state's political culture, but this reshaping probably was not as great as its proponents had intended or its antagonists feared. Although organized labor in Nebraska suffered a series of defeats in this era, it remained a significant ecomonic and political force. Years later, with the exodus of the packing industry from Omaha and the decline of the labor movement generally, the losses were worse. Employers once again took advantage of the situation, and the erosion of union membership continued here and elsewhere.

Yet at the same time, a growing number of public employees and teachers in Nebraska have organized. Ironically, they often have utilized the CIR, a mechanism developed in an antilabor era, in their collective bargaining efforts. Perhaps the facilitation of public-sector bargaining is another legacy, indirect to be sure, of the employer offensive of 1946–49.

Gambling and Politics in Nevada

JEROME E. EDWARDS

The rise of gambling in Nevada since 1945 has dominated its politics. Never antagonistic to each other, the realms of gambling and of politics developed a symbiotic relationship, as politicians recognized gambling's growth and, finally, its indispensable importance to the state.

Ever since the beginnings of the mining frontier in 1859, gambling has been part of the Nevada scene. The development of the Comstock lode brought in a population composed largely of unmarried, unrooted men with money and time on their hands. In 1869, the legislature legalized gambling over Gov. H. G. Blasdell's veto. Legalized gambling was also a popular feature of the Tonopah and Goldfield mining rushes of the first decade of the twentieth century. It came to be accepted as part of the fabric of Nevada life, as it was part of the fabric of life in many of the more rough-hewn areas of the American West. Indeed, George Wingfield, who was to dominate the Nevada political and economic scene for a quarter of a century before his banks closed in 1932, got his financial start as a professional gambler, playing a mean game of poker in various clubs.[1]

In 1909, the Nevada legislature, reacting to rising pressure from women's, educational, religious, and other reform groups, turned its back on its raucous past by outlawing gambling. Yet despite these restrictions, the atmosphere in Reno, Las Vegas, and smaller towns remained wide open. Life went on much as always. Legal card games were available in the front rooms of clubs, while everything else went on in the back. As long as mining and ranching remained the mainstays of the Nevada economy gambling was part of the scene. Unlike any other western state, Nevada never outgrew its nineteenth-century past, and its population remained predominantly male and single, relatively unchurched, rootless, and exceedingly small.[2] By 1930 it had only 91,058 people spread over 110,540 square miles (less than the population of Camden, New Jersey, or

Tacoma, Washington), most of whom lived in small towns. It was by far the least populous state of the Union.

When gambling was relegalized in March 1931, it seemed a most natural thing to do. Opposition was pro forma. Norman Biltz, then close to Nevada kingpin George Wingfield, later declared, "All the legal brains of the State of Nevada—I say all the principal ones—went to work to draft a gambling bill." The statute was accepted with complete equanimity. Soon after the passage, writer Henry F. Pringle commented, "The vast majority of Reno's citizens are well satisfied with the new regime, and her business men appear to stand unanimously behind open gambling and open prostitution." The general feeling was that relegalization merely made legal what had been barely pushed underground. It was an affirmation of a way of life, and a cheap way to pick up some much-needed tax dollars for starved city and county coffers (especially in a time of economic depression). Beyond that, there were few plans.[3]

The American Guide Series volume on Nevada, published in 1940 under the auspices of the Work Projects Administration and sponsored by Jeanne Wier, director of the Nevada State Historical Society, reflected this widespread complacency with gambling.

> Though visitors occasionally put up large stakes, the local citizens stick to small amounts and, with many opportunities to observe the workings of the law of averages, are restrained in their gambling. Young Nevadans show relatively little interest in the sport when they reach the age that permits them to place counters on the roulette boards and pull slot machine handles. Further, the State is completely free of racketeers, in spite of the large sums handled by some of the clubs, and no Nevada prosecuting attorney has had a chance to make a name for himself by exposing corrupt relations between politicians and gambling club owners.[4]

In short, Nevada gambling would be honest, and the state and its people would be untainted by the institution. "But Nevada is large," the American Guide Series volume went on the say, "its people content with their way of life, so it is unlikely that even large numbers of visitors will change its essential quality." A decade later, Joseph McDonald, the editor of Reno's *Nevada State Journal*, wrote in the *Annals of the American Academy of Political and Social Science* that there was "probably no other state in the United States today that could successfully control wide-open gambling." Besides, if there were scandals, shootings, and racketeering, legalized gambling "would go out in a hurry, as it did in 1909 when shortsighted gamblers tried to control the state's politics."[5] Nevadans seemed disembodied from the institution they were nurturing in their midst; and if it did turn bad, the state could just abolish it, none the worse for the experience. McDonald's implicit assumption was that gambling could be controlled (although at the time he wrote there was no regulation). The good ol' boys of politics were in control. They would know what to do.

In 1945, gambling, which had previously been ineffectively regulated by the cities and counties, was put under state control, thus becoming a state political problem. Just as Nevada's twentieth-century experience with gambling was shaped by its nineteenth-century past, so had Nevada, by 1945, evolved a distinctive political style. What made it distinctive was Nevada's small population. By the beginning of the postwar era, *after* a considerable boom in southern Nevada during World War II, the state still had an estimated population of only 148,000.[6] Its population was dispersed, clustered mostly in small towns. Politics could still be run from the standpoint of knowing as many of one's constituents as possible. In 1944, only some 5,400 people voted for president in the state. As late as 1952, outsider Tom Mechling ran for U.S. Senate, trying deliberately to shake the hand of every registered voter.[7] Nevada politics, in terms of scale, was more akin to the politics of a Chicago alderman ward than of a larger state. An experienced politician (with some prompting by aides) could address voters by their first names, ask how the kids were, comment on local issues, and so on. It was very personal, because everyone knew everybody. Then, too, the political and financial elite knew each other. There was not the distance between leadership and people, or among leaders, that was typical of a society with a much larger population and a more complex infrastructure.

With this small population, there were few competing power centers. The rural counties ("cow counties"), with their mostly shared values, dominated the state legislature. Financial and political power was centered in the one city with national fame and metropolitan pretensions— Reno, with 21,000 people in 1940. The aspirations and desires of emergent Las Vegas were of little account, at least in 1945.

The elite of Reno and Nevada lived in a small and cohesive area, all within a half-mile of each other, in the city's southwest side. They patronized many of the same businesses, attended the same social and club functions, and could see each other on a daily basis if they so desired. Not only were they neighbors, most of Nevada's elite had known each other for a relatively long period. Many of the leaders had come out of the Tonopah-Goldfield mining boom of the first decade of the twentieth century, having moved to Reno after the boom's decline. By 1945 they were also getting along in age. Not all the leaders liked each other, but they had known each other for some time.

This network of personal relationships was enhanced by the weakness in Nevada of the two-party system. The division between Republican and Democrat in the state at this time was not an especially deep one. What was important was to elect strong leaders of either political party to the U.S. Senate who could argue for Nevada interests and then to keep reelecting them. The leaders of both parties were generally conservative. There was a community of interest and of values that transcended party lines. These values included a belief in the vulnerability of Nevada to outside forces, particularly to the federal government (which possessed most of the land); a belief in Nevada's development, a development they envisioned themselves as leading; and a devotion to silver as almost an article of faith.[8]

At this time the preeminent leader of the Nevada political scene was Patrick A. McCarran.[9] Elected to the U.S. Senate as a Democrat in 1932, he gained primacy in the party by 1938 and served until his death in 1954 as a "political boss" of Nevada. He practiced the closest thing to machine politics that his state ever saw. He built up his organization by assiduous devotion to the needs of his constituents, by doing personal favors for people (and no favor was too mundane), dispensing patronage, and asking for nothing in return but instant and undivided loyalty. His organization straddled both political parties. To friends and loyalists, he was benevolence personified; to his political enemies, he could be vengeful—for he did not easily forgive their sins. He categorized people in personal terms. To his way of thinking, Nevada politics consisted of the "good guys" (his friends in both parties) versus the "bad guys" (his enemies in both parties). Under his tutelage, Nevada politics was gossipy and nonideological; little thought was given to reform or even to how the state was changing and what to do about it. If a bureaucracy were to be developed, its chief purpose would be to give him its undivided loyalty; of secondary interest was the bureaucracy's need to effect or administer a program.

McCarran was not against economic development for his state, but he thought in terms of traditional ranching and mining industries. He was not against federal pork by any means, but he wanted to control the dispensation of the federal largesse. His close associates, such as Norman Biltz and lobbyist John Mueller, also thought in traditional terms, and in this they reflected the thinking of the Reno financial crowd, who wanted the state to be developed by suitable people (i.e., the present circles of the wealthy). Biltz in particular desired a relatively slow growth for Nevada, and postwar Las Vegas made him "nervous."[10] McCarran knew that a rapid growth in population would be a threat to the perpetuation of his machine. In 1952, an embittered, complaining, aging McCarran wrote his wife, "There is a great movement of new people into the state. There are four thousand people living in Clark County [Las Vegas] and as many more here [Reno]. They are on wheels, so to speak and really don't belong here."[11] Fundamentally, McCarran's power was based on keeping his state small, and he could not reconcile himself, as an old man, to its rapidly changing nature.

If he thought of gambling at all, it was as just another adjunct to his political machine. As with every other person or entity in the state, he would grant it favors and expect loyalty in return. He helped loosen wartime restrictions on scarce construction materials so Benjamin ("Bugsy") Siegel could build the Flamingo, the first postwar hotel erected on the highway to Los Angeles.[12] He was repaid for encouraging the burgeoning gambling enterprises: In 1952, after the editorial jibes of Herman ("Hank") Greenspun's *Las Vegas Sun* got too exasperating, McCarran (or his office) organized a casino advertising boycott of the newspaper, apparently with the expectation of grinding the newspaper down to submission or bankruptcy. The gambling owners obeyed, and in one morning the newspaper lost 30 percent of its advertising revenue.

Gus Greenbaum and Benny Binion, two gamblers with illustrious racketeering pasts, laid it straight to Greenspun. In Greenbaum's words, "Hank, you've got to lay off. The Old Man has the power of life and death over us." Later, Moe Dalitz, formerly of the Cleveland Mob, added, "Why did you have to attack the Old Man? . . . You've put us in a terrible position. You know as well as I that we have to do what he tells us. You *know* he got us our licenses. If we don't go along, you know what will happen to us." When giving a deposition on the case, McCarran was forced to admit that he had received many services from the hotels and casinos absolutely free. In 1944 and 1950 he had obtained free campaign headquarters space in Las Vegas at the El Cortez hotel. He added, "As a rule, when I would go into any one of these hotels in the dining room, when I would ask for the check, any one of those hotels would say there is no check."[13] (It might be added that it was, and is, standard Nevada casino

and hotel procedure that politicians are "comped," that is, given comple-
mentary meals, rooms, and liquor.)

But gambling, and Las Vegas, could not be held down. The state was
changing, by the mid-1950s far more than the state political leadership
realized or desired. The unprecedented growth could not have been
predicted, and certainly was not by Senator McCarran and his cohorts.
The success of Harolds Club in Reno demonstrated that mass advertising
techniques worked. Gambling became something to be merchandised.[14]
In Clark County, the construction of Hoover Dam attracted thousands of
tourists. During World War II, Las Vegas became a boom town because of
Basic Magnesium, Inc. (BMI) and the thousands of soldiers being trained
at the U.S. Army Gunnery School. Many of the workers and soldiers
enjoyed the gambling available in town.[15] Beginning in 1946 with Bugsy
Siegel's Flamingo and continuing with the Thunderbird in 1948, the
Desert Inn in 1950, the Sahara in 1952, the Riviera, the Dunes, and the
New Frontier in 1955, great hotel-casinos were built on the rapidly
developing Las Vegas Strip. These establishments created a new type of
gambling experience—one no longer tied in with the traditional western
experience but, instead, evoking exotic (African, Caribbean, or South
Seas) themes. Glitzy entertainment featuring Hollywood stars was offered.[16] Many of the strip hotels were controlled by the Mafia, a fact of life
ignored by the politicians. In turn the mobsters, refugees from police
raids on illegal operations in other states, sought sanctuary in Nevada, and
brought with them their expertise, essential for such a rapidly emergent
industry, and otherwise unobtainable investment and construction money.
They were the entrepreneurs who truly developed Nevada in the twentieth
century.

Gross revenues from gambling operations in Nevada soared from
$21,575,472 in 1946 to $55,235,560 in 1952 and an astonishing
$145,037,000 in 1958.[17] By the latter year gambling had emerged as
Nevada's leading industry, and the ripple effects on Nevada's tiny population and economic base were profound. Gambling brought new residents,
and Nevada was now the fastest growing state relative to its size in the
Union. The number of people in Nevada rose from 110,247 in 1940 to
285,278 in 1960; Clark County shot up from 16,414 to 127,016, and Las
Vegas displaced Reno as Nevada's largest city, although Reno still remained the economic and political power center.

The old political types just had to adjust. Gambling had now become
indispensable to Nevada's economy, and in a sense the state was hostage to

the new forces enveloping it. Gambling no longer was an adjunct to the political machine; it was now the controlling force. Even McCarran somewhat reluctantly had to recognize how important gambling had become and admit that its eradication would ruin the state. After the sensational hearings of the Special Senate Committee to investigate Organized Crime Activities, chaired by Senator Estes Kefauver of Tennessee, which revealed the extent of mob influence in Nevada, a determined effort was made in the Congress to tax the state's gambling right out of existence.[18] In a long, revealing letter to Joseph McDonald, McCarran stated well the ambiguity of the situation, and why he had to try to save Nevada's own "Peculiar Institution."

> The Committee on Ways and Means of the House of Representatives announced to the open session of the House of Representatives that they would bring in a bill with a 10 per cent tax on the gross receipts of gambling. That was inserted in the Congressional Record and it was no idle threat. Ten per cent of the gross receipts of gambling in the state of Nevada would close every gambling house, regardless of where it is located or how it is conducted. Virginia Street would be in mourning and the gleaming gulch of Las Vegas would be a glowing symbol of funereal distress. . . . In the last few years the State of Nevada has woven gambling in its various forms into the warp and woof of the State's economic structure.

Curiously, McCarran seemed not only somewhat surprised at the ascendancy of gambling in Nevada but also perturbed. He had battled long for the agriculture and mining interests of his state. His deep commitment to economic progress in the West inclined him toward manufacturing rather than tourism. But here was something else—unforeseen, rather inconvenient, and not entirely defensible—which *had* to be supported because the alternative was unthinkable:

> The State has builded its economy on gambling. Indeed so much so, that I'm afraid we have blinked our eyes at that which to my mind is the stronger form of economy, namely, payrolls on legitimate business and payrolls coming from industry at its lowest ebb. Our agricultural industry has been hard hit by the fact that the livestock population of the state has dwindled. Our tax agencies have looked to the more lush source from whence to derive additional taxes to maintain the State's machinery. . . . I hope the time will come when the financial structure of the State of Nevada will not rest on gambling. I hope the time will come when we point with pride to industries of all kinds in the State of Nevada, with payrolls that will sustain the economy of Nevada. But that isn't today, Joe, and it won't be tomorrow.[19]

Old money found the adjustment to the new ecomonic realities not totally unpleasant. Gambling was economically convenient and lucrative, so it was easy to cash in and join the process. Norman Biltz, among others, was forced to accommodate, as it became apparent that in Nevada joining with the gamblers was necessary for maximization of investment and profits. In 1955 Biltz decided, along with partners Stanley Dollar and John Mueller, to build a hotel in Reno that would not offer gambling. It would have "a lovely lobby and all the things that these people who are against gambling say they want and will support." The Holiday was built and proved a disaster. "You could shoot a cannon through the place," said Biltz later. "I think on a good night we might have had five per cent occupancy." Fortunately, the building had been designed so gambling could be put in if necessary, which was soon accomplished. "The Holiday for the last three or four years has run about ninety-five per cent occupancy, instead of five," added Biltz. "And I don't hear any more from the die-hards about building them another place without gambling."[20]

In the 1950s the older political and economic forces governing Nevada accommodated themselves to the force of gambling; rather belatedly, and only after McCarran's death in 1954, did the state leadership realize that to save gambling from hostile, outside elements, they would have to regulate it. Although the state of Nevada took nominal control of gambling in 1945, no attempt at effective regulation was made for another decade. Until 1955, it was enough happily to collect taxes, and in effect, anyone who wished a license could receive one. The state denied any racketeer influence in Nevada gambling. But the cloud lingering over the state from the Kefauver investigations suggested that if Nevada did not effectively monitor and regulate the industry, the federal government would come in and tax it out of existence. For the most part, effective state regulation obtained the approval of the gamblers. (Grandfathering in the mobsters who had previously dominated the industry undoubtedly helped.) In 1955 Republican Gov. Charles Russell signed the law creating the State Gaming[21] Control Board to monitor and license gambling operations. At first the board was subsidiary to the State Tax Commission, but in 1959, under the leadership of newly elected Democratic Gov. Grant Sawyer, an independent State Gaming Control Commission was formed. State supervision of gambling promised protection against a potentially vengeful federal government. Nevada gambling and the state government, with the support of its people, thus became partners in order to sustain the industry.

The support of the voters was key. Partly this demonstrated the growing importance of the gambling industry as an employer. But the support was almost universal. Moral stricture against gambling got nowhere in Nevada, perhaps reflecting the low representation, and imperceptible influence, within the state of those Protestant denominations that had traditionally condemned gambling. Arguments that official gambling was dominated by the underworld were virtually ignored by the press and denied by the state. Fundamentally, gambling suited the public convenience. From the beginning, it had overwhelming public support in Nevada, as evidenced by confidential surveys commissioned by the Thomas C. Wilson Advertising Agency for Harolds Club over a twenty-year period. The surveys were conducted by Facts Consolidated, a Los Angeles research firm. In 1948, the survey asked people how Nevada's "progress" was affected by the gambling laws. Progress was helped by gambling, answered 83 percent, while only 14 percent believed that it was hindered. The 1948 survey also inquired as to what effect gambling had on taxation, to which 89 percent replied that it "helped" taxation. The survey also asked whether the 1931 statute relegalizing gambling should be repealed. Only 9 percent favored repeal, while 82.5 percent wanted legalized gambling to remain. Later surveys suggested that popular support for gambling actually increased with time. By 1962, only 5 percent of the respondents polled thought that gambling should be repealed.[22]

Some of the respondents indicated that Nevada should offer a low-tax package in order to attract the wealthy to the state. Legalized gambling was popular because it put much of the tax burden upon the tourist. Although gambling brought growth, and with the growth came increasing government responsibilities, the idea was prevalent that gambling also decreased the tax burden for most individuals, keeping everyone ahead of the game.

After 1960 the gambling industry continued its astonishing growth. In 1955, gross gambling revenues had been $94,368,588; in 1965 they were $301,245,000; in 1975, $1.1 billion, $3.2 billion in 1985, and over $5.0 billion in 1990.[23] Such growth became its own chief reward, and the amazing material success of Nevada gambling drew appreciative response from the American business community and from other states. Gambling continued to bring in residents, and Nevada remained the fastest-growing state in terms of percentages for each decade from 1960 to 1990. The 1960 population of 285,278 grew to 1,201,833 by 1990. Furthermore, no other state saw a more radical geographical redistribution of its inhabitants. Clark County, with 127,016 inhabitants in 1960, soared by 1990 to 741,459—then 61.7 percent of the state's population. Yet the vast majority of Nevada's land area remained almost unsettled; a group of thirteen counties, with an area greater than that of the United Kingdom, still had fewer than one person per square mile.

The changes in the gambling industry from 1960 to 1990 were fundamental. Perhaps the most important factor was the Corporate Gaming Act of 1969, which allowed major publicly held corporations, such as Hilton and Metro Goldwyn Mayer (MGM), to come to Nevada. Bank financing for new construction became available, and the mob's control of Las Vegas diminished. Las Vegas became a major convention center, visited even by the Southern Baptists in 1987.[24] By 1992, of the ten largest hotels in the United States, nine were in Las Vegas, and even larger ones are either under construction or on the drawing boards.[25] The importance of gambling to the state was almost absolute in 1989: of 537,433 people employed in Nevada statewide, nearly 70 percent (372,000) worked in gambling or associated industries. In Clark County, those with occupations in gambling or related industries accounted for 78 percent of the work force.[26]

Political changes were as fundamental as the demographic and economic changes. The most important political changes were occasioned not only by the evolution of the state, but by a forced restructuring of the state legislature.

Previously, the rural counties had controlled the state legislature. Of all the counties in the state, they were the least dependent on gambling. Before 1965, the fifteen counties in the state other than Washoe and Clark held fifteen out of seventeen seats in the state senate. Three Nevada counties had fewer than 1,000 people in 1960, and yet, as ordained by the state constitution,[27] they were represented equally (one seat per county) with Clark County, home of 127,016 people. The state assembly made a stab at apportionment by population, but since each county was guaranteed a minimum of one assembly seat, the rural counties remained overrepresented. This was an exceptionally self-perpetuating system; Nevada's constitution allowed no realistic alternative.

The rural counties could have used their political power against the casino interests, but these small counties had been bought off in the closing days of the 1957 legislative session by an amendment to a gambling bill offered in conference committee by Sen. Errit Cord, who represented tiny Esmeralda County. Cord's amendment distributed the table tax equally to each county; and it was estimated that in the amendment's first year of operation, each county would receive $39,000 with the annual booty to grow handsomely over the years. This tax distribution saved several counties from bankruptcy and possible dissolution. As Norman Biltz remarked concerning the deal, "Little Esmeralda County's got so much money with four hundred registered voters in Esmeralda; they got money running out of their ears." So the small counties also had a stake in the gambling system.[28]

The casino owners might as well have saved their money, because the days of rural control of the legislature were numbered. In a 1962 decision *(Baker v. Carr)* and a 1964 decision *(Reynolds v. Sims)* the U.S. Supreme Court stated that the method of apportioning the state legislature adopted by states such as Nevada was unconstitutional. Henceforth, *both* houses of a state legislature had to be apportioned on the basis of population. The upshot of the decisions was that the Nevada legislature had to be reapportioned, and of course this meant that the real power center of the state swung toward Las Vegas. A Las Vegas woman, Flora Dungan, went to federal court in 1965 and sued the governor, Grant Sawyer, stating that the Nevada legislature, according to *Reynolds v. Sims*, would have to be reapportioned. In this case, *Dungan v. Sawyer* (1965), the lower federal court agreed.

So in 1966 the Nevada legislature most unwittingly reapportioned itself. Other bodies such as the University of Nevada Board of Regents were also forced to reapportion to reflect changing population trends, but the legislature was most greatly affected. In 1965, the rural counties had 15 out of 17 state senators. By the 1980s Clark County alone had 12 out of 21 senators. In the assembly, Clark County's strength went from 12 assembly people out of 37, to 24 out of 42. To look at it another way, the state senator from the central district represents an area larger than the state of New York, and the senator from the northern district represents an area larger than either Ohio or Tennessee. Clark County's domination of the state legislature is absolute, if one looks just at the numbers. In 1990 Clark County had 61.7 percent of the state's inhabitants. No other state, except for Hawaii, is equally dominated by a major metropolitan area. The implication of the Supreme Court decisions was that dynamic growth and population figures were to become the sole determinants of representation and power in state government; other interests were brushed aside, and from the standpoint of Nevada's chief industry, there was no competing power to counteract its influence. Clark County legislators certainly retained normal divisions of party and ideology, but all of Clark County's political representatives had a common interest in the protection and encouragement of gambling. The industry's triumph in the state was ensured by the U.S. Supreme Court reapportionment decisions. Ironically, the democratic reforms of the 1960s tightened the grip of gambling on the state.

The changing nature of legislative power helped ensure that Nevada's future would be tied in with gambling. Previously that had not been clear. The wild surge of growth that gambling had enjoyed during the 1950s was lost in the following decade. No major hotel had been built on the strip since 1958, and annual percentage increases in gambling revenue appeared to be slowing down. With only a 5.2 percent increase, 1965 was the worst year of growth for the industry since 1950. In 1966, an article appeared in the *Atlantic Monthly* by Edward F. Sherman, a legal aide to Gov. Grant Sawyer, entitled "Nevada, The End of the Casino Era." Its closing words declaimed, "Nevada has embarked on the road to becoming just another American state. Difficult days are ahead for its gambling industry, and the transition pains of the post-Casino Era may be unpleasant. But the Casino Era is drawing to a close, and few Nevadans will mourn its passing."[29]

Sherman was a terrible prophet. In 1969, the reapportioned legislature passed the Corporate Gaming Act, which revamped the economic structure of the gambling industry—and with it, gambling's image. Corporate financing became available, and Nevada banks deepened their stake in the state's chief industry. Even the federal government, previously inimical to Nevada's peculiar institution, did what it could to aid and abet its growth. The federally funded Southern Nevada Water Project passed Congress in 1965, due chiefly to the efforts of Sen. Alan Bible. This opened up almost limitless amounts of Colorado River water for thirsty Las Vegas. By increasing the water supply, the federal government issued a virtual blank check to underwrite Las Vegas's growth, so much of it dependent upon the extensive use of water for its casinos, golf courses, fountains, newly created lakes, and sumptuous greenery.[30]

The political leaders could only approve. Their ties to the industry grew ever closer. In August 1975, the Commission of the Review of the National Policy Toward Gambling, which had been created by Congress in the Organized Crime Act of 1970 to study all aspects of gambling in America and to recommend policy to the states and the federal government, met in Carson City and Reno to see how Nevada was regulating its chief industry.

Thirty-eight Nevada leaders (representing the worlds of government, business, education, gambling, religion, and journalism) testified, virtually all emphasizing the beneficial, rosy aspects of gambling's impact upon the state. Twenty-four years before, the Kefauver committee had been irascible and confrontational; by contrast, the Commission of the Review of the National Policy Toward Gambling was most cooperative, and the general atmosphere was that of a love fest. Many points were constantly reiterated, as if there had been a previous collusion of testimony, or perhaps everyone simply shared the same values and outlooks. An official effort seemed to have been made to give the commission only one side of the story. No controversial casino owners, such as Benny Binion or Moe Dalitz, were invited to the hearings. Such leaders as Sen. Howard Cannon and Gov. Mike O'Callaghan emphasized the stringent nature of Nevada's gambling regulation and attempted to fit the industry into the greater American business and cultural mainstream. The commission members ate it all up, and their final report highly commended Nevada gambling.[31]

Not surprisingly, with such a dominant industry, the lines drawn between the political world and the world of gambling became quite blurred. Perhaps it could not have been otherwise. An incident in November 1978 involving Robert List, the governor-elect, illustrated the increasingly close connection between the two worlds. List was accused by the North Las Vegas *Valley Times* of having received more than two thousand dollars (in List's words "a few hundred dollars") in free rooms and meals from the Stardust Hotel while he was state attorney general—in fact, at the same time his office was conducting a major investigation of skimming at the hotel and was in court against one of the hotel's chief executive officers, Frank Rosenthal, in a licensing dispute. While receiving the "comps," List also collected a per diem reimbursement from the state for precisely the same expenses. Confronted with these double-dipping and conflict-of-interest charges, List replied that this "was common practice in accordance with state procedures."[32] List was only embarrassed—if that—by the incident and went on to serve a full term as governor.

Far more nationally publicized, and also illustrative of the ambiguous lines between the gamblers and the politicians, was an event concerning Sen. Paul Laxalt. Laxalt, who had been an effective and popular governor from 1967 through 1970, decided to retire to private life instead of standing for reelection. Later, he successfully ran for the U.S. Senate in

1974, and was reelected to that office in 1980. He became, for a while, the most famous of Nevadans, not for his position or influence in the Senate, but rather because of his close friendship with Pres. Ronald Reagan, whose trusted adviser he became.

On 1 November 1983, articles in the highly respected *Sacramento Bee*, and *Bee* papers in Fresno and Modesto, discussed at length the nature of Laxalt's ownership, financing, and construction of the Ormsby House casino-hotel in Carson City, which he had undertaken after leaving the governorship. Most of the *Bee's* information was undisputed. Laxalt, a man of admittedly modest means, had put up a total of $938 for the multimillion dollar venture, as had his brother Peter. All the rest of the money was supplied by banks, most notably the Chicago First National bank, which at one point gave notice that it was ready to lend $950,000 to Laxalt for five years without security. According to the story, the Ormsby House was plagued by financial problems, and the Laxalts eventually sold their interest in the hotel-casino, well after Paul's election to the Senate. When Laxalt sold, the hotel was indebted to Chicago First National for $7.3 million. Claiming insider information from the Federal Bureau of Investigation (the source for which it refused to divulge), the *Bee* alleged that a major cause for the Ormsby House's financial failure was skimming of up to $2 million, although the *Bee* did not link that directly to the Laxalts.[33]

Senator Laxalt himself made this into a major story by suing Mc-Clatchey Publications (the owner of the *Bee* newspapers) for $250 million. He did not dispute most of the story's details, but demanded that the newspaper apologize for and retract any implication that the Laxalts had skimmed money from the operation. In the end, Laxalt settled for nothing, except for a formal statement from the *Bee* that the newspaper never meant to imply that Laxalt had participated in, or had knowledge of, any skimming.[34] After the settlement, Laxalt made an abortive try for the Republican presidential nomination in 1988, an attempt that soon collapsed, partly because of the negative image connected with his Nevada associations. At the least, the story illustrated the ease with which Nevada politicians went into the gambling industry while out of office. The reverse was true as well. Robert Cashell, the owner of Boomtown near Reno, served as a member of the University of Nevada Board of Regents for six years and was lieutenant governor of the state from 1985 through 1988.

The extent to which casinos provided campaign funding is not altogether clear, but their role was obviously important. When Paul Laxalt ran for the U.S. Senate in 1974, his campaign spent approximately $500,000, mostly raised in Nevada, and more than half of that came from the casinos. Six years later, these contributions to Laxalt more than doubled. When questioned by national reporters on the propriety of this, Laxalt stated, "A politician taking money from gambling in Nevada is like one taking campaign money from the auto people in Michigan. Gambling is our legal business."[35] True enough, but no other state is quite so dominated by a single industry as is Nevada. The influence of gambling money is felt even in races for the state judiciary. In 1984, Judge Charles Thompson of the state district court in Las Vegas, spent $154,000 on his reelection effort. One of the chief issues in the campaign was his issuance of a restraining order against strikers in a hotel-casino dispute. Far outspending his opponent, he received $7,500 in political contributions from the Golden Nugget casino in Las Vegas; $5,500 each from the Four Queens and from Sam's Town; $5,000 from the California Hotel; and $3,000 each from Caesar's Palace and the Las Vegas Hilton.[36] A legislative newsletter from Common Cause in Nevada documenting 1992 candidate expenditures (not including funds received by the political parties) shows well the importance of casino giving to all state races, including those for state supreme court. Casino political gifts for state senate and assembly seats throughout Nevada are widespread; a Las Vegas or Reno casino will typically give political money not only for its particular district race but for races everywhere in the state. Casino campaign donations far exceed those from any other interest group—labor, legal, medical, or educational.[37]

The residents of Nevada do not question, and have not questioned, this dominance. If the state has become handmaiden to a single industry, it is because its people recognize the economic indispensability of it; it has become an integral part of the state's landscape. Residents cannot conceive of a society with greater economic diversity and more competing interests. There is an old, traditional view, still popular in the state, that the real Nevada is the Nevada of wide open spaces, sagebrush, mining towns, singularly beautiful mountains, productive cattle and sheep ranches, and simple frontier virtues. But the real Nevada, at least measured by any meaningful economic index, is far more gritty: it is the Nevada of the strip and its glitter, downtown Reno, South Tahoe's towering hotel-casinos, and likely the next gambling center, Laughlin.[38] The old-time Nevadans sold their patrimony long ago. Meanwhile, the smooth talking politicians glide comfortably between the two camps, drawing their money from the one and pitching their rhetoric to the other.

Two-Star General, Three-Time Loser: Patrick Hurley Seeks a Senate Seat in New Mexico

RICHARD LOWITT

J. S. McCall, a lawyer in Carlsbad, wrote former governor Richard Dillon in October 1945, "I have heard it rumored that General Hurley might be persuaded to run for the U.S. Senate next year." Both men were active in Republican party affairs and both thought Patrick J. Hurley, with "his splendid record as Secretary of War, his military record in two wars along with his record in civilian life as a lawyer all coupled with his ability makes a splendid candidate and the finest timber possible for the Senate." Dillon, in fact, had been talking to other Republican leaders and reported that all were convinced that Hurley could win a Senate seat and that "he would likely pull over the Republican ticket" in the 1946 election.[1]

Unable to elect a governor since Dillon won a second term in 1928 and a senator since Bronson Cutting won reelection in 1934, the Republican party, thanks in large part to New Deal relief and other programs, appeared destined to a permanent minority role, much like the party throughout the "solid South." After Cutting's death in a May 1935 plane crash, New Mexico could not boast a Republican holding a major elective public office. Hurley's candidacy offered the party an opportunity to emerge from the political wilderness by reviving the two-party system in the state.

At the time McCall wrote to Dillon, Hurley was in Washington on leave from his post in Chungking as the American envoy to Chiang Kai-shek's government. James J. Byrnes, secretary of state, and Pres. Harry S Truman wished Hurley to return to his post. Hurley, weary of the diplomatic infighting in the embassy owing to his unstinting support of Chiang Kai-shek's hostility toward members of the Chinese Communist Party seeking recognition in his government, contemplated resigning his post. As the situation worsened in China, with Communist forces engaging Chiang's troops and the Russians reportedly assisting the Chinese Communists in Manchuria and North China, Hurley apparently gave up any hope he might have had of witnessing a unification of the contending forces. Moreover, criticism of his role in China was beginning to surface in the American press, and Hurley, wanting to defend his support of the Nationalist government against charges that American assistance was serving to stifle democratic aspirations in China, on 27 November 1945 released a press statement containing a review of his wartime experience and a statement of resignation. Hurley was now free to seek a seat in the U.S. Senate.

Despite his illustrious career, Hurley had never won an elective office. He was defeated in a race for a seat in the Oklahoma State Senate in 1910. He decided to try again, this time representing New Mexico. If elected he could expound his views on American foreign policy, and on the people who made it, in an arena where he could make a difference. In doing so he would be defending his role in China during World War II.[2] But first he had to be nominated and then elected. Three times he was nominated and three times he failed to win election. In 1946 he lost to Dennis Chavez by less than 5,000 votes and claimed "there were frauds in the election just concluded." In 1948 he lost to Clinton Anderson, who stepped down as secretary of agriculture to make the race. Hurley lost by over 28,000 votes. He now had to wait and bide his time until 1952, when once again he would contest Dennis Chavez for a Senate seat.

However, Hurley now faced a problem he had not previously encountered. With the Republican party in control of the governor's office for the first time in over two decades, Edwin L. Mechem, who would be seeking reelection, was not sure that he wanted to share the top of the ticket with a two-time loser more interested in national affairs than local politics. For the first time Hurley would have to fight for the senatorial nomination and wage a primary campaign. All of this became clear on 21 November 1951, when Hurley went to the room of Albert Mitchell, the Republican National Committeeman, at the LaFonda Hotel. After Mitchell and Hurley had had lunch, Governor Mechem and two of his close political associates entered the room. Discussion centered on opposition to Hurley within the Republican party, of which Hurley was aware. Dennis Chavez would be seeking reelection, and Hispanic party members would support him "on purely racial grounds," as had happened in 1946. Indeed prominent Hispanic Republicans, like Maurice Miera and Manuel Lujan, already had indicated their intention to support Chavez. Miera explained to Hurley that "the natives would never have another United States Senator" if Chavez were defeated. After these preliminaries, Fred H. Maxey, chief of the revenue bureau, informed Hurley "if you want the Republican nomination at this time, you will have to pay for it." Maxey specified "that the Republican nomination will cost you $100,000 — $50,000 to be paid well in advance of the primary and the other $50,000" after he received the nomination. Maxey made it clear that "in addition to guaranteeing you the nomination we will go through with the organization behind you and we think we can assure you election to the Senate." Maxey concluded by insisting that contributions made directly to Hurley's campaign should be turned over immediately to him in his capacity as campaign manager.

Hurley admitted to being "shocked, surprised, humiliated." Endeavoring to maintain a calm exterior, he said "categorically and definitely the answer to your proposal is no." While the discussion made it evident to Hurley that he would meet intense Republican hostility to his candidacy, he believed that he could win in the primary if he "filed by petition."

Appalled at "the thick-headed immoral, illegal, attitude of these leaders of the Republican Party," Hurley recognized that in this campaign he would have a Democratic opponent, Dennis Chavez, and numerous internal opponents at the top level of the Republican party.[3]

On 19 January 1952 Hurley formally announced his candidacy for the U.S. Senate "subject to the Republican Primary and Convention." He concluded his statement by saying, "I supported Edwin L. Mechem for governor through the last campaign. I will support him wholeheartedly in this year's campaign." But now for the first time in two decades factional fights in the party came to the fore. Hurley had two opponents in the primary.[4]

He campaigned hard to win delegates first to the Republican Primary Convention and then to secure the Republican nomination by winning the primary. Unfortunately both of Hurley's opponents also won enough delegates at the primary convention to put their names on the ballot with his, but his name would head the list of senatorial candidates in the primary election to be held on May 6.[5]

Observers predicted that the scramble for the Republican senatorial nomination would develop into a rough primary battle in which Hurley, dynamic and quick-tempered, would be challenged by party leaders denouncing him as a politically ambitious prima donna and ruthless campaigner. What Hurley feared most was that "at least 3,000 state officials and employees while they are being paid by the taxpayers would participate in the campaign" against him. Hurley was confident that if no pressure were put upon them, he could count on the support of many of them. This situation provided him with an issue that he could exploit: government by the people or by a political machine.[6]

Despite heated exchanges and maneuvering among party leaders, in mid-April political observers generally conceded that Hurley held a commanding lead. They proved correct. Hurley won the primary and won handily in counties where party leaders close to Mechem had been expected to "exercise the most control over the voters." Hurley, who had alienated prominent party leaders by calling them "Chavez Republicans," now had to seek their support for the fall campaign. He believed that he could overcome this handicap once the party united in the presidential campaign behind Dwight Eisenhower and Richard Nixon. Party leaders wanted to see a Republican victory in the fall as badly as Hurley wanted a Senate seat.[7]

In October, Hurley benefited from Eisenhower's appearance in the state. Hurley introduced him before a capacity crowd at the University of New Mexico stadium in Albuquerque. Also helpful to Hurley was an appearance by U.S. Senator Robert A. Taft and funding provided by the Republican Senatorial Committee. As the campaign reached its climax, most observers concluded that the presidential vote was the key to the Chavez-Hurley race, which was considered too close to call.[8]

And when it was over, it was still too close to call. Eisenhower carried the state and Mechem handily won a second term as governor, but it took several days of tabulation before Dennis Chavez moved into the lead. Late reporting returns from the largely Hispanic northern counties slowly nudged Chavez ahead. As in 1946 Chavez defeated Hurley by a scant 5,000 votes, 122,543 to 117,168. Hurley, however, did not accept Chavez's victory. Saying that the fight had just begun, Hurley obtained court orders impounding ballot boxes in four northern counties and charged that there were violations of both federal and state laws. He intended to challenge the election and called for both a state and federal investigation of fraud in the Senate race.[9]

Hurley's decision to contest the election launched a series of investigations that were not fully resolved until April 1954, seventeen months after the election. The twists and turns of these investigations brought to public attention seamy aspects of New Mexico politics. While talk of vote fraud was common throughout New Mexico since the days of the Santa Fe Ring during the territorial period, never before was the public made so thoroughly aware of the sordid details as over the course of those seventeen months. Shortly after the election, the Federal Bureau of Investigation (FBI) launched a preliminary inquiry, questioning politicians and election officials to determine if there were violations of either state or federal election laws. Hurley, pleased that an investigation was getting underway, remained convinced that he was elected and added, "I want to enfranchise the majority of the voters of New Mexico who have been disfranchised by corrupt political machines."[10]

Next, the State Canvassing Board and finally the Senate itself, as the final judge of its own membership, would consider the matter. The Senate Committee on Privileges and Elections could either dismiss Hurley's challenge as without merit or, if it recommended unseating Chavez, forward its report to the whole Senate for a vote. The membership of the State Canvassing Board was two-to-one Democratic, with Governor Mechem the lone Republican member.

By the end of November the contest headed for the courts as Hurley strove to prevent the State Canvassing Board from sending election returns stored in Santa Fe back to the counties for canvassing. Despite the efforts of Hurley's lawyers, a recount of 65,000 ballots in 231 voting divisions boosted Chavez's majority by an additional 295 votes. (On 29 November, prior to the recount, the State Canvassing Board had certified Chavez as the victor by 5,071 votes.) Hurley thereafter wrote Chavez that he would carry the fight to the U.S. Senate. In response, Chavez asserted that if the dispute went to the Senate, the outcome would be "equally disappointing" to Hurley.[11]

With a Republican president and a Republican-controlled Congress, Hurley had grounds for believing that he could unseat Chavez and realize what he had fought three campaigns to achieve, a seat in the U.S. Senate. However, he must have been disturbed by a story circulating in Capitol corridors about a deal struck by Senate leaders in which the Democrats agreed not to approve the report examining the dubious financial transactions discovered in Joseph McCarthy's banking and brokerage accounts and thereby not challenge his right to a second term in the Senate, if the Republicans agreed to accept Chavez. Hurley advised friends "definitely that there is no such deal and will not be." Republicans, he said, "are playing for keeps this time" and would have some Democratic support. What gave Hurley further assurance that his case would be heard was the appointment of a Senate Elections Investigating Subcommittee to further probe it.[12]

On 17 April 1953, the subcommittee issued its preliminary report, a scathing statement calling for a full-scale ballot count in the Hurley-Chavez contest. Hurley supporters were delighted. The full-scale investigation, Sen. Frank Barrett warned, would take time. Thomas C. Hennings, the Democratic member of the three-member subcommittee, dampened somewhat the enthusiasm of Hurley's friends by remarking that in his opinion "illegal acts were committed by both sides." Among the findings of the investigators were a failure to provide voting booths in many precincts, evidence of unqualified voters, and discrepancies in vote totals. In addition, ballot burning, coercion, and intimidation of voters were also mentioned. As a first step, Barrett said the subcommittee would attempt to have the attorneys for Hurley and Chavez agree on procedures for the ballot recount, which the chief investigator intended to get underway promptly.[13]

Robert Hansen, a reporter for the *Denver Post*, called the preliminary report the initial phase of what could be "the most comprehensive vote fraud investigation in the nation's history," the outcome of which would play a significant role in resolving domestic and foreign policy issues confronting the nation. So tight was the Republican balance in the Senate—forty-eight Republicans to forty-seven Democrats, plus Wayne Morse, who recently renounced his allegiance to the Republican party—that if Hurley was successful in his bid to oust Chavez, the balance would shift forty-nine to forty-six, excluding Morse. Much, therefore, was riding on the outcome of this investigation, which increasingly attracted national attention and brought top political reporters to the state. Besides reporters and Senate investigators (a seventeen-person task force), the FBI reportedly had fifteen agents, virtually every one in New Mexico, at work probing federal vote fraud complaints. In addition, both Hurley and Chavez had forces in the field. Hurley's team consisted of about forty private investigators, attorneys, former law enforcement officers, and a clerical staff. By April more than $50,000 from private and national Republican party funds had been poured into Hurley's effort. Although the Chavez camp generally discounted the investigation, it too began to bolster its cause.[14]

The Senate subcommittee's probe became in effect a minefield that could detonate furious political brawling. In Congress, party tensions were aroused early in May when a resolution authorizing $100,000 to recount the votes was sidetracked after intense partisan debate on the Senate floor. In Washington, both contestants were backed much more vigorously than they were by their own party leaders in New Mexico. In Hurley's case, it was clear that top Republican leaders from the outset were not enthused about his candidacy. In turn Hurley had accused Governor Mechem and Harry Robins, the state Republican chairman, of supporting Chavez. In all, the contest, particularly Judge Bill Scoggin's order that 18,000 ballots in his judicial district be burned, helped blacken New Mexico's political reputation. [15]

In July, because of pessimism about the Senate approving additional funds, it appeared that the inquiry might be drawing to an end. A resolution providing $160,000 for the investigatory subcommittee ran into Democratic opposition. With Senator Taft recovering from surgery, the slim Republican majority no longer existed. Moreover, many senators were disturbed over reports of what appeared to be a deliberately slow pace involving interminable haggling over each ballot. Fearing termination of funding, on 18 July 1953, the chief counsel of the Sub-Committee on Privileges and Elections, Wellford H. Ware, issued a summary report. Ware indicated that when completed, "Our investigation will prove that due to the intentional and flagrant violations of the secrecy of the ballot more than 6,102 votes will be gained by Patrick J. Hurley," enough to overturn Chavez's majority of 5,366. [16]

By the end of July the Senate Privileges and Elections Committee had already spent a quarter of a million dollars, and the Republican National Committee had contributed an additional $27,500, to which Hurley himself had subscribed an unknown amount. A staff of thirty-three Senate investigators worked out of headquarters established in Albuquerque's Medical Arts Center, with furniture supplied by the General Services Administration. In addition, both Hurley and Chavez each employed a staff of eight challengers. Yet thus far, despite the huge effort, though numerous discrepancies were made public, no evidence of widespread fraud had been unearthed in the process of recounting votes. [17]

In early September, Ware, nevertheless, was promising to produce evidence of considerable fraud in northern New Mexico counties. But his promise proved to be empty. At the end of the month the subcommittee announced that the investigation had ended. Members of the investigative staff would return to Washington to write the report. The subcommittee had completed a recount in only twelve of New Mexico's thirty-two counties. Although Ware still had about $75,000 available to continue the investigation, most observers concluded that Hurley's cause was hopeless and that it would be a waste of time, effort, and taxpayers' money to continue an investigation that thus far had yielded inconclusive results that did not seriously challenge Chavez's lead over Hurley.[18]

The Senate, which would ultimately decide the fate of Chavez and Hurley, possibly tipped its hand when it voted only $37,500 out of a $160,000 appropriation request to continue the investigation through the fall. The Senate was then evenly divided — 47 Democrats, 47 Republicans, 1 independent (Wayne Morse), and 1 vacancy (Robert A. Taft had died on July 31); the Democrats assuredly would fight all the way to keep every seat they could. Several Republicans also indicated support for Chavez. History also favored Chavez. Out of 121 contested Senate elections, only 21 members had been expelled, 15 by a two-thirds vote, the others by a majority vote declaring their seats vacant. If the Senate eventually declared Chavez's seat vacant, Governor Mechem would appoint a successor; as Mechem and Hurley were at odds throughout the campaign, Hurley could not gain the seat by appointment. Moreover, interest in the controversy, as reflected by columnists and newspapers, was fading rapidly. What interest there was in the subcommittee's investigation turned into disappointment when the meager results of the recount became known. A lethargic public was concluding that the controversy was much ado about nothing, or at best very little.

Hurley, too, was worried about the outcome. His dilemma was that no one ever charged Chavez with fraud. The only charge was that fraud was responsible for Hurley's defeat. To unseat Chavez it would be necessary to prove that there was an organized campaign of fraud designed to defeat Hurley.[19]

Hurley's last chance depended on the subcommittee report, which by November 1953 was in its final stages of preparation. "Every effort," Hurley wrote, "has been made to keep the people from knowing the truth." The report, Hurley hoped, would show "that I defeated Senator Chavez."[20]

And it did. Released on 18 December 1953, the subcommittee's report recommended that about 30,000 votes be thrown out because of lack of secrecy in the balloting. If the report's recommendations were adopted by the Senate, Hurley would replace Chavez, giving the Republicans a one-vote majority. But in December the report was a long way from adoption. It needed approval of the Rules Committee to get on the floor, where it then would have to survive an angry partisan debate. Of the suspect 30,000 votes, about 20,000 were cast for Chavez, 10,000 for Hurley.[21]

The conclusion of the contest, the main brawl, seemingly would get underway in January, when Congress reconvened. Hurley, pleased with the report, was firm in his conviction that there was enough evidence to show that Chavez was defeated and that he was elected. As if to bolster his case, in January the subcommittee by a two-to-one vote decided to investigate further possible violations of New Mexico ballot secrecy laws. Three staff members returned to New Mexico for six more weeks of inquiry. The investigators returned, it was rumored, to bring into question several thousand more votes so that Senate Republicans could drive toward a decision of "no election" in the Hurley-Chavez dispute. Such a verdict would allow Governor Mechem to name a senator to serve only until the election of a successor in November 1954. This approach, if more than a rumor, was at best a gamble, as the Democrats now held a majority of forty-eight to forty-seven in the Senate and Wayne Morse, the Oregon independent, and William Langer, a North Dakota Republican, reportedly supported Chavez.[22]

By the end of January press reports suggested that Republicans were giving up the effort to unseat Chavez despite their urgent need for another Senate seat. They were now outnumbered in the Senate, and Republicans were fearful that the entire Eisenhower legislative program, which could hinge on the outcome of the fall elections, would be jeopardized by a losing fight to replace Chavez. If Chavez were unseated, Governor Mechem, who purportedly was planning to run for Senator Clinton Anderson's seat, would name a Republican replacement. To avoid further political chaos in New Mexico, which could impair his ambitions, Mechem let it be known that he did not like the prospect of a bitter fight to oust Chavez. Besides affecting Mechem's prospects, such a fight could end the truce that had prevailed in the first session of the Eighty-third Congress where Democrats claimed credit for getting many administration measures passed. In all, as the investigators in New Mexico recounted votes, the complex political balance in Washington seemingly indicated that Hurley's chances of a Senate seat were fading. He had become a pawn in a political game over which he had no control.[23]

While the investigators continued their probe, Senate Democrats in March, believing they had the votes to win, called for a showdown on the Republican effort to unseat Senator Chavez. He had been serving for more than a year on a "without prejudice basis" while the Republican-controlled elections subcommittee investigated the contest and spent over $200,000 in the process. If a report were not forthcoming, Senate Democrats said they would offer a resolution to restrict the Rules

Committee, which would present the report of the subcommittee, from further consideration of the issue.[24]

The Democratic threat prompted the subcommittee to release its findings and to recommend that the election be called no contest, that the seat be declared vacant, that the governor appoint a successor to Senator Chavez to serve until someone was elected in the fall. Hurley, not sanguine about the prospect of Governor Mechem selecting him, complained, "The record shows that I was elected" and, he added, "The Republican Party just didn't have the guts to hold what the record shows."[25]

The showdown was now clearly in sight. The subcommittee report recommending Chavez's ouster was signed by its two Republican members, Chairman Frank A. Barrett and Charles E. Potter. Thomas Hennings, the Democratic member, filed a dissenting report. If the Senate adopted the report, Chavez was out. Hennings, however, hoped that once the members considered his dissenting report, Democrats would muster a substantial majority behind Chavez. If the Rules Committee turned down the subcommittee recommendations, the matter would die there. If the recommendations went forward, a simple majority vote would suffice for a Senate decision. At this point most observers believed that Chavez would keep his seat.[26]

A resolution emanating from the Rules Committee on 16 March 1954 placed the matter on the calendar for consideration by the full membership. With presentation of the long-delayed minority report of Senator Hennings on 20 March, the way was finally cleared for a Senate vote. Whereas the majority report examined the conduct of the election, Hennings attacked the conduct of the recount, concluding that there was "no legal or moral basis" for the move to unseat Chavez. On Monday, 22 March, debate got underway on the resolution declaring a vacancy in a New Mexico Senate seat.

It was an auspicious debate; Vice-President Nixon presided. Majority leader William Knowland sat through the opening hours. Seated near Barrett were Wellford Ware (subcommittee counsel) and other aides. Several packing crates filled with records of the contest were stacked nearby. Barrett was not granted permission to bring Harry Bigbee, Santa Fe attorney for Hurley, onto the floor for consultation. Senator Chavez spent most of the afternoon seated near Hennings, who discussed his report in a three-hour speech. Nearby, available for handy reference, were several piles of law books. All of Chavez's aides were on the floor. In the gallery with his wife and daughter Imelda was his chief lawyer, Arthur T. Hannett, a former governor of New Mexico. Both New Mexico congressmen, Antonio Fernandez and John Dempsey, were on the floor. Ready to be of assistance was Clinton Anderson accompanied by his chief aide. Only Hurley and his wife, in residence at their Washington home, were nowhere in evidence.[27]

After the debate the following day, 23 March, the vote was held. Five Republicans and Wayne Morse joined with the forty-seven Democrats in voting against the recommendation of the Rules Committee stating that no one was elected to the Senate in New Mexico in 1952. The five Republicans were George Aiken, John Sherman Cooper, Frederick Payne, Margaret Chase Smith, and H. Alexander Smith. Two other Republicans, Thomas Kuchel and William Langer, were paired in favor of Senator Chavez. All were regarded as among the more liberal of their colleagues on the Republican side of the aisle. Every Democratic member was on hand and all voted against the recommendation, except Chavez, who refrained from voting. In the diplomatic gallery, observing the voting and listening to the debate, was Hurley accompanied by his wife and daughter. The vote climaxed fourteen months of investigation and two days of Senate debate. After it was all over, colleagues crowded around Chavez and shook his hand. Chavez later issued a statement thanking the Senate for "vindicating him." It was, he said, "a proud and joyous occasion." He remarked, "The senator from New Mexico was not on trial today, but truth and decency were on trial and, as always, in the end they prevailed." No one bothered to ask Patrick Hurley what he thought.[28]

After three campaigns Hurley had enough of partisan politics. Neither the subcommittee that made the investigation, nor the majority of the Senate Rules Committee, much to Hurley's regret, directed any charges against Senator Chavez personally. But they did say, in strong language, that they had found "flagrant violations" of constitutional rights and "general misconduct" of the balloting, so much that it became "impossible to distinguish the free and honest vote." Hurley possibly found some slight satisfaction, given these conclusions, in the knowledge that Chavez won a victory with little honor in it and that the whole affair was a discredit to the state of New Mexico and its election officials. If the state started to set its political house in order, then Hurley's electoral failures might not have been in vain.[29]

In November the election controversy officially came to an end when the federal government turned back to the state the ballots and election materials impounded during the investigation. On Monday, 22 November 1954, diesel oil was poured on the ballots with a state official standing by to watch. As they went up in smoke, so did the tattered remnants of Hurley's hopes for a Senate seat. Three times he tried and three times he failed. Twice, in 1946 and 1952, he had good reason to believe that fraudulent electoral practices deprived him of the seat. When he contested the election, the outcome was determined by considerations central to a struggle over matters confronting the U.S. Senate and the Eisenhower administration, considerations that had little to do with Hurley. He became a pawn and was sacrificed in a conflict he had not anticipated. Out of it all came an increased awareness of the necessity for electoral reform in New Mexico. And Hurley, like an old soldier, slowly faded from public view until his death in Santa Fe on July 30, 1963. Despite his shabby treatment, he remained ever loyal to the Republican cause, contributing funds whenever called upon — with one exception. He would not contribute nor say one word in support of Edwin L. Mechem in his various campaigns. He considered Mechem "the outstanding election corruptionist in the most corrupt elections in New Mexico."[30]

CHAPTER 12

A Part of the Nation and Apart from the Nation: North Dakota Politics Since 1945

DAVID B. DANBOM

On 1 January 1945, North Dakota's congressional delegation was solidly Republican. So was its governor and all but a handful of its legislators.

The state and its congressmen were known for staunch isolationism in foreign policy. Gerald Nye, defeated for reelection to the Senate in 1944, had been one of the most prominent leaders of the America First Committee. Sen. William ("Wild Bill") Langer continued this tradition by being one of the only two senators to vote against American membership in the United Nations.

In domestic policy, the congressional delegation reflected the state's heritage of agrarian radicalism. Congressman William Lemke and Senator Langer had been early members of the Nonpartisan League (NPL). During the 1930s, Lemke supported radical measures of farm relief, such as the Frazier-Lemke Bankruptcy Act, designed to prevent farmers from losing their property. As governor in 1933, Langer had declared a moratorium on farm foreclosures and had embargoed the shipment of wheat out of the state to drive prices higher. Congressman Usher Burdick, another NPL veteran, had led the radical North Dakota Farm Holiday Association during the depression.

North Dakota had a reputation for sending mavericks, true "sons of the wild jackass," to Washington, and the delegation that took the oath in 1945 was no exception. Lemke had accepted the presidential nomination of Father Charles Coughlin's Union party in 1936. Burdick's different drummer led him to crusade for the release from prison of Ezra Pound, the poet

Author's note: I gratefully acknowledge the comments of Mike Jacobs, John Monzingo, Larry Peterson, and Jack Zaleski on an earlier version of this chapter.

who championed Fascist Italy during World War II, and to be one of the two members of the House of Representatives to vote against the Communist Control Act of 1954. Langer's senatorial career featured a series of bizarre stands, including opposition to the confirmation of Earl Warren as Chief Justice of the Supreme Court on the grounds that a North Dakota jurist had never been appointed to that body.

In January 1993, North Dakota sent an entirely Democratic delegation to the 103d Congress. This marked the fourth Congress in a row in which no North Dakota Republican had served. A Republican governor was inaugurated in 1993, but his party had held that office for only four of the previous thirty-two years. Moreover, most of the state's constitutional officers sworn in in 1993 were Democrats, and that party held the state senate.

The state's Congressmen no longer advocate idiosyncratic views on foreign policy. They are in the Democratic mainstream, mildly dovish but generally supportive of a strong defense and of America's position as a world leader. Unlike their predecessors, these leaders did not come out of the agrarian radical tradition. Born during or after World War II, they have not experienced the political and economic struggles of the 1930s. These Congress members also diverged from those prior to 1945 in that none could remotely be considered a maverick. It would be unfair to characterize these men as colorless, and Sen. Byron Dorgan is frequently quoted on economic issues, but none would come first to the mind of a Washington reporter looking for a good story to enliven a slow news day.

The dramatic differences between the delegation of 1993 and that of 1945 reflect momentous changes in North Dakota politics. Some of these changes involve matters of political style. Some of them involve significant political realignments in the state. Others involve the decreasing relevance to North Dakotans of particular issues. The most important changes in North Dakota politics, however, involve an altered relationship to the federal government and altered expectations from that relationship.

The political culture in which Langer, Lemke, Nye, Usher Burdick, and their contemporaries thrived was shaped by social, economic, and geographic realities of North Dakota in its early years. Physical isolation and a colonial economic relationship with the rest of the country were important factors. Way out on the northern edge of the United States, sparsely populated, and distant from centers of economic, cultural, and political power, North Dakota conceived itself from its earliest years as outside of the national mainstream. This outsider mentality was furthered by the fact that the early population was overwhelmingly composed of immigrants and the children of immigrants, mostly from isolated and peripheral places in Europe such as Norway and Russia.

North Dakota's isolation contributed to a high degree of suspicion of national institutions and trends, and sometimes to what might even be called a siege mentality. Ironically, this sense of apartness encouraged behaviors that exacerbated the state's isolation.

An important component of North Dakota's sense of isolation and its suspicion of outside forces was its colonial economic status. North Dakota depended on outside capital to finance its agriculture and commerce, on railroads owned by outsiders to export its raw agricultural products and import manufactured goods, on outside consumers to buy North Dakota wheat and beef, and on outside manufacturers and workers to produce essential goods — the clothes they wore, the stoves that warmed them, and the plows that turned their soil.

North Dakotans believed, with no little justice, that they were mistreated junior partners in these economic relationships. Real interest rates were high, railroads usually enjoyed monopoly status and levied charges accordingly, and farmers took what was given for their products and paid what was demanded for what they bought.

The state was unsure of how to respond to this situation. Conservatives suggested that North Dakota must create a friendly atmosphere for capital if it was to overcome its colonial status. Radicals believed that the state must seize command of its economic fate by economic cooperation and public ownership of essential facilities, and that it must join with other similarly oppressed states to change the rules by which the national economy operated.

In the first half of the state's history, the radicals seemed to have the upper hand. A series of agrarian protest movements swept the state, climaxed by the rise of the Nonpartisan League, which gained control of the state government in 1916. Dominated by A. C. Townley, a former member of the Socialist Party, the NPL pushed through a number of radical measures, including creation of a state-owned bank and a state-owned grain elevator and flour-milling complex. These institutions were imaginative responses to the state's problems, but their unintended effect was to push North Dakota further outside of the mainstream of a country devoted to private property.

Further peripheralizing the state was its isolation in foreign policy. Living in the middle of the North American continent, far from any potential enemy, North Dakotans had difficulty grasping how European or Asian developments might threaten them. More important, the ethnic composition of the state militated against actions directed against Germany. Germans-from-Russia and Reich Germans are two of the three largest ethnic groups in the state, and their emotional ties to their homeland were strong. Norwegians, the other large ethnic group, were not committed to Germany, but their attitudes toward European conflicts reflected the neutrality of Norway and the antimilitarism of their ancestors, many of whom came to America to escape conscription. Thus North Dakotans found themselves out of step with a country that went to war with Germany twice in less than a quarter of a century.

The political culture of an isolated, outsider state provided opportunities for certain types of politicians to thrive. North Dakotans admired those who stood strongly for the state's idiosyncratic points of view, whether they were effective legislators or not. Attacks on big business, bankers, Wall Street, even on the New Deal for doing too little for agriculture all played well in North Dakota. Congressmen who stood up to the majority were admired, almost regardless of their stands. Bill Langer's defense of Joe McCarthy and Usher Burdick's championship of former communists—though seemingly very different—were both admired, often by the same people. Constituents favored isolationism in foreign policy especially when it could be connected, as Gerald Nye connected it, with criticism of big business.

Mavericks such as Langer and Lemke thrived in this political environment, where routine legislative duties, while not irrelevant, were distinctly secondary to defending constituents against hostile government actions, tilting with the interests, and playing a flamboyant role for the audience at home.

While the political culture of North Dakota changed slowly and incompletely, the national policy environment changed significantly, and in ways that affected the state dramatically. Before 1933 federal programs had a minimal impact on North Dakota, but the New Deal marked the beginning of a high level of governmental activism. Federal farm programs, targeted at basic commodities such as wheat, made North Dakota farmers dependent on the government for a substantial portion of their incomes. Governmental expenditures on infrastructure development funneled millions of dollars into the state. Federal relief programs—on which half of the citizens of the state depended for at least partial support during that desperate year of 1936—helped people survive the depression and the drought.

Although North Dakotans were slow to realize it, federal programs were changing their lives. The mildly redistributionist character of most federal expenditures narrowed the income gap separating North Dakota from most of the rest of the country. And the farm programs, which diminished risk by placing a floor under prices, gave North Dakotans something to conserve when it became apparent during World War II that the programs would probably become permanent.

The first major North Dakota political figure to grasp the implications of these developments for the state was Milton Young, who served in the Senate from the fall of 1945 until his retirement in 1981.

Young was very different from Langer, his senior colleague. While Langer was flamboyant and aggressive, Young was colorless and reticent (a trait that may have been encouraged by a speech impediment). Langer's forte was debate; Young functioned most effectively in committee. Langer was a maverick with roots in agrarian radicalism, while Young was a thoroughly conventional and conservative midwestern Republican.

Young's conservative ideology did not blind him to the practical realities of operating in the new world of federal activism. He used his seat on the Senate Agriculture Committee to protect and enhance programs pertaining to North Dakota's premier crop, earning the affectionate sobriquet "Mr. Wheat." He assiduously pursued funds for infrastructure development and recognized the opportunities that the cold war presented North Dakota. Young's efforts were crucial in securing major air force bases at Grand Forks in 1956 and Minot in 1957.

North Dakotans' eagerness to secure military bases symbolized one important way in which they moved closer to the national mainstream: after 1945, they were no longer isolationist in foreign policy. In a world of high-speed aircraft and intercontinental ballistic missiles, foreign threats to security no longer seemed so distant or abstract. But the main reason North Dakotans changed their minds was that the enemy changed. North Dakotans were much more comfortable and even enthusiastic about their nation's hostility toward the Soviet Union than they were when Germany was the enemy.

Another way in which North Dakota became more conventional after World War II was by developing a genuine two-party system. For most of the forty years after the rise of the NPL in 1915, North Dakota had been a state with one major party, the Republicans, including two major factions—Leaguers and conservatives. The major election in most years was thus the Republican primary. A handful of Democrats sat in the legislature, where they were viewed as curiosities, and the rare Democrat who won a statewide race usually did so only because he received support from one disgruntled Republican faction or the other.

The NPL had operated in the Republican party because most North Dakotans considered themselves Republicans in 1915 and because in the early twentieth century the GOP could justifiably claim to be the party of progressive governmental activism. As the Democratic party increasingly assumed the mantle of progressivism, however, and as the national Republican party became more staunchly conservative, that position seemed increasingly anomalous.

During World War II, liberal Leaguers began to press for a shift of the NPL from the Republicans to the more ideologically compatible Democrats. At the same time, the conservative Republican Organizing Committee, led by Milton Young, began working for the permanent exclusion of the NPL from the party.

This process was not unique to North Dakota. Progressives in Wisconsin and Farmer-Laborites in Minnesota were also moving into the Democratic orbit, but the transition was somewhat slower in the Peace Garden state. In 1956, the NPL decided to file its candidates under the Democratic party column, and in 1960, at a raucous and sometimes violent NPL convention in Bismarck, members voted to merge formally with the Democrats.

The merger of the Democratic party and the NPL quickly bore fruit. In 1958, Usher Burdick's son, Quentin, general counsel of the North Dakota Farmers Union, became the first Democrat ever elected to the U.S. House of Representatives. In 1960, he won a special election to fill the Senate seat vacated by Bill Langer's death, launching a career in the upper chamber that lasted until Burdick's own death in 1992. In 1960, North Dakota also selected a Democratic governor, William Guy.

Once they began voting Democratic, North Dakotans discovered they liked it. In 1980, they filled the state's sole U.S. House seat with Democrat Byron Dorgan, formerly state tax commissioner; and in 1986, they replaced one-term Republican Sen. Mark Andrews with Kent Conrad, Dorgan's understudy at the tax commission. When Dorgan moved up to the Senate in 1992, the voters filled the House seat with Democrat Earl Pomeroy, who had been insurance commissioner.

Although it is still called the Democratic–Nonpartisan League (D-NPL) party, the party demonstrates fewer and fewer vestiges of the agrarian radicalism with which the NPL was associated. Most North

Dakota Democrats are centrists—fiscally moderate or conservative and mildly progressive on social issues. Like the national Democratic party, the D-NPL has worked to energize minority voters. American Indians are an important part of their constituency; Richard LaFromboise, Louise Defender Wilson, and other Indians hold positions of leadership in the party. They have also been receptive to women, some of whom have achieved important policymaking roles. Following Ruth Meiers's election as the lieutenant governor in 1984, Tax Commissioner Heidi Heitkamp was elected to the important post of attorney general in 1992; and Sarah Vogel became agriculture commissioner in 1988, securing reelection four years later.

All of this might suggest that North Dakota has become a Democratic state, but that is not really the case. North Dakota has gone Republican in every presidential election since 1964. Part of the reason for this loyalty is undoubtedly cultural. Despite any allegiance to the state Democratic party, many socially conservative North Dakotans reject the national Democratic party's representation of African Americans, Hispanic Americans, feminists, homosexuals, organized workers, and other nonmajority groups. These voters are more inclined toward the national Republican party.

Cultural factors do not explain the continuing strength of the Republican party at the local level, however. Throughout the era of genuine two-party competition, the Republicans have dominated the state legislature, usually controlling both houses. Three of the state's four largest cities have Democratic mayors, but Republicans have generally dominated local government, holding the lion's share of county and town offices.

What the Democrats have most remarkably enjoyed has been dominance of the congressional delegation. Hard work and attractive candidates have played a part, but the Democrats' main strength lies in the fact that North Dakotans perceive them as the "conservative" party: they are more likely than the Republicans to "conserve" the redistributive federal programs on which North Dakotans have come to depend over the last half century.

Quentin Burdick's career serves as a case study in Democratic conservatism. On issues of national importance Burdick was a liberal, usually taking the opposite stand from that of Milton Young, his colleague for twenty years. He was a champion of the War on Poverty, a staunch supporter of the welfare system, and a consistent friend of labor and civil rights. He was, in short, a typical liberal Democrat. But, like Young, he recognized that his role was analogous to that of the ambassador of a client state to a wealthy patron. North Dakotans would judge him not by the stands he took on national issues but by his ability to bring home the bacon.

Like Young, Burdick kept a low profile on the Senate floor, concentrating on committee work. He paid careful attention to the agriculture program, to public works, and to whatever else might benefit his state. He was so successful in directing resources to North Dakota that the *Denver Post* announced his death with the headline "King of Pork Dies."

The efforts of Young and Burdick and most of the other congressmen who worked in the activist environment of postwar Washington are clearly reflected in North Dakota's position today. Every year North Dakota gets two to four dollars from the federal government for every one it sends in. The state is consistently among the leaders in federal expenditures per capita. In most years more than 20 percent of farm income is provided by the federal government. In 1988, federal disaster aid for drought-stricken farmers totaled over $400 million, and this in a state with only 650,000 people. During the 1980s state government general fund revenues coming from the federal government exceeded 20 percent. In 1985 the 15,000 military personnel in the state brought more than $250 million in wages into local economies.

North Dakotans view themselves as independent people, and they worry about the budget deficit. They are sometimes embarrassed by particularly flagrant examples of pork-barrel benefits to their state, as when Quentin Burdick attempted to secure federal funds for restoration of bandleader Lawrence Welk's childhood home as part of a Germans-from-Russia interpretive center. Moreover, federal programs can be a mixed blessing. Money often comes with onerous strings attached, and programs may exacerbate some state problems while relieving others. The Conservation Reserve Program, for example, put money in farmers' pockets; but by taking as much as 25 percent of the land in some counties out of production, it sped the demise of many rural communities.

On balance, though, North Dakota is better off that it was when grandstanders like Langer and Lemke railed against the government and its wicked ways. Their successors understood that the role of the federal government had changed, and they made the practical adjustments necessary to help North Dakota benefit in the new environment. In the process, they moved the state closer to the national mainstream. Being an outsider carries psychic rewards, but insiders get most of the material benefits.

The shifts in behavior of North Dakota voters and their representatives in Congress have made the state more a part of the nation, but in some ways it is still apart from the nation. The old outsider political culture, nurtured by isolation, hardship, and ethnicity, has not completely passed away. Many of the conditions that fostered North Dakota's outsider identity are still present. The state remains relatively isolated, and the economy is still colonial. Despite continuing economic development efforts, North Dakota still lives by producing wheat, beef, coal, oil, and other commodities for export, while it imports manufactured goods.

The outsider political culture continues to be reflected in the tendency of North Dakotans to suspect others. The state's national politicians are careful to portray themselves as defenders of North Dakota against the machinations of larger and more sophisticated states and against conniving politicians and corrupt institutions. In his 1992 campaign, for example, incumbent Sen. Kent Conrad stressed his success in preventing Sen. Robert Dole from diverting North Dakota drought aid to Kansas.

Blaming others for the state's problems is a reflection of the vitality of the outsider culture. Japan is a favorite whipping boy, of course, as is Canada for supposedly taking unfair advantage of free trade to the detriment of North Dakota farmers. Sometimes contemporary North Dakota politicians remind one of old-style leaders like Langer, as does Byron Dorgan when he excoriates the "junk bond kings" of Wall Street for destroying the U.S. economy.

On the local level, the survival of the traditional political culture of North Dakota is much clearer. North Dakota is part of the Populist and Progressive tradition of an accessible, responsive, and malleable government. It is also part of the commonwealth political tradition, with its stress on the civic responsibilities of voters and its high expectations for elected officials.

Some of the most remarkable and attractive aspects of North Dakota politics derive from these enduring traditions. North Dakotans have not dropped out of the political process. Voter turnout is very heavy (65 percent or better in presidential election years)—in part because of same-day voter registration but mainly because most North Dakotans have a strong sense of civic identity and civic duty.

North Dakotans are close to their public officials. The state leads the nation in elected officials per capita, meaning that, for many, legislators and county commissioners are literally friends and neighbors. The people of the state want their elected officials to be accessible. During the legislative session, which occurs once every two years for a maximum of eighty days, most representatives and senators go home every weekend to explain to their constituents what is transpiring in Bismarck. North Dakota's governor is the only one in the nation who has no bodyguard, and the only one whose home phone number is listed in the local directory. This can cause some inconvenience for the governor—as when a drunken Floridian called Governor Guy in the wee hours of the morning to settle a bar bet regarding the existence of North Dakota—but the people of the state would have it no other way.

Congressmen must be accessible, too. They must come home regularly to conduct town meetings and listen to local problems, and their service to constituents must be prompt and efficient. One of the keys to Langer's political success was his almost legendary attentiveness to constituent needs, and his effective successors have marked his example well. In larger states people are concerned when their representatives in Congress are anonymous, but North Dakota's leaders get in trouble at home when they are perceived as attending too closely to national issues. Gerald Nye's defeat in 1944 was due less to his isolationism than to North Dakotans' perception that America First had commanded too much of his attention. Mark Andrews became a leader among moderate Republican senators and achieved important reforms in defense procurement, but he was defeated in 1986 in part because North Dakotans thought such activities distracted him from his primary purpose of ministering closely to their needs.

North Dakotans' frequent use of the initiative and referendum, encouraged by permissive petitioning requirements, also reflects their insistence on an accessible and responsive government, as well as their western skepticism regarding the performance of elected officials. The initiative has been used in recent years to restructure the tax system, legalize charitable gambling, and place term limits on congressmen and state legislators. The referral process has been used on numerous laws, and has resulted in the outlawing of parking meters in the state, cancellation of a series of tax increases, and disapproval (followed six years later by approval) of legislation permitting retail stores to open on Sundays.

The initiative and referendum process has fostered a colorful group of leaders with personal followings. Robert McCarney in the 1960s and 1970s, and Kent French and Russell Odegard in the 1980s and 1990s, have sometimes sparked legislative action by threatening to initiate and impeded it by threatening to refer. Legislators express frustration with the initiative and referendum process, but recognize that North Dakotans, with their attentiveness to civic affairs and their demand for governmental responsiveness, would not likely favor a constitutional restriction on these devices.

As they pertain to the federal government and national politics, then, North Dakota politics and politicians have become more conventional, closer to the national mainstream, more a part of the nation. That change has been facilitated by an altered international scene, by the development of a genuine two-party system, and the emergence of political personalities unscarred by the titanic political battles of the first four decades of the twentieth century. And it has been necessitated by the rise of an activist federal government in the 1930s and the changing relationship between that government and the states.

Yet at the same time, especially on the state level, the flavor of the old political culture endures. And so it will endure, as long as North Dakotans retain their peculiar ideas about the nature and function of government, as long as they insist on accessible and responsive public officials, and as long as they perceive themselves as relatively isolated from the rest of the nation. A part of the nation, North Dakota in subtle ways remains apart from it.

CHAPTER 13

"The More Things Change . . .": Oklahoma Since 1945

DANNEY GOBLE

A major theme in western state history is that politics in the entire region has undergone profound change in recent decades. Historians might dispute the exact date of change's conception and the length of its gestation, but nearly all affirm the primacy of change itself. So popular has been that thesis that it has become the organizing theme in textbooks of regional history. For example, Michael P. Malone and Richard W. Etulain, who date the change to the Second World War's end, draw upon an impressive variety of monographs to proclaim that "the postwar decades brought with them . . . sweeping changes in the western political order . . . [as] the old patterns of the postfrontier era crumbled."[1]

Nearly anyone familiar with the broad contours of politics in Oklahoma would agree with the application of that judgment to the Sooner State. Change has been a major theme in the state's postwar politics, and many of its dimensions do represent the generally unmourned passing of the rowdy disorder so prevalent in earlier decades. "Old-time rustics"—the phrase is Malone and Etulain's[2]—like "Alfalfa Bill" Murray no longer strut and storm across Oklahoma's political stage. Voters are less likely to confuse public policy with political drama. Not many Sooners still traipse to the polls determined to stamp the Democratic rooster. Public officials have had to become far more familiar with accounting procedures and bureaucratic rules and far less accustomed to lining their own pockets with public funds.

Under modern circumstances, Oklahomans are sorely embarrassed to have a member of the legislature refer to "chinks" and "slopes" during formal debate and another justify his habit of carrying a loaded pistol on the floor with the excuse that militant lesbians have threatened his life. They similarly regard as a momentary curiosity the news that their fellow citizens of one judicial district have overwhelmingly elected a dead man.

Such items still occasionally make their way into wire service reports, but they are regarded as singular oddities, not as compelling evidence that (as *Time* magazine once put it) there is always an "aroma in Oklahoma" when it comes to politics.[3]

At a more substantive and structural level, the single greatest change in the postwar patterns of Sooner politics is also the most visible. After decades of one-party rule, Oklahoma has emerged as a two-party state. It is a change typical to many western states, particularly states of the southwest, and it came to Oklahoma in a manner familiar to regional historians. In a "trickle down" fashion, early GOP success at the presidential level eventually opened the path to improved Republican fortunes for in-state contests.

In 1952, Dwight Eisenhower began the process when he easily captured Oklahoma's electoral college votes, becoming the first Republican to do so since Herbert Hoover bested Al Smith in 1928.[4] At the time, no one thought that Eisenhower's victory was any more of an omen than Hoover's had been. After all, the 1928 result had turned on the losing candidate's religion just as the 1952 outcome had drawn upon the winning candidate's war record, both personal rather than partisan circumstances. Eisenhower carried Oklahoma a second time in 1956. That victory again received not a partisan or even bipartisan explanation but a nonpartisan one. Similarly, scholarly interpretations tended to coincide with Democratic excuses when Richard Nixon put Oklahoma in the Republican column a third consecutive time in 1960. Students and practioners alike emphasized the impossible religious cross that John Kennedy had shouldered as a Catholic nominee.

For those reasons, many regarded Lyndon Johnson's restoration of Oklahoma to the Democratic column in 1964 a return to normal voting habits if not to normalcy. Few noted, however, that Johnson's 56 percent of the Oklahoma vote was 6 points below his national share and a pale reflection of the big totals that previously had gone to the state's Democratic winners, even those who had run in far less favorable circumstances against far more credible opponents. Perhaps that is why so many were quick to discount Richard Nixon's victories in 1968 and 1972, even though the second smashed the record that Franklin Roosevelt had set in 1936. But Gerald Ford in 1976? Ronald Reagan in 1980 and 1984? George Bush in both 1988 and 1992—particularly in the latter, when he comfortably beat the governor of a neighboring state who enjoyed the nearly unanimous support of every prominent state officeholder?

At some undefined point, all of the separate explanations had become excuses. Surely, not luck, not circumstance, not personality, not even all these combined could account for the complete record. In eleven consecutive presidential contests, the Republicans had raced away with Oklahoma's electoral votes ten times. Not even the traditional Republican bastions of Kansas, Maine, or Vermont have been kinder to the GOP than Oklahoma has been since 1952.[5]

That record had powerful explanations with consequences that in time spilled over to other contests. One was that many voters who had voted for Ike or Nixon doubtless regarded themselves loyal Democrats, just not Democrats of the "yellow-dog" breed. Nonetheless, the facts were that they had broken with ingrained tradition, they had turned their backs on the party of their fathers, and the country had not gone to hell. Neither had the hands that marked Republican ballots withered at their sides. Once done, it became steadily easier to use those hands to vote for other Republicans, including Republicans seeking other offices. In time, it became possible even to admit to themselves that they were Republicans in behavior, perhaps even in name. Thus, as political scientists noted, the percentage of eligible voters who registered on the Republican side (though always a minority) steadily increased, and Republican primary turnout persistently rose toward the numbers voting in Democratic primaries.[6]

A second explanation was that Eisenhower's nomination, Kennedy's Catholicism, and much else in that long string of apparently isolated circumstances was due to a profound change in national politics, particularly at the presidential level. The basic pattern was that the national Republican party—particularly its "presidential wing"—was moving steadily toward the center of the political spectrum (even Ronald Reagan was far more conservative in rhetoric than in deed) while the national Democratic party was lurching leftward. The latter was particularly true after two generation-shaping events of the 1960s. The civil rights movement spawned an ever-larger assault upon traditional ways in the name of minority rights, and the war in Vietnam stamped the national Democratic party as the party of flabby international idealism and emaciated national defense. In those circumstances, the Democratic party could nominate candidates like George McGovern, and Oklahomans could vote Republican, even when the immediate alternatives were apparently less clear-cut.

Such were the circumstances that made it possible to build a viable Republican alternative within the state. And Henry Bellmon did just that.

A Noble County farmer of limited political experience (Bellmon had served a single term before losing his legislative seat in the 1948 Republican primary to an eighty-year-old retired dentist), Bellmon accepted the thankless job of Republican state party chairman in 1960. Though the party was in the process of winning its third consecutive presidential contest in Oklahoma, signs of its organizational impotence were everywhere. Moving into party headquarters, a bare three-room suite staffed by a single secretary, Bellmon discovered that real power in the party rested with a self-appointed "finance committee," a handful of reactionary anti–New Dealers who kept a hammerlock on party purse strings and a death grip on party purposes. At the grassroots level, the party did not have even a county chairman in several of the state's seventy-seven counties. The average age of its nearly three hundred state committee members was almost seventy, and a good number of them had not been seen in years.[7]

From that beginning, Bellmon effected a revolution in party affairs. Breaking the hold of the old guard, Bellmon took control of party finances while also increasing them by hiring a public relations firm to draw in small contributions from thousands of previously ignored voters. Those who thereby gained a stake in Republican fortunes also won a voice in party councils. New chairmen emerged in every county, including some that had had none in living memory. Fifteen new regional task forces coordinated their efforts. Two hundred new state committee members dropped overnight the committee's average age by more than thirty years. A well-publicized re-registration effort immediately increased the party's registered voters by 20 percent. The party began to recruit and train potential candidates and scheduled a series of seminars that emphasized the need to master complicated state issues rather than rely on knee-jerk conservative dogma. While rebuilding the state party, Bellmon also defied the national leadership by insisting that Nixon's 1960 campaign be turned over to it, not to another Democratic-dominated "independent" organization like those that had had charge of the Eisenhower campaigns within the state.

All of that was in place by 1962, when Henry Bellmon became the first Republican to be elected governor of Oklahoma. True, he had some luck. William P. Atkinson, his Democratic opponent, had won his own nomination by being the last man standing after an unusually bloody Democratic primary. But no mistake should be made about it. This was not an election that Democrats lost nor even one that Henry Bellmon won. This was a party victory. Indebted to much, including to the earlier presidential wins, Henry Bellmon's election in 1962 marked a fundamental change in Sooner politics precisely because it resulted from a fundamental change within one element of the state's political structure. The Republican party of Oklahoma finally had shed the legacy of the Great Depression both in the minds of the voters and in its own internal structure.

A series of campaigns over the next three decades proved the permanence of that change. Because Oklahoma's governors were then ineligible for self-succession, the Republicans had a spirited primary race in 1966 for a nomination that had suddenly become worth having. Nearly 100,000 Sooners—more than half again the number that had voted in any previous Republican primary—nominated Dewey Bartlett. An independent-minded state senator from Tulsa, Bartlett's most notable legislative contribution had been his authorship of several bills striking down the worst remnants of Oklahoma's segregation statutes. Bartlett easily won the general election by an even larger margin than Bellmon's. After a constitutional amendment allowed gubernatorial self-succession, Bartlett came within a hair's breadth of becoming the first Oklahoma governor to serve two terms. Instead, he lost to David Hall in 1970 by barely 2,000 votes out of more than 712,000 cast. Nearly every observer credited Bartlett's defeat to overconfidence. No previous Republican had even been exposed to the disease. In time, an Oklahoma Republican did serve two gubernatorial terms. Henry Bellmon, after twelve years in the U.S. Senate, reclaimed the governor's office in 1986. At that point, Sooner Republicans had managed to win three of the eight races since 1962.

The party's record in U.S. Senate contests was even more impressive. After serving his first gubernatorial term, Bellmon waited two years before challenging A. S. Mike Monroney, a respected Washington veteran with twenty years of congressional service. It was not even close. Bellmon won by more than 50,000 votes. Neither was it close in 1972 when Bartlett joined Bellmon in the Senate by beating Ed Edmondson, another twenty-year Democratic veteran as the Second District's representative. Bellmon won a second term in 1974, as Bartlett likely would have had not cancer forced his retirement in 1978. As it was, Republicans did not have long to wait. In 1980, Don Nickles, a young state senator from Ponca City with exactly two years experience in office, was elected to the U.S. Senate by a margin of nearly 100,000 votes. Nickles's two subsequent victories were considerably less surprising but no less impressive. What was particularly impressive was that the party that had managed to win only three Senate races over the first sixty-one years of Oklahoma's statehood[8] had won six of nine in the succeeding twenty-four years.

The resurrection of party competition in Oklahoma is one of those changes that is both visible and measurable. What is far less apparent and nearly impossible to quantify may be more important. The context of political competition has itself changed. For most of the state's history, Oklahoma's political history has been the story of clashing conflicts rooted in primitive but powerful divisions. Campaigns, issues, policies— all too often these reflected the crudest divisions of economic exploitation, racial bigotry, and religious fanaticism. Unruly legislators ceased brawling with each other only long enough to make common cause against governors, whom they assaulted with interminable investigations that continued even after they had removed two successive governors. Governors fought back while opening a second front against other elected officials in the executive branch, the tussles more often involving personal pique than substantive principle. The state of Oklahoma relished picking fights with other states as well as with federal authority, at times backing its words with military pretensions. Running through all of that was the stain of administrative mismanagement and plain old corruption, their only redeeming virtue being that they often were unalloyed with hypocrisy.

Sooner politics of recent decades has been far less explosive, if far less colorful. One is tempted to say that the state has matured, a metaphor that often enters social science jargon as "modernization."[9] Either term captures the spirit of the changes involved. Because effective management of a modern state requires skills more administrative than thespian, political evolution has rendered vestigial aspiring politicians' gifts for drama. Expensive media-dominated campaigns targeted at a metropolitan electorate require calculated blandness rather than the rabble-rousing techniques of old. Policymaking demands the cautious assembly of coalitions rather than the mobilization of the discontented. Federal spending has become far too important to both the state's economy and its budget to be jeopardized with fruitless confrontations over ideology or prerogative.

In some respects, the specific changes can be seen and explained, even measured. One is the professionalization of the executive branch. Distrustful of power in the governor's office (or anywhere else, for that matter), the authors of the 1907 constitution declared that the governor would exercise "the Supreme Executive power." Then, they sapped that power by grafting onto the executive branch a briar patch of elected secondary officials. Moreover, subsequent constitutional amendments and statutes further diluted the executive's power by creating what amounted to a fourth branch of government: an array of agencies, boards, and commissions, each clothed with executive authority but few subject to the governor's immediate power. As late as 1966, Oklahomans still were electing twenty-one executive officers, including the clerk of the state supreme court and the chief mine inspector—and the four assistant mine inspectors as well. The number of quasi-independent administrative boards increased with virtually every legislative session, not slowing even as they passed two hundred.[10]

Over the next few years, Oklahomans finally shortened their ballot, meeting a common goal of several generations of unheeded reformers. In striking measure, they did so in response to a single statesman: Wilbur Wright. An unintended reformer (who was no kin to the pioneering aviator), this Wilbur Wright was a retired watch repairman whose name had appeared on Democratic ballots since 1938.[11] Previous electorates had ignored it, generally in favor of yet more famous names. Enough weary and confused voters noticed it in 1970 to give him a job: state labor commissioner. In midterm, Wright hastily resigned the office to avoid a criminal investigation over his filing of obviously fraudulent travel claims. His name then even better known, he returned at the first opportunity, and Oklahomans easily reelected him to his old job in 1974. Again, the prospect of criminal charges drove Wilbur Wright from office—and drove Sooner voters to their senses. In 1975, they voted overwhelmingly to amend the constitution to make the office appointive, applying the same principle to three other positions and consolidating two others. Whatever the motive, it was a few steps toward a modernized executive branch. More came later. By 1990 only nine executive offices remained on the Oklahoma ballot.[12]

Still heading the list was the office of governor, its powers generally strengthened over the recent years. Now able to appoint many secondary officials, the governor also was eligible (after 1966) to serve a second consecutive term. After much wrangling with the legislature and agency heads, a modified cabinet system in 1987 began to establish some gubernatorial control and coordination over the array of administrative agencies. If still a long way from the White House model, Oklahoma's governor's office compared well with that of most other states as a powerful and professionalized institution.[13]

Legislative changes nicely mirrored the evolution in the executive branch. Again, the most significant change came not from reformers and—most assuredly—not from the legislators themselves. It came from federal judges who had grown weary and frustrated with the state's refusal to acknowledge the twentieth century. Although the 1907 constitution had mandated legislative reapportionment following each decennial census, district lines had changed only once—after 1910's census, and then slightly. Subsequent censuses over the next half-century resulted in no changes at all. They did, of course, record a massive relocation of population within the state. Since 1907, Tulsa, for example, had grown from a small trading village to the self-proclaimed "Oil Capital of the World." Though Houston might contest that honor (not to mention the challenge from Dhahran), tiny Fairfax, Gore, or Tishomingo could not. Yet through the mid-1960s Tulsa controlled one seat in the forty-four-member state senate, the same number that served Fairfax, Gore, or Tishomingo.[14] Little wonder, then, that only one state (Tennessee) had a more malapportioned state legislature than did Oklahoma when the federal courts finally stepped in. After years of legislative posturing, foot-dragging, and subterfuge, federal judges in 1964 ordered both legislative houses be immediately apportioned on a strict "one-person, one-vote" basis. The judges themselves drew the new district lines.[15]

The court-ordered reapportionment brought a permanent change to the legislative body. One consequence was soon visible. After the 1970 census, the legislature turned to political scientists with the University of Oklahoma's Bureau of Government Research. Equipped with maps, census data, and computers, the professors made their recommendations and the politicians accepted them with a minimum of fuss and almost no changes. That the legislature's dogs did not even bark was the surest sign of change. Other changes came swiftly. After 1966, legislators met in annual sessions. No longer part-time employees, they were no longer paid part-time salaries. A 1968 amendment removed the constitutional salary cap ($15 per day for up to seventy-five legislative days) and opened the path to professional salaries. Their work environment became more professional as well. Post-reapportionment chambers streamlined their committee systems and created joint committees with oversight respon-sibilities during the months between formal assemblies. A legislative council reappeared and hired a full-time staff of professional experts charged with research and the drafting of bills.[16]

Reform of the state judiciary and local governments completed the process of maturation. These, too, came less from a commitment to good government than to the shocking discovery of how very bad Oklahoma's government was.

In the judiciary's case, the discovery was a scandal involving one retired member of the state supreme court and two sitting justices. After a series of spectacular criminal trials in 1965, all three were convicted of bribery charges involving systematic corruption that had stretched over years and had influenced an indeterminable number of cases. The scandal led to imprisonment for the judges and their accomplices and to the first substantial reform of the Oklahoma judiciary since statehood. The state bar, legal educators, and aroused citizens seized the opportunity to modernize the state's method of judicial selection. Gone was the old practice of popular election on partisan tickets. In its place was a complex mechanism designed to free the judicial process from the worst abuses of partisan elections, including the collection of campaign funds that had provided the pretense for the recent crimes. Thereafter, the governor made appellate appointments from a list of candidates nominated by a bipartisan commission. Voters entered the equation only with periodic later elections on whether to retain each judge—the choice universally taken.[17]

Reform of Oklahoma's local government, particularly as practiced by the state's 231 elected county commissioners, was slower coming. That it came at all was easy enough to understand. Though each county's 3 elected commissioners were supposed to act as a single board administering public policy, the reality was that local government in the state always had resembled a feudal order with 231 separate, independent, and virtually sovereign principalities.[18] Elected from separate geographical districts, each commissioner was pretty much free to proceed at will within district boundaries. Colleagues willingly granted each commissioner's independence as the price necessary to maintain their own. Because the commissioners generally were responsible for paying the salaries of other county officials, the latter were even less likely to challenge their sovereignty. Neither did the legislature show much interest in supervising the commissioners' affairs. Particularly in the state's rural counties—the same counties that controlled the legislature through the long decades of malapportionment—county commissioners were forces taken seriously. It was they who had the most direct and immediate contact with voters. A friendly county commissioner could turn out a big vote on election day. So could an unfriendly one. It, therefore, behooved those who wrote state laws to keep the commissioners as friendly as possible.

The coin that purchased and sealed these mutual understandings usually was state tax money, most notably that share of state highway revenues allotted to maintain county roads. Though the commissioners had broad authority, most residents thought of them as road builders. Collectively, they spent millions of dollars annually to maintain more than eighty thousand miles of county roads and hundreds of rural bridges. Nearly all of that money came from state appropriations. All of it ended up in the pockets of suppliers, contractors—and commissioners. Nearly every citizen at all informed about local government knew that commissioners routinely received a 10 percent kickback on every piece of lumber, foot of pipe, and gallon of road oil bought. Citizens talked openly about the flat-fee kickbacks that commissioners took on leases of heavy road-building and maintenance equipment. On dozens of Main streets, there was talk about the local commissioners taking fifty-fifty splits with suppliers who billed the county for nonexistent or undelivered materials.

Many people talked, and many complained. The latter usually were "good government" types and a few metropolitan editors, people with little standing and even less influence in rural Oklahoma. The complainers included neither suppliers nor contractors nor commissioners nor those dependent on them: local sheriffs, county attorneys, and powerful state legislators. Even governors who dared make the practices public and demand reform learned to regret their indiscretion.[19]

As was so often the case in Oklahoma, change came from outside the system. The particular outsiders were agents of the Federal Bureau of Investigation, the Internal Revenue Service, and the U.S. Department of Justice. Beginning in the spring of 1981, newspaper headlines began to record indictment after indictment, trial after trial, and conviction after conviction. By 1984, the feds had convicted more than 200 people, including 110 incumbent commissioners and 55 former ones. Sixty of the state's seventy-seven counties saw at least part of their local officialdom leave the courthouse for the Big House.

Under the circumstances, the only surprising thing was that the reforms that inevitably followed were so minor, aimed almost exclusively at the immediate problem of purchasing procedures. In finally imposing the barest of restraints on its county commissioners, Oklahoma had left untouched what many took to be the heart of the problem: an archaic structure of local government mixed with a public tolerance of political corruption. Standing red-faced before one of the largest and most odious political scandals of the twentieth century, the state sent a few miscreants to jail, usually to the federal corrections facility at El Reno, Oklahoma. There, they would be accessible to their friends, families, and former constituents. Structural reform, obviously overdue, turned out to be minimal.[20] It was a nice commentary on the extent of political change in Oklahoma.

Perhaps for that reason, we should reexamine some of the other "sweeping changes in the western political order." In Oklahoma, where the wind does come sweeping down the plains, it undeniably has left changes in its wake. But Oklahoma's wind also stirs up a great deal of dust, and that can have the effect of obscuring how many things have not changed at all.

Take, for example, the rise of a modern two-party system in Oklahoma. It is true that the recent Republican domination of Oklahoma's presidential and senatorial voting is unprecedented in state history. And it is also true that the three Republican gubernatorial victories since 1962 are the only three in the state's history. But what about other contests? And what effect has partisan competition had in shaping public policy?

The first question is easily answered. Almost everywhere *except* at the very top of the ticket, Oklahoma remains very much a Democratic state. Once voters get past the glamour races, they still generally go straight down the Democratic ticket. Except for its top-of-the-ticket successes, the Republican party has won only 5 statewide races in the past thirty years. That is not a very impressive total—not when the state has elected 102 secondary statewide officers over that time span and when 37 Democrats won their state offices without the bother of facing a Republican opponent. Since World War II, Oklahoma's delegation in the U.S. House of Representatives usually has included a single Republican member—just as it has for all of the state's history except for the Great Depression's worst years. In legislative races, the party's share of seats has actually averaged less than it had been before a steady diet of "Hoover stew" nearly starved the GOP out of the statehouse. In fact, the last three decades of alleged Republican power in Oklahoma compare rather poorly to the first three decades of this century, when Republicans may not have done as well in the prestige races but did much better in other respects. When Republicans won in those years, they won up and down the ticket. They also exercised real power, twice controlling the state's congressional delegation and twice controlling the state house of representatives. Neither has even been conceivable in the more recent past.

And what has been the effect on public policy? That is harder to measure. But start with the fact that the GOP has held on average only about a quarter of the seats in the lower house and a fifth in the upper chamber. Most of those seats represent districts with little partisan competition—just as most of the Democratic seats do. Under those circumstances, there has been little incentive (and little encouragement) for Republican lawmakers to enter bipartisan coalitions to advance a positive program. The consequence has been that the Republican role in policymaking has been almost exclusively negative. The joke is that Republican lawmakers even answer the roll call by saying "No." They have occasionally been able to attract enough Democratic nay-sayers to block change, but they have almost never been capable of promoting change.

The best example came in the second Bellmon administration. Elected as the state's economy was reeling from the collapse of oil prices, Bellmon entered office with the prospect of a $350 million budget shortfall. With funding already slashed, particularly in higher education, the governor proposed a series of modest tax increases as a levy to block the fiscal flood. After acrimonious debate—debate that made the old "postfrontier" style of political discourse seem tame indeed—the legislature granted most of the increases but did so over strong and vocal Republican opposition. Bellmon next called a special legislative session and presented it with an education reform bill. One Republican agreed to introduce the governor's bill, but every one of the others prepared to vote with Democrats to adjourn *sine die*. The governor avoided that embarrassment only when Democratic Speaker Steve Lewis stepped forward with his own school reform bill, which Bellmon hastened to endorse. With no other item on the agenda, the special session spent nearly a year before barely passing the package. On the critical vote in the state senate, Henry Bellmon got exactly one vote from the party that he had built.[21] One wonders what good it had done him and what difference it had made to the state.

Other changes of political structure similarly have had few obvious consequences for public policy. Changes in the legislature's mechanisms, for example, have been far more notable than any changes in its products. Not even reapportionment has had visible consequences at all consistent with the expectations of its supporters and the fears of its opponents.[22] In fact, it would be difficult to demonstrate that any of the changes in Oklahoma's political practices have had much positive impact on state policy. By most measures, the state's position relative to the other forty-nine states has barely changed since 1960. Discernible movement often has not been favorable. In 1960, for example, Oklahoma ranked thirty-eighth in total educational spending per pupil, and the state paid the nation's twenty-eighth highest average teacher salary. In 1991, after just over three decades of political change, total educational spending had slid to forty-third, driving average teacher salaries down to forty-eighth. A cynic might note that Oklahoma is now among the national pacesetters only in such dubious categories as its incarceration rate (fifth in 1991) and legislative salaries (ninth in 1991), hoping that the two achievements are not causally related.[23]

That changes in the structure of state politics have been unaccompanied by any obvious changes in state policies ought not be surprising. Political scientists have long understood that differences in states' policies only dimly reflect differences in their political practices. Party competition may be more or less intense, state governors more or less powerful. State legislatures may be more or less malapportioned, their procedures more or less professional. What is decisive, it turns out, is none of these.[24] When budgets are written, when priorities are ranked, when conflicts are resolved, something altogether different comes into play. Sometimes, the difference that makes the difference lies in things much more difficult to locate and measure. Sometimes, the difference lies amid things that are remarkably impervious to changes at all.

In Oklahoma's case, the most obvious of these is the state's constitution. Written in the winter of 1906–1907, few documents more fully captured the spirit of their age.[25] It was an age of reform, and nearly every version of it made its way into the charter. The result was a fifty-thousand-word document that was widely praised in its day as an instrument of advanced democracy.[26] That day has long since passed. What has not passed is the cumbersome government structure that the constitution has bequeathed to the state. Because its authors feared the accumulation of power, they dispersed it into so many constitutional nooks and crannies that it would be impossible for anyone to govern too poorly. Alas, however, it has meant that neither can anyone govern very well. Because they feared that their pet notions might be rejected by later legislatures or courts, they also packed the constitution with details more statutory than fundamental.[27] That has meant that the inevitable recasting of those principles has required subsequent constitutional amendments—amendments that only have made the document yet more cumbersome and that themselves have usually required further amendments.[28]

Such observations are hardly new. From time to time, outsiders and
Oklahomans have examined the state's constitution, both generally reach-
ing the same conclusion. In the middle of the Great Depression, Gov. E.
W. Marland commissioned the prestigious Brookings Institution to study
Oklahoma's government and the constitution on which it rested. The
detailed report—all 483 pages of it—affirmed a central observation:

> The difficulty in Oklahoma is that frontier democracy coincides with a modern
> industrial system. . . . Oklahoma is advanced materially but retarded socially.
> It is [economically] developed but governmentally immature. Its basic need is to
> catch up with itself. . . . The Constitution, therefore, must be viewed as one of
> Oklahoma's fundamental problems; and, in some directions, no substantial
> progress can be made until constitutional obstacles have been removed.[29]

Since those words were written, nearly every subsequent study has cited
that comment and elaborated on it. The result is an impressive collection
of constitutional studies.[30] The studies continue, but so does the constitution.

For all the criticism, the constitution continues because Oklahomans
have agreed that it should. The original document declared that the people
should vote "at least once in every twenty years" on the calling of a new
constitutional convention. Like many of its other provisions, however, this
was not self-executing. It requires that the legislature submit a referendum on the subject. Only three times—in 1926, 1950, and 1970—has the
legislature bothered to do so, and each time voters decidedly rejected the
proposal.

That is not to say, however, that Sooners have been unwilling to tinker
with the work of their forefathers. On the contrary: through 1989 Oklahomans had voted 274 times on amending their constitution—133 amendments winning approval, 55 of them since the 1970 vote rejecting a new
convention. Moreover, the pace of change was growing swifter. In 1990,
Oklahomans added eight more constitutional amendments. Two of those
affected Article 10 ("Revenue and Taxation"), bringing to well past forty
the steadily lengthening chain of amendments to amendments to amendments. The result for that one article was measurable. In its much-
amended form it had come to nearly twenty closely printed pages, just
about one-fifth of the constitution's substantive length. Unchanged has
been the basic problem: an enormously cumbersome and archaic structure
of government that makes any real political change unlikely if not
impossible.

However obvious has been Oklahomans' attachment to their inherited constitution, that is not the most remarkable element of the state's political persistence. For all the differences that are apparent between the state's politics before and after the Second World War, there are also continuities that scarcely have been interrupted by global war or by any of the other supposedly transforming events of the recent past. The most powerful of those date to the close of the nineteenth century, when Oklahoma was not yet a state but two distinctly different territories.

Roughly the western half of the modern state was settled under the federal Homestead Act. Beginning in the famous land runs of 1889 and thereafter, whites (and some African Americans) took claims to quarter sections and town lots. Particularly in the territory's northern section, those first settlers tended to come from Kansas or other midwestern states.[31] They brought with them the cultural traditions of their native region. Their favored churches were Methodist, Presbyterian, or Camp-bellite. Their politics was Republican. Most were land-owning farmers whose prosperity depended on their investments in land, machinery, and people. This was the history shared by thirty-seven of the state's present seventy-seven counties, the thirty-seven that old maps designate as comprised by Oklahoma Territory.

The forty counties of eastern and south-central Oklahoma share a different history. Once designated Indian Territory, these had been the domain of the so-called Five Civilized Tribes—the Cherokee, Choctaw, Chickasaw, Creek, and Seminole nations. At the turn of the century, federal authorities abolished those governments and forced severalty land allotments among tribal citizens. Most soon lost their land. Those who took it were called (even by themselves) "grafters."[32] They and those who came to work the land that the grafters accumulated tended to come from the old Confederacy, with all that implied. Most were Baptists. Nearly all (nearly all of the whites, anyway) were Democrats. The great bulk worked land that they did not own, raising cotton, the region's chief crop until well into the 1930s. In that portion of Oklahoma, the economy was bound by a chain of exploitation rather than with investment, including investment in people.

Those two territories combined to become the present state in 1907, and their separate histories presumably became of only historical curiosity. In fact, however, the contemporary state continues to reflect those original differences. Even now, the area settled by midwestern entrepreneurs remains markedly different from that exploited by grafters and farmed by tenants.[33] Despite a near balance of natural resources, the two remain economically distinct. For one thing, western Oklahoma is far more prosperous. Of Oklahoma's fifteen counties of highest per capita income, thirteen lie in the old Oklahoma Territory. Only the former Indian Territory's Tulsa and Washington counties make the list, both because they provide the headquarters of major oil companies. The remainder of the old Indian Territory has never escaped its past. For all of its natural beauty, the former Indian Territory now gives Oklahoma twenty-five of its thirty-two counties of lowest per capita income, including every one of the poorest seventeen.

The two territories also remain culturally distinct. Visitors are struck by eastern Oklahoma's resemblance to the states of the American south, contrasted with the more western flavor of Oklahoma Territory. That particular difference is not amenable to precise measurement, but others are. The former Oklahoma Territory, in which the original settlers early on placed a premium on education, continues to provide twenty-one of the thirty counties that rank highest in state school testing programs. The old Indian Territory provides twenty-three of the thirty-two lowest-scoring counties.

If anything, the political consequences of those original patterns are even stronger. Partisan lines have proven to be particularly persistent since many Sooners continue to vote just as their great-grandparents did. For all but the worst years of the Great Depression, the state's northwestern quadrant has been faithfully Republican, and its southeastern section has been unfailingly Democratic. The balance of power always has lain with the counties that straddle a diagonal that runs from the state's northeastern corner to its center before turning due west to reach the Texas Panhandle. Originally, these were the decisive counties because these were where the flows of immigrating population were most balanced. Subsequently, these have been the counties most subject to metropolitan growth, including a recent arrival of considerable numbers of out-of-state newcomers. Thus, nearly every election in the state's history has seen each party draw on the same dependable sources and battle over the same contested territory, that battle determining who wins and who loses. The only difference that recent decades have made is that the battles there have (sometimes) had slightly different outcomes.

The most powerful political fact in Oklahoma is also the most persistent; and it, too, is rooted in a geographical expression of the state's peculiar history. Not until 1990 did Oklahoma elect its first governor

(David Walters) from its western half.[34] Before that, every chief executive had come from the east, all but three of them from the old Indian Territory.[35] In the legislature, leadership in both chambers has been all but monopolized by representatives from the old Indian Territory. That was true before World War II as well as after it, and it was true before reapportionment and after, too. From the very beginning, the state's strongest representation in Washington also has normally come from the Indian Territory side. World War II did nothing to change that, as is evidenced by the immediate postwar prominence of Sen. Robert S. Kerr (born in Ada) and present status of Sen. David Boren (of Seminole). Of course the Oklahoman who rose to higher federal office than any other was Carl Albert, Speaker of the House and most distinguished son of Bugtussle in the old Choctaw Nation.

So strong and so persistent has been the political supremacy of the old Indian Territory that one is tempted to conclude that there must be something peculiar in the water of eastern Oklahoma. The difference owes less to drinking water than to political culture. Like its economic and cultural distinctions, modern Oklahoma's political differences also have roots in different territorial experiences. Those who settled the Indian Territory brought with them more than certain economic, cultural, and partisan preferences. More than in its west, Oklahoma's east was settled by those schooled in what Daniel Elazar has labeled a "traditional" political culture.[36] A variant of the predominant political culture of the southern states, eastern Oklahoma's reigning political culture has always shared qualities associated with the south: Democratic local dominance, low voter turnout, highly personalized politics, tolerance of corruption, distrust of centralized authority, and friends-and-neighbors campaigning. Not least of its qualities has been that political power tends to accumulate in a few families or a few professionals who make politics their entire career.

Western Oklahoma's political culture is closer to Elazar's description of an "individualistic" political culture. Originating in the Midwest and later flourishing in many of the western states, that political style tends to be both more partisan and more ideological. Voter turnout tends to be high, since politics is assumed to be of value to all. Its chief purpose, however, is to maintain an unfettered marketplace, and government's role is primarily economic: the encouragement of private initiative and wide-spread access to the marketplace. Beyond that, government really has very little to do. Those who seek power often do it reluctantly. Proud of their amateur status, they temporarily pursue causes before returning to "the real world," chiefly independent business.

When products of those two cultures contest for power, the advantage lies with the professionals. Winning is their only real cause, and in Oklahoma they do that better than anybody else. Once they have power, they know what to do with it. That, however, is no guarantee that they will govern well.

One thing is certain. The state that they govern is a state riddled with contrasts and similarities. It is a state that knows both change and continuity. It is, in other words, a state shaped by its own history, free to change but never free to escape its past. What state is not? After all, what else is history?

CHAPTER 14

The Battle to Control Land Use: Oregon's Unique Law of 1973

E. KIMBARK MACCOLL

"There is a shameless threat to our environment," declared Gov. Tom McCall to the opening session of the Oregon state legislature in January 1973. Oregon's status as "the environmental model for the nation" was menaced, he warned, by "unfettered despoiling of the land, sagebrush subdivisions, coastal 'condomania,' and the ravenous rampage of suburbia in the Willamette Valley" —the most productive farmland in Oregon.[1]

With this and subsequent messages to the legislature, McCall set the stage for one of the most unusual legislative battles in the state's 114-year history. Its outcome gave the state responsibility for enforcing environmental goals that were set locally. Local planning had to conform to state policies.

Oregon's first effort at what today is called land-use planning had resulted in the passage of legislation in 1911 to protect the state's beaches for public use and enjoyment. Under prodding from Gov. Oswald West, a Democrat, the state asserted public ownership of all beach areas up to the mean high-water mark. The Beach Bill of 1967, sponsored by Governor McCall and State Treasurer Robert Straub, further defined the rights of public access and prohibited future development that might damage the coastline. Four years later, the legislature passed the Oregon Coastal Conservation and Development Commission Act, which established an official oversight agency for an area of "critical concern." For the first time, "the state acknowledged the responsibility it shares with coastal cities and counties to protect coastal resources through comprehensive planning and management."[2]

Protecting the coast was only one of several concerns that prompted many Oregonians to take action in the 1960s. As early as 1961, the state legislature had attempted to protect prime agricultural lands by "authorizing lower tax assessments for land in exclusive farm use zones." Like programs in forty-one other states that encouraged farmers not to sell to speculators and developers, Oregon's law had proved to be ineffective in slowing "leapfrog subdivisions around growing cities of the Willamette Valley."[3]

Another subject of deep concern to Oregonians was water resources, especially the Willamette River. Following the enactment of the Oregon Clean Water Act of 1965, Congress passed the Federal Water Resources Planning Act in July of the same year. Almost two years later, Pres. Lyndon Johnson ordered the establishment of the Pacific Northwest River Basins Commission, the first such commission in the nation. Stimulated by federal action and supported by Governor McCall, the legislature passed the Willamette River Park Systems Act in the spring of 1967. This act led to the establishment in 1973 of the Willamette Greenway system, and was dedicated to preserving the river's natural state from Portland to Eugene (a hundred miles to the south) by keeping nearby homes and farm buildings out of sight from the river. The state also received authorization to purchase large areas adjoining the river for public recreation.[4]

Concern for protecting and enhancing Oregon's water quality led to the creation of the Department of Environmental Quality (DEQ) in 1969. Charged with additional responsibilities for air quality and for managing the proper disposal of solid and hazardous wastes, the DEQ functioned under the authority of the Environmental Quality Commission, the DEQ's policy and rule-making board of citizens appointed by Governor McCall.

Much of the incentive for these actions, apart from a growing national awareness, was Oregon's expanding population, which had grown from 1.5 million in 1950 to 2.1 million in 1970. The nation's tenth-largest state in land area, in 1970 Oregon's population was two-thirds urban, with nearly half living in the Portland metropolitan area. Approximately 10,000 acres of Willamette Valley farmland were being converted to urban use each year, out of only 2 million agricultural acres in the entire valley. Related to this development was the likelihood of greatly increased pollution.[5]

A similar loss of farmland was occurring all over the state. In collaboration with Oregon State University's Department of Agriculture, county extension agents were working with county planning commissions to encourage them to zone their land for exclusive farm use. The secretary of state, Clay Myers, spoke repeatedly on the issue. To the Farm and Land Brokers section of the Oregon Association of Realtors he put the question, "What do we want the Willamette Valley to be like in the decades ahead?"

He called for tighter zoning, effective planning, and "regional agencies" to administer a program to save the best agricultural lands. Similar concerns began to percolate through the legislature, where an Interim Committee on Agriculture decided to examine the "long range impact of urbanization on agricultural lands." The leading legislators were farmers.[6]

SENATE BILL 10: A FIRST EFFORT

The time seemed propitious for official corrective action. In 1969, Governor McCall told the legislature, "An urban explosion for environmental pollution is threatening the livability of Oregon in such a manner that effective land-use planning and zoning have become of statewide, not merely local, concern." A legislative act, Senate Bill (SB) 10, required (rather than allowed) cities and counties to develop comprehensive plans and zone all land within their borders by 31 December 1971. If satisfactory progress were not made by that date, the governor was authorized to assume personal responsibility. The bill set general goals (the legislature rejected more specific ones), and no standards were set for evaluating the comprehensive plans. Furthermore, no staff or money was provided for the job.[7]

Despite its limitations, SB 10 broke new ground nationally. Oregon became the first state to require *all* local governments to zone their land and to develop comprehensive plans. Neither Hawaii's land-use law of 1961 nor Vermont's environmental-control law of 1967 was comprehensive: both focused largely on selected critical areas. California was the first state to require local governments to adopt comprehensive land-use plans, but only its coastal areas were included. Although some of Oregon's 240 cities and 36 counties did not fully comply with SB 10, its implications spread fear among many landowners who believed their property rights were in jeopardy. An initiative petition, placed on the May 1970 ballot, sought to overturn the law by restricting planning authorities' powers and limiting the government's ability to interfere in the use of rural lands. Its defeat, by 55 to 45 percent, brought sighs of relief to the planners. Running for reelection that spring, the governor had actively campaigned against the repeal measure, saying on more than one occasion, "Repeal SB 10 and you might as well throw me out, too. I refuse to preside over the deterioration of Oregon's quality environment."[8]

A journalist by profession, McCall had grown up in central Oregon, surrounded by the state's natural beauty. Ranch life nurtured his strong spirit of independence (not uncommon among Oregon's politicians), which, blended with his sense of humor, was to produce some of the most colorful rhetoric in the Pacific Northwest's political history. He inherited several personal traits from two illustrious grandfathers: Samuel McCall, two-term governor of Massachusetts, and Thomas Lawson, a Boston copper speculator and author (after whom the Oregon governor was named). A lifelong Republican in the family tradition, he rose to the leadership of the more progressive ranks within the GOP, becoming an outspoken critic of a fellow governor, Ronald Reagan of California. McCall was elected governor of Oregon in November 1966 after serving two years as secretary of state.

With the defeat of the measure to repeal SB 10, coupled with his reelection, McCall felt that he had been given a mandate to continue the land-use reforms begun three years earlier. He realized that massive public involvement and an educational program were essential. He had two years in which to prepare, because, as matters stood, with conservative Republicans controlling the state senate and house, "no corrective legislation was going to make it through the '71 session."[9]

His major cohorts in the land-use-planning fight were Hector Macpherson and Joseph T. ("Ted") Hallock, state senators; Robert Logan, director of local government relations for the Executive Department; L. B. Day, a former director of the Oregon Department of Environmental Quality; and Clay Myers, secretary of state.

It was the weaknesses in SB 10's implementation that had motivated Macpherson to run for the state senate in 1970. A Republican representing the Albany region of the mid-Willamette Valley, the mild-mannered legislator, described by one commentator as "a raw-boned, somewhat cerebral dairy farmer," had become a self-taught expert on land-use planning. In 1963 he formed the Linn County Planning Commission, of which he became the first chairman in 1965.[10]

His senatorial colleague Ted Hallock presented a marked contrast to Macpherson, both in personality and political partisanship. A ten-year Portland legislator, a highly decorated World War II bombardier (the subject of a *New Yorker* magazine profile), a national award-winning radio broadcaster, and a public relations expert, the liberal Democrat was described by friend and foe alike as "intense, brilliant, stubborn, acerbic and single-minded." He was likened by one associate to "a cigarette which has been smoked so fast and hard that the paper is intact, but it is burned out on the inside."[11]

The main insider working closely with Macpherson was Robert K. Logan, a former city manager whom Governor McCall had recruited as a staff planner. Logan, a quiet, somewhat self-effacing bureaucrat, helped Macpherson lay out the basic strategy for the campaign and later played a crucial role in developing public support for the governor's program. "Tom McCall was a risk taker," Logan has remarked; one of the risks the governor took was to push for a land-use plan for the Willamette Valley, with its more than eight hundred units of government. McCall never became too involved in the details. He had absolute faith in his staff and gave its members complete support.[12]

L. B. Day, a graduate of Willamette University in Salem, had become a senior official of the mid-Willamette Valley Teamsters Union, closely tied to the canning industry. He had served three terms in the Oregon House, having switched from the Democratic to the Republican party in 1967. A multifaceted legislator whose "colorful and aggressive style quickly separated his admirers from his opponents," he was known for his booming voice and direct questions, and for never tolerating governmental abuses. "Controversy is what makes government so damned good," he once pronounced, and no bill would be more controversial in 1973 than Oregon's land-use law. Two years earlier, McCall had appointed Day the first director of the Oregon Department of Environmental Quality.[13]

The fifth member of the command was Secretary of State Myers, whom McCall had appointed to office in January 1967. Myers, a fifth-generation Oregonian, had long been a vocal advocate of land-use planning. As a leader of the Republican party's progressive wing who was by nature an independent, he had become a close confidant of McCall and had been instrumental in persuading him to run for governor in 1966.[14]

With the aid of Logan and Myers, McCall appointed the Willamette Valley Environmental Protection and Development Planning Council, a citizens' group headed by Myers, who said the group's aim was to "stimulate public awareness of the problems and decisions involved in planning the growth and development of the Willamette Valley for the next three decades."[15]

"The project," as it became known, consisted of two phases: a study by Lawrence Halprin & Associates, landscape architectural consultants in San Francisco, that would indicate alternative patterns of growth for the valley by the year 2002; and a plan to get the public involved by means of a booklet and a slide show on Halprin's scenarios. Logan prepared the booklet (entitled *The Willamette Valley: Choices for the Future*), developed the strategies for its use, and assisted Myers as project manager.[16]

1971: A MILESTONE YEAR

Although no action on land-use reform per se emerged from the 1971 legislative session, several important environmental bills did win passage with strong support from the governor. Known as the "B" bills, they included the nation's first bottle bill, requiring deposits on soft-drink and beer cans and bottles, and a ban on pull-tabs; the bicycle bill, which set aside a mandatory percentage of highway revenues for bicycle paths; a bill providing bonds for pollution abatement; a new beach bill, extending public authority from the mean high-water mark to the line of vegetation; and a billboard-removal law, for the replacement of billboards with standard logos along federal and state highways. The legislature also enacted the Oregon Coastal Conservation and Development Commission Act, as already mentioned, and established the Department of Environmental Quality.[17]

In retrospect, 1971 was a milestone year in Oregon's environmental reform program, and a triumph for Governor McCall in the first year of his second and final term. It was also the year in which a book on land-use control had a significant impact throughout the country. *The Quiet Revolution in Land Use Control*, by Fred Bosselman and David Callies, "heavily influenced" Senator Macpherson, to whom it was introduced in 1972 by the new staff attorney for the Oregon Student Public Interest Research Group, Henry Richmond, a graduate of the law school at the University of California, Berkeley. Richmond, asked to participate in Macpherson's preparations for the 1973 legislative session, became greatly involved in promoting SB 100; in the process, he developed a lasting friendship with McCall. He and the governor later established 1000 Friends of Oregon, a citizens' watchdog group that follows the implementation of SB 100.[18]

Early in 1972, Macpherson decided to form his own committee to develop legislation for the 1973 session. In the 1971 legislative session, his bill to make land use a major study never got past the Ways and Means Committee for its funding, as neither Speaker of the House Robert Smith (an eastern Oregon Republican) nor Senate President John Burns (a conservative Democrat from Portland) considered it a priority. Burns had been elected president by a coalition of conservative Democrats and

Republicans. Macpherson had warned him, "I don't give a damn what you do, I'm going to go ahead!" Fortunately, the governor provided critical staff support and funding.

Macpherson enlisted the help of Logan, at the Executive Department. Logan was delighted, since he was as determined as Macpherson to get the job done.[19] They then decided to set up two committees: one, the Land Use Policy Committee, to be chaired by Macpherson and to work on broad-based legislation; the other to concentrate on strengthening the exclusive farm-use zoning and on modernizing the subdivision laws.

Macpherson's committee, to which Richmond had offered his services, was itself broad based. It included "a city councilman, two mayors, three county commissioners, environmentalists, two developers, a realtor, a county agent, three county planning commission members, a college professor who was an expert in land-use planning, a representative of the Associated Oregon Industries, and representatives of the Home Builders and the Oregon Planners Association." Senator Hallock was too busy to become involved, but "promised to support any legislation developed." Macpherson's creation of an unofficial interim committee to take testimony and draft proposed legislation angered Senate President Burns, who, feeling that Macpherson had gone over his head, carried a grudge into the 1973 session.[20]

Macpherson and his action committee used the Model Development Code from *The Quiet Revolution* in preparing their legislative package. The book also influenced Myers and Logan in their report for the Willamette Valley Environmental Protection and Development Planning Council, which McCall was to make public at the end of September 1972. The book's authors expounded a broader view of land values than the traditional one that "land's only function is to enable its owner to make money. . . . It is essential," they wrote, "that land be treated as both a resource and a commodity. . . . This concept . . . underlies our whole philosophy of land use regulation." In essence, they called for a new "land ethic," whereby land values would reflect society's willingness to promote individual land ownership.[21]

PREPARING FOR BATTLE: SUMMER AND FALL 1972

In July 1972, in a major speech to the Oregon Newspaper Publishers Association, Clay Myers addressed what he termed the "greatest threat to our way of life." Citing a swelling stream of immigrants crossing [Oregon's] borders," he warned that "some of our best recreation land [is] being snapped up by out-of-state developers."[22]

Governor McCall dwelt on the same theme as he prepared for a "legislative assault" on "grasping wastrels." By executive order, he had already established fourteen regional councils of government, whose formation met federal grant requirements for transportation planning, river clean-up, and sewage treatment. He had also requested that the Department of Revenue make a cursory check of land sales east of the Cascade Mountains. He discovered that some 160,000 acres of arid rangeland, desert, and plains had already been subdivided into 43,000 parcels. "These kinds of subdivisions . . . made up the bulk of an estimated 1,000 illegal land promotion schemes, which were unrecorded and unregulated," according to one commentator.[23]

On 29 September 1972, the governor and his secretary of state released a letter to all Oregonians. McCall described the "long and tedious" two-year effort as he unveiled Project Foresight. He discussed the major points of the Halprin study, which presented two choices for each of the following subjects: land use; transportation; open space and recreation; employment and income; pollution, energy, and power; and governmental interrelationships. The first choice was to "do nothing"; the second, to take action to control growth.[24]

Both Myers and McCall wanted to focus the public awareness and concern created by Project Foresight on the 1973 legislative session. They hoped the session would produce a "package of laws and resolutions" that would expedite the decisions necessary to " 'save' the Willamette Valley—and ultimately every area of the state" and expected Halprin's scenarios to raise the environmental consciousness of those whom the program reached. As Macpherson noted, "In late 1972, land-use planning was a hot issue." To Logan, preparing the Oregon land-use package was a legislative tour de force unprecedented in the state. "We took an issue with no previous legislative or public support and in just two years it became a bandwagon," he recalls. "I had so many fronts going I felt like an Israeli general."[25]

For three days, beginning on 20 November 1972, more than six hundred people attended the Governor's Fifth Conservation Congress, organized by Logan in Portland with speakers from all over the country. Representatives from forty-five business, civic, conservation, and governmental organizations were there. McCall did not specifically mention the forthcoming legislative session in his welcome address, but he focused on the issues that would face the legislature as he tried to forge a consensus of disparate interests. On 9 December, over five hundred people went to an environmental legislative workshop at Lewis and Clark College in Portland. As reported in a new monthly newsletter named *Feedback*, response to the workshop was extremely enthusiastic.[26]

Feedback itself became a crucial weapon in Logan's arsenal, another of his self-described "wild" activities. According to Logan, in 1972 the U.S. Department of Housing and Urban Development (HUD) gave Oregon $300,000 more than the state had expected to receive as a federal planning grant, a windfall that was not reported to the legislature. Logan was on good terms with HUD officials, who were angered by Washington State's failure to establish regional councils of government, as Oregon had. The $300,000 was actually part of Washington's designated planning funds, and Logan's office immediately put the sum to work, financing conferences and publications, including the *Willamette Valley: Choices for the Future* pamphlet, and *Feedback*, which summarized statewide land-use activities and was distributed free of charge.[27]

To establish the newsletter, Logan created a nonprofit corporation in Salem, chaired by Carl Halvorsen, a prominent Portland businessman. Most of the public believed that *Feedback* had been founded by a group of Willamette Valley citizens. No one asked about funding for it, although Governor McCall knew the source of the money. Logan supported a staffed office near the Capitol on $30,000 a year for two years. Macpherson was delighted by his activities, but "wondered what Logan would be doing next."[28]

Few people outside of Logan's office other than Governor McCall knew that the original Halprin study, the pamphlet, and the subsequent slide show (McCall's Project Foresight) had been financed by Logan's office. The Halprin study had never been completed. Logan and his staff rewrote and published it in Salem and then summarized it in pamphlet form.[29]

Over a period of more than seven months, Project Foresight reached approximately twenty thousand valley residents. At each slide show, interested viewers could have their names added to the mailing list for *Feedback*. The list exceeded seven thousand names. According to Logan, Project Foresight succeeded in ways its creators had not anticipated, creating "widespread valley support for statewide land use planning legislation in 1973."[30]

THE BATTLE BEGINS: JANUARY 1973

The 1973 session of the Oregon legislature, opened by Governor McCall's blockbuster speech, found the Democrats in control of both houses for the first time in ten years. On the surface, there appeared to be bipartisan support in both houses for strengthening state oversight of local land-use planning. But many objections began to be heard, not only from legislators but from interest groups throughout the state. Hostility was vehemently expressed by rural Clackamas and Washington County landowners outside of the Portland metropolitan region, by local officials statewide who felt their authority was being threatened, and by coastal residents who feared a loss of property values by proposals to restrict development.

Two candidates emerged as the leading contenders for senate president: Sen. Ted Hallock of Portland, and Sen. Jason Boe of Reedsport, one of the coastal areas of concern. Neither Boe nor Hallock liked each other, although Hallock had done public relations work for the Oregon Optometric Association, of which Boe was a member. When Hallock conceded his support to Boe, the new senate president felt obligated to toss him a bone in the form of appointment as chairman of the Senate Environmental and Land Use Committee. Boe purposely loaded the seven-member committee with three other Democrats unsympathetic to Macpherson's legislative package: former Senate President John Burns; Mike Thorne, from a wealthy eastern Oregon wheat-growing family; and Jack Ripper, from the southern Oregon coast, an area that feared state intrusion. Besides Macpherson, the Republican members were Victor Atiyeh, of suburban Washington County, and George Wingard, a builder from Eugene, who was close to Macpherson and could be expected to support him. The lineup was crucial because Oregon's legislature had always had a strong committee system, which worked over the bills before they were submitted to legislative vote. The bills were usually altered, "sometimes beyond recognition," according to Macpherson. They could also die in committee and never reach the floor.[31]

Although numerous bills related to land use were introduced, SB 100 was the critical measure. Carrying Hallock's and Macpherson's names as cosponsors, fifteen hundred copies of the bill were printed. All were gone in two days. Hallock found himself in the cross fire, a position he seemed to enjoy. The veteran six-term legislator, with his urbane and persuasive talents, ran the hearings on a rigorous schedule with supreme efficiency.

Every conceivable interest was represented. The liveliest attacks came not from the lobbyists, however, but from the committee's own members. Hallock was fed up with critics who demanded "local control," which he felt was a "phony issue" designed to worry the Democrats.[32] This was ironic, as the whole thrust of SB 100 came from the bottom up, from local involvement in the creation and implementation of goals to the state's role in enforcing compliance. Although 90 percent of all decisions were to be made at the local level, it was the state's ultimate authority that aroused the most fears.

A key provision of the bill called for the establishment of a new state agency, the Department of Land Conservation and Development, which would be responsible to the Land Conservation and Development Commission (LCDC), consisting of seven appointed members. These seven commissioners (one from each of the then four congressional districts and three from the state at large) would be charged with generating and enforcing land-use planning goals after holding statewide meetings of citizens and governmental officials. Two provisions of the bill drew the loudest complaints: the authority granted to the fourteen appointed regional councils of government, which would be the local planning agencies; and the listing of specific "areas of critical state concern," such as recreational sites or estuaries, which would be subject to state regulation.

To keep the legislature involved, the bill also provided for a permanent Joint Legislative Committee on Land Use, an oversight committee consisting of four house and three senate members, including the chairs of the House and Senate environment and land use committees of the Fifty-seventh Legislative Assembly. The elected chairman, Ted Hallock, has recalled that the inclusion of sections 23 and 24 in SB 100 was "really a fluke." It was the first time in his memory that the legislature had ever created a permanent interim committee. (Hallock ran it until he retired from the state senate nine years later.) It rarely met; most of its business was conducted between Hallock and the chair of the LCDC.[33]

By mid-February, SB 100 was in deep trouble. "It had almost crumbled," remembered Don Barney, the Portland lobbyist. The governor had become so pessimistic and frustrated that he said to Hallock, "Give me $500,000 for SB 100 and I'll sign the son-of-a-bitch." If the legislature appropriated the money for the Department of Environmental Quality (DEQ), McCall planned to work through the department by executive order to carry out the original bill's intent through state zoning, using whatever powers he could muster.[34]

Ironically, the bill's near defeat at that point, the *Oregon Times* reported, occurred "just as other established citizen groups were joining the Oregon Environmental Council in support of the bill." Among those groups, the influential Oregon League of Women Voters became active advocates. At a work session on 18 February, "an interesting thing happened," according to the *Times.* Lobbyists from Weyerhaeuser, Associated Oregon Industries, Oregon Home Builders, Oregon Wheat Growers, and Associated Oregon Counties commented on the bill for the first time. Hallock knew that some drastic action was needed.[35]

Devising an unusual strategy, he converted the lobbyists into an ad hoc committee for the purpose of proposing an acceptable draft that *would* pass. He appointed L. B. Day as chairman, knowing that he would run a tight operation and produce as strong a bill as could get passed. At the first meeting, Day locked the door and "raged until hoarse," glaring at the members and telling them that in the interest of Oregon, they "couldn't stand in the way of this bill."[36]

"Inside of ten days, L. B. had pulled off a near miracle," wrote Charles Little, an observer from the Conservation Foundation of Washington, D.C., who spent six weeks in Oregon following the bill's stormy course. Counties were to replace "councils of government" (COGs) as the review bodies, although counties would be permitted to form their own voluntary councils. While specific "areas of critical concern" were deleted, the LCDC, in developing goals and guidelines, could propose such areas to the legislature as they logically emerged from the process. "Activities of state concern," such as the siting of public facilities, remained under the LCDC's oversight. Citizen participation in drawing up comprehensive plans and drafting zoning ordinances became mandatory. Finally, the governor's authority to assume ultimate planning responsibility was replaced by that of the LCDC, which would become the enforcer.[37]

Many of the bill's staunchest supporters were dismayed by the new SB 100, but Hallock defended the changes. "There was no way we could pass the bill with COGs included," he recalled. Too many people mistrusted the levels of government that McCall had established five months earlier to meet federal grant requirements. Hallock knew that regional government had to be divorced from land-use planning, at least at that stage. At the urging of Portland Mayor Neil Goldschmidt and City Commissioner Lloyd Anderson, he amended the bill to allow Portland, instead of Multnomah County, to retain its review authority within its jurisdiction. In a rare appearance before a legislative committee, the governor urged the senators to accept the revised bill. "In most respects," he said, "it is more satisfactory than the original bill."[38]

VICTORY: SENATE BILL 100 APPROVED

McCall's endorsement was strengthened by the support of the Oregon Environmental Council, representing some eighty conservation groups statewide. Even the powerful utility companies came on board. According to the *Oregon Times*, they "had been bought off by a committee amendment removing power plant siting from the list of 'activities of statewide significance.' " Senator Atiyeh, the conservative Republican representing Washington County on Hallock's committee, "was mollified" by an amendment reducing LCDC "approval" of an activity of statewide significance to "review and comment." Atiyeh's other amendment, restricting citizen standing in the appeals section, was also approved.[39]

On 6 April 1973 the bill passed out of Hallock's committee by a vote of six to one, John Burns casting the only nay vote. On the senate floor, twelve days later, it passed eighteen to ten. Most of the no votes came from the eastern, southern, and coastal regions of the state. There was still one more hurdle—the house side of the legislature. Hallock implored Nancie Fadeley, the representative from Eugene and chair of the House Environmental and Land Use Committee (Hallock's counterpart), not to tamper with the bill—"not to change one comma." Changes by her committee or on the house floor could have doomed the entire bill. "I decided I wouldn't risk it," she told Betty Merten, reporter for the *Oregon Times*, even though Fadeley would have preferred a stronger bill, akin to the original one. Unchanged, SB 100 passed the house forty to twenty, with Macpherson sitting on the house floor by invitation of the house leadership, which wanted him present to answer any questions. This was one more of the unusual actions accompanying the bill's transit through the legislature.[40]

On 29 May 1973, Governor McCall happily signed the pioneering measure, comprising fourteen pages and fifty-eight sections. As Hallock quipped toward the end of the session, "Macpherson was the father of land use in Oregon, L. B. Day was the godfather, and I was the obstetrician." While the bill was not what he had hoped for initially, he was proud of it. But some of his fellow legislators remained confused over just what they had achieved. As the Salem *Oregon Statesman* editorialized, "Members . . . are having trouble explaining to one another exactly what [SB

100] would accomplish." Calling it a "patchwork of political compromises," the *Statesman* said that "its language is so unclear as to leave serious doubts about its real authority." Macpherson and Hallock had purposely kept the bill general, with no specific goals or areas of concern, to prevent it from failing. As Hallock told Merten, "The choice was to have this bill or nothing."[41]

According to McCall's biographer, Brent Walth, the governor worried about SB 100's lasting strength. He fretted about the LCDC and the fact that the bill "was tremendously hedged." He also worried about leaving land use to another governor after his second term ended in January 1975.[42]

THE NEXT CHALLENGE: THE GOALS

Six months elapsed before Governor McCall appointed the members of the LCDC. By mid-August he had received seventy-six nominations for forty candidates. Delaying the process was the circulation of over four thousand referral petitions to repeal SB 100 through a special election early in January 1974. Before passage of the bill, Hallock had unsuccessfully attempted to preserve an emergency clause in the bill that kept opponents from immediately challenging the measure. McCall had been worried about this eventuality, but the referral's backers failed to collect the required 26,656 signatures. It was the first of many similar failed attempts in subsequent years.[43]

The first chairman of the LCDC was L. B. Day, "the saviour of SB 100," in Macpherson's opinion. As director of the Department of Environmental Quality, he had headed the agency everyone loved to hate. The DEQ was about to be replaced by the LCDC "as a favorite whipping boy." Day was to chair most of the goal-setting statewide meetings. Macpherson has aptly described him: "A big man, hawk-nosed, sonorous, testy with bureaucrats and politicians but kindly to inexpert citizens, he loomed over the meetings, popping Malox and seemingly kept alive by a row of filled coffee cups."[44]

The other members of the commission were Portland lawyer Stephen Schell, a land-use expert and ardent conservationist who had worked with Bob Logan; Dorothy Anderson, a lobbyist for the Oregon League of Women Voters; Albert Bullier, Jr., past president of the Oregon Association of Realtors; Richard Gervais, a businessman and former mayor of Bend, in central Oregon; Paul Rudy, the head of the University of Oregon's Marine Biology Center; and James Smart, a prominent Willamette Valley farmer with county planning experience. McCall chose his former director of state planning, Arnold Cogan, an engineer and urban planner by profession, to be director of the new Department of Land Conservation and Development. He took office in February 1974, concurrent with the first meetings of the LCDC.[45]

Cogan quickly realized that he had assumed a herculean task. The LCDC had eleven months in which to identify and adopt goals "dealing with the state's major land use concerns and conflicts." Cogan and the LCDC were to design and conduct three rounds of statewide community meetings during 1974, with additional rounds to follow in 1975, all devised to provide "a maximum opportunity for citizens of the state to become involved in preparing the goals and guidelines."[46]

As Cogan has recalled, "We were a beleaguered agency with a small staff, inadequate budget, no place to call home, and little help and support" other than that offered by the governor and by Logan in the Executive Department. Following the passage of SB 100, the House Ways and Means Subcommittee refused to appropriate any funds for implementation of it. Toward the end of the session, however, the legislature did pass an alternative funding bill, but it provided only $100,000—barely enough to keep the agency operating. At a special session in February 1974, additional, but still inadequate, funds from state and federal sources were appropriated. Day wanted to raid a portion of the federal money in Logan's budget, an action that Logan adamantly resisted with McCall's backing, even though Day had previously assured Cogan that the governor favored the transfer. Cogan quickly discovered that Day liked to "play games and create problems for which he already had solutions."[47]

Cogan and his staff had hardly moved into their small office before it was time to hold the first citizen-involvement workshops. In April and May of 1974, they held twenty-eight community workshops for more than three thousand citizens "to express their viewpoints on the state goals." With two rented vans and cars containing members of the commission, they scheduled daily meetings from dawn to dusk in different cities—an exhausting pace for all but Day, who seemed to thrive on the experience.[48]

After completion of the first draft of the goals, another seventeen public hearings were held. By the deadline of 13 December 1974, the commission had held seventy-six public hearings. Over ten thousand Oregonians were involved one way or another—through meetings, direct mailers, and television programs. McCall alone taped more than forty separate public-service announcements tailored to each part of the state.[49]

On 1 January 1975, the Land Conservation and Development Commission adopted fourteen goals and guidelines, giving local governments one year in which to comply—a period that proved entirely unrealistic. The costs were so overwhelming that the 1975 legislature appropriated $5.9 million, of which $4.4 million was distributed to local governments to help pay the costs of implementing the goals. It took many more millions of dollars and numerous deadline extensions before Oregon's thirty-six counties and 241 cities were finally brought into compliance with state goals in mid-1986.[50]

Of the goals advanced by the LCDC, the most important and controversial dealt with agricultural lands, forest lands, and urbanization. Taken together, these three goals mandated that cities and counties cooperate in drawing urban growth boundaries to engird land already urbanized as well as any necessary for expected growth until the year 2000. Agricultural lands beyond the urban growth boundaries were to be zoned for exclusive farm use. The less specific forestland goal required the preservation of timberlands in a similar way. Defining the productive levels of land used for agriculture and timber production became critical issues for the LCDC in subsequent years. The last five goals, approved by the LCDC in December 1976, pertained to critical areas purposely left out of SB 100: the Willamette River Greenway, estuarine resources, coastal shorelands, beaches and dunes, and ocean resources. In 1979 the legislature created the Land Use Board of Appeals, which gave Oregon the fastest land-use process in the nation.[51]

A BRIEF SUMMARY

One of Tom McCall's last acts as governor was to form the nonprofit group 1000 Friends of Oregon on 8 January 1975. "This organization," he said, "gives the people of Oregon a powerful tool to make good land-use planning a reality." He created an advisory board, which he chaired until his death eight years later. Ten of Oregon's leading citizens agreed to join him. Twelve other citizens formed the first board of directors. Under the able and dedicated direction of Henry Richmond, 1000 Friends became the watchdog of Oregon land-use planning, "working daily to see that the city and county comprehensive plans were followed as they were intended, and properly updated as needed." According to McCall, the LCDC and 1000 Friends were in "the tradition of the Oregon system, . . . under which thousands of volunteers over the years have been appointed to boards, and commissions, and task forces . . . to inject the citizen into his own form of government."[52]

Oregon's land-use program was "the first of its kind, presenting a model for other states to follow." McCall knew that it would be challenged in future years. Ballot measures to repeal SB 100 failed by large margins in 1976, 1978, and 1982, and in 1984 a similar measure failed to obtain enough signatures even to get on the ballot. In every legislative session to the present day, challenges have arisen that have forced some modifications strongly condemned by 1000 Friends as attempts to weaken the existing rules and procedures. One group of land-use experts noted in 1984, "The biennial sessions . . . often appear to be a cross between Baghdad's bazaars and a used-car market with the trading, shouting, and backslapping that goes on. . . . LCDC is . . . subject to these kinds of pressures during its rulemaking."[53]

As early as 1974, Arnold Cogan, director of the Department of Land Conservation and Development, felt pressure from some of the major land-owning companies in the state, particularly the Western Environmental Trade Alliance and the Georgia Pacific Corporation. According to Cogan, Bill Moshofsky, the former vice-president of Georgia Pacific (America's largest lumber producer), "still leads the fight against land-use planning in Oregon" through his group Oregonians in Action, which is dedicated to giving counties greater flexibility in the uses of their land. The cry for "local control" still rings out, even though it was the lack of control over development pressures that led to the passage of SB 100 twenty years ago.[54]

Current advocates of relaxed land-use regulation have strong support in the southern and eastern regions of Oregon, where "locally based growth factors are consonant with the populist spirit that has helped shape the West." As Hector Macpherson used to say, "Scratch a farmer, and you'll find a subdivider." Oregon got the jump on its western neighbors, who are now just realizing that environmental quality concerns must be taken seriously. Yet most observers of Oregon politics agree that SB 100 could never be passed in 1994.[55]

Although Oregon has had a more activist legislature than have most western states, it has always provided any governor who was so inclined with the opportunity to dominate the political arena. No governor of the state has ever taken such skillful advantage of his or her opportunities as McCall did, with his broad environmental reform program. He formulated the policies and managed them from the executive office with the backing of a dedicated and energetic staff, often relegating the details to key assistants whom he implicitly trusted. Caring little for partisan politics and willing to take risks, he worked in a situation where the legislative majority and the governor were of different parties, an occurrence "common in the West," as one writer has noted. Without a Democratic legislature in 1973, Governor McCall and Secretary of State Myers, both Republicans, could not have succeeded. The working relationship between Democratic Senator Hallock and Republican Senator Macpherson and with their Republican governor was unique, at least in Oregon's history. Personal rapport, common values, and joint commitment to a cause provided the essential ingredients for success.[56]

To what extent will Oregonians remain committed to environmental values even if they have to sacrifice some economic growth? For more than a decade, Oregon, Washington, and California have ranked at the top of the nation as the best managers of the environment, while the remaining western states have ranked in the bottom half. The strength and effectiveness of Oregon's future land-use control program will depend heavily on the character, values, and commitment of its governors. McCall's example will be hard to emulate. As one observer put it, Tom McCall was willing "to throw his whole political self into the battle to protect the public weal."[57]

CHAPTER 15

South Dakota Governance Since 1945

HERBERT T. HOOVER AND STEVEN C. EMERY

South Dakota ranks sixteenth among the fifty states for its acreage but, in recent years, fortieth for a population, which is restricted by a heavily agricultural economy in a region of limited rainfall. The nearly 50 million acres contained by the present state boundaries supported no more than 25,000 American Indians and fewer than 1,000 non-Indians as Dakota territorial government came into place in 1861. While the tribal census statistics changed little, the aggregate grew to 328,808 by the time of statehood in 1889, and to 629,849 by the year 1930. Thereafter an exodus caused first by the Great Depression and then by the lure of wartime employment reduced the population to 589,702 in fifteen years. Since 1945 there has been a gradual increase to approximately 700,000 at the 1990 census (at least 10 percent of American Indian heritage, mainly Sioux).[1]

Non-Indian and tribal South Dakotans have shared experiences largely in their struggle for subsistence on the land under inhospitable climatic conditions and, for somewhat different reasons, mutual dependence on federal programs, services, and employment. Otherwise, the lives of white people and those of most tribal members have been very different, even though Indians have all been classified as citizens since 1924.

In the realm of governance, the partisan behavior of non-Indians has been similar to that of peoples in neighboring states. Soon after the establishment of the territorial Dakota Republican party (in 1866) and the organization of the Democratic party (in 1868), local observers reported that more than 80 percent of the voters registered as Republicans, and they dominated politics for nearly a century. Until the 1960s Republicans won three-fourths of all elections in South Dakota, with margins of victory ranging up to 92 percent. Since statehood in 1889 Democrats have elected only four governors (in 1926, 1932, 1958, and 1970); on only three occasions have they controlled a majority of seats in the senate at Pierre

(1959–61, 1971–75, and 1993 to present); and only once have they gained equality with Republicans in the state house of representatives (1973–75). Parity of strength between the two major parties during the mid-1970s — when each claimed about 46 percent of the electorate—was short-lived. In 1978 Republicans won majorities of seats in both houses of the legislature as well as the governorship, and thereafter remained in control at Pierre until they lost a majority of seats in the Senate during the election of 1992. State government has been mainly the province of Republicans all along, and they have exercised control over most agencies of local government, as well.

Their predominance has not gained expression in doctrinaire conservatism; on the contrary, Republican officials have supported socialistic endeavors of various kinds. Pursuing governmental assistance of a nature earlier recommended by Populists, Peter Norbeck and William McMaster — both progressive Republican governors — during the years from 1917 to 1925 gained approval from legislators to purchase a coal mine in North Dakota, open a cement plant at Rapid City, sell gasoline and lubricants, offer crop insurance, and loan some $59 million to farmers and ranchers through a "rural credits" program. By the mid-1930s state officials withdrew from most of these enterprises, but they retained the cement plant, which recently has reported annual profits as great as $10 million. Under Republican leadership the state of South Dakota operated game lodges and resorts; and in the 1980s, purchased decayed railroad trackage, improved it at considerable expense, and subsidized the Burlington line to keep rolling stock in operation for the transportation of agricultural products. All along, municipalities owned and operated liquor stores, power plants, airports, and telephone systems. Never has a free enterprise credo encumbered the governmental ownership and operation of business ventures in South Dakota.

In other ways, however, administrators and legislators in Pierre since World War II have exercised conservatism in the management of fiscal affairs. One was steadfast adherence to a constitutional restriction on deficit spending. Economic distress coupled with fear that legislators might exceed revenues with expenditures caused delegates at the constitutional convention to place a ceiling of $100,000 on indebtedness, as a general obligation of the state. By constitutional amendment in 1918, progressive Republicans modified the restriction to allow officials to borrow as much as one-half of 1 percent of the assessed valuation of property in the state to sponsor particular improvements. Governors Norbeck and McMaster quickly put taxpayers at risk with bonded indebtedness to fund the socialistic programs mentioned above. As a result, the people of South Dakota lost $263,000 on crop insurance; $174,000 on the coal mine; and nearly the entire $59 million on the rural credits plan, because officials loaned funds to farmers and ranchers with little concern about the stability of their operations or the value of the land they used as collateral. After the sale of foreclosed real estate, South Dakota suffered a net loss of more than $40 million, which officials retired through relentless effort during the period 1927–54.[2] Because of that experience, they restricted further bonded or federally secured indebtedness to projects reasonably assured of repayment through lease or rental fees, such as the construction of public buildings. Cardinal rules in state finance have been unwavering observance of the constitutional restriction on general obligation indebtedness, guarded use of bonded indebtedness, and budgetary constraint to preserve surplus funds in the treasury sufficient to deal with emergencies.

South Dakota Republicans were equally conservative about raising revenue through the use of taxes on real estate, spending, and licensure. Modest income and personal property taxes installed while Democrat Tom Berry was governor in the 1930s were repealed in 1943 and 1978, respectively. Regressive taxes plus profits from public enterprises ($8.5 million in fiscal year 1991–92) and, recently, levies on gambling receipts ($33 million in 1991–92) have been the mainstays in revenue raised by the legislature within the state.

The legacy of Republican resistance to deficit spending and progressive taxation caused *Money Magazine* to rank South Dakota sixth below the most desirable state in an evaluation of tax burdens on individuals and corporations across the fifty states and the District of Columbia in 1992. The consequence of policies that earned such a favorable report has been heavy reliance upon federal subsidies, which have come to South Dakotans in various ways. Since 1945 federal dollars have been increasingly critical in legislative allocations at Pierre. From approximately 20 percent of the state budget in 1952 the amount grew to 39.5 percent in 1992. Subsidies for use in legislative allocations have come either as grants-in-aid (requiring state matching funds) or as unrestricted gifts. Largest among them have been funds for highway construction and maintenance and for aid to public education. Additional grants have provided assistance to senior citizens, dependent children, and the visually impaired, and have subsidized American Indian education, airport construction, public health, flood containment, fire control, and other needs.

Along with grants have come two other kinds of federal assistance. Most critical have been agricultural price supports and conservation payments. In the fiscal year 1990–91, aggregate federal assistance to farmers and ranchers in South Dakota totaled $436,180,886.[3]

The other type of federal subsidy has come through the operation of agencies that have employed South Dakotans and purchased from them various goods and services. Most prominent since 1945 have been those of the U.S. Postal Service, U.S. Army Corps of Engineers along the Missouri River, U.S. Air Force at Ellsworth Strategic Air Command Base at Rapid City, National Park Service in the Badlands and at Mount Rushmore, U.S. Forest Service in the Black Hills, and U.S. Bureau of Indian Affairs and Internal Revenue Service, with offices centered at Aberdeen.

Voters understood, in other words, that conservative fiscal behavior among state officials depended on the election to Congress of senators and representatives of liberal spending dispositions. They agreed with officials at Pierre, too, that fiscal conservatism depended on governmental efficiency and so cast their votes by referendum in favor of reorganization for many agencies. Twice there were studies that contained recommendations for change—in 1922, and in 1954 by a Little Hoover Commission—but officials took no significant action. Finally, during the 1970s, Democrats drew on recommendations from the Little Hoover Commission to formulate plans for thoroughgoing reorganization in the executive and judicial branches of state government.

The legislature changed only by the creation of the Legislative Research Council in 1951, acceptance of annual sessions in 1962, and reorganization of districts according to census data every ten years to accommodate a drift of population from rural to urban constituencies. But the executive branch underwent extensive change. The Commission on Executive Reorganization, formed in 1971, advanced a plan that brought the adoption of five constitutional amendments by the electorate, all from 1972 to 1974, which led to the consolidation of 160 functionally overlapping agencies into sixteen executive departments, headed by secretaries who form the governor's cabinet, plus a special commission to manage the cement plant in Rapid City. Administrative reorganization also included the establishment of the Office of Executive Management, containing four bureaus; and inspired an increase in the terms of governors and other constitutional officers from two to four years, in time for the election of 1976.

Next came the overhaul of the judicial branch. Reorganization, mandated by the legislature in 1973, eliminated all district, county, and municipal courts as well as the office of justice of the peace. A new system evolved to include a supreme court comprising five judges, initially appointed by the governor but retained in office by (nonpartisan) election to eight-year terms; circuit courts of general jurisdiction comprising thirty-six judges for eight judicial districts, similarly elected to eight-year terms; and magistrate court judges, installed by appointment, with jurisdiction limited to misdemeanor criminal and minor civil suits, distributed across the eight judicial districts.

With reorganization in the judicial system came some adjustments in the agencies of law enforcement. To serve needs beyond those provided by municipal police and county sheriffs, there appeared a system comprising officers in the Division of Criminal Investigation (commonly known as the DCI, or "Little FBI"), under the Office of the Attorney General; the State Highway Patrol, under the Department of Public Safety; and the Conservation Officer staff, whose members replaced game wardens, under the Department of Wildlife, Parks and Forestry. Federal employees included Federal Bureau of Investigation officers; a Secret Service officer, permanently stationed in Sioux Falls; and a U.S. marshal at Sioux Falls, serving by political appointment, supported by a dozen deputies scattered across the state who held civil service appointments.

Reorganization in the 1970s included the modernization of equipment, especially that used by officers in the State Highway Patrol, an agency established during the 1930s and much in need of improvement. For the first time, officers were issued lightweight flack jackets; .357-magnum instead of .38-caliber revolvers; burn-resistant jackets; hand radios, night sticks, riot batons, and mace; jackets with nonchoke collars; and caps instead of hats with neck bands that could be used to choke officers during struggles.

Some historians and political scientists have argued that administrative reorganization should parallel judicial reorganization to consolidate local institutions of government. At the end of the 1970s there remained 1,733 agencies: 1 state, 67 county (3 unorganized); 311 municipal; 1,009 township; 198 school district; and 147 special district units (including 59 for soil conservation, 21 for sewage processing, 18 for flood control, and 12 for irrigation).

County and municipal governments evoked little comment. The county system contained few problems with overlapping jurisdictions or inefficiency. After 1962, municipal governments possessed the power of "home rule" to exercise maximum flexibility in function and organization. Municipal attrition progressed by gradual elimination through the consolidation of farms and ranches and a corresponding drift of population toward larger towns and cities.

Townships were subjects of some discussion. Following administrative reorganization in the 1970s South Dakota remained one of only sixteen states to retain township governments, with functions restricted mainly to property assessment hearings, road maintenance, and weed control. Despite obvious merit in the transfer of township functions to county commissioners, the instinct to retain some control over affairs at the community level has kept township governance in place.

Recently voters took action, however, which forced adjustments in rules to control the tenures of elected officials. After they approved the extension of terms for state officials from two to four years, voters became increasingly critical about the distraction of politicians by plans for reelection. Their concern was first expressed in 1988, when the legislature petitioned Congress to restrict the tenures for all its members to twelve years, then initiated change through referendum during the election of 1992.

Beginning with incumbents as well as newcomers installed in office on 1 January 1993, U.S. Senators and representatives from South Dakota serve consecutive terms limited to twelve years; and state legislators as well as all elected (constitutional) administrative officials (except the public utilities commissioner) serve terms of continuous tenure limited to eight years. The critical phrase in the amendment approved by the electorate is "consecutive service." On the completion of twelve consecutive years in the U.S. House of Representatives, for example, a South Dakotan could twice seek election to the U.S. Senate, and if successful enjoy twenty-four years of uninterrupted service in Congress, then immediately run for additional terms in the U.S. House of Representatives. Similarly, a person could move from one to another office in state government, winning election to each for a total of no more than eight consecutive years, and enjoy uninterrupted public service for a lifetime. The point of the amendment is not to restrict the tenures of elected officials to eight or twelve years, but rather to prevent any official except the public utilities commissioner from treating a single elective office as a sinecure.

Beyond the management of fiscal policy and the modernization of governmental agencies, in this state with a limited population so heavily dependent on federal support, legislators and administrators alike have done more "housekeeping chores" and dealt with fewer major responsibilities than have their counterparts in more heavily populated states. Yet some items of public interest have placed great demands on public officials. After World War II, for approximately thirty years no responsibility was more critical or expensive than the completion of a modern system of roads that could meet the needs of communication, agribusiness, and tourism.

Federal officials created an opportunity for highway improvement with their decision to contain the Missouri River, through the Flood Control Act of 1944 and subsequent legislation that authorized the acquisition of Missouri River Valley land. Frequently throughout the history of the state gorging ice and raging floods inundated the Missouri Valley and interrupted traffic for months at a time. Congress allocated tens of millions of dollars to purchase "taking areas" and install four massive rolled-earth dams, which came into place during the period of 1954–66. The cost to South Dakotans was mainly in the surrender of valley land. The durability of the dams and the lakes they created as well as their ecological consequences remain open to question; but their practical value to life in South Dakota never has been a subject of debate, among most non-Indians at least, in large degree because the dams facilitated the completion of a suitable network of highways and roads. Further, they diminished the hazard of floods, stimulated tourism, generated hydroelectric power, and contained water for irrigation and urban use.

Road improvement was a public charge long in need of attention. For a quarter-century after statehood, responsibility fell exclusively on officials in local government agencies, who created disconnected, unsurfaced trails and maintained them very little. Expressions of desire for a consolidated effort toward improvement came first from local groups through a "good roads" movement that began in 1912. From then to mid-century, state and local officials matched federal funds and used New Deal programs to subsidize networks of trunk routes and local roads connected by six bridges across the Missouri River.

Through the 1950s expenditures for road improvement and expansion exceeded all other demands on legislative resources, which came mainly from special allocations or sales and use tax receipts. During critical years of maximum construction, the federal portion offered to support construction on primary and secondary roads within the state was approximately 73 percent; and on interstate freeways, some 91 percent. Congress paid most of the cost for construction on highways across four earthen dams along the Missouri River. Nevertheless, between the years 1953 and 1965, annual investments by the state on roads rose from $25,809,000 to $69,511,000.

By the end of the 1970s the road system neared completion. It encompassed 9,278 miles classified as trunk highways; 20,838 as county roads; 48,095 as township roads; and 2,845 as urban roads.

Just after roads on the agenda of urgent business following World War II was the management of a public educational system far more complex and expensive than state and local officials could justify for such a limited population. (In addition, there existed two other school systems: one established by Christian denominations for non-Indian parishioners that included primary schools, academies, and colleges; another created by Christian denominations as well as by federal officials for American Indians. Spread across the state in various enclaves, tribal and non-Indian peoples alike wanted access to all levels of education in close proximity to their homes.)

The system under public control was by far the largest, hence the one most in need of reorganization. At mid-century, public officials funded and managed 3,395 independent or common school districts to provide elementary education for 86,487 pupils and to operate 283 secondary schools for 28,401 students. Justification for consolidation and modernization was obvious, but resistance was strong. Schools long had provided South Dakota communities social activities and entertainment as well as practical instruction. Educational institutions were keys to economic survival for many small towns.

Despite pressure from opposing forces, inevitably state officials forced change in the interest of economy as well as educational program improvement. During 1955 legislators passed a law to encourage voluntary reorganization by districts. In 1960 the State Board of Education ordered every teacher to acquire a four-year degree by 1968. In 1967 legislators required that all communities be annexed to schools with accreditation by the year 1970. The combination of these actions reduced the number of country schools to approximately 1,000 by 1970. Within two decades of the 1955 legislation the number of school districts declined from 3,288 to only 198. Although still more complex than taxpayers easily could sustain, by the end of the 1980s the system was suitably consolidated, its programs adjusted to national academic standards, and the number of units classified as country schools reduced to fewer than 50.

After mid-century the higher educational system became a point of equal concern, not only because of the cost of its operation, but also due to crises pertaining to accreditation and academic standards. In 1969, Richard Gibb, commissioner of higher education, devised a plan for reorganization, but pressure from local interests diminished its implementation to the attachment in 1971 of Dakota State College at Madison and Southern State College in Springfield as branches to the University of South Dakota. A short time later Gov. Richard Kneip sponsored a movement to create a single university system, on the Wisconsin model, but it failed due to resistance from parochial representatives. At length, the Board of Regents settled for the moderate consolidation of programs across the system and an increase in student-to-teacher ratios with hope of reducing faculty costs.

In 1984 Gov. William Janklow reduced the system somewhat. He closed the Springfield university branch and saved the town by converting the campus into a co-correctional, medium-security state prison, and he converted the Madison branch into a computer training center. Yet there remained under regents' control the University of South Dakota at Vermillion; South Dakota State University (A&M) at Brookings; Dakota State College at Madison; Northern State College, mainly for teacher training, at Aberdeen; Black Hills State College, mainly for teacher training, at Spearfish; South Dakota School of Mines in Rapid City; and the schools for the deaf and for the visually impaired in Sioux Falls and Aberdeen. (By 1990 the legislature renamed all colleges under its control to include "university.")

Inordinate complexity resulting in cost inefficiency is the primary reason that public education remains the most expensive enterprise supported by state government. For fiscal year 1992–93, aggregate educational allocations drew some $293,000,000 from state general funds, of which $121,303,693 went into higher education, matched by $113,420,000 in federal funds. The total cost of funding all sixteen state administrative departments and their respective services came to only $121,612,000 in state funds, against $253,321,000 in federal funds. Social services cost $76,823,956 in state funds, against $226,327,734 federal funds. The judicial branch drew $16,910,210 from general state revenues.

Road construction, educational management, an array of social services, and administrative efficiency have been the main concerns of public officials in South Dakota since World War II. Otherwise, for two decades or so, legislators and administrators at Pierre concentrated on housekeeping functions, occasionally tinkering with the delivery of services and reacting to demands for policy changes suggested by national trends. Legislators demonstrated their bent toward McCarthyism in 1955, for example, by requiring a loyalty oath of all public employees, and they kept this requirement in effect to the year 1974. They funded bonuses for both World War II and Korean War veterans. They maintained the state's "right-to-work" law with judicial support to stifle the growth of labor unions. They reacted to the matter of capital punishment with a lapse in executions that lasted from 1947 to 1993. South Dakota was among the last states to require a driver's license (in 1953) and licensure through examination (in 1959).

Early in the 1970s, when Republicans and Democrats attained approximately equal strength in Pierre, legislators became increasingly responsive to national as well as regional needs. In 1993, Mary Edelen, former state representative, reviewed prevailing issues since the legislative agenda began to grow:

> A case in point has been the abortion rights issue. Following the U.S. Supreme Court decision, in *Roe v. Wade* during 1973, which legalized access to abortion, the 1973 Legislature passed a 19-section bill, specifying when and how the procedure could be performed in the state. An emergency clause was added, so it went into effect immediately upon the signature of the Governor. Nearly every session since 1973, legislators have debated this controversial issue with great emotion and public outcry.

> [Following judicial reorganization in 1975 came the revision of] the South Dakota Criminal Code in 1977. The Legislature approved a bill that redefined the crime of incest as rape in 1984. The same year it approved Martin Luther King, Jr., day as a working holiday, and later changed it to a non-working holiday. Since then through legislative action, the state has joined the Southwestern Low-Level Radioactive Waste Disposal Company, with several other western states; and has approved scratch-and-match lottery, video lottery, and high-stakes gambling in Deadwood.

> In 1991 a bill was approved to fund the Veterans Bonus for men and women who served in the Vietnam War, and extended benefits to those who served in Lebanon, Grenada, Libya, Panama, and the Persian Gulf.

> Recently the Legislature has authorized the state's public schools to loan textbooks to children who attend private schools or alternative instruction in the home; expanded a two-year into a four-year medical school at the University of South Dakota; approved victim/witness legislation; established a Children's Trust fund; and approved mandatory child restraints in automobiles for children under the age of five, while at the same time refusing to adopt mandatory seat belts for adults.

The legislature has been on the ground floor in the country in adopting legislation in many areas. Some of these include mediation for farmers who are about to lose their farms, a state subsidy for ethanol production, and loans for new businesses and industrial plants. The legislature changed the interest-rate laws to enable Citibank to set up a credit card business in the state, worked to solve the medical malpractice crises, and approved several Tribal/State Relations bills in hopes that better communication could be established between the tribes and state officials.[4]

Public officials have earned fairly high marks for their attempts to address major issues in state and local governance, but they have faltered in the resolution of problems in their relationship with leaders of Indian tribes on nine reservations in South Dakota.[5] There was a window of opportunity to assert control after 1953, when Congress passed House Concurrent Resolution 108 to facilitate an end to federal supervision over tribal affairs on the assumption that state governments might fill the void. An effort by the South Dakota Legislature to do so failed in 1964, however, when by referendum voters rejected the assumption of state jurisdiction. Since missing that opportunity, state officials have faced increasing conflict over jurisdiction at the cost of almost continuous litigation.

An underlying cause for discord has been a feeble grasp of how tribes fit into the political system of the United States, and the range of jurisdictional authority retained by tribal leaders as a result. Non-Indians have been taught that powers not delegated to the United States under the Constitution are reserved by the states, under whose aegis there exist county, township, municipal, school district, and special district jurisdictions. Few have learned, however, that federal treaties, statutes, and precedents have also preserved rights for the tribes that cannot be infringed by state or local governments.

Tribal leaders have never contested the loss of power to govern on large tracts of land *legally* ceded to the United States — for instance, most of the land in eastern South Dakota — but they have defended rights of governance within reservation boundaries created by treaties or "congressional Agreements." Most troublesome have been the issue of tribal jurisdiction over "fee lands" (owned by individuals free of federal restrictions) within reservation boundaries and the application of tribal jurisdiction across reservations pertaining to such matters as taxation, traffic control on country roads and state highways, representation on school boards, and wildlife use and management. Short of congressional intervention, the only means of dealing with disputes between tribal leaders and state

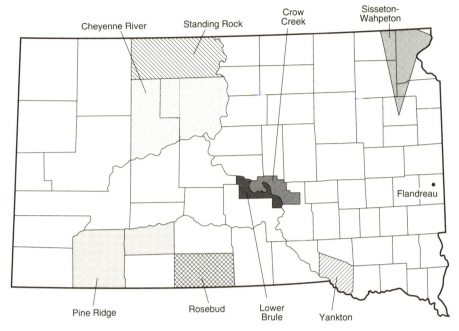

South Dakota Indian Reservations

officials have been (most often) litigation in federal courts or (less frequently) informal agreements formulated by tribal and state officials with approval from the U.S. Department of the Interior.

At litigation, attorneys general representing South Dakota use various arguments. One is that tribal members are subject to state jurisdiction because they are citizens of the state as well as of the United States. Another is that tribal governance deprives non-Indians and members of other tribes who reside within reservation boundaries of rights due them as citizens because they cannot vote in tribal elections. Attorneys general also insist that state agencies are entitled to exercise authority over such matters as taxation and wildlife management across South Dakota, reservation boundaries notwithstanding.

Tribal attorneys respond with various historical examples. They employ phrases from treaties (some treaties involving the Sioux date back to the year 1815). They cite precedents in federal actions to defend tribal rights against infringement by external political forces, and call attention to how steadily tribal leaders have managed the affairs and protected the interests of their constituents.

Federal officials have supported tribal rights in most instances, as a trust responsibility, when conflicts appeared over a variety of issues. They have supported tribal claims to wildlife jurisdiction, rooted in treaties ratified as early as 1825, as matters of custom and expectation that, without interruption, have been exercised to the benefit of the tribes in various ways. Individually, tribal members have never ceased to hunt and fish for their livelihood, and some have hunted and fished for profit from the sale of hides and meat. Culturally, many have cherished control over natural bounty as a key to the survival of philosophy and spirituality. Collectively, residents of some reservations have come to rely on the sales of licenses and services to outsiders as sources of revenue—recently more than $200,000 a year for the Lower Brule tribe. From appearances, litigation over this single issue will continue until Congress intercedes, or until state and tribal leaders find some compatible way to share jurisdictional authority—such as a five-year agreement recently negotiated between Michael Jandreau, Lower Brule tribal chairman, and Governor Janklow, which permitted both tribe and state to sell hunting licenses without either conceding jurisdictional authority to the other.

Other issues of similar interest abide. There has been conflict over the sale of automotive license plates, maintenance and policing of roads, and operation of tribal casinos. Some disputes have evoked interesting solutions from the courts. Recently a federal judge heard protests from tribal leaders on Lake Traverse Reservation because their constituents could not gain representation on Roberts County school boards. He settled the matter with a decision out-of-court that ordered the establishment of a "cumulative voting system," allowing every voter to "aggregate his votes for one or more candidates" in order to facilitate the election of Sissetons and Wahpetons to the school boards.

Separate from the political arena of conflicting jurisdictions is an environment of governance for tribal members alone on the nine reservations of South Dakota, in which there is no place for participation by state and local governmental leaders. Operating in isolation under protection by the United States, tribal officials have shouldered two general responsibilities.

One has been cooperation with federal officials in the search for economic resources sufficient to satisfy the needs of their constituents.

Contrary to a popular misconception among non-Indians, tribal members never have been more reliant on federal funds than have non-Indians in the state. Until the end of the 1920s there came to Indian people "payments" in literally hundreds of thousands of vouchers issued from agency officials or U.S. Treasury Department checks. Instead of beneficence, they represented proceeds from the sale of land and individual labor. After these resources all but disappeared, tribal members received New Deal support in the 1930s, then Great Society "grants relief" in the 1960s with no greater preference than that extended to other groups in need. Since 1945 Indians have paid taxes on all incomes, expenditures, and properties (except restricted land), and with some federal assistance relocated from rural areas on the reservations to urban settings off the reservations in search of education and employment. Tribal leaders shared with federal officials responsibility for the economic welfare of those who chose to retain reservation residence. Farming, ranching, small business, craft work, public employment, community projects supported by grants, entitlements available to all United States citizens, and recently casino gambling operations have been the primary means.

The other general responsibility has been the supply of governmental services to tribal members. This might be illustrated with a profile of any one of nine reservation governments. The one at Cheyenne River Reservation is distinctive for its service to descendants from four of the seven Lakota tribes (Minneconjou, Sans Arc, Two Kettle, and Blackfoot Sioux), who have retained the greatest per capita acreage in Sioux Country on one of the region's most isolated reservations.

For Cheyenne River Lakotas there exists a governmental system based on a constitution and bylaws approved in 1935, with several amendments, which operates according to the principle of the separation of powers. The Cheyenne River Sioux tribe (*Wakpa Waste Oyate*, translated Good River People) is a subdivision of the *Oceti Sakowin* (Seven Council Fires of Tetonwan Lakota of the Great Sioux Nation). It is located in north-central South Dakota on a portion of what formerly was called the Great Sioux Reservation. The boundaries of the present-day Cheyenne River Sioux Reservation were established by Article 2 in the congressional Agreement of March 2, 1889 (25 Stat. 888). The reservation, which is about the size of the state of Connecticut, has approximately 9,000 residents, about 6,000 of whom are American Indian—the great majority being tribal members and spouses of tribal members. For reservation residents, the Cheyenne River Sioux Tribal Council has provided a system of government, and also has "established courts for the adjudication of claims [and] disputes" (Article 4 of the Tribal Constitution and By-Laws.)

The elected council legislates by passing ordinances, written in response to needs expressed by lobbyists and expert witnesses. It charters agencies to deliver essential services. The agencies' responsibilities include a tribally controlled community college; housing; a buffalo herd; transportation and construction; nutrition; women, infants, and children; energy assistance; telephone communications; disbursement, payroll, and financial management; a repayment cattle program; information management, mainly by computer; personnel; central records; higher educational support; gaming (soon to be expressed by the operation of a casino); alcoholic beverage control; and tribal planning.

The council also addresses matters of infringement on tribal interests. Starting in 1944 there was the Missouri River Flood Control Act, which did not contain a clear expression of congressional intent to allow the taking of Indian lands under federal law. This act and its progeny spelled doom for the tribe's best agricultural, grazing, and timber lands along the Missouri River.

At the Cheyenne River Reservation, tribal officials spent much of their time through the 1950s dealing with problems related to the United States' acquisition of lands for the construction of the Oahe Reservoir on the "taking area" (area taken to accommodate the reservoir). Negotiations regarding tribal claims took approximately four years. The tribe was also confronted by the need to prepare for the inundation of the Old Agency, a historic community on the Missouri River, when the floodgates were closed on the Oahe Reservoir.

Other grave concerns of the time included maintaining federal recognition of the tribe and the potential loss of treaty-based federal services. Two opposing goals—maintaining federal recognition while demonstrating to federal officials that "progress" was being made toward assimilation in the agency boarding school and elsewhere—were delicately balanced by traditionalists and traditional-minded tribal council members.

Probably the most significant issue faced by the *Wakpa Waste Oyate* is the Black Hills Claim, coupled with a claim for unceded hunting lands, sometimes called the Article 16 lands because a recognized claim to ownership was assured by Article 16 of the Fort Laramie Treaty of 1868. Decades of preparation produced claims dockets 74-A and 74-B. With these at hand, the U.S. Court of Claims recommended and Congress approved monetary compensation for the Great Sioux Nation tribes by the

United States (in *United States v. Sioux Nation*, 1980). By 1993, with interest this amounted to more than $300 million. The Cheyenne River Tribal Council has formally stated its opposition to accepting the funds, with the official position that the tribe never will accept the money because of the significance of *He Sapa* (the Black Hills) to Lakota traditionalists and other tribal members.

During the late 1970s and early 1980s, the issue of who had authority within the exterior boundaries of a reservation was challenged by the state of South Dakota on several reservations including Rosebud and Lake Traverse. In *Solem v. Bartlett* (1984) a Cheyenne River Sioux tribal member had committed a crime on Indian land within the reservation and subsequently was prosecuted by the state and sent to the state penitentiary. On appeal, he raised the issue of whether the state court had properly asserted subject-matter jurisdiction over the case when the crime had been committed by an Indian in Indian Country. Lawyers representing the Office of the State Attorney General argued that the Cheyenne River Reservation's northern and western boundaries (established by the congressional Agreement of March 2, 1889) had been diminished by the Homestead Act of 29 May 1908. Fortunately for the tribe, in the *Solem* case the U.S. Supreme Court held that the exterior boundaries of the Cheyenne River Reservation were not diminished by the 1908 Homestead Act.

The 1970s were in some ways cathartic. Externally, tribal leaders prepared to stand their ground against past or present intrusions on tribal land or jurisdiction. Internally, the Cheyenne River Sioux cleansed themselves of some of the anti-Indian sentiment that had been instilled by missionaries, federal officials, and teachers and administrators from U.S. Bureau of Indian Affairs (BIA) or mission schools. Once that happened, strong efforts emerged to teach the Lakota language and culture in schools and elsewhere. Additionally, after the enactment of Public Law 93–638, in 1975, the tribe initiated efforts to contract for services formerly provided by the BIA. Those contracts remain in place. For example, the tribe contracts with the BIA to provide law enforcement services to the reservation. In addition, the tribe operates a judiciary as part of the tribal governmental services contract.

The Cheyenne River judicial system consists of a superior court, which adjudicates civil cases including small claims, lawsuits, and decisions of the tribal council and all tribal administrative bodies; a criminal court, which hears criminal misdemeanor cases arising from offenses committed by tribal members and non-member Indians within exterior reservation boundaries; and a juvenile court, which decides all cases dealing with child welfare, including those transferred to the court from state courts pursuant to the Indian Child Welfare Act as well as cases involving juveniles who have committed infractions or offenses. A tribal appellate court hears appeals from the three other courts, freed from interference by tribal council members through a constitutional amendment approved during June 1992.

Serving the judicial branch are the tribal attorney general and the tribal attorney, who are responsible for maintaining conformity to constitutional authority and tribal laws in relationships with external forces as well as with members of the tribe. Also under the judicial branch is a tribal police force, which functions outside the ken of council influence as an agency of the court to enforce the law.

Adjudication within the tribe takes place in courts through a process similar to that used by the eight state circuit courts. Comparative studies indicate that penalties for infractions of tribal laws are less severe than are those assigned in the non-Indian system, inasmuch as they include fewer instances of incarceration and more public service or settlement by counsel and compromise.

Litigation against intrusions by external forces is a primary responsibility of the attorney general, whose attention usually is divided by several cases of infringement. Early in the year 1993 the tribe was involved in four federal cases of litigation. During March, its attorneys appeared in the U.S. Supreme Court regarding the extent of tribal civil regulatory jurisdiction over non-Indians hunting and fishing on lands taken for the construction of the Oahe Reservoir as well as on the reservoir itself—up to the historic midchannel as defined in Section 4 of the Agreement of 2 March 1889. The Supreme Court decided the case during June 1993. Supreme Court justices refused to allow the extent of jurisdiction requested by state officials, yet remanded the case to the federal circuit court at St. Louis with instruction for a review of the extent of tribal jurisdiction previously allowed by this circuit court. Judges at St. Louis heard arguments from both sides during May 1994 and deliberated during the summer months. Their decision will have profound impacts on the management of wildlife by tribes across the country.

Operating a tribal government is an extremely complex matter. Many different tribes and tribal leaders look to the Cheyenne River Sioux Tribe for direction. Noteworthy is its stability; through four-year terms for both the tribal council and the chairman as well as staggered terms on the council, at all times at least half the Council has two years of experience.

The structure of a typical, modern tribal government in South Dakota is similar to that of a non-Indian government agency, but the tenor of governance is very different because it represents an uninterrupted legacy reaching back to a time preceding the existence of written records. When modern constitutional governments appeared during the 1930s—on Lake Traverse Reservation in 1931, Yankton Reservation in 1932, and Cheyenne River as well as other reservations under the Indian Reorganization Act after 1934—they revitalized an abiding authority of tribal government. Continuously since the 1930s, elected tribal officials have enlarged the scope of their jurisdiction to include many functions that previously had been seized by federal agency employees. Currently they act with protection under a trust responsibility of the United States (secured by treaties, congressional statutes, and binding precedents) that cannot be altered except by congressional action with the consent of the tribes.

In various ways, since World War II trends and problems of governance in South Dakota have been similar to those in many heartland and western states. For the existence of a dual system of government, however, South Dakota is atypical. Perhaps nowhere else in the West have conflicting interests of non-Indian against Indian systems of governance been as intense and perplexing.

CHAPTER 16

The Texas Gubernatorial Election of 1990: Claytie Versus the Lady

BEN PROCTER

In 1989, at the beginning of the dog days of summer, Texas politics were pretty spirited. The state legislators were in special session, their antics once more reminding Texans of the cynical New York jurist's observation in 1866 that "no man's life, liberty, or property are safe while the legislature is in session." Any number of lawmakers were fearfully concerned about the abortion issue, especially because antiabortion leaders were demanding a special session on the topic. Many others considered education most vital, especially the problem of fair financing between the rich and poor counties—a question for which there were as yet no viable solutions. And still others, while professing the need for ethics reform and the curtailment of lobbying, became involved in a scandal known as "Chickengate," in which Lonnie ("Bo") Pilgrim, an East Texas poultry magnate, had naively walked onto the floor of the Senate and, in full view of the public and capitol press corps, had presented ten-thousand-dollar checks to five state senators. Republican Gov. Bill Clements thus summed up the 1989 special session as "a failure."[1]

But what really attracted the attention of Texans was the 1990 governor's race. Although election day was sixteen months away, the participants were already lining up to do battle. Whether Democratic or Republican, they made up a formidable group, representing money and power as well as running the gamut from liberalism to conservatism. They were, in the main, white, Protestant, and male—except for one female aspirant. Their years of experience in the public and private sectors were impressive, if not intimidating. They were confident in their own ability to govern and, more important, their opportunity to win.

The Democrats had an impressive trio of candidates. Seemingly, the front runner was Attorney General Jim Mattox. He had $3.7 million in his campaign chest—much more than any other Democratic opponent and more than enough for the primary on 13 March 1990. Mattox boasted that he could raise $6 million more for the general election. At age forty-six, he had already proven himself to be an activist, a can-do public servant in the Populist tradition. He attacked huge corporations for not giving their fair share of revenues to the state, demanded that hundreds of fathers meet their responsibilities by paying child support, and brought suit against building developers and insurance companies on behalf of the average person. As a consequence, he was often in the headlines, creating favorable publicity both for Mattox the public servant and Mattox the candidate. Surely of equal significance, he was a hard worker and a tireless campaigner; he had not lost a race in seventeen years.

Mattox was, as Daniel Cavazos of the *San Antonio Light* observed, a man of "many edges" — nearly all of them rough. He was a street fighter, a "take-no-prisoners" campaigner who welcomed confrontation and seemed to thrive on "mudslinging and cheap shots." He was from a broken home in Dallas, his alcoholic father having abandoned his mother and three small children. Jim Mattox was thus forced, at age twelve, to help support the family by working as a dishwasher, busboy, waiter, even a door-to-door teenage salesman of Bibles in the tough area of East Dallas. With the help of his mother he worked his way through Baylor University and Southern Methodist University Law School, achieving distinction as "a bright, outgoing, and politically attuned" classmate. Showing little interest in social niceties, Mattox was direct in conversation, forthright about his purposes, unwavering in the achievement of his goals.[2]

State Treasurer Ann Richards was a candidate of equal political stature and of greater national exposure — and therefore one to be reckoned with. As the keynote speaker at the National Democratic Convention at Atlanta in July 1988, she had achieved celebrity status by mocking the Republican presidential nominee, George Bush, with the memorable quip (among others), "Poor George, he can't help it; he was born with a silver foot in his mouth." For almost a year she had been gearing for the governor's race, being the first Democrat to announce her candidacy. She assembled an excellent campaign staff that was competent, experienced, and loyal. In many ways she and Mattox were much alike. She, too, was a winner, having held public office continuously since 1976, first as a Travis County commissioner (Austin) and then, after 1982, as state treasurer. And during all that time she had built a reputation as an "exacting boss," an efficient manager both of organizations and people, a person of "warmth and caring" who could, however, verbally excoriate an opponent with ridicule and invective. At age fifty-six, Richards was ten years older than Mattox, but was no less indefatigable as a campaigner and just as single-minded in reaching her objectives.

Yet Richards had a number of obstacles to overcome in order to reach the governorship. In a state of huge distances, conservative by tradition and, in certain areas, "macho" in speech and attitude, Richards was a liberal Democrat who had become somewhat of a heroine in the feminist movement. Her candidacy challenged the idea of male dominance in state politics. After all, while Miriam A. ("Ma") Ferguson was elected to two terms as governor (1925–27 and 1933–35) with the help and support of James ("Jim") Ferguson, her husband and former governor, many Texans had comfortably voted for her because of her campaign slogan: Two for the Price of One. Richards, however, was a divorced, silver-haired grandmother who, despite having a family of four devoted children, could "terrify men" with her acid tongue. Many Texans would never forgive her for humiliating George Bush. Some well-heeled Democratic supporters refused to contribute the kind of funds necessary to a statewide campaign; so Richards had to depend on numerous small contributors (enlisting over 11,000 by the end of 1988) and on fund-raising events in New York City, Washington, and Hollywood.[3]

Mark White was the third of this Democratic triumvirate. Even though a late starter—he did not begin airing his possible candidacy until August 1989 and did not formally announce until the end of November—White had to be taken seriously by both Mattox and Richards. As far as name recognition, he was easily the winner, having run three statewide campaigns over the past twelve years. He was a tall, good-looking man approaching age fifty, comfortably self-assured and in line with the Texas political establishment, usually taking a moderate to conservative stance on issues. Between 1973 and 1979 he achieved some favorable recognition as secretary of state under Gov. Dolph Briscoe. Then he was elected attorney general, again fashioning a good record. In 1982 he decided to run against Bill Clements, the state's first Republican governor in over a hundred years; and in a bitter, bloody campaign White narrowly defeated him. But in 1986 Clements had "his revenge," especially with Texans having suffered through four years of economic recession and higher taxes, as well as a stressful and highly controversial revamping of public school education, including a "no pass, no play" rule for students and competency examinations for all teachers (proposed by businessman H. Ross Perot and attorney Tom Luce of Dallas).

White, however, had a certain amount of "political baggage." Even though hoping to receive much of the "moderate" and all of the "conservative" Democratic votes, he was arriving on the scene at a late date; in other words, some of his potential supporters and financial backers had already committed themselves by the time he announced his intention to run. The same was true in regard to organization; other candidates, both Democratic and Republican, had already hired many of the best political professionals and campaign workers. Possibly the greatest problem for the White campaign, though, was the candidate himself. His motivation for running seemed to be ego and a need to vindicate his single term as governor. Some political experts observed that White, unlike Mattox and Richards, was not willing to do whatever was necessary to win.[4]

The Republican candidates, although unable to match the Democrats in public experience, were equally imposing. State Railroad Commissioner Kent Hance, age forty-seven and a graduate of the University of Texas Law School, was the obvious frontrunner, as verified by the polls. Over the past six years he had run three statewide races; therefore, he had the greatest name identification. He also had the most outstanding political record. As a former Democratic state senator and Boll-Weevil (conservative) congressman from Lubbock, he aspired to be a U.S. senator, but in a hotly contested Democratic primary in 1984 he suffered a disappointing and narrow defeat. Then in 1985 he switched parties, only to lose in the Republican gubernatorial primary in 1986. But Hance did not fade into political oblivion: he was appointed by Gov. Bill Clements to fill a vacancy on the Texas Railroad Commission in 1987 and the next year became the first Republican ever elected to that panel.

Yet Hance did not have merely an Achilles heel, one political commentator pointed out, but a whole foot. Just prior to joining the Republicans in 1985, he displayed a lack of veracity by announcing that he was "a John Kennedy Democrat" and that he would "never switch parties or wives." He also had a tendency to be, as several reporters noted, "a first-class demagogue." He tended to prey on Texan prejudices and fears, making his opposition to some unpopular issue the centerpiece of his campaign. Thus Hance, even though described as "quick-witted" and "funny," was considered an aggressive campaigner with an unflattering mean streak.[5]

Clayton Williams, however, was something else. A fifty-eight-year-old multimillionaire businessman from Midland, with extensive operations in banking, cattle, real estate, and oil, he seemed the embodiment of frontier Texas, the image of "big oil, masculine ideals, and flamboyant egos." His heritage was deeply rooted in state tradition and history. His grandfather had pioneered the trans-Pecos West country around Fort Stockton late in the nineteenth century—he had wrested the land from the formidable Comanches and the cruel ravages of the desert. Williams credited his father and mother with teaching him "the old ways," a respect for family, institutions, and the land. Williams believed that many aspects of modern urban life were destroying the fabric of which Texas was made. Late in 1985 his fourteen-year-old son, Clayton Wade, became heavily involved with drugs and soon thereafter underwent a difficult period of rehabilitation. This personal experience galvanized Williams's convictions. In June 1990 he announced his intention to run for governor, to fight a "holy war" against drugs, to "make Texas great again" by giving "back to our kids the Texas my father gave to me."

But Clayton Williams, of the infectious smile and big ears and glistening white teeth, all resting under a cowboy hat, had frailties both personal and political that would severely test his candidacy; yet he remained confident and undaunted. To address the problems of name recognition and inexperience in dealing with the public in general and the media in particular, he hired the best TV and political consultants that his money could buy. He then proceeded to finance a multimillion-dollar campaign. But what troubled the Williams campaign was the candidate himself. Although personable and charming in his sometimes unassuming naivete, Williams had, if anything, too much confidence—the ego and impetuosity that often accompany extreme wealth. The big question was, Could his advisors restrain the unorthodox candidate, who had several large statues of John Wayne in his Midland business complex, who reveled in a Texas A&M University degree by unabashedly yelling the "gig 'em Aggies" chant, who had made headlines for one of his causes in 1985 "by leading a posse of ten cowboys on horseback up the steps of the Capitol," who was intrigued by the novelty and glamor of this new adventure? It was not likely. But, after all, Clayton Williams was paying for the ride.[6]

Jack Rains of Houston, soon to be fifty-two, had the makings of a strong contender, but his "great crusade" in behalf of Texas education never got off the ground. Although appointed secretary of state by Governor Clements in 1987, Rains had low name recognition with Texas voters. Like Williams, he was a graduate of Texas A&M and a successful business executive, having founded 3D/International, a mammoth architectural and engineering firm. Despite such experience and training, he had a tendency to be, as one capitol correspondent noted, politically "impulsive and accident-prone." For instance, Rains announced, as the bedrock of his gubernatorial campaign, a "ten-point program for better education" and then, inexplicably, listed only nine points. He also tried the "folksy" approach, appointing Bum Philips, the popular former head coach of the Houston Oilers, his campaign treasurer. As for fund raising, Rains was disappointed in his efforts to secure large campaign contributions from financial heavyweights in Houston as well as the many Texas Republicans with whom he had worked.[7]

Forty-nine-year-old Tom Luce of Dallas would round out the principal Republican contestants. Most political pundits considered his background and abilities the most impressive of the four, but such credentials have not often been convincing to Texas voters. A graduate of Southern Methodist University, with degrees both in business and law, Luce had fashioned an enviable reputation locally and across the state. As the top attorney in the 150-person Dallas law firm Hughes and Luce, he had successfully represented Ross Perot in several government ventures. He had also served with distinction under three governors. In 1981 he was appointed by Governor Clements to a War on Drugs Committee that, in turn, prompted the state legislature to pass major antidrug legislation. In 1984, under Governor White, he was, as one capitol correspondent stated, "the architect of the sweeping . . . education reforms." With Clements again in 1987, he headed a state commission that secured federal funding for the Superconducting Super Collider near Waxahachie. Because of his sterling performances in the private and public sectors, Clements and Perot persuaded him to announce on 15 September, despite a poll showing that only 1 percent of likely GOP primary voters would support him. And, although he was entering the race late and was described as a "bland" and "uninspiring" stump speaker, Luce was confident that Texans would reward his service to the state and that Clements and Perot would draw supporters as well as provide ample financial backing.[8]

With such an impressive array of gubernatorial candidates Texas voters anticipated a flurry of political activity for the remainder of 1989. They were disappointed not in the amount of energy exerted and the dollars spent but in the dearth of issues addressed.

On the Democratic side, Richards initiated a dialogue that seemed to establish an issue agenda. At Wichita Falls on 11 July 1989 she first of all endorsed a prochoice stance. Then she proposed that three topics should dominate the governor's race. Ethics reform should be of primary concern; hence, she challenged all candidates to release their income tax returns, as she had just done. Second, the next governor must spur the economy and "sell the state like it has never been sold before." And lastly, she intended to revitalize education so that the children of Texas would be "given the opportunity to go as far as their ability takes them." At Laredo on 20 July she added one more goal—reform of the state prison system.[9]

Richards's campaign tactics served to provoke Jim Mattox. Richards claimed this agenda as her own, but except for a few minor details, Mattox had also supported all these issues. Consequently, he decided to establish his own arena for combat, his "comfort zone" for dominance—and victory. Mattox first sought to solidify his base of support. In July and August, in his duties as attorney general, he pleased public school teachers by upholding the state law providing for a career ladder; he demonstrated his concern for the average Texan by forcing the chair of the Texas Public Utilities Commission to resign because "the entire concept of regulating utilities . . . [was] a public sham"; and he brusquely threatened two hundred men involved in paternity suits to plead guilty and pay or face penalties. Then he did what he knew best: attack and attack again. To members of the American Federation of Labor–Congress of Industrial Organizations (AFL-CIO) in Houston, whose early endorsement (by a two-thirds majority) was a terrific boost to his candidacy, Mattox boasted that "only he . . . not Richards . . . was tough enough to be governor."[10]

Thus, from Labor Day to the end of 1989, the Democratic gubernatorial campaign deteriorated from accusation to ignominy. Since Mark White mysteriously vacillated until the middle of November from "rumor to run" to a "strong possibility," Mattox had no qualms about trying to destroy his only sure opponent. His actions prompted Molly Ivins of the *Dallas Times Herald* to describe him as "a man so mean he wouldn't spit in your ear if your brains were on fire." On 12 September Mattox accused the Richards campaign of tactics reminiscent of Watergate—of trying to plant a spy in his staff—and demanded an apology. From late September into October he argued that each candidate's health and social habits— alluding to Richards' previous bouts with alcoholism—should be of concern to Texas voters. After the press (almost statewide) rebuked him, calling him "the black knight in Texas politics," he tried to divert such unfavorable publicity. On 10 October Mattox officially announced for governor and launched a twenty-four-hour tour throughout the state. A key plank of his campaign was a state lottery, which would raise money for public education and a "war on crime." Then, to clean up his image with the public and press, he pledged with Richards on 18 October to run a positive campaign — "to stick to issues and avoid personal attacks." But after a *San Antonio Light* poll on 29 October gave Richards 42 percent to his 8 percent, Mattox returned to his old, aggressive tactics in every speech and interview.[11]

Richards was by no means passive. With the help of an able staff, she waged her own war of attack and counterattack. In meetings with Mexican Americans and AFL-CIO members, with whom Mattox had a majority, Richards campaigned vigorously, hoping to maintain more than a third of their support in order to block endorsements. And when Mattox pushed these groups for a simple majority ruling, she characterized him as "a bully." Furthermore, Richards answered every one of Mattox's charges — and leveled some of her own. At a meeting in San Antonio of the Texas Association of Broadcasters, Richards belittled a grim-faced Mattox (who had spoken previously) for promoting a lottery with a "catchy sound bite" designed to elect a governor. "But God forbid [that it be] Jim Mattox," she asserted, because "one must have wisdom to govern." But Richards was not yet done with her adversary. In her campaign autobiography, entitled *Straight from the Heart*, she charged that Mattox, to further his own candidacy, had "sought to scuttle her keynote address to the Democratic National Convention." She also infuriated Mattox with a campaign mailing that featured an endorsement from Sarah Weddington, the defense attorney in the *Roe vs. Wade* case, and listed Mattox with three Republican candidates as opponents of a woman's right to choose. In this manner — through innuendo and one-upsmanship and invective — the Democratic candidates continued to wrangle through the Christmas season of 1989. Nor would the situation improve when Mark White officially joined the fray on 29 November.[12]

Meanwhile, the Republican candidates were equally busy — and becoming increasingly contentious. Late in July the four main contenders began to stir, especially after Clayton Williams received some favorable publicity. On 25 July Jack Rains officially entered the race and monopolized front-page headlines throughout the state for almost a week. As a consequence, Kent Hance geared up his political organization. On 15 August he officially announced for governor, declaring that he was ready to spend $3 million on behalf of a "New Vision for Texas" (his campaign theme). And that meant not only "sweeping changes in the state's education and criminal justice systems" but tax breaks to revitalize the economy and state legislation to restrict abortion. But, most important,

Hance—looking for a crowd-pleasing issue or "straw man" to knock down—came out staunchly for a constitutional amendment to ban a state income tax. And despite an occasional headline that Tom Luce was considering the race for governor, that Rains was organizing his campaign, or that Williams was speaking before carefully chosen, "friendly" groups, the Hance campaign proceeded splendidly through August and the first week of September.[13]

Then came Clayton Williams's media blitzkrieg, which completely unhinged his opponents and reintroduced many Texans to the Texas myth. From mid-September to 1 November his campaign aired five slick, highly effective television commercials. Always in view was Clayton Williams, with ears and smile and cowboy hat. And always in the background were reminders and symbols of the Texas past, complete with campfire and horse and family album. The most effective commercial, which would quickly become a political TV classic, portrayed teenage drug offenders, in convict garb, laboring with sledgehammers in the barren wastes of the Big Bend country. Williams, like a frontier marshal enforcing justice in the Old West, announced, "When our kids get on drugs, that's when Clayton Williams is going to introduce them to the joys of bustin' rock." Still another, equally well done, dealt with state government spending and cost overruns. With the state senate chamber as a backdrop and images of legislators debating, Williams explained the wastefulness of the present state finances—75 printing shops, 40 airplanes, 21,000 automobiles—and proposed a 7 percent budget cut. And, if the "liberal" politicians in Austin thought that they could bypass him as governor, he quipped, "Then they just don't know Clayton Williams."[14]

The forthcoming results were an advertiser's dream. Through numerous thirty-second TV appearances, Clayton Williams fast became a familiar member of many Texas families. "The joys of bustin' rock" and "then they just don't know Clayton Williams" soon were popular catch phrases that Texans relished repeating. In response, Rains began airing TV commercials after 7 October; Luce was relegated to the status of a candidate with an identity crisis; and Hance tried to persuade voters that Williams lacked experience and that the expensive war on drugs, together with a proposed 7 percent budget cut, would unquestionably produce a state income tax. By the end of October, polls showed Williams pulling even with Hance, while Rains and Luce were registering under 5 percent. By the end of 1989 Williams was definitely the front runner.[15]

At the beginning of 1990, with approximately ten weeks until the 13

March primary, the major candidates approached their campaigns with renewed vigor. They all decided that TV and radio were the best ways to reach seventeen million people spread across 254 counties. And they were prepared to invest $50 million if necessary. After all, Clayton Williams had bounded from last to first in the Republican polls after a $2 million media assault of only six weeks. The candidates were still concerned with fund-raising activities, events drawing free media coverage, and endorsements by individuals, organizations, and newspapers; but more than anything else they were searching for the topic, the political gimmick, that would capture the imagination of the voters.[16]

The three Democratic candidates were seasoned campaigners with experienced handlers. During much of January they and their staffs geared up for a final victorious onslaught. Jim Mattox, in the role of attorney general, generated a tremendous amount of news coverage. He was also determined to secure Hispanic and labor endorsements, a move that Ann Richards and Mark White were barely able to prevent by joining forces. In pursuit of those voters on 19 January Mattox (running a poor third in the polls behind White and Richards) seized on what he considered a winning theme—tough-on-crime television commercials. In one, Mattox candidly announced, "As attorney general, I've carried out the death penalty thirty-two times." In another, he told how, as an assistant Dallas County district attorney late in the 1960s, he successfully prosecuted a rapist. Then Mattox concluded, "My opponents say I'm too tough. I learned something twenty years ago. When you're fighting criminals, you've got to be tough."

Mark White's handlers also became convinced that Mattox had touched upon the major concern of Texas voters; after all, Clayton Williams had them repeating "the joys of bustin' rock." So White was persuaded to commit his resources during the six weeks before the primary to a macabre, tasteless commercial. With police mugshots of nineteen prison inmates as a backdrop, White marched before the TV camera and said,

> These hardened criminals will never again murder, rape, or deal drugs. As governor, I made sure they received the ultimate punishment—death. And Texas is a safer place for it. But tough isn't enough. The criminals know how to tangle up the courts and delay executions. To bring them to justice takes strength and dedication, because if the governor flinches, they win. Only a governor can make executions happen. I did, and I will.

In stark contrast to what "Saturday Night Live" satirically described as "Stop me before I kill again commercials," Ann Richards poured money into ads emphasizing home and family, in which she was surrounded by her grown children, with granddaughter Lily Adams on her lap. And it worked. By the middle of February she was leading in most polls, with White and Mattox lagging 7 or 8 percentage points behind.[17]

Then came three Democratic face-offs with the candidates, which columnist Carolyn Barta of the *Dallas Morning News* said was like "seeing the Texas chain-saw massacre." In the first debate at Houston on February 7 all three acquitted themselves reasonably well. They all vowed not to raise taxes; they discussed the merits of a state lottery, with White and Richards denouncing "as a lie" a Mattox TV commercial implying that he was "the only candidate supporting a Texas lottery to raise revenues." And they agreed upon a prochoice stand. But in one exchange Richards made what Mattox described (and White concurred) as a "white feminist fringe" slip. In discussing the issue, Richards said, "I cannot arrive at any conclusion but that no legislator, no judge, and no bureaucrat has any business in determining whether a white woman has an abortion or not."[18]

So the battle was joined, with all three Democratic candidates becoming infected with the "sleaze virus." Mattox exultantly exploited the "white woman" comment, asserting that such a mind-set was typical of Richards. For instance, he noted that in a 1976 speech she had referred to a Mexican American as a "wetback." Both Mattox and White realized, however, that the greatest chink in the Richards armor had to do with a possible history of drug abuse. Hence, they opened up their medical records and demanded that she do the same. When Richards countered by announcing that she had "taken no mind-altering chemicals for ten years," they continued to hammer her, as one writer put it, "with all the sanctimoniousness they could muster." In the second Democratic debate in Dallas on 2 March, they pressed her "to answer the question," because, as Mattox pragmatically asserted, "Clayton Williams will do more than just bust rocks. He'll bust our party and . . . the candidates that are in our party." In reply, Richards still maintained her stance of having answered the question "repeatedly." Any other response, she believed, would further enlarge the parameters of the controversy.[19]

Ann Richards was in trouble politically — and she knew it. With polls on 25 February showing that White had passed her and that Mattox was moving up, she decided that issues alone would not sustain her at this juncture in the campaign. Whether acting out of desperation or from conviction, Richards went on the offensive on 5 March, lashing out at her two opponents. At a news conference in Austin she stated that she would "reveal no more about her personal life." Then she announced: "I have been sober for ten years. Have Jim Mattox and Mark White been honest for ten years?" More specifically, she asserted, "These failed politicians of the past . . . [were] unfit to run" because both had "enrich[ed]" themselves "at public expense." At the same time Richards aired statewide TV spots that continued this attack on their integrity. And at the third and last TV debate on 7 March she defended herself against the charges of "gutter politics" by a visibly angry Mark White and an acerbic Jim Mattox. When they both volunteered to take a drug test, she quipped that a "lie detector test" would be more appropriate. Then she deftly explained, "Everybody knows that ten years ago I went to a hospital . . . where I was treated for alcoholism, and have had a wonderful ten years and a joyful recovery. I have made speeches all over the country about the joys of recovery, and the fact that if you need help, and you can get help, you can have a better life." Richards thus shifted the focus from "illegal drug use" to "recovery," concluding that to the question "about exactly what I did and when I did it, . . . my response has been . . . to get help, and you can put your past behind you."[20]

For that important week prior to the primary Richards did put her past behind her. She redirected the focus of the campaign, and to her advantage. White was unsettled by this attack on his character; rather than concentrating on getting out his voters, he changed his schedule, the *Dallas Morning News* noted, "to answer allegations." Mattox was outwardly unaffected; he understood this type of campaign and met the challenge with a massive TV onslaught. On 13 March, Texans delivered the verdict as to the effectiveness of the three campaigns. Richards led with 39.3 percent to a surprising 37 percent for Mattox and a disappointing 19 percent for White. One battle had ended, but another was about to begin. The runoff was a month away.[21]

The Republican campaign during the ten weeks prior to the 13 March primary was equally heated and venomous at first. The major problem for Williams's three opponents was how to slow down, if not derail, his political onslaught. It would surely be difficult. On 16 January he loaned himself $3.2 million to finance the last eight weeks of the campaign. His handlers also protected him from direct confrontations with his opponents whenever possible and came up with publicity stunts that he could appreciate and be comfortable with. For instance, on 31 January, he led a group of retired Texas Rangers in a convoy of eighteen-wheelers on a two-hundred-mile trip from Grand Prairie (just west of Dallas) to Austin. On the Capitol walkway, with cameras flashing, he was "in his element," vowing "to deregulate trucking in Texas" because transportation fees were outrageously high. Not only was he siding with the average working Texan, but he was also taking a shot at his nearest rival, Railroad Commissioner Hance.[22]

All three Republican adversaries were confident that "Claytie," as he liked to be called, would stumble; but to make sure, they were ready to give him a nudge, if not a shove. Kent Hance was not discouraged. On 6 January he announced that Marine Lt. Col. Oliver North of the Reagan administration Iran-Contra operation had agreed to attend two fundraisers in February. Two days later he began operating a pay-per-call solicitation drive that would allow voters, for a mere $5.95 per call, to give money to the campaign as well as endorse his candidacy. Although Jack Rains tried to focus on substantive issues, Hance, together with Luce, uncovered evidence that Williams had been involved in two fistfights a few years previously, noting that addressing problems in that fashion may have been appropriate in 1890 but was now unbecoming for a chief executive. In turn, Luce attacked Williams for using slogans instead of "talking substance," especially in regard to 7 percent budget cuts in state spending and the financing of a monumental drug program. When all four men met in Houston for a TV debate on 7 February, Williams was, as he put it, "under constant fire." But short answers and pleasant euphemisms and a "wide grin" served him well. Typical of the evening was his remark to the press, "I didn't realize I had so many faults until it became known I was a front-runner."[23]

On 14 February the Republican race for governor became a rout. Thirty miles south of Abilene, four of Williams's longtime business associates died in a plane crash. He immediately canceled all personal appearances for the week and suspended all of his commercials; he then went to be with the wives and families and friends of the victims. Finally after five days, during which time all Texans wondered whether he would continue the campaign, he announced that because "the heartache and grief were so overwhelming . . . I considered dropping out of the governor's race." But since the friends who had died in the crash were the ones who first offered "counsel and encouragement" when he was deciding to run, he would keep faith with their wishes and "be back in the saddle."

From that moment forward Williams gained increasing momentum. Within a week he was leading Hance statewide by 20 percentage points and in the El Paso area alone by 42 percent. Newspaper analysts discussed his "mystique" and described him as a "political phenomenon," a "rising star in Texas politics" — indeed "a Texas version of Ronald Reagan." And his three opponents in the next television debate on 1 March were, the *Houston Post* reported, "all perfect gentlemen." Thus, on 13 March, Texas voters confirmed the verdict rendered four weeks earlier. Williams won a landslide victory with 61 percent of the vote, and Texas Republicans were giddily anticipating a fall coronation.[24]

But the voters would first have to select a Democratic opponent. Both Mattox and Richards agreed on election night that they would run "an upbeat" race, that is, unless "attacked." On 22 March, however, all such hopes vanished when Mattox, in a WOAI-AM radio interview, announced that Richards "should answer the questions concerning her own drug usage and she should talk about such things, for instance who supplied her or what she did, how often she did it, what kinda drugs were used — issues such as that." The "demolition derby" was on — and continued unabated. Both camps realized that TV was essential to getting their messages across; therefore, they were determined to raise $1 million for the runoff (which they did in three weeks). Mattox hammered at Richards incessantly, even claiming that she had used cocaine. He next questioned whether she was "tough enough" to be governor, since she was obviously "ducking debates" on this issue. A week prior to the election, he bolstered his campaign by receiving the endorsement of Mark White, who likened Richards to "Nazi war criminal Heinrich Himmler" for her "cold-blooded" campaign against him. In turn, Richards claimed that Mattox was unethical; he was still refusing to release previous income tax statements. And as for his "multiple addiction" charges "without proof," she replied, "Jim Mattox is a desperate man" who is trying to "find an issue that will be as full of tar and mud as he can get it." Then both capped their mud-slinging campaigns with a barrage of thirty-second TV commercials. In one of them Mattox pictured Richards's face with questions superimposed in bold type, which an off-stage announcer repeated: "Did she use marijuana, or something worse like cocaine? Not as a college kid but as a 47-year-old elected official sworn to uphold the law." Richards's advertisement, in contrast, depicted the caricature of an animated Jim Mattox "with his arms going in circles, hurling mud all over a picture of Richards and her granddaughter Lily." Then an off-stage voice said, "Jim Mattox. He's at it again. The same old politics. Mudslinging and negative campaigning."[25]

This old-fashioned Texas mudslide continued until 10 April, although Mattox sensed the bitter outcome before then. To *Fort Worth Star-Telegram* reporter Joe Cutbirth, he summed up the long campaign this way: "Texas Democrats," he lamented, "didn't care about competence or record; they just wanted to elect a woman." And, whether correct or not in that evaluation, he was surely right as to outcome. On 10 April, Richards won impressively by 57 to 43 percent. The race for governor was dubbed "Claytie Versus the Lady."[26]

For almost two weeks after the 13 March primary Williams basked in the spotlight of political victory, ecstatic and exultant in his new-found prominence, confident of and trusting in the continuation of what several journalists had called a near-perfect campaign. All three of his opponents — Hance, Luce, and Rains — endorsed him immediately and pledged their support. Mark White, as well as many conservative Democrats, were furious with Richards and not terribly pleased with Mattox; hence, Williams was enthusiastically seeking both their endorsement and support. The news media were also effusive in their praise and glowing in their reports; after all, he was good copy.[27]

Late in March, however, Williams began to experience hostility from the news media that caused the wheels of his well-oiled political machine to wobble, if not almost collapse. In Washington on 20 March he candidly replied to a question regarding his choice of a Democratic opponent, "Jim Mattox," because "I would be more uncomfortable and cautious running against a woman." Thus the next day's headline read, "Williams Admits He'd Prefer a Male Opponent." Then, on 25 March, Williams provided the media with enough ammunition to last for weeks. At a public relations photo opportunity, bringing scores of journalists, photographers, and TV crews to a roundup on his 26,438-acre ranch near Alpine, Williams startled his handlers by exposing personal thinking and attitudes (unrehearsed and live) more in sync with the West's historic past than with modern Texas. Around a chuckwagon campfire early that morning, Williams, decked out in the working gear of a cowboy, moved about drinking coffee and cordially chatting with his guests while waiting for a dense fog to lift. Then he unwittingly shared an old West Texas witticism with them. "The weather is like rape," he announced for all to hear. "If it's inevitable, just relax and enjoy it." In the furor that followed, Williams repeatedly apologized for his "insensitivity," for his "terrible mistake" in trying to be humorous, but to no avail. The news media and women's groups continually reminded him of this egregious error, and his handlers nervously began to program their candidate against another similar occurrence.[28]

Yet Williams, despite such gaffes, maintained his popularity with Texans; in fact, polls had him ahead of Richards by as much as 22 percentage points during May and June. With these statistics in mind, his advisers laid out a strategy for victory. They definitely were determined to avoid political pitfalls. That meant a carefully arranged schedule but, more important, no debates with Richards. Williams also must not appear to be hostile because, judging from Jim Mattox's experience, voters react "more negatively to a male candidate who attacks a woman than to a woman candidate who attacks a man." At the same time, Williams must not give Richards the opportunity to stress his inexperience in government and his naivete regarding some issues. His handlers decided that Williams should focus on "home and apple pie" concerns, such as no new taxes, while allowing Republican "attack dogs" to cast aspersions and innuendoes at Richards. Then for the last four months of the campaign, with the aid of substantial monetary contributions, they would flood the news media with commercials that would continue to present Claytie as a family member who treasured the "old values."[29]

With this agenda laid out, Williams seemed to follow the guidance of his professional advisers rather dutifully, without many slips and not much political damage. Late in April he candidly admitted to a *Houston Post* journalist (who had supposedly received a tip from the Richards' camp) that prostitutes had "serviced" him when he was sixteen, and also at Texas A&M University. He then explained that "it's part of growing up in West Texas" and that "it was kind of what boys did at A&M." But, he announced, "I've never claimed to be a perfect man. If doing drugs ten years ago [obviously referring to Richards] is all right, then certainly I think going to a Mexican border town forty years ago is all right." Again in July to a reporter of *U.S. News & World Report*, who questioned his use of the word "serviced," he ingenuously stated, "In the world I live in of bulls and cattlemen, you talk about the bull servicing the cow. I was trying to find a nice, polite term for [a crude term for sexual intercourse beginning with f]."[30]

Such explanations seemed to satisfy most Texans, if not the news media. Through the summer, therefore, Williams was able to follow a prepared script and maintain an imposing lead. During May and June he participated in several huge fundraisers (grossing over $4 million) in Dallas and Houston with either Pres. George Bush or Vice-Pres. Dan

Quayle. He addressed friendly audiences, such as the independent oil and gas producers and, except for one scheduling mishap on 26 May, was never on the same platform with Richards. He also endorsed a constitutional amendment outlawing the desecration of the American flag at a Veterans of Foreign Wars convention, no new taxes to a "select 500" at the Petroleum Club in Fort Worth, and a prolife stance to an antiabortion assemblage. Late in July, during a two-day "Claytie Country Caravan" through rural East Texas, he denounced Richards's values as being out of step with those of most Texans. Then the Williams's camp launched a two-pronged offensive. First was a barrage of thirty-second TV commercials featuring Williams in cowboy gear, with cows and horses in the background. In one ad he looked squarely into the camera and asked Texans "to give this fella a whack at that budget. I'll find enough money to build some prisons, hire some lawmen, and save some to boot." In another he bragged about founding "twenty-six companies" and creating "100,000 jobs in fifty Texas towns and cities," intimating that he would achieve comparable results as governor. And secondly, to keep Richards off balance and on the defensive, the state Republican party aired widespread radio commercials, accusing Richards of "favoring a state income tax" and "supporting the liberal agenda of the gay and lesbian caucus." Williams disavowed any complicity in these attacks but expressed "confidence" that the party could "document its charges."[31]

In combatting this Republican onslaught, Richards had major problems to overcome. She had to reorganize her staff and establish her campaign goals, first among them raising money (at least $6 million) in order to be competitive on TV during the last two months of the campaign. She needed not only to secure her Democratic grass-roots base but enlarge it considerably by galvanizing the women of Texas into solid support. The voters were to be sold on Richards's experience in government, her knowledge of financial matters, her desire to help all Texans. And, equally important, they must unmask the media myth of Clayton Williams. Or, as one adviser put it, Richards's staff needed to "make people see Clayton Williams himself, rather than Clayton Williams starring as John Wayne."[32]

With these objectives in mind, the Richards camp worked to slow down the Williams juggernaut and, if possible, take the offensive. The progress of the campaign was at first discouraging. During much of April, Richards personally telephoned a number of key Mattox and White supporters, asking them to take leadership roles in her campaign. She appointed trusted individuals, such as Lena Guerrero, to build a massive get-out-the-vote program and others, equally as competent, to shore up her strength in rural counties as well as solidify her growing strength with women. Eventually, in July, she selected Lt. Gov. Bill Hobby of Houston, former mayor Henry Cisneros of San Antonio, and former U.S. congresswoman Barbara Jordan as her campaign cochairs. On numerous political stops (from April through July) Richards stressed abortion rights, better schools, higher pay for teachers, and the promotion of state businesses nationwide, but seemingly with minimal results. Then in July, with Williams's million-dollar TV campaign and the state Republican party assault on her values, she found herself on the defensive and her campaign going nowhere. In several polls she was anywhere from 13 to 26 percentage points behind.[33]

Richards and her staff realized that the campaign had to reach a new level of intensity, one that would unsettle her opponent and disrupt his obviously effective strategy. Their plan was to attack Williams as Richards's "invisible" opponent. Whenever possible Richards needled him, challenging him to debate her—to "quit hiding behind the skirts of various women" and "his goofy grin" and to "come out and fight like a man." And with Republicans claiming that "Richards is an honorary lesbian," she had no qualms in questioning any aspect of his career and character, including his virility.[34]

Hence the attacks on Williams became increasingly harsh and personal. Beginning in August the Richards camp unleashed a series of devastatingly clever radio and TV commercials undermining Williams's media image as well as his reputation as a successful businessman. The first TV spots combined a picture of Richards, and then an off-stage announcer said: "Behind the screen on Claytie TV . . . It's a lot different. . . . Over three hundred lawsuits documented in court records and newspapers. Mountains of debt. Millions in junk bonds. Allegations of fraud and price fixing. His own employees had to sue him for back pay. And that's just the public record. His court records are sealed in secrecy and he refuses to disclose his income taxes." And then the announcer asked: "What else is behind the screen? Stay tuned." Two weeks later Richards launched a new series of ads on 22 August that portrayed her opponent as an antienvironmentalist and a polluter. One commercial said, in part, "The state of Texas has had to stop Clayton Williams seven times for his oil pollution. Who'll stop him if he's governor? Stay tuned"; from another thirty-second spot, "He has been repeatedly cited for polluting our environment. A record so bad the Railroad Commission says Williams . . . 'has a history of violating pollution rules.' . . . One of his oil spills endangered [the city of] Brenham's water supply. Stay tuned."[35]

Although Williams asked for "a truce" on negative campaigning, Richards was not about to let up: "Your pattern of activity over the past three months has been to appear to take the 'high road' while letting the Republican Party and your surrogates wage a hateful, vitriolic campaign. I do not intend to be fooled again." Richards thus continued to goad him at every turn, asking why he was "afraid" to debate her and whether or not he would disclose his income tax returns. When a Travis County grand jury began investigating alleged illegal insurance activities by his Clay-Desta National Bank, she reminded voters that Bill Clements, the present governor, had also been involved in a major scandal (within a week after his election in 1986). And as for Williams's support of a voucher system for Texas schools, Richards ridiculed him as "a man that doesn't have the foggiest idea of what's going on in a public school."[36]

Into September the ridicule and invective raged. As the candidates stepped up the tempo, Richards's strategy of dispelling the Clayton Williams myth began to succeed. Or as Richards later recollected: "We knew, we knew that [given sufficient time and enough prodding] he was going to blow!" And Williams did; the gaffes began to multiply. At Duncanville on 31 August he bragged to a large crowd of supporters that he was going to "head and hoof [hogtie] Ann Richards and drag her through the dirt." In reply, the Richards camp announced that "it's not the first time that Clayton Williams has likened women to cattle." On learning that Richards had announced at a party celebrating the tenth anniversary of her sobriety that one poll showed her only 6 percentage points behind, Williams quipped to reporters, "I hope she didn't go back to drinking again." Williams later said that he had made "a poor choice of words."[37]

Several political analysts predicted that the election was still Williams's to win or lose. A *Dallas Times Herald* poll had him 15 points ahead on 1 October. But as one pundit sarcastically quipped, "He snatched defeat out of the jaws of victory." On 11 October Williams and Richards appeared jointly—the first time in over four months—before the Greater Dallas Crime Commission. With a crowd of one thousand watching as Richards approached the dais, Williams turned to a friend and said, "Watch this!" Disdainfully he refused to shake her extended hand and said, "I'm here to call you a liar today." She replied, "I'm sorry, Clayton," but he angrily continued, "That's what you are. You've lied about me. You've lied about

Mark White. You've lied about Jim Mattox. I'm going to finish this deal today and you can count on it."[38]

Williams was right, but not in the way he had envisioned. From that day forward the gubernatorial contest changed momentum. Newspapers across the state blistered him for bad manners, for not being "a gentleman," for embarrassing a woman. Henry Cisneros, who had been relatively quiet in the campaign, "stumped" the Rio Grande Valley, calling on Hispanic men "to defend a lady's honor." Bob Bullock, Democratic candidate for lieutenant governor, who had earlier distanced himself from Richards, now became her champion in a "holy cause." While campaigning in South Texas, he announced, "You men, now you listen to me! In Texas a man shakes a woman's hand! I'm here to tell you Clayton Williams is no man!" And the Richards camp capitalized on the faux pas with two TV commercials. One, entitled "Clayton Williams, in His Own Words," quoted four gaffes. Then the voice-over quizzically said, "Governor Williams?" The other was a most appealing scene, picturing Richards with her aged father. Looking straight into the camera, she lamented, "When my father was in his seventies, his health insurance was canceled. And he has no recourse, no place to go, because health insurance in this state is not regulated." She then promised, as governor, that such injustices would cease. And no matter that Clayton Williams launched several new TV ads, no matter that President Bush, Vice-President Quayle, and other Republican luminaries campaigned for him in Texas. Nonetheless, Williams was now fighting just to maintain his standing. During the last week in October several polls indicated that the race was too close to call.[39]

Then, in its last ten days of the campaign, the Williams campaign became a model of what a candidate should never do. In the course of a televised interview in Dallas he revealed that he had already voted absentee; therefore, the questioner asked, "How did you vote on Proposition 1?" To the amazement of both panelists and viewers, he professed ignorance of its contents, even though the amendment had to do with changing the timing of gubernatorial appointments. After the taping he compounded his error by announcing: "I wasn't highly informed on Proposition 1, but my wife was. She told me what to do." Three days later, even as the shock of this comment reverberated across the state, Williams voluntarily revealed to a reporter what Richards had been trying to find out since June—that he had "paid no income tax in 1986 . . . it was a bad year." Later in the day, while visiting his alma mater, Texas A&M

University, Williams attempted to smooth over the gaffe by saying that he had "paid millions of dollars in taxes, but not in 1986."[40]

Nothing more was needed. Richards's staff immediately prepared a radio commercial that charged Williams with using "loopholes in the law to avoid paying taxes" and that "millions of average Texans paid taxes . . . our share . . . and his." The commercial concluded, "Ms. Richards pays her taxes just like you. And she'll be a governor on our side."[41]

Even before election day on 6 November the outcome was assured. In North Dallas, the Republican Women's Caucus announced that Richards was their choice, partly over Williams's antiabortion stance and partly because of his offensive comments during the campaign. Governor Clements ridiculed Williams for his ignorance of the issues. Tom Luce, who had masterminded the state public education system, opposed Williams's voucher system. Even Mark White, who had sworn never to vote for Richards, announced that he was backing the Democratic ticket. Soon after the polls closed the numbers verified the obvious trend. Richards won with 52 percent of the vote, and for the first time in Texas history a woman had captured the governorship solely on her own credentials.[42]

CHAPTER 17

The Emergence of a Republican Majority in Utah, 1970–1992

THOMAS G. ALEXANDER

Between 1970 and 1992, the structure of Utah politics changed from relative parity between the Republican and Democratic parties to domination by the GOP. Far from resulting simply from a single factor such as the oft-cited power of the Church of Jesus Christ of Latter-day Saints (LDS, or Mormon), the change followed an extremely complex set of transformations in the economic and political culture of the state and the region.[1] In general, however, the influences most responsible were closely associated with the evolution of Utah from a colony under the domination of eastern capitalists and the federal government to a semiautochthonous state in which local people controlled an appreciable percentage of business enterprise.

The changes themselves have had at least two important results. First, the people of Utah generally approved of the changes; and, as ordinarily happens in political democracies, they registered that approval by voting for the party in power. In doing so, the majority of Utah voters adopted the Republican party's culture, which emphasized political and social conservatism. Second, as the leadership of the LDS church generally approved of the conservative political and social culture, they gained support from those people in the state who favored the changes as well. At the same time, those who disliked the new culture or who favored reforms not possible under that political culture attributed the changes to the influence of the LDS church rather than to the alteration of underlying conditions. In the process a new religiously based political alignment has replaced the former political system in which members of all religious traditions worked through both major parties. The new realignment seems almost like a reincarnation of the system of the nineteenth century in which the most active Mormons joined the People's party and everyone else supported the Liberal party.[2]

Republican party domination in Utah is a recent phenomenon. After achieving statehood in 1896 until the realignment of the 1970s and 1980s, Utah generally followed national trends.[3] After electing a Republican governor and legislative majority in the special election of 1895 called to inaugurate statehood, Utahns (along with the remainder of the Mountain West) flipped into the Democratic column in the elections of 1896 and 1898. In 1896 Utah cast 83 percent of its vote for Democrat William Jennings Bryan, the largest margin received by any presidential candidate in the state's history, at the same time sweeping Democrats into both houses of the state legislature, the federal House of Representatives, and the open U.S. Senate seat. This resulted from the depression of the early 1890s and the antagonism of the national Republican party to the free coinage of silver, crucial in a state with a colonial economy reliant on extractive industries including a massive—but depressed—mining industry.

Unlike the change in Utah politics since 1970, however, the votes of the late 1890s did not constitute a fundamental shift in political culture. Following the return of good times by 1900, Utah moved with the rest of the nation into the Republican column until the teens. Between 1900 and 1912, Republicans dominated the legislature, the governorship, and the congressional delegation. The emergence of the Progressive movement after 1910 eroded Republican party strength until a 1916 landslide carried Democrat Simon Bamberger, a Jewish immigrant businessman, into the governor's chair. Following the red scare after World War I, the Republican party controlled the legislature throughout the 1920s, though it lost the governorship in 1924 to Democratic businessman George H. Dern, who continued to serve until 1933 when he became Franklin Delano Roosevelt's secretary of war.

Reacting to the hard times of a depression that generated 36 percent unemployment in the Beehive State, Utahns swept the Democratic party into power in 1932. The New Deal coalition continued to control the state government and the congressional delegation until a postwar reaction in 1946 restored balance.

Most important for the analysis of recent events, however, during the depression of the 1930s, Utah citizens handed the LDS church some of its most striking political defeats. Removing Republican LDS Apostle Reed Smoot from the U.S. Senate in the 1932 elections, Utahns in 1933 cast the deciding votes in a referendum repealing the Eighteenth Amendment, in spite of official LDS support for Prohibition. In 1936, Utahns gave 69 percent of their votes to presidential candidate Franklin D. Roosevelt in the face of an editorial campaign against him in the LDS-owned *Deseret News* and antagonism against New Deal programs by church President Heber J. Grant and First Counselor J. Reuben Clark.

The 1946 election marked the reemergence of essential parity between the two parties. In 1946, Republican antigovernment maverick J. Bracken Lee won the governorship; and the GOP captured a majority in the state house of representatives as well as one of the congressional seats. Between 1946 and 1974, the Republican party captured the state house of representatives eight times, the Democratic party prevailed six times, and in the 1951 house the two parties shared equal representation. The Democratic party captured the state senate seven times, and the Republican party controlled it six times. Two Democrats (Herbert B. Maw, a former University of Utah professor and Democratic holdover; and attorney Calvin L. Rampton, Utah's only three-term governor) and two Republicans (Lee, a political maverick from Price, and George P. Clyde, a hydraulics engineer and former Utah State University dean) sat in the governor's chair during the period. Five Republicans served a total of thirty-two years and five Democrats served an aggregated twenty-eight years in the U.S. House. Three Republicans and two Democrats held seats in the U.S. Senate. Between 1946 and 1972 Utah generally voted with the national majority in presidential elections and in majorities quite near national figures. The major exception was in 1960, when 55 percent of Utah voters supported Richard Nixon while John Kennedy took a narrow national victory.

A sort of a balance wheel seemed to function. When the Republican party won overwhelming control of the state house of representatives (as in its 86 percent showing in 1966), the majority eroded within four years, eventually returning the Democratic party to power in 1970. The last time, however, that the Democratic party won a majority in either house of the state legislature was in the 1974 election, when it gained 53 percent of the seats in the house and a one-seat majority in the senate.

Between 1976 and 1993, the Democratic party failed to elect a majority in either house of the legislature, and after 1980 it lost every gubernatorial bid. Its power in the state eroded like a riverbank in the face of a surging Republican flood. The shift to the Republican party in presidential politics became just as evident. Between 1964 and 1972, Utah followed the national trend in each quadrennial election. In 1976 however, 65 percent of Utah voters supported Gerald Ford, who lost nationally in a close race with Georgia Gov. Jimmy Carter.

After the 1976 election, the erosion of Democratic strength seemed abundantly evident. In 1980 and 1984, 72 and 73 percent of Utah voters supported Republican Ronald Reagan, the highest since Bryan's victory in 1896, topping even Franklin Roosevelt's showing in 1936.[4] In gubernatorial politics, election results since 1976 tell a similar story. The election of moderate Democratic attorney Scott M. Matheson in 1976 over a badly divided Republican ticket masked the underlying strength of the GOP tide.[5] Matheson won again in 1980, but since 1984 Republicans have held the governor's post continuously. The closest contest came in 1988 when a former contractor, Republican incumbent Norman H. Bangerter, carried only 41 percent of the vote against 39 percent for Salt Lake City's Democratic Mayor Ted Wilson, and 21 percent for antitax Republican businessman Merrill Cook, who ran as an independent. Bangerter, who had previously served as senate president, got the undeserved nickname "old pump and tax" because he helped to solve severe problems caused by Great Salt Lake flooding by pumping excess water into the west desert and because he recommended a tax hike in 1987 to provide much-needed funding for Utah's public schools.[6]

With some exceptions, Utah's congressional delegation has reflected the Republican domination. In 1974, former Salt Lake City mayor and businessman Jake Garn defeated Democratic Second District congressman and attorney Wayne Owens with 50 percent of the vote in a hard-fought contest for the U.S. Senate. Garn went on to gain national notoriety as the nation's only astronaut-senator. In 1976, conservative Republican attorney Orrin Hatch with 54 percent of the vote beat incumbent Democratic moderate Senator Frank Moss, also an attorney.

Until the 1980 census gave Utah a third congressional seat, the state had had two congressmen since 1912. During the 1970s, Utah's First Congressional District included northern, central, and eastern Utah, and the Second District consisted of Salt Lake County and the tier of counties stretching southward along the state's western border. After 1980, Salt Lake County enclosed the entire Second Congressional District, but because the county's population was so large, both the First Congressional District (which included northern Utah and the counties running along the state's western border) and the Third Congressional District (which reached from Utah County across the central and eastern counties to the Colorado and Arizona borders) included parts of Salt Lake County.

Most of the federal congressional elections have gone to the Republican party. Since he defeated incumbent Democrat Gunn McKay in 1980,

Republican businessman Jim Hansen has held the First District seat. In 1976 the Salt Lake City police caught one-term Democratic Congressman Allen Howe propositioning a decoy posing as a prostitute. Refusing to drop out of the race as more savvy colleagues advised him, Howe lost to Republican businessman Dan Marriott. The Republicans continued to hold the Second District seat until 1986, when Wayne Owens defeated Salt Lake County Commissioner Tom Shimizu. Owens held the seat until 1992, when he ran unsuccessfully for the U.S. Senate seat vacated by his former opponent Garn. In the 1992 election, however, Democratic businesswoman Karen Shepherd defeated Republican attorney Enid Greene for Owens's seat.

After winning handily in 1982 in the first election in the Third Congressional District against inept token opposition, Howard Nielsen, a Brigham Young University professor and conservative Republican, held the seat until he retired in 1990. In 1990, however, conservative Democratic tax attorney Bill Orton beat conservative Brigham Young University Professor Karl Snow and a badly divided Republican party. In 1992 Republican Richard Harrington's attempt to portray Orton as a spend-and-tax liberal Democrat failed, and Orton won easily with a whopping 59 percent of the vote.[7]

Before 1976, votes in Utah's counties seem to have balanced the two parties.[8] Since the mid-1970s, however, changes in party strength have altered the geographic composition of the state's politics among the state's most populous and fastest-growing counties. The most significant changes have taken place along the urbanized Wasatch Front. From a strongly Democratic county, Weber County has become independent. Once independent but Democratic-leaning Salt Lake County has become merely independent. Both Utah County, formerly independent-Democratic, and Davis County, formerly independent, have become strongly Republican. Washington County, formerly an independent stronghold in Utah's otherwise heavily Republican "Dixie" (as Utah's southwestern corner is called), has become strongly Republican as well. In fact, Carbon is the only county the Democratic party can count on. Even formerly strongly Democratic Tooele County may be seen as independent-Democratic. The one county that may have shifted from its previously Republican orientation to become independent is rural Grand in southeastern Utah, largely because of a rapidly growing environmentalist contingent.[9]

The changing composition of contributions to Utah's state election campaign fund reflects the shift toward the Republican party as well. Utah taxpayers can check a box on their state income tax returns to direct the state to contribute $1 to an election fund. Unlike the federal system, which is nonpartisan, Utah voters must designate the party to receive their contribution. In 1974, 51 percent of the $101,500 total went to the Democratic party, 39 percent to the Republican party, and 9 percent to the American party. In 1976 for the first time contributions to the Democratic party fell behind those to the Republican party (45 percent to 48 percent, although the total—$34,900—was lower). Since that time, the Democratic party has consistently received less than the Republicans. In 1987, for instance, the Republican party received 56 percent of the total while the Democratic party got 44 percent.[10]

Why has this happened? Certainly the fundamental reason has been the general economic prosperity and the shift toward a semiautochthonous economy during a period of Republican administrations in Utah and the nation. Utah suffered from the stagflation and succeeding recession that began in 1979 during the Carter administration and left the state with a rising unemployment rate that reached 9.2 percent in 1983. The Reagan reelection campaign undoubtedly benefited from the decline in unemployment to 6.5 percent in 1984. Thereafter, Utah's unemployment rate continued to decline to 4.9 percent in 1988 and to 4.6 percent in 1989. Even during the national recession of 1991–92, Utah's unemployment rate ranged consistently below 4.9 percent until late 1992 when it briefly topped 5 percent. At the same time, the national unemployment level ranged consistently above 7 percent, reaching 7.7 percent in the summer of 1992.[11]

In large part, Utah's vigorous performance resulted from a basic alteration in the structure of the economy.[12] Between 1900, when the LDS church withdrew as a major force in Utah's economic growth, and World War II, when the federal government invested heavily in defense industries in Utah, the Beehive State's colonial economy prospered at the sufferance of absentee—generally eastern—capitalists. In the process, the Guggenheims, Rockefellers, and Hearsts invested heavily in Utah's mining industry; the monopolistic American Sugar Refining Company bought a controlling interest in the beet sugar industry; and a national utility holding company acquired Utah Power and Light.

During World War II a second strain of colonialism infected Utah as the federal government became a major absentee employer. By 1950 Utah looked like the typical postwar colonial mountain state. The state relied heavily on extractive industries such as mining, which employed 5.3

percent of the labor force, and agriculture, where 12.4 percent worked; transportation (especially railroads), which employed 9.7 percent; and government, which employed 9.4 percent.[13] Ogden and northern Davis County, in 1950 still significant centers for the colonialist Southern and Union Pacific railroads, were virtual federal colonies heavily reliant for their prosperity upon defense installations such as Hill Air Force Base and Utah General Depot. Manufacturing in Utah, which employed 12.2 percent of the labor force, consisted principally of the primary processing of the products of Utah's mines and farms—particularly copper, lead, sugar beets, and truck crops. Salt Lake County depended on trade, mining, and the products of the county's smelters. Utah County was heavily dependent on Geneva Steel Corporation (a subsidiary of USX), Brigham Young University, and agriculture.

With the exception of Tooele County, which had a heavy defense commitment in Tooele Army Depot and Dugway Proving Grounds and an active mining and smelting industry, and Carbon and Emery counties, which boasted significant coal production, the rest of Utah relied heavily on crop agriculture, ranching, trade, and some oil and uranium extraction. Irrigated commercial agriculture—sugar beets and truck crops—and dairy production dominated in Cache and Box Elder counties in northern Utah. In the rural counties of eastern Utah and those south of the Wasatch Front, farmers generally relied on general agriculture and on ranching. Exceptions were Sanpete County, where in addition a thriving turkey industry had begun to develop, and the Uinta Basin and southeastern Utah, where oil and uranium added a dimension to the economy.

By 1988 all of that had changed. Extractive industries like agriculture and mining had declined in importance in the state. Only 1.5 percent of Utahns—less than half the national average—worked in agriculture. Mining had declined to 1.2 percent of the nonagricultural labor force. While still employing Utahns at a rate well above the national average, mining no longer dominated the economy as it had before 1950. Employment in transportation and communications had declined from 11.3 percent of the nonagricultural labor force to 6 percent. Only government employment at 21.6 of nonagricultural labor remained as a major vestige of the colonial pattern. But government employment represented the new colonial economy dominated by Washington rather than the old colonial pattern controlled by Wall Street.

During the 1970's, Utah's economy began to turn a corner. A new, increasingly self-directed economy emerged as Utah entrepreneurs began to generate much of the state's growth internally. By the late 1980s Utah had developed a postindustrial and postcolonial economy that others might have envied.

An analysis of the twenty-four largest employers in the state published in September 1992 reveals the dimensions of the new semiautochthonous pattern.[14] Of the top twenty-four, three are federal installations (Hill Air Force Base, Internal Revenue Service Center, and Tooele Army Depot), representing the new colonial economy, with a total employment of 27,342. Of the remaining twenty-one, however, only five firms — Thiokol, Delta Air Lines, U.S. West, Kennecott, and Hercules — with a total of 19,200 employees are based outside of Utah. They are the major vestiges of the old colonial economy. The other sixteen largest employers, with a total of 94,431 workers, are local.

Most significant has been the growth of a group of electronics and other high-tech firms in Wasatch Front cities. One of Utah's largest employers, WordPerfect Corporation in Orem, the largest developer, manufacturer, and supplier of word-processing programs in the world, started in 1979. Employing only 16 people in 1982, WordPerfect's work force had grown to nearly 2,300 by 1990.[15] Provo is the home of 1983-founded Novell, which employed 1,200 in 1990 and has become one of the nations's major computer network developers and suppliers. Evans and Sutherland of Salt Lake employed 1,300 people in the design of computer hardware and software for use in graphics applications and flight simulation. In 1990 Iomega employed nearly 1,000 at its plant in Roy, where it produced and supplied various types of computer hardware, especially its Bernoulli removable hard disks and tape-backup systems. Unisys, located in Salt Lake City (although the company isn't based there), employed nearly 2,300 in the development of hardware and software for mainframe computers and communications systems for the Department of Defense and other agencies. These developments have benefited from the location of three of Utah's other major employers, Brigham Young University, University of Utah, and Utah State University, each with excellent computer science, scientific, and engineering programs.[16]

Responding to changes in the economy represented by these high-tech businesses, the composition of manufacturing employment changed dramatically. Although the percentage of those employed in manufacturing remained at about the same level over the forty years from 1950 to 1990, the type of manufacturing changed dramatically. In 1950 virtually all major manufacturing resided in the colonial economy and consisted principally of the primary processing of metals and agricultural products. By 1990 electronic and aerospace manufacturing came to predominate. The production of electronic equipment expanded from 1.8 percent to 13.2 percent of manufacturing earnings. At the same time the manufacture of transportation equipment—largely aerospace related—expanded from 14.6 percent to 21.3 percent of manufacturing earnings.[17] Much of the aerospace manufacturing has been carried on by two colonial companies at plants in Box Elder and Salt Lake counties: Thiokol, a major—if somewhat controversial—contractor on the space shuttle, near Tremonton; and Hercules, in West Valley City.

Some of the heavy manufacturing previously dominated by outside companies has closed or, like Geneva Steel, has been acquired by local entrepreneurs. Although not actually a part of the emerging semi-autochthonous economy, those companies that have moved sizable operations to Utah in recent years have contributed to its independence.[18] Until the 1970s, Salt Lake City offered flights to anywhere in the world—as long as a passenger was willing to change planes in Denver, a United Airlines hub. Then Atlanta-based Delta Air Lines, one of the world's major carriers, acquired Western Airlines and located one of its national hubs in Salt Lake City. This decision together with service by a large number of national and regional carriers has increased the accessibility of Utah's Wasatch Front market to business travelers and tourists.

Moreover, these developments have spawned a host of locally owned companies providing services to other Utah businesses and households. Particularly significant has been the expansion of finance, insurance, and real estate, which grew from 3.4 percent of nonagricultural employment in 1950 to 5.1 percent in 1988. A second—and clearly the most important—change has been the rapid growth of service industries, which expanded from 10.9 percent of the nonagricultural labor force in 1950 to 23.6 percent in 1988. Although it may be fashionable to ridicule the growth of service industries as creating minimum wage jobs flipping hamburgers at McDonald's and changing sheets at Holiday Inn, the conditions of Utah's developing indigenous economy reveal a much different pattern. A survey of change in the service sector between 1977 and 1982 showed that instead of fast-food employees, the major growth had taken place in legal services, accounting, and engineering, architectural, and surveying services.

Over the same period Utah's economy has diversified in part through expanded tourism. Although Temple Square in Salt Lake City, with the

Mormon Tabernacle and Temple, is the state's major tourist attraction, Utah has five national parks, six national monuments, and two national recreation areas. The state boasts fourteen ski areas, which employed approximately 12,300 people during the 1990–91 season. A number of these such as Snowbird, Alta, Park City, and Deer Valley—all within an hour's drive of Salt Lake International Airport—have attracted hundreds of affluent high rollers.[19]

Spurred by this rapid internal economic development, the state's population grew nearly 18 percent between 1980 and 1990, topping 1.7 million, and making Utah the ninth-fastest-growing state in the nation.[20] Most important, that growth came principally in urban areas, as the countryside continued to lose population.

Conventional wisdom has it that urban areas tend to be Democratic and Republicans live in rural areas and suburbs. In Utah that generalization is only partly true—Republicans live everywhere. After alternating with the remainder of the nation in urban growth until 1940, following World War II, Utah far outstripped the nation in city expansion. The 1990 census revealed Utah as the eighth most urbanized state in the nation with 84.4 percent of its population living in urban areas, largely along the Wasatch Front.[21] Moreover, the most urbanized regions of the state have shifted most rapidly into the Republican column. The entire Wasatch Front from Utah County through Cache County has become a nearly unbroken string of cities with Republican majorities.

While the Republican party has benefited from the unprecedented economic growth, the Democratic party has hurt itself in Utah by considerable ineptitude among both its national and local leadership. The activities of the Carter administration provide a case study in national bungling.

In Utah—indeed in all of the arid west—water is the mother's milk of politics. In Utah, opposing federal reclamation projects is akin to attacking Michelangelo's Pieta with a hammer and chisel. Environmentalists can point out that the projects constitute a mainstay of welfare capitalism and an enormous federal subsidy for the West, but that carries virtually no weight in the arid states.

In Utah the darling of urban residents is the Central Utah Project, designed to divert water from the Colorado Basin to the Wasatch Front. Irrelevant to Utahns is the charge—basically true—that much of the project was a fraud: supporters champion its high subsidies as a means of helping poor farmers, but most of the water is used in Utah's expanding cities, and some farmers may actually lose water to the project.

Recognizing the inefficiency and high cost of this and other projects, the Carter administration proposed cancellation of a number of reclamation projects including the Central Utah Project. When the proposed cancellations produced the predictable backlash, the administration back-pedaled, but that just added to an image of ineptitude reinforced by the failure to deal effectively with the occupation of the American embassy in Iran and with the stagflation.

Not all of the Democratic party's problems have been made in Washington. Utah Democrats share the blame for their poor performance. Allen Howe's decision to continue his campaign for Congress in 1976 in spite of charges of propositioning a police decoy provides one example. Congressman Wayne Owens, whose support for urban programs and environmentalism played well in the Second Congressional District, has never won a statewide race. In 1992 his campaign faltered in part because he had written overdrafts during the House of Representatives banking scandal of 1991–92. At the same time, he lost in a number of counties in part because of his strong support of a larger total of wilderness areas than the Bureau of Land Management had proposed, which was perceived as a threat to rural businesses such as grazing and logging.

Moreover, the state Democratic party has had an extremely difficult time promoting unity and loyalty in political campaigns. During the 1992 campaign, powerful Democratic insiders Dan Berman, an attorney, and Kem Gardner, a prominent businessman, ran full-page advertisements blasting Owens for his attacks on Robert Bennett, his Republican opponent. In 1992, also, Stewart Hansen's decision to run as an unabashedly prochoice candidate in an overwhelmingly Mormon, and antiabortion, state hurt the party considerably. Those Democrats who did well in the election tended to distance themselves from Hansen's third-place campaign. Oklahoma satirist Will Rogers's jest that he belonged to no organized political party—he was a Democrat—seems a fact of life in Utah.[22]

At the same time, a number of volatile political issues have created problems for both the Republicans and the Democrats, but most generally for the Democrats. Utah's unprecedented urban growth has produced a number of issues that the conservative Republican governments of the 1970s and 1980s failed successfully to address; but these issues have not hurt them at the polls because their justification for not solving the problems has been to avoid raising or reforming taxes.

Adequate funding for education has been the single most difficult problem Utah has faced. At 21.8 per 1,000 people in 1990, Utah had the third-highest birthrate in the nation after the District of Columbia and Alaska—a rate much higher than the national average of 16.7 per 1,000. At the same time Utah's family size at 3.15 was well above the national average. There is little wonder that between 1980 and 1990, the number of school-age children in the state actually grew from 24 to 26.6 percent of the population.[23]

With large numbers of children flooding its schools, Utah financed its public education through high class sizes and low teacher salaries. In 1989, with 24.8 students per teacher, Utah had the highest pupil-teacher ratio in the nation. With a per pupil expenditure of $2,579, Utah ranked dead last.[24] By the 1992–93 school year, Utah had reduced its class size but only to 22.78 students per teacher, which was still above the national average.[25] The average salary of $28,825 for teachers in 1991–92 ranked Utah forty-sixth among the fifty states and District of Columbia.[26]

Utah has not suffered as some states might have under the pressure of underfunded education because the strongly profamily Mormon culture has served as a surrogate for adequate funding. The relatively homogeneous population (72 percent Mormon) used their small resources to great advantage by supporting education through a strong sense of community, strong family values, and positive cultural attitudes. As a result, in 1989 Utah's high school graduation rate was 82.1 percent (9th in the nation) and its dropout rate was only 17.9 percent (forty-third in the nation). Moreover, average scores of Utah high school graduates on both the American College Test (ACT) and Scholastic Aptitude Test (SAT) ranked above the national average.

At the same time, the majority of active Mormons tend to feel a sense of security not present in less cohesive communities.[27] The strong sense of community among Mormons creates some problems for Utah's larger society. Cultural cohesiveness among Mormons tends to leave Protestants, Catholics, Jews, and the unchurched with a sense of alienation from the Mormon majority.

Moreover, the conservative culture has cost all the people of Utah dearly. While struggling to fund education and other public services, the state government has spent a great deal of time and money addressing the social agenda of conservatives, particularly in paying for lawsuits and referenda. Perhaps the best example has been the battle over abortion. After it seemed probable that the Supreme Court majority that supported abortion rights in *Roe v. Wade* (1973) had eroded, conservatives in Utah lobbied for the passage of antiabortion legislation. The 1991 legislature passed one of the strictest prolife laws in the nation, allowing abortions only in the case of rape, incest, danger to the mother's life, and severe fetal deformity. Threatening at first to punish both pregnant women and doctors, the legislature amended the act to limit punishment only to physicians. After spending more than $750,000 defending the law, the state suffered a defeat in December 1992 when U.S. District Judge J. Thomas Greene ruled that Utah could not ban abortions before twenty-one weeks of gestation or require notification of the father. Since then, however, continued defense of the law promises to cost the state more because a group of obstetricians have filed a notice of appeal from Greene's ruling, which still leaves them at risk of prosecution for decisions to give primary concern to the health of the mother after twenty-one weeks of gestation.[28]

In spite of the rapid economic development during the 1980s, the money to pay for education, other state services, and the conservative social agenda comes from a population whose income is below the national average. In 1990, Utah's per capita income at $14,083 placed it forty-eighth in the nation. With larger than average households, income per household averaged $45,160, which placed Utah thirtieth. This was still below the national average of $50,540. Moreover, the per household income trailed behind all the states of the West except New Mexico, Oregon, Montana and Wyoming.[29]

At the same time, because of the state's conservative political culture, Utahns did not share the rewards or the burdens of growth equally. In practice, the poorest people bore the highest costs of rapid growth while the greatest rewards accrued to the most wealthy.[30] Because of a highly regressive structure, the tax burden falls inordinately on the poor. The largest sources of revenue for state and local government are property taxes, which are used for local purposes, and the sales tax and individual income tax, which are used principally for state purposes.[31] At more than $700 million in fiscal year 1986–87, sales taxes generated the largest single block of statewide revenue in Utah. In Utah, sales taxes of 6 to 6.25 percent are added to virtually all purchases except drugs and homes.[32]

Moreover, the legislature, succumbing to the blandishments of welfare capitalism, has indulged business with favorable policies not available to individuals. Certain firms are exempt from sales taxes, and cities have lured businesses by tax-increment financing that taxes the buildings constructed by the favored corporations at the same rate as undeveloped land, shifting the burden of growth to established homes, businesses, and the sales tax. Redevelopment agencies declare poor neighborhoods blighted, allowing large developers to expel poor people from their homes and to disrupt small enterprises through the exercise of eminent domain and forced sales at "fair market" prices.

While the tax burden fell disproportionately on the poor, hardship caused by funding shortfalls for such public needs as education caused by the relatively low per capita state taxes was borne by children and their teachers. For the 1990 fiscal year, the Census Bureau estimated that Utah taxes at $1,020 per capita ranked thirty-sixth among the fifty states compared with a national average of $1,211 per capita. This placed the state tax burden of Utahns lower than any of the western states except Oregon.[33]

As the Republican party gained overwhelming majority status in the state, interest groups that might have pressed for a progressive restructuring of the tax system in order to provide additional funding for the poor and disadvantaged and for education have been either uninterested or ineffective in pressing for reform. Conservative forces opposed to raising taxes or to shifting the tax burden more equitably to the wealthy and to business have prevailed in the limited debate on additional taxes. Various interest groups tend to checkmate each other; their efforts seem to result in maintenance of the status quo. Studies of various lobbying groups since the 1960s rate the Utah Public Employees Association, the Utah Educational Association, and local governments as most effective, but none of these have lobbied for structural reform to redistribute the tax burden, although they have succeeded in getting additional funding for their interests. Other effective lobbies, however, have successfully fought against additional taxes and against tax reform. These include oil and gas interests, utilities, banking, business groups, the Independent party, and the Utah Taxpayers Association, a business lobby with a secret membership list that seldom finds any tax it cannot oppose.[34]

At the same time that conservative elements have dominated Utah politics (as they have the politics of other states in the West), the LDS church has added a dimension to the politics of the Beehive State unusual in the United States. The only state in the union that comes close to Utah's 72 percent domination by one religion is Rhode Island, which is 60 percent Catholic. After Mormons divided into the two major political parties in the 1890s, leaders in the LDS church continued to intervene in politics by lobbying openly for and against various pieces of legislation and by throwing their support behind various—generally Republican—candidates.

In the late 1960s, however, the church leadership began to avoid intervening directly in partisan political contests, and in 1974, the First Presidency and Council of the Twelve essentially institutionalized that policy by setting up a committee to monitor public policy. The committee initiates, supports, or opposes measures but takes no position on candidates. In the process, they labeled policies on which they chose to take a stand as "moral" issues. At first called the Special Affairs Committee, then the Public Affairs Committee, this organization was headed by members of the Council of the Twelve—the church's second governing body.

Since the organization of this committee, the church leadership has taken stands against a number of issues. These include the basing of the MX Missile on mobile tracks in Utah, the Equal Rights Amendment (which the majority of Utahns favored until the church announced its opposition), liquor by the drink (on which the legislature has compromised for economic reasons), abortion on demand, and pari-mutuel betting (which went down to defeat in a referendum in November 1992).[35]

Ironically, the power of the Mormon culture is so pervasive in Utah that the members of the Public Affairs Committee rarely have to lobby directly on questions in which the church leadership takes an interest. Instead, they either receive calls from political leaders, or the politicians understand because of the pervasive culture how the church will stand on a "moral" issue.[36] The major exception was the Equal Rights Amendment, against which the church leadership mounted a nationwide campaign.

With church leadership declining to take stands on most issues and no longer backing particular candidates, one might have expected the creation of a two-party political system in which representatives of both parties generally voted in line with their religious culture on moral questions but opposed each other on economic, social, and political matters. That has not been the case. Because the political realignment that brought the Republican party into control of the state took place during a period of prosperity and fundamental economic change, Utah is effectively a one-party state dominated by an antiprogressive coalition. Unwilling to reform the system, the Republican party has been more concerned with finding enough money under the existing system for education, public works, and the poor and has effectively sidetracked any efforts for basic reform.

Ominously, a recent tendency for Mormons to join the Republican party en masse has raised the distinct possibility of a return to the religiously divided politics of the nineteenth century, when all Mormons were members of the People's party and all non-Mormons joined the Liberal party. Research has shown that by the late 1980s upward of 70 percent of the Mormon vote was going to the Republican party and roughly the same proportion of non-Mormons voted Democratic. Moreover, active (strongly observant) Mormons tend to be the most Republican group in the state. In effect, the political division of the state has tended to separate the active Mormons and some conservative non-Mormons into the Republican party, and active Protestants, Catholics, Jews, the irreligious, inactive Mormons, and some active Mormons into the Democratic. Unless the situation changes, because of the high percentage of Mormons in the state, these conditions spell not only the possibility of religiously based parties but continued minority status for the Democrats.[37]

These circumstances promise continued difficulty for Utah's political culture. Announced cuts in federal defense budgets are sure to undercut further both the old and the new colonial component of Utah's economy. Such cuts may also increase State unemployment. Ironically, such unemployment will probably benefit the Republicans more than the Democrats since for the foreseeable future they will take place while the Democratic party governs in Washington; and, if Utah's experience with the Carter administration is any indication, the Clinton administration will get the blame for job losses at the major new colonial installations such as Hill Air Force Base and Tooele Army Depot and at old colonial businesses such as Thiokol and Hercules. Shifts of employment to the emerging semi-autochthonous economy may reduce unemployment eventually, but it seems unlikely that the Democratic party will benefit.

In addition, the Republican party's aversion to serious tax reform based on the ability to pay, coupled with a weak labor movement (which has failed to attract women and has operated under a state right-to-work law since 1954), is producing an increasingly unequal distribution of the wealth. Without a viable Democratic alternative or a strong progressive movement in the Republican party, that situation is unlikely to change.

Moreover, the tendency for active Mormons to join the Republican party in increasingly large numbers lessens the possibility of intraparty interaction and compromise between representatives of various religious groups, which in turn offers the distinct possibility of increased bigotry and intolerance on the part of both the Mormon majority and the non-Mormon minority. This seems even more likely in light of a proposed constitutional amendment (favored by a majority of Utahns) that would scrap the strict separation of church and state written into Utah's 1895 Constitution. It passed the 1993 state senate and fell short of the necessary two-thirds majority by only four votes in the house.[38]

At present, while the state is riding a wave of unprecedented economic prosperity, additional funding to solve the state's problems is still unlikely, and widening social and religious division are distinct possibilities. Given the lack of state funding, educational problems and other difficulties such as environmental deterioration (especially air pollution), pressure on the public transportation system, deteriorating roads and highways, urban crime, pockets of poverty, unmet medical needs, and homelessness present unsolved challenges. Whether the conservative majority in Utah will address these problems or another realignment takes place remains to be seen.

CHAPTER 18

Grand Coulee Dam, the Columbia River, and the Generation of Modern Washington

ROBERT E. FICKEN

The main current of modern Washington history runs through the Columbia River. Deep canyons and fearsome rapids made the great stream, in its 1,200-mile-long natural state, an obstacle to settlement. Built just in time for the Second World War, Grand Coulee and Bonneville dams transformed the economy of the entire state. Drawing heavily on what the liberal journalist Richard Neuberger termed "the incredible electric wealth of the Columbia," aluminum mills, aircraft plants, and the Hanford Engineer Works led directly to additional dam construction.[1] The "ferocious, rip-roaring old Columbia," as one observer happily wrote, was "properly harnessed and . . . put to work" as the driving force of up-to-date industrial enterprise.[2] In the process, Washington fell into a position of dependence on the federal government, to the mortification of regional groups hoping to exploit the state's water resources.

On the eve of the Second World War, Washington State's economy focused on timber west of the Cascades and agriculture east of the mountains. Most workers labored in forest, mill, or field, reflecting a pattern dating back to the settlement era of the mid-nineteenth century. Industry, for all practical purposes, consisted of the production-for-export of lumber, pulp, and paper. Aircraft factories and shipyards employed altogether a few thousand people. The nearest aluminum plant was in California.[3] The winds of international discord soon combined with a newly available surge of electricity to sweep away the old economic system.

Contrary to Donald Worster's "hydraulic society" interpretation, under which federal bureaucrats and corporate managers imposed irrigation on the American West, development of the Columbia River proceeded from local initiative.[4] Building on the turn-of-the-century suggestions of assorted engineers, journalists, and desert visionaries, two plans emerged in 1918 for the reclamation of over a million acres on the Columbia Plateau. The first, promoted in Wenatchee, Ephrata, and other dust-blown towns of the Big Bend, recommended building a mammoth dam at the mouth of the Grand Coulee and pumping impounded water into the coulee, which thereby became an awesome natural reservoir.[5] The second, formulated in Spokane with the influential support of the Washington Water Power Company, involved construction of a gravity canal from a dam at Albeni Falls on the distant Pend Oreille River.[6] In July 1920, the state Columbia Basin Survey Commission, controlled by Spokane interests, reported in favor of the gravity project. Gen. George W. Goethals of Panama Canal fame soon endorsed the recommendation, on the basis of a cursory review and in return for a handsome fee.[7] Washington officials, unfortunately, depended on federal financing. The Bureau of Reclamation, aware that the state's report was based more on politics than objective calculation, refused involvement in the proposed irrigation undertaking.[8]

Direct federal involvement with the Columbia Basin Project began only in 1929. Remembering that an earlier congressional act authorized "multipurpose" studies of navigable rivers, Republican Sen. Wesley L. Jones asked the U.S. Army Corps of Engineers to produce a detailed plan for the development of the Columbia.[9] Following the dictates of a senior legislator and poaching on what had previously been regarded as the bureaucratic preserve of the Bureau of Reclamation, the military responded with the major study that became known as the 308 Report. Completed in 1931, the examination concluded on the basis of objective criteria that the Grand Coulee scheme was the superior means of irrigating the basin, especially because the sale of electricity might subsidize the construction of reclamation works. The other prominent feature of the report was a framework of eight dams, from Grand Coulee furthest upstream to the Columbia Gorge, designed for maximum utilization of the river's potential for water power.[10] Obsessed with the Great Depression, Pres. Herbert Hoover objected to the findings, citing the great cost involved and the persistent national farm surplus problem. Similar concerns led the War Department to officially reject the advice of its field engineers.[11]

Political calculation and vision, rather than rote engineering analysis, motivated Franklin D. Roosevelt, the Democratic candidate for president in 1932. Speaking in Portland, Oregon, at the height of the campaign, he pledged to build the nation's "next great hydroelectric development" on

Columbia Basin Project, Washington
Copyright 1944, Rufus Woods, *The 23-Years' Battle for Grand Coulee Dam* (Wenatchee, Wash.: *Wenatchee Daily World*, 1944), 30.

the Columbia River. The speech, literally electric in its impact, sparked new hope on the part of longtime Grand Coulee advocates and an Oregon-based drive for construction of a dam at Bonneville.[12] A new Columbia Basin Commission, appointed by Gov. Clarence Martin, took up the task of securing federal funds for construction of the Grand Coulee project by the state of Washington.

Meeting with Washington Sen. Clarence Dill in April 1933, President Roosevelt redesigned Grand Coulee according to his own political con-ceptualization. As a means of limiting cost, he insisted that the project must initially be a low dam, with the previously planned high dam to be completed at some future date. Reclamation, moreover, was eliminated by presidential fiat, "deferred until such time as existing lands suitable for agriculture have been taken up."[13] Politics also figured in the decision to build both Grand Coulee and Bonneville, the former benefitting Washing-ton and the latter Oregon, and the grant of construction responsibility to, respectively, the Bureau of Reclamation and the U.S. Army Corps of Engineers. Although objecting to the alterations in Grand Coulee, Wash-ington's Columbia Basin Commission was dependent on federal funding and had no choice but to accede to Roosevelt's wishes.[14] Similar fiscal calculation dictated a state surrender when Secretary of the Interior Harold Ickes, custodian of the $63 million allocated to Grand Coulee, ordered a federal takeover of the project in October 1933.[15]

After lengthy preparatory work, construction of Bonneville and Grand Coulee began in 1934. The former, 175 feet high, was completed in the spring of 1938, with five of the ten scheduled generators on line. A change order issued by the Department of the Interior in 1935, meanwhile, provided for an efficient transition from Roosevelt's low dam to a high dam at Grand Coulee.[16] Finished in the fall of 1941, with three generating units in place, the structure soared 500 feet above the riverbed and impounded the Columbia for 150 miles to the Canadian border. The final official cost, $196 million, represented a threefold increase over the $63 million Roosevelt originally approved.[17]

Local supporters of Grand Coulee, though forced to acquiesce in the federalization of the project, still hoped to secure their longtime goals. For them, the dam was a product of the Progressive era, a vestige of early-century reform transformed into concrete and steel. Washington State Progressivism had aimed to curtail outside political and corporate domi-nance by implementing direct democracy, regulation of business, and conservation.[18] Utilizing an inexhaustible resource and encouraging the agricultural and industrial development of an entire region, Grand Coulee Dam served a similar purpose. Washington, particularly the four Big Bend counties, might thereby avoid the fate of Montana and other plundered western states. "Whole sections of the United States . . . have been LOOTED and the people robbed of their birthright," pointed out Rufus Woods, a Wenatchee publisher and leader of both the Progressive movement and the campaign for dam building on the Columbia. "It is for us to decide," Woods insisted on behalf of Pacific Northwest residents, "whether the billion dollar wealth of the Columbia shall be looted and decimated, or whether . . . we shall have a program of ORDERLY DEVEL-OPMENT."[19]

In the view of Woods and other dam proponents, "orderly development" was bound to bring about stability and balance east of the Cascades. Currently, the region adjacent to Grand Coulee depended almost entirely on irrigated orchards, carrying (as the *Wenatchee Daily World* warned in an editorial) "all its eggs in one basket." Apple growers prospered in some seasons but suffered in others when markets were overstocked and prices fell below the cost of production. To be sure, the reclamation features of the Grand Coulee project, when finally implemented, looked to a substantial increase in agricultural output. The focus, however, would be on sugar beets, at least according to the Rufus Woods prescription, providing a much-needed complement to apples.[20]

Crop diversification was by no means the only benefit to be realized from construction of Grand Coulee. Abundant and inexpensive electricity, booster organizations believed, would lead to the industrialization of a rural and isolated region previously supported by single-crop agriculture. Sugar beets, for example, might be processed in Quincy, Ephrata, Moses Lake, and the other towns of the Big Bend. (Rufus Woods expected the first 400,000 acres watered by the Columbia Basin Project to support eight to ten factories.) The timber and mineral wealth locked away in the Cascades, moreover, became exploitable by local manufacturers when combined with power from the Columbia. The near future, thanks to utilization of the river, would include the production of lumber, aluminum, steel, and fertilizer.[21]

Grand Coulee was the key to a fully independent, economically integrated region, to the achievement of time-honored Progressive goals. Water stored behind the dam meant new and productive homes for thousands of reclamation settlers. Industry developed on the basis of hydroelectricity represented markets and a source of manufactured products for farmers. Rapid population growth guaranteed more political clout for a previously trod-upon section of the Pacific Northwest. To secure these goals, local residents must retain effective control of the river in general and of Grand Coulee in particular—they must fight to secure and retain the benefits of dam building. Already, the necessary reliance on federal funding compromised this fundamental condition. "In the long run, nothing is free," warned the *Wenatchee Daily World* as it bemoaned the centralizing effect of the "mad scramble" of states, counties, and municipalities to "share in the unprecedented bounty" of the New Deal.[22] Dams came with a price, and the price was the inevitable undermining of the original sponsors' aspirations.

Other obstacles also frustrated the expectations of groups supporting Grand Coulee. The impending completion of Bonneville Dam raised the question of power distribution. Unwilling to assign the task to an existing agency or to create the proposed Columbia Valley Authority, Congress in 1937 established the Bonneville Power Administration (BPA) as a "provisional" sales agency.[23] J. D. Ross, the head of the BPA, quickly secured approval of a transmission line between Bonneville and the Grand Coulee construction site, thereby bringing about the "consolidation of the two Federal plants into one." Over the long haul, Ross intended to create a Pacific Northwest energy grid, combining the region's public and private generation facilities. So far as eastern Washington was concerned, these plans represented a dangerous scheme, for the transmission lines allowed distant locations to consume electricity that might otherwise be used in the immediate vicinity of Grand Coulee.[24]

Rufus Woods and his friends expected industry to locate near the dam, attracted to the remote upper Columbia country by the availability of cheap electric power. Ross, however, argued that electricity should be sent to existing centers of population and manufacturing. Following his line, the BPA adopted a "postage-stamp" rate structure. Regardless of distance from the generating station, customers paid $17.50 per kilowatt-year for primary energy. Thus manufacturers had no incentive, complained a bitterly disappointed Woods, to build plants in the Big Bend. Policies made in far-off Portland, the headquarters of the BPA, denied local residents the rewards of their victory in securing construction of Grand Coulee.[25]

Together, the centralizing tendencies of federal funding, regional transmission networks, and postage-stamp power rates compromised the local autonomy precepts of booster organizations. For the moment, however, the fundamental question was whether or not Bonneville and Grand Coulee were viable economic undertakings. Prior to shifting from the Seattle Municipal Lighting Department to the BPA, Ross insisted that there was no market for the electricity to be generated at Grand Coulee.[26] Corps of Engineers studies provided apparently objective support for such forecasts. "On account of uncertainty as to how long it will take . . . to absorb the very large blocks of power" scheduled to come on line from Bonneville and Grand Coulee, Col. Thomas Robins, the officer in charge of army engineering efforts in the Pacific Northwest, advised indefinite postponement of all preliminary work for new dams. "Further development of the Columbia River in the interests of power," wrote Robins, "will not be required for many years to come."[27] In December 1934 the Pacific Northwest Regional Planning Commission, an offshoot of the New Deal National Resources Planning Board, endorsed this finding.[28]

World War II kept Bonneville and especially Grand Coulee from becoming embarrassments for the Roosevelt administration. Massive federal defense expenditures, commencing with the Munich Agreement, stimulated industrial growth and began the economic transformation of the Pacific Northwest. "Never before in peace time," the *Wenatchee Daily World* observed in mid-1940, "has any nation attempted to force so much money into the channels of business in such a short time."[29] Increased production at Boeing in Seattle created a growing regional demand for the light metals required in the manufacture of airplanes. In December 1939, the Aluminum Company of America (Alcoa) announced plans for a manufacturing complex on the lower Columbia, to be run by Bonneville electricity. Aluminum producers and other interests intent upon profiting from the defense boom were, as Rufus Woods wrote, "positively avid for cheap electric power."[30] The preparedness drive eliminated the concern over energy markets and set the stage for further development of the Columbia.

Cheap Columbia River power drove regional industry to new heights in the months prior to Pearl Harbor. The basic BPA $17.50 rate served, according to the National Resources Planning Board, as "the chief drawing card" in attracting new aluminum plants to the Pacific Northwest.[31] Enormous energy requirements—17,000 kilowatt-hours of electricity went into the production of a ton of metal—meant that the cost of transporting bauxite ore from distant mines was more than offset by bargain Bonneville electricity. Despite opposition from monopoly-conscious Alcoa, the federal government funded manufacturing complexes for Spokane, Longview, and Tacoma, adding to the drain on the river produced by the original Alcoa facility at Vancouver. The valley of the Columbia, enthused Rufus Woods, "soon will be the aluminum capital of the world!"[32]

By the time Grand Coulee began producing energy for industry in the fall of 1941, the region was on the verge of an energy crisis. New generators had already been ordered to supplement the three 108,000-kilowatt units originally installed at the coulee. Construction of a second powerhouse, to accommodate even more generating capacity, was authorized. The belief that fifteen years, at minimum, would be required to absorb the project's electricity, was replaced by a call from Paul Raver, Ross's successor as BPA administrator, for at least one new Columbia River dam.[33] The BPA and the Federal Power Commission initiated studies to determine which of the 308 Report projects ought to be given priority. In February 1942 the BPA recommended that construction planning be started at the Foster Creek and Priest Rapids sites and that the privately owned Rock Island Dam be enlarged.[34]

Industrial production and the pressure on existing energy sources mounted in the aftermath of Pearl Harbor. In late December 1941 Congressman Charles Leavy predicted that America's active involvement in the world conflict was bound to bring "some tremendous developments" to Washington.[35] Building upon the base erected by the preparedness campaign, the federal government expended billions of dollars in the Pacific Northwest. Regional shipbuilding employment passed the 200,000 mark by mid-1943. Fifty thousand workers toiled at Boeing Company in 1944, a year in which the firm's airplane sales to the military exceeded $600 million. Five aluminum reduction plants and a single rolling mill produced, depending on the study cited, between 37 percent and 45 percent of the nation's supply of the strategic metal. The demand for civilian labor overwhelmed the supply of men and women, forcing up wages and doubling personal income in the region.[36]

New opportunities arose in the early months of 1943 from reports of a "mysterious" government undertaking. The army, according to stories circulating throughout the state, had "taken over 650,000 acres" between the lower Yakima River and the Columbia, giving local residents "thirty days to evacuate."[37] The site was isolated, adjacent to abundant supplies of fresh water, and near Grand Coulee, making it an ideal location for the production of plutonium for the Manhattan Engineering District's atomic bomb project.[38] The drain on energy was expected to be enormous. "They will immediately take all the surplus power from Grand Coulee Dam," reported one journalist after an off-the-record conversation with government engineers. Once up and running, in fact, the Hanford Engineer Works used the entire output of two Grand Coulee generators.[39]

Electricity from the Columbia River made the aluminum industry, Boeing's expanded production, and Hanford possible. Pending installation of the fourth, fifth, and sixth generators, two units were shifted to Grand Coulee from California's Shasta Dam in 1942, allowing for a major boost in output. By 1944, the Grand Coulee project alone produced one-third of the energy consumed in the Pacific Northwest. With Bonneville, it drove the aluminum plants of Washington and Oregon and supplied the needs of the region's shipyards. According to one calculation, two of every five planes turned out in the United States during the war were credited to the Columbia. Overall, claimed Raver of the BPA, "fully 85 percent" of the power generated by the federal dams went directly into the defense effort.[40] With reason, many observers claimed that Grand Coulee was responsible for victory over Germany and Japan.[41]

Pressed by the demands of war, the Corps of Engineers commenced detailed survey work at Foster Creek, the dam site downstream from Grand Coulee, in 1943. The resulting plan, completed in final form in August 1945, called for the expenditure of $104 million on a 200-foot-high structure.[42] Meanwhile, Congress authorized construction of an army dam at Umatilla Rapids, below the mouth of the Snake, in 1944.[43] Operating on the principle that "storage is the key to complete development of the Columbia River," military engineers also contemplated dam building on the stream's high mountain tributaries. By impounding water for release during normal low-flow periods, storage projects would maximize year-round production at all downstream generating stations.[44] Opposition in British Columbia to a cross-border reservoir, however, stalled the proposed Libby dam on the Kootenai River in northwestern Montana.[45] Residents of Idaho and Montana, antagonized by the prospective flooding of land for the benefit of power consumers in Washington and Oregon, fought off dam building on the Clark Fork–Pend Oreille system.[46]

Homefront prosperity and the campaign for new dams produced little celebration among the original backers of Grand Coulee. Accentuating prewar trends, decisions by the Roosevelt administration defense bureaucracy added to the frustration felt on the upper Columbia. By the time the project began generating electricity in late 1941, a second transmission line ran alongside the connection to Bonneville authorized by Ross. The first of four planned lines to Spokane was near completion, and work was underway on a cross-Cascades power linkage to Tacoma. Wenatchee, hometown of Rufus Woods and the metropolitan center for the counties closest to Grand Coulee, was, in contrast, not connected to the dam. "Millions of dollars are spent to take the power away," lamented the Woods newspaper, "and apparently it's all going to be taken away."[47]

Only one war plant, a small ferro-silicon operation located a few miles from Wenatchee, was opened along the upper Columbia.[48] The various war mobilization agencies instead concentrated factories at tidewater on the lower river and on Puget Sound. Large supplies of electricity were already available in those sectors, thanks to the BPA, while labor was more easily recruited and housing more readily provided in existing urban areas. "Virtually all the small communities of our state . . . are being depleted of man power," Woods complained to Secretary of the Interior Harold Ickes, "while the metropolitan centers are taking . . . the big defense projects." So long as the $17.50 postage-stamp rate remained in force, moreover, the trend was unlikely to be reversed. "We have gone right smack into centralization," Woods observed as federal money followed federal electricity to the cities.[49]

War mobilization generated major demographic shifts. Most of the quarter-million people migrating to the Pacific Northwest in search of defense work settled in urban locations. Seattle's population increased by 20 percent. Bremerton, location of the Puget Sound naval shipyard, doubled in size. Rural residents also moved out. The four Big Bend counties lost 18,000 inhabitants between April 1940 and February 1943. Despite significant growth in Ephrata, the site of a military training facility, the population of Grant County declined by half. Two-thirds of the citizens of Douglas County, along the east bank of the Columbia, left for the coast and jobs with Boeing or in the shipyards of Puget Sound.[50]

"Disgusted with the way that the Columbia River is being handled," Woods fought a homefront battle for the recovery of Grand Coulee's lost electricity. "This great old Columbia valley," he argued, focusing on the cause of and solution to his region's retarded wartime development, "is now at the cross roads." Down one path lay a course devised by the federal government, which had already seized the Grand Coulee Dam and placed its output in the hands of the BPA. Down the other might be found independence, to be attained by "keep[ing] a handle on this tremendous potential resource of the future." Decisions made in Portland and in the nation's capital, including those dealing with rates and transmission lines, invariably worked to the disadvantage of Wenatchee and its upriver hinterland. Unless this trend was soon reversed, Woods predicted, the upper Columbia "will be in the same fix" as the Old South, an impoverished land exporting cheap raw materials and importing expensive manufactured products.[51]

Three-fourths of the Columbia's potential energy was located within sixty-eight miles of Wenatchee, claimed Woods. The community and the surrounding counties therefore had a right to preferential treatment in the matter of rates and to ultimate separation from the BPA. Present and future development "should be guided by the people of the immediate area concerned," Woods explained to the BPA's Raver. "The people who are vitally interested . . . will do a better job because it is before them by day and by night." Grand Coulee, after all, had been promoted by and in behalf of local organizations. Hence the irony and the bitterness when the benefits went to Portland and Spokane, to Seattle and Tacoma, urban areas that had opposed construction. "Those cities still laugh at us," wrote Woods's close associate Kirby Billingsley, "they take the power and thumb their noses at us in [the] Columbia Valley." The BPA, exclaimed another unhappy observer, was "selling Grand Coulee down the river."[52]

The effort to secure a reversal in the downstream power flow was undermined by the expectation that peace would bring a return of depression conditions and a collapse in the demand for electricity. Expert analysts anticipated a 90 percent drop in regional shipyard employment and a substantial reduction in the Boeing work force. Although the National Resources Planning Board predicted an increase in aluminum output, the federal government ordered a cutback in production at the end of 1943.[53] Testifying before the Columbia Basin Commission, private utility executives forecast a massive postwar energy surplus, to prevail for at least a decade after the Axis surrender. The BPA expected a million persons in its service area to be unemployed by 1947. According to Homer T. Bone, retiring in 1944 after two terms as U.S. senator from Washington, the central problem facing the Pacific Northwest was how to make up for the closure of defense industries.[54]

Confounding expectations, the postwar slump was brief and followed by a regional economic boom. Population growth—Washington added a half-million permanent residents between 1940 and 1946—and the frenzied purchase of electrical appliances, available in quantity for the first time since Pearl Harbor, accounted for much of the stimulus. The commencement of the cold war prevented wholesale demobilization of the armed forces and massive cutbacks in defense spending. Hanford, expanding in top-secret fashion, maintained a steady drain on the Columbia River. Instead of being decommissioned, the aluminum industry was reorganized under government auspices, with Reynolds Metals Company and Kaiser Aluminum Company emerging as major competitors of Alcoa. So important was aluminum production that 40 percent of the electricity from Grand Coulee and Bonneville went into the postwar manufacture of light metal. No longer concerned with the prospect of an energy surplus, in August 1946 the BPA declared an impending power shortage.[55]

An attempt to encourage the rational planning, construction, and operation of existing and new water projects revealed the continuing importance of local autonomy to supporters of Grand Coulee in Washington State. Twenty agencies in three cabinet departments currently claimed some degree of responsibility for the Columbia River. The "duplication of governmental units has become a fine art," noted journalist Richard Neuberger of the existing situation on the stream.[56] Democrats and Republicans alike agreed on the basic remedy. "To insure the greatest possible development of the basin," stated U.S. Sen. Warren G. Magnuson of Washington, "it is necessary that inter-agency jealousies be submerged and the efforts of all pooled." The creation of a single river authority, affirmed Congressman Walt Horan, was "inevitable."[57]

Legislation introduced in the spring of 1945 by U.S. Sen. Hugh Mitchell of Washington provided for a presidentially appointed Columbia Valley Authority (CVA) under the effective control of the secretary of the interior.[58] The bill sparked immediate opposition from threatened agencies such as the Corps of Engineers and the Bureau of Reclamation as well as private utilities and conservative Republicans. Rufus Woods, Kirby Billingsley, Walt Horan, and other prodevelopment leaders also opposed Mitchell. "That matter of turning the Columbia over to Washington D.C. is all wrong," protested Woods. A CVA, if it were "in the right place with the right men," though, would be acceptable to this group.[59] Horan's alternative measure for a valley authority with coequal roles for the federal government and the Pacific Northwest states brought "the *control* of the Columbia as *close* to the people" as political circumstances allowed and drew support from traditional Grand Coulee backers.[60]

Debate over the CVA continued for the remainder of the Truman administration, with the combatants unable to resolve the question of local control. Congress, in the meantime, authorized the Corps of Engineers Foster Creek dam in 1946 but failed to appropriate funds for construction. Development organizations on the upper Columbia, who expected the project to make up for the power lost from Grand Coulee, blamed several factors for the failure to secure money. The army supposedly lacked genuine interest in Foster Creek, preferring to concentrate on Umatilla—now renamed after Oregon's late Senator Charles McNary—and on a series of navigation-enhancing dams proposed for the lower Snake River.[61] The Bureau of the Budget, intent on reducing spending to some approximation of prewar levels, argued against funding new water projects in the West. A general feeling on Capitol Hill that Washington State had received more than its fair share of federal money since 1933 posed an additional obstacle.[62]

National political developments, specifically the Republican triumph in the 1946 congressional elections, further complicated the situation. Republican legislators hostile to public power and federal development works held key leadership positions in both houses of the Eightieth Congress. Democratic Senator Magnuson detailed the "over-all private utility strategy" in a series of "no illusions" reports to friends east of the Cascades.[63] Bills requiring the sale of federally generated electricity at the bus-bar and eliminating important subsidies for dam construction drew heavy support from the representatives of midwestern and eastern states. Republicans also tried to repeal the authorization of Foster Creek, on the basis of a contention that the single-purpose project was unconstitutional.[64] For exposing these attempts to hamstring the state's economic future in the interest of private profit, Rufus Woods was virtually read out of his party by conservative Republicans. He was no New Dealer, retorted Woods, but a "Theodore Roosevelt republican" devoted out of "common sense" to the "thesis" that the Columbia River "must be developed by government."[65]

Dramatic events revived the movement for federal development of the Columbia in 1948. The crisis in Berlin confirmed fears that the cold war was not a short-term phenomenon, pointing up the need for expanded power generation in support of defense industry.[66] Rapid melting of an abnormally heavy snowpack produced disastrous flooding along the river in May and June, with at least thirty fatalities and property losses in excess of $100 million. In the aftermath, Paul Raver of the BPA called for the implementation of "adequate flood control" measures and construction of an "integrated system" of multipurpose dams. Senator Magnuson de-

manded that federal agencies tame the rampaging Columbia.[67] President
Truman's upset electoral triumph in November, accompanied by the
reassertion of Democratic control over Congress, amounted, in the view
of Rufus Woods and other boosters, to an endorsement of new dam
building in the Pacific Northwest.[68]

A postelection regional electricity brownout, produced by the impact
on stream flow of an early winter, clinched the case for renewed river
development. Lights were turned off, business operations curtailed, and
laborers thrown out of work. This state of affairs, according to Rufus
Woods, was scandalous: "here we are on the greatest power pool in
America . . . and talking about [a] shortage of power." Dams ought to be
built "SOMEWHAT IN ADVANCE OF DEMAND," yet "foolish, foolish"
followers of the private utility line in Congress had "opposed construction
of Foster Creek" and other much-needed generating facilities. McNary
Dam, the only new plant currently underway, was not scheduled for
completion until 1954, adding to the sense of emergency. Following the
thinking of Woods, Senator Magnuson, Congressman Henry M. Jackson,
and other members of the Washington delegation demanded the immediate undertaking of Foster Creek.[69]

In fact, $2 million were provided for preliminary work at the dam site in
a supplementary appropriation bill approved by Congress in early 1949.
The regular federal budget, passed later in the year, included an additional
$5 million for what was now renamed Chief Joseph Dam.[70] The project,
completed in 1958 with sixteen installed generators, was by no means the
only immediate result of Berlin, the flood, and Truman's victory. New
generating units, the tenth and eleventh overall, went into service at Grand
Coulee in 1949. The Corps of Engineers prepared plans for a storage dam
at Albeni Falls on the Pend Oreille River, a development finished in 1952.
Pending resolution of the cross-border reservoir issue, the army also
readied the Libby project on the Kootenai. The Oregon congressional
delegation launched a campaign for a major dam at The Dalles on the
Columbia. Washington and Idaho organizations did the same on behalf of
Ice Harbor and Hells Canyon on the Snake. Core drilling and other
exploratory investigation began above Wenatchee at Rocky Reach and
Wells, sites originally examined in the 308 Report.[71]

Massive augmentation of the regional power supply failed to reverse the
troublesome trend toward centralization. Rufus Woods and his associates
on the upper Columbia continued to oppose a CVA operated from outside
the region, especially because of growing fear that water might be

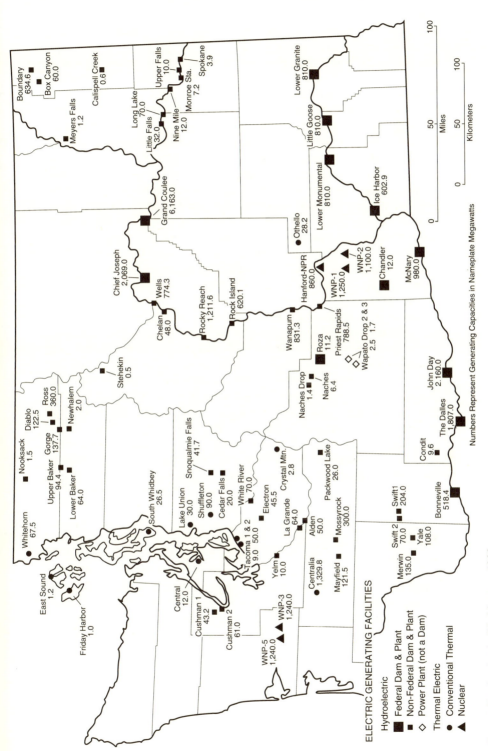

ELECTRIC GENERATING FACILITIES

Hydroelectric
■ Federal Dam & Plant
▪ Non-Federal Dam & Plant
● Power Plant (not a Dam)

Thermal Electric
◇ Conventional Thermal
▲ Nuclear

Numbers Represent Generating Capacities in Nameplate Megawatts.

Energy Production in Washington, 1988
Numbers represent generating capacities in megawatts.

diverted to California.[72] The failure to secure a politically viable valley authority meant that existing agencies, notably the BPA, the Corps of Engineers, and the Bureau of Reclamation, remained the key factors on the river. In early 1949, the Corps and the Bureau of Reclamation reached a "shotgun wedding" accord, apportioning responsibility for all proposed federal dams on the Columbia and its tributaries and providing for a "pooling" approach to the financing of construction.[73] Seeing in the agreement a last chance for salvation of their longtime aspirations, local autonomy forces supported Senator Magnuson's bill authorizing the dams and establishing a Basin Account. The Basin Account would allow revenue from one project to support the building of the next, providing a sustained and self-funding program independent of congressional or bureaucratic obstructionism. Opposed by the farm lobby, the utility industry, Oregon, and Republicans generally, the Magnuson measure died in the summer of 1950, ignored by a Congress preoccupied with Korea and McCarthyism.[74]

Defeat of the Basin Account approach meant that, except for public utility district (PUD) projects, dam building in the Columbia drainage continued to be the preserve of entrenched federal agencies, dependent on congressional appropriations. River development remained embroiled in politics and bureaucratic rivalry. Between 1950 and the early 1960s, the Corps of Engineers completed Chief Joseph, McNary, John Day and The Dalles dams on the main Columbia. Opposition from the Atomic Energy Commission, which feared "adverse effects" on the Hanford nuclear reservation, prevented construction of the army-approved Ben Franklin dam near Richland.[75] The Grant County PUD, meanwhile, undertook development of the Wanapum and Priest Rapids sites upstream from Hanford. Further upriver, the Chelan County PUD built Rocky Reach Dam, and the Douglas County PUD constructed Wells Dam.[76] On the storage front, military engineers were finally able to proceed with the long-delayed Libby project on the Kootenai River after the conclusion of a diplomatic agreement between the United States and Canada in 1961.[77]

Construction of these dams reflected the ever-mounting postwar demand for electricity in the Pacific Northwest. Per capita energy usage in the region increased from 1,501 kilowatt-hours in 1940 to 7,100 kilowatt-hours in 1955, with the latter figure three times greater than the national average. Residential customers made up one-quarter of the market, but manufacturing placed the heaviest strain upon existing power plants. One-third of the nation's aluminum supply came from Washington and Oregon in the mid-1950s. The insatiable strategic industry took half the regional output of electricity and was directly responsible for one-third of the total sales made by the BPA.[78]

Installed hydroelectric capacity in the Pacific Northwest as of 1958 was 8.1 million kilowatts, two-thirds from the federal dams of the Columbia drainage basin. An additional 5.5 million were in process of installation in that year, and a further 2.9 million kilowatts were either licensed or authorized for construction.[79] More development was needed, however, according to the Corps of Engineers. Computer projections forecast a two-thirds growth in the population of Washington and Oregon between 1955 and 1980. Residential demand for electricity was expected to double and industrial requirements to increase by 450 percent. By 1970, manufacturers in the Northwest needed two-and-a-half times the energy utilized in the mid-1950s. Overall peak demand by all consumers was calculated at 27.4 million kilowatts for 1980.[80]

Maximum exploitation of all remaining dam sites, the Corps of Engineers reported in 1958, fell far short of meeting anticipated growth in the demand for energy. "Thermal generation" (i.e., nuclear power) advised the military, would supplant hydroelectricity early in the twenty-first century.[81] "In the future," according to the regionwide River Basins Commission, a federal task force appointed in the mid-1960s, "the major part of the Pacific Northwest's base load will be met by nuclear power plants." Urged on by the BPA, private utilities in Seattle and Portland developed plans for such installations. On an especially grandiose note, the Washington Public Power Supply System (WPPSS), a consortium of public utility districts, secured financing for five plants. Accelerating costs, environmentalist opposition, and mounting safety concerns prevented the nuclearization of the region. Only one WPPSS facility was completed, and the agency became mired in a financial scandal of historical proportions.[82]

Further unexpected problems came from the impact of dam building on the salmon of the Columbia. Studies at McNary Dam in the mid-1950s revealed an 11 percent loss at that site alone on the downstream migration. Fishery organizations placed little faith in the Corps of Engineers and the Bureau of Reclamation and opposed new projects on the river and its tributaries.[83] Senior army officials insisted that salmon protection was of secondary importance to energy generation and denounced defenders of the environment as "wildlife extremists" and "hysterical authors."[84] Nonetheless, political pressure forced the agencies to expend millions of dollars on hatcheries and research, to "make up," as one engineer privately conceded, "for the delays of the past." Fishery continued to suffer, however, with the salmon and steelhead catch during the 1960s barely one-seventh of the tally recorded in the era of the First World War.[85] The threat posed by dams to a major commercial and recreational resource, together with the rise of a regional environmental movement in response to that threat, made for an increasingly complex and emotion-laden developmental picture on the Columbia.

The history of Columbia River development is replete with irony and unanticipated result. Grand Coulee Dam, setting the process in motion, was supposed to water land and encourage the growth of Big Bend industry, advancing locally devised objectives under the control of local interests. Instead, the project emerged from the political process as the property of the United States, constructed and operated by the Bureau of Reclamation and subject to the dictates of the Bonneville Power Administration. With the smaller Bonneville Dam in tow, Grand Coulee became an integral part of the military-industrial complex created during the Second World War and perpetuated during the cold war. Supposed to advance peaceful purposes, its energy was drained off and made over into aluminum, aircraft, and plutonium.

Grand Coulee in particular, and utilization of the Columbia River in general, built modern Washington on a foundation of international discord. The state, historically isolated and dependent on the export of products direct from the forest and the soil, was transformed into a center of industry and advanced technology. The lumberjack and the field hand were replaced as regional symbols by the airplane plant worker and the scientist. In the process, Washington became heavily reliant on federal largesse, defense contracts, military base expenditures, and research contracts.[86] Another phenomenon of the late twentieth century, the environmental movement, grew in response to the impact of river development on salmon and, because of Hanford, on the earth, the air, and the water. Grand Coulee, a project supposed to guarantee regional autonomy, led instead to the sacrifice of local aspirations to the national interest. Political and economic power flowed from the Pacific Northwest to a distant and mysterious "other Washington."

CHAPTER 19

"Politics Is Personal": Postwar Wyoming Politics and the Media

PHIL ROBERTS AND PEGGY BIEBER-ROBERTS

"Everything in Wyoming is political," goes the oft-quoted saying, "except politics. Politics is personal." The remark explains much of the uniqueness of Wyoming politics from World War II to the 1970s. In a state characterized by a tiny population huddled in small towns thinly spread across some 97,000 square miles, all successful politicians have been individuals who knew their constituents, many on a first-name basis. Weak parties and general consensus on most major issues contributed to this politics of personality. For example, Democratic U.S. Sen. Gale McGee, a Vietnam war hawk, and Congressman Teno Roncalio, a fellow Democrat but outspoken opponent of the war, were both reelected in the same year. And both won in a state where the Republicans enjoyed a huge registration edge.

An outside observer would be hard pressed to explain these results by relying on conventional demographic analysis. The state is overwhelmingly white, and a class structure is virtually nonexistent.[1] Organized religion has not been a factor in the state's politics.[2] Two of the most popular politicians since the 1930s were Roman Catholics: Republican Frank Barrett, who served as congressman, governor, and U.S. senator; and Democrat Joseph C. O'Mahoney, who represented Wyoming in the U.S. Senate from 1933 to 1960 with one two-year break.

Although party identification may be a factor in very close contests, the two political parties in Wyoming have shared similar conservative assumptions on issues of economics and libertarian views on civil rights and individual freedoms. The overriding issue since World War II has consistently been ecomonic development, but until the gubernatorial campaign of 1966, both parties embraced the assumption that government should encourage it. Only after the explosive development of the mineral industry, primarily coal, after 1974 when mineral development threatened to overwhelm the traditional industries of agriculture and tourism, did politicians in both parties propose ways of controlling the impact of it. These threats to the economic balance caused legislators in both parties to join in voting for popular legislation to boost severance taxes on mineral companies and industrial siting laws to protect the environment.

That is not to say that the mineral companies did not have strong allies. Avowedly pro-mining candidates won the Republican gubernatorial nominations in 1974 and 1978 with the strong backing of the industry.[3] The support, however, was filtered through local managers and spokesmen. Dominated by outside capital, these firms made decisions affecting Wyoming very far from the high plains of the state.

The mineral companies are not alone in this outside control, however. While much of the rest of the West has been escaping from what Bernard DeVoto decried as "colonialism" almost a half-century ago, by the early 1980s, Wyoming seemed increasingly colonial. Independent banks and member banks of a bank holding company owned and headquartered in the state once added voices to the financial affairs of the state. After the energy bust of the early 1980s, these banks were owned and controlled by directors in distant cities on the West Coast and in the Midwest and Northeast. But nowhere was the drift toward deeper colonialism more apparent than in the news media. The symbiotic tie between media owners and prominent politicians has disappeared in the newer, more colonial Wyoming. Small weeklies were purchased by out-of-state newspaper chains, and the three remaining chains controlled by Wyoming groups stepped away from political partisanship.[4] This was a striking change from the political scene at the end of the World War II.

Powerful personalities dominated the Wyoming political scene at the war's end, and none were any more forceful than two newspaper owners who exercised considerable influence in their respective political parties. Tracy McCraken, the owner of a statewide chain of dailies including both dailies in the state capital, was at the height of his influence after the war. Not only did he control papers in all but two of the seven largest towns in the state, he served at various times as Democratic national committeeman and state party chairman. Adding to his influence was his ownership of radio stations and, after 1954, Wyoming's first television station.[5] McCraken's counterpart on the Republican side was James B. Griffith, publisher of a weekly newspaper in the small eastern Wyoming town of Lusk. Griffith backed a succession of Republican candidates in successful campaigns for statewide office and served as state party chairman.

Just as the national partisan press gradually gave way to bland corporate ownership in the decades following the war, Wyoming papers passed out of the hands of these publisher-politicians. By the time of Tracy Mc-Craken's death in December 1960 (six months after "putting Kennedy over the top" as chairman of the Wyoming delegation to the national convention in Los Angeles), Wyoming's independent, often fiercely partisan, family-owned papers were disappearing. By the time the 1980s energy bust descended on the state, most newspapers were owned by chains, many by firms headquartered in other states. The McCraken papers, never strong in statewide coverage and distribution, lost considerable influence about 1965 when the *Casper Star-Tribune*, controlled by Howard Publications of Oceanside, California, opted to begin a statewide distribution system. (The firm bought out local minority shareholders in 1972.)

Perhaps fortunate for the financial health of special interest lobbies, television never has been a significant factor in electoral politics. The two major stations in the state, in Casper and Cheyenne, serve relatively small areas of the state. More homes receive over-the-air signals from stations in Utah, South Dakota, Montana, Colorado, Nebraska, and Idaho, depending on a viewer's location. Even more significant, 120,000 Wyoming homes are wired for cable television, a postwar innovation pioneered nationally in Casper, Wyoming.

Media consolidation and chain ownership were not unique to Wyoming. Nevertheless, the changes came at the very time that other sectors of the economy were increasingly dominated by outside interests. Unlike other parts of the West as the 1970s began, Wyoming was not becoming more economically independent. It was becoming, in fact, more colonial.

The three main industries since statehood have been agriculture, mineral production, and tourism. Since territorial days, agriculture often meant the Wyoming Stock Growers Association, a group whose members made up a disproportionate share of the legislature for much of the first century of statehood.

Mineral production, until the 1970s, meant coal and oil. The major coal mines were owned by the Union Pacific Coal Company, a division of the railroad that remained the largest private landowner in the state. A few mines, such as those at Kemmerer and near Sheridan, were owned by smaller corporations, most of which were headquartered in the East. The oil industry, too, was dominated for much of the first half of this century by two companies: Standard Oil of Indiana and Ohio Oil. A few small independent producers managed to prosper during the post–World War II years, but most operations were controlled by multinationals that sent relatively low-ranking managers to oversee their Wyoming operations.

Of the three major industries in the first six decades of this century, tourism remained the least controlled by outside interests, although outside companies held the key concessions in Yellowstone National Park. Hotel/motel chains and fast-food restaurants were slow to locate in Wyoming.

Economic data for the 1950s and 1960s show a period of stagnation. The population during both decades barely grew. When railroads completed the shift away from coal-burning locomotives, the economies of coal mining towns such as Rock Springs and Rawlins declined. The massive oil discoveries in the Middle East brought steep declines in oil exploration and prices. At the same time, cattle ranchers felt the cost squeezes and the increasing competition from alternative sources of meat. Tourism alone seemed prosperous although the primary destination point throughout the period was Yellowstone National Park, where a federally sanctioned concessionaire prospered while towns along the main routes vied as overnight stopovers for park-bound auto travelers.

The key to electoral success in congressional office from Wyoming was to cater to the needs of the three industries and, at the same time, denounce federal government interference in state affairs. The pattern had been set and perfected by Sen. Francis E. Warren, who spent a lifetime in the U.S. Senate, holding the mark for longevity until it was surpassed by Carl Hayden of Arizona. Republican Warren and his Democratic colleague John B. Kendrick, who held similar views toward constituent service and federal interference, both passed from the scene by the beginning of the New Deal.[6] Kendrick was replaced by Joseph C. O'Mahoney, a former editor of the *Wyoming Eagle* and Kendrick aide, who kept an eye out for the interests of Wyoming's three main industries while, at the same time, championing most New Deal programs. O'Mahoney demonstrated his independence of Washington, however, in 1937 by opposing Roosevelt's plan to increase the membership of the Supreme Court. While the position may have lost him friends in the New Deal, it guaranteed him strong support back home. Wyomingites liked having their congressional delegation stand up to the federal government. O'Mahoney served another sixteen years until he was defeated by Gov. Frank Barrett in the Eisenhower landslide of 1952. He was returned for a final term two years later.

It was during O'Mahoney's long tenure that Tracy McCraken became the state's leading Democratic party spokesman. While he used the influence of his newspaper chain to support particular Democratic party candidates, he did not engage in any meaningful debate on issues. T. A. Larson in his *History of Wyoming* could have been describing McCraken's tenure as party leader when he characterized politics in Wyoming as a "game played seriously by a few hundred people, most of them men. In even-numbered years they maximize their efforts and activate temporarily a few thousand recruits."[7]

McCraken's evening paper in Cheyenne, the *State Tribune*, was editorially Republican despite the owner's close affiliation with the Democratic party. Its editor consistently endorsed Republicans. McCraken's morning paper, the *Wyoming Eagle*, remained Democratic.

While McCraken's *Eagle* was the flagship voice of the Democratic party, the main Republican spokesman was J. B. Griffith, who published the Lusk *Herald* in a small eastern Wyoming ranch community. Griffith had come into prominence when he successfully led the campaign of rancher Nels Smith to victory over two-term governor Leslie Miller in 1938.[8] In gratitude, Smith appointed Griffith state land commissioner in 1939. Griffith shared McCraken's love for the "game" of politics even though he owned just one paper, compared to McCraken's statewide chain of dailies. In 1942, Smith lost to the secretary of state, Democrat Lester C. Hunt, who remained governor throughout the war years. At the same time, Griffith helped his fellow townsman and political ally Frank Barrett win the state's only congressional seat. In none of these races did candidates of either party question the general assumptions about catering to the state's major industries. In all cases, economic development meant gaining federal support for the three major industries and making state government their partner in growth.

Governor Hunt was a former Lander dentist who had gained fame in the middle 1930s when, as secretary of state, he commissioned the bucking horse logo for the state's license plate. When World War II ended, Hunt feared Wyoming would experience the same kind of economic collapse it had suffered after World War I. Consequently, he was reluctant to request increased state appropriations for any purpose. War industries had not located in Wyoming as they had in other western states. The economy remained tied to the three basic industries of minerals, agriculture, and tourism. Politics remained a game driven by personality.

In the 1940s and 1950s, McCraken expanded his empire by purchasing daily newspapers in key Wyoming cities and adding broadcast stations to his operation. Unlike many of his less-affluent predecessors in the Wyoming newspaper business, McCraken was a businessman, first, and a political kingmaker, second. To understand McCraken's political influence in the postwar years, one must look back to a major financial and political coup in 1937, when McCraken's much smaller *Wyoming Eagle* forced a merger with what had been the most powerful statewide daily, the *Wyoming State Tribune*.[9] By the end of World War II, McCraken had control of the larger Republican daily and newspapers in a half dozen other Wyoming towns.

Observers initially predicted that the *State Tribune*'s editorial pages would make the inevitable switch to Democratic support. But McCraken, the businessman, took a nonpartisan approach. The *Tribune* was to remain staunchly Republican editorially for the rest of McCraken's life and beyond.

Democratic party nominees continued to be men who held the same basic assumptions about the three Wyoming industries as McCraken held. As the 1950s began, however, some issues crept into the politics of personality although none was to threaten the continued concern for the health of the three major industries.

Like several of his predecessors, including Warren and Kendrick, Hunt resigned from the governorship in mid-term to take a seat in the U.S. Senate. Meanwhile, Frank Barrett left Congress after four terms and, with Griffith's editorial help, won election to the governorship. Two years later, he, too, moved to the U.S. Senate following an upset win over Senator O'Mahoney in the 1952 general election.[10]

Barrett and Hunt shared similar assumptions about federal assistance to Wyoming's main industries. Both courted the stock growers and the oil industry and generally voted in their interests. The two men split over the tactics of Joe McCarthy. Barrett supported the Wisconsin senator even when the Senate voted for censure. By early 1954, Hunt was becoming increasingly troubled by McCarthy's actions, worried about his own health, and disturbed by his son's minor legal problems. The Democratic party, nationally and in Wyoming, expected him to seek reelection. On an April morning in 1954, Hunt brought a rifle to his Senate office and committed suicide. His death sent shock waves through the Wyoming political scene. O'Mahoney, who was still very popular statewide and was McCraken's choice for the seat, helped settle the confusion. He ran for the seat and was returned to the Senate after spending two years out of office.[11]

Four years later, the Democrats reached a postwar pinnacle when a popular young University of Wyoming history professor, Dr. Gale McGee, upset Barrett's reelection bid to the Senate. As McGee was joining fellow Democrat O'Mahoney in the U.S. Senate, Rawlins lawyer J. J. ("Joe") Hickey took back the governor's office from the Republicans by defeating incumbent Milward Simpson. In most respects, personality and not issues drove these campaigns. Along with the inevitable aid from McCracken's papers, McGee relied on a nonpartisan base of former students whom he had inspired during his dozen years of university teaching.

Simpson had gained a reputation for free spending during his four years as governor. He acted somewhat out of character for a Republican in other matters, too. He openly opposed capital punishment, declaring he would commute such sentences to life in prison. Hailing from the Yellowstone Park area town of Cody where he once edited the local newspaper (in which he maintained an ownership interest), Simpson was angered by what he believed was poor service and unfair prices set by the Yellowstone concessionaire chosen by the National Park Service. He asked the legislature to authorize state purchase of the Yellowstone concessions. The tourism industry was uncomfortable with Simpson's radical plan, and the legislature refused to let this experiment in socialism proceed. Instead, legislators opted for increased state outlays for the Wyoming Travel Commission so that the agency could attract more tourists for longer stays.

In the view of some observers, Simpson lost in 1958 because he had become mired in a dispute over where the proposed interstate highways would intersect in northern Wyoming. When he opted not to overrule the supposedly nonpartisan state highway department's proposal favoring a location near Buffalo, he angered Sheridan County voters, who then sat out the fall election. The balance was tipped toward Hickey, who proved to be more fiscally conservative than Simpson and equally defiant of federal government "interference." The most celebrated nonissue of Hickey's administration was the media-charged demand from federal highway officials that Wyoming's highways be striped with white paint instead of the traditional yellow. In a symbolic display of state's rights, the Wyoming legislature ordered state highway officials not to comply, even at the risk of losing federal highway funds. The issue was eventually settled quietly.

Like the senatorial election of 1954, the 1960 race was memorable for tragedy. Senator O'Mahoney, who had suffered a stroke in 1959 and remained in poor health, did not seek another term. Republicans nominated forty-two-year-old congressman Keith Thomson, a businessman and journalist by training, who defeated a Casper lawyer in the November general election. Wyoming Republicans, disappointed with the election of young John F. Kennedy to the presidency, felt some consolation with young Thomson's victory. They prophesied that, with any luck, he could challenge Warren's senatorial longevity mark.

Barely two weeks after the general election, Thomson, on vacation near Cody, had a heart attack and died. He had not yet even been sworn into office. In a move that some observers believe brought long-term disaster to the Democratic party, Governor Hickey resigned from his office, allowing his fellow Democrat Secretary of State Jack Gage to become acting governor. Gage then appointed Hickey to serve out the two years in the U.S. Senate until an election could be held. The move angered Republicans, who characterized it as tantamount to electoral theft.[12]

On 26 December 1960, before Hickey was sworn in to the Senate and less than a month before John F. Kennedy was to be inaugurated, Democratic power broker Tracy McCraken died of a heart attack at a ranch west of Cheyenne. Two months before the election, old Republican kingmaker Griffith had died, bringing to an end the game of personality politics he had so ably played for a generation against his old rival McCraken.

Even though the Democrats again held both U.S. Senate seats and the governorship, the 1962 elections promised to undo much of the party's strength. When the election results came in, Hickey lost by a wide margin to Milward Simpson, the same man he had defeated for governor six years earlier.

Meanwhile, Senator McGee continued building a reputation for bringing home the federal bacon. In 1959, through the influence of Lyndon Johnson, the Senate leader, McGee became the only freshman senator named to the powerful Senate Appropriations Committee. Even though he was hardly the darling of the radical right, McGee served his constituency, convincing ranchers and oilmen that he could be counted on to support their interests.

Unlike other states that have strong manufacturing bases, Wyoming's labor unions have never been strong. Organized labor in Wyoming, devastated by the closing of coal mines and the scaling back in railroad employment, lost a sharp challenge in 1963 when the legislature passed the "right-to-work" law. Passage came on a one-vote margin following strong lobbying by Gov. Clifford P. Hansen, who called in the National Guard to keep order outside the capitol during debate on the bill.

Milward Simpson opted not to seek reelection to a full six-year term in 1966. Governor Hansen won the Republican Senate nomination and faced popular Congressman Teno Roncalio in the fall general election.

As the campaign of 1966 opened, the state's economy remained static. There appeared to be great potential for mineral development, although the few companies taking advantage of the low property taxes and absence of state income taxes were mostly multinationals. Individual and family-owned ranches were facing increasing pressures from corporate operations.

Wyoming personality-politicians since World War II had worried about overreliance on the three very cyclical main industries. They had reason for concern, as the boom-and-bust cycle in those industries demonstrated. While most might have wished for spectacular and sustained economic growth, few expected it would ever happen. An exception was Ernest Wilkerson, a Casper lawyer and businessman who had been a financial backer of the *Casper Morning Star* when it began publishing in 1949. The *Star* was bought out six years later by the *Casper Tribune-Herald*, ending Wilkerson's direct connection to the media. Further, the Casper Democrat remained outside McCraken's circle of Democratic party allies.

Wilkerson mounted an "issues campaign" and won the 1966 Democratic party nomination for governor on the platform "Wyoming's wealth for Wyoming's people." Concerned with the increasing concentration of absentee ownership in the mineral industry, Wilkerson argued that if the state was to prosper, the mineral industry should be expected to carry some of the burden in the form of mineral severance taxes. No politician since before the Second World War had ever so directly challenged one of the state's three main industry groups. National mineral companies reacted with alarm and sent representatives on speaking tours to counter Wilkerson's claims. Some threatened to cease operations in Wyoming altogether if such a tax was instituted. Others passed out bumper stickers to company employees with slogans such as Wyoming's Oil Is Our Bread and Butter.

With Cliff Hansen, the incumbent, running for the Senate, the Republicans chose Torrington lawyer Stan Hathaway as their gubernatorial nominee. Known for his no-nonsense straight talk, Hathaway gained strong support from the frightened mineral industry. Hansen narrowly defeated Roncalio. Hathaway had an easier victory over Wilkerson, but as the next three years were to demonstrate, Wyoming politics would never be the same.

Party kingmakers, Republican Griffith and Democrat McCraken, had maintained a general consensus on issues affecting the major state industries while playing the game of politics. But politics in Wyoming was shifting away from personalities. With what the absentee-owned corporations viewed as threats to their Wyoming operations, they became increasingly involved in partisan races. Newspapers, once owned by proudly political publishers who often seemed more concerned with party victory than the bottom line, were bought out by chains, little concerned with politics except for the ways in which it might affect the economic condition of their investments. The political landscape was no longer shaped by the locally controlled media. The media became a conduit for economic interests residing far beyond the state borders.

Economic conditions remained stagnant in the late 1960s despite "guns-and-butter" prosperity in much of the rest of the country. After opposing any severance tax during the 1966 campaign and the ensuing two years of his first term, Hathaway reluctantly signed a modest severance tax bill passed by the 1969 legislature. Passage came just in time. Five years later, when Hathaway refused to seek a third term, opting for a brief tenure as President Gerald Ford's secretary of the interior, another boom period in minerals had begun.

Four Republicans, each representing important divisions in the state party, dueled for the gubernatorial nomination. The losing candidates included Riverton newspaper publisher Roy Peck (a longtime proponent of industrial development) and Sheridan rancher Malcolm Wallop, who later defeated McGee for the U.S. Senate. The Republican nominee, ultraconservative trucking company owner Dick Jones, lost in the general election to Kemmerer lawyer Ed Herschler.

Democrat Herschler began an unprecedented three full terms in 1975. In Herschler's administration, mineral severance taxes were increased and some of the revenues were designated to alleviate "impact" in coal-mining communities. A permanent mineral trust fund was set up to ensure some economic security when the inevitable bust cycle occurred. The Department of Environmental Quality, formed in Hathaway's administration, was given increasing responsibility over mining operations.

Herschler's administration, despite its support for higher severance taxes and stiffer environmental laws, sought a balance among the three main industry groups. A rancher and former legal counsel for the Union

Pacific Railroad, Herschler did not elicit the fears Ernest Wilkerson had from the mineral industry even though their well-paid lobbyists worked to diminish severance taxes. The state media, despite increasing chain ownership, generally applauded Herschler's tax policies that had been drafted to provide much-needed public services to municipalities and counties.

In a rare demonstration of solidarity, the railroads and Wyoming ranchers united to defeat a proposed "coal slurry" pipeline. Ranchers feared serious depletion of groundwater; the railroad did not welcome an alternative source of transport for its most important cargo, Wyoming coal.

The Herschler administration joined in the denunciation of the pipeline project, but it did not ignore "economic development." Worried that too much reliance on the mineral industry might lead to difficulties in the future, Herschler tried to lure all manner of industry to the state. The international trade office sent boosters to Europe and Asia in attempts to gain wider markers for Wyoming's agricultural products and energy resources. When voters in Nevada and Utah protested placement of the MX missile system in their states, Herschler embraced the project, with the overwhelming approval of the state's media.

Meanwhile, the state's congressional delegation had turned decidedly Republican. When Roncalio announced his retirement in 1978, President Ford's young chief of staff Dick Cheney returned to Wyoming and won the state's sole congressional seat. Two years earlier, Malcolm Wallop scored an upset win over Senator McGee, who most observers believed had lost touch with his constituents. The senator had dropped his effective but politically pointless motto McGee for Me in favor of a Washington-generated campaign slogan, He Has Clout. He campaigned sporadically in the state, relying on out-of-state consultants who recommended that he tend to his senatorial duties rather than make the customary statewide personal appearances so expected by Wyoming voters.

Ironically, Republican Wallop was endorsed by environmental groups who favored his voting record on such issues in the state senate over McGee's lukewarm environmental pronouncements. His environmentalist proclivities, however, were not reflected in his Senate record, one that became increasingly conservative in the Reagan years. When Senator Hansen opted to retire, the Republicans nominated Al Simpson, the son of former governor and senator Milward Simpson.

Following his defeat, McGee was named ambassador to the Organization of American States by President Jimmy Carter. After Reagan's election, McGee remained in Washington as a consultant until shortly before his death in 1992.

In the closing years of his final term, Herschler watched the Wyoming economy hit the inevitable bust cycle. By 1984, the state's population was in decline and the energy industry, buffeted by international price cuts, began closing mines, shutting in oil wells and laying off workers. The state media reacted with some alarm, with a few recommending that Herschler institute plans for ambitious economic diversity. Attempts to woo industries ranging from a Budweiser brewing plant to makers of mechanical bulls met with little success.

When Herschler announced he did not intend to seek a fourth term, Republicans were relieved. They had not held the governorship in twelve years and all indications pointed to a GOP victory. A liberal Republican emerged from the hard fought primary with the party nomination. He was Pete Simpson, whose more conservative younger brother Al was becoming nationally known from his seat in the U.S. Senate. The Democratic nomination went to a relatively unknown Casper lawyer, Mike Sullivan, who gained the nomination almost by default. Despite the predictions of media analysts, Sullivan, the more conservative of the two men, scored a major upset, sending Pete Simpson back to his post as University of Wyoming vice-president for development.

Unlike the economic good times experienced by Wyomingites during much of his predecessor's tenure, Governor Sullivan faced an economic downturn rivaling even the Great Depression in its severity. The population of the state declined as unemployed workers sought jobs in other states. Banks closed at near record rates and real estate markets were flooded with homes in such energy-dependent towns as Casper and Rawlins.

Sullivan, like his predecessors, pursued a policy of enticing industry into the state. An ill-conceived loan program, initiated in his immediate predecessor's waning days, tried to pour low-interest state loans into very high risk ventures. The setbacks did not jeopardize Sullivan's reelection campaign against the Republican nominee, Mary Mead, daughter of former governor and senator Cliff Hansen. In 1992, Sullivan became the first sitting governor to endorse the candidacy of Bill Clinton. Even though the economy was an important issue in Wyoming, the state's most influential newspaper, the *Casper Star-Tribune* endorsed the incumbent president. Even Governor Sullivan's active campaign was not enough for the Democratic nominee. George Bush carried Wyoming by a wide margin.

In 1933, Wyoming politicians, publishers, and voters still yearned for the advantages to be gained from economic development. But the usual ambivalence about population growth and destruction of a way of life became more sharply evident. New residents, many attracted to the state because it was not economically well developed, opposed government economic development plans. At the same time, resentment over increasing colonialism and federal government interference continued to grow in Wyoming. When an influential committee of leading decision makers convened as the Wyoming Public Policy Forum in late 1992, participants noted that no federal government officials were among their number. Further, no publishers or broadcasters were represented. The media, once the source of homegrown political power, were no longer run by Wyomingites. The editorial direction, if any, was directed from beyond the state's borders, just like decision making in the state's three main industries. The editors, once the political kingmakers, were mostly young, ambitious employees of out-of-state corporations. Promotions meant moving to other newspapers owned by the chains in other states. To many longtime Wyomingites, these developments indicated that colonialism was more pervasive in 1993 than at any time in the state's history. In the political arena where McCracken and Griffith once battled editorially, outsiders with little interest in Wyoming politics churned out the mostly interchangeable press product of the 1990s.

Notes

CHAPTER 1

1. Institute of Business, Economic and Government Research, "The Petroleum Industry in Alaska," *Monthly Review of Alaska Business and Economic Conditions* 1 (1964): 1.

2. Brent R. Bowen, *Defense Spending in Alaska* (Fairbanks: University of Alaska, Institute of Social, Economic and Government Research, July 1971), 1.

3. Institute of Business, Economic and Government Research, "Alaska's Economy in 1967," *Monthly Review of Alaska Business and Economic Conditions* 5 (1967): 2.

4. Herb Hilscher and Miriam Hilscher, *Alaska, USA* (Boston: Little, Brown and Company, 1959), chapter 16 title.

5. Federal Energy Regulatory Commission Hearings, Trans-Alaska Pipeline System, prepared direct testimony of Henry W. Coulter (docket no. OR 78–1), presented on behalf of the state of Alaska, Washington, D.C., 16 December 1981, 5–6. [transcript]

6. *Iron Age* 208 (July 1971): 41.

7. Federal Task Force on Alaskan Oil Development, *A Preliminary Report to the President,* Washington, D.C., 15 September 1969.

8. Barry Lopez, *Arctic Dreams* (New York: Charles Scribner's Sons, 1986), 397.

9. George Collins and Lowell Sumner, "The Northeast Arctic: The Last Great Wilderness," *Sierra Club Bulletin* 38 (October 1953): 25.

10. U.S. Congress, House Interior and Insular Affairs Committee, Subcommittee on Merchant Marine and Fisheries, Hearings, S. 1899, A Bill to Authorize the Establishment of the Arctic Wildlife Range, Alaska (Washington, D.C.: Government Printing Office, 1960): par. 2, 413–14.

11. Fairbanks Chamber of Commerce to the Bureau of Land Management BLM (Anchorage office), 30 January 1958, BLM file, Arctic National Wildlife Range (ANWR), box 13, Alaska Conservation Society Papers, University of Alaska, Fairbanks.

12. Bil Gilbert, "Power and Light on a Lonely Land," *Pipeline* (1974), clipping, Oil and Gas File, box 43 (105), Fairbanks Environmental Center Collection, University of Alaska, Fairbanks.

13. Federal Task Force on North Slope Oil Development, *Preliminary Report,* 20.

14. *Alaska Industry* 2 (October 1970): 11.

15. *Alaska Industry* 2 (September 1971): 4.

16. U.S. Department of the Interior, Draft Environmental Impact Statement for the Trans-Alaska Pipeline System, sec. 102 (2)C of the National Environmental Policy Act of 1969, Washington, D.C., 15 January 1971, 142.

17. U.S. Congress, Senate, Committee on Interior and Insular Affairs, Hearings, Trans-Alaska Pipeline System, Draft Environmental Impact Statement (Washington, D.C.: Government Printing Office, 1971), 2: 618, 630; 3: 783 (hereafter cited as Hearings, TAPS, Draft EIS).

18. Hearings, TAPS, Draft EIS, 2:3, exhibit 4; 1:41.

19. Bill Walters of ARCO, as quoted in *Oil Daily* 17 (September 1971): 91. (Atlantic Richfield merged with Atlantic Refining in 1966 to become ARCO.)

20. Kenneth Brower, *Earth and Great Weather: The Brooks Range* (San Francisco: Friends of the Earth, 1971), 165.

21. Hearings, TAPS, Draft EIS, supplemental testimony, 7:3, exhibit 56(b).

22. As quoted in Richard Corrigan, "Environment Report: Fishing Town Joins Legal Fight to Stop Trans-Alaska Pipeline Project," *National Journal* 3 (3 July 1971): 1402.

23. U.S. Department of the Interior, *Final Environmental Impact Statement, Proposed Trans-Alaska Pipeline.* National Technical Information Service, Springfield, Va. (March 1972), 7:M-5-3-6. Further dissent from the Department of the Interior's official stance appeared shortly afterward in Richard D. Nehring, "Future Developments of Artic Oil and Gas: An Analysis of the Economic Implications and Alternatives," Office of Economic Analysis, Department of the Interior, Washington, D.C., 10 May 1972; and Jack O. Horton, "An Alternative to the Trans-Alaska Pipeline," undated memorandum, reproduced in the record of U.S. Congress, Joint Economic Committee, Hearings, Natural Gas Regulation and the Trans-Alaska Pipeline, 7–9, 22 June 1972 (Washington, D.C.: Government Printing Office, 1972): 344–45.

24. Hearings, TAPS, Draft EIS, 1971, 4:4–5.

25. *Congressional Record,* 93d Cong., 1st sess. (17 July 1973): 24323.

26. Brock Evans to Ken Farquarson, Sierra Club of British Columbia, 30 May 1973, Alaska File, box 8, Sierra Club office files (San Francisco), Bancroft Library, University of California, Berkeley.

27. *Fairbanks Daily News-Miner,* 13 July 1973.

28. *Congressional Quarterly Almanac* 29 (1973): 603.

29. Harvey Manning, "Which Way Out?," *Not Man Apart* 3 (July 1973): 8.

30. Joint Economic Committee, Hearings, Natural Gas Regulation and the Trans-Alaska Pipeline, 344–45.

31. *Fairbanks Daily News-Miner,* 15 March 1973.

32. *Congressional Record,* 93d Cong., 1st sess. (12 November 1973): 36599.

33. Official state of Alaska figures quoted in Art Davidson, *In the Wake of the Exxon Valdez* (San Francisco: Sierra Club Books, 1990), 84.

34. Bernard DeVoto, "The West Against Itself," *Harper's* 194 (January 1947): 13.

CHAPTER 2

1. Mary Austin, *The Land of Little Rain,* originally published in 1903, was reprinted in 1988 by Penguin Books, with an introduction by Edward Abbey.

2. Edward Abbey, *The Journey Home: Some Words in Defense of the American West* (New York: E.P. Dutton, 1977), 147.

3. Ibid., 147–48.

4. Robert F. Berkhofer, Jr., "Space, Time, Culture, and the New Frontier," *Agricultural History* 38 (1964): 21–30.

5. William E. Smythe, *The Conquest of Arid America* (Seattle: University of Washington Press, 1969). This reprint of the 1905 edition includes a new introduction by Lawrence B. Lee.

6. Ibid., xxvii.

7. Karen L. Smith, *The Magnificent Experiment: Building the Salt River Reclamation Project, 1890–1917* (Tucson: University of Arizona Press, 1986), 9–10.

8. Ibid., 25–34.

9. Ibid., 157.

10. Jack Williams, "Postlude: The Future," in *The Taming of the Salt* (Phoenix: Salt River Project, 1979): 128–30.

11. See Joseph E. Stevens, *Hoover Dam: An American Adventure* (Norman: University of Oklahoma Press, 1988).

12. Abbey, *Journey Home,* 148. For a recent history of Phoenix, see Bradford Luckingham, *Phoenix: The History of a Southwestern Metropolis* (Tucson: University of Arizona Press, 1989). Luckingham has also written a brief history of Phoenix, Tucson, Albuquerque, and El Paso in *The Urban Southwest: A Profile History of Albuquerque, El Paso, Phoenix, and Tucson* (El Paso: Texas Western Press, University of Texas, 1982).

13. John A. Folk-Williams, Susan C. Fry, and Lucy Hilgendorf, *Western Water Flows to the Cities* (Washington, D.C.: Island Press, 1985), 17.

14. This list is based on a case study of agricultural water quality problems by Brian P. Borofka, C.S. Cousins-Leatherman, and Richard D. Kelley, "Developing a State Ground Water Policy in the Corn Belt: The Iowa Case," in ed. Deborah M. Fairchild, *Ground Water Quality and Agricultural Practices* (Chelsea, Mich.: Lewis Publishers, 1987), 392.

15. Philip L. Fradkin, *A River No More: The Colorado River and the West* (New York: Alfred A. Knopf, 1981), 197–98.

16. Rich Johnson, *The Central Arizona Project, 1918–1968* (Tucson: University of Arizona Press, 1977), 20.

17. Ibid., 226–27.

18. Marc Reisner, *Cadillac Desert: The American West and Its Disappearing Water* (New York: Viking, 1986), 304–305.

19. Ibid., 314.

20. Ibid., 309–10.

21. Frank Welsh, *How to Create a Water Crisis* (Boulder: Johnson Books, 1985), 43–48.

22. Ibid., 142–45.

23. Paul Lowes, "Sitting on Gold: The Yavapai Resistance to Orme Dam" (Unpublished paper prepared for a class in American Indian history at Arizona State University, July 1989). Copy in the possession of the author.

24. Ibid.

25. Peter Iverson, *Carlos Montezuma and the Changing World of American Indians* (Albuquerque: University of New Mexico Press, 1982), 184–85.

26. Lowes, "Sitting on Gold."
27. Ibid.
28. Ibid.
29. Robert H. White, *Tribal Assets: The Rebirth of Native America* (New York: Henry Holt and Company, 1990), 146–49.
30. Ibid., 150.
31. Ibid., 154–59, and Ak-Chin Indian Community, "Water Settlement Celebration, January 9, 1988."
32. White, *Tribal Assets*, 159–60.
33. Ibid., 163–65; Ak-Chin, "Water Settlement." For a useful discussion of recent negotiations on Indian water rights, including a discussion of Ak-Chin, see Thomas R. McGuire, "Getting to Yes in the New West," in ed. George Pierre Castile and Robert L. Bee, *State and Reservation: New Perspectives on Federal Indian Policy* (Tucson: University of Arizona Press, 1992), 224–46.
34. McGuire, "Getting to Yes," 232.
35. Ibid., 232–33; Ak-Chin, "Water Settlement"; John A. Folk-Williams, *What Indian Water Means to the West* (Santa Fe: Western Network, 1982), 13–14. See also Thomas R. McGuire, "Illusions of Choice in the Indian Irrigation Service: The Ak-Chin Project and an Epilogue," *Journal of the Southwest* 30(2): 200–21.
36. Ak-Chin, "Water Settlement"; White, *Tribal Assets*, 168–72.
37. Ak-Chin, "Water Settlement."
38. Susan Edmond, "Pinal County Devising Plan to Fix CAP Mess," *Arizona Republic*, 20 June 1993 (reprinted from *Casa Grande Dispatch*).
39. Tony Davis, "Can Some Good Come Out of the CAP?," *High Country News*, 17 May 1993 (reprinted from *Tucson Weekly*).
40. Edmond, "Pinal County"; Davis, "Can Some Good."
41. Reisner, *Cadillac Desert*, 314–15; Steve Yozwiak and Paul Brinkley-Rogers, "Fight for Water Is Fight for Life: State Senators Tackle Urban-Rural Tug of War," *Arizona Republic*, 25 March 1990.
42. Davis, "Can Some Good."
43. Edmond, "Pinal County." For another plan sympathetic to farming interests, see Michael J. Brophy, "The Central Arizona Project—A Project in Crisis and a Future in Jeopardy" (Unpublished paper, 3 April 1992). Copy in possession of the author.
44. Davis, "Can Some Good."
45. On the "progress" in Santa Fe from one golf course to six, see Bruce Selcraig, "Fore! in Santa Fe," *High Country News*, 17 May 1993. Donald Snow, associate editor of *Northern Lights* and a resident of Missoula, muses, "As I myself have learned here on the threshold of middle age, all things merge into one, and a golf course runs through it." Snow, "A Golf Course Runs Through It," *Northern Lights* (Spring 1993), 3.

CHAPTER 3

1. Jackson K. Putnam, "The Pattern of Modern California Politics," *Pacific Historical Review* 61 (February 1992): 23–27; and Putnam, "The Progressive

Legacy in California: Fifty Years of Politics," in ed. Tom Sitton and William Deverell, *California Progressivism: Revisited and Revised* (Berkeley and Los Angeles: University of California Press, forthcoming).

2. Part of his success was due to his crafty exploitation of California's notorious crossfiling law, which enabled him to win reelection in 1946 without a Democratic opponent, and his founding and direction of the California Republican Assembly, a private political organization that allowed Republicans to get around cumbersome restrictions on party activities. See Jackson K. Putnam, *Modern California Politics,* 3rd ed. (San Francisco: Boyd and Fraser, 1990), 28–34; Leo Katcher, *Earl Warren: A Political Biography* (New York: McGraw-Hill, 1967), 82–86; John D. Weaver, *Warren: The Man, the Court, the Era* (Boston: Little, Brown, 1967), 101, 148; Janet Stevenson, *The Undiminished Man: A Political Biography of Robert Walker Kenny* (Novato, Calif.: Chandler and Sharp, 1980), chap. 7; and Earl Warren, *The Memoirs of Earl Warren* (Garden City: Doubleday, 1977), 159–71.

3. Warren repeatedly used the word "pragmatic" to describe his actions as governor. Warren, *Memoirs,* chap. 8. On his activism and his dealings with the legislature, see Katcher, *Earl Warren,* 177, and Richard Harvey, *Earl Warren, Governor of California* (Jericho, N.Y.: Exposition Press, 1969), 97–98.

4. Putnam, "Progressive Legacy," 21. Warren also pushed through some tax increases, and the state budget went past the billion dollar mark during his administration. Putnam, *Modern California Politics,* 34.

5. Warren did secure passage of some of his health care proposals by increasing the Aid to the Blind program and by expansion of the unemployment insurance program. Putnam, *Modern California Politics,* 35–36; Warren, *Memoirs,* 186–89; Katcher, *Earl Warren,* 186–90; Weaver, *Warren,* 136–40; and Harvey, *Earl Warren,* 119–32.

6. Norris Hundley, Jr., *The Great Thirst: Californians and Water, 1770s–1990s,* (Berkeley and Los Angeles: University of California, 1992), 268–71.

7. Putnam, *Modern California Politics,* 37–38; Warren, *Memoirs,* 232; Harvey, *Earl Warren,* 157–60.

8. Warren opposed antipicketing, antifeatherbedding, and right-to-work bills. He secured expansion of the unemployment insurance and workers' compensation systems and attempted unsuccessfully to have farm workers included in the latter. He angered the unions, however, with his stances on the issues of "hot cargo," jurisdictional strikes, and state senate reapportionment, but he seems not to have forfeited many labor votes in the process. Putnam, *Modern California Politics,* 37–38.

9. Ingrid W. Scobie, "Jack B. Tenney and the 'Parasitic Menace': Anti-Communist Legislation in California, 1940–1949," *Pacific Historical Review* 43 (1974): 188–211; Edward L. Barrett, Jr., *The Tenney Committee: Legislative Investigation of Subversive Activities in California* (Ithaca: Cornell University, 1951); Robert L. Pritchard, "California Un-American Activities Investigations: Subversion of the Right?," *California Historical Society Quarterly* 49 (1970): 309–27; Edward R. Long, "Earl Warren and the Politics of Anti-Communism," *Pacific Historical Review* 51 (1982), 51–70; and Putnam, *Modern California Politics,* 38–41. Edward Long's article takes a more critical view of Warren's actions here than does this author.

10. Putnam, *Modern California Politics,* 40, 123.

11. Ibid., p. 43; Royce D. Delmatier, Clarence F. McIntosh, and Earle G. Waters, eds., *The Rumble of California Politics, 1848–1970* (New York: John Wiley and Sons, 1970), 330; Herbert L. Phillips, *Big Wayward Girl: An Informal Political History of California* (Garden City: Doubleday, 1968), 172–73.

12. Putnam, *Modern California Politics,* 42; H. Brett Melendy and Benjamin F. Gilbert, *The Governors of California: Peter Burnett to Edmund G. Brown* (Georgetown, Calif.: Talisman Press, 1965), 433–34. On the establishment and later destruction of the Short-Doyle Act, see Gale Cook, "A Promise Unfulfilled," *California Journal* 20 (May 1989): 194–97.

13. In addition to the above sources by Putnam, Phillips, Melendy and Gilbert, and Delmatier, McIntosh, and Waters, see Gladwin Hill, *Dancing Bear: An Inside Look at California Politics* (Cleveland: World Publishing Co., 1968), chap 11; and especially Totton J. Anderson, "The 1958 Election in California," *Western Political Quarterly* 12 (1959): 276–300.

14. Putnam, *Modern California Politics,* 45–48; Delmatier, McIntosh, and Waters, *Rumble,* 331–42; Jacqueline R. Braitman, "Elizabeth Snyder and the Role of Women in the Postwar Resurgence of California's Democratic Party," *Pacific Historical Review* 62 (May 1993). I am indebted to Ms. Braitman for providing me with an advance copy of this article, an earlier version of which she read as a paper at the Pacific Coast Branch of the American Historical Association annual meeting in Kona, Hawaii, July 1991. For a long-range look at the rise of the state Democratic party, see Michael P. Rogin and John L. Shover, *Political Change in California: Critical Elections and Social Movements, 1890–1966* (Westport, Conn.: Greenwood, 1970), chap. 5.

15. The Republicans had been in power since the election of 1898 except for the abortive reign of Culbert L. Olson (elected in 1938). Olson's administration was so ineffective that he hardly interrupted the Republican hegemony. Putnam, *Modern California Politics,* 24–28; Robert E. Burke, *Olson's New Deal for California* (Berkeley and Los Angeles: University of California Press, 1953).

16. Brown's legislative achievements are laid out in Delmatier, McIntosh, and Waters, *Rumble,* 341–45, 348–54; Putnam, *Modern California Politics,* 48–54; and Phillips, *Big Wayward Girl,* chaps. 27, 28, 31.

17. There were also some minor but significant innovations such as smog control and consumer protection legislation, the latter mainly attributable to Unruh. Delmatier, McIntosh, and Waters, *Rumble,* 348; Melendy and Gilbert, *Governors,* 443, 446; Phillips, *Big Wayward Girl,* 188.

18. In addition to the above sources see Roger Rapoport, *California Dreaming: The Political Odyssey of Pat and Jerry Brown* (Berkeley: Nolo Press, 1982), 75.

19. A thorough account of the origins and development of this act can be found in Edmund G. Brown et al., *California: The Dynamic State* (Santa Barbara: McNally and Loftin, 1966), chap. 5.

20. In addition to the sources in n. 16, see ibid., chap 4, and, most important, Hundley, *The Great Thirst,* 277–87. This system is now usually referred to as the State Water Project.

21. Governmental reorganization was a major facet of the early shaping of the

neoprogressive agenda. Jackson K. Putnam, "The Persistence of Progressivism in the 1920's: The Case of California," *Pacific Historical Review* 35 (November 1966): 399–400, 410.

22. Melendy and Gilbert, *Governors*, 446–47. An interesting critique of this effort was made by Ron Seyb, "It's Ideas That Count: Pat Brown Reorganizes California's Executive Branch" (Paper read at the Western Political Science Association Annual Meeting, Seattle, Washington, 21 March 1991).

23. Phillips, *Big Wayward Girl,* chap. 31; Delmatier, McIntosh, and Waters, *Rumble,* 354–57.

24. Phillips, *Big Wayward Girl,* 229; Ed Gray, "Jesse Unruh, 'Big Daddy' of California," *The Nation* 196 (9 March 1963); Helen Fuller, "The Man to See in California," *Harpers* 242 (April 1971); James R. Mills, *A Disorderly House: The Brown-Unruh Years in California* (Berkeley: Heyday, 1987). The latter is informative but heavily biased against Brown and in favor of Unruh.

25. V. O. Key, Jr., "A Theory of Critical Elections," *Journal of Politics* 17 (February 1955).

26. Kurt Schuparra, "The 1958 California Election and the Origins of the State's Conservative Movement" (Paper presented at Pacific Coast Branch of the American Historical Association Annual Meeting, Loyola Marymount University, Los Angeles, August 1993). I am indebted to Mr. Schuparra for giving me an advance copy of this paper.

27. Kurt Schuparra, "Barry Goldwater and Southern California Conservatism: Ideology, Image and Myth in the 1964 Republican Presidential Primary," *Southern California Quarterly* 74 (Fall 1992): 277–98.

28. Putnam, *Modern California Politics,* 54–58; Delmatier, McIntosh, and Waters, *Rumble,* 357–64.

29. The Democrats held onto the attorney general's office and retained leads in the state senate of 21 to 19 and in the assembly of 42 to 38.

30. For accounts of Reagan's speeches and the main outlines of his conservative political philosophy see Lee Edwards, *Ronald Reagan: A Political Biography* (Houston: Nordland, 1980), chap. 7; Bill Boyarsky, *Ronald Reagan: His Life and Rise to the Presidency* (New York: Random House, 1981), chap. 7; Lou Cannon, *Reagan* (New York: Putnam's, 1982), chap. 8; and Paul D. Erickson, *Reagan Speaks: The Making of an American Myth* (New York: New York University Press, 1985).

31. Putnam, *Modern California Politics,* 5–60; Cannon, *Reagan,* 119–24.

32. Cannon, chaps. 10–13. By far the best accounts of Reagan's adventures in the field of public finance are Garin Burbank, "Speaker Moretti, Governor Reagan, and the Search for Tax Reform in California," *Pacific Historical Review* 61 (May 1992), 193–214, and Burbank, "Governor Reagan's Only Defeat: The Proposition 1 Campaign in 1973," *California History* 72 (Winter 1993–94), 360–73, 395–97.

33. Opposing views of Reagan and the universities can be found in W. J. Rorabaugh, *Berkeley at War: 1960's* (New York: Oxford University Press, 1989) and Garin Burbank, "Governor Reagan and Academic Freedom at Berkeley, 1966–1970," *Canadian Review of American Studies* 20 (Summer 1989): 17–30.

34. The Rumford Act had been repealed by the passage of ballot measure Proposition 14 in the election of 1964. The latter in turn was invalidated by the courts, thus reinstating Rumford. Putnam, *Modern California Politics,* 61; Cannon, *Reagan,* 111.

35. Cannon, *Reagan,* 124–25; Putnam, *Modern California Politics,* 61, 65, 70. This was especially true regarding Reagan's stance on the aforementioned Redwoods National Park. Although he attacked it in his 1966 campaign and in the early days of his administration, he supported passage of it in 1968. Cannon, *Reagan,* 124, 349, 351, 352; Melody Webb, "Parks for People: Lyndon Johnson and the National Park System" (Paper presented at Frontier and Region Conference on the American West in Honor of Martin Ridge, Huntington Library, San Marino, California, 13 April 1993). Dr. Webb told me that day that she considered Reagan's support essential to the bill's passage in Congress. This episode neatly demonstrates the difference between Reagan, the ideological campaigner, and Reagan, the pragmatic governor.

36. Cannon, *Reagan,* 128–32.

37. An outstanding analysis of this subject is Garin Burbank, "Governor Reagan and California Welfare Reform: The Grand Compromise of 1971," *California History* 70 (Fall 1991), 278–89, 328–30.

38. Governors who did this and governed effectively as a result were Frank Merriam (1934–1938) and Goodwin Knight (1953–1958). Two who refused to do so and were gubernatorial failures were Friend W. Richardson (1923–1926) and Culbert L. Olson (1939–1942). Putnam, "Pattern of Modern California Politics," 28–29, 31–34, 37–38.

39. Ibid., 43.

40. Ibid.; Cannon, *Reagan,* 125.

41. Lou Cannon, *President Reagan: The Role of a Lifetime* (New York: Simon & Schuster, 1991), is replete with examples of Reagan's inattention and unawareness on crucial issues.

42. Putnam, *Modern California Politics,* 63. Some right-wing extremists such as Senator John Schmitz, a John Birch Society member, did not forget and attacked Reagan as a sellout to the liberals. An associate of Schmitz named Kent Steffgen, satirizing Reagan's political autobiography *Where's the Rest of Me,* published a book entitled *Here's the Rest of Him* (Reno: Foresight Books, 1968) in which he charged that Reagan's "remainder" was politically liberal. The book tended to sink without trace in an ocean of pro-Reagan media publicity, however.

43. Putnam, *Modern California Politics,* 70–71.

44. My apologies to George Dangerfield, whose *The Strange Death of Liberal England* I regard as a classic of modern political history. The "proud of his credentials" quotation is from Ed Salzman, *Jerry Brown: High Priest and Low Politician* (Sacramento: California Journal Press, 1976), 14.

45. For Brown's background and early campaigns see Salzman, *Jerry Brown;* Rapoport, *California Dreaming;* John C. Bollens and G. Robert Williams, *Jerry Brown in a Plain Brown Wrapper* (Pacific Palisades, Calif.: Palisades, 1978); John J. Fitzpatrick, "His Father's Son," *New West,* 16 January 1978; Mary E. Leary, *Phantom Politics* (Washington, D.C.: Public Affairs, 1977); J. D. Lorenz, *Jerry*

Brown: The Man on the White Horse (Boston: Houghton-Mifflin, 1978); Robert Pack, *Jerry Brown: The Philosopher Prince* (New York: Stein and Day, 1978); and Gary Wills, *Lead Time: A Journalist's Education* (Garden City: Doubleday, 1983), chap. 16; *California Journal* 9 (June 1978), entire issue.

46. Putnam, *Modern California Politics*, 74, 76–77, 81; Rapoport, *California Dreaming*, 180; and Bollens and Williams, *Jerry Brown*, chap. 7.

47. Putnam, *Modern California Politics*, 74–75; Lorenz, *Jerry Brown*, 122.

48. Putnam, *Modern California Politics*, 75–76; Bollens and Williams, 18, 107, 120–22, 124–25; Larry Liebert, "The S. F. Zen Center—Brown's Recruitment Depot," *California Journal* 9 (January 1978): 5–8.

49. Putnam, *Modern California Politics*, 77–85; Ed Salzman, "The Brown Record," *California Journal* 9 (June 1978): 173–76.

50. Putnam, *Modern California Politics*, 85; Ed Salzman, "Life After Jarvis," *California Journal* 9 (August 1978), 264–67; Ed Salzman, "Brown's Second Spirit," *California Journal* 9 (December 1978): 384–85.

51. Putnam, *Modern California Politics*, 82–83, 85–87; Ed Salzman, "Brown's Republican Budget," *California Journal* 10 (February 1979): 50–52; Ed Salzman, "Typhoid Jerry," *California Journal* 10 (April 1979): 131–32.

52. Putnam, *Modern California Politics*, 87–96; Ed Salzman, "Shedding the 'Flake' Image," *California Journal* 10 (June 1979): 192–93; Ed Salzman, "The Predictable Jerry," *California Journal* 10 (October 1979): 340–42; Charles Brereton, "New Hampshire: Blastoff for Reagan, Meltdown for Brown," *California Journal* 11 (April 1980): 167–68; Ed Salzman, "Brown's Political Future," *California Journal* 11 (June 1980): 216–18; Michelle Willens, "Whither Jerry Brown?" *California Journal* 11 (November 1980): 415–516; Eric Brazil, "Medflies and Politics," *California Journal* 12 (April 1981): 137–39; Ed Salzman, "Brown's Last Budget," *California Journal* 13 (February 1982): 61–63; Ed Salzman, "Judging Jerry," *California Journal* 13 (June 1982): 189–94; Michelle Willens, "Struggle for the Senate," *California Journal* 13 (July 1982): 253–55.

53. Putnam, *Modern California Politics*, 96; James R. Carroll, "Tom Versus Duke," *California Journal* 13 (July 1982): 229–31; Donald H. Harrison, "Deukmejian's Dilemma," *California Journal* 13 (December 1982): 433–37; Robert S. Fairbanks, "Election post mortem, 1982," *California Journal* 13 (December 1982): 437–41.

54. Putnam, *Modern California Politics*, 95, 113; Andrea Margolis and Richard Zeiger, "Bleeding Hearts, Stone Hearts: A California Journal Survey of Legislative Voting Records," *California Journal* 18 (January 1987): 30–33.

55. The governor proposed a fiscal "rollover" of about one billion dollars from the 1983–84 budget to the following year's budget. Although traditionalists, ironically mostly right-wing Republicans, had always held this to be unconstitutional, the California constitution was vague on the subject. "That Balanced Budget Mandate," *California Journal* 14 (January 1983): 6, and Robert Fairbanks, "That Unbalanced Budget," *California Journal* 14 (February 1983): 45–47.

56. Richard Zeiger, "A Bittersweet Farewell: George Deukmejian Kept His Word, but Was It Good Enough?" *California Journal* 21 (January 1991): 7–13.

57. Ibid., 7; Putnam, *Modern California Politics*, 98–99. For two very cogent

articles on Deukmejian's crime policy by Vincent Schiraldi, see *Los Angeles Times,* 9 December 1987, pt. 2, 15 and 22 March 1993, B11.

58. Putnam, *Modern California Politics,* 99–103; Richard Zeiger, "The Supreme Court Election," *California Journal* 18 (September 1986): 423–27; "The 1986 Election: The Supreme Court," *California Journal* 17 (December 1986): 588; Zeiger, "Duke's Landslide," *California Journal* 17 (December 1986): 579–81. A very thoughtful treatment of the supreme court elections by one of the losers is Joseph R. Grodin, *In Pursuit of Justice: Reflections of a State Supreme Court Justice* (Berkeley and Los Angeles: University of California Press, 1989): chap. 10.

59. Putnam, *Modern California Politics,* 103–109.

60. Ibid., 111–16; Ted K. Bradshaw and Charles G. Bell, eds., *The Capacity to Respond: California Political Institutions Face Change,* Public Affairs Report no. 29 (Berkeley: University of California, Institute of Governmental Studies, February 1988).

61. Putnam, *Modern California Politics,* 110–11, 114–15. A. G. Block, "Budget Deadlock Takes State to the Brink," *California Journal* 21 (September 1990): 420–24.

62. The Republicans likewise remained overwhelmingly conservative though divided between mere political, laissez faire conservatives and cultural, especially radical religious, conservatives. "Who's Left — Who's Right?," *California Journal* 22 (March 1991): 138–40; A. G. Block "The Broken Elephant: Fall of Assembly Republicans," *California Journal* 22 (October 1991): 444–49; Eleanor Shapiro and A. G. Block, "Uncivil War," *California Journal* 23 (June 1992): 296–300.

63. Richard Zeiger, "Pete Wilson Inherits a State in Disarray," *California Journal* 21 (December 1990): 560–64; Gerald C. Lubenow, ed., *California Votes: The 1990 Governor's Race* (Berkeley: IGS Press, 1991).

64. Wilson proposed a program to deal with social problems in health, welfare, and educational fields by "preventive" rather than remedial measures. Sound though limited in its potential reach, it was quickly engulfed by the fiscal crises. Richard Zeiger, "Pete Wilson After One Year," *California Journal* 22 (December 1991): 541–44.

65. For a dramatic account of the perverse atmosphere in the contemporary state legislature, see Robert A. Jones, "California's Bitter Season," *Los Angeles Times Magazine,* 27 September 1992, 14–18, 40–41.

66. Block, "Broken Elephant"; Zeiger, "Pete Wilson."

67. Zeiger, "Pete Wilson"; Robert Shapiro, "Boosting the Sales Tax: Who Gets Hurt?," *California Journal* 22 (June 1991): 283–86; Steven A. Capps, "Wilson, Lawmakers Unleash Monster Budget," *California Journal* 22 (September 1991): 392–96; "Pete Wilson's Record," *Los Angeles Times,* 27 December 1992, A26.

68. A. G. Block, "The Reapportionment Failure," *California Journal* 22 (November 1991): 503–505; Zeiger, "Pete Wilson," 543.

69. Jones, "California's Bitter Season."

70. Wilson got his way on the abstruse funding formula for public schools but made concessions on other issues. *Los Angeles Times,* 6 September 1992, A3–6, A1, 24, B1, 5–6. Richard Zeiger, "Blundering Toward a Budget," *California Journal* 23 (September 1992): 425–30.

71. Tupper Hull, "Workers' Compensation Gets No Reform," *California Journal* 23 (November 1992): 535–38.

72. The Democrats also won the other U.S. Senate seat with Barbara Boxer's victory and won five of the seven new congressional seats allotted the state after the 1990 census. They formally lost two seats in the state senate, but two seats were won by independents who often voted with the Democrats and three seats were left vacant, with Democrats strong in two of these districts. "Election 1992," *California Journal* 23 (December 1992), entire issue.

73. *Los Angeles Times,* 9 January 1993, B10; 12 January 1993, B10; 29 January 1993, B10; 1 March 1993, A3; 24 March 1993, A1, 18–19; 16 April 1993, A3, 34; 22 April 1993, A14; 23 April 1993, A3, 41; 5 May 1993, A3, 24; 15 May 1993, A32; 15 May 1993, A30; Mary Beth Barber, "Year of Action?" *California Journal* 24 (May 1993): 12–13.

74. *Los Angeles Times,* 7 June 1993, A3.

75. On December 1, 1993, Clayton R. Jackson, a major lobbyist and Paul Carpenter, former Democratic senator and State Board of Equalization member, were convicted of fraud. On February 17, 1994, Patrick Nolan, a Republican assemblyman and former minority leader, pleaded guilty to related crimes and resigned his office. *Los Angeles Times,* 2 December 1993, A1, 34, 35; 18 February 1994, A1, 26.

76. *Los Angeles Times,* 22 June 1993, A1, 20, 21; 23 June 1993, A1, 14; 1 July 1993, A3, 25; 5 July 1993, A3; 27 August 1993, A30; 9 September 1993, A3, 23; 13 September 1993, A1, 26–27.

77. *Los Angeles Times,* 21 May 1993, A1; 19 September 1993, A3, 19. Laura A. Locke, "Proposition 174, Vouchers Lose Big," *California Journal* 24 (December 1993): 21–22.

78. *Los Angeles Times,* 21 August 1993, A29; 21 September 1993, A1, 21.

79. This statement does not apply to the issues of illegal immigration and crime. On the former, the governor took extreme positions, even to the extent of proposing a constitutional amendment denying citizenship to children of illegal immigrants born in the United States, and called on Democratic leaders to "kiss [his] behind" for opposing him on the issue. On the question of violent crime, both the governor and the democratically dominated legislature allowed themselves to be stampeded into passing a draconian, expensive, dysfunctional, probably unenforceable, and possibly unconstitutional "three strikes and you're out" law. *Los Angeles Times,* 10 August 1993, A1, 16; 19 August 1993, A3, 19; 23 August 1993, A3; 13 March 1994, M1, 4, 6.

CHAPTER 4

1. Laws and organizations were crucial to agricultural development in the west. The Mining Act (1866) established that state rather than federal law would define water rights. The Desert Land Act (1877) provided land to those who would work the parcels by developing irrigation systems. The Carey Act (1894) opened up more land, with the stipulation that a private or public irrigation system had to be planned before the land could be sold to individual farmers. Problems arose,

however, when speculators built the requisite irrigation facilities and retained essential water rights. Even though the states found various ways to protect farmers' water rights, the Reclamation Act (1902) was passed to provide federal financing for irrigation projects that was to be repaid by irrigators.

The development of irrigation organizations can also be traced across time. In fact, there is a strong relationship between the dominant type of irrigation provider and legislation: mutual ditch companies still exist but were the dominant organization before the Reclamation Act; irrigation districts, authorized in Colorado in 1901, were the preferred organization in the early Reclamation era; conservancy districts, authorized in Colorado in 1937, became dominant organizations because they were given authority to impose taxes in order to repay federal water projects. Vernal Aulston, "Colorado Water Conservancy Districts: An Old Institution in a New Policy Arena" (Plan B Paper, Department of Political Science, Colorado State University, Ft. Collins, 1992), 3–18.

2. Daniel Tyler, *The Last Water Hole in the West* (Niwot: University Press of Colorado, 1992), 4–93.

3. Donald Worster, *Rivers of Empire* (New York: Pantheon Books, 1985), 3–60 329–35.

4. Tyler, *Last Water Hole,* 426.

5. John Walton, *Western Times and Water Wars* (Berkeley and Los Angeles: University of California Press, 1992), 307.

6. Tyler, *Last Water Hole,* 61.

7. Walton, *Western Times,* 332.

8. Tyler, *Last Water Hole,* 426.

9. David H. Getches, "Pressures for Change in Western Water Policy," in *Water and the American West,* ed. David H. Getches (Boulder: University of Colorado School of Law, 1988), 157.

10. Walton notes that opponents can fight the state's domination and policy prescriptions with ideology, cultural explanation, examples of injustice and of collective action to promote change. Local communities or ethnic and ideological groups may continue to resist even after losing major battles to a dominant political force. *Western Times,* 307, 331–34.

11. Helen Ingram, *Water Politics, Continuity and Change* (Albuquerque: University of New Mexico Press, 1990), 9; Robert Gottlieb, *A Life of Its Own: The Politics and Power of Water* (San Diego: Harcourt Brace Jovanovich, 1988), 47.

12. Gottlieb, *A Life of Its Own,* 121; Charles F. Wilkinson, "To Settle a New Land: An Historical Essay on Water Law in Colorado in the American West," in *Water and the American West,* ed. David H. Getches (Boulder: University of Colorado School of Law, 1988), 10.

13. Ingram, *Water Politics,* 8.

14. Ibid., 121; Gottlieb, *A Life of Its Own,* 246.

15. Daniel McCool, *Command of the Waters* (Berkeley and Los Angeles: University of California Press, 1987), 132–34.

16. Ibid., 142–44.

17. Ibid., 146–55.

18. Ingram, *Water Politics,* 5.

19. Michael R. Moore, "Native American Water Rights: Efficiency and Fairness," *Natural Resources Journal* 29 (Summer 1989): 766.

20. Ingram, *Water Politics*, 26.

21. Ibid., 66–8.

22. Steve Hinchman, "Animas–La Plata: The Last Big Dam in the West," *High Country News* 25 (22 March 1993): 10.

23. Ingram, *Water Politics*, 69–73.

24. Ibid., 131.

25. Ibid., 74–82.

26. Ibid., 129.

27. Mark Obmascik, "More than Just a Squawfish at Stake in Animas Project," *Denver Post*, 20 May 1990, 7C.

28. Hinchman, "Animas–La Plata," 12; Ingram, *Water Politics*, 128; Gottlieb, *A Life of Its Own*, 67.

29. Hinchman, "Animas–La Plata," 13–14.

30. Obmascik, "More than Just a Squawfish," 7C.

31. Environmentalists filed a suit to block construction, seeking a supplemental environmental impact statement (EIS) study that would incorporate changes in the status of wildlife that have occurred since the original EIS. Mark Obmascik, "Suit Seeks to Halt Huge Water Project," *Denver Post*, 26 February 1992, 1B. When the supplemental analysis was completed in October 1992, the Environmental Protection Agency (EPA) said the analysis was inadequate and raised several specific objections. "EPA Calls for Revision of Environmental Study," *Rocky Mountain News*, 17 December 1992, 36. The Bureau of Reclamation began preparing a revised analysis due to be published in 1995. Brian A. Ellison, Denver Regional Office of General Accounting Office, telephone interview by author, 10 June 1994.

32. Hinchman, "Animas–La Plata," 11–2.

33. Ingram, *Water Politics*, 127; Obmascik, "More than Just a Squawfish," 7C; Gottlieb, *A Life of Its Own*, 220.

34. James L. Cox, *Metropolitan Water Supply: The Denver Experience* (Boulder: University of Colorado, Bureau of Governmental Research and Service, 1967), 34.

35. Tyler, *Last Water Hole*, 206–207; Cox, *Metropolitan Water Supply*, 102.

36. Kenn Ellison, Denver Regional Council of Governments, telephone interview by author, 26 July 1989; Larry Kallenberger, Colorado Department of Local Governments, telephone interview by author, 3 August 1989; J. Gordon Milliken, "Water Management Issues in Denver, Colorado, Urban Area," in *Water and Arid Lands of the Western United States*, ed. Mohamed T. El-Ashry and Diana C. Gibbons (Cambridge: Cambridge University Press, 1988), 340–44, 371; Cox, *Metropolitan Water Supply*, 123–42.

37. Brian Ellison, "The Denver Water Board: Bureaucratic Power and Autonomy in Local Natural Resource Agencies" (Ph.D. diss., Colorado State Univerity, 1993), 106–107.

38. Milliken, "Water Management Issues in Denver," 354.

39. Bob Weaver, consultant to Environmental Caucus, telephone interview by author, 4 August 1989.

40. Brian Ellison argues in "The Denver Water Board" (Ph.D. diss., Colorado State University, 1993), 127, that the alliance's principal players—Dan Luecke of Environmental Defense Fund, Bob Weaver of Trout Unlimited, and Carse Putsmueller of the National Audubon Society—had the expertise to challenge the project's technical merits.

41. Charlie Jordan, Denver Water Department, telephone interview by author, 28 July 1989; Milliken, "Water Management Issues in Denver," 371.

42. Ellison, "The Denver Water Board," 127.

43. John Aloysius Farrell, "Denver Plays Its Water Card," *Denver Post Magazine,* 22 June 1986, 17–23.

44. John K. Andrews, Independence Institute, telephone interview by author, 7 August 1989; Rich Ferdinandsen, Jefferson County commissioner, telephone interview by author, 11 August 1989; Miller Hudson, Citizens for Metro Cooperation, telephone interview by author, 9 August 1989; Monte Pascoe, member of Denver Water Board, telephone interview by author, 2 August 1989.

45. Ellison, "The Denver Water Board," 126–28.

46. Dick Foster, "Two Forks Death May Trigger Water Wars," *Rocky Mountain News,* 2 December 1990, 70.

47. Moore, "Native American Water Rights," 765–68.

48. McCool, *Command of the Waters,* 254.

49. Dirk Johnson, "Tribes Face New Battle for Progress," *Denver Post,* 5 January 1992, 1C.

50. Ibid.

51. McCool, *Command of the Waters,* 245–51.

52. Ingram, *Water Politics,* 132.

53. Ingram, *Water Politics,* 131; Gottlieb, *A Life of Its Own,* 220–221.

54. Obmascik, "More than Just a Squawfish," 7C.

55. "New Study Not Expected to Kill Animas–La Plata," *Rocky Mountain News,* 18 April 1992, 24; "EPA Calls for Revision," 36.

56. Hinchman, "Animas–La Plata," 12.

57. Ingram, *Water Politics,* 132.

58. Getches, "Pressures for Change," 144.

59. Tyler, *Last Water Hole,* 81–186.

60. Ibid., 57–59.

61. Ibid., 376–81; Ingram, *Water Politics,* 15, 130; McCool, *Command of the Waters,* 217–20.

62. McCool, 218–19.

63. Wilkinson, "To Settle a New Land," 2.

64. A water partnership called American Water Development, Inc. (AWDI) purchased the Baca Ranch in the San Luis Valley. AWDI requested a permit to pump 200,000 acre-feet of water to be sold to front-range water cities to make a profit for the partnership. San Luis Valley citizens strenuously objected and fought the attempt in court. In a major victory for San Luis interests and environmentalists, the Colorado Supreme Court denied AWDI's claim for water and ordered the partnership to pay $2.7 million in legal fees. John Sanko, "Court Denies Claim to San Luis Water," *Rocky Mountain News,* 10 May 1994, 8A.

65. Aurora, a fast-growing Denver suburb, bought 8,250 acre-feet of water from the Rocky Ford Ditch Company. This purchase has dried up 4,000 acres of agricultural land in the Arkansas basin, threatening some communities' very existence. Wilkinson, "To Settle a New Land," 10.

Likewise, when Margaret Carpenter, the mayor of suburban Thornton, concluded that environmentalists would make it too difficult to build the Two Forks dam, she sought to buy water rights secretly from indebted farmers served by the Northern Colorado Water Conservancy District (NCWCD). The purchases were made in secret because NCWCD's charter prohibited the district from delivering water outside its boundaries. When the NCWCD found out that Thornton intended to pipe the water sixty miles south, the district responded fiercely to prevent the water from leaving the district. Tyler, *Last Water Hole,* 448–50. Water court judge Robert Berhrman approved Thornton's right to about 75 percent (50,000 acre feet) of water. Despite earlier opposition, NCWCD officials are satisfied with the decision. Mike Patty, "Water Decision Spills No Tears," *Rocky Mountain News,* 19 August 1993, 28A. The diversion of the water will force the conversion of approximately 12,000 acres (2 percent of the district's irrigated land) to dry-land crops. J. Lewandowski, "Water a Running Concern," *Coloradoan,* 10 April 1994, A1.

66. Getches, "Pressure for Change," 155.

67. Milliken argues that had the DWB played a stronger role promoting a metropolitan water planning and cooperation, a more rational water system would have been in place to respond to the demands of a growing area. Milliken, "Water Management Issues in Denver," 340. Likewise Cox argues that, in part, these water districts and municipal water departments came into being because (1) the DWB's refused to provide water to suburban communities during the drought of the 1950s, forcing communities to create agencies of their own; (2) the DWB was willing to provide water to special water agencies even during surplus years; (3) Denver charged higher rates to suburban agencies, who resented this and preferred spending money on their own facilities rather than paying higher water prices; and (4) Denver refused to let water agencies mix Denver water with the suburban provider's existing supplies, encouraging the agencies to either abandon their treatment facilities or provide all of their own water. Cox, *Metropolitan Water Supply,* 148–56.

68. Milliken, "Water Management Issues in Denver," 346.

69. Getches, "Pressure for Change," 155.

70. Ingram, *Water Politics,* 130–32.

71. Ibid., 24.

72. Ibid., 130; Gottlieb, *A Life of Its Own,* 246; McCool, *Command of the Waters,* 221.

73. Gottlieb, *A Life of Its Own,* 247.

74. William P. Browne, *Private Interests, Public Policy, and American Agriculture* (Lawrence: University Press of Kansas, 1988), 187.

75. Browne, *Private Interests,* 192–251.

76. Ibid., 134.

77. Ibid., 170–77.

78. Ibid., 249.
79. Ibid., 208.
80. Ibid., 250.

CHAPTER 5

1. Mark Hoffman, ed., *The World Almanac and Book of Facts, 1991* (New York, 1991), 624; State of Hawaii Department of Health, *Report to the Legislature: State Health Insurance Program* (Honolulu, January 1992).
2. *San Jose Mercury News,* 8 November 1992, 6C.
3. U.S. Congress, Senate, *Law Enforcement in the Territory of Hawaii,* 72d Cong., 1st sess., 1932, Doc. 71.
4. "ILWU 'History,'" *Honolulu Record,* 5 August 1954, Samuel King Papers, Gov., Misc., IWLU File, Hawaii State Archives (hereafter cited as HSA).
5. Sanford Zalburg, *A Spark is Struck!* (Honolulu, 1979), 139–55.
6. Letter from Eric Beecroft to H. Rex Lee, 22 October 1946, U.S. Department of Interior, Office of Territories Classified Files, RG 126 File 9-4-55(4), Labor Conditions General, National Archives.
7. Letter from A. G. Budge to Eric Beecroft, 17 October 1946; unsigned letter [Julius Krug] to John Steelman [22 October 1946]; memorandum from Roy E. James to E. Arnold, 30 October 1946, U.S. Department of Interior, Office of Territories Classified Files, RG 126 File 9-4-55(4), Labor Conditions General, National Archives; Zalburg, *A Spark is Struck!,* 154.
8. U.S. War Department, General and Special Staff, G2 Regional File, 1933–44, Islands, Hawaiian, RG 165, Box 1921, Hawaiian Islands, File 2020, Socialism, Radicalism, Communism, 15 June, 1939, National Archives; memorandum, FBI director to attorney general, 23 October 1947: "Report of Special Agent [name blacked out], dated Nov. 28, 1939, at Honolulu, entitled 'Communist Activities in the United States,'" FBI File 97-10, Index no. 100-3-110-95.
9. FBI "Report of Special Agent, Nov. 28, 1939 . . . .," FBI File 97-10, Index no. 100-3-110-95; Zalburg, *A Spark is Struck!,* 171, 195–96, 223–27; letter from Ingram Stainback to Oscar Chapman, 15 September 1947, Oscar L. Chapman Papers, Harry S Truman Library, Independence, Mo.; letter from J. Harold Hughes to Tom C. Clark, 4 February 1948, J. Howard McGrath Papers, Truman Library, Independence, Mo; transcript of telephone call from Julius Krug to James P. Davis, 26 September 1947, Julius Krug Papers, Library of Congress Manuscript Division; H. A. B[utler] Staff, October 1947, Communism, Hawaii Confidential Report, Hugh A. Butler Papers, Box 227, Nebraska Historical Society, Lincoln; letters from Ingram Stainback to J. A. Krug, 14 and 15 October 1947, Ingram Stainback Papers, U.S. Department of the Interior, Sept. 1947–Mar. 1948, HSA; letter from J. A. Krug to Jack W. Hall, 25 October 1947, U.S. Department of the Interior, Office of the Secretary, Central Classified Files, 1907–53, RG 48 File 9-4-15, Labor Conditions.
10. 79th Cong. 2d sess. (1946), Committee on Territories, *Subcommittee Report on Official Trip to Conduct a Study and Investigation of the Various Questions and Problems Relating to the Territory of Hawaii re: H. Res. 236,* 3–11; 80th Cong., 2d

sess. (1948), Senate Subcommittee on Territories and Insular Affairs, *Report, Statehood for Hawaii to Accompany H.R. 49,* 5–6.

11. Letters from Stainback to J. Krug, 15 September and 14 October 1947, RG 126, File 9-4-116, Communism; letter from Ingram Stainback to Tom Clark, 17 october 1947, Stainback Papers, U.S. Department of Justice, 1942–47, HSA.

12. Report, Honolulu Special Agent [name blacked out], "Communist Party, U.S.A., 13th District, Honolulu Field Division," 4 February and 29 October 1947, FBI File 97-10, Index no. 100-3-110-64, 100-3-110-126; Butler Staff, [Report], October 1947, Communism, Hawaii Confidential Report, Butler Papers, Box 227.

13. Memorandum, Communist Party, U.S.A., 13th District, Honolulu Field Division, FBI director to attorney general, 9 June 1948, FBI File 97-10, Index # 100-3-110-146; letter from William Borthwick to Oscar Chapman, 12 January 1949, Department of the Interior, RG 126, File 9-4-49, Part 5, Governmental Status — Statehood General.

14. Memo, Robert Shivers [ca. 4–5 Aug. 1949], Joseph Farrington Papers, Del., 81st Cong., Allen, July 1949, HSA; letter from Charles Kauhane to Oscar Chapman, 2 September 1949, RG 48 Cent. Class File 9–4–2, Part 3, Administrative General; letter from Harry B. Kronick to Sen. J. Howard McGrath, 25 July 1949; letter from Charles Kauhane to Oscar Chapman, 26 July 1949, and from Chuck Mau to William M. Boyle, Jr., 15 November 1949, RG 126 File 9–4–116, Political Affairs — Democratic Party of Hawaii; letter from Jack Burns to Mr. Secretary, 25 April 1951, U.S. Department of the Interior Office of Territorial and International Affairs, Territory of Hawaii Files, Hawaii, Organization and Management; interview, Lawrence Fuchs with Dan Aoki, Honolulu, 12 November 1958; Special Agent Joseph O. Logue, Report on Communist Party . . . Honolulu . . . , 10/13, 16–19/50, FBI, File 100-3-110-329, p. 22; Zalburg, *A Spark is Struck!,* 295–302.

15. Letters from Hugh Butler to Sen. Eugene Millikin, 29 December 1948, and to Joseph O'Mahoney, 20 November 1948 and 16 May 1949, Butler Papers, Nebraska State Historical Society, Box 241; *U.S. News & World Report,* 10 August 1959, 57–58.

16. Justus F. Paul, "The Power of Seniority: Senator Hugh Butler and Statehood for Hawaii," *Hawaiian Journal of History* 9 (1975), 140–45.

17. Report, Honolulu Special Agent, 27 April 1950, FBI File 97-10, Index no. 100-3-110-[?]; Memorandum, Emile Bilodeau to John W. Gibson, Hawaii — Interim Report 13-N, A-General — UnAmerican Activities & Statehood, U.S. Department of Labor, RG 174, Box 96, File of Philip M. Kaiser; letter, James Coke to Hugh Butler, 8 May 1950, Butler Papers, Box 26, unmarked file; Zalburg, *A Spark is Struck!,* 298–304.

18. *Honolulu Advertiser,* 21 February 1984, IV-6; 26 July 1957, A-1, A-10; 27 July 1957, A-1, A-4, A-7; Betty F. Buker, ed., *Men and Women of Hawaii* (Honolulu: Honolulu Star-Bulleting Printing Co., 1972), 76; interview, H. Brett Melendy and Rhoda Hackler with Mrs. John A. Burns, Kailua, Hawaii, 24 September 1980; letters, J. Burns to Brian Casey, 22 July 1957, and to James N. Morita, 30 July 1957, John A. Burns Papers, Honolulu; interview, Lawrence Fuchs with Judge Calvin MacGregor, Honolulu, 14 November 1957; interview, H. Brett

Melendy and Rhoda Hackler with William Quinn, Honolulu, 25 September 1980.

19. Harry Hansen, Luman H. Long, George DeLury, Mark Hoffman, eds. *World Almanac, 1960–1990* (New York, 1960–1990). s.v. "Elections."

20. *New York Times,* 14 December 1992, C10.

21. University of Hawaii, *The Community Colleges* (Honolulu, 1972).

22. Conversations with general contractors, Honolulu, 1974.

23. *New York Times,* 14 December 1992, C10; interview, H. Brett Melendy with Edward White, provost, Kauai Community College, 1973.

24. Hawaii, Department of Health, *State Health Insurance Program,* (January 1992) 28–29.

25. Letter, Luz G. Abcede, administrator, State Health Program to Dr. H. Brett Melendy, 10 December 1992; John C. Lewin, director of health, State of Hawaii, "Reflection on National Health Care Reform Based on Hawaii's Experience," (Honolulu: Hawaii State Health Program, March 1992), 4.

26. *Business Week,* 19 March 1979, 158 and 161.

27. U.S. Bureau of Census, *1990 Census of Population: General Population Characteristics, Hawaii* (Washington, D.C.: Government Printing Office, 1992), 1–2; Harry Hansen, ed., *World Almanac, 1965* (New York, 1965), 221.

28. *San Francisco Chronicle,* 26 January 1977, 1; *New York Times,* 13 June 1971, 50; 28 June 1977, 16.

29. George E, Delury, ed., *World Almanac, 1978,* 687, and *1991,* 624; *San Francisco Chronicle,* 19 March 1978, B4.

30. Walter F. Frear, *Mark Twain and Hawaii* (Chicago: Lakeside Press, 1947), 242–43.

CHAPTER 6

1. Carlos A. Schwantes, *In Mountain Shadows: A History of Idaho* (Lincoln: University of Nebraska Press, 1991), 252.

2. James A. Aho, *The Politics of Righteousness: Idaho Christian Patriotism* (Seattle: University of Washington Press, 1990), 21.

3. *Los Angeles Times,* 13 July 1988.

4. *Washington Post,* 27 October 1992.

5. Randy Stapilus, *Paradox Politics: People and Power in Idaho* (Boise, Idaho: Ridenbaugh Press, 1988), 18.

6. Aho, *Politics of Righteousness,* 7.

7. See "Warriors of Hate Find No Homeland in Idaho," *New York Times,* 2 January 1988. According to one Idaho activist working against the white supremacists, "Now we're known for the Nazis, but eventually we'll be known as the community that faced the Nazis and won."

8. 61 LW 4575 (1993).

9. 61 LW 4576.

10. See, *State v. Mitchell,* 485 N.W.2d 807 (1992), and 61 LW 4576 (1993).

11. 61 LW 4577.

12. 61 LW 4578.

13. Ibid.

14. *New York Times,* 12 June 1993.

15. *Idaho Statesman,* 31 March 1983.

16. Idaho Code Sec. 18-7901-7904 (1983).

17. 112 S.Ct. 2538 (1992).

18. 597 N.E.2d 450 (1992).

19. 485 N.W.2d 807 (1992).

20. *State v. Sullivan,* No. 19194 (4th Jud. Dist. Ct. Id., Oct. 28, 1992).

21. *Idaho Statesman,* 14 November 1992.

22. U.S. Department of Justice, Idaho Advisory Committee to the United States Commission on Civil Rights, *Bigotry and Violence in Idaho* (Washington, D.C.: Government Printing Office, 1986), 12 (hereafter cited as Idaho Advisory Committee report).

23. *Lewiston Tribune,* 10 December 1982.

24. Idaho Advisory Committee report, 12.

25. See Idaho Advisory Commission report, 61, app. C.

26. Aho, *Politics of Righteousness,* 55.

27. Anti-Defamation League (ADL) of B'nai B'rith, *ADL Facts,* "The 'Identity Churches': A Theology of Hate" (New York, 1983), 6.

28. See Leo P. Ribuffo, *The Old Christian Right: The Protestant Far Right from the Great Depression to the Cold War* (Philadelphia: Temple University Press, 1983).

29. Aho, *Politics of Righteousness,* 55.

30. *Idaho Statesman,* 14 September 1980. See Aho, *Politics of Righteousness,* 24.

31. L. J. Davis, "Ballad of an American Terrorist," *Harpers,* (July 1986): 56.

32. ADL, "A Theology of Hate," 5–6.

33. *Deseret News,* 17 January 1988.

34. Southern Poverty Law Center (SPLC), Montgomery, Alabama, "Klanwatch Intelligence Report" (February–March 1986), 5.

35. See ADL, "A Theology of Hate"; Center for Democratic Renewal (CDR), Atlanta, Georgia, "The Monitor" (March 1986).

36. Richard Butler, *Deseret News,* 17 January 1988.

37. Davis, "American Terrorist," 57.

38. SPLC, "Klanwatch Intelligence Report," 5.

39. CDR, "The Monitor" 5.

40. SPLC, "Klanwatch Intelligence Report," 5.

41. Aho, *Politics of Righteousness,* 57.

42. Davis, "American Terrorist," 58.

43. *Idaho Statesman,* 14 September 1980.

44. *Deseret News,* 17 January 1988.

45. Aho, *Politics of Righteousness,* 58.

46. *Idaho Statesman,* 14 September 1980.

47. Aho, *Politics of Righteousness,* 7, 58; CDR, "The Monitor" (August 1986).

48. *Washington Post,* 27 October 1992. "Aryan National — such a grandiloquent name, such a microscopic sect. But if you want to know something about extremism in North Idaho, this is a place to start. This is one of the granddaddies of Idaho fanatical creeds."

49. CDR, "The Monitor," (March 1986): 6.

50. In one interview, Butler referred to Hitler as "a holy man." *Deseret News,* 17 January 1988.

51. *Idaho Statesman,* 15 July 1982.

52. *Idaho Statesman,* 15 July 1982.

53. Idaho Advisory Commission report.

54. These annual festivals of hate, or "Rambo-charged conventions of hate-mongers," otherwise known as "Butler's bigot barbecues," provided fuel for greater visibility of the Aryan Nations and its increasingly aggressive tactics. See Susan S. Lang, *Extremist Groups in America* (New York: Franklin Watts, 1990), 66–67.

55. "Shotgun News," 15 January 1981.

56. Aho, *Politics of Righteousness,* 7.

57. The sobriquet "the Order" evidently was taken from a novel, *The Turner Diaries,* written by William Pierce, a former instructor of physics at Oregon State University who became prominent in the Washington, D.C.–based National Alliance. In his novel, written under the pseudonym Andrew MacDonald, Pierce posits the formation and successful operation of a right-wing, white supremacist revolutionary cell known as the Order. The group eventually overthrows the United States government and declares war, not on Moscow but on Tel Aviv.

58. Anti-Defamation League (ADL) of B'nai B'rith, *Special Report,* "'Propaganda of the Deed': The Far Right's Desperate Revolution," (New York: May 1985), 1.

59. See Davis, "American Terrorist," 54.

60. See Idaho Advisory Committee report for a survey of these and related activities.

61. ADL, "'Propaganda of the Deed,'" 1.

62. Ibid., 5.

63. *Idaho Statesman,* 16 April 1985. See Idaho Advisory Committee report.

64. Aho, *Politics of Righteousness,* 61.

65. "The Monitor" (January 1986): 2.

66. *Idaho Statesman,* 30 September 1986; *Seattle Times,* 30 September 1986 and 3 October 1986.

67. "A Unique Coalition Combats Bigotry," *Seattle Times,* 20 October 1988.

68. See *New York Times,* 6 March 1988 and 27 March 1988.

69. *Idaho Statesman,* 11 November 1988. In the spring of 1992, it was disclosed that a group called the New Order, or the Bob Mathews Brigade, had drafted a plan to murder Marshall Mend, founder of the Kootenai County Human Relations Task Force, and Bill Wassmuth of the Northwest Coalition Against Malicious Harassment. The plot was uncovered by an FBI informant, and according to Wassmuth, those involved were deported to Italy and Canada. See *Chicago Tribune,* 30 August 1992, and *Seattle Times,* 17 February 1992.

70. SPLC, "Klanwatch Intelligence Report" (October 1989): 3.

71. SPLC, "Klanwatch Intelligence Report" (June 1990): 1–2.

72. SPLC, "Klanwatch Intelligence Report" (June 1991): 4.

73. U.S. Commission on Civil Rights, *Intimidation and Violence: Racial and*

Religious Bigotry in America (Washington, D.C.: Government Printing Office, 1983), 27.

74. *New York Times,* 15 October 1992.

75. "Hate Groups Hanging on in Idaho Haven," *New York Times,* 15 October 1992. Also *New York Times,* 23 June 1993. See *Washington Post,* 27 October 1992: "How and why is it that a little God-gorgeous finger of the continental United States, sitting up there between Montana and Washington, formed by glaciers, cut by gin-clear winters, should have become these past several decades a nesting ground for so many stripes of resister, protester, evader, constitutionalist, survivalist, Bircher, Kluxer, Aryan?," C1.

76. Stapilus, *Paradox Politics,* 1.

77. "As far as most of the world knows, North Idaho is an uncivilized fragment of Northwest geography that is home to racists and fringe cult figures. . . . North Idaho has become a cruel national joke, a stereotypical haven for weirdos and racists." *Seattle Times,* 30 August 1992.

78. *Seattle Times,* 30 August 1992, 24.

79. In 1987, New York City gave the city of Coeur d'Alene the Raoul Wallenberg Award for its zealous and successful opposition to the white supremacy movement in northern Idaho.

80. " 'Even though we have the most comprehensive set of laws against hate crimes of any state in the nation, the racists continue to recruit on a message that this state will somehow welcome them,' said Tony Stewart, head of the Kootenai County Task Force on Human Relations, in Coeur D'Alene. 'It's a cloud that we've been under for a long time.' " *New York Times,* supra note 75.

81. *Seattle Times,* 15 March 1993.

82. *Chicago Tribune,* 7 July 1991. According to one leading member of the Aryan Nations, "You don't have to be a racist to be against elite environmentalists and big government."

83. See *Idaho Statesman,* 9 July 1993, and *New York Times,* 9 July 1993. Harris was acquitted on all charges. Weaver was tried and found guilty on the earlier gun charges. Weaver was acquitted of the murder and conspiracy charges in the July 1993 trial; however, he was sentenced to prison on convictions of lesser offenses that stemmed from the stand-off with law enforcement authorities.

84. See *New York Times,* 9 July 1993.

85. See "Fugitive in Idaho Cabin Plays Role of Folk Hero," *New York Times,* 25 August 1992.

86. See "Idaho Siege Might Fuel Neo-Nazis," *Chicago Tribune,* 30 August 1992.

CHAPTER 7

1. Gerald D. Nash, *The American West Transformed: The Impact of the Second World War* (Bloomington: Indiana University Press, 1985), vii–viii. For other good general treatments of the post–World War II West, see Richard White, *"It's Your Misfortune and None of My Own": A New History of the American West* (Norman: University of Oklahoma Press, 1991), and Michael P. Malone and Richard W.

Etulain, *The American West: A Twentieth-Century History* (Lincoln: University of Nebraska Press, 1989).

2. Generally, "prior appropriation" doctrine declares water to be the public property of the state and recognizes the right of a person to use some portion of a stream flow. The state usually establishes a hierarchy of "beneficial" water uses, and a water user receives a right granted either through the state engineer's office or the courts. The right is dated, and this date determines when a person receives water in relation to other water users of the same source, "first in time, first in right." "Riparian" doctrine, in contrast, assures the owner of a stream bank the use of the flow passing by or through the land. Originating in common law, this doctrine guarantees a riparian owner the right to stream flow undiminished in quantity and unaffected in quality regardless of the uses of this same water by any other upstream riparian owner. At the same time, a riparian owner is required to return the same water to the stream materially undiminished, generally ruling out consumptive uses of water.

3. Wells A. Hutchins, *The Kansas Law of Water Rights* (Topeka: Division of Water Resources and Kansas State Water Resources Board, 1957), 44.

4. R. V. Smrha, "George Knapp and the Kansas Water Rights Act," *Kansas Water News* 9 (April 1966): 4.

5. Hutchins, *Kansas Law of Water,* 29.

6. "Drouth" is a Kansas idiom for "drought," and throughout this chapter "drouth," not "drought," will be used.

7. Hutchins, *Kansas Law of Water,* 70.

8. Joseph L. Arnold, *The Evolution of the 1936 Flood Control Act* (Fort Belvoir, Va.: Office of History, United States Army Corps of Engineers, 1988), 16–22.

9. Philip E. Meyer, "Tuttle Creek Dam: A Case Study in Local Opposition" (Master's thesis, University of North Carolina, 1962), 7–14.

10. The Pick-Sloan Plan derived its name from Col. Lewis Pick of the Army Corps of Engineers and Glenn Sloan in the Bureau of Reclamation, both of whom had drawn up plans for flood control and hydroelectric projects in the Missouri Basin. The enthusiastic approach to dam building employed by both the corps and bureau is detailed by Marc Reisner in *Cadillac Desert: The American West and Its Disappearing Water* (New York: Penguin Books, 1986), 189–94. This institutional invigoration would move the Tuttle Creek project out of the corps's broom closet and into the light.

11. Avery served five terms in Congress followed by one term as governor of Kansas. Ironically, Avery lost most of his farm to the Milford Reservoir on the Republican River.

12. The history of the Feather River Project sustains this Kansas supposition. See Norris Hundley, Jr., *The Great Thirst: Californians and Water, 1770s–1990s* (Berkeley and Los Angeles: University Press of California, 1992), 276–77, 286–87.

13. Homer E. Socolofsky and Huber Self, *Historical Atlas of Kansas* (Norman: University of Oklahoma Press, 1972; rev. ed., 1988), 6.

14. Huber Self, *Environment and Man in Kansas: A Geographical Analysis* (Lawrence: Regents Press of Kansas, 1978), 57–60.

15. David E. Kromm and Stephen E. White, "The High Plains Ogallala Region," in *Groundwater Exploitation in the High Plains*, ed. David E. Kromm and Stephen E. White (Lawrence: University Press of Kansas, 1992), 16.

16. Donald Green, "A History of Irrigation Technology Used to Exploit the Ogallala Aquifer," in *Groundwater Exploitation in the High Plains*, ed. David E. Kromm and Stephen E. White (Lawrence: University Press of Kansas, 1992), 41–42.

17. David E. Kromm and Stephen E. White, "Groundwater Problems," in *Groundwater Exploitation in the High Plains*, ed. David E. Kromm and Stephen E. White (Lawrence: University Press of Kansas, 1992), 46.

18. "Zero Depletion: Plan to Limit Water Use Divides Kansans," *Wichita Eagle-Beacon*, 26 May 1991.

19. Ibid.

20. "Robert Hess Helped Keep Water Flowing to a Thirsty City," *Wichita Eagle-Beacon*, 23 February 1922.

21. *Cities of Hesston and Sedgwick, and Harvey Hensley, Cities of Burrton and Halstead v. R.V. Smrha, Chief Engineer, Division of Water Resources, Kansas State Board of Agriculture, Topeka, Kansas, The City of Wichita, Kansas, and The City of Newton, Kansas*, 184 Kan. 223 (1959).

22. "A Market for Water Is Born," *Wichita Eagle-Beacon*, 4 November 1990.

23. Ibid.

24. "Battle Line Being Drawn for Intrastate Water Struggle," *Wichita Eagle-Beacon*, 30 January 1989.

25. "Milford Delay Necessitates Greater Efforts to Save Water," *Wichita Eagle-Beacon*, 4 November 1992.

26. "Spreading Brine Poses Danger to Water Supply," *Wichita Eagle-Beacon*, 13 November 1988; and "Nitrate Contamination Pits Pretty Prairie Against State," *Wichita Eagle-Beacon*, 30 September 1991.

27. For a discussion of consumer-based environmentalism, see Samuel Hays, *Beauty, Health, and Permanence: Environmental Politics in the United States, 1955–1985* (New York: Cambridge University Press, 1987); and "Wichita's Water Gluttony Could Be Costly," *Wichita Eagle-Beacon*, 9 October 1992. Hays believes that the post–World War II American middle class has been largely concerned with economic consumption rather than economic production. Clean air, clean water, sustainable water supplies, and so forth, become more important than the building of dams to increase water supplies, which is of a production mentality.

28. John L. Zimmerman, *Cheyenne Bottoms: Wetland in Jeopardy* (Lawrence: University Press of Kansas, 1990), 132–36, and "Life in Contested Waters," *Wichita Eagle-Beacon*, 7 March 1991.

29. Zimmerman, *Cheyenne Bottoms*, 111–15.

30. James Sherow, *Watering the Valley: Development Along the High Plains Arkansas River, 1870–1950* (Lawrence: University Press of Kansas, 1990), 158–59.

31. Zimmerman, *Cheyenne Bottoms*, 128.

32. "Water Decision Upsets Farmers," *Wichita Eagle-Beacon*, 23 February 1992.

33. Ibid.

34. Ibid.

35. "Agricultural Interests Oppose Special Fees for Water Plan," *Wichita Eagle-Beacon,* 16 February 1989.

CHAPTER 8

1. U.S. Department of Commerce, Bureau of the Census, *1990 Census of Population, General Characteristics, Montana* (Washington, D.C.: Government Printing Office, 1992), 1. The *Missoulian* (Missoula, Montana), 8 February 1993.

2. For another reference to the state as a town with long streets, see William Kittredge, *Hole in the Sky: A Memoir* (New York: Alfred A. Knopf, 1992), 225.

3. Howard, *Montana, High, Wide, and Handsome* (New Haven: Yale University Press, 1943); Toole, *Montana, An Uncommon Land* (Norman: University of Oklahoma Press, 1959); *Montana: A State of Extremes* (Norman: University of Oklahoma Press, 1972).

4. For the size of the ACM, see David M. Emmons, *The Butte Irish: Class and Ethnicity in an American Mining Town, 1875–1925* (Urbana: University of Illinois Press, 1989), 237. On how the AMC reached its size and power, see Michael Malone, *The Battle for Butte: Mining and Politics on the Northern Frontier* (Seattle: University of Washington Press, 1981).

5. Howard, *High, Wide, and Handsome;* Toole, *Uncommon Land;* Toole, *State of Extremes.* See also Neal R. Peirce, *The Mountain States of America: People, Politics, and Power in the Eight Rocky Mountain States* (New York: W. W. Norton, 1972), 90–119.

6. Michael Malone, "Montana as a Corporate Bailiwick: An Image in History," in *Montana Past and Present,* papers read at Clark Library Seminar of 5 April 1975, William Andrews Clark Memorial Library, Los Angeles (Berkeley and Los Angeles: University of California, 1976), 57–76. A. G. Mezerik, *The Revolt of the South and the West* (New York: Duell, Sloan and Pearce, 1946), 45–46 (Malone quotations); Howard, *High, Wide, and Handsome,* 84; Toole, *State of Extremes,* 121–22.

7. Michael Malone, "The Close of the Copper Century," *Montana The Magazine of Western History* 35 (Spring 1985): 69–72; Malone, "The Collapse of Western Metal Mining: An Historical Epitaph," *Pacific Historical Review* 55 (August 1986): 455–64.

8. Thomas M. Power, *The Economic Pursuit of Quality* (Armonk, N.Y.: M. E. Sharpe, Inc., 1988), 106–68; Albert Borgmann, *Crossing the Postmodern Divide* (Chicago: University of Chicago Press, 1992), 132.

9. "Close of the Copper Century," 72.

10. Toole devotes more than half of both of his books to Butte, the Company, and its allegedly nefarious dealings. For the history of ACM after 1913, see George Hildebrand and Garth L. Mangum, *Capital and Labor in American Copper: A Study of the Linkages Between Product and Labor Markets* (Cambridge: Harvard University Press, 1992), 69–71.

11. Hildebrand and Magnum, *American Copper,* 71; Montana Department of Commerce, *Montana Statistical Abstract, 1984: A Supplement to Economic Conditions in Montana, 1984.* (Helena, 1985), 85.

12. Hildebrand and Magnum, *American Copper,* 144–47, 148–52, 210–22; see

also Vernon H. Jensen, *Nonferrous Metals Industry Unionism, 1932–1954: A Study of Leadership Controversy* (Ithaca: Cornell University Press, 1954).

13. For Butte strikes, see Emmons, *Butte Irish*, 364–83, 398–99; Michael Malone, Richard Roeder, and William Lang, *Montana: A History of Two Centuries*, rev. ed. (Seattle: University of Washington Press, 1991), 328–30. For Butte and other strikes, see Hildebrand and Magnum, *American Copper*, 131–35, 217–18, 230–44. For Colorado, see George Suggs, *Colorado's War on Militant Unionism: James H. Peabody and the WFM* (Detroit: Wayne State University Press, 1972); David Montgomery, *The Fall of the House of Labor: The Workplace, the State, and American Labor Activism, 1865–1925* (Cambridge: Cambridge University Press, 1987), 110, 318, 338, 346. For Arizona, see James Brykit, *Forging the Copper Collar: Arizona's Labor-Management War of 1901–1921* (Tucson: University of Arizona Press, 1982).

14. On the reduction of the Butte work force occasioned by open pit mining, see Peirce, *Mountain States*, 101.

15. Malone, Roeder, and Lang, *Montana*, 325, 347, 366–68; Peirce, *Mountain States*, 99; John McNay, "Breaking the Copper Collar: The Sale of the Anaconda Newspapers and the Professionalism of Journalism in Montana" (M.A. thesis, University of Montana, 1991); Richard Ruetten, "Anaconda Journalism: The End of an Era," *Journalism Quarterly* (Winter 1960): 3–12.

16. For the legislative council, see Malone, Roeder, and Lang, *Montana*, 391. On the fall of the Montana Twins and the abandonment of the hospitality rooms, see Peirce, *Mountain States*, 95, 96, 98; Malone, "Bailiwick," 71. For the Steelworkers Union, see Hildebrand and Magnum, *American Copper*, 233, 245, 247, 250. The constitutional convention is covered in Ellis Waldron and Paul Wilson, *Atlas of Montana Elections, 1889–1976* (Missoula: University of Montana Publications in History, 1978), 259–60; *Time*, 10 April 1972. See also "1889–1970: The Montana Constitution. Resource or Burden?" Pamphlet file, Toole Archives, University of Montana.

17. Hildebrand and Magnum, *American Copper*, 150–51; Malone, Roeder, and Lang, *Montana*, 325–28.

18. Malone, Roeder, and Lang, *Montana*, 325–27; Montana Department of Commerce, *Montana Statistical Abstract: A Supplement to Economic Conditions in Montana, 1984* (Helena, 1985), 10–11; Bureau of the Census, *1990 Census*, 1.

19. Howard, *High, Wide, and Handsome*, 85.

20. On the Milwaukee Railroad, see Malone, Roeder, and Lang, *Montana*, 343. Population figures are from Montana Department of Commerce, *Statistical Abstract*, 10–11, 14–15. Peirce writes about the declining number of Montana farmers in *Mountain States*, 110. The Poppers were covered in a story in the *Missoulian*, 13 January 1992.

21. Montana Department of Commerce, *Statistical Abstract*, 10–11; Bureau of the Census, *1990 Census*, 1.

22. For "blue eyed Arabs," see Malone, Roeder, and Lang, *Montana*, 397–98. Montana Department of Commerce, *Statistical Abstract*, 341–46, 361–63, 366, 373–77.

23. Montana Department of Commerce, *Statistical Abstract*, 391, 394. Last

figures are from Bureau of Business and Economic Research, *Montana Forest Products Industry: A Descriptive Analysis, 1969–1988* (Missoula, 1990), 9; and Western Wood Products Association, *Statistical Yearbook of the Western Lumber Industry* (Portland, 1992), 5. *Missoulian*, 15 February 1993.

24. Interview with Marc Racicot, *Montana Business Quarterly*, 30, 4 (Winter 1992): 13.

25. Toole, *Uncommon Land*, 256–58; Power, *Economic Pursuit*, 127–28, 139–43.

26. Montana Department of Commerce, *Statistical Abstract*, 91–94; U.S. Department of Commerce, Bureau of the Census, *Statistical Abstract of the United States, 1992*, 112th ed. (Washington, D.C.: Government Printing Office, 1992), 437.

27. Historians should pay more attention to the so-called urban safety valve and its divergent effects on different states. The significance of a large and economically diversified city within a state was noted by Professor Paul Polzin, director of the University of Montana Bureau of Business and Economic Research. Interview, 14 January 1993.

28. For the Nicklaus-designed golf course, see the ARCO advertisement in the *Missoulian*, 22 January 1993.

29. *Great Falls Tribune*, 16 August 1988.

30. Waldron and Wilson, *Montana Elections*, 259–60, 262.

31. Ivan Doig's best-known tribute to Montana is *This House of Sky* (New York: Harcourt Brace Jovanovich, 1978); Norman Maclean's is *A River Runs Through It* (Chicago: University of Chicago Press, 1976). William Kittredge and Annick Smith were the compilers of *The Last Best Place* (Helena: Montana State Historical Society Press, 1988). Also deserving of a place is William Bevis, *Ten Tough Trips: Montana Writers and the West* (Seattle: University of Washington Press, 1990). Borgmann, *Crossing*, 20–27, 116–38.

32. William Kittredge traces the evolution from farm to agribusiness on his family's Oregon ranch in *Hole in the Sky*.

33. Borgmann, *Crossing*, 142–43.

CHAPTER 9

1. For an overview of Omaha labor history, see William C. Pratt, *Omaha in the Making of Nebraska Labor History* (Omaha: Ad Hoc Committee for the Study of Nebraska Labor History, 1981).

2. See Ronald M. Gephart, "Politicians, Soldiers and Strikes: The Reorganization of the Nebraska Militia and the Omaha Strike of 1882," *Nebraska History* 46 (June 1965): 89–120; Mary Cochran Grimes, "The Governor and the Guard in the Omaha Tram Strike of 1935," *Nebraska History* 69 (Fall 1988): 120–30.

3. See William C. Pratt, "The Omaha Business Men's Association and the Open Shop, 1903–1909," *Nebraska History* 70 (Summer 1989): 172–83.

4. George R. Leighton, "Omaha, Nebraska: The Glory Is Departed—Part II," *Harper's Monthly Magazine* 177 (August 1938): 326.

5. For a survey of Nebraska labor history and legislation, see Russell Lowell

Beebe, "History of Labor Organization and Legislation in Nebraska to 1918" (M.A. thesis, University of Nebraska, 1938).

6. Jonathan Ezra Garlock, "A Structural Analysis of the Knights of Labor: A Prolegomenon to the History of the Producing Classes" (Ph.D. diss., University of Rochester, 1974), 326–28.

7. *Unionist* (Omaha), 4 April 1947. Central labor bodies were then located in Beatrice, Fremont, Grand Island, Hastings, Lincoln, Norkfolk, Omaha, and Scottsbluff. In addition, the Congress of Industrial Organizations (CIO) had a central body in Omaha–Council Bluffs (Iowa).

8. Gary Garrison, "Omaha's Building Trades Strike of 1917: The Business Men's Association Labors Against Union Organization" (Seminar paper, University of Nebraska, Omaha, 1973); William C. Pratt, "The Omaha Business Men's Association and the Open Shop, 1903–1922" (Paper presented at the Missouri Valley History Conference, 14 March 1987).

9. James A. Stone, "Agrarian Ideology and the Farm Problem in Nebraska State Politics with Special Reference to Northeast Nebraska, 1920–1933" (Ph.D. diss., University of Nebraska, 1960), 265.

10. Norris eventually came to eschew conventional partisan politics altogether, promoting a nonpartisan legislature for Nebraska and seeking reelection to the U.S. Senate in 1936 and again in 1942 as an independent. For Norris's senatorial career, see Richard Lowitt, *George W. Norris: The Persistence of a Progressive, 1913–1933* (Urbana: University of Illinois Press, 1971); Richard Lowitt, *George W. Norris: The Triumph of a Progressive, 1933–1944* (Urbana: University of Illinois Press, 1979). While Farmer-Laborism had a following in a number of states, its most successful outpost was Minnesota. See Richard M. Valelly, *Radicalism in the States: The Minnesota Farmer-Labor Party and the American Political Economy* (Chicago: University of Chicago Press, 1989). Perhaps it should be pointed out, however, that a state could have a prolabor administration and still have a weak labor movement. The open shop prevailed in Minneapolis, despite a Farmer-Labor governor, until the mid-1930s. See Lois Quam and Peter J. Rachleff, "Keeping Minneapolis an Open-Shop Town: The Citizens' Alliance in the 1930s," *Minnesota History* 50 (Fall 1986): 105–17. Even in Minnesota, the labor movement seemingly needed a boost from the New Deal to succeed. The relative ineffectiveness of prolabor administrations at the state level after World War I is a promising topic for further research.

11. An article in a local labor paper, with the headline "Anything to Say This Week, Senator Norris?" reveals Teamster impatience with Norris's neglect of state labor issues. It reads in part: "How about working for a little 'T.V.A.' for the workers of Nebraska, Senator Norris? How about helping the Nebraska workers, the most progressive force in the state, to bring about a bit more economic justice, to win higher wages and better working conditions that can bring a bit more food and clothing and happiness to the workers and the mothers and children of Nebraska?" *Farmer-Labor Press* (Council Bluffs), 3 January 1939. This article appeared in a special issue of the paper edited by the Omaha Teamsters near the end of a long strike. Lowitt notes, "Sympathetic though he was, Norris expressed dissatisfaction with some positions taken by organized labor. More often he tried to

be of help, as in the case of a teamsters' strike in Omaha when he successfully prodded conciliators in Washington to bring the parties together." Lowitt, *George W. Norris: The Triumph of a Progressive,* 269.

12. *The Unionist,* 3 May 1940; "Labor Backs Senator Norris, *The Unionist,* 30 October 1942. At its 1942 convention, the American Federation of Labor (AFL) in Nebraska had referred to Norris as "the greatest legislator that has ever sat in the halls of our National Congress."

13. According to the *Omaha World-Herald,* the Nebraska American Federation of Labor (AFL) had "a membership of between 50 thousand and 60 thousand Nebraskans." *Omaha World-Herald,* 3 June 1947 (evening edition). Earlier, a packinghouse union spokesman reported, "7500 UPWA members in Omaha." *Omaha World-Herald,* 2 November 1946 (evening edition). CIO ranks also included brewery workers in Omaha and rubber workers in Lincoln.

14. For discussion on antilabor efforts at the state level, see Harry Millis and Emily Clark Brown, *From the Wagner Act to Taft-Hartley: A Study of National Labor Policy and Labor Relations* (Chicago: University of Chicago Press, 1950); Lucille B. Milner and Paul Brissenden; "Union Regulation by the States," *New Republic* 108 (14 June 1943): 790–92; E. Merrick Dodd, "Some State Legislatures Go to War—On Labor Unions," *Iowa Law Review* 29 (January 1944): 148–74.

15. "The term right-to-work itself is a misnomer and a good example of artful propaganda. These laws do not and were never intended to guarantee a right to work or a right to a job." James R. Eissinger, "The Right-to-Work Imbroglio," *North Dakota Law Review* 51 (Spring 1975): 573.

16. *Omaha Bee-News,* November 19, 1929, as quoted in *Unionist,* 12 September 1930. The Bricklayers Union also wanted a union foreman to be used on this job.

17. *Open Shop* 3 (September 1, 1922): 1.

18. A recent letter in a North Dakota newspaper suggests this attitude: "A right-to-work state such as North Dakota does not guarantee a living wage, health or retirement benefits, safe working conditions or job security. The right-to-work law allows employers to fire employees at a minute's notice with little recourse." *Minot Daily News,* 6 July 1993.

19. Millis and Brown, *From the Wagner Act;* Milner and Brissenden, "Union Regulation"; Dodd, "Some State Legislatures."

20. Dodd, "Some State Legislatures," 174.

21. *Lincoln Star,* 30 March 1943; *Nebraska State Journal* (Lincoln), 30 March 1943; *Unionist,* 2 April 1943. Swarr apparently did not mention any decisions by name, but Millis and Brown cite two 1940 "cases involving antipicketing statutes and ordinances" where the Supreme Court "had held that picketing is protected as a form of free speech." Millis and Brown, *From the Wagner Act,* 330.

22. *Nebraska State Journal* (Lincoln), 12 March 1946; *Unionist,* 15 March 1946.

23. *Omaha World-Herald,* 26 April 1946, (evening edition).

24. *Omaha World-Herald,* 3 May 1946 (evening edition).

25. *Unionist,* 16 August 1946.

26. Bill Wax, "Lloyd E. Skinner Career Characterized by Stewardship," *Midlands Business Journal* (Omaha), 2 April 1982. Clipping file, Historical Society of Douglas County, Omaha.

27. *Unionist,* 15 March 1946 and 14 June 1946.

28. Wax, "Lloyd E. Skinner Career."

29. *Omaha World-Herald,* 3 May 1946; *Polk's Omaha City Directory 1946* (Omaha: R. L. Polk & Co., 1946).

30. Labor representatives, from the first time they heard of the right-to-work campaign, asserted that its moving force was from outside Nebraska. *Nebraska State Journal,* 12 March 1946.

31. *Unionist,* 5 July 1946.

32. *Lincoln Star,* 3 July 1946; *Unionist,* 12 July 1946.

33. *Unionist,* 20 September 1946; 11 October 1946; 1 November 1946.

34. *Omaha World-Herald,* 25 October 1946 (evening edition).

35. *Nebraska Agriculture,* 12 September 1946. According to a source from within the Nebraska Small Business Men's Association (NSBMA), "Charles Marshall, president of the Nebraska Farm Bureau Federation, is making a tour of Western Nebraska speaking in favor of the amendment." *Omaha World-Herald,* 25 October 1946 (evening edition). The school amendment called for state aid to local school districts.

36. *Omaha World-Herald,* 9 October 1946 (evening edition). A labor spokesman reported a more ominous wording on these signs: "Out along Nebraska highways this week billboards carried the words, 'Run the Labor Leaders and Racketeers Out of Nebraska. Vote "X" Yes 302.'" *Unionist,* 4 October 1946. Skinner denied that this wording was used on the billboards.

37. Near the end of the campaign, the labor movement circulated a leaflet that "quoted editorials of Nebraska State Journal, Beatrice Times, Grand Island Independent and Columbus Daily Telegram in opposition to the proposed anti-union shop amendment. Due to typographical error another editorial was shown under the heading 'From the Journal—Stockman.' This heading was in error. It should have read 'From the Nebraska Union Farmer.' We regret that in this one respect a mistake was made." *Grand Island Daily Independent,* 4 November 1946.

38. Abstracts of Votes Cast, Election Records, Secretary of State Collection, Nebraska State Historical Society, Lincoln.

39. *Unionist,* 13 June 1947.

40. Telephone conversation with Lloyd Skinner, February 1984.

41. *Grand Island Daily Independent,* 7 November 1946.

42. *Omaha World-Herald,* 3 January 1949 (evening edition).

43. For the teachers' pension measure, see *Omaha World-Herald,* 23 January 1947; *Nebraska State Journal,* 14, 16 April 1947.

44. *Omaha World-Herald,* 22 March 1947 (evening edition).

45. Ibid.; *Nebraska State Journal,* 22 March 1947.

46. *Lincoln Star,* 7 and 8 April 1947.

47. *Lincoln Star,* 7 April 1947.

48. *Lincoln Star,* 15 April 1947.

49. *Omaha World-Herald,* 15 April 1947 (evening edition).

50. *Omaha World-Herald,* 17 and 21 April 1947 (evening edition).

51. *Omaha World-Herald,* 3 June 1947 (evening edition), *Nebraska State Journal,* 3 June 1947. Although Guenther had been reinstated as president, he later

was defeated in his bid for reelection at the 1947 state AFL convention. *The Unionist,* 12 September 1947.

52. For a review of 1947 state labor legislation, see "States Lead in Legislation," *Business Week,* 14 June 1947, 90–97.

53. Ibid., 90.

54. William C. Pratt, "Workers, Bosses, and Public Officials: Omaha's 1948 Packinghouse Strike," *Nebraska History* 66 (Fall 1985): 294–313.

55. Ibid., 302–303.

56. *Omaha World-Herald,* 1 May 1948.

57. *Unionist,* 4 June 1948.

58. *Omaha World-Herald,* 2 May 1948 (morning edition).

59. Pratt, "Workers, Bosses, and Public Officials," 305.

60. *Omaha World-Herald,* 26 May 1946 (morning edition, Clipping file, Historical Society of Douglas County); *Omaha World-Herald,* 4 November 1948 (evening edition).

61. *Omaha World-Herald,* 3 January 1949.

62. A number of efforts have been undertaken in the Nebraska legislature to repeal the right-to-work amendment or modify it so as to allow the agency shop, an arrangement which "would permit an agreement between a union and an employer that would require all employees to share the union's cost of representing them, whether or not they are members of the union." *Omaha World-Herald* 6 April 1979 (evening edition). Clipping file, Historical Society of Douglas County, Omaha.

63. Keith Lumsden and Craig Petersen, "The Effect of Right-to-Work Laws on Unionization in the United States," *Journal of Political Economy* 83 (1975): 1242.

64. *Lincoln Star,* 10 April 1947; Pratt, "Workers, Bosses, and Public Officials," 302.

65. Robert Anderson, Swarr's son-in-law, indicated that Swarr authored both the 1946 right-to-work amendment and the 1949 antipicketing law. Telephone conversation with Robert Anderson, February 1984. Swarr's involvement with the right-to-work and antipicketing measures testifies to the continuity between the earlier Omaha Business Men's Association and the NSBMA. In early 1949, the *Omaha World-Herald* reported the merger of the two groups and quoted the president of the older employer organization, "There is no use having two organizations to do the same thing." *Omaha World-Herald,* 8 January 1949 (evening edition).

66. *Lincoln Star,* 24 March 1949; *Omaha World-Herald,* 24 March 1949 (evening edition); *Unionist,* 25 March 1949. L.O. Schneiderwind, NSBMA president, died later the same day he testified for the antipicketing measure. He was succeeded as NSBMA president by Lloyd Skinner. *Omaha World-Herald,* 29 April 1949 (evening edition).

67. *Lincoln Star,* 24 March 1949; *Unionist,* 25 March 1949.

68. *Omaha World-Herald,* 13 and 26 April 1949 (evening editions); 13 May 1949 (evening edition).

69. *Omaha World-Herald,* 8 November 1950 (evening edition). Buffett attracted 63 percent of the vote in the 1950 election.

70. The 1949 antipicketing law was later utilized during packing strikes in Omaha and Dakota City. See *Omaha World-Herald,* 21 July 1982 (morning edition). The U.S. Circuit Court of Appeals case that struck down most of its major provisions arose out of a 1986 strike at the Dakota City Iowa Beef Processing (IBP) plant. See *United Food and Commercial Workers International Union, AFL-CIO, et al. v. IBP, Inc., et al.,* 857 Fed.R.2d 422. For local union reaction to this decision, see *Omaha World-Herald,* 10 September 1988 (morning edition).

71. Interview with Hubert ("Red") Lockard, 26 February 1981. Lockard was a longtime leader of United Packinghouse Workers of America (UPWA) Local 8, which represented workers in the Omaha Armour plant. In 1956 the U.S. Supreme Court ruled that Nebraska's right-to-work law did not apply to railroad workers covered by the 1951 Railroad Labor Act. This decision overturned a Nebraska Supreme Court ruling. *Omaha World-Herald,* 21 May 1956 (evening edition). Clipping file, Historical Society of Douglas County, Omaha. According to the *World-Herald,* the decision "blew a gaping hole in the 'right-to-work' laws of Nebraska and 17 other states."

72. James W. Kuhn, "Right-to-Work Laws—Symbols or Substance?" *Industrial and Labor Relations Review* 14 (July 1961): 587–94; Lumsden and Petersen, "The Effect of Right-to-Work Laws on Unionization in the United States."

73. *Omaha World-Herald,* 15 April 1947 (evening edition).

74. David George Wagaman, "Public Employee Impasse Resolution: A Historical Examination of the Nebraska Experience with Some Comparisons to the New York State Experience" (Ph.D. diss., University of Nebraska, Lincoln, 1977); David G. Wagaman, "The Evolution of Some Legal-Economic Aspects of Collective Bargaining by Public Employees in Nebraska Since 1919," *Nebraska History* 58 (Winter 1977): 475–89; Janet Stewart Arnold, "The Historical Development of Public Employee Collective Bargaining in Nebraska," *Creighton Law Review* 15 (1981–82): 477–97. A 1987 law, LB 661, provides an impasse resolution mechanism for state employees that normally eliminates the need to utilize the Court of Industrial Relations (CIR) in contract negotiations. It seems unlikely that this law would have been adopted if a large number of state employees had not already been covered by collective bargaining.

75. Telephone interview with Jerry Wilson, director of Member Rights/Negotiations, South Dakota Education Association, 13 July 1993; telephone interview with Kenneth Melius, executive director, South Dakota State Employees Association, 22 July 1993; telephone interview with Laura Ripplinger, office manager, North Dakota Public Employees Association–American Federation of Teachers, July 1993; telephone interview with Nancy Sands, UniServ director, North Dakota Education Association, 23 July 1993; telephone interview with James Fotter, president, Wyoming Education Association, 12 August 1993; telephone interview with Robert Reynolds, assistant director, Wyoming Public Employees Association, 12 August 1993. My comments on public-sector collective bargaining are limited to state employees and state college and university faculty. Public school teachers and city and county workers often have collective bargaining in Nebraska and these other states. Kansas is another right-to-work neighbor. Its state employees (and the faculty at one state university) are covered by collective bargaining

by collective bargaining agreements, but its labor law does not provide for binding arbitration in the case of an impasse. Thus, as is the situation in public sector bargaining in the Dakotas and Wyoming, the employer can impose its last offer. Telephone interview with Paul Dickhoff, director of negotiations, Kansas Association of Public Employees, 10 September 1993. This contrasts with Nebraska legislation, which provides for binding arbitration in the event of an impasse. Nebraska's 1987 law allows for a legislative review of wage settlements and arbitration awards for state employees, but to date the unicameral has not overturned any of them. The legislature has no such review power over state college and university settlements.

CHAPTER 10

1. C. Elizabeth Raymond, *George Wingfield: Owner and Operator of Nevada* (Reno: University of Nevada Press, 1992), 12–13, 26–35.

2. Jerome E. Edwards, "From Back Alley to Main Street: Nevada's Acceptance of Gambling," *Nevada Historical Society Quarterly* 33 (Spring 1990): 18–20.

3. Norman H. Blitz, "Memoirs of the Duke of Nevada" (Unpublished oral history, Reno Library, University of Nevada, 1967), 119; Henry F. Pringle, "Reno the Wicked: The American Capital of Divorce and Gambling," *Outlook* 158, 29 July 1931, 403.

4. Writers Program, Works Progress Administration, *Nevada, a Guide to the Silver State* (Portland: Binfords and Mort, 1940), 4.

5. Joseph F. McDonald, "Gambling in Nevada," *Annals of the American Academy of Political and Social Science* 269 (May 1950): 30, 34.

6. U.S. Bureau of the Census, *Statistical Abstract, 1951* (Washington, D.C.: Government Printing Office, 1951), 28, quoted in Gerald D. Nash, *The American West Transformed: The Impact of the Second World War* (Bloomington: Indiana University Press, 1985), 222.

7. Jerome E. Edwards, *Pat McCarran: Political Boss of Nevada* (Reno: University of Nevada Press, 1982), 170.

8. See Jerome E. Edwards, "Wingfield and Nevada Politics — Some Observations," *Nevada Historical Society Quarterly* 32 (Summer 1989): 133–34.

9. The chief political study of Pat McCarran is Edwards, *Pat McCarran.*

10. Freeman Lincoln, "Norman Blitz, Duke of Nevada," *Fortune* 50 (September 1954): 141.

11. Patrick McCarran to Mrs. McCarran, 4 November 1952, McCarran Collection, Nevada Historical Society, quoted in Edwards, *Pat McCarran,* 180.

12. James F. Smith, " 'Bugsy's' Flamingo and the Modern Casino Hotel," in *Gambling and Public Policy: International Perspectives,* ed. William R. Eadington and Judy A. Cornelius (Reno: University of Nevada, Institute for the Study of Gambling and Commercial Gaming, 1991), 502.

13. Edwards, *Pat McCarran,* 115–62.

14. Russell R. Elliott, *History of Nevada,* 2d rev. ed. (Lincoln: University of Nebraska Press, 1987), 282–83; Gilman Ostrander, *Nevada, the Great Rotten*

Borough, 1859–1964 (New York: Knopf, 1966), 208–11; see also Harold S. Smith, Sr., *I Want to Quit Winners.* (Englewood Cliffs, N.J.: Prentice-Hall, 1961), 169, 171.

15. Eugene P. Miehring, *Resort City in the Sunbelt: Las Vegas, 1930–1970* (Reno: University of Nevada Press, 1989), 26, 29, 38–40; John M. Findlay, *People of Chance: Gambling in American Society from Jamestown to Las Vegas* (New York: Oxford University Press, 1986), 114–17, 125–27.

16. Moehring, *Resort City in the Sunbelt,* 46–50, 74–80; Deke Castleman, *Las Vegas* (Oakland: Compass American Guides, 1991), 73–101.

17. Elliott, *History of Nevada,* 408.

18. Edwards, *Pat McCarran,* 148–55.

19. Pat McCarran to Joseph F. McDonald, 3 July 1951, McCarran Collection, quoted in Edwards, *Pat McCarran,* 152–55.

20. Lincoln, "Norman Biltz, Duke of Nevada," 140–41; Biltz, "Memoirs of the Duke of Nevada," 227–28.

21. Significantly Nevada officials adopted the word *gaming* rather than *gambling* to describe Nevada's chief industry. Indeed *gambling,* which is the older word, was initiated by Reno entrepreneur William F. Harrah in the late 1940s in his advertising. It sounded "better . . . a little neater." *Gaming* sounded more innocent and also more like an industry, comparable to automotive, steel, and banking enterprises. *Gambling,* through the traditional view of conservative Protestant denominations, was already associated with eternal damnation.

22. Thomas C. Wilson Opinion Survey, Manuscript Division, Nevada Historical Society, Reno.

23. Elliott, *History of Nevada,* 408.

24. *Las Vegas Sun,* 9 April 1989.

25. See David Spanier, *Welcome to the Pleasuredome: Inside Las Vegas* (Reno and Las Vegas: University of Nevada Press, 1992), 12–13.

26. *Nevada Business Journal* 4 (July 1989), 10.

27. The one-county, one-seat provision for the Nevada State Senate had been legislatively mandated for the 1919 session. It was made part of the Nevada Constitution in 1950. William D. Swackamer, *Political History of Nevada.* 8th ed. (Carson City, 1986), 159, 213.

28. Biltz, "Memoirs," 119–20.

29. Edward F. Sherman, "Nevada, the End of the Casino Era," *The Atlantic* 218 (October 1966): 116.

30. Based on a manuscript to be published by the University of Nevada Press (1994), Gary Elliott, "The Developing Empire: Senator Alan Bible and the New American West, 1934 to 1974."

31. See United States Commission on the Review of the National Policy toward Gambling, "Transcript of Proceedings, the Nevada National Hearings," (3 typed volumes, unpublished, photocopied). Hearings—Carson City, 18 August 1975, Las Vegas—19–21 August 1975; United States Commission on the Review of the National Policy toward Gambling, *Gambling in America, Final Report* (Public Gaming Research Institute: Rockville, Md., 1976).

32. *Nevada State Journal* (Reno), 18 November 1978.

33. *Sacramento Bee,* 1 November 1983, 2 November 1983, *New York Times,* 21 October 1984, 21 December 1985.

34. *New York Times,* 28 September 1984.

35. *New York Times,* 21 October 1984.

36. Michael W. Bowers, "Judicial Selection in Nevada: Choosing the Judges," *Halcyon/1989, a Journal of the Humanities,* 98.

37. *Common Cause/Nevada,* Spring Edition, 1993, Legislative Newsletter.

38. "Emergent Laughlin" is a border town across the Colorado River from Bullhead City, Arizona. By 1990 it had three one-thousand room hotels. See Deke Castleman, *Las Vegas,* 223–26.

CHAPTER 11

1. J. S. McCall to Dick Dillon, 20 October 1945; Dillon to McCall, 22 October 1945. Patrick J. Hurley Papers, box 158, Western History Collection, University of Oklahoma, Norman.

2. Russell D. Buhite, in the incisive and well-written monograph *Patrick J. Hurley and American Foreign Policy* (Ithaca: Cornell University Press, 1973), reviews Hurley's lengthy and controversial career as secretary of war during the Hoover administration and as an itinerant envoy, serving with the rank of major general during the Second World War in the Southwest Pacific, Russia, the Middle East, and finally China.

3. After leaving the meeting on 21 November 1951, Hurley drafted a preliminary memorandum of what had occurred. Two days later he fleshed out this memorandum in a statement for his confidential files. Hurley Box no. 161 for both items (hereafter Hurley followed by box number).

4. Patrick J. Hurley press release, 19 January 1952, Hurley 169; Mel Mencher, "In the Capital," *Albuquerque Journal,* 21 January 1952; *Albuquerque Tribune,* 8 February 1952, Hurley 473.

5. "Santa Fe Feud Marks GOP Convention," *Raton Range,* 29 February 1952, Hurley 474. Hurley won 381 votes; 370 went to Wesley Quinn and 212 to John Knorr, Hurley's two opponents. See stories in *Raton Range,* 3 March 1952, and *Springer Tribune,* 6 March 1952, on the preprimary convention, Hurley 474.

6. "Republican Senatorial Race," *Albuquerque Journal,* 22 March 1952, Hurley 474; "Statement by Patrick J. Hurley," 22 March 1951, Hurley 168. Hurley did not release this statement to the press.

7. For story on the Republican party organization, see "In the Capital," *Albuquerque Journal,* 3 April 1952, Hurley 479. For the heated exchanges, see stories in the *Santa Fe New Mexican,* 14 and 16 April 1952; see "In the Capital," *Albuquerque Journal,* 20 April 1952, for an evaluation of the campaign. Hurley 473 for all items. "Prattle," *New Mexico State Record,* 8 May 1952, provides an analysis of the primary election. Once the primary was over, Republican leaders, "convinced we have the best chance in years to win the general election," papered over their differences. *Albuquerque Journal,* 17 May 1952, Hurley 473. Hurley to E. H. Bradshaw, 23 May 1952; Hurley to Mrs. Ward Williams, 28 May 1952; Hurley to Henry Luce, 17 June 1952. Hurley 168 for all correspondence.

8. "Memo for the Press: Eisenhower Meeting," 10 October 1952, Hurley 168; *Clovis News Journal,* 14 October 1952, Hurley 473; Stephan Alex to Everett Dirksen, 15 October 1952, Hurley 169. For stories on the close Senate race, see George Rothwell Brown article in the *Chicago Herald American,* 23 October 1952, Hurley 473; *Albuquerque Tribune,* 30 October 1952; *Roswell Record,* 31 October 1952, Hurley 476.

9. Hurley's decision to challenge the election commanded national press coverage. *Gallup Independent,* 5 November 1952; *Roswell Record,* 5 November 1952; *Albuquerque Tribune,* 5 November 1952; *El Paso Herald-Post,* 5 November 1952; *Santa Fe Record,* 6 November 1952; *New Haven Courier-Journal,* 7 November 1952. Hurley 476 for all items.

10. *Albuquerque Journal,* 11 November 1952; *Las Vegas Optic,* 11 November 1952, Hurley 476. *Las Cruces Sun News,* 13 November 1952; *Farmington Times,* 12 November 1952, Hurley 476.

11. *Santa Fe New Mexican,* 24 November 1952, Hurley 476; *Santa Fe New Mexican,* 14 December 1952; *El Crepusculo,* Taos, 13 December 1952, Hurley 477; *Los Angeles Examiner,* 14 December 1952, Hurley 170. Of New Mexico's 894 voting divisions, 231 were involved in the recount. The canvasing board ordered that poll books and tally books (not actual ballots) be returned for completion and correction by election officials in the voting divisions.

12. Albert G. Simms to Hurley, 21 January 1952 (*sic*); Hurley to Simms, 27 January 1953, Hurley 170; see also Marquis Childs, "Why Senator McCarthy Escaped Being Challenged," *Philadelphia Bulletin,* 6 January 1953, Hurley 475.

13. *Albuquerque Journal,* 18 April 1953; Charles Lucey article in *El Paso Herald-Post,* 18 April 1953, Hurley 479. Lucey, a Scripps-Howard staff writer, covered this story until the conclusion of the contest. I relied heavily on his insightful articles.

14. Two articles by Robert Hansen in *Denver Post,* 5 April 1953. Hansen's article on Chavez's response to Hurley's charges, *Denver Post,* 6 April 1953, Hurley 485. This dispute marked the third Senate-contested election in New Mexico's history. The preceding one occurred in 1934, when Chavez contested Bronson Cutting's victory. It ended with Cutting's death in a plane crash and Chavez's appointment in his place.

15. Don Irwin article, *New York Herald Tribune,* 8 May 1953; *Albuquerque Tribune,* 6 May 1953 — both Hurley 479. Robert S. Allen in *New York Evening Post,* 18 May 1953, Hurley 480; "State Taking Beating" *Carlsbad Current-Argus,* 27 May 1953, Hurley 482. For an account of the burning of 18,000 ballots covering a three-county area on the order of Judge Scoggin, see Charley Lucey article in *Albuquerque Tribune,* 27 May 1953, Hurley 481.

16. Stephan Alex to Harold Rainville, 20 June 1953; Alex to Robert Humphrey, 20 June 1953, Hurley 170. Ruth Finney article, *Albuquerque Tribune,* 10 July 1953, Hurley 480; "Summary Report of the 1952 New Mexico Senatorial Election: July 18, 1953," a copy of which can be found in Hurley 170. The committee, when the report appeared, had completed its recount of the ballots from Bernalillo County and was beginning its count of Rio Arriba County. Results from only eighty-seven precincts had been reviewed.

17. Drew Pearson, "Staff of 33 Probes New Mexico Senatorial Vote," *Tampa Tribune*, 26 July 1953, Hurley 480.

18. Robert Hansen, "New Mexico's Battle of the Ballots," *Denver Post*, 6 September 1953; *Santa Fe New Mexican*, 20 September 1953; *Washington Post*, 21 September 1953; *New York Times*, 20 September 1953, all Hurley 481.

19. Hurley to Dwight D. Eisenhower, 5 September 1953, Hurley 170. Hurley reportedly blamed all of his troubles on Governor Mechem — a further indication of Hurley's desperation. See Will Harrison, "Inside the Capitol," *Roswell Record*, 2 November 1953, Hurley 170.

20. Hurley to Stanley Kemp, 19 November 1953; Hurley to Romain C. Hassrick, 19 November 1953; Hurley to Carl Gilbert, 10 December 1953, Hurley 170.

21. "Release to Press by Subcommittee on Privileges and Elections," 18 December 1953, Hurley 170; *Albuquerque Journal*, 19 December 1953.

22. Hurley to James G. Stahlman, 31 December 1953, Hurley 170; *Carlsbad Current-Argus*, 6 January 1954, Hurley 483; Will Harrison article, *Santa Fe New Mexican*, 10 January 1954. Harrison discussed the complicated and delicate situation affecting the balance of power in the Senate. In that chamber Clinton Anderson was seeking to delay the admission of Hawaii into the Union until the Hurley-Chavez dispute was resolved. It was assumed that Hawaii's senators would be Republicans. See Ruth Finney articles in *Albuquerque Tribune*, 18 and 25 January 1954, Hurley 483.

23. Raymond J. Blair article, *New York Herald Tribune*, 25 January 1954; *Albuquerque Journal*, 25 January 1954; Ruth Finney article, *Albuquerque Tribune*, 25 January 1954. Hurley 483.

24. *Albuquerque Tribune*, 9 March 1954; *Santa Fe New Mexican*, 9 March 1954; *Las Cruces Sun News*, 9 March 1954; *Albuquerque Journal*, 10 March 1954, Hurley 483. In a March 14 radio broadcast Drew Pearson said that a total of $217,000 was spent investigating the election.

25. Hurley to Joe Kirkpatrick, 11 March 1954; Hurley to James W. Lewis, 11 March 1954, Hurley 170. Charles Lucey article, *Washington Daily News*, 10 March 1954; *Santa Fe New Mexican*, 11 March 1954, Hurley 483.

26. Two articles, one by Charles Lucey, in *Albuquerque Tribune*, 12 March 1954; *Tucumcari News*, 11 March 1954; *Albuquerque Journal*, 12 March 1954; *Santa Fe New Mexican*, 11 March 1954; William S. White article, *New York Times*, 14 March 1954. Robert S. Donovan article, *New York Herald Tribune*, 14 March 1954, Hurley 483. Donovan made much of the fact that this contest was the fourth disputed election in New Mexico since it became a state.

27. A copy of "Senator Hennings Minority Views," 83d Cong. 2d sess., Report 1081, pt. 2, can be found in Hurley 170; *Albuquerque Journal*, 23 March 1954, Hurley 484.

28. *Washington Post and Times Herald*, 24 March 1954, story by Robert G. Albright; J. A. O'Leary article, *Washington Evening Star*, 23 March 1954; *Albuquerque Journal*, 24 March 1954; *Santa Fe New Mexican*, 24 March 1954; Ruth Finney article, *Albuquerque Tribune*, 24 March 1954, Hurley 484.

29. Statement by Patrick J. Hurley, 24 March 1954, Hurley 170. Hurley was pleased with the attention the contest received, explaining, "The editorial com-

ment throughout the nation is overwhelmingly favorable to me." However, he felt that the Washington columnists seemed "to justify the action of the Senate on a partisan basis." See Hurley to James W. Lewis, 31 March 1954, Hurley 170.

30. Hurley to W. Harold Brenton, 4 November 1955; Hurley to James W. Lewis, n.d. (rough draft prepared in 1956), Hurley 170. See also Jack Harrison Pollack, "How Crooks Steal Your Votes," *Readers Digest* (September 1956), a copy of which is in Hurley 170. Pollack argued, citing the 1953 campaign as "one of the most notorious abuses of paper ballots," that ballot thievery was "more prevalent than ever today" and that voters had to be alert to help assure that their vote was counted accurately and honestly.

CHAPTER 13

1. *The American West: A Twentieth Century History* (Lincoln: University of Nebraska Press, 1989), 264.

2. Ibid., 273.

3. "Aroma in Oklahoma," *Time,* 19 July 1954, 18.

4. The most convenient source for election returns is *The Directory of Oklahoma: State Almanac* (Oklahoma City: Oklahoma Department of Libraries). Published biennially, current editions contain detailed election data for every statewide election since 1980. Equally complete data for earlier elections are available in the 1981 and earlier editions.

5. Only Arizona, which has gone Republican in every presidential election since 1948, has been more faithfully Republican.

6. An incomparably complete study of modern Oklahoma's voting behavior is Samuel A. Kirkpatrick, David R. Morgan, and Thomas G. Kielhorn, *The Oklahoma Voter: Politics, Elections and Parties in the Sooner State* (Norman: University of Oklahoma Press, 1977).

In the late 1950s, the ratio of party registration was approximately five-to-one Democratic. Although Oklahoma's closed primary system still encourages voters to register Democratic if they intend to cast a meaningful vote in most local races, the ratio is now under two-to-one. Similarly, the ratio of Democratic to Republican first primary voters in 1958 was thirteen-to-two. In 1990, it was five-to-two.

7. With his daughter, Pat, Bellmon has recently written his memoirs, *The Life and Times of Henry Bellmon* (Tulsa: Council Oak Books, 1992). It is an account as plainspoken as the career that it records. The only scholarly study of Bellmon's early career firmly places it in the context of state politics of the early postwar years: Wayne F. Young, "Oklahoma Politics with Special Reference to the Election of Oklahoma's First Republican Governor" (Ph.D. diss., University of Oklahoma, 1964).

8. Each of those earlier victories had occurred under very peculiar circumstances, none more so than in 1942, when the GOP's successful nominee was and remained a registered Democrat. The three earlier elections are discussed in James R. Scales and Danney Goble, *Oklahoma Politics: A History* (Norman: University of Oklahoma Press, 1982), 97–102, 130–34, 224–30.

9. Jason Finkle and Richard Gable, eds., *Political Development and Social*

Change (New York: John Wiley and Sons, 1971); Myron Weiner, ed., *Moderniza-tion: The Dynamics of Growth* (New York: Basic Books, 1966); and Samuel P. Hayes, "Modernizing Values in the History of the United States," *Peasant Studies* 6 (1977): 68–79.

10. Oklahoma's contemporary state government is analyzed thoroughly in David R. Morgan, Robert B. England, and George G. Humphreys, *Oklahoma Politics and Policies: Governing the Sooner State,* Politics and Governments of the American States series (Lincoln: University of Nebraska Press, 1991). Chapter 7 discusses the state's executive branch, "a many splintered thing" which—by the authors' admittedly uncertain count—includes 246 agencies, boards, and commissions.

11. Wright's name first appeared on Oklahoma's record 531-square-inch ballot of 1938. Other names on that same ballot were Patrick Henry, Mae West, Oliver Cromwell, Sam Houston, Huey Long, and Will Rogers. Of the group, only Rogers won.

12. Ironically, one of the nine was state labor commissioner, which voters had again made elective in a constitutional amendment approved 8 November 1988. Whatever that says about the voters' memories, it does comment on the awkward evolution, discussed below, of the state's constitution.

13. Morgan, England, and Humphreys, *Oklahoma Politics and Policies,* 105–106, 115–16.

14. Tulsa could not even begin to compete with the three small towns for the *effectiveness* of representation. Fairfax, Gore, and Tishomingo were the respective hometowns of three of the state's senatorial potentates: Clem McSpadden, Ray Fine, and Joe Bailey Cobb.

15. To cite the most extreme case, one voter in the sparsely populated Panhandle had had approximately the same influence in selecting state senators as did eighty in Oklahoma County. The entire complex story is recounted in George J. Mauer, "Political Equality and Legislative Apportionment in Oklahoma, 1907–1964" (Ph.D. diss., University of Oklahoma, 1964) and Richard D. Bingham, "Reapportionment of the Oklahoma House of Representatives: Politics and Process," Legislative Research Series no. 2 (Norman: Bureau of Government Research, University of Oklahoma, 1972). See also Samuel A. Kirkpatrick, *The Legislative Process in Oklahoma: Policy Making, People and Politics* (Norman: University of Oklahoma Press, 1978), 40–49.

16. Julius Allen Singleton, "The Effects of Reapportionment on the Oklahoma House of Representatives" (Ph.D. diss., Texas Tech University); Kirkpatrick, *The Legislative Process in Oklahoma,* 40–49.

In the early 1970s, the prestigious Citizens Committee on State Legislatures ranked the fifty state legislatures on the bases of their adoption of "modern" practices. By that measure, Oklahoma's overall rank was fourteenth. *The Sometime Governments: Critical Study of the 50 American State Legislatures* (New York: Bantam Books, 1971), 52–53. Updated information using essentially the same scale is available in Morgan, England, and Humphreys, *Oklahoma Politics and Policies,* 86–99.

17. John W. Wood, "Reform of Judicial Selection Procedures in Oklahoma,"

Oklahoma Government Bulletin 2, no. 1 (February 1964); Alan Durbin, "Popular Election of the Oklahoma Supreme Court," *Oklahoma Government Bulletin* 4, no. 1 (Spring 1966); Morgan, England, and Humphreys, *Oklahoma Politics and Policies*, 124–26.

18. Bertil L. Hanson, "County Commissioner of Oklahoma," *Midwest Journal of Political Science* 9 (1965): 388–400.

19. Old "Alfalfa Bill's" boy and eventual successor, Johnston Murray, was one of the few chief executives who at least spoke openly about the commissioners' practices. According to the younger Murray, these were high on the list of misdeeds that "shame my state and keep it in the category of the retarded." He did, however, wait until his term had expired (and he had moved to Texas!) before making the charge in a classic account of misrule in the Sooner state: "Oklahoma's in a Mess," *Saturday Evening Post,* 30 April 1955, 20–21, 92, 96–97.

A few years after Governor Murray published his parting shot, J. Howard Edmondson made reform of the commissioners' road-building spending a campaign pledge. Overwhelmingly elected in 1958 on the basis of that and other equally fundamental reforms (including forced reapportionment of the legislature), Edmondson battled fruitlessly with the commissioners and their legislative allies, finally forcing the question to a public vote. The powers arrayed against change marshaled a massive rural vote to defeat the proposition by nearly two-to-one.

20. Robbie Jameson, *The Oklahoma County Commissioner Scandal: Reaction and Reform* (Norman: Bureau of Government Research, University of Oklahoma, 1986); and Frank S. Meyers, "Political Science and Political Corruption: The Case of the County Commissioner Scandal in Oklahoma" (Ph.D. diss., University of Oklahoma, 1985); Morgan, England, and Humphreys, *Oklahoma Politics and Policies,* 194–200.

21. Bellmon, *The Life and Times of Henry Bellmon,* 338–41, 352–70.

22. Kirkpatrick, *The Legislative Process in Oklahoma,* 39–40.

23. David R. Morgan, *Handbook of State Policy Indicators,* 3d ed. (Norman: Bureau of Government Research, University of Oklahoma, 1978), 47, 50; Edith R. Horner, ed., *Almanac of the 50 States,* (Palo Alto, Calif.: Information Publishers, 1993); Kathleen O'Leary Morgan, Scott Morgan, and Neal Quinto, eds., *State Rankings, 1992: A Statistical View of the 50 United States* (Lawrence, Kans.: Morgan Quinto Corp.).

Among the western states, only California pays a higher legislative salary than Oklahoma's $32,000 per year. However, every western state is among the forty-five states that pay a higher average salary to their full-time state and local public employees, who in Oklahoma average earning $10,000 annually less than their part-time lawmakers.

24. Thomas Dye, *Politics, Economics, and the Public* (Chicago: Rand McNally, 1966); Herbert Jacob and Michael Lipsky, "Outputs, Structure, and Power: An Assessment of Changes in the Study of State and Local Politics," *Journal of Politics* 30 (1968): 510–38; David R. Morgan, *Handbook of State Policy Indicators,* 4th ed. (Norman: University of Oklahoma, Bureau of Government Research, 1982), 1–15.

25. The most thorough account is Danney Goble, *Progressive Oklahoma: The Making of a New Kind of State* (Norman: University of Oklahoma Press, 1980).

26. Charles Beard, "The Constitution of Oklahoma," *Political Science Quarterly* 24 (1909): 95–114.

27. Among the oddest provisions of the state's constitution are those declaring that the flash point of kerosene shall be 110 degrees centigrade and setting the rate charged by passenger trains at two-cents per mile. The first remains as surely one of the most peculiar requirements of any state's charter of basic governing principles. The second provision, never enforced, finally was deleted by one of the state's many constitutional amendments in 1986–several years after the last passenger train ran in Oklahoma.

28. The tortured history of Articles 27 and 28 illustrates the need for continual redrafting through constitutional amendment. Article 27, allowing for the sale of alcohol but including all sorts of legislative details, entered the constitution on 7 April 1959. Over the next seventeen years, Oklahomans voted four times on amending the details. The first came at the same election in which the original article was approved! In 1984, voters repealed the entire article, replacing it with the current twenty-eighth article—it, too, crammed with legislative detail. Within twenty-six months, they were voting to amend *that* article.

29. Brookings Institution, *Report on a Survey of the Organization and Administration of Oklahoma* (Oklahoma City: Harlow Publishing Company, 1935).

30. Studies of Oklahoma's constitution—all directed at its substantial revision—could fill a small library. The most complete are H. V. Thornton, ed., "Oklahoma Constitutional Studies of the Oklahoma Constitutional Survey and Citizen Advisory Committees" (Unpublished ms., 1948); American Assembly of Columbia University, *Final Report: Oklahoma Conference on State Government* (n. p., 1957); League of Women Voters Education Fund, *Study of the State Constitution, Parts I and II* (Washington, D.C., 1966); Oklahoma Legislative Council, *Revising the Oklahoma Constitution: Report and Recommendations of the Special Committee on Constitution Revision to the Executive Committee, State Legislative Council to the First Session, Thirty-second Oklahoma Legislature* (n. p., 1968); and Constitution Revision Study Commission, "The Constitution of the State of Oklahoma: Recommendations for Revision," *Oklahoma City University Law Review* 16 (1991): 513–750.

31. Solon J. Buck, "The Settlement of Oklahoma," *Transactions of the Wisconsin Academy of Sciences, Arts, and Letters* 15 (1907): 259–76.

32. Angie Debo, *And Still the Waters Run: The Betrayal of the Five Civilized Tribes* (Princeton: Princeton University Press, 1940).

33. This and the following paragraph are based on an unpublished paper prepared by Larkin Warner, Regents Professor of Economics at Oklahoma State University, in 1989. Professor Warner's statistics, some of which are used here, are taken from United States Department of Commerce and the Hudson Institute's 1990 study, *The Future of Oklahoma* (Indianapolis).

34. In this case only, Interstate 35 defines the line between western and eastern Oklahoma.

35. Of the three, one (Henry S. Johnston of Perry) was impeached, one (E. W.

Marland of Ponca City) never held a subsequent office, and one (Henry Bellmon of a Billings farm located one and one-quarter miles east of Interstate 35) was a Republican.

36. Daniel Elazar, *American Federalism: A View from the States* 3d ed. (New York: Harper and Row, 1984), chap. 5.

CHAPTER 14

1. *Oregonian,* 9 January 1973; State of Oregon, Legislative Assembly, *Journals and Calendars of the Senate and House,* 57th sess., 1973, J313.

2. Richard Benner, "LCDC Develops Coastal Goals," *1000 Friends of Oregon Newsletter,* 1 October 1975, 3.

3. H. Jeffrey Leonard, *Managing Oregon's Growth* (Washington, D.C.: Conservation Foundation, 1983), 6; Janet McLennan, "A Decade of Growth," *Landmark, A Quarterly Journal of 1000 Friends of Oregon* 2 (1985): 3.

4. Pacific Northwest River Basins Commission, Urban and Rural Lands Committee, *Ecology and the Economy* (Vancouver, Wash., November 1973), iv; Leonard, *Managing Oregon's Growth,* 5.

5. Charles E. Little, *The New Oregon Trail* (Washington, D.C.: Conservation Foundation, 1974), 13; Douglas Peeples, "Open Spaces," *Metropolis* (January 1972), n.p.

6. Hector Macpherson, "Toward a Statewide Land Use Law," in "The Use of Land in Oregon, 1973–1993" (Unpublished, 1000 Friends of Oregon); Clay Myers, speech to the Farm and Land Brokers Program of the Oregon Association of Realtors, 12 September 1968, Myers Papers; Myers, interview with author, 11 April 1993.

7. Macpherson, "Statewide Land Use Law"; Macpherson, oral history interview with Carl Abbott, 16 December 1992 (Oregon Historical Society).

8. Macpherson, "Statewide Land Use Law"; Henry R. Richmond, "Tom McCall—In Memoriam," *1000 Friends of Oregon Newsletter* (Winter 1983): 2; Tom McCall and Steve Neal, *Tom McCall: Maverick, An Autobiography* (Portland: Binford and Mort, 1977), 196–97.

9. Macpherson, "Statewide Land Use Law."

10. Little, *New Oregon Trail,* 9; Macpherson and Ted Hallock, oral history interview with Carl Abbott, 16 December 1992 (Oregon Historical Society).

11. Anecdote told to Richmond, as quoted by John Painter, Jr., *Oregonian,* 11 April 1982.

12. Robert K. Logan, telephone conservation with author, 25 February 1993; see also Logan, *The Oregon Land Use Story* (Salem: Executive Department, Local Government Relations Division, January 1974).

13. *Oregonian,* 26 October 1986, from an obituary following Day's death at age fifty.

14. Myers interview.

15. *Oregon Journal,* 30 September 1972.

16. Ibid.; Logan, telephone conversation, 25 February 1993; Myers interview.

17. Little, *New Oregon Trail,* 8.

18. Fred Bosselman and David Callies, *The Quiet Revolution in Land Use Control* (Washington, D.C.: Government Printing Office, 1971).

19. Macpherson, "Statewide Land Use Law"; Little, *New Oregon Trail,* 10; Logan, telephone conversation with author, 23 February 1993.

20. Little, *New Oregon Trail,* 10; Macpherson, "Statewide Land Use Law"; Hallock, telephone conversation with author, 23 February 1993.

21. Bosselman and Callies, *Quiet Revolution,* 314–15.

22. 20 July 1972, Myers Papers.

23. Little, *New Oregon Trail,* 11–12.

24. Lawrence Halprin & Associates, *The Willamette Valley: Choices for the Future* (Salem: State of Oregon, 1972); State of Oregon, Executive Department, Local Government Relations Division, *The Willamette Valley: Choices for the Future,* pamphlet prepared by Robert K. Logan (Salem, 1972); *Oregon Journal,* 30 September 1972. McCall's letter appears at the beginning of *Oregon Land Use Package* (Salem: Executive Department, July 1973), n.p.

25. *Oregon Journal,* 30 September 1972; Macpherson, "Statewide Land Use Law"; Leonard, *Managing Oregon's Growth,* 8; Little, *New Oregon Trail,* 11; Logan, telephone conversation, 25 February 1993.

26. "A Discussion Forum on Land-Use Planning," November 20–22, 1972, Division of Continuing Education, Oregon State System of Higher Education.

27. Logan, telephone conversation, 25 February 1993.

28. Ibid.

29. Ibid.

30. Logan, *Oregon Land Use Story,* 8; Logan, telephone conversation, 25 February 1993.

31. Hallock, telephone conversation, 23 February 1993; Macpherson, "Statewide Land Use Law."

32. Hallock, oral history interview.

33. Hallock, oral history interview; Hallock, telephone conversation with author, 3 March 1993.

34. Betty Merten, "The Story of Senate Bill 100: A Torture Trail to Land Use Planning," *Oregon Times* (September 1973): 25; Hallock, oral history interview; Hallock, telephone conversation, 3 March 1993.

35. Merten, "Senate Bill 100," 25; Hallock, oral history interview; Hallock, telephone conversation, 3 March 1993.

36. Merten, "Senate Bill 100," 19; Hallock, oral history interview; Brent Walth, telephone conversation with author, 1 March 1993. Walth is the author of an unpublished biography of Tom McCall.

37. Little, *New Oregon Trail,* 19.

38. Hallock, oral history interview; Little, *New Oregon Trail,* 20; *Feedback,* 14 March 1973.

39. Merten, "Senate Bill 100," 26.

40. Hallock, oral history interview; Macpherson, "Statewide Land Use Law."

41. State of Oregon, Legislative Assembly, *Enrolled Senate Bill 100,* 57th sess., 1973, chap. 80; Hallock, oral history interview; Merten, "Senate Bill 100," 27; *Feedback,* 18 May 1973.

42. Walth, telephone conversation with author, 1 March 1993.

43. *Feedback,* 16 September 1973; Myers interview.

44. Macpherson, "Statewide Land Use Law."

45. Arnold Cogan, "Goals for the Future," in "The Use of Land in Oregon, 1973–1993"; Cogan, interview with author, 15 January 1993.

46. Cogan, "Goals for the Future."

47. Ibid.

48. Ibid.

49. Ibid.

50. Ibid.; *1000 Friends of Oregon Newsletter* (October 1975): 2.

51. Leonard, *Managing Oregon's Growth,* 12–13; McLennan, "Decade of Growth," 3–7.

52. Richmond, "Tom McCall—In Memoriam," 2; McLennan, "Decade of Growth," 6; Henry R. Richmond and Carolyn Gassoway, "Conversation with Tom McCall," *1000 Friends of Oregon Newsletter* (October 1976): 6.

53. Edward J. Sullivan, Norman Williams, Jr., and Bernard H. Siegan, "The Oregon Example: A Prospect for the Nation," *Environmental Law* (Summer 1984), iv, 847. During the last decade, Maine, Vermont, Rhode Island, New Jersey, Florida, Georgia, and Washington have followed Oregon's precedent by enacting statewide land-use or growth-management laws.

54. Cogan, "Goals for the Future."

55. Eric B. Herzik, "The Economic Environment," in *Politics and Public Policy in the Contemporary American West,* ed. Clive S. Thomas (Albuquerque: University of New Mexico Press, 1991): 74; Leonard, *Managing Oregon's Growth,* 26.

56. Raymond W. Cox III, "Gubernatorial Politics," in *Politics and Public Policy,* 266.

57. Richmond, "Tom McCall—In Memoriam," 2.

CHAPTER 15

1. Mainly, Herbert T. Hoover authors the segment in this chapter pertaining to state government, and Steven C. Emery authors the segment about reservation government. Themes and data come from tribal files and from numerous documentary and published sources. Historical perspective as well as detail can be found in Herbert S. Schell, *History of South Dakota* (Lincoln: University of Nebraska Press, 1975); and in Herbert T. Hoover and Larry J. Zimmerman, eds., *South Dakota Leaders* (Vermillion: University of South Dakota Press, 1989). More penetrating analysis of non-Indian political history is included in Alan L. Clem, *Prairie State Politics* (Washington, D.C.: Public Affairs Press, 1967); and in William O. Farber, Thomas C. Geary, and Loren M. Carlson, *Government of South Dakota* (Vermillion: Dakota Press, 1979).

Additional political analysis with annual statistics exists in articles prepared every year for encyclopedia publications. This chapter draws heavily upon the following sources, all s.v. "South Dakota": Collier's *Yearbook,* 1945–59, 1968–89; Britannica *Yearbook,* 1960–67; Americana *Annual,* 1990–93. Valuable, too, is a substantial collection of information gathered by the Legislative Research Council (LRC) since its establishment at Pierre in 1951. On request, staff members respond to specific inquiries and provide a bibliography of LRC publications.

Further investigations of particular issues in the political history of the state may be accomplished by the use of several collections on the campus of the University of South Dakota: Governmental Research Bureau files and occasional publications, in the Political Science Department; Business Research Bureau files and occasional publications, in the School of Business; and special collections, which include rare books and periodicals as well as archives, preserved by the I. D. Weeks Library.

2. Some discrepancy exists in records regarding the net loss to taxpayers, probably due to different calculations of interest paid over time on the loan. A minimum estimate of the loss is $40 million.

3. U.S. Department of Agriculture, *FY 1991 and 1992 ASCS/CCC Federal Assistance, South Dakota, Summary of Programs* (Washington, D.C.: U.S. Government Printing Office, 1992).

4. Mary Edelen of Vermillion drew upon her memories and files from eighteen years of service in the South Dakota House of Representatives to prepare this summary of legislative accomplishment for the period 1973–93. She also reviewed and edited other contents, not only from her perspective as a legislator, but also with her insight as a professional historian.

5. Gov. George Mickelson stimulated communication by including Indian cultures and perspectives in state centennial observances, and continued to promote tribal interests until he died in an airplane accident in 1993. He had been traveling in the effort to preserve a meat-packing plant at Sioux Falls.

CHAPTER 16

1. 1 Tucker 248 (N.Y. Surr. 1866); *Austin American-Statesman*, 15, 21, 31 July 1989; *Dallas Morning News*, 16, 20, 21 July 1989; *Houston Chronicle*, 21 July 1989; *Amarillo Daily News*, 19 July 1989; *Bryan-College Station Eagle*, 22 July 1989.

2. *Fort Worth Star-Telegram*, 7 January 1990; *Austin American-Statesman*, 8 January 1990; *Dallas Morning News*, 26 January 1990; *San Antonio Light*, 28 January 1990; Celia Morris, *Storming the Statehouse: Running for Governor with Ann Richards and Dianne Feinstein* (New York: Charles Scribner's Sons, 1992), 54, 55, 57, 61–64.

3. Morris, *Storming the Statehouse*, 20–25, 29–56; Ann Richards with Peter Knobler, *Straight from the Heart: My Life in Politics and Other Matters* (New York: Simon & Schuster, 1989); *Austin American-Statesman*, 13 August 1989; *Houston Post*, 8 October 1989.

4. *Austin American-Statesman*, 30 November 1989; *Dallas Morning News*, 3 December 1989; *San Antonio Light*, 10 December 1989; *Fort Worth Star-Telegram*, 7 January 1990; *Amarillo Sunday News-Globe*, 10 September 1989; *Abilene Reporter News*, 22 October 1989.

5. *San Antonio Express*, 13, 17 August 1989; *Dallas Morning News*, 8 August,

5 November 1989; *Dallas Times Herald,* 26 October 1989; *Fort Worth Star-Telegram,* 7 January 1990.

6. "Meet the Governor: Clayton Williams," *Texas Monthly* (October 1990), 122, 125, 148, 150, 152, 154, 156; *Fort Worth Star-Telegram,* 7 January 1990; *Wall Street Journal,* 22 February 1990.

7. *Dallas Morning News,* 26 July 1989; *Houston Post,* 26 July 1989; *Fort Worth Star-Telegram,* 7 January 1990; *San Antonio Light,* 4 February 1990.

8. *Houston Post,* 15 September 1989, 28 January 1990; *Dallas Morning News,* 13 August, 15, 20 September 1989. *Fort Worth Star-Telegram,* 7 January 1990; *Dallas Times Herald,* 27 August 1989.

9. Wichita Falls Times, 12 July 1989; *Laredo Morning Times,* 21 July 1989; *Dallas Morning News,* 26 July, 1, 5 September 1989; *Austin American-Statesman,* 20 August, 3 September 1989; *Dallas Times Herald,* 29 August 1989; *Houston Post,* 28 August 1989.

10. *Fort Worth Star-Telegram,* 20, 21, 24, 29 July 1989; *Dallas Times Herald,* 20, 30, 31 July 1989; *Houston Post,* 27 July, 11, 22 August 1989; *Houston Chronicle,* 27, 28, 31 July, 28 August 1989; *San Antonio Express,* 30 July, 1 August 1989; *San Antonio Light,* 30 July 1989; *Dallas Morning News,* 27, 31 July, 2, 3, 11 August 1989; *Austin American-Statesman,* 30 July 1989; *Abilene Reporter News,* 23 August 1989.

11. *Houston Chronicle,* 4, 6, 27 August, 5, 17, 18, 24, 26 September, 16, 26 November 1989; *Austin American-Statesman,* 10 August, 26 September, 7, 30 November 1989; *Dallas Morning News,* 17 August, 12, 17, 18, 22, 24, 26, 27, 28 September, 18, 19, 22, 24 October, 1, 12, 13, 18 November 1989; *San Antonio Express,* 8 September, 19 October 1989; *Fort Worth Star-Telegram,* 12, 25, 26 September, 10, 20, 29 November 1989; *Houston Post,* 11, 12, 26 September, 11, 27 October 1989; *El Paso Times,* 12 September 1989; *San Angelo Star-Telegram,* 31 August 1989; Morris, *Storming the Statehouse,* 61–65, 67–70.

12. *Houston Post,* 27 July, 16 August, 12, 26 September, 9, 27 October, 3, 13 November 1989; *Houston Chronicle,* 27 August, 12, 24 September, 5, 16 October, 7 November 1989; *Austin American-Statesman,* 30 July, 13 August, 16 October 1989; *Dallas Morning News,* 3, 28 September, 5, 12, 14, 16, 23 October, 12 November, 3 December 1989; *Fort Worth Star-Telegram,* 12 September, 10 November 1989; *San Antonio Express,* 3 September 1989; Morris, *Storming the Statehouse,* 2–3, 39–56; Richards, *Straight from the Heart,* 11–32.

13. *Dallas Morning News,* 23, 25, 26 July, 5, 16, 28 August, 5, 7 September 1989; *Houston Post,* 27, 30 August, 7 September 1989; *Amarillo Daily News,* 28 July, 16, 17 August 1989; *San Angelo Star-Telegram,* 28 July 1989; *Corpus Christi Caller,* 29 July 1989; *Beaumont Enterprise,* 27 July 1989; *Wichita Falls Times,* 30 July, 18 August 1989; *Laredo Morning News,* 29 July 1989; *Austin American-Statesman,* 8, 16 August 1989; *Abilene Reporter News,* 3 August 1989; *Lubbock Avalanche Journal,* 9, 16 August 1989; *San Antonio Express,* 17, 23 August 1989; *Dallas Times Herald,* 27 August 1989.

14. *Dallas Morning News,* 12, 16 September 1989; "Williams," *Texas Monthly,* 149; *Houston Post,* 16 September 1989; *Houston Chronicle,* 9, 16 September 1989; *Fort Worth Star-Telegram,* October 14, 1989; *San Antonio Express,* 1 October 1989.

15. *Dallas Morning News,* 15, 20 September, 7 October, 4, 5, 12, 29 November 1989; *Houston Chronicle,* 18 September 1989; *San Antonio Light,* 29 October, 28 November 1989; *Dallas Times Herald,* 5 November 1989; J. Michael Kennedy, "Cowboy and the Girl," *Los Angeles Times Magazine,* 21 October 1990; *Waco Tribune Herald,* 15 December 1989; *Lubbock Avalanche Journal,* 15 December 1989.

16. As conclusive evidence for statements in this paragraph, see five large volumes of photocopied Texas newspapers from 1 January to 15 March 1990 at the Texas Legislative Library, Austin. For the $50 million TV estimate, see *San Antonio Express,* 25 December 1989; *Austin American-Statesman,* 7 January 1990.

17. *Austin American-Statesman,* 7, 12, 22 January 1990; *Houston Post,* 4, 13, 14, 19, 24 January 1990; *Dallas Morning News,* 12, 13, 14, 17, 18, 20, 24, 26, 29 January, 4, 11 February 1990; *Dallas Times Herald,* 13, 20 January, 8, 11, 13, 14 February 1990; *Houston Chronicle,* 14, 16, 17, 19, 20, 28 January, 11 February 1990; *San Antonio Express,* 25 December, 16 January 1990; *San Antonio Light,* 19, 21 January, 14 February 1990; *Fort Worth Star-Telegram,* 13, 14, 18, 19, 21, 24 January, 1, 4, 11 February 1990; Morris, *Storming the Statehouse,* 67–72, 83.

18. *Houston Post,* 7, 8, 10 February 1990; *Dallas Times Herald,* 8, 11, 14 February 1990; *Dallas Morning News,* 8, 11, 12 February, 12 March 1990; *Houston Chronicle,* 8, 9, 11 February 1990; Morris, *Storming the Statehouse,* 79–80.

19. *Dallas Morning News,* 16, 17, 19, 23, 27, 28 February, 3, 4 March 1990; *Dallas Times Herald,* 8, 11, 16, 24 February, 1, 4 March 1990; *Houston Chronicle,* 9, 11, 16, 18, 24 February, 3, 5 March 1990; *Houston Post,* 10, 28 February, 4 March 1990; *Austin American-Statesman,* 3 March 1990; Morris, *Storming the Statehouse,* 73–86.

20. *Houston Post,* 25, 28 February, 6, 7, 8 March 1990; *Houston Chronicle,* 25 February, 3, 5, 6, 7, 8 March 1990; *Dallas Times Herald,* 1, 4, 6, 7, 8 March 1990; *San Antonio Express,* 6, 7, 8, 9 March 1990; *Dallas Morning News,* 25 February, 6, 7, 8, 9 March 1990; *Austin American-Statesman,* 6, 7, 8 March 1990; Morris, *Storming the Statehouse,* 88–90.

21. *Dallas Morning News,* 9, 10, 12 March 1990; *Austin American-Statesman,* 12, 13 March 1990; Morris, *Storming the Statehouse,* 90–93. For election results, see all major newspapers for March 14 and 15, 1990.

22. *Houston Post,* 17 January, 1 February 1990; *Fort Worth Star-Telegram,* 17, 19 January, 1 February 1990; *Fort Worth Star-Telegram,* 17, 19 January, 1 February 1990; *Austin American-Statesman,* 4 February 1990; *Dallas Morning News,* 14 January, 2 February 1990.

23. *San Antonio Light,* 7 January 1990; *Dallas Morning News,* 10, 11, 14, 20 January, 7, 8, 9, 12 February 1990; *Houston Post,* 9 January, 10 February 1990; *Houston Chronicle,* 11, 18 January 1990; *San Antonio Express,* 16 January, 10 February 1990; *Bryan-College Station Eagle,* 14 January 1990.

24. *Austin American-Statesman,* 15, 19, 20 February, 6, 12, 14 March 1990; *Houston Chronicle,* 15, 16, 18, 24, 27, 28 February, 2, 3, 14 March 1990; *Houston Post,* 15, 20, 21, 22, 23 February, 1, 2, 4, 6, 7, 11, 14 March 1990; *Dallas Morning News,* 15, 19, 22, 26, 28 February, 2, 6, 7, 9, 12, 14 March 1990; *San Antonio Express,* 15 February, 1, 4, 9, 12, 14 March 1990; *El Paso Times,* 24 February 1990;

Abilene Reporter News, 27 February 1990; *Dallas Times Herald,* 15, 18, 20, 24, 27 February, 1, 2, 4, 9, 11, 14 March 1990.

25. *Dallas Morning News,* 14, 15, 17, 22, 23, 24, 28, 29 March, 1, 3, 4, 5, 6, 9 April 1990; *Austin American-Statesman,* 14, 15, 16, 18, 22 March, 3, 4 April 1990; *Houston Chronicle,* 22, 23, 29, 30 March, 1, 4, 5, 7, 9 April 1990; *Houston Post,* 14, 17, 22, 28, 29 March, 2, 3, 4, 5 April 1990; *Dallas Times Herald,* 14, 22, 28, 29 March, 4, 5, 8 April 1990; *Fort Worth Star-Telegram,* 15, 18, 24 March, 1, 6, 8 April 1990; Morris, *Storming the Statehouse,* 94–103.

26. *Dallas Morning News,* 11, 12 April 1990; *Houston Chronicle,* 11, 12 April 1990; *Dallas Times Herald,* 11 April 1990; Morris, *Storming the Statehouse,* 103–105.

27. *Dallas Morning News,* 14, 15, 16, 19, 20, 22 March 1990; *Houston Post,* 15, 16, 20, 21, 22 March 1990; *Austin American-Statesman,* 15, 16, 18, 22 March 1990; *San Antonio Express,* 15, 18 March 1990; *Houston Chronicle,* 14, 15, 16, 21 March 1990; *Fort Worth Star-Telegram,* 14, 16, 18, 20 March 1990; *Dallas Times Herald,* 14, 15, 20, 21 March 1990.

28. *Dallas Times Herald,* 21, 26, 27 March 1990; *Houston Chronicle,* 21, 25, 26 March 1990; *Dallas Morning News,* 21, 25, 26, 27, 28 March, 1 April 1990; *Houston Post,* 26, 27, 28 March 1990; *Austin American-Statesman,* 26, 27, 29 March 1990; *Fort Worth Star-Telegram,* 21, 26, 27 March 1990.

29. *Houston Post,* 16, 23 April, 24 May 1990; *Fort Worth Star-Telegram,* 15 April 1990; *Abilene Reporter News,* 27 February, 19 May 1990; Morris, *Storming the Statehouse,* 105–10.

30. *Dallas Times Herald,* 23 April 1990; *Dallas Morning News,* 23, 27 April, 24 May 1990; *Houston Post,* 23 April 1990; *Austin American-Statesman,* 23, 24 April 1990; *Fort Worth Star-Telegram,* 23, 24 April, 18 July 1990; *U.S. News & World Report,* 16 July 1990, 41; Morris, *Storming the Statehouse,* 111–12.

31. *San Angelo Star-Telegram,* 17 April, 5 June, 29 July 1990; *Dallas Morning News,* 27 April, 4, 7, 9, 15, 17, 18, 19, 22, 24, 27, 30 May, 15, 24, 26, 27, 28 June, 10, 14, 16, 17, 18, 19, 28, 29, 30 July, 4 August 1990; *Dallas Times Herald,* 4, 17 July 1990; *Fort Worth Star-Telegram,* 10 May, 12, 21 June, 1 July 1990; *Beaumont Enterprise,* 23 July 1990; *El Paso Times,* 29 July 1990; *Austin American-Statesman,* 16 April, 23 May, 12, 19, 27 June, 10, 20, 25 July, 5 August 1990; *Houston Post,* 22, 27 April, 17, 19, 27 May, 19, 20, 27, 28 June, 5, 12, 17, 19, 28 July, 1 August 1990; *Houston Chronicle,* 11, 16, 19 May, 4, 24 June, 2, 19 July, 2 August 1990; *San Antonio Express,* 20 May, 3, 27 June, 6 July 1990; *San Antonio Light,* 2 May, 3, 13 June, 7 August 1990.

32. Morris, *Storming the Statehouse,* 110–15; *Fort Worth Star-Telegram,* 15 April, 1 May 1990; *Houston Post,* 16 April 1990; *Houston Chronicle,* 15 April 1990; *Austin American-Statesman,* 3 May 1990; *Abilene Reporter News,* 19 May 1990.

33. Morris, *Storming the Statehouse,* 115–17; *Dallas Morning News,* 28 April, 15 June, 26 July 1990; *Corpus Christi Caller,* 1 May 1990; *Houston Chronicle,* 24 May, 9, 13, 20 June, 2 July 1990; *Beaumont Enterprise,* 31 May, 19 July 1990; *Bryan-College Station Eagle,* 3 June 1990; *Fort Worth Star-Telegram,* 9, 10 June, 27 July 1990; *Houston Post,* 10 June 1990; *San Antonio Express,* 12 July 1990; *Lubbock Avalanche Journal,* 10 June 1990; *El Paso Times,* 29 June 1990.

34. Morris, *Storming the Statehouse*, 117–27; *Houston Chronicle*, 20 June, 13 July 1990; *San Antonio Express*, 14 June, 6 July 1990; *Houston Post*, 17, 20 June, 13 July 1990; *Waco Herald Tribune*, 5 July 1990; *Dallas Morning News*, 13 July 1990; *Dallas Times Herald*, 4, 13, 25 July 1990; *Austin American-Statesman*, 5 August 1990.

35. *Houston Post*, 3 August 1990; *Austin American-Statesman*, 3, 5, 23 August 1990; *Fort Worth Star-Telegram*, 5 August, 2 September 1990; *Dallas Times Herald*, 12, 23 August 1990; *Dallas Morning News*, 14, 17, 21 August 1990; *San Antonio Light*, 16 August 1990; *Amarillo Daily News*, 4 September 1990; Morris, *Storming the Statehouse*, 123, 126–30.

36. *Austin American-Statesman*, 23 August 1990; *Amarillo Daily News*, 4 September 1990; *Houston Chronicle*, 12, 14, 20, 21 September 1990; *Dallas Morning News*, 15, 18, 20, 23 September 1990; *Houston Post*, 8, 25 September 1990; *San Antonio Express*, 2 October 1990; Morris, *Storming the Statehouse*, 145–53.

37. Morris, *Storming the Statehouse*, 156–59; *Houston Post*, 22 September 1990; *Austin American-Statesman*, 28, 29 September 1990; *Dallas Morning News*, 22, 24 September 1990; *Fort Worth Star-Telegram*, 22 September 1990; *Houston Chronicle*, 29 September 1990; *Dallas Times Herald*, 29 September 1990; *San Antonio Express*, 29 September, 14 October 1990.

38. Morris, *Storming the Statehouse*, 158–59; *Dallas Times Herald*, 3, 12 September 1990; *Dallas Morning News*, 12 October 1990; *Austin American-Statesman*, 12, 13, 15 October 1990; *Houston Post*, 12 October 1990; *San Antonio Express*, 12 October 1990; *Fort Worth Star-Telegram*, 12 October 1990.

39. Morris, *Storming the Statehouse*, 152, 158–61; *Dallas Times Herald*, 13, 19, 20 October 1990; *San Antonio Express*, 14, 17 October 1990; *Austin American-Statesman*, 19, 26, 27 October 1990; *Dallas Morning News*, 16, 19, 20, 24, 25, 30 October 1990; *Fort Worth Star-Telegram*, 16, 17 October 1990; *Houston Chronicle*, 13, 16 October 1990; *Houston Post*, 15, 16, 17, 19, 23 October 1990; *Galveston Daily News*, 18 October 1990.

40. *Dallas Morning News*, 31 October, 3, 4 November 1990; *Fort Worth Star-Telegram*, 31 October, 3 November 1990; *Dallas Times Herald*, 31 October, 1, 3 November 1990; *Houston Post*, 31 October, 1, 3 November 1990; *San Antonio Express*, 3 November 1990; Morris, *Storming the Statehouse*, 161–65.

41. *Houston Chronicle*, 24 October, 7 November 1990; *Dallas Times Herald*, 30 October 1990; *Dallas Morning News*, 1, 4, 7 November 1990; *Fort Worth Star-Telegram*, 31 October 1990: Morris, *Storming the Statehouse*, 166.

42. *Dallas Morning News*, 1 November 1990; *Houston Chronicle*, 24, 25, 31 October 1990; *Dallas Times Herald*, 29, 30, 31 October 1990; *Austin American-Statesman*, 2 November 1990; and all Texas newspapers for 7, 8 November 1990.

CHAPTER 17

1. For an extreme assertion that the Mormons dominate the state, see John Heinerman and Anson Shupe, *The Mormon Corporate Empire* (Boston: Beacon Press, 1985).

2. During the late 1970s and early 1980s, only California, Washington,

Montana and Hawaii among the western states continued traditional support of the Democratic party. Ronald J. Hrebenar and Robert C. Benedict, "Political Parties, Elections and Campaigns, II," in Clive S. Thomas, ed., *Politics and Public Policy in the Contemporary American West* (Albuquerque: University of New Mexico Press, 1991), 150–56.

3. The statistics in the following discussion are taken from *Statistical Abstract of Utah, 1990* (Salt Lake City: University of Utah Bureau of Economic and Business Research, 1990) and the statistical tables in Richard D. Poll, Thomas G. Alexander, Eugene E. Campbell, and David E. Miller, eds., *Utah's History,* 2nd ed. (Logan: Utah State University Press, 1989).

4. For election information see Richard D. Poll, Thomas C. Alexander, Eugene E. Campbell, and David L. Miller, eds. *Utah's History.* 2d ed. (Logan, Utah: Utah State University Press, 1989), 700–701. Information on the 1992 election comes from *Deseret News,* 4 November 1992.

5. For memoirs of the Rampton and Matheson administrations, see Calvin L. Rampton, *As I Recall,* ed. Floyd A. O'Neil and Gregory C. Thompson (Salt Lake City: University of Utah Press, 1989) and Scott M. Matheson and James Edwin Kee, *Out of Balance* (Salt Lake City: Peregrine Smith Books, 1986).

6. *Salt Lake Tribune,* 20 December 1992.

7. *Salt Lake Tribune,* 13 December 1990; *Deseret News,* 4 November 1992.

8. James B. Mayfield, "Electoral Patterns, 1895–1980," in Deon C. Greer, Klaus D. Gurgel, Wayne L. Wahlquist, Howard A. Christy, and Gary B. Peterson, eds., *Atlas of Utah* (Provo: Brigham Young University Press; Ogden: Weber State College, 1991), 169–77.

9. This assessed the changes based on an analysis of gubernatorial and U.S. House elections between 1976 and 1988.

10. *Statistical Abstract of Utah, 1990,* 307.

11. *Statistical Abstract of Utah, 1990,* 101; Utah State Data Center, *Utah Data Guide: A Newsletter for Data Users* (Salt Lake City: Utah Office of Planning and Budget, July 1992), 11; *Daily Herald* (Provo), 7 January 1993.

12. *Statistical Abstract of Utah, 1990,* 103.

13. Leonard J. Arrington, *The Changing Economic Structure of the Mountain West,* 1850–1950, Utah State University Monograph Series 10:3 (Logan: Utah State University Press, 1963), 49.

14. *Salt Lake Tribune,* 7 September 1992. These are the top employers and their 1992 employment figures: Hill Air Force Base, 17,512; State of Utah, 13,080; Intermountain Health Care, 12,806; University of Utah, 11,657; Brigham Young University, 7,500; Internal Revenue Service Center, 6,380; Smith's Food and Drug, 6,200; Thiokol, 6,000; Granite School District, 5,700; Jordan School District, 5,496; Delta Air Lines, 4,300; ZCMI, 3,950; WordPerfect, 3,800; Utah Power, 3,700; Salt Lake County, 3,600; LDS Church, 3,500; Davis School District, 3,450; Tooele Army Depot, 3,400; Utah State University, 3,250; U.S. West Communications, 3,150; First Security Corporation, 3,069; Kennecott, 2,900; Hercules Aerospace, 2,850; Geneva Steel, 2,700. Note: I have considered Utah Power a local corporation as its principal headquarters are in Salt Lake City and its operations are located exclusively in the Mountain West.

15. Jan Eyeless Crispin-Little, "WordPerfect Corporation," *Utah Economic and Business Review* 48 (October 1988); Jan Eyeless Crispin-Little, "Software Companies Lead Growth in Utah's High Technology Industry," *Utah Economic and Business Review* 52 (March 1992).

16. Ibid. For examples of other internally financed companies, see Jan Eyeless Crispin-Little and John Brereton, "Utah's Emerging High Technology Companies," *Utah Economic and Business Review* 49 (May–June 1989). As foreign competition began to reduce the United States' share of the electronics market, Utah experienced some decline in employment. James A. Wood, "Utah's Electronics Industry," *Utah Economic and Business Review* 50 (September 1990).

17. James A. Wood, "Manufacturing in the West Since World War II," *Utah Economic and Business Review* 51 (March 1991).

18. Ibid.

19. Boyd L. Fjeldsted and Frank C. Hachman, "Results of the 1990–91 Utah Skier Survey," *Utah Economic and Business Review* 51 (August–September 1991).

20. Utah State Data Center, *Utah Data Guide* 10 (January 1991): 7.

21. Others, in descending order, are District of Columbia, 100 percent urban; California, 91.3 percent; New Jersey, 89 percent; Rhode Island, 87 percent; Hawaii, 86.5 percent; Nevada, 85.3 percent; New York, 84.6 percent. The nation as a whole was 73.7 percent urban.

22. For an additional example see party leaders' failure to appreciate Bill Orton's success. *Salt Lake Tribune,* 8 January 1993.

23. Utah Data Center, *Utah Data Guide* 10 (July 1991): 5; *Statistical Abstract of the United States, 1992,* 181.

24. *World Almanac and Book of Facts, 1992,* 214.

25. *Salt Lake Tribune,* 31 January 1993.

26. *Daily Universe,* 31 February 1993.

27. On the role of the Mormon ward, see Douglas D. Alder, "The Mormon Ward: Congregation or Community," *Journal of Mormon History* 5 (1987): 61–78,

28. *Salt Lake Tribune,* 11 February 1993; *Provo Herald,* 11 February 1993.

29. Utah State Data Center, *Utah Data Guide* 10 (July 1991): 8.

30. *Salt Lake Tribune,* 1 September 1992. Increase or decrease in per family (not per capita) income, 1979–89; bottom fifth, $12,907 to $13,318 (3.2 percent); second fifth, $27,166 to $25,391 (− 6.5 percent); third fifth, $36,954 to $36,883 (− .02 percent); fourth fifth, $49,147 to $49,811 (1.4 percent); top fifth, $79,708 to $84,011 (5.4 percent).

31. For fiscal year 1986–87, the state obtained $719 million from property taxes, $701 million from sales taxes, $533 million from individual income taxes, $69 million from corporate income taxes, $121 million from motor fuel taxes, $90 million from unemployment compensation taxes, and $28 million from vehicle registration. Utah Foundation, *Statistical Abstract of Government in Utah* (Salt Lake City, 1988), 39.

32. The information on the sales tax rate was supplied by Jim Sutherland of the Utah County Auditor's Office. Income tax rates in 1988 ranged from 2.75 to 7.75 percent. The highest marginal rate bore on incomes over $7,500, and the personal exemption is not indexed while all federal deductions are allowed. *World Almanac*

and Book of Facts, 1992, 188; Utah Foundation, *Statistical Abstract of Government in Utah,* 42.

33. *World Almanac and Book of Facts, 1992,* 154.

34. Ronald J. Hrebenar, Melanee Cherry, and Kathanne Greene, "Utah, Church and Corporate Power in the Nation's Most Conservative State," in Ronald J. Hrebenar and Clive S. Thomas, *Interest Group Politics in the American West* (Salt Lake City: University of Utah Press, 1987), 109–11.

35. For a discussion of some of these matters, see Robert Gottlieb and Peter Wiley, *America's Saints: The Rise of Mormon Power* (New York: Putnam, 1984); and Mike Carter, "Mormon Political Clout a Fact of Life in Utah," *Provo Herald,* 17 January 1993.

36. Thomas G. Alexander and James B. Allen, *Mormons and Gentiles, A History of Salt Lake City* (Boulder: Pruett, 1984), 295. For an example of support for this position by the Roman Catholic Church, see *Provo Herald,* 17 January 1993. See also Ronald J. Hrebenar, Melanee Cherry, and Kathanne Greene, "Utah: Church and Corporate Power," 114–15, 121–22.

37. David B. Magleby, "Religion and Voting Behavior in a Religiously Homogeneous State" (Unpublished paper presented at the annual meeting of the American Political Science Association, 1987), 25.

38. Tom Goldsmith, "Prayer Debate Needs 'Graciousness,'" *Salt Lake Tribune,* 11 February 1993; *Salt Lake Tribune,* 6, 16 February 1993.

CHAPTER 18

1. Richard L. Neuberger, *They Never Go Back to Pocatello: The Selected Essays of Richard Neuberger,* ed. Steve Neal (Portland: Oregon Historical Society Press, 1988), 35.

2. *Wenatchee Daily World,* 19 December 1949. The sense of a "wild" river "tamed" by engineers was a common theme of the New Deal–World War II era. See, for example, Richard L. Neuberger, *Our Promised Land* (1938; Moscow: University of Idaho Press, 1989), chaps. 3–4. For a contrary expression of preference for "the Columbia as it was more than as it is," see Stewart Holbrook, *The Columbia* (1956; San Francisco: Comstock Editions, 1990), 329.

3. National Resources Planning Board, *Pacific Northwest Region: Industrial Development* (Washington, D.C.: Government Printing Office, 1942), 19, 21–22, 30; Statement on Industry, 29 May 1943, enclosed in R. F. Bessey to Rex Willard, 31 May 1943, National Resources Planning Board Records, RG 187, Federal Records Center, Seattle. For details on the historical Washington economy, see Robert E. Ficken, *The Forested Land: A History of Lumbering in Western Washington* (Seattle: University of Washington Press, 1987); Robert C. Nesbit and Charles M. Gates, "Agriculture in Eastern Washington, 1890–1910," *Pacific Northwest Quarterly* 37 (1946): 279–302.

4. See, in general, Donald Worster, *Rivers of Empire: Water, Aridity, and the Growth of the American West* (New York: Pantheon Books, 1985), esp. 269–72 for factually distorted coverage of dam building on the Columbia. Also see Donald Worster, "New West, True West: Interpreting the Region's History," *Western*

Historical Quarterly 18 (1987): 141–56.

5. *Wenatchee Daily World,* 18 July 1918; Bruce Mitchell, "Rufus Woods and Columbia River Development," *Pacific Northwest Quarterly* 52 (1961): 139–44. There were no dams on the Columbia at this time. "Hydro Electric Plants . . . Above the Mouth of the Snake," September 1921, Seattle District Records, U.S. Army Corps of Engineers, RG 77, Federal Records Center, Seattle.

6. Marvin Chase to A. P. Davis, 10 February 1919, Columbia Basin Survey Commission Records, Washington State Archives, Olympia; Bruce C. Harding, "Water from Pend Oreille: The Gravity Plan for Irrigating the Columbia Basin," *Pacific Northwest Quarterly* 45 (1954): 52–60.

7. *The Columbia Basin Project* (Olympia: Frank M. Lamborn, Public Printer, 1920); George W. Goethals, "Report on Columbia Basin Irrigation Project," 20 March 1922, Willis Batcheller Papers, University of Washington Library, Seattle.

8. Opposition in Idaho and Montana to the storage of water for use in the gravity scheme also stalled progress. For a sampling of Reclamation Service thinking, see D. C. Henny, James Munn, and C. T. Pease to Chief Engineer, 13 December 1920, Department of the Interior Records, Office of the Secretary, 1907–36, RG 48, National Archives.

9. Wesley L. Jones to Roy R. Gill, 25 January, 26 February, 22 March 1929, Wesley L. Jones Papers, University of Washington Library, Seattle.

10. The report was published as *Columbia River and Minor Tributaries,* 73d Cong., 1st sess., 1933, H. Doc. 103. A revised list prepared by senior corps officials increased the number of dams to ten. The tally included the first Columbia River power dam, built at Rock Island near Wenatchee by the Puget Sound Power & Light Company in the early 1930s.

11. "Brief of Conversation with President Hoover," 8 October 1931; "Report on Meeting with the President," October 1931; James O'Sullivan to Rufus Woods and William Clapp, 6, 18, 26 March, 7 April 1932, Rufus Woods Papers, *Wenatchee World;* Charles Hebberd to Gill, 6 November 1931, Roy R. Gill Papers, Washington State University Library, Pullman.

12. *The Public Papers and Addresses of Franklin D. Roosevelt,* 13 vols. (New York: Random House 1938–50), 1:727–42. Also see Philip J. Funigiello, "The Bonneville Power Administration and the New Deal," *Prologue* 5 (1973): 89.

13. A. S. Goss to Clarence D. Martin, 17 April 1933, James O'Sullivan Papers, Gonzaga University Library, Spokane. C. C. Dill to Martin, 17, 19, 21, 26 April 1933; Dill to O'Sullivan, 19 April 1933; Franklin D. Roosevelt to Dill, 20 April 1933, Clarence D. Martin Papers, Washington State University Library, Pullman. Roosevelt's letter to Dill, detailing the points discussed, has been published in Edgar B. Nixon, ed., *Franklin D. Roosevelt and Conservation, 1911–1945,* 2 vols. (Hyde Park, N.Y.: Roosevelt Library, 1957), 1:158–59.

14. Woods to E. F. Banker et al., 10 November 1933; Banker to W. Gale Matthews, 2 May 1933; Matthews to Harvey Smith, 28 April 1933, Columbia Basin Commission Records, Washington State Archives, Olympia; Willis Batcheller to O'Sullivan, 21 April 1933, O'Sullivan Papers.

15. Minutes, 20, 31 October 1933; O'Sullivan to Martin, 28 October 1933. All Columbia Basin Commission Records; O'Sullivan to Woods, 28 October 1933,

O'Sullivan Papers; Woods to Dill and John Bowen, 26 October 1933; Woods to Batcheller, 6 November 1933, Woods Papers; Dill to Martin, 28 October 1933, Martin Papers.

16. Elwood Mead to Harold L. Ickes, 19, 27 December 1934, 11, 20 May, 4 June 1935, Department of the Interior Records, Office of the Secretary, 1907–36. On construction of the dams, see Richard Lowitt, *The New Deal and the West* (Bloomington: Indiana University Press, 1984), 157–70.

17. S. O. Harper to Marshall Dana, 6 July 1935, National Resources Planning Board Records.

18. There is an extensive literature on the state's Progressive movement. See, in particular, Howard W. Allen, *Poindexter of Washington: A Study in Progressive Politics* (Carbondale: Southern Illinois University Press, 1981); Robert D. Saltvig, "The Progressive Movement in Washington" (Ph.D. diss., University of Washington, 1966); William T. Kerr, Jr., "The Progressives of Washington, 1910–12," *Pacific Northwest Quarterly* 55 (1964): 16–27.

19. *Wenatchee Daily World*, 24 September 1934, 6, 9 April, 22 July, 19 November, 13 December 1935.

20. *Wenatchee Daily World*, 21 May 1929, 6 August 1937, 25 May, 27 October 1938, 13 January, 14, 19 June, 19 October 1939. The Wenatchee Valley produced one-eighth of the nation's commercial apple crop. This important and volatile Washington industry has yet to receive detailed study from historians. For an introduction to the subject, see John Fahey, *The Inland Empire: Unfolding Years, 1879–1929* (Seattle: University of Washington Press, 1986), chap. 6.

21. *Wenatchee Daily World*, 20 January, 26 February, 5 August 1937; 13, 25 January, 5, 23 March, 9 April, 5 September, 17, 19 November 1938, 9 August 1939; Woods to Charles Leavy, 22 January, 5 June 1940, Woods Papers.

22. *Wenatchee Daily World*, 13 December 1935. Washington ranked ninth among the states in per capita New Deal spending between 1933 and 1939, and first in a tally restricted to states with population in excess of a million. Leonard Arrington, "The New Deal in the West: A Preliminary Statistical Inquiry," *Pacific Historical Review* 38 (1969): 311–16, and "The Sagebrush Resurrection: New Deal Expenditures in the Western States, 1933–1939," *Pacific Historical Review* 52 (1983): 1–16.

23. Charles McKinley, *Uncle Sam in the Pacific Northwest: Federal Management of Natural Resources in the Columbia River Valley* (Berkeley and Los Angeles: University of California Press, 1952), 157–62; Herman C. Voeltz, "Genesis and Development of a Regional Power Authority in the Pacific Northwest, 1933–43," *Pacific Northwest Quarterly* 53 (1962): 65–69.

24. Memo, "Interconnection of Coulee and Bonneville Plants," 18 March 1936; J. D. Ross memo, "Grand Coulee–Bonneville Base," 5 May 1937; J. D. Ross to Morris L. Cooke, 12 November 1936; Ross to Homer T. Bone, 3 June 1937; Ross to C. E. Magnusson, 16 June 1937; Ross to Leavy, 25 February 1938, Seattle Lighting Department Records, University of Washington Library. Leavy to O'Sullivan, 1 March 1940; Leavy to W. E. Southard, 18 March 1940, O'Sullivan Papers. Matthews to Woods, 26 January 1938, Woods Papers. On construction of the transmission network, see "Columbia River and Tributaries," 87th Cong., 2d

sess., 1961, H. Doc. 403, vol. 2, app. C, pt. 1, 4–5; pt. 3, 1; McKinley, *Uncle Sam in the Pacific Northwest*, 170–72. On Ross's career with the Bonneville Power Administration (BPA), see Funigiello, "Bonneville Power Administration and the New Deal," 89–93.

25. In an effort to appease critics, the BPA reserved a small portion of Grand Coulee's output for use at the dam site at a rate of $14.50 per kilowatt year. Woods to Arthur Langlie, 4 October 1944, Woods Papers; *Wenatchee Daily World*, 2 September 1940; B. H. Kizer to Bone, 13 March 1941, National Resources Planning Board Records. BPA rate policies are summarized in Paul J. Raver's speech to Seattle Rotary Club, 4 December 1940, Warren G. Magnuson House Papers, University of Washington Library, Seattle. Also see McKinley, *Uncle Sam in the Pacific Northwest*, 167–68; Funigiello, "Bonneville Power Administration and the New Deal," 89–93.

26. Ross to Ralph A. Horr, 25 January 1934; Ross to Ross Tiffany, 4 August 1934; Ross to Charles H. Ireland, 18 August 1934, Seattle Lighting Department Records; Woods to Ross, 27 November, 6 December 1934, Woods Papers. Ross changed his tune upon taking over the BPA. "No great hydro plant ever goes begging," he informed President Roosevelt in May 1938. Ross to Roosevelt, 31 May 1938; Roosevelt to Ross, 3 June 1938. Rivers and Harbors Files, Records of the Office of Chief of Engineers, 1923–42, RG 77, National Archives.

27. Thomas Robins to Chief of Engineers, 30 June 1937, in 75th Cong., 1st sess., H. Doc. 704; Thomas Robins to Chief of Engineers, 3 March 1934, Report of Technical Advisory Committee, 24 March 1934, "Proceedings of Conference on Power Use," 14 December 1934, all in North Pacific Division Records, U.S. Army Corps of Engineers, RG 77, Federal Records Center, Seattle.

28. Proceedings of Conference on Power Use, 14 December 1934, North Pacific Division Records. Woods to Dana, 20 December 1934; 1 January 1935; Kizer to Dana, 19 December 1934; O'Sullivan to Dana, 18 December 1934. National Resources Planning Board Records. Also see Lowitt, *New Deal and the West*, 138–39; McKinley, *Uncle Sam in the Pacific Northwest*, 459–61.

29. *Wenatchee Daily World*, 5 June, 2 August 1940.

30. *Wenatchee Daily World*, 7 September, 5, 27, 30 December 1939; 7, 21 March, 4 April, 3 June, 27 August 1940. Ickes to Joseph Guffey, 26 September 1941; Statement on Industry, 29 May 1943. National Resources Planning Board Records. Leavy to O'Sullivan, 16 July 1940, O'Sullivan Papers. Also see Gerald D. Nash, *World War II and the West: Reshaping the Economy* (Lincoln: University of Nebraska Press, 1990), 94.

31. National Resources Planning Board, *Pacific Northwest Region*, 29.

32. A kilowatt-hour is the power needed to light a 1000-watt bulb for an hour. *Wenatchee Daily World*, 4 March, 12 April, 17 July, 19, 22 September 1941; 21 September 1944; "Columbia River and Tributaries," app. C, pt. 6, 3; "Columbia River and Tributaries, Northwestern United States," 81st Cong., 2d sess., H. Doc. 531, 3156; Gerald D. Nash, *The American West Transformed: The Impact of the Second World War* (Bloomington: Indiana University Press, 1985), 29; Nash, *World War II and the West*, 91–101; McKinley, *Uncle Sam in the Pacific Northwest*, 182.

33. J. D. Ross had died in March 1939. *Wenatchee Daily World*, 29 July, 30

September 1941, 2 October, 22 December 1941. Woods to Paul Piper, 17 December 1945; Piper to Woods, 4 August, 1, 8 October 1941. Woods Papers.

34. Bonneville Power Administration Service Report, 12 February 1942, Magnuson House Papers; C. R. Moore to Division Engineer, 27 February 1942, Rivers and Harbors Files.

35. Leavy to Woods, 30 December 1941, Kirby Billingsley Papers, North Central Washington Museum, Wenatchee.

36. Statement on Industry, 31 May 1943, National Resources Planning Board Records; Nash, *American West Transformed,* 17, 79; Nash, *World War II and the West,* 101; National Resources Planning Board, *Pacific Northwest Region,* 4–5, 19, 29–30; "Columbia River and Tributaries," app. C, pt. 5, 23; pt. 6, 4; *Employment Trends in Basic Industries, Sept. 1940–Aug. 1945* (Olympia: State Department of Conservation and Development, 1947), 10; "Columbia River and Tributaries, Northwestern United States," 65, 3110, 3154.

37. Karl Stoffel to Kirby Billingsley, 12, 16, 18, 29 March 1943, Woods Papers; Billingsley to Walt Horan, 9 March 1943; Billingsley to Stoffel, 16 March 1943, Billingsley Papers.

38. Introductory entry, F. T. Matthias Diary, U.S. Army Corps of Engineers History Office, Fort Belvoir, Va. Also see Michele Stenehjeim Gerber, *On the Home Front: The Cold War Legacy of the Hanford Nuclear Site* (Lincoln: University of Nebraska Press, 1992), 22–26.

39. Billingsley to Stoffel, 16 March 1943, Billingsley Papers; Marc Reisner, *Cadillac Desert: The American West and Its Disappearing Water* (New York: Viking, 1986), 170. On the vital importance of electricity to the selection of Hanford for the Manhattan Project, see War Production Board to Bonneville Power Administration, 11 May 1944; Leslie R. Groves, "Memorandum for Undersec-War," 11 August 1944. Manhattan Engineering District Records, RG 77, National Archives.

40. Grand Coulee's capacity was approximately four times that of Bonneville. Bessey to Willard, 27 May 1943, enclosing "Memorandum on Hydroelectricity, May 25, 1943," National Resources Planning Board Records; *Wenatchee Daily World,* 6 August 1942, 20 February, 23 November, 28 December 1943, 26 July, 12, 21 September, 13 October, 29 November, 8 December 1944; Frederick Simpich, "Wartime in the Pacific Northwest," *National Geographic,* 82 (1942), 436.

41. Billingsley to Hugh B. Mitchell, 21 May 1946, Hugh B. Mitchell Papers, University of Washington Library, Seattle. On the general subject of the role of power in war mobilization, see Philip J. Funigiello, "Kilowatts for Defense: The New Deal and the Coming of the Second World War," *Journal of American History* 56 (1969): 604–20.

42. "Conrad P. Hardy to DivEngineer," 15 August 1945, file 1505–22, Upper Columbia Basin, Seattle District Office, Corps of Engineers. For local reaction to the Foster Creek plan, see Woods to Horan, 3 July 1945; Horan to Woods, 5 November 1945, Woods Papers; Horan to Robins, 2 November 1945; Robins to Horan, 15 November 1945, Walt Horan Papers, Washington State University Library, Pullman.

43. On Umatilla dam planning, see William F. Willingham, *Army Engineers*

and the Development of Oregon: A History of the Portland District, U.S. Army Corps of Engineers (Washington, D.C.: Government Printing Office, 1983), 150.

44. "B. E. Torpen Memorandum, Storage for Power, Columbia River Basin," August 1945, file 1505–22, Upper Columbia Basin.

45. Background of International Columbia River Investigations, n.d., Acc. 68A–1926, Records of the Office of Chief of Engineers, 1943–   , Washington National Records Center; Paul J. Raver, "The Challenge to Statesmanship," *Pacific Northwest Quarterly* 49 (1958): 99; W. O. Silverthorn to L. L. Wise, 7 January 1955, Columbia Basin Inter-Agency Committee Records, University of Washington Library, Seattle; "Interim Report on Kootenay River to the International Joint Commission," 1 November 1950; L. H. Hewitt to G. L. Beard, enclosing preliminary notes, 1 July 1949, both file 1505–22, Libby Project, Seattle District Office, Corps of Engineers.

46. Compton I. White to Woods, 25 May, 9 June 1943; Woods to D. L. Marlett, 8 June 1943; to George H. Campbell, 14 June 1943; to A. F. Winkler, 14 June 1943, Woods Papers; J. P. Alvey to Mitchell, 13 June 1946, Mitchell Papers.

47. *Wenatchee Daily World,* 8 October, 30, 31 December 1941, 3 May 1943.

48. Woods to Billingsley, 25 April 1942; to T. A. Love, 9 March 1943; to Paul J. Raver, 23 March 1944, Woods Papers; Billingsley to Tom Welborn, 6 December 1943; Billingsley to Joesph G. Knapp, 5 February 1944; Raver to J. V. Rogers, 15 June 1942; Abe Fortas to Billingsley, 27 June 1942, Billingsley Papers.

49. Woods to Ickes, 18 August 1941; Woods to Emil Hurja, 7 August 1941, Woods Papers; *Wenatchee Daily World,* 12 August, 9 October 1941.

50. Bessey to Willard, 27 May 1943, enclosing "Memorandum on Population, May 25, 1943," National Resources Planning Board Records; *Wenatchee Daily World,* 2 February, 1 August 1942, 29 March, 3 November 1943.

51. *Wenatchee Daily World,* 16 February, 30 April, 1 May, 19 June, 30 November, 5, 29 December 1942, 6, 18 February, 16 April, 28 May, 25 June, 5 July 1943; Woods to Piper, 17 December 1945; Woods to Goss, 15 April 1942; Woods to White and Reginald S. Dean, 3 December 1942; Billingsley to Stoffel, 7 October 1943, Woods Papers; Billingsley to Bone, 7 July 1943, Billingsley Papers.

52. *Wenatchee Daily World,* 4 June, 30 November 1942, 9 April, 24, 25 June 1943; Woods to Raver, 21 July 1943; Billingsley to Rogers, 7 May 1942, Woods Papers; Billingsley to Bone, 16 June 1942; Billingsley to Fortas, 18 June 1942; Stoffel to Billingsley, 19 October 1943, Billingsley Papers.

53. "Statement on Industry," 29 May 1943, National Resources Planning Board Records; Woods to Lewie Williams, 19 April 1943; Horan to Billingsley, 3 January 1944, Woods Papers; Billingsley to Horan, 7 January 1944, Billingsley Papers; *Wenatchee Daily World,* 6, 13 October, 22 November, 14 December 1943, 18 January, 26 August 1944. The revelation that the Reconstruction Finance Corporation had funded the development of aluminum production in Canada by a corporate cousin of Alcoa sparked outrage in the Pacific Northwest. See Nash, *World War II and the West,* 103–14.

54. *Wenatchee Daily World,* 21 January 1946, 17 February 1948, 27 January 1949; Bone to Billingsley, 3 November 1944, Billingsley Papers.

55. *Wenatchee Daily World,* 5 July 1945; 14 June, 6, 19, 21, 26 August 1946; 20,

22 January, 1 March, 30 December 1948, 4 January, 20 April, 30 July 1949; memorandum, 12 September 1947, Columbia Basin Commission Records. On the disposition of the wartime aluminum plants, see Nash, *World War II and the West,* 114–21.

56. John Gunther, *Inside U.S.A.* (New York: Harper & Brothers, 1947), 132. The Neuberger quote is from St. Louis *Post-Dispatch,* 15 May 1949, clipping in Henry M. Jackson House Papers, University of Washington Library, Seattle.

57. Warren G. Magnuson to Charles J. Bartholet, 20 September 1949, Arthur Langlie Papers, University of Washington Library, Seattle; Horan to Welborn, 16 November 1944; Horan to Norman Mackenzie, 27 December 1944; Horan to Billingsley, 11 April 1945, Horan Papers.

58. Drafted by Interior Department lawyers, the measure placed the prospective Columbia Valley Authority (CVA) under the jurisdiction of a National River Basin Development Board, chaired by the secretary. C. G. Davidson to Billingsley, 13, 18, 21, 26, 31 January, 7 February 1945; Mitchell to Billingsley, 24 March 1945, all Billingsley Papers; McKinley, *Uncle Sam in the Pacific Northwest,* 550–56.

59. Woods to Ed Davis, 10 October 1944; Woods to Langlie, 4 October 1944; Woods to Hal Holmes, 29 November 1944; Woods to Martin, 29 November 1944; Woods to Magnuson, 23 January 1945; Woods to Rex L. Nicholson, 21 May 1945; Woods to Goss, 25 September 1948; Woods to Horan, 11 April, 18, 20 June, 10 September 1945; Woods to Mackenzie, 16 April 1945; Woods to Dill, 17 April 1945; Woods to Mitchell, 20 September 1945; 7 April 1949, Woods Papers; Woods to O'Sullivan, 29 November 1944, Woods O'Sullivan Papers; Billingsley to Horan, 21 November 1944; Billingsley to Hu Blonk, 1 January 1945; Billingsley to Davidson, 29 January 1945, Billingsley Papers. For general coverage of the CVA fight, see Elmo Richardson, *Dams, Parks and Politics: Resource Development and Preservation in the Truman-Eisenhower Era* (Lexington: University of Kentucky Press, 1973), chap. 1.

60. Horan to Billingsley, 24 November 1944, 20 March, 23 May 1945, Billingsley Papers; Horan to Woods, 15 March 1945; Woods to Horan, 17 April, 18, 20 June 1945, Woods Papers; McKinley, *Uncle Sam in the Pacific Northwest,* 562.

61. Horan to Raymond A. Wheeler, 9 February 1948; Horan to Woods, 28 February 1948; Billingsley to Horan, 26 February 1948, Horan Papers; Horan to Henry M. Jackson, 11 October 1948, Jackson House Papers; James O'Sullivan Report, 29 February 1948, Billingsley Papers; Woods to O'Sullivan, 28 February 1948, O'Sullivan Papers.

62. Magnuson to Welborn, 15, 25 July 1946, Warren G. Magnuson Senate Papers, University of Washington Library, Seattle; Horan to Billingsley, 29 December 1947, 5, 19 March, 21 July 1948, Billingsley Papers; Horan to Woods, 28 February 1948; Horan to Hebberd, 5 March 1948, Horan Papers.

63. Magnuson to Billingsley, 29 March, 20 June 1947, Billingsley Papers.

64. Much of the legal argument supporting these measures was supplied by Seattle Chamber of Commerce Secretary Floyd Hagie, a determined champion of the private utilities. Magnuson to Billingsley, 20 June 1947, Billingsley Papers; Magnuson to Woods, 23 July 1949; Woods to George A. Dondero, 29 May 1947; Woods to Horan, 15 April, 16 June 1947; F. O. Hagie to Woods, 2 January 1947;

O'Sullivan to Woods, 11 January 1947, 26, 27 January 1948, Woods Papers; McKinley, *Uncle Sam in the Pacific Northwest,* 115, 209–10.

65. *Wenatchee Daily World,* 11 January 1947; Woods to Billingsley, 23 January 1950; Billingsley to Horan, 8 January 1947, Billingsley Papers; Stoffel to H. F. Morse, 23 January 1947, Woods Papers; Stoffel to Langlie, 27 January 1949; Harry P. Cain to Langlie, 12 March 1949, Langlie Papers.

66. Horan to Billingsley, 1 August 1948, Billingsley Papers.

67. *Wenatchee Daily World,* 15 June 1948; Magnuson to Wheeler, 17 August 1948, Magnuson Senate Papers. For details on the flood, second only to the disaster of 1894 in the recorded history of the Columbia, see "Columbia River and Tributaries, Northwestern United States," 79–80; Willingham, *Army Engineers and the Development of Oregon,* 151–58.

68. *Wenatchee Daily World,* 6, 9, 11 November, 6 December 1948.

69. *Wenatchee Daily World,* 11, 29, 30 December 1948; 4, 17, 27 January, 22 February 1949; Woods to Charles Cone, 24 December 1948, Woods Papers.

70. Chief Joseph, the legendary Nez Perce leader, spent the final years of his life at Nespelem on the adjacent Colville Reservation. Friends of Rufus Woods campaigned to have the project named for the Wenatchee publisher. He, in turn, preferred that the honor go to missionary Marcus Whitman. Woods to Rogers, 1, 21 March 1949; Billingsley to Rogers, 22, 24 May 1949, all Department of Conservation Records, Washington State Archives; to Chester Kimm, 27 March 1949; Bill Royce to Billingsley, 10 May 1949, Billingsley Papers; Horan to Kimm, 30 December 1948; Horan to Frank Bell, 12 January 1949, Horan Papers; James W. Wallace to Mitchell, 28 July 1950, Mitchell Papers.

71. The 308 Report preference for the Chelan over the Wells site was reversed in 1949. Hewitt to Division Engineer, 1 October 1947, file 1505–22, Albeni Falls Project, Seattle District Office, Corps of Engineers; Hewitt to Roger B. McWhorter, 3 May 1949, acc. 68A–1926, Records of the Office of Chief of Engineers, 1943–   ; Hewitt to Beard, 1 July 1949, file 1505–22, Libby Project; "Columbia River and Tributaries, Northwestern United States," 135–39, 148–50, 459–68, 479–87, 600–602; Herbert G. West to Billingsley, 19 October 1950, Billingsley Papers; Woods to Rogers, 27 September 1949, Department of Conservation Records.

72. Woods to Fred Haley, 11 May 1949; Woods to Horan, 18, 31 January, 20 June 1949; Woods to Raver, 6 April 1950; Woods to Magnuson, 21 February 1949; Woods to Mitchell, 20 December 1948; 7 April 1949, Woods Papers. On the post–1948 CVA situation, see McKinley, *Uncle Sam in the Pacific Northwest,* 563, 643–53.

73. "Agreement on Principles and Responsibilities," 11 April 1949, Bureau of Reclamation and Corps of Engineers; Horan to Langlie, 13 May 1949; Michael W. Straus to Langlie, 11 May 1949, Langlie Papers; Straus to Julius A. Krug, 5, 13, 27 January 1949; Davidson to Straus, 22 December 1948; Krug to Lewis Pick, 23 March 1949, Department of the Interior Records, Office of the Secretary, 1937–53, RG 48, National Archives; Krug to Mitchell, 25 May 1949, Mitchell Papers; Memorandum, "The Corps of Engineers '308' Report," n.d.; press releases, 17, 20 June 1949, Jackson House Papers; McKinley, *Uncle Sam in the Pacific Northwest,* 638–43.

74. Magnuson to Woods, 9 March 1950; Billingsley to Woods, 6 August 1949, 31 January, 2 February 1950; Billingsley to Rogers, 25 September 1949; 29 January, 6 February, 24 April 1950, Woods Papers; Horan to Billingsley, 28 November 1949; Norman Schut to Billingsley, 7 March 1950; Rogers to Billingsley, 14 October, 9 November 1949; 7 July 1950, Billingsley Papers.

75. The project was named after adjacent Benton and Franklin counties, rather than Benjamin Franklin. "Columbia River and Tributaries," 1:228, 230–32; Plan of Survey, Ben Franklin Project, 29 April 1960, file 1517–08, Survey Reports, Seattle District Office, Corps of Engineers.

76. The Chelan Public Utility District (PUD) also acquired Rock Island Dam from the Puget Sound Power & Light Company. Pacific Northwest River Basins Commission, Columbia–North Pacific Study, app. 2, The Region, October 1970, 31; Columbia River and Tributaries (CR&T) Study, Reach Inventory, April 1975, 10–34. These studies were examined in the Seattle office of the Corps of Engineers.

77. Pacific Northwest River Basins Commission, Comprehensive Framework Study, 110; Portland *Oregonian,* 16 March 1961, clipping in Northwest Public Power Association Records, University of Washington Library; Allen F. Clark, Jr. to William F. Cassidy, 18 January 1961, file 1517–08, Survey Reports.

78. At 1.5 million tons for 1955, national aluminum production was two-thirds greater than the peak wartime year. One-third of the aluminum produced in the Northwest went into military usage, reflecting the linkage between the Cold War and the regional economy. "Columbia River and Tributaries," 1:10–11, 13, 46, 48; vol. 3, app. C, pt. 5, 37–38, 45, 170, 183; pt. 6, 1, 3–7, 13.

79. "Columbia River and Tributaries," 1:45; vol. 2, app. C, pt. 1, 2–4.

80. "Columbia River and Tributaries," 1:1, 10–11, 50; vol. 2, app. C, pt. 1, 10–11, 13, 16–17; pt. 5, 170, 183. Runaway growth caused regional booster organizations to demand comprehensive Corps of Engineers studies on a regular five-year basis. Gus Norwood to Clark, 11 June 1958, Northwest Public Power Association Records.

81. "Columbia River and Tributaries," 1:50–54; vol. 2, app. C, pt. 4, 1–6.

82. Puget Sound Task Force, Pacific Northwest River Basins Commission, App. 9, Power, March 1970, 2, 55, 74, 79–80, 101; Pacific Northwest River Basins Commission, Comprehensive Framework Study, 268–69. On the nuclear power fiasco, see Daniel Jack Chasan, *The Fall of the House of WPPSS* (Seattle: Sasquatch Publishing, 1985) and the series of *Washington Post* articles for 2–5 December 1984.

83. "Columbia River and Tributaries," 1:94; Don W. Clarke to Jackson, 10 March 1949, Jackson House Papers; Milo Moore to Ralph A. Tudor, 30 June 1945, Magnuson Senate Papers; Anthony Netboy, *Salmon of the Pacific Northwest: Fish vs. Dams* (Portland: Binford & Mort, 1958), 52–61.

84. "Columbia River and Tributaries, Northwestern United States," 310; "Robert P. Young to Chief, EngDiv," 15 June 1959; to Henry C. Dworshak, 30 June 1959, file 1517–08, Survey Reports; Roy S. Kelley speech to Walla Walla Chamber of Commerce, 24 February 1970, Catherine May Papers, Washington State University Library, Pullman.

85. E. C. Itschner to Magnuson, 10 March 1953, Magnuson Senate Papers; "Columbia River and Tributaries," 1:95–96; Netboy, *Salmon of the Pacific Northwest,* 63–65; Willingham, *Army Engineers and the Development of Oregon,* 199–201; Pacific Northwest River Basins Commission, app. 2, The Region, 32.

86. See the discussion in Robert E. Ficken and Charles P. LeWarne, *Washington: A Centennial History* (Seattle: University of Washington Press, 1988), 183–86.

CHAPTER 19

1. It could be argued that families who own large ranches occupy near feudal status in some communities. In the territorial and early statehood period, the Wyoming Stock Growers Association wielded significant influence over state affairs. The three "Grand Old Men" of Wyoming politics, Francis E. Warren, Joseph M. Carey and John B. Kendrick, were all association stalwarts. Members of the organization continued to hold a disproportionate number of seats in the state legislature until recent years.

2. Adherents of the Latter-Day Saints (LDS; Mormon) faith predominate in some areas in the extreme western part of the state and the Big Horn Basin. Mormons never have been elected to the governship or to any of the congressional offices, although members of that faith have served as state treasurer and state superintendent of public instruction.

3. State Senator Dick Jones, the owner of a trucking firm in Park County, was the Republican nominee in 1974. John Ostlund, a Gillette businessman and rancher, was the 1978 nominee.

4. One chain was controlled by Roy Peck and Robert Peck of the *Riverton Ranger.* Roy Peck, an unsuccessful candidate for the Republican gubernatorial nomination in 1974, died suddenly in Cheyenne in 1982 while serving in the state senate. His brother Robert, the current state senator from Fremont County, continues to operate the family-owned newspaper group. A second chain, Sage Publishing Company, was headed by Bruce Kennedy, who was killed in an automobile accident in 1992. The McCraken chain, noted later, is the third Wyoming-controlled group. For additional information on the history of Wyoming newspaper ownership, see Carolyn Tyler, ed. *Wyoming Newspapers: A Centennial History* (Cheyenne: Wyoming Press Association, 1990).

5. Soon after McCraken died, the U.S. Department of Justice instituted antitrust proceedings against Cheyenne Newspapers, Inc., the family-owned company, charging it with holding a media monopoly in the state's capital city. The firm owned the two daily newspapers, the only television station, the cable television system, and the largest radio station. For more on the litigation, see Peggy Bieber-Roberts, "Media Monopoly in Cheyenne" (Unpublished M.A. thesis, University of Wyoming, 1985).

6. Warren was the last territorial governor and the first state governor. Soon after statehood, Warren resigned from the governorship to accept legislative selection to the U.S. Senate. Unlike many of his "stalwart Republican" colleagues, Warren was able to retain his seat even after the Seventeenth Amendment forced him to seek popular election. Joseph M. Carey, the first U.S. senator from

Wyoming, was an arch-rival of Warren's. When he was rebuffed by Warren's organization for the Republican gubernatorial nomination in 1910, Carey accepted the Democratic nomination and won even though he did not officially change his party affiliation from Republican to Democrat.

7. T. A. Larson, *History of Wyoming* (Lincoln: University of Nebraska Press, 1965; rev. ed. 1978), 542.

8. The Smith administration may have demonstrated the ultimate in personality-driven politics. The handsome rancher who some said "looked like a governor" turned out to be a poor administrator who often acted according to the prejudices of others. His manipulations of the University Board of Trustees in an ultimately successful attempt to oust the university president, Arthur G. Crane, cost him politically. When he sought reelection in 1942, his heavy-handed meddling in agency personal matters had alienated even members of his own party.

9. Local Democrats, including Kendrick, had simply handed the *Wyoming Eagle* over to McCraken following a successful campaign when it became apparent that it would be an expensive liability to maintain during the two years until the next election. McCraken transformed the *Eagle* from the political sheet for Senator John B. Kendrick and other Democrats into a business. The *Tribune* could boast of its statewide readership, but there were no statewide businesses to provide the advertising base. In a sense, management of the *Tribune* always expected local Cheyenne merchants to subsidize the readership because few readers in distant places such as Sheridan, Cody, and Evanston could be expected to be regular customers in Cheyenne stores. McCraken's daily *Eagle* was specifically targeted toward local customers. It shamelessly boosted local businesses in news and editorial pages and offered attractive ad rates. At the same time, McCraken cannily let his *Eagle's* bigger rival spend its resources on statewide circulation.

10. For a study of the 1952 senatorial election, see Barton R. Voigt, "Joseph C. O'Mahoney and the 1952 Senate Campaign" (Unpublished M.A. thesis, University of Wyoming, 1973).

11. On Hunt's suicide and the events leading up to it, see Rick Ewig, "McCarthy Era Politics: The Ordeal of Senator Lester Hunt," *Annals of Wyoming* 55 (Spring 1983): 9–21.

12. For a biography of Gage, see Kathleen M. Karpan, "A Political Biography of Jack R. Gage" (unpublished M.A. thesis, University of Wyoming, 1975). Interestingly, Karpan was elected Wyoming Secretary of State in 1986, the highest position to which Gage was elected.

The Contributors

Thomas G. Alexander is Lemuel Hardison Redd, Jr., Professor of Western American History at Brigham Young University. He has published widely in Western and Mormon history and is the author of *A Dependent Commonwealth: Utah's Economy from Statehood to the Great Depression.*

Peggy Bieber-Roberts is Assistant Professor of Mass Communication at the University of Wyoming, specializing in media and politics. She holds the Ph.D. from the University of Washington. A former Wyoming legislative reporter and owner/publisher of a city magazine, she has written extensively on Wyoming media history.

Peter Coates is Lecturer in U.S. History at the University of Bristol, United Kingdom, specializing in environmental history. He received the 1993 W. Turrentine Jackson Award of the Western History Association for his book on conflicts between conservationists and developers in Alaska.

David B. Danbom is Professor of History at North Dakota State University. His most recent book is *Our Purpose to Serve: The First Century of the North Dakota Agricultural Experiment Station.* He is past president of the Agricultural History Association and is presently associate editor for the North Dakota Institute of Regional Studies.

Sandra K. Davis is Associate Professor of Political Science at Colorado State University, specializing in American politics and environmental policy. she has written articles on water policy, public lands issues, and citizen participation.

Jerome E. Edwards is Professor and Chair of the Department of History at the University of Nevada, Reno. He has written several books, including *Pat McCarran, Political Boss of Nevada.* His current research focuses on the evolution of gambling in Nevada.

Steven C. Emery, an enrolled member of the Cheyenne River Sioux Tribe, is Attorney General of the tribe. He holds the J.D. from Harvard University. He and his brother, who is also an attorney, are responsible for the tribe's legal affairs.

David Emmons is Professor of History at the University of Montana. He is the author of *The Butte Irish: Class and Ethnicity in an American Mining Town, 1875–1925*, which was awarded the 1990 Robert Athearn Prize by the Western Historical Association.

Robert E. Ficken is an independent scholar residing in Issaquah, Washington. He is the author or coauthor of a number of books on Pacific Northwest history, including *The Forested Land: A History of Lumbering in Western Washington, Washington: A Centennial History,* and *Rufus Woods, the Columbia River and the Building of Modern Washington.*

Danney Goble, Historian in the Carl Albert Center, University of Oklahoma, is a specialist on Oklahoma since territorial days. He is the author or coauthor of several books, including *Little Giant: The Life and Times of Speaker Carl Albert* and *The Story of Oklahoma,* both published by the University of Oklahoma Press.

Herbert T. Hoover is Professor of History at the University of South Dakota. He is the author or editor of numerous books and articles on Indian-white relations in historic Sioux Country, South Dakota, and the upper Missouri River drainage basin.

Peter Iverson is Professor of History at Arizona State University. He is the author or editor of several books on American Indians and the West, including *When Indians Became Cowboys: Native Peoples and Cattle Ranching in the American West,* published by the University of Oklahoma Press.

Richard Lowitt is Professor of History at the University of Oklahoma. His most recent book is *Bronson M. Cutting: Progressive Politician.*

E. Kimbark MacColl received his Ph.D. at the University of California, Los Angeles. He has published several books on the history of Portland, where he is active in both civic and academic affairs while directing The Georgian Press Company.

H. Brett Melendy is Professor Emeritus, University of Hawaii and San Jose State University, and is director of the Territory of Hawaii History Project.

He is the author of monographs and articles on Asian immigration to the United States and on California and Hawaii politics.

William C. Pratt is Professor of History at the University of Nebraska at Omaha and a trustee of the Nebraska State Historical Society. Much of his research concerns farm and labor movements in the Upper Midwest.

Ben Procter is Professor of History at Texas Christian University. He has published extensively on Texas history. His most recent book is *Just One Riot: Episodes of Texas Rangers in the 20th Century.*

Jackson K. Putnam is Emeritus Professor of History at California State University, Fullerton. He is a keen student of California politics, a field in which he has published widely. His most recent book, *Modern California Politics,* is now in its third edition.

Phil Roberts is Assistant Professor of History at the University of Wyoming, specializing in the history of Wyoming and the American West. He holds the Ph.D. from the University of Washington and the J.D. from the University of Wyoming. A native of Lusk, Wyoming, he has practiced law, edited newspapers, and worked in public history.

Stephen Shaw is Associate Professor of Political Science at Northwest Nazarene College, Nampa, Idaho. He received his Ph.D. from the University of Oklahoma and is the author of *The Ninth Amendment: Preservation of the Constitutional Mind.*

James E. Sherow is Assistant Professor of History at Kansas State University, specializing in environmental, U.S., Western, and Kansas history and in ethno-history. He is the author of *Watering the Valley* and is presently working on an environmental history of the central High Plains between 1780 and 1870 and an environmental history of Kansas.

Homer E. Socolofsky is Emeritus Professor and University Historian at Kansas State University. He is past president of the Agricultural History Society and a leading historian of Kansas. His research focuses on Great Plains agriculture and the disposal of its public lands.

Index